This volume is part of the first ever comprehensive edition of the works of Immanuel Kant in English translation. The purpose of the Cambridge edition is to offer translations of the best modern German editions of Kant's work in a uniform format suitable for Kant scholars. When complete (fourteen volumes are currently envisaged), the edition will include all of Kant's published writings and a generous selection of his unpublished writings such as the *Opus postumum, handschriftiche Nachlass,* lectures, and correspondence.

Kant's views on logic and logical theory play an important role in his critical writings, especially the *Critique of Pure Reason.* However, since he published only one short essay on the subject, we must turn to the texts derived from his logic lectures to understand his views. The present volume includes three previously untranslated transcripts of Kant's logic lectures: the *Blomberg Logic* from the 1770s; the *Vienna Logic* (supplemented by the recently discovered *Hechsel Logic*) from the early 1780s; and the *Dohna-Wundlacken Logic* from the early 1790s. Also included is a new translation of the *Jäsche Logic,* compiled at Kant's request and published in 1800 but which also appears to stem in part from a transcript of his lectures.

Together these texts provide a rich source of evidence for Kant's evolving views on logic, on the relationship between logic and other disciplines, and on a variety of topics (e.g., analysis and synthesis) central to Kant's mature philosophy. They also provide a portrait of Kant as lecturer, a role in which he was both popular and influential.

In keeping with other volumes in the series, there is substantial editorial apparatus, including a general introduction, linguistic and factual notes, glossaries of key terms (both German–English and English–German) and concordances relating Kant's lectures to Georg Friedrich Meier's *Excerpts from the Doctrine of Reason,* the book on which Kant lectured throughout his life and in which he left extensive notes.

THE CAMBRIDGE EDITION OF THE WORKS OF IMMANUEL KANT

Theoretical Philosophy, 1755–1770
The Critique of Pure Reason
Theoretical Philosophy after 1781
Practical Philosophy
Aesthetics and Teleology
Religion and Rational Theology
Anthropology, History, and Education
Natural Science
Lectures on Logic
Lectures on Metaphysics
Lectures on Practical Philosophy
Opus postumum
Notes and Fragments
Correspondence

IMMANUEL KANT

Lectures on logic

THE CAMBRIDGE EDITION OF THE WORKS OF IMMANUEL KANT

IMMANUEL KANT

Lectures on logic

TRANSLATED AND EDITED BY
J. MICHAEL YOUNG
University of Kansas

Published by the Press Syndicate of the University of Cambridge
The Pitt Building, Trumpington Street, Cambridge CB2 1RP
40 West 20th Street, New York, NY 10011-4211, USA
10 Stamford Road, Oakleigh, Victoria 3166, Australia

First published 1992

Printed in the United States of America

Library of congress cataloging-in-publication data

Kant, Immanuel, 1724–1804.

[Lectures. English. Selections]

Lectures on logic / Immanuel Kant ; translated and edited by J. Michael Young.

p. cm. – (The Cambridge edition of the works of Immanuel Kant)

ISBN 0-521-36013-7

1. Logic Modern – 18th century. I. Young, J. Michael. II. Title. III. Series: Kant, Immanuel, 1724–1804. Works. English. 1992.

B27581992

160–dc20 91-34583

CIP

A catalog record for this book is available from the British Library.

ISBN 0-521-36013-7 hardback

Contents

PART II

A. The Vienna logic

B. The Hechsel logic (in part)

CONTENTS

PART III

The Dohna-Wundlacken logic

(Contents as in manuscript of original text)

PART V
Appendixes

General editors' preface

Within a few years of the publication of his *Critique of Pure Reason* in 1781, Immanuel Kant (1724–1804) was recognized by his contemporaries as one of the seminal philosophers of modern times – indeed as one of the great philosophers of all time. This renown soon spread beyond German-speaking lands, and translations of Kant's work into English were published even before 1800. Since then, interpretations of Kant's views have come and gone and loyalty to his positions has waxed and waned, but his importance has not diminished. Generations of scholars have devoted their efforts to producing reliable translations of Kant into English as well as into other languages.

There are four main reasons for the present edition of Kant's writings:

1. Completeness. Although most of the works published in Kant's lifetime have been translated before, the most important ones more than once, only fragments of Kant's many important unpublished works have ever been translated. These include the *Opus postumum,* Kant's unfinished *magnum opus* on the transition from philosophy to physics; transcriptions of his classroom lectures; his correspondence; and his marginalia and other notes. One aim of this edition is to make a comprehensive sampling of these materials available in English for the first time.

2. Availability. Many English translations of Kant's works, especially those that have not individually played a large role in the subsequent development of philosophy, have long been inaccessible or out of print. Many of them, however, are crucial for the understanding of Kant's philosophical development, and the absence of some from English-language bibliographies may be responsible for erroneous or blinkered traditional interpretations of his doctrines by English-speaking philosophers.

3. Organization. Another aim of the present edition is to make all Kant's published work, both major and minor, available in comprehensive volumes organized both chronologically and topically, so as to facilitate the serious study of his philosophy by English-speaking readers.

4. Consistency of translation. Although many of Kant's major works have been translated by the most distinguished scholars of their day, some of these translations are now dated, and there is considerable terminological disparity among them. Our aim has been to enlist some of the most accomplished Kant scholars and translators to produce new translations, freeing readers from both the philosophical and literary preconceptions of previous generations and allowing them to approach texts, as far as possible, with the same directness as present-day readers of the German or Latin originals.

In pursuit of these goals, our editors and translators attempt to follow several fundamental principles:

1. As far as seems advisable, the edition employs a single general glossary, especially for Kant's technical terms. Although we have not attempted to restrict the prerogative of editors and translators in choice of terminology, we have maximized consistency by putting a single editor or editorial team in charge of each of the main groupings of Kant's writings, such as his work in practical philosophy, philosophy of religion, or natural science, so that there will be a high degree of terminological consistency, at least in dealing with the same subject matter.

2. Our translators try to avoid sacrificing literalness to readability. We hope to produce translations that approximate the originals in the sense that they leave as much of the interpretive work as possible to the reader.

3. The paragraph, and even more the sentence, is often Kant's unit of argument, and one can easily transform what Kant intends as a continuous argument into a mere series of assertions by breaking up a sentence so as to make it more readable. Therefore, we try to preserve Kant's own divisions of sentences and paragraphs wherever possible.

4. Earlier editions often attempted to improve Kant's texts on the basis of controversial conceptions about their proper interpretation. In our translations, emendation or improvement of the original edition is kept to the minimum necessary to correct obvious typographical errors.

5. Our editors and translators try to minimize interpretation in other ways as well, for example, by rigorously segregating Kant's own footnotes, the editors' purely linguistic notes, and their more explanatory or informational notes; notes in this last category are treated as endnotes rather than footnotes.

We have not attempted to standardize completely the format of individual volumes. Each, however, includes information about the context in which Kant wrote the translated works, an English–German glossary, an index, and other aids to comprehension. The general introduction to each volume includes an explanation of specific principles of translation and, where necessary, principles of selection of works included in that volume. The pagination of the standard German edition of Kant's works, *Kant's Gesammelte Schriften,* edited by the Royal Prussian (later German) Academy of Sciences (Berlin: Georg Reimer, later Walter deGruyter & Co., 1900–), is indicated throughout by means of marginal numbers.

GENERAL EDITORS' PREFACE

Our aim is to produce a comprehensive edition of Kant's writings, embodying and displaying the high standards attained by Kant scholarship in the English-speaking world during the second half of the twentieth century, and serving as both an instrument and a stimulus for the further development of Kant studies by English-speaking readers in the century to come. Because of our emphasis on literalness of translation and on information rather than interpretation in editorial practices, we hope our edition will continue to be usable despite the inevitable evolution and occasional revolutions in Kant scholarship.

Paul Guyer
Allen W. Wood

Acknowledgments

Early work on a translation of the *Jäsche Logic* was supported by the General Research Fund at the University of Kansas. The majority of the work on the translations was supported, however, by a grant from the National Endowment for the Humanities, an independent federal agency.

Karl Ameriks, who is editing texts that deal with metaphysics for another volume of the Cambridge edition, gave me early encouragement and advice. He and Steve Naragon also provided me with a draft of their glossary, which I consulted as I developed my own.

Reinhard Brandt and his colleagues at the Kant Archive in Marburg provided me with much assistance. Werner Stark, in particular, offered useful advice, and he helped me procure a prepublication copy of Pinder's edition of the *Hechsel Logic.* (For permission to use that edition I thank Felix Meiner Verlag, Hamburg, which will soon publish it, and which holds the copyright to it.) Werner Stark and Anke Lindemann-Stark gave generously of their time to help me compare the Academy edition of the *Vienna Logic* and the *Dohna-Wundlacken Logic* with microfilm copies of the manuscripts.

Norbert Hinske in Trier also provided much assistance and advice. I profited greatly, too, from the published volumes of his *Kant-Index,* as well as from information that he provided about texts not yet covered by the *Kant-Index.* Terry Boswell spent several hours helping me to check the Academy edition of the *Blomberg Logic* against the photocopy of the manuscript that Hinske possesses in Trier.

In deciphering particularly troublesome passages, and in tracking down obscure references, I had help from numerous colleagues at the University of Kansas. I should mention, in particular, Dan Breslauer, Henry Fullenwider, Oliver Phillips, and Alfonso Verdu.

Last but by no means least, I had invaluable help from Karin Plewka. Ms. Plewka, whose participation was made possible by the grant from the National Endowment for the Humanities, did the initial translations of most of the Latin passages. She also reviewed my translations of all the German texts, helping me to decipher many difficult passages. Finally, she developed much of the information contained in the explanatory endnotes.

I owe a deep debt of thanks to all the persons I have named. It goes without saying that I am responsible for the flaws that remain.

Translator's introduction

I. THE IMPORTANCE OF KANT'S LOGIC LECTURES

Kant's views about the nature of logic, and about various points of logical theory as well, figure prominently in his Critical works. This is especially true in the first and most fundamental of those works, the *Critique of Pure Reason*. Indeed, Kant characterizes the *Critique* – or the major portion of it, at least – as an essay in transcendental logic. This means, on the one hand, that the work is to be understood as containing something different from logic, something that does not deal merely with the canons of all thought, but with the concepts and principles governing knowledge of objects in space and time. It also means, however, that both in the broad sweep of its architectonic and in the detail of much of its argument the *Critique* assumes familiarity with Kant's views on logic; for transcendental logic, though different from logic proper, is supposed to build upon the latter. In dividing transcendental logic into an Analytic and a Dialectic, in deriving the table of categories, in classifying the dialectical inferences of pure reason, and in numerous other instances as well, Kant simply assumes that his readers are familiar with his views on logic.

In spite of this, Kant's views on logic have received comparatively little attention, especially in the Anglo-American philosophical community. There are at least two reasons for this. In the first place, Kant's approach to logic falls within what can broadly be called the Aristotelian tradition, which has in important ways been superseded. It is true that Kant does not accept the tradition uncritically. He insists, for example, that logic must treat hypothetical and disjunctive judgments, not just categoricals, as basic forms of judgment. He also rejects the Aristotelian doctrine of the four syllogistic figures as a false subtlety. It is likely, too, that these criticisms are symptomatic of deeper differences between Kant's view of judgment and inference and the view of Aristotle. Nonetheless, Kant's criticism of the tradition is developed only imperfectly. He does not succeed, for example, in formulating a principle that will cover hypothetical and disjunctive syllogisms as well as categorical ones; indeed, contrary to his own insistence, he often speaks as though there were only categorical judgments and categorical syllogisms. Even if he had managed to extend traditional logic in the ways he intended, moreover, Kant's logic would still have lacked the clarity, the generality, and the power of modern quantification theory.

In the second place, modern readers have generally been skeptical about Kant's claim to have built his transcendental logic on a framework provided by formal logic. They have been skeptical, not just about whether Kant succeeds in doing this, but also about whether it is possible, or even important, that he should succeed. This skepticism stems in part from widespread rejection of Kant's view that philosophy has to be done systematically, on the basis of an architectonic. But it also rests on the evident failure of some of Kant's attempts to work out detailed connections between logic and transcendental logic. To mention only the most conspicuous example, Kant claims that the categories, which are concepts belonging to transcendental logic, derive from the functions of thought in judgment, and that these latter are identified in logic proper. His claim has been met with numerous objections both of principle and of detail, and no one has yet provided a convincing response to these objections.[1]

Both of these points warrant discussion. Fundamentally, however, both are correct. Kant is not a major contributor to the development of formal logic. He fails, too, in his most conspicuous efforts to build his transcendental logic on clues provided by formal logic. The fact remains, nonetheless, that Kant's views on logic deserve study.

The point is not simply that one cannot appraise Kant's views without first understanding them. It is also that many of his views on logic are important, both for understanding Kant and for understanding the topics that are central to his Critical philosophy. Apart from the questionable ways in which Kant tries to draw on formal logic in the first *Critique*, the fact remains that much of the central argument of that work is deeply influenced by his views on logic and logical doctrine. To mention just one example, Kant's views about analysis and synthesis, which permeate the argument of the *Critique* and which have been the subject of much critical discussion, can be understood only in light of his views concerning concepts and judgments. And even if Kant fails to develop a satisfactory formal logic, his reflections on fundamental notions in logic – the notions of a concept and of judgment, for example – deserve consideration by anyone interested in the philosophy of logic or the theory of knowledge.

Gaining an understanding of Kant's views on logic is not easy, however. Kant himself wrote only one work in logic, an early essay entitled *The False Subtlety of the Four Syllogistic Figures* (2:45–61). The other published logical work associated with his name, a manual for use in teaching logic that was published in 1800, was written not by Kant himself but by a former

[1] The most serious effort to defend Kant's derivation is made by Klaus Reich in *Die Vollständigkeit der kantischen Urteilstafel* (*The Completeness of the Kantian Table of Judgments*), Berlin: Richard Schoetz, 1932. Though widely admired for its subtlety and depth, Reich's work has not convinced many that Kant's derivation is successful.

student, Gottlob Benjamin Jäsche. As Jäsche tells us in his preface to the manual, he prepared the manual at Kant's request. In doing so, moreover, he had at his disposal Kant's personal copy of Georg Friedrich Meier's *Excerpts from the Doctrine of Reason*, the book on which Kant lectured throughout his entire career, and in which he had written extensive notes. These notes were used by Kant as the basis for his lectures, and they provided Jäsche with a wealth of materials from which to prepare the desired manual. None of this implies, however, that the manual that Jäsche produced should be accepted uncritically as a presentation of Kant's views. Indeed, there are many reasons to treat Jäsche's manual with caution.

In the first place, the notes in Kant's copy of Meier's text had been compiled over a period of forty years. Not surprisingly, they therefore contained conflicting views and varying formulations. They were also difficult to decipher. Kant had had blank pages interleaved between the pages of Meier's work, and his notes filled these blank pages. They also filled the margins of Meier's work itself, even the spaces between the lines. Many notes were written between or even on top of one another. Many were broken off, and although they may have been continued elsewhere, the connections were frequently indicated only imperfectly. Many notes, finally, are highly abbreviated. Deciphering Kant's notes was thus a formidable task. Deciding which were earlier and which later, and which might therefore be regarded as presumptively more authoritative, was still more difficult. Erich Adickes, who edited all of Kant's handwritten materials for the Academy edition, claimed to be able to classify them into more than thirty different chronological periods.[2] Developing this classification required years of concentrated, difficult labor, however. Even then, his classifications were in many cases only tentative, and his results have been disputed.[3]

Jäsche plainly succeeded in deciphering many of Kant's notes, and he incorporated many into the text that he published as *Immanuel Kant's Logic*. Nonetheless, a great deal of the text is attributable to Jäsche. He tells us in his preface that he is responsible for much in the "presentation and ordering" of the materials. In particular, he divided the text into a lengthy introduction (dealing with a wide range of issues that are related to logic but do not properly belong to it) and a relatively brief main part (dealing with logic proper), although he took his cue from Kant's own remarks concerning the limits of logic proper. Unfortunately, Jäsche does

[2] See the Introduction to Volume 14 of the Academy edition, esp. 14:xxv–liv.

[3] See Otto Schöndörffer, "Bemerkungen zu Kants handschriftlichem Nachlass. (Akademieausgabe Bd. XIV u. XV.)," *Altpreußische Monatsschrift* 53 (1916), 96–150, and "Bemerkungen zu Kants handschriftlichem Nachlass. Teil II (Akademieausgabe Bd. XVI)," *Altpreußische Monatsschrift* 56 (1919), 72–100. See also Adickes's response in his *Vorwort* to Volume 17 of the Academy edition.

not tell us anything more about how he proceeded. Neither does he say that he altered and edited many of Kant's notes, although study of those notes indicates that this is so.[4] Finally, Jäsche does not say that he has drawn upon any materials other than Kant's notes. There is reason to believe that he had at his disposal at least one transcript of Kant's logic lectures, however, and that he used it. Benno Erdmann reported in 1880 that a transcript bearing the name Hoffmann agreed with the manual that Jäsche produced "on all essential points almost word-for-word." He even maintained that "Jäsche used Kant's personal copy [of Meier's *Excerpts*] only for revision of his own source, [which was] one or more of the transcripts of the lectures."[5] Since the transcript was apparently destroyed during World War II, further investigation of Erdmann's claim is now impossible. Nonetheless, the prevalent view among those who have worked on the logic materials is that Jäsche probably drew upon at least one such transcript, perhaps one that he had prepared, but more likely one or more of the many available in Königsberg.[6]

One cannot simply assume, then, that Jäsche's manual is a reliable statement of Kant's views. In addition to the points noted above, we have no evidence that Kant took any role in the preparation of the manual or that he reviewed it.[7] The manual must be interpreted with care, therefore, and it has to be appraised in light of other available materials. Indeed, to gain a reliable picture of Kant's views on logic one has to consult all of the available materials.

The materials in question fall into three categories. In the first are items that Kant himself prepared for publication: his 1762 essay on the syllogistic figures and his numerous remarks about logic in other published works, especially in the *Critique of Pure Reason*. These will be available in other volumes of the Cambridge edition. In the second category are the handwritten notes that Kant provided to Jäsche, which are published in Volume 16 of the Academy edition. Because of their often fragmentary character, as well as their dependence on each other and on

4 For a summary of questions about the authenticity of Jäsche's manual and some examples of differences between Jäsche's text and Kant's own notes, see Terry Boswell, "On the Textual Authenticity of Kant's *Logic*," *History and Philosophy of Logic* 9 (1988), 193–203.

5 In his review of Moritz Steckelmacher's *Die formale Logik Kants in ihren Beziehungen zur transcendentalen* (Breslau, 1879), in the *Göttingsche gelehrte Anzeigen*, 19 May 1880, pp. 609–34; quoted by Werner Stark in "Neue Kant-Logiken," in *Kant-Forschungen*, Bd. 1, ed. by R. Brandt and W. Stark, Hamburg: Felix Meiner, 1987, p. 127.

6 For discussion of this question see Werner Stark, "Neue Kant-Logiken," pp. 127–8, as well as notes 13, 21, 96, and 157.

7 In a declaration entitled *Nachricht an das Publicum, die bey Vollmer erschienene unrechtmäßige Ausgabe der physischen Geographie von Im. Kant betreffend* (*Declaration to the Public Concerning the Illegitimate Edition of the Physical Geography published by Vollmer*), 29 May 1801 (12:398), Kant states that he did authorize Jäsche to prepare the manual. He does not say that he has reviewed what Jäsche produced.

Meier's text, these notes do not lend themselves well to translation. In the third category, finally, are the texts stemming from Kant's logic lectures. These include the various surviving transcripts of his lectures. They also include the manual prepared by Jäsche, which, in light of its origin, might even be viewed as a privileged transcript, and which I will refer to not as Kant's *Logic* but as the *Jäsche Logic.* The texts contained in the present volume all belong to this third category, which I have titled, accordingly, *Kant's Logic Lectures*.

The texts included in this volume stem from four different periods of Kant's career. Part I contains the *Blomberg Logic*, which is based on Kant's logic lectures in the early 1770s. Part II includes the *Vienna Logic* and a portion of the *Hechsel Logic*, which are closely related texts stemming from lectures given around 1780, when the *Critique of Pure Reason* was being completed. Part III contains the *Dohna-Wundlacken Logic*, a transcript deriving from lectures given in the early 1790s. Part IV, finally, consists of the *Jäsche Logic*, published in 1800 and presumably derived from Kant's lectures late in his career.

Given the dates of lectures on which these texts are based, they provide a record of what Kant taught about logic over roughly the last twenty-five of the forty years that he lectured on the subject. The record, inevitably, is imperfect. At the same time, however, it is extensive and it seems to be largely reliable. One cannot look to it, in general, for precise, carefully worded formulations of fundamental points. One can glean from it a good knowledge of the topics that concerned Kant and of the views he took toward them. One can also find reasonably good evidence of how Kant's lectures related to Meier's text at various important stages of his career. The texts in question provide insight, accordingly, into how Kant's views on logic (and a variety of other subjects) developed. None of them, not even the *Jäsche Logic*, can be taken as a definitive statement of Kant's views. In the field of logic, however, there simply is no such definitive statement to be had. One has to take the full range of materials described, read as extensively as possible, and attempt to build a coherent picture of Kant's views through the accretion of detail.

Besides helping to illuminate Kant's views on logic, the texts translated here are also important in other ways. For one thing, as a glance at the lengthy Introduction to the *Jäsche Logic* makes evident, Kant spent a great deal of time in his logic lectures talking about matters which, on his own account, do not belong to logic proper. Indeed, one of Kant's principal, recurrent concerns was to distinguish logic from other subjects and to make plain its limits. He insisted that logic is to be understood only as a canon for the sciences, not as an organon. Logic provides us with norms to which all cognition ought to conform, he argued, and we may therefore speak of various "logical perfections" that cognition should have. We should not assume, however, as his rationalist predecessors had, that logic provides *all* the norms for cognition, and that it can therefore characterize *all* the perfections that a cognition ought to have. Because knowledge requires intuition, according to Kant, and because intuition is sensible, not intellectual, one must recognize that we cannot have knowledge of things, nor even frame distinct concepts of them, without relying on sensible intuition. One must distinguish, accordingly, between the analysis of concepts, which allows us to render distinct those concepts that are given, and the synthesis of intuition, which allows us to make or fabricate distinct concepts (e.g., in mathematical disciplines). Analysis rests on the principle of contradiction, which is a logical principle; in a sense, therefore, logic can tell us all that we need to know about how knowledge resting on such analysis is possible. Synthesis, on the other hand, which provides the basis for the perfection of cognition in mathematics and natural science, has to be treated in a discipline other than logic. That discipline is what Kant eventually came to call "critique." Not surprisingly, then, one finds in the transcripts of Kant's logic lectures a wealth of materials that shed light on Kant's dissatisfaction with rationalism and on his developing conception of a Critical theory of knowledge.

Besides logic and the theory of knowledge, Kant also touched on many other subjects within the framework of his logic lectures. There are discussions of the distinction between the logical and the aesthetic perfection of cognition, which frequently include remarks on aesthetics and on literature and the arts. There are discussions of the distinction between the theoretical and the practical, and these often lead to remarks on topics in moral philosophy. There are discussions, too, of history, including the history of science and of philosophy, as well as of politics, religion, and law. In these various discussions one sees Kant reflecting on the broad range of topics that fall within his Critical philosophy. One also sees him tailoring his lectures to his auditors, many of whom sought careers in government service or in the ministry.

In the transcripts of Kant's logic lectures, finally, one finds a portrait of Kant as thinker and as teacher, one that supplements what we know of him from the works that he himself prepared for publication. The portrait is often lively, for Kant lectured in a free, spontaneous way. He used his lectures, too, not merely to convey information and doctrine, but to explore problems, including those that were central to his ongoing philosophical development. He also spent a good deal of time developing examples and illustrations. The transcripts therefore contain much valuable detail. They help to show what Kant knew of mathematics and natural science, of literature and history, of the history of philosophy. They often clarify condensed, difficult passages in Kant's published works. They also shed light on Kant's views about education, both his official pronouncements and his actual practice, making plain, for instance, how important he considered it to think for oneself. Finally, these texts provide what the self-imposed restraints of the major Critical writings preclude, namely, examples of Kant's wit, and of his ability to give to ideas what he himself would call popular as well as scholastic perfection.

2. THE LOGIC LECTURES THEMSELVES

In May of 1755, after successfully defending his work *De Igne* (*Concerning Fire*), Kant received the degree of *Magister*, roughly equivalent to the present Ph.D. The following September he defended a dissertation *Principiorum primorum cognitionis metaphysicae nova delucidatio* (*A New Elucidation of the First Principles of Metaphysical Cognition*). With successful defense of the latter work, an equivalent to the present *Habilitationsschrift*, he attained the right to offer lectures at the University in Königsberg. His career as a lecturer began immediately thereafter, in the winter semester of 1755–6, with lectures on logic, metaphysics, and mathematics. It continued without interruption for forty years, through the summer semester of 1796.

Throughout these forty years Kant offered lectures on a wide variety of subjects. Besides the three just mentioned, these also included moral philosophy, natural law, philosophical encyclopedia, natural theology, pedagogy, anthropology, physical geography, theoretical physics, and mathematics. Kant devoted considerable time and energy to his lectures, too. During his years as a docent, he lectured an average of sixteen hours per week. Nor did he diminish his activity after his appointment as Professor of Logic and Metaphysics in August of 1770. In the winter semester of 1776–7, for example, he lectured at least twenty-six hours per week.[8] The subjects on which he lectured most frequently were metaphysics (at least thirty-four times), logic (at least thirty-two times), physical geography, which Kant was the first to treat as a free-standing discipline (at least thirty times). He also lectured frequently on anthropology (at least nineteen times), moral philosophy (at least twelve times), and natural law (at least twelve times).[9] As his students attest and as the published announcement of his lectures for the winter semester of 1765–6 makes plain (2:303–13), besides giving considerable time to his lectures, Kant also gave a good deal of thought to their purpose, and hence to both their form and their content.

[8] See Karl Vorländer, *Kants Leben*, 4th, improved edition, Hamburg: Felix Meiner, 1986, p. 42.

[9] The figures are taken from Emil Arnoldt, *Kritische Exkurse im Gebiet der Kantforschung* (*Critical Excursus in the Area of Kant Research*), originally published in 1894 but reprinted in an expanded version in Arnoldt's *Gesammelte Schriften*, Berlin: Bruno Cassirer. The figures given here are from the expanded version, in vol. IV (1908) and vol. V (1909). In each case the figure given is the number of times that Arnoldt was able to establish that the lectures in question were actually held. In many cases lectures were announced but not provably held. Arnoldt's work contains a vast amount of information about Kant's activity as lecturer, as well as about the origin and the composition of the *Critique of Pure Reason*.

Kant's lectures were well attended all through his career. Even before his first lecture he had a reputation as a penetrating thinker and a man of encyclopedic learning. According to his biographer Borowski, Kant's very first lecture therefore drew an overflow crowd.[10] Over the course of his career he frequently had a hundred or more auditors. For the logic lectures in particular he typically had eighty or more students, and even when the numbers were lowest – as in the summer semester of 1796 – he had roughly forty.[11] For the most part, too, his lectures drew high praise. Students, many of whom entered the university at the age of only fourteen or fifteen, and many of whom did not seek careers in academic life, found the logic lectures quite difficult.[12] Nonetheless, Kant is praised for the seriousness with which he approached his subject and for the care that he gave to making it intelligible. He is praised, too, for his wit and humor, and for the importance he gave to trying to teach his listeners to think for themselves. "Think for oneself – investigate on one's own – stand on one's own feet – these were expressions that repeatedly occurred in his lectures," says Borowski.[13] Only in the last years of his career, as his physical powers dwindled, does one find unfavorable comments on his lectures.[14]

Like all professors in Prussian universities at the time, Kant was required to take a published text as the basis for his lectures.[15] He did not follow his text slavishly, however, but lectured instead in a free, informal way. Kant often stated his own views directly. Sometimes, however, he stated the views of the author on whom he was lecturing. Sometimes, too, he sought simply to raise questions and develop problems. He developed many examples and illustrations, and often he reflected on these at length. Frequently, too, he mentioned relevant authors and referred to relevant facts. His aim throughout, as he often stated, was not to teach his students philosophy, but instead to show them how to philosophize. In reading the transcripts of his lectures, it is important to keep these facts in mind. One should be acquainted with the text on which the lectures are based. One should also remember that when Kant is reported as saying something, it is not always his own view he is stating.

[10] See the description in Ludwig Ernst Borowski, *Darstellung des Lebens und Charakters Immanuel Kants*, reprinted (along with other biographies by R. B. Jachmann and A. Ch. Wasianski) in *Immanuel Kant: Sein Leben in Darstellungen von Zeitgenossen*, Darmstadt: Wissenschaftliche Buchgesellschaft, 1968, p. 85.

[11] The figures come from the expanded version of Arnoldt's *Kritische Exkurse*, in vol. V, p. 332.

[12] Kant often recommended that students attend someone else's lectures on the subject first, e.g., those of Karl Ludwig Pörschke. See Vorländer, *Kants Leben*, p. 123.

[13] Borowski, op. cit., p. 86.

[14] See, for example, the comments of Fichte and Reusch, quoted in Vorländer, pp. 162–3.

[15] An exception to this rule was made only for Kant's lectures on physical geography, for which no suitable text was available.

Throughout the forty years that he lectured on logic Kant took as the basis for his lectures Georg Friedrich Meier's *Auszug aus der Vernunftlehre* (*Excerpts from the Doctrine of Reason*, Halle, 1752),[16] a shortened version of his *Vernunftlehre* (*The Doctrine of Reason*, published in Halle in the same year). In the beginning Kant seems to have followed Meier's text closely. Even in the early 1770s, as the *Blomberg Logic* shows, he still discussed virtually every paragraph of Meier's work. As the later transcripts make plain, however, he departed from Meier increasingly as the years went by. Indeed, students attending his logic lectures in the 1790s apparently thought it unnecessary to have a copy of Meier's text.[17]

3. THE TRANSCRIPTS OF KANT'S LOGIC LECTURES

Kant had a long career as a lecturer, and his lectures spanned a wide range of subjects. The students who attended his lectures, like all students of that period, depended on transcripts or notes as a basis for study. As Kant's reputation spread, there was also considerable interest in Kant's lectures among people who could not attend them, and this was another source of demand for such transcripts. Not surprisingly, therefore, numerous transcripts of Kant's lectures were prepared, especially of those – like the ones on logic – that were frequently offered and heavily subscribed. What is surprising, perhaps, is that we know so little about the transcripts that have survived. In most cases, even though the title page of a manuscript may bear a name, it is unclear who actually wrote the transcript. In most cases, too, though the title page may bear a date, it is far from obvious on which semester's lectures the transcript is based. None of the manuscripts we have appears to be an original transcript. At best they are fair copies. In most cases they appear to be further removed from the original lectures than that, being copies of fair copies, or copies of copies. In some cases a manuscript may derive from more than one original transcript, perhaps even from transcripts based on lectures in different semesters.

Just as it is often unclear who wrote the original transcript, so is it often unclear who actually prepared the copy that we have. Such copies were apparently produced widely in Königsberg, sometimes by students for their own use, often by students or others – professional copyists and

[16] Jäsche says that Kant had used Meier's text since 1765 (9:3), apparently meaning to imply that he had used a different text prior to that. In the published announcement of his lectures for the winter semester of 1765–6, Kant does say that he will use Meier's text (2:310). It appears that he also used it before 1765, however, and probably right from the outset.

[17] See the comments of von Purgstall, quoted by Kowalewski in his Introduction to *Die philosophischen Hauptvorlesungen Immanuel Kants*, 1924, p. 30.

possibly servants as well – for sale to third parties. Such, at least, is what the internal evidence in the manuscripts suggests. The mistakes made within the manuscripts are in many cases those associated with copying (e.g., repetition of entire lines). There are complex relations between the content of the various manuscripts, too, which seem to be explicable only on the assumption that the practice of copying was widespread. As Erich Adickes said after working extensively on a wide variety of transcripts, "one transcript *x* will go its own way in certain sections (a), will agree more or less word-for-word with transcript *y* in other sections (b), and with transcript *z* in yet other sections (c), while *y* and *z* altogether diverge from one another."[18]

According to recent research, there is evidence for the existence of more than twenty transcripts of Kant's logic lectures, of which eleven are known still to exist.[19] Of these eleven, seven were included in Volume 24 of the Academy edition, published in 1966 under the editorship of Gerhard Lehmann. Also included in that volume were previously published fragments of two manuscripts that apparently were destroyed in World War II (those bearing the names of Hintz and Hoffmann), so that the total number of transcripts in that volume comes to nine. Six of the nine are reasonably extensive. Of these I have selected three – the *Blomberg Logic*, the *Vienna Logic*, and the *Dohna-Wundlacken Logic* – for translation in this volume. As noted earlier, I also include a portion of the *Hechsel Logic*, which was not included in the Academy edition because it was not discovered until the early 1980s.

I decided at the outset to translate a small number of complete texts rather than excerpting passages from all the available texts. The principal reason for this decision was that it is always difficult to interpret excerpts, especially ones from transcripts such as these. One wants the entire text so that one can familiarize oneself with the writer's style, with the care and depth that are typical of the text, with what is said about other issues, etc. But other reasons also played a role in my decision. I wanted to present as full a picture as possible of Kant's views on logic at different stages of his career, and I wanted to provide texts that do not simply present Kant's views on logic but also show the character of his lectures.

Part I of this volume contains the *Blomberg Logic*, which is apparently based on lectures given early in the 1770s. Internal evidence – a quotation from Kant's Inaugural Dissertation of 1770, and the mention of other works published as late as 1770 – makes it plain that the text itself cannot be earlier than this. The lectures on which the text is based may perhaps be somewhat earlier, though the developed state of Kant's views

[18] Erich Adickes, *Untersuchungen zu Kants physischer Geographie* (*Investigations into Kant's Physical Geography*), Tübingen, Verlag von J. C. B. Mohr [Paul Siebeck], 1911), p. 35.
[19] Werner Stark, "Neue Kant-Logiken," in *Kant-Forschungen*, pp. 123–64.

suggests that they were not much earlier. The title page bears the name of H. U. v. Blomberg. It seems clear, however, that the person in question – Heinrich Ulrich Freiherr von Blomberg (1745–1813) – could not have transcribed the lectures himself, since he had completed his studies in Königsberg by 1764. It is not clear who actually wrote the manuscript, nor how it came into Blomberg's possession.[20] In any case, the transcript gives a very thorough account of Kant's lectures, divided into sections that are labeled so as to indicate the paragraph of Meier's text that is under discussion at each point. The transcript does not present as lively a portrait of Kant's lectures as does the *Philippi Logic*, which likewise stems from the early 1770s. It is also repetitious and wordy, especially in the section on prejudices. What would be flaws in a work prepared for publication are sometimes advantages in a transcript, however. The coverage of topics is thorough. Also, the repetitions frequently provide evidence for the correctness of various formulations, and they help with the interpretation of problematic passages. In addition, the Blomberg transcript is written for the most part in sentences that are complete, or ones that at least require little in the way of conjecture, whereas the *Philippi Logic* is more often telegraphic.

Part II contains the *Vienna Logic* and a portion of the *Hechsel Logic*, both based on lectures in the early 1780s, when the *Critique of Pure Reason* was being readied for publication. The *Vienna Logic* does not bear the name of any individual. The title page describes it as "written by a society of auditors" who remain unknown to us. Lehmann gave the transcript its name simply because the manuscript was located, then as now, in the library of the University of Vienna. It is a reasonably extensive transcript, even though it breaks off before the completion of the lectures. It offers a great deal of valuable material related to the *Critique of Pure Reason* – more than is provided, for example, by the *Pölitz Logic*, which is based on lectures from the same period.

Lehmann argued, on the basis of minimal internal evidence, that the *Vienna Logic* is based on lectures given in the mid-1790s, at the very end of Kant's activity as a lecturer. More recent research by Tillmann Pinder, which broadens the range of evidence brought to bear on the question, and which also distinguishes carefully between the dating of the manuscript and the dating of the lectures from which the manuscript derives, shows Lehmann's view to be incorrect.[21] What allows Pinder to draw this conclusion is that the *Vienna Logic* belongs to a group of texts – including the *Hechsel Logic*, the *Pölitz Logic* (24:497–602), and the *Hoffmann Logic* (24:944–52) – which are related to one another in the complex ways suggested above. In

[20] See Lehmann's introduction to Vol. 24 (24:976–7).

[21] Tillmann Pinder, "Zu Kants Logik-Vorlesung um 1780, anläßlich einer neu aufgefundenen Nachschrift," in *Kant-Forschungen*, Bd. 1., pp. 79–114.

several cases, portions of one text are either identical with, or very similar to, corresponding portions of another. Given these links between the texts, and given that for some of the transcripts there is evidence dating the lectures on which they are based, Pinder was able to build a convincing case that all four transcripts derive from lectures given "around 1780." His research also yields an added benefit. He established that the second half of the *Hechsel Logic* was apparently identical, word for word, with the second half of the *Vienna Logic*. The *Vienna Logic*, however, breaks off in the midst of Kant's treatment of judgment, and a sizeable portion of it is therefore missing.[22] Given its relation to the *Hechsel Logic*, however, one can reasonably surmise that the last third of the Hechsel text was virtually identical with the missing section of the *Vienna Logic*. One can use the Hechsel text, accordingly, to supplement the *Vienna Logic*, as I do here in Part II.

Part III contains the *Dohna-Wundlacken Logic*, which according to its title page is based on Kant's logic lectures in the summer semester of 1792. The manuscript itself does not bear any name. According to Kowalewski, however, who published an edition of the text in 1924,[23] it was prepared by the Count Heinrich Ludwig Adolph Dohna (1777–1843), who came to Königsberg in the fall of 1791 and attended Kant's logic lectures the following summer. It seems clear that the logic transcript was actually in Dohna's possession. Apparently Dohna did not himself write the manuscript, however, and it is uncertain who did.[24] In any case, the transcript seems plainly to be based on lectures in the early 1790s. Though relatively brief, it is condensed in style and reasonably thorough. As printed in the Academy edition, which was based entirely on Kowalewski's edition, the text appears to be divided into sections, each of which is based on a different lecture, with many of the sections even being dated. In fact, this is illusory. The manuscript is written as a continuous text. The dates given, ostensibly as the dates of the various lectures on which the text is based, appear in the manuscript only as marginal notes. The division into sections occurred when Kowalewski inserted the dates and other notes into the body of the text. One cannot assume that the text provides a lecture-by-lecture transcript of what Kant said, therefore. Nonetheless, it provides a condensed, clear representation of Kant's lectures, if not in the summer of 1792, then probably in the early 1790s.

[22] Actually, the manuscript breaks off twice, once at 24:937, toward the end of the discussion of judgments, and a second time shortly thereafter (24:940), in the midst of the discussion of immediate inferences. This last segment is in a different hand and in a very abbreviated style. I omit it, providing instead the corresponding section of the *Hechsel Logic*.

[23] A. Kowalewski, *Die philosophischen Hauptvorlesungen Immanuel Kants* (*Immanuel Kant's Principal Lectures in Philosophy*), 1924. Also included in this volume are two further transcripts, one of Kant's anthropology lectures, one of his metaphysics lectures.

[24] This is the view of Werner Stark of the Kant Archive in Marburg. See also Stark, "Neue Kant-Logiken," note 144. The Kant Archive has a microfilm of the Dohna manuscript, to which Lehmann did not have access as he prepared Volume 24.

Part IV, finally, contains the manual that Jäsche published in 1800. Given what has been said of the origin of this text, it should be apparent that we cannot trace it to lectures given in any one semester. It is reasonable to think of it, nonetheless, as representative of Kant's views toward the end of his career.

4. NOTES ON THE TRANSLATIONS

The translations included in this volume are all based on critical editions that have been or soon will be published. In the case of the *Hechsel Logic*, my translation is based entirely on the edition prepared by Tillmann Pinder, to be published by Felix Meiner.[25] For all the other texts, I have taken the Academy edition as my basis. I have made use, however, of other sources, including the relevant volumes of Norbert Hinske's *Kant-Index*[26] and microfilms and photocopies of the manuscripts. Details may be found below.

My principal aim in translating these texts has been to render them as literally as possible, so that the English reader will have a reliable representation of what the German text says, and a good feel for what that text is like. As far as possible, I have translated technical terms by single English words. (Glossaries are provided in the Appendix.) This often results in ungainly English. To take a conspicuous example, it is natural to translate the German term *Erkenntnis* sometimes as "knowledge," sometimes as "cognition," sometimes even as "branch of knowledge." It is natural, similarly, to translate *erkennen* sometimes as "to know," sometimes as "to cognize," sometimes as "to recognize." In the interest of literalness I have translated these terms consistently as "cognition" and "to cognize." The English is often ungainly, but the reader will know what term is present in the German text, and the connections between the various passages in which Kant uses these terms will therefore be evident.

In the interest of literalness I have also tried to avoid interpreting as I translate. This is a goal that can only be approached, of course, never completely attained. Still, where the text is ambiguous, unclear, or awkward in German, I have tried to render it that way in English. I make exceptions only when interpretation is needed in order to render the text intelligible or to establish a clear meaning in English. In such cases I generally indicate – by using square brackets to mark interpolations and alterations, or by quoting the German text in the footnotes – the interpretive aspect of the translation. When I translate a technical term in a

[25] I was able to obtain a copy of Pinder's edition with the assistance of the Kant Archive in Marburg.

[26] Norbert Hinske, *Kant-Index, Band 2: Stellenindex und Konkordanz zu "Immanuel Kant's Logik" (Jäsche-Logik)*, Frommann-Holzboog: Stuttgart-Bad Cannstatt, 1986, and *Band 3.1: Stellenindex zur "Logik Blomberg,"* 1989.

nonstandard way, or use a technical term in English to translate something other than its standard counterpart in German, this is likewise indicated in the footnotes. (Often, for instance, *Kenntnis* is written in the manuscripts when *Erkenntnis* is plainly meant.)

For the most part, the transcripts translated here consist of complete, grammatical sentences or reasonable approximations thereto. Punctuation and capitalization are frequently faulty, however. In general, where such flaws will not hinder understanding I have left them in the text, but there are two broad exceptions: First, many sentences in the manuscripts, especially in the *Blomberg Logic,* do not begin with initial capitals; in the translation, such sentences have been capitalized to improve readability. Second, many of the lists in the manuscripts are numbered or lettered in irregular ways; the numbering or lettering, and the punctuation, have been regularized. Where other alterations were needed to make the text intelligible, or to render it clearly in English, I have marked them by putting them in square brackets. I could find no sensible way to reproduce the delightful vagaries of eighteenth-century German orthography. The quotation of terms and phrases in the footnotes will give the reader some idea of the irregularities present in the texts, however.

One problem that confronts the translator, especially in the case of the transcripts, is how to decide whether a word in the text is regarded by the author as German or as foreign. In the case of printed texts like the *Jäsche Logic,* German words are characteristically printed in Fraktur, while words regarded as foreign are set in Roman type. In the case of handwritten texts there is a similar distinction between German script and Roman script. The use of Roman letters is quite irregular, however, especially in the handwritten texts, and it does not always correlate with whether a word is regarded by the author as German or as foreign. Frequently, for example, the stem of a word is written in Roman letters, but the ending is German and may be written in German script. In such cases the word is plainly being treated as though it were German. For reasons like these Erich Adickes, in editing Kant's handwritten materials for the Academy edition, did not attempt to reproduce the differences between the two scripts. Instead, he classified words as foreign (and printed them in Roman type) when their endings indicated that they were being treated as such. When words of foreign origin had German endings, Adickes treated them as German words (and printed them in Fraktur).[27]

I have adopted Adickes's principle. Words whose endings indicate that they were regarded as German are translated into English and printed here in regular type. Words whose endings indicate that they were regarded as foreign are left in the original language and are printed here in italics. Not surprisingly, most such words are Latin. Where their meaning

[27] In Volume 24 Lehmann prints all words in Roman type.

is plain, either from context or because they have obvious cognates in English, I leave them untranslated. Otherwise I provide translations in the footnotes. For the most part I have corrected and standardized the spelling of Latin terms, though I have left some common variants in spelling (e.g., the use of "j" for "i"). I have also followed the now-usual convention of capitalizing the initial words of Latin sentences, and of putting free-standing Latin nouns in the nominative case. (When embedded in a German sentence such nouns are declined.)

Guidelines developed for the Cambridge edition call for the use of italics *both* to indicate that a term is foreign (non-German in the original, non-English in the translation) *and* to indicate emphasis. For texts like the ones in this volume, where foreign terms – especially Latin – are used extensively, this has required the adoption of two special conventions. First, since all foreign terms are in italics, a convention is needed to indicate which of them were emphasized in the original text. Letter spacing is used for that purpose. (Thus "*p r i n c i p i u m*" indicates that the Latin term was emphasized in the original, while "*principium*" indicates that it was not.) Second, since several foreign terms – most prominently Latin adverbs like "*subjective*" and "*absolute,*" but also Latin nouns like "*species*" and "*nexus*" – have direct English cognates, a convention is required to indicate that such terms are not emphasized English terms (translating emphasized German), but instead are foreign, both in the original text and in this volume. A subscripted letter – "L" for Latin, "F" for the few such French terms that occur – is used where necessary to mark such terms as foreign. (I omit subscripts in the case of "*a priori*" and "*a posteriori,*" which are always regarded as Latin in the texts, and wherever context makes it clear that the term is regarded as foreign.)

On other matters I follow the general guidelines for the Cambridge edition. I attempt to preserve the appearance of the text on the page, including of course the paragraph structure. I also preserve sentence structure when possible, though I place more importance on trying to convey the sense of a sentence accurately than on preserving its structure. Emphasis in the texts (indicated by spaced type in printed German texts and by underlining in manuscripts) is shown by italics, as indicated above. Dark-letter type is reproduced with boldface. Explanatory notes are printed at the end of the volume. Notes on the text – translations of foreign terms, quotations of the text, indications of variations between the edition and the manuscript – are printed at the bottom of the page as footnotes.[28]

One question that faces the translator of materials on Kant's logic is

[28] Since the distinction between German words and foreign words rests on Adickes's interpretive principle, I use only regular type – no italic – in the quotations of the text that appear in the footnotes. Where there is emphasis in the original text, however, I indicate this in quotations from that text by using italics.

how to translate the terms *Grund*, *Folge*, and *Konsequenz*. I translate the first consistently as "ground," even though this often produces ungainly English, and the second as "consequence." To mark the distinction between the second term and the third, I translate *Konsequenz* with the Latin term *consequentia*. (One could translate *Konsequenz* as "consequence" and *Folge* as "consequent," but then one would either have to translate *Folge* as "consequent" in all contexts, or translate it sometimes as "consequent" and sometimes as "consequence." Neither alternative is appealing.)

Another characteristic of the transcripts, especially of the Blomberg text, is that key terms are often followed by one or more synonyms, usually in Latin. Where such synonyms can be rendered without redundancy I leave them in the text. Where this is impossible, I translate the entire group of synonymous terms by a single English word, but then indicate in the footnotes what words are actually in the text. Such passages are especially interesting for the light that they shed on the relations between Kant's Latin, which was essentially that of the rationalist tradition, and his German.

As far as the explanatory notes at the end of the volume are concerned, I have taken a minimalist approach. In those passages devoted to the history of philosophy or of logic I have made sure that names are given in a standard English spelling, so that readers can readily find more information about the figures mentioned. For seventeenth- and eighteenth-century figures who are mentioned in the text but who may not be familiar to Anglo-American readers, I have tried to provide dates of birth and death and in some cases a small amount of information. For references to books published in these two centuries I have tried to provide the place and date of publication. In a few cases where the text is especially puzzling or problematic, or where references are quite obscure, I have provided explanatory notes.

A few additional comments are needed concerning individual texts:

(I) My translation of the *Blomberg Logic* is based on the Academy edition (24:7–301), and the page numbers in the margins are those of this edition. I have made heavy use, however, of Volume 3.1 of Hinske's *Kant-Index* (referred to in the footnotes simply as "KI"). Where Hinske reports significant differences between the Academy edition ("Ak") and the manuscript ("MS"), I note these differences in the footnotes. For many passages Hinske suggests readings of the manuscript different from those of the Academy edition, and for many problematic passages he offers conjectures as to how they might be read. I have accepted many of his suggestions, and in each case I indicate this in the footnotes. Also indicated in the footnotes are corrections and conjectures of my own.

(II) My translation of the *Vienna Logic* is also based on the Academy edition (24:787–940), whose pagination I provide in the margins. The volume of Hinske's *Kant-Index* that deals with the *Vienna Logic* has unfortunately not been published yet. Hinske has given me a brief list of documented errors and of conjectures, however, and where I make use of this list I indicate this in the notes. For passages that seemed to me dubious, I compared the Academy edition with a microfilm of the manuscript at the Kant Archive in Marburg. In almost all cases the Academy edition proved correct – unsurprisingly, perhaps, since the manuscript is quite legible. The few significant differences I discovered are indicated in footnotes. For numerous passages I have had to conjecture alternative readings in order to make sense of the text. These conjectures are also indicated in the notes.

In translating the *Hechsel Logic* I have relied entirely on the soon-to-be-published critical edition by Tillmann Pinder. I have not seen the manuscript or a copy of it. The page numbers I provide in the margins are not those of Pinder's edition, however, which is not yet in print, but of the original manuscript. Hechsel's text is filled with errors of spelling and grammar, and with many obvious mistakes and incoherencies as well. I have relied heavily on Pinder's corrections and conjectures, as the footnotes to my translation will show. I have not cited all the errors noted by Pinder, however; I omit those that deal merely with orthographic variation, for example. Where Pinder notes an error or makes a conjecture that affects the meaning of the text, however, and I follow him, I note this in the footnotes.

(III) When the Academy edition was prepared, Lehmann did not have access to the original manuscript of the *Dohna-Wundlacken Logic* or to a copy of it. Instead, he worked entirely from Kowalewski's edition. Since the Academy edition (24:676–784) is far more readily available today than Kowalewski's is, I have based my translation on it and have provided the page numbers of that edition in the margins. I have compared the Academy edition with the Kowalewski edition (referred to in the footnotes as "Ko"), however. I have also had the benefit of several suggestions from Norbert Hinske. Finally, for passages that seemed dubious, I compared the Academy edition with a microfilm of the manuscript at the Kant Archive in Marburg. Although the script is difficult to read, there were surprisingly few cases where the Academy edition was mistaken or where Lehmann's reading of difficult passages seemed wrong. There are several cases, however, where I have had to conjecture a reading of the text in order to make sense of it. All corrections and conjectures are indicated in the footnotes, as are also the instances I have discovered where the Academy edition differs from the manuscript, or from Kowalewski's edition, or both.

(IV) In the case of the *Jäsche Logic*, the textual problems are mercifully few. The first edition was published in Königsberg in 1800 by Friedrich Nicolovius. The text as printed was in reasonably good shape, as indicated by the fact that a published list of printer's errors was quite brief. Max

Heinze, who edited the text for Volume 9 of the Academy edition, modernized the punctuation and spelling. Heinze also heeded the list of printer's errors, though only for 9:60 ff., since he obtained the list only after typesetting was already under way. I have taken Heinze's edition (9:1–150) as the basis for my translation, and I provide the page numbers of that edition in the margins. I have made use of Volume 2 of Hinske's *Kant-Index* (referred to in the footnotes simply as "KI"), which contains the published printer's errors, and which also notes a few mistakes in the Academy edition. I have also made a partial comparison of the Academy edition with a first edition of the text, verifying mistakes noted by Hinske, and looking especially for differences in emphasis. Where my translation is based on a reading that deviates from the Academy edition this is indicated in the footnotes.

The *Jäsche Logic* has been translated into English three times before.[29] One translation, which I have not seen, was done by John Richardson in 1819. A second, of the Introduction only, was done by Thomas Kingsmill Abbott in 1885.[30] A third, of the entire work, was done by Robert Hartman and Wolfgang Schwarz in 1974.[31] The latter two translations are readily available. Abbott's translation, though not bad, is so loose and so old-fashioned in its terminology that I have not made any use of it. The translation by Hartman and Schwarz is far better. I place less importance than they do on maintaining sentence structure, more on trying to convey the sense of each sentence. I differ with them, too, on the best translations for various technical terms. I consider it important, finally, to have a translation of the *Jäsche Logic* that is consistent with those of the various transcripts included here.

The Appendixes contain German–English and English–German glossaries. They also include a concordance of the contents of Meier's text, Kant's handwritten reflections on that text, and the *Jäsche Logic*. This concordance is derived from the table of contents that Adickes developed for Volume 16 (16:xi–xiv) and from correlations between Kant's reflections and the *Jäsche Logic* that Adickes identified and included in the text of Volume 16 (after the headings for individual sections). Also included in the Appendix is a concordance indicating how the transcripts translated here correlate with the text of Meier's *Excerpts from the Doctrine of Reason*. Except for the information about the *Hechsel Logic*, which I have abstracted from Pinder's edition of the text, this concordance is derived from the one provided by Lehmann for Volume 24 of the Academy edition (24:1085–98).

[29] See Boswell, "On the Textual Authenticity of Kant's *Logic*," p. 193.

[30] *Kant's Introduction to Logic and His Essay on the Mistaken Subtilty of the Four Figures*, London: Longmans, Green, 1885 (reprinted New York: Philosophical Library, 1963).

[31] *Immanuel Kant: Logic*, Indianapolis: Bobbs-Merrill, 1974.

PART I

The Blomberg logic

Collegium of Professor Kant
concerning Meier's
Excerpts from the Doctrine of Reason

transcribed
by H. U. v. Blomberg

Introduction to the doctrine of reason according to the thoughts of Professor Kant

All our cognitions are acquired

1. through experience
2. through our own practice and
3. through instruction.

From learning arises the spirit of imitation.[a] This learning happens in childhood. There is of course a certain skill that one brings about for oneself through imitation; but he who imitates shows the least degree of capacity.

The first origin of our cognitions[b] is empirical. Many things arise through imitation and many cognitions through imitation.[c]

We see what others have shown us and we imitate.

The 2nd kind is the practice of our acquired skill. Through frequent employment[d] of our insights and talents we attain a greater cognition and new insights, and these can be increased still further by means of our own experience.

The last thing is to attain a cognition through universal rules[;] these are derived from reason.

The first method of attaining cognitions must be abandoned just as soon as the capacities achieve a faculty of cultivating[e] themselves. One must seek to think for oneself, to judge for oneself.

This kind of practice with our capacities demands the very same degree, even if one thinks in opposition to what others have thought.

The natural understanding has its own laws, according to which alone it can proceed. These are called natural laws.

Besides natural laws there are also precepts for the artificial[f] understanding. The first is to proceed completely without laws, and to make use

[a] "Nachahmung."
[b] "Kenntniße."
[c] "Imitation."
[d] "Ausübungen."
[e] "excoliren."
[f] "gekünstelten."

neither of natural [laws][g] nor of precepts. If, next, one wants to cultivate 17 one's own reason, one first makes use of the natural laws of reason. This happens when one thinks often, or through practice or frequent attempts, when one considers an object according to both particular and universal laws.

The 2nd use of the understanding takes place according to artificial[h] rules, or according to precepts, and from this arises the artificial understanding.

One only learns to walk by first being led[;] so too does one learn to think by first of all imitating[;] after that one begins to use his feet himself and alone. Thus we begin to judge for ourselves and to use our understanding through frequent and repeated attempts to judge for ourselves.

The merely natural laws are cultivated by means of experience, but for the artificial use I have to have other rules. One must first imitate[,] then practice by oneself, and finally one acquires precepts.

Through imitation we can acquire crafts, but through precepts a science. Versification can be compared, as it were, with crafts.

We learn to judge finely[i] by rules, but to write poetry finely[j] through frequent practice.

All cognition takes place according to rules: These are either merely natural or artificial.

Natural rules concern the common and healthy understanding and healthy reason.

The artificial rules are the rules of learnedness. We acquire their first use not by imitation but by frequent use of our reason[;] the common understanding is thereby cultivated.

The common use of the understanding is that with objects of experience.

The artificial [use] is that according to precepts and rules.

People talk much now about the healthy understanding[;] they prize it too highly. Some have believed that healthy reason differs from the sciences merely in degree. But this gives no distinct boundary where one stops and the other begins. Healthy reason and learnedness are distinct not merely in degree but also in species[;] there are 2 particular sources of 18 each kind.

A learned man is one whose learnedness is not grounded on common experience. According to the common mode of speech, understanding is called a common understanding insofar as it is found in most in the same degree.

It is a healthy understanding, however, when it is correct. It is not healthy by degrees; rather, correctness is when the understanding and

[g] Ak, "Natürlichen Gesetze"; MS, "Natürlichen" (KI, lxvi).

[h] "künstlichen."

[i] "Schön zu urtheilen."

[j] "schön zu dichten."

reason judge according to laws that agree with experience. But when there are no other *principia* besides experience[,][k] then a healthy reason still remains a common reason. There is also an instructed understanding, which could not have been acquired through common experience; and this is a science. There is a *logica* of the common understanding and of healthy reason and a *logica* of learnedness. It serves to enrich the common and healthy understanding, and to cultivate this healthy reason for learnedness.

The *logica* of healthy reason will have one's own experience as its *principium* and thus be empirical; it will not contain the rules for how we ought to think but rather will indicate the rules according to which we commonly think. There are 2 sorts of rules[:] A.) the rules according to which one proceeds[;] these are laws of appearance, and *subjective*[.][l] These subjective laws are the laws of reason, according to which it commonly proceeds in judging and thinking. B.) *Objective* laws, according to which the understanding ought to proceed. These are called *dogmata*$_{L}$.

Subjective laws bring about errors. One extends healthy reason by attending to the rules according to which the understanding ought to proceed.

We extend objective laws through doctrines, but to cultivate healthy reason one need not give any universal rules or precepts; learned reason is not grounded on empirical *principia*.

Common understanding is the understanding for judging according to laws of experience; common reason, however, [is] reason by which we infer according to the laws of experience. This reason is called common, then, because it is the least degree, with all objects that come before us. On the occasion of experience we always have a measuring stick by which we compare sizes with one another. We proceed thus when we want to find the average size; we take that, namely, of which we want to find the average size, e.g., man[;] we reckon every man's size according to the measuring stick, add these together, divide it by the number of men whom we have ever[m] seen in our lives[;] from this the average size then emerges, which is adequate for every man. Thus too is the average size of the understanding elicited from the understanding with which one is acquainted through common experience. The common understanding is the measure. The common and healthy understanding is a small but correct understanding, and its cognition has great usefulness. In an area of farmers there are not nearly as many errors as in a district of learned men that is just as large. For the farmer always goes by the guiding thread of experience[;] he judges about little, but judges correctly about that

19

[k] Ak, "sind."; MS, "sind" (KI, lxvi).
[l] Ak, "*Subjectiv.*"; MS, "*Subjectiv*" (KI, lxvi).
[m] Reading "jemahls" for "niemahls," with Hinske (KI, lxxiii).

little. The employment of common and healthy reason is also easy[;] all cognition from experience has more life, more that is intuitive, than that which has arisen from universal concepts. The *first advantage* of common reason is *simplicity*. The 2nd is *correctness*. The 3rd *usefulness*. The 4th *ease* and the 5th *clarity* and *liveliness*. For cognitions arise with the light with which empirical representations are endowed. Accordingly, healthy reason will suffice for belles lettres.[n]

Taste really requires no learnedness at all to be quite perfect. In fact, learned taste is false, spoiled taste.

What is beautiful must please universally and please everyone. For passing judgment on beauty, experience is required, and the judgment of the beautiful and the ugly is made in consequence of common and healthy reason. Common and healthy reason lies at the basis of all learnedness; it becomes ridiculous if it is not grafted onto this stem. In history we do not need common understanding[;] so is it, too, with many mathematical propositions. But in the philosophical and all other sciences, where mere imitation of another understanding is not sufficient, but rather the spirit of genius itself is necessary, the common understanding is indispensable.

The use of all the cognitions of the learned, and their application, is
20 possible only through healthy reason. Someone can be a learned man without a healthy understanding, to be sure, but this is a ridiculous pedant. All learnedness is either *historical* or *rational*. Cognition which is derived from common reason as regards its form, but from common experience as regards its matter, is *historical*. Historical learnedness includes history, geography, etc. A historically learned man can also make reflections, but these belong then to rational learnedness. The matter in rational learnedness can also be grasped by common reason and experience. But the form is wholly different. Men find more amusement in the faculty of being able to give themselves a pleasure than in the pleasure itself. When I draw[o] the particular from the universal I need understanding, but when I infer the universal from particular cases, then I need another method. The understanding cognizes everything *a priori*, healthy reason *a posteriori*. We have cognitions that are empirical, since we ascend from below, and in rational ones we descend from above. The logic that is an organon of rational learnedness does not concern historical but rational cognitions. The logic that is an organon can prescribe rules to a learnedness that is already present, and then it is called *logica critica*, or it can prescribe rules through which one can achieve learnedness, and then it is called *logica dogmatica*[.] All logics are not dogmatic but critical. Philosophy involves more genius than imitation.

The whole of nature moves according to rules[;] thus water moves

[n] "schönen Wissenschaften."
[o] "abziehe."

according to hydraulic rules, nature operates according to rules, even inconstant weather has its certain rules, although we may not notice them. Animals move according to rules of which they often are not at all conscious. Man acts according to rules and in particular makes use of the understanding according to certain propositions and rules. How often do men act according to rules, too, without being conscious of them? E.g., they speak their mother tongue. Employment of our powers often occurs without our being conscious of it, and this is (1.) because this already lies in our nature. (2.) It often occurs by imitation, by means of an example which we imitate, in order gradually to make use of our understanding as we see that others make use of it. (3.) One's own use. Our own practice brings us to the skill to use the understanding without being conscious of its rules. 21

As man learns to walk, so does he also learn to think. This understanding thus educated[p] [is called] *sens commun.*[q] When it is correct it is called the healthy understanding, because the skill of using it is subjected to a common use. The frequent use of our understanding among the objects of experience finally makes us fit to use it correctly. It can become correct, then, through mere practice and use. The healthy understanding should be common[;] hence the understanding that goes further than its senses teach it in experience is not common[;] that would be the learned use of the understanding. The healthy understanding is concerned with experience, then; it must proceed according to rules of which it is itself not conscious.[r] Thus it is not undisciplined[;] it is only that it does not know these rules *in abstracto* but rather *in concreto*. Some *occupations* involve a healthy, alert understanding, then.

The causes of things do not strike the senses as much as their effects do. Hence one must also be acquainted with the rules according to which one can use the healthy understanding. In many cases one cannot rely on his own practice; but the only instructor of the common understanding is experience. First of all, then, the healthy understanding and healthy reason are greatly needed, then, to provide a basis for all abstract higher cognitions[;] we commonly oppose healthy reason to the affected learnedness of proud erudition. But this will not do, for learnedness always presupposes the healthy understanding, [as] art does nature. They are *distinctae*, to be sure, but not *oppositae*. It has become the fashion, however, to praise the healthy understanding to the detriment of the honor of the sciences. It is of course no criticism if one says that someone lacks science, but if someone does not have a healthy understanding he is a natural minor, a child. At the least, then, we demand of everyone healthy understanding.

[p] "gebildete."

[q] Ak, "Sens commun; MS, "*Sens commun*" (KI, lxvi).

[r] Reading "nicht selbst bewußt" for "selbst bewußt," with Hinske (KI, lxxiii).

There are certain *average types* of perfections[;] e.g., the beauty of a woman is, as it were, a merit, ugliness offends, but tolerable looks are an average thing, which one expects of people, as it were. People are distinguished by beauty and ugliness in particular. So is it too with people's size. 22 Our eyes form a certain *idea* of the average, and what is extraordinary, people in most cases agree on this. Thus one speaks, e.g., of a man's wealth. The average between riches and poverty we call *being well-off*[.] In all our concepts, then, we make the average a measuring stick. So too is the healthy understanding the average among people's capacities. Healthy reason is not supposed to go a step further than experience leads it. The healthy understanding does not cognize or judge *in abstracto* but *in concreto*[;] it draws its judgments from experience. However it can also cognize universally[,] *a priori*[,] and *in abstracto* much that experience teaches us. The healthy understanding is thus the faculty of judging correctly *in concreto*. Often quite reasonable people cannot judge at all *in abstracto*, since just as often they think *in concreto*. So it is in moral cases, e.g., by means of an example in a case one cognizes things *in concreto*. The understanding that can judge *in abstracto* is called the more refined, scientific understanding. The natural faculty of judging is the understanding, the faculty of inferring is reason. Through experience one becomes clever but not learned. Cleverness does not consist in science[;] one can be and become clever without any learnedness. The healthy understanding and reason show their value especially in *praxis*$_{L}$. No science can in the least replace[s] or compensate for a certain lack of the healthy understanding and its application *in concreto*, although it can well replace much else. Our universal judgments alone cannot help us. With all rules I have to know (1.)[t] whether they may be applied to the case.

(2.) As to how I am to apply them here, there can be very learned people lacking all healthy understanding. In the use of the understanding there is thus something that nature has reserved for genius, as it were, and which no art can replace.

Through an excess of learnedness people often become all the more absurd and completely unfit for judging *in concreto*. The healthy understanding, which is small but correct, involves (1.) *simplicity*. It remains on the ground[u] of experience and does not love chimerical ideals. This very simplicity makes the understanding all the more correct, certain, and reliable than science. An academy of sciences in Paris concocts 1000 23 times more errors than a village full of farmers. (2.) Its cognitions are *intuitive* through examples and instances. It represents for us the *objecta in natura*, while the more refined understanding only shows the shadows of

[s] Reading "im geringsten ersezen" for "im geringsten nicht ersezen."

[t] Reading "wißen, 1: ob" for "wißen, ob," with Hinske (KI, lxxiii).

[u] "an dem boden."

things. The healthy understanding is the *controleur*[v] of learnedness. The common healthy understanding grows without instruction. Thus are common, living languages distinguished from learned, dead languages.

To state universal rules by which one may pass judgment on the infallibility of a witness involves more than simply common and healthy understanding[;] it involves art and learnedness. Languages were there before their grammars, speakers before rhetoric, poets before poesy.

If I have universal cognitions[w] of the understanding, and universal rules for it, too, then I still must have in addition understanding, in order to judge whether this or that actually stands under this rule or not. All doctrine in the whole world is just a universal complex[x] of rules for using the powers of the understanding, but there still has to be[y] an understanding, which only nature can give. Persons who possess learnedness but lack a healthy understanding are far more absurd than the wholly ignorant. From this arises *pedantry*, however. An obstinate dummy cannot be called a pedant. Learnedness must always be there, but the ability to apply cognized universal rules to particular cases *in concreto* must be lacking. Although a pedant, with all his science, still possesses a kind of dumbness, of course. So is it with all making of witty observations in society[,] even with compliment-making in accordance with universal precepts. The Chinese have books of compliments[.] Universal rules always bear witness to the weakness of our understanding. Like a beginner's lexicon of a language[.] There is much regularity without consciousness of the rules; so is it with the healthy understanding. But the use of the understanding in accordance with rules of which one is conscious is called *science*. There are cases where someone without science can go further than someone else with science, but also where the greatest healthy understanding cannot go as far as science alone. Thus in mathematics, surveying, one cannot get along by means of the mere understanding[;] there must always be some science there. So is it with the apothecary's art, too. To pass judgment on morality, on right and wrong,[z] on the other hand, no science or learnedness is needed. Otherwise the human race would be very imperfect. Here the common understanding is the judge of science. 24

In all sciences a precept serves to develop our capacities for all cases. But with all instruction in art it is always necessarily left to the subject's understanding whether, and to what degree, these universal precepts are applied in individual cases. Thus one cannot possibly become clever in accordance with universally valid rules and precepts, since cleverness

[v] French: supervisor, controller.

[w] "Kenntniße."

[x] "ein allgemeiner Inbegriff."

[y] Ak, "so muß"; MS, "es muß" (KI, lxvi).

[z] "des Rechts und Unrechts."

really consists in being able to subsume individual cases in common life under the universal rules of such life.

The discipline that contains the rules of the good use of the understanding and of reason in general is called *logica.* It does not determine any individual cases[.] In all other sciences, logic is applied. Logic is related to the whole use of the understanding just as *grammatica* is to a language. Grammar always has a source for the correctness of its rules, but the proof lies in experience.

Logic shows the rules for the use of the understanding and reason, which can themselves be cognized *a priori* and without experience, since they do not depend on it. The understanding here has insight into its own rules and makes thereof a discipline, an instruction, which can be known *a priori*, however, and therefore it is called a doctrine.

In logic not only is reason applied, actually, but reason is its object, the object of its consideration *in usu.*

There are many cognitions whose form is not rational, and in that case it is not a doctrine of reason. So is it, e.g., with the science of taste.

Philosophia is in general the science of reason[a] of the qualities of things. On the first point it differs from the historical, on the second from the mathematical sciences. It is called a science of reason, however, because it expounds cognitions *in abstracto.*

For establishing a first science, such as, e.g., logic is, nothing is required but the common healthy understanding.

The special and fully appropriate name for logic is science of reason,[b] 25 because this is its object. The many other *scientias rationales* should be called reason's sciences.[c]

Logic is called a science because its rules can be proved by themselves[,] apart from all use[,] *a priori.* On this account neither grammar nor aesthetics is a science. And there really and properly is no science of the beautiful at all; rather, whatever we know of the beautiful is nothing but a *critica.*

Logica will thus have no other grounds or sources than the nature of human understanding. For any cognition at all, and thus for logic, there are always (1.) . . . a) *objective* and b) *subjective* grounds. In every science one rightly studies the object, what belongs to its greatest perfection, but also . . . (2.) the subject, i.e., the means[,] the *substrata*$_L$[,] for attaining the object. And so in sciences of the understanding I have to study man first and foremost[;] but since this happens seldom or among few, there arise thence, e.g., the many errors in morals in particular, which most moralists

[a] "Vernunft-Wißenschaft."
[b] "Vernunft-Wißenschaft."
[c] "Wißenschaften der Vernunft."

commit,[d] who can speak admirably of virtue, to be sure, and can praise, recommend, and describe it, but who are not in a position to develop the appetite and love for employing it[,] to produce it in their audience, because they have not studied man.

Logica is a good *philosophia* concerning the good use of reason, and of its rules. Thus it considers not just the nature of human reason alone but also in particular its precepts as well.

Psychologia develops the nature of the human understanding based on experience and considers it. It too will have its sources, then, i.e., we will have to learn some subjective laws of the use of reason from psychology and experience.

Thus we can take as the object of our consideration 1st the subjective laws of our understanding, in accordance with which we actually make use of our understanding,

That science which examines the subjective laws of the rules of our uses of understanding and reason is called *psychologia.*

Logic does not really contain the rules in accordance with which man actually thinks but the rules for how man ought to think. For man often uses his understanding and thinks otherwise than he ought to think and use his understanding.

26

Logic thus contains the objective laws of the understanding and of reason. Thus the portrayal of a good republic is often so opposite to an actually existing republic that it contains precisely the opposite of the latter.

Thus we have basically only 2 objective doctrines, for there are only 2 objective powers of the soul[:] *Power of cognition* and *faculty of desire.* Thus logic as well as morals has as its object a *praxis*$_{\text{L}}$, an employment, the use of our understanding, the application of our free faculty of choice. But they are not for this reason called practical sciences.

We can have a theoretical [and][e] also a practical logic and morals. Disciplines are practical when their effects are practical.

Logic is not merely a critique, it is an actual doctrine, which can be proved. Its rules are taken *in abstracto* and proved. Not every doctrine is practical, however[;] it can be a pure theory. Now if logic is a mere theory of the conditions under which a cognition is perfect according to laws of the understanding and of reason, then it is not[f] a means of *execution*;[g] it would be a *theory* but not an *organon.*

There is a logic that is called a *scientia propaedeutica*, an introductory science.

[d] Reading "die meisten Moralisten begehen" for "die meisten Moralisten."

[e] Ak, "und auch"; MS, "auch" (KI, lxvii).

[f] Reading "kein Mittel" instead of "ein Mittel," with Hinske (KI, lxxi).

[g] "*Execution.*"

And thus it will serve us as a means of critique or as an organon[;] but it is not an organon,[h] it only sharpens the understanding in judging concerning cognitions[.]

Logic contains the rules of the use of our understanding and of our reason, then. Thus everything else stands under it. It opens the way to all other sciences.

[h] Reading "Mittel der Critic oder als ein Organon, das ist sie aber nicht" for "Mittel der Critic, aber nicht als ein Organon, sie," with Hinske (KI, lxxi).

Introduction to the doctrine of reason according to the Author

§ 1

There are many rules of movement, and of the understanding[;] every ship, every fish, follows the rules of movement. We ourselves are subject to these laws. We observe them in walking and in other movements. Nature has implanted these laws in men and animals. But in the case of 27 these laws we do nothing more than fulfill them unknowingly, like the animals.

It would be needless to seek to scout out these laws and not to take a single step without reflection. As the fish in its swimming observes these rules most exactly by means of practice, so can we too, just by means of practice only, acquire a skill in observation of them[.] How quickly do we know how to help ourselves when we are about to fall? But we would lack this capacity if we sought first to reflect on what position we should take.

Borellus[1] has written a book on rule-governed movement.

Besides the laws and rules of movement, however, there are also rules and laws of the understanding. We arrange all our judgments in accordance with these laws. As a child in walking learns to observe the laws of movement, so too, in judging, does it seek to form itself according to those laws of the understanding. All this it does unknowingly, and it acquires the skill merely through practice.

For common cognition it is not necessary that we be conscious of these rules and reflect on them. If we were to do that we would lose very much. But if our understanding wants to have ascended to learned cognition, then it must be conscious of its rules and use them in accordance with reflection, because here common practice is not enough for it. These rules, which the understanding has to observe in learned observation or cognition, are prescribed to us by logic, which we are now about to expound.

The author defines it quite correctly: it is a science that treats of the rules of learned cognition and of learned exposition. A shorter definition would be: Logic is a science that teaches us the use of the understanding in learned cognition.

It is also called *philosophia instrumentalis*, because it can be seen, as it were, as an *instrumentum* of all further philosophical sciences.

Through frequent observations we have scouted out the rules of the understanding. Aristotle established some; but these were nothing but road signs toward errors. It took great effort to forget such false propositions, to give the understanding its natural perfection again, and to investigate its true rules.

28

§ 2

A correct logic is like a straight line, so that one must not deviate from it either to the right or to the left. It would be desirable that logic be brought to such correctness and perfection.

The author indicates to us in this *paragraphus* whence we must derive its rules, if we want to make it that perfect.

Contributing to this are, namely,

1. experiences of the effects of human reason[.] Bacon of Verulam[2] (see his life in Formey's *Hist. of Philosophy*,[3] p. 293 ff. and in Gentzkenius's *Historia Philosophica*,[4] p. 156, 157) first showed the world that all philosophy consists of phantoms of the brain if it does not rest on experience.

It would be just as necessary to write an experimental logic as physics, in which one should investigate how man can err through prejudices, and overhastiness, and in other ways too, so that rules can be prescribed for him as to how he ought to guard against that.

One should make observations, furthermore, as to how we can judge most correctly, and also prescribe rules on this in logic.

2. We have to look at the nature of the human understanding, so that one can set up rules appropriate to it.

It would be foolish to set up logic for rational beings in general, or even for angels, and to think, in doing so, that it could be useful to us too. It would be just as if I were to give to a cripple, who has to walk with crutches, rules and precepts for how he should walk and run like someone healthy. 3. Our rules have to be governed by those universal basic truths of human cognition that are dealt with by *ontologia*. These basic truths are the *principia* of all sciences, consequently of logic too. We must remember also that here at the beginning of *philosophia* we are not yet in a position to provide a perfect *logica*[;] that requires insights that one can only use with an audience already familiar with the whole of philosophy. Here we will be concerned to give only provisional rules for learned cognition, which will make it easier to learn the remaining sciences.

§ 3

29

The purpose of the doctrine of reason can be divided into the *immediate* and the *mediate* purpose. The *immediate* one is the improvement of learned cognition, the *mediate* one that of common cognition. This last can happen if, in daily intercourse, one seeks to improve men's concepts, in doing which one must not make use of scholarly *termini* if one does not want to be called a pedant.

As far as the immediate purpose of logic is concerned, namely, the improvement of learned cognition, this concerns those who are learned by profession, as well as others. Through it everyone can improve his learned cognition as much as he will. Those who are learned by profession differ from others by means of certain *termini technici*, and also through the fact that learnedness is the noblest employment, although it is often pursued by others, e.g., by kings, only as an avocation.[i]

Since the number of the sciences is now so great, it would be fair for each to have his special field assigned to him, because it is impossible to perfect oneself in all sciences.

Among those persons who are not learned by profession one could reckon women, who, in accordance with their capacities, can also occupy themselves with learnedness.

There are sciences which require a sharp mind, much reflection, and profundity. These are for the male sex. On the other hand there are sciences that require wit and a kind of feeling, and these are proper for women.

§ 5

Here philosophy is discussed. Its object is the universal qualities and characters of things. It is well to notice, however, that philosophy does not look to see *quotiens aliquid positum sit*,[j] but rather only *quod positum sit*.[k] It considers only qualities, it only asks, what is posited? *Mathese*, on the other hand, investigates how many times the thing is posited, and investigates the *quantitates* of things, how great they are. Philosophy, furthermore, does not consider all qualities, not the whole character of things, but only those that are met with in many things and on account of this are called universal.

30

Philosophy is a science, but one must not think on that account that things must always be demonstrated and defined in philosophy. Mathematics has that feature.

[i] Reading "Nebenwerk" for "Nebenwerkzeug," with Hinske (KI, lxxiii).

[j] how often something is to be posited.

[k] what is to be posited.

Our author's definition, which he gives for philosophy, is the following: philosophy, he says, is a science of the universal characters of things, insofar as they are known without belief. It is also customary to say: *philosophia est scientia, quae circa rerum rationes*[l] *versatur*[;][m] but because philosophy occupies itself not only with the grounds of things but also frequently simply with their characters, one easily sees that this definition is incorrect. Philosophy involves a higher use of reason[;] but it is hard to determine where philosophy begins and where it ends, just as it is hard to determine[n] the boundary, e.g., between poverty and wealth. A person is rich, it is said, e.g., if he has 50,000 or 20,000 Rthlr.,[o] but with what amount of money does he cease to be rich, and when does he become rich? – The boundaries between stinginess and thriftiness are just as hard to determine. At some point philosophy must be distinct from the common use of reason, poverty from wealth, miserliness from thrift, but where this point is it is hard to say.

Now we will consider the author's restrictions[;] he says: the characters of things must be cognized in philosophy without belief.

Our cognition is of three kinds. We cognize something

1. through *experience*, which happens with occurrences and in general with many objects of history.
2. through *reason*, which abstracts universal cognitions[p] from individual things, and
3. through *belief* in the testimony of another. In this latter way we know that Paris, London, etc., are in the world, although we have not seen any of them. We do not doubt this at all, either, because we rely on the testimony of others who have been there. In philosophy there is no belief[;] here no one must rely on the testimony of others[;] even if someone were to swear to the immortality of the soul, we would not believe him or trust him without proofs, because in philosophy there is no belief. How does someone who is a blind follower of someone else deserve the title of a *philosophus*? Pythagoras's pupils accepted everything their teacher said to them only for five years, and these supposed philosophers do this their whole life long, and always say ἀυτός ἔφα.[q]

31

If there were nothing at all but belief in philosophy, it would not be possible that now this man, now that one, should be placed on the throne of the sciences, and that such changes of fashion in the learned horizon would go on. Just as great men keep people who are learned for them, who pursue the sciences, give advice, give them sympathy, etc., etc., while they concern themselves merely with their digestion. Thus Wolffius and other

[l] Ak, "rationis"; MS, "rationes" (KI, lxvii).
[m] Philosophy is the science that deals with the grounds of things.
[n] Reading "schwer zu bestimmen" for "zu bestimmen," with Hinske (KI, lxxiii).
[o] Reichsthaler.
[p] "Kenntniße."
[q] he himself said it.

true philosophers did the preliminary work and laid the ground for a few supposed philosophers, and these latter do not need to do more than acquaint themselves with it.

If we want to subdivide *philosophia*, we have to[r] presuppose that the activities of our soul consist of cognition, feeling, and desire. The science which deals with the use of the understanding is .... *logica*,
which discusses the universal objects of the understanding is .... *metaphysica*,
which deals with corporeal objects is .... *physica*,
which deals with feeling is .... *aesthetica*,
and the science which has to do with our actions and desires is called .... *morals*,
or .... *philosophia practica*.

The first *philosophia* no doubt began where objects could no longer strike the senses, and this kind of objects were no doubt the objects of religion.

As for the *history* of *philosophy*, the following is to be noted: the Chaldeans had a philosopher in Zoroaster, and among the Persians a Zoroaster is likewise known, who is completely distinct from the Chaldean, however. The *philosophia* of the Chaldeans was very obscure and uncertain. (Thus theology first extended philosophy, *ad pag.* 44.)[5] It stretches back into the farthest reaches of antiquity, and what one can find out about it proceeds from very doubtful reports. One must therefore be very cautious if one does not want to mix up the doctrines of the ancients with the inventions that were widespread[s] in later times. The religion of those peoples was a mixture[t] of the most nonsensical[u] superstition, a crude, horrible idolatry. The priests deceived the foolish people by all kinds of tricks.[v] Soothsaying, spells, interpretations of dreams, childish and extravagant ceremonies constituted the whole of it. If there was still something good under this crude shell, it is impossible to pick it out now. This philosophy thus has the reputation for the most perfect foolishness, but it must have been a dangerous foolishness too; for from the earliest times of the Roman monarchy on, the arts of the Chaldeans were banned as suspicious[w] and godless. Yet in spite of such obscurity in the Chaldean philosophy, it was still very famous throughout antiquity. Its followers divided into various sects, among which were: Sipparenes,[x] Babylonians, Orchenes, Borsip-

32

[r] Ak, "müßten;" MS, "müßen" (KI, lxvii).
[s] Reading "ausgebreiteten" instead of "ausgearbeiteten," with Hinske (KI, lxxi).
[t] Reading "Gemenge" instead of "Grenze," with Hinske (KI, lxxi).
[u] Reading "widersinnigsten" instead of "wiederspänstigen," with Hinske (KI, lxxi).
[v] Reading "Kunst-Griffe." instead of "Kunst-Griffe" with Hinske (KI, lxxi).
[w] Reading "verdächtig" instead of "verderblich," with Hinske (KI, lxxi).
[x] Reading "Sipparener" for "Hipparener," with Lehmann (24:990).

penes, etc.[6] Zoroaster is reputed to be the originator of magic, i.e., the father of the crudest of all deceptions, of the most shameful[y] superstition[;] he is said to have been killed by fire from heaven. The priests are supposed to have instructed Belus in *astronomia* and *physica*[.] Berossus, Marmaridius, Zabratus,[z] and Teucrus are known to us merely by name.

All the philosophies of the most ancient peoples were to be found among the priests. The Egyptians and Persians had probably been the first whose understanding overstepped its limits and who began to make *speculationes. Astrologia, cosmologia*, arose before the physical sciences. The foremost object of their investigation was the origin of things, for these are without doubt the most important questions, and those that must have occurred to people after they first cared for the needs of their bodies. However, this first inquiry will of course have contained more superstition than philosophy. This much is certain: Before *philosophia* had utterly and completely separated itself from the power of the government and from the authority of the clergy in a nation, no philosophy could really be produced.

The originator of Persian *philosophia* was Zerdush[7] or Zoroaster. He lived at the time of the Babylonian captivity; he was the chief of the religion. He brought together his doctrines in a work called *Zend Avesta.* His *Oracle* is a book forged by the neo-Platonics. The Persians' priests

33 were called *magi*$_{\mathrm{L}}$, and their sovereign *archimagus*. The doctrines of their *philosophia* were the following. The highest god is the intellectual fire: to produce the world, there proceeded from this two mutually opposed[a] basic beings or[b] *principia*. The supreme being, from which all others proceed, on which the law of emanation also depends, is called M i t h r a. The 2 basic beings are Ormazd, a very pure, active, spiritual[c] light, and Ahriman, the passive and material darkness, which is born of the limitation of light[d] and bound up with it as a necessary consequence. From the intermingling of these 2 basic beings all sublunary beings proceeded, and so the origin of evil must be explained on earth. There will come a time, however, when darkness will be conquered and destroyed by light. In their opinion the soul came from the gods and, like them, was immortal. Their moral doctrines recommended chastity, righteousness, fairness, escape from the appetites. This they expressed thus: Thou must follow the light

[y] Reading "Betrügereyen, und des schändlichsten" instead of "betrügereyen schändlichsten," with Hinske (KI, lxxi).

[z] Reading "Marmaridius, Zabrates" instead of "Marmaridius Zabratus," with Hinske (KI, lxxi).

[a] Reading "zwey einander widrige" instead of "andere wiedrige," with Hinske (KI, lxxi).

[b] Reading "oder" instead of "und," with Hinske (KI, lxxi).

[c] Reading "geistiges" instead of "günstiges," with Hinske (KI, lxxi).

[d] Reading "Einschränkung des Lichtes" instead of "Einschränkung," with Hinske (KI, lxxi).

and preserve thyself from the plague of darkness or from the begetting of matter.

Among the Chinese we note three great philosophers: Confucius, Keilau, and Janzu, whom they worshipped as a 3-headed idol.[8] They held Pythagoras's opinion concerning the transmigration of souls, worship sun, moon and stars, and not infrequently even the devil, so that he will not harm them. Therefore they set his image on the forward part of their ships, and wear terrifying heads on their clothing. Among the Chinese all *philosophia* is nothing but morals, some astronomy and mathematics, and a kind of political science[e] and way of governing. Confucius was a Solon to the Chinese.

Among the Jews before the destruction of Jerusalem we note some sects, such as

1. the *Sadducees*, who stem from Antigonus of Sokho. Starting from discontent with the doctrine of good works, by which one can gain nothing with God, he came to the complete opposite, and said: one must serve God without any hope of such reward. Zadok and Boethus understood this doctrine wrongly[;] therefore they denied resurrection of the body and all rewards after this life.
2. the Karaites, or scribes,[f] who rejected all allegorical interpretations of the text and, by the way, accepted all the propositions of the Sadducees. They adhered to the school of Shammai.
3. the sect of the *Pharisees*[;] it gets its name from the Hebrew word *parasch*,[g] which means the separated people. For they believed themselves very different from the common people, partly through their science, which consisted, however, only in false explanations of the law, partly through meritorious deeds, which, however, were nothing more than observations of external ceremonies and superstitious actions. Their doctrine was supported above all by the school of Hillel. 34
4. the sect of the *Essenes*. They departed most of all from Jewish customs. The persecutions of the Syrian kings, or rather Cambyses' invasion, gave them their start. Their way of life was very similar to the orders of monks. They served God in a largely only spiritual way[;] they had established hours in which they attended to certain duties.
5. the sect of *therapeutics*. They flourished in Egypt and were completely monk-like.[h]

From the times after the destruction of Jerusalem and of the temple we note the rabbis called Gamaliel and Judah the Pious, the most distinguished originators of Talmudic doctrine. The cabalistic doctrine is in the secret books Sefer ha-Peli'ah, Sefer ha-Bahir, and Sefer ha-Zohar. The rabbis Akiva and Simeon bar Yohai, propagated it, but as a secret doc-

[e] "Staats-Wißenschaft."

[f] "die *Karäer*, *Karaiten* oder Schriftgelahrte."

[g] Ak, "*peruschim*"; MS, "*parasch*" (KI, lxvii).

[h] Inserting a paragraph break, with Hinske (KI, lxxi).

trine. Finally the *philosophia* of Aristotle became mixed with them, although all the rabbis opposed this. We find proofs for this in the work *Kuzari.*[i] The famous rabbi Moses Maimonides was well trained in this. This mixed doctrine has much similarity with the positive and moral *theologia*[j] that was grounded on the interpretation of divine law. Rabbi Saadiah brought this into a system. Moses Maimonides gave it a more philosophical[k] direction, and made of it 13 articles of belief, which he named roots. The Jews in Egypt, finally, adopted the allegorical method and even the philosophy of this country, namely, the concept of the emanations, which arose from the intermingling of the opinions of Zoroaster, Pythagoras, and others. They sought to combine all this as well as possible with their opinions. Among the therapeutics this doctrine was already in full swing, and Philo followed it. In the 2nd century, the Jews' fear of being scattered prompted them to formulate this doctrine in writing,[l] and thus they propagated these errors further and further. On this, see more in Formey's *History of Philosophy* pp. 72, 184.[9]

35 The philosophy of the ancients contains the defect that they did not make observations as we do now. It went thus with *mathematicae*, where the ancient writings are just as invaluable, except that one did not combine mathematics with observations of nature, which afterwards became a cause of so many discoveries, however.

The ancients did not have any geography, or at least only a very imperfect one.

It was among the Greeks that philosophers were instructed concerning all propositions and doctrines and the art of governing and the purpose of their people, and there that they did something to perfect these. However rough the philosophy that came to the Greeks, it was just that cultivated when handed over by them to other peoples. In all sciences of the understanding and of taste, the merit of the Greeks is thus the greatest. The government of the Greeks was formed by schools of philosophers. Among them, however, we note especially the so-called *7 wise men*. These are:

1st *Thales*, who among them all deserves to be called a wise man on account of his mathematics.

2nd *Solon*[,] a belletrist,[m] good poet, skilled general, and excellent lawgiver. His motto was: Bear in mind the end.

3rd *Chilon* was visible and honorable among the Lacedaemonians on account of his justice and patience. His motto was: do not learn too much, rather, learn to know thyself.

[i] "Cuzzeri."

[j] Reading "Positiv- und Moral-Theologia" instead of "Positiven Moral-Theologia," with Hinske (KI, lxxi).

[k] Reading "Philosophischere" instead of "Philosophische," with Hinske (KI, lxxi).

[l] Reading "schriftlich abzufaßen" instead of "abzufaßen," with Hinske (KI, lxxi).

[m] "ein schöner Geist."

4th *Pittacus* of Mytilene[,] a courageous and good soldier[;] his motto was: heed the time.[n]

5th *Bias* of Priene in Ionia. A righteous, magnanimous, virtuous, and clever man. His *symbolum* was: Love as if you could hate.

6th *Cleobulus*, born in Rhodes. He learned wisdom among the Egyptians. His daughter, Cleobulina, was heiress to his virtues and sciences[;] nothing, he said, is better than moderation.

7th *Periander*[,] a prince of the Corinthians.

Democritus deserves to be called the first philosopher. He was the instructor of the great and famous Epicurus, who is among the ancients what Cartesius represents among the moderns, and who improved the 36 previous method of philosophizing. In Lucretius we find propositions from the Epicurean philosophy. But since Lucretius, as is known, was occasionally absurd, he can of course have corrupted the propositions.

Pyrrho was a man of great insights. He had the saying: *non liquet*[,][o] which he constantly shouted at the impudent sophists to damp their pride[;] he was the founder of the skeptics, who were also called *zetetici*.[p] This sect finally took doubting so far, and became so excessive, that it finally began to doubt everything, even, indeed, mathematical propositions.

Socrates devoted himself to practical philosophy, which he proved especially by his conduct.

Pythagoras placed much importance on numbers[;] he held the number 10 to be the most perfect number, but others held it to be the fourth, and they thought on account of this that God had made 4 elements. He wanted to think everything out by means of numbers. Therefore he said, among other things: *animal est numerus se ipsum movens*.[q]

Plato was very rhetorical, and obscure, and in such way that he often did not understand himself.

Aristotle developed a blind trust in himself, and he harmed *philosophia* more than he helped it.

Zeno was the founder of the stoical sect.

The Romans, finally, produced no particular major sects but rather followed the Greeks.

The Arabs brought forth Aristotle's doctrine again, and the *scholastici* also followed them. On some points modern times have advantages over ancient times[;] these latter were lacking in empirical cognitions. Thus the *eventus*[r] in nature of the ebb and flow, which was discovered in modern times, was unknown to Aristotle.[10] But the means now available for achieving this also did not exist in those times. E.g ., to travel so quickly[;] and

[n] "kenne die Zeit."

[o] It is not clear.

[p] From ζητητικός, disposed to search or inquire.

[q] An animal is a self-moving number.

[r] occurrence.

due to this lack, the extension of empirical cognition[s] was held back particularly; and these are excellent sources, after all, from which reason ought to draw.

The ancient *philosophi* were in general either (1.) *skeptical philosophers*, and these were *misologists* or reason-haters, or *dogmatists*[,] and all these had their designation according to their *principia*[.] Among them, however, moral philosophy, natural science and acquaintance [with nature] were poor and false.

37 *Baco de Verulam*, who pointed out the importance of the effort of bringing observations of nature under certain propositions. (And up until now the external observations and external natural phenomena have been sufficiently extended, but not the internal.)

Cartesius, *Malebranche*, *Leibniz*, and *Wolffius*, the last of whom, through his industry, produced a *systema* of philosophy, were in recent times the ones who improved philosophy, and were its true fathers.

All the efforts of our philosophy are

1. *dogmatic*
2. *critical.*

Among critical philosophers *Locke* deserves priority. *Wolff*, however, and the Germans generally, have a methodical philosophy.

Finally, Crusius has become famous[;] he has some good but very much that is incorrect, and he errs particularly in wanting to prove many propositions merely from the nature of the understanding.

As far as *logica* is concerned, Aristotle was the first to expound it, and he also invented the 4 syllogistic figures.

The *logica* of the scholastics consisted merely of subtleties.

Locke's book *de intellectu humano* is the ground of all true *logica*.

At the time of the Reformation, in France, Petrus Ramus wrote a logic.[11] He taught his countrymen, the French, to pronounce the *quin*, *quisquis*, *quanquam* not in accordance with the French but in accordance with the Latin dialect. A great dispute arose over this between him and the teachers at the Sorbonne, so that as this matter came to the government, many were removed from office merely on account of wrong pronunciation. After him Wolff, and also Crusius, wrote a *logica*, the latter of which cannot make the learning of the sciences easier, however, but rather is so obscure that another logic is required in order to understand it.

Now, finally, the critical philosophy thrives most, and in this the English have the greatest merit.

For the most part the dogmatic method has fallen into disuse in all

[s] "Erfahrungs-Erkenntniß."

sciences; even morals is not expounded dogmatically any more, but more often critically.

§ 6

38

Logic deals with the rules either of certain, or of probable, learned cognition[;] the latter is called *logica probabilium*. In common life we act more according to probability than according to certainty, for which reason the *logica probabilium* would be very useful.

Bernoulli[12] wrote one, to be sure, but it is nothing but a mathematics that is applied to cases of chance. He shows, e.g., how one can throw 8 times according to the rules of probability.

The *logica probabilium* has merely examples and has its use in funeral funds. The one we are talking about here, however, ought to extend to the experience of all men, and such a one is not available.

Crusius's *logica* of the probable is held by many to be good; but it contains only universal considerations, which gain regard because of their learned tone.[13]

Just as it is easier to make a circle than an ellipse, and easier to give the rules for virtue than those for inconstancy, so can one more easily find the rules for certain cognition than those for probable cognition. The grounds for certainty are determined, but those for probability are not. Now it ought to be shown, however, how great they should be if something is to be probable, which is hard to determine.

§ 7

Logic can be subdivided into

1st *theoretical*
2nd *practical logica.*

Theoretical logica only shows us the rules for learned cognition, while the *practical* applies these rules to particular cases.

§ 8

In this *paragraphus* the author speaks of the usefulness of the doctrine of reason. It furthers 1st the learning of the sciences generally. This is to be understood only for logic in the objective sense, namely, for a logic that is really constituted as it properly ought to be. A *logica*, however, that is as obscure and as excessively refined as that of Crusius cannot have this usefulness.

39

It improves the understanding and reason, 2ndly, just as he who understands a language according to its rules cannot err as easily as he who has learned it only *ex usu*. Thus he is also not as certain of the thing as the former, and he hardly knows how to get along in matters that he has not yet encountered. Since someone else, on the other hand, can arrange everything according to the rules that the language prescribes for him, he who has in view the rules by which he ought to form his understanding, and who applies them properly, also does not fall into error as easily as he who knows nothing of these rules.

Logic furthers, e.g., *virtue*. In doubtful matters one can in fact proceed according to the rules of logic and judge whether the thing is really good or not. It has this useful effect on *virtue directe*[;] it furthers *virtue indirecte*, as it does all speculative sciences and cognitions, by abstracting a man from sensible charms when he has acquired a taste for it, and even by giving him a kind of decency. If man is to occupy himself with speculation he must be calm, decent, and satisfied with things outside himself, and with the help of logic this can become customary with him.

The doctrine of reason itself
The first principal part
Of learned cognition

THE FIRST SECTION

Of learned cognition universally in general

§ 10

In this *paragraphus* the author wanted to give a definition of representation, but because he could not do it he helped himself out with a rhetorical flight, as commonly happens when one can say nothing certain. He says at the end that a representation acts like a picture that shows the pictorial skill of the soul in its interior.[t] What representation is cannot really be explained. It is one of the simple concepts that we necessarily must have. Every man knows immediately what representation is. Cognitions and representations are of the same sort. Concepts are somewhat different from them, however, as we shall see in what follows. Cognition and representation are taken in logic to be of the same sort. Every representation is something in us, which, however, is related to something else, which is the object. Certain things represent something, but we represent things. Logic does not teach us how we ought to represent something by means of consciousness, but rather it presupposes the consciousness of something as a psychological matter. 40

§ 11 et 12

In every cognition whatsoever we find something material. But also something formal.

The object as we represent [it] is the *material*,[u] while the manner of the representation is called the *formal*. If, e.g., I represent virtue to someone, then I can look in part to what I represent, in part to how I represent it[;] the latter is the *formal*[,] the former the *material* in the representation.

[t] "in ihrem innwendigen."

[u] Reading "das *Materiale*" for "das *Object*."

Logic has to do for the most part with the formal in cognition. Cognitions can have various forms in one *materia*, however. There are whole sciences whose philosophy differs from the common understanding not in matter but only in form, in distinctness[;] thus it is, e.g., with morals.

§ 13

When we distinguish a representation and its object, with which it is concerned, from other representations, then we are conscious of the representation. *Consciousness* accompanies each of our states[;] it is, as it were, the intuiting of ourselves.

Nonetheless, we are not conscious of most of our representations, of the strongest and the most powerful. Who should represent that? We can prescribe rules only for those representations of which we are conscious.

41 We cannot speak of *consciousness* in more detail here. The doctrine concerning it really belongs to *metaphysica*. And to have a correct concept of it, much is taken as a ground from *metaphysica*.

§ 14

Here confused and distinct representations are discussed. If, in a composite representation, I distinguish from one another the parts of which it consists, that is a distinct representation. But if I do not distinguish its partial representations from one another, then it is a *confused representation*. E.g., if I see a cheese mite, my representation of it is in the beginning confused. But if I take a *microscopium* in hand and become aware in it of a jaw full of teeth, 2 rows of feet, 2 black eyes, then I represented all of that previously. But I was not able to distinguish these partial representations of the limbs from the whole body. My cognition becomes distinct by means of the *microscopium*, however, in that by means of it I represent the individual parts of the cheese mite, and distinguish these from the whole body. In just the same way, when I consider the Milky Way with the naked eye I distinguish nothing from anything else. I am not conscious, in my representation, of any of the parts. But if I look at the Milky Way through a *tubus*, then I see that it consists of fixed stars. I represent these fixed stars as parts of the Milky Way and distinguish the representation of one fixed star from the representation of another; and therefore I have a distinct representation, because what is required for this is just that I should distinguish the partial representations from one another, and the partial representations of the fixed stars are partial representations of the Milky Way.

A simple representation, and simple cognitions, cannot be or become confused, nor distinct either. Confusion and distinctness are to be found only in composite cognitions.

One principal property of logic will thus be to explicate a confused cognition and to make it distinct.

Indistinctness is opposed to distinctness, but confusion to order. Something can be confused, regardless of the fact that I am conscious of the partial representations, and that it does have distinctness. A distinct representation is not always orderly. The more we reduce our representations to simple ones, the more we remove confusion. 42

In distinct representations the material is just like that in confused ones. In one case we represent just as much as in the other. In confused representations, just as much as in distinct ones, we have partial representations. For if we did not have them, we would not have the total one either.

In confused representations, however, we do not distinguish the partial representations. A cognition can be distinct only insofar as it is a total representation. Likewise, only a total representation can be confused. A simple representation is neither confused nor distinct. For in such a representation I cannot distinguish one partial representation from another. The distinct as well as the confused occurs only in total and composite representations:

Distinctness can occur

1st *in intuiting*, when we can distinguish well the mark of that which we intuit. That is distinctness in intuition.

2nd *in thinking*, when we combine clear concepts and representations with intuiting. Often one can intuit something distinctly without thereby thinking of something distinctly.

We achieve distinctness in intuition through more attention *per synthesin*; distinctness in concepts, however, involves the analysis of what I think, what I already actually conceive[v] in thoughts[,] i.e., the distinctness of the understanding *per analysin*. All of morals involves merely concepts of the understanding. Empirical distinctness is attained *a posteriori* by attention to the objects of experience. Distinctness of reason, however, is attained *a priori* by attention to the actions of my understanding.

§ 15

A ground is that from which something can be cognized, and a consequence is what can be cognized from the ground. We can make use of this definition here. In *metaphysica*, however, we will not be satisfied with it. A ground from which, in what follows,[w] everything can be understood, thus one from which nothing is lacking, is a sufficient ground, and an insufficient ground is one where only something can be cognized. E.g., when we 43

[v] "Concipire."

[w] "in der Folge."

say that the moon has inhabitants because mountains and valleys are present on it, this is an insufficient ground. From this one sees only that it is possible and probable that there are inhabitants of the moon. But if, e.g., a businessman has 100,000 Rthl. in wealth and one says that he has made 50,000 Rthl. through trade and he inherited 50,000[x] Rthl., then this is a sufficient ground. The relation of the ground and of the consequences is their connection[.] E.g., a tree is connected with its fruit[;] the tree is the ground, the fruit the consequence.

§ 16

Every truth has its ground, i.e., [that] by which one can distinguish it from the false and hold it to be true. This is here in *logica*. Sufficient grounds are properly spoken of in *metaphysica*.

§ 17

If I merely know the ground of a consequence, the cognition is not yet on that account rational. E.g., when one assigns saltpeter as the ground of a thunderstorm. When one has distinct insight into how the consequence arises out of the ground, however, e.g., how out of the saltpeter the thunderstorm arises, then our cognition is rational. The author speaks here of rational cognition[y] without having previously spoken of distinct cognition. He ought to have called it a cognition of reason,[z] which itself arises out of reason.

§ 18 et 19

All the perfections of cognition are

1st *aesthetic*, and consist in agreement with subjective laws and conditions.
2nd *logical*, and consist in agreement with objective laws and conditions.

All the *requisita* of these perfections of cognition are:

44

1. *sensation*[,] how I am affected by the presence of the object.
2. *the power of judgment.*
3. *mind*[.][a]
4. *taste.*

A cognition agrees with the subject when it gives us much to think about and brings our capacity into play. This requires especially ease,

[x] Ak, "500000"; MS, "50000" (KI, lxvii).
[y] "der vernünftigen Erkenntniß."
[z] "eine Vernunft-Erkentnniß."
[a] "*Geist.*"

intuition, and this requires *similia*, examples, instances. But sensation has only the 2nd position, intuition the 1st. For we cannot judge by means of sensation, but we can by means of intuition, and just for that reason the former has the lowest position in what has to do with aesthetic perfection, the latter the highest.

With cognition there are two sorts of perfections: (1.) that it agrees with the constitition of the thing.

2nd that it has an effect on our feeling and our taste. The former is a *logical* perfection, the latter an *aesthetic*, but both are formal. We have one logic that makes and can make our cognitions[b] logically perfect, another that makes and can make our cognition[c] aesthetically so. The former teaches us to make representations that conform to the constitution of the thing, which the logic that we now intend to treat does. The latter, however, which contains aesthetics, must deal with those representations that have effect on our feeling. Logical perfection involves the distinctness of the representation, and also that it must be rational[;] the latter is treated in § 14.

We can say that cognition or representation in which reason is applied, in which I cognize the grounds, is rational; but the logical perfection of a representation requires particularly its *truth*. Another means to objective perfection is distinctness. Thus a demonstration, e.g., is logically perfect if the proofs adduced are sure, distinct, certain, and they agree with the properties of the thing. But a proof can be easy, too, although this property does not actually relate to the object but rather to the subject. With various subjects, one and the same proof can therefore be hard for one to grasp, yet easy for another.

45

Ordinaire$_F$, one has to sacrifice some logical perfection if one wants to attain an aesthetic perfection, and one has to give up some aesthetic perfection if one wants to attain a logical perfection. Something can never be really distinct without being somewhat hard, nor ever really lively without being somewhat indistinct, *et vice versa*.

No one has yet been able accurately to combine, to determine, and to discover the correct measure of aesthetic perfection with logical perfection. That involves much delicacy. What promotes our life, i.e., what brings our activity into play, as it were, pleases. Something becomes easy for us if it is in order. Order is thus a means for the agreement of our cognition with the object with which it is concerned. Furthermore, the new pleases us especially, and no less does the incomprehensible too, just because it is incomprehensible, if only it is true as well. In general, everything wonderful [pleases]. Surprise[d] always has something pleasant

[b] "Kenntniße."

[c] "Kenntniß."

[d] "Die Befremdung."

for sensibility, but also something displeasing for the understanding. Therefore do we listen so gladly to the most wonderful stories. An aesthetic perfection is a perfection according to laws of sensibility. We make something sensible when we make the object awaken and excite a sensation, and when I make something capable of intuition. The greater art of taste consists in now making sensible what I first expounded dryly, in clothing it in objects of sensibility, but in such a way that the understanding loses nothing thereby. A perfection gets its worth from being communicable. At the ground of everything that has to do with taste lies a sociability,[e] and through this taste elevates itself very much; he who only chooses that which pleases himself and no other has no taste at all. Thus taste cannot possibly be isolated[,] idiosyncratic. The judgment concerning taste is thus never a private judgment[;] from this we see[:]

1st Taste must relate to the judgment of all. Taste is a judgment of the most universal approval.

2nd Taste involves something sociable, social.[f]

Sociability gives life a certain taste that it otherwise lacks, and this taste is itself social. When what pleases me sensibly must also please others straightforwardly, then this means: I have taste. There are some men who have nothing social, although they can otherwise be honest people.

46 People who live in isolation[g] all have no taste. In the human soul there exists a certain *principium* that would very much deserve to be studied, namely, that our mind is communicative,[h] so that man gladly communicates as well as accepts communication. Therefore do men communicate with one another so gladly, and seldom does man sense proper pleasure when he cannot communicate, and communicate his thoughts and inclinations, to someone. Our knowledge is nothing if others do not know that we know. Thus it is that man tests his judgment on the judgment of others, and it pleases him at once if it agrees with his. It is therefore completely absurd to say: taste is a certain private judgment by a man concerning what he enjoys, what pleases him. Such a man has no taste at all. Taste also has certain universal laws, but can these laws be cognized *in abstracto a priori*? No. But *in concreto*; because the laws of taste are really not laws of the understanding, but universal laws of sensibility. Taste itself is an object concerning which we can engage in reasoning to some extent.[i] But this reasoning does not constitute taste, but rather only increases it.

[e] "eine Geselligkeit."

[f] "etwas geselliges, gesellschaftliches."

[g] "Solitarii Sonderlinge."

[h] Reading "Communicable, und mittheilend" for "Communicable, und mithleidend," with Hinske (KI, lxxiii).

[i] "von welchem wir manches vernünfteln können."

The judgment of taste is: One judges concerning this or that thing by means of and according to its look.

If a man has taste, then he sees what he chooses. That pleases almost everyone, and thoroughly[.]

The norm, the guideline (how something ought to be) of taste, does not lie in the universal rules of reason, but instead is found nowhere but in real works of taste. Hence there must be lasting models of taste, or taste will soon come to an end. Likewise there must be lasting models of writing style in a dead (learned) language, for these alone are unchangeable, i.e., the Latin and Greek language. Much can be clarified and cognized *a priori* but yet cannot subsequently be employed.

Man is polished, refined, not by means of instruction but rather by means of social intercourse, and especially with well-mannered, well-raised women.

Genius and taste are to be wholly distinguished from one another. Genius works, so to speak, in the rough, but in things excellent. It is desirable for school instruction 47

1. to work in what is rough but sublime
2. and then to polish.

But there everything has to be and become polished equally, and more attention is given to petty things and secondary matters than to the principal matters, and force is even used as well. *Genius*, on the other hand, is seldom cultivated. But the damage that such school methods cause in these matters is very great. E.g., in elegant Latin. One never looks to the thoughts, but always just to expression, to the words.

Only through intercourse and society does man become polished. Models, models worthy of imitation, are needed to form and preserve taste. The archetype of all perfections exists only in thoughts, however. It is an *archetypon*, and merely an ideal. True beauty must be sketched, as it were, by means of a sensibility. Morals contains the *archetypon* of ethical perfection.

When, in a representation, reason is not applied[j] particularly, then this is not a rational cognition[, but] it is not on that account irrational either. E.g., when I know into what countries Europe is divided, I do not use reason for this but only memory, and on this account it is not a rational cognition. But what is not a rational cognition is not then irrational, but rather this holds only for that which is against reason. E.g. If I have acquainted myself with the movement of the planets without using reason, it is not a rational cognition that I have of this, but neither is it an irrational one.

A cognition that is not rational, where I do not need reason but only

[j] "adhibiret."

memory, in which case I do not see how something derives from its ground, is a historical cognition.

A perfect historical cognition, says the author in the 19th §, is a *cognitio pulchra sive aesthetica*.[k] It is wrong, however, for him to take beautiful and aesthetic to be the same, for aesthetics includes not only the beautiful but also the sublime. A historical cognition is one that is not rational. When the author speaks of a perfect historical cognition, therefore, and takes it to be an aesthetic cognition, he can understand by this nothing but a 48 cognition which, though it is not rational, can still have a perfection. But he thereby explained himself very badly. For who can see from this what sort of a perfection this is supposed to be. This amounts to my wanting to say: A periwig is that which, even if it is not exactly a hat, nor a cap, can nevertheless be placed on the head just as well.

We have spoken first of the aesthetic perfection of a cognition and have said that it consists in the effect on our feeling. From this we can easily gather what an aesthetic cognition is, namely, one that affects our feeling (by means of pleasure or displeasure). Historical cognition is a cognition that is not rational. E.g., when someone has much acquaintance with natural history, and he does not cognize this in connection with its grounds, then he does not have rational but only historical cognition. In other cases, historical cognition means a cognition that relates only to individual things, and it is opposed to the dogmatic. But it is not taken in this sense here. The author holds every perfect historical cognition to be beautiful. But a cognition can be historical without being beautiful. We can know from Homer everything mythological, even all the travels of Ulysses, etc., and more, so that we have a quite perfect historical cognition[;] and nevertheless it will not be beautiful if it has no effect on our feeling, if we regard everything coldly and we sense nothing along with it. Such a cognition is only beautiful and aesthetic, as we said above, if it has an influence on our feeling of pleasure and displeasure. In a cognition, the beautiful is diminished when the rational and distinct is furthered. Just as a woman's beauty vanishes when one considers it through a *microscopium*. The best expressions, those that strike us most, lose their force when one analyzes them and cognizes them more distinctly by means of the understanding. Often our understanding rejects something, e.g., various kinds of clothes, that accords with our taste and stirs our feeling. Hungarian clothes are much more conformable to the understanding than the French[;] they would be better, more comfortable, etc. *Item*[l] it is more conformable to the understanding that the door not be located in the middle of the house and thereby make the rooms small[;] but our feeling requires necessarily that everything be symmetrical and that the door, e.g.,

[k] cognition that is beautiful or aesthetic.

[l] Likewise.

not be located at the corner of the house. Feeling is stirred by confused cognition, and on that account it is very hard to observe it, so that in general a science of it, i.e., *aesthetica*, has very many difficulties. Baumgarten[14] first made a science of it. 49

§ 20

Rational cognition has advantages over historical cognition, in that it requires the understanding and reason. But sometimes historical cognition has advantages over rational. Historical cognition must provide the ground for all rational cognition. The brooder who shuts himself up in his room and wants to attain much rational cognition will not get far if he has not first acquired historical cognition by means of experience from books, or from intercourse, from the society of other people. Historical cognition is given to me *a posteriori*[;] it contains everything that pertains to rational cognition. It shows how something is, but rational cognition shows how something ought to be (thus it is, e.g., in morals). It only makes distinct what historical cognition indicates. It alters only the *formal*. Without historical cognition reason has no *materialia* to make distinct. It is a great error in our upbringing to occupy ourselves with rational cognition too early, without yet having a sufficient historical cognition. Rational cognition, however, is not more perfect than historical cognition in all relations, in all cases. E.g., if someone is to be excited, rational cognition will have little or no effect.

In regard to common life, historical cognition likewise has more use, just as the farmers in a state are more useful than all the *mathematici* and *astronomi*. –

There is no man who does not have metaphysical judgments. A science will in general consist of cognitions that constitute a whole.

§ 21

Philosophical cognition has the same object that historical and rational cognition has. Only the form is different. It is indeterminate where philosophical cognition begins and rational ends.

In the same way, e.g., degree is undetermined in the case of the affects. A greater degree of sensible desires is an affect. But how great this degree would have to be is uncertain. 50

With philosophical cognition, now, one seeks, from the characters of things, to have insight into the connection of their grounds and consequences. Some are of the opinion that they have philosophy, although they really lack it, and others actually have it without thinking so. Those who memorize *definitiones* from Wolff and other philosophers think they have philosophy. They only have a merely historical cognition and actually cannot philosophize at all, and think for themselves, or judge, concerning objects. They lack the skill of at least judging a thing philosophically.

§ 22

In this *paragraphus* the author speaks of the perfections of cognition. He also explains what perfection is. The concept of perfection actually belongs to *metaphysica*, and here it is introduced in the wrong place. All perfection, however, is

1st practical
2nd theoretical

Theoretical perfection is actually concerned with the quantity of [cognition], as, e.g., its extensiveness, fruitfulness. But practical fruitfulness, on the other hand, is more a perfection as to quality, as, e.g., its importance, and beauty, and therefore it is

1. *logical*
2. *aesthetical*

Beauty is properly a matter of art. But art presupposes practice.

In all perfection what matters is always that one has before one's eyes a purpose, a model, a proto- and an archetype. Regarding this, one can properly judge, and say whether one thing, and which thing, is more perfect than another. Thus it is in general with the nature of man. Anyone who has seen many men forms for himself an archetype, a model of the 51 size, of the beauty of a man, which contains the mean on all points and for all kinds of the human form. E.g., among many erroneous copies of a man, the original in most cases makes and preserves the mean.

But from the putting together of many partial beauties a perfectly beautiful thing cannot possibly be brought out. Many beautiful, varied clothes, sewn together, would look awful. (*Nulla dies sine linea[.] Apelles.*[15]) E.g., the artist, the painter, etc., cannot possibly put together an archetype of a painting, but must rather create it. Logical perfections are ones that are perceived only when one regards the thing distinctly. Aesthetic perfections, however, are ones that are sensed by means of confused concepts. The beauty of all good poetic representations, e.g., of paradise lost, [has] an aesthetic perfection. It is sensed only in confused concepts, and it loses its value just as soon as the concept is made distinct.

There are

1st *beautiful objects*,
2nd *beautiful representations of objects*

The ugliest woman can be beautifully painted, i.e., excellently rendered, and the most beautiful woman can be uglily painted, i.e., terribly rendered and distorted. Beautiful objects can occur only in objects. No judgment at all can be made, however, concerning a beautiful cognition. For that we have examples, to be sure, but they are not archetypes. Models, however, are examples that come closest to the archetype.

In mathematics, propositions and theses have logical perfections[;] here concepts are distinct. When the poet has made for me the best, most stirring, most lively representations of spring, when he has spoken of lowing, grazing herds, of tenderly rustling zephyrs, of fragrant meadows, etc., etc., then my cognition is aesthetically perfect. It is beautiful, but not distinct. I have not thereby attained any distinct insight concerning the ground and the causes of spring. This the *astronomus* can and must explain for me from the course of the sun. The French observe for the most part only aesthetic perfection. When they investigate the grounds of something, and want to have distinct concepts of a thing, then they turn to the beautiful, stirring, and pleasing, and thereby they do great harm to logical perfection. There are learned men who are nothing but artists of reason,[m] and imitative philosophers of this sort are commonly very stubborn about holding to their opinions once adopted. On the other hand, other learned people are, as it were, so to speak, masters and lawgivers of reason. 52

Learning that is historical in form but rational in matter is called a historical cognition. There are many Ciceros in philosophy, many, indeed, who do not know at all what sort of difference there is between philosophy and the science of philosophizing.

§23

The imperfections of cognition are also either *logical* or *aesthetic*. If the imperfections are found in confused concepts, then they are *aesthetic*. If they are present in distinct concepts, however, then they are logical imperfections. E.g. A Swiss poet says that as the Rhone runs through Lake Geneva and yet stays clear, so should the truly virtuous go, uninjured and unsoiled, through the masses of the wicked. Here there is a logical imperfection. On closer investigation one finds that the Rhone runs filthy through Lake Geneva, so that it is made clear and pure by the lake.

As beauty consitutes [everything] in aesthetic perfection, a cognition is dry, e.g., in mathematical considerations. But when a cognition is to be beautiful, but this purpose is not attained, then it is ugly. This occurs, however, in all writers who want to be witty, but who are not and cannot be.

We notice aesthetic imperfections far more than logical ones. For they are immediately opposed to our feeling. –

[m] "Vernunft-Künstler."

An historical cognition is historical either

1. *materialiter*
2. *formaliter*

To *imitate* someone else's science, furthermore, is called *copying*. There are sciences that can be learned, which are *historical* as to form but *rational* as to matter. Some sciences of reason are like this. So is it, e.g., with mathematics. Thus sciences can be acquired, indeed, even communicated, to the degree of perfection conformable to their nature. There are sciences to be imitated [or] to be learned,[n] but also sciences of genius, which cannot be learned.

53

Philosophy, and the art of philosophizing, cannot possibly be learned, but mathematics surely can[.] Thus I cannot teach any man new thoughts, wit, spirit, naiveté in expression, as I teach him to write or to calculate. A philosophy would be learned in a certain time, to be sure, if I were to acquire it in such a way that I copied it as it was given to me[;] but then we would do no more than philosophize as much as we had memorized. But we would certainly not be in any position to philosophize in the least about what had been learned.

The principles of mathematics, on the other hand, are in most cases *intuitive*, and their application takes place, likewise, according to a certain *intuitus*; but this is impossible in philosophy.

The character of a true philosopher is such that he does nothing but exercise his natural powers and capacities, by means, of course, of the searching investigation of critique.

Philosophy can never be learned in half a year, as is commonly believed. Philosophy belongs rather as a study for men who occupy high office, have experience, although we think that philosophy is much easier than jurisprudence and medicine.

Philosophy cultivates the universal capacities of nature by means of reason and surpasses all effects of these capacities. The investigation that goes beyond all cognition inquires after the sources of the concepts of the understanding, and their first origin. And this investigation is one of the most important, and from this it follows necessarily that one does not in the least learn to philosophize when one copies and learns quite exactly the philosophy of others. One can rather profit far more if one accustoms oneself to, and learns the science of, being able to criticize and judge the philosophy of others. My philosophy must be grounded in myself, and not in the understanding of others. It must not bind me to any original model. The method of teaching philosophy is thus twofold:

54

1st the one that cultivates the philosophical spirit, and does not let itself be learned or imitated.

[n] "Wißenschaften der Nachahmung der Erlernung."

2nd that which follows a certain *autor* faithfully, comments on him, and which tries to use memory as an aid in philosophy.

This might do in mathematics, but not in philosophy.

§ 24

A cognition can be merely learned, or learned and beautiful at the same time. In the first, one merely has distinctness as one's purpose, and this cognition is dry. That cognition which not only teaches the understanding but also stimulates feeling and attracts is at once beautiful and learned.

The latter cognition is, however, hardest to attain, and far harder than the former. For if one goes only slightly too far with beauty, one immediately does damage to logical perfection. If, on the other hand, one really wants to further logical perfection, then one becomes dry and loses the beautiful.

To observe scholarly and beautiful cognition in an oral cognition, and still more in a written one, can thus actually be called the true touchstone of the learned. But who possesses this?

A perfect historical cognition, if it is to be really beautiful, is perfect not in regard to its matter but rather to its form. E.g., an extended science of geography is in itself historically very useful, and perfect, but still not on that account beautiful. Instead, with the beautiful it always depends rather on the formal, on the manner of the cognition. If, e.g., Voltaire expounds exactly the same historical cognition as Hübner,[16] the material in the two expositions will be one and the same, but the formal will be quite different[;] with the first it will be quite other than with the latter, namely, it will be beautiful, and it will excite feeling.

The material, as, e.g., the distinctness and the correctness of the cognition, can in the one case be just as it is in the other. But the form[,] what excites, delights and flatters our feeling, is different. Distinctness, then, and correctness, concerns the material, and consequently belongs to logical perfection as one of its properties. The excitement, however, and delight that pleases immediately at once concerns the formal, and consequently belongs as a property to aesthetic perfection. 55

In every aesthetic perfection I cognize things confusedly. Much acts on me at once, and affects me. E.g., if in the *theatrum* a hero appears suddenly[,] terrifyingly[,] frightfully[,] and with a huge retinue, then our soul is overcome by that which is exciting[.] The understanding, on the other hand, omits much that seems to it superfluous. It seeks rather only to make its cognition as distinct as possible, and just on this account in most cases ignores all taste, all flattering adornments[;] all make-up is left off, and that which appears aesthetically very beautiful we regard as quite miserable when we consider it again through the understanding alone.

The French nation has the peculiarity that it looks more, and most of all, to the aesthetic[,] to external ornament. The English nation, on the other hand, cultivates logical perfection instead. Therefore it happens, too, that our understanding commonly learns not much, or little, from French books (though some are also excluded from this). One remembers well, when one has read them, that one was delighted with them as with a [piece of] music; but one knows at the same time that the understanding has learned nothing from them, which does not often occur in the case of English books.

§ 25–26

These two paragraphs contain perfections of cognition in itself. Extensiveness[,] among other things, whereby many objects are cognized, is certainly a perfection[;] e.g., he who has made progress in true geography, who knows many cities, countries, rivers, etc., by name and location, can be a master of the so-called name-geography.[o]

In the 26th § the author speaks of the quantity of cognition as likewise a perfection. In every quantity whatsoever there is always a multitude, but there is not quantity in every multitude. In every quantity I can consider

56 the *extensive* and the *intensive*. In the first case, when I consider the *extensive* in a quantity, I look to the multitude of units[,] to their number, how many of them there are. But in the other case, namely, when I consider intensive quantity, I look particularly to the quantity of each unit. And so it is too with cognition. If I consider, namely, only the multitude of the objects that I cognize, then I look merely to the extensive quantity of the cognition. But when I cognize a single object wholly and really perfectly, then the cognition is great[p] *intensive*$_L$. In the latter it is really a matter of degree, of how I cognize the unit.

§27

Truth is a perfection that is included in the logical as well as in the aesthetic perfection of cognition. It is a principal logical perfection, on which the others all depend. When I cognize the thing as it actually is, then my cognition is true. For aesthetic perfection, truth is also required. Therefore Milton is reproached for representing death and sin as persons, as it were, because this is not appropriate to their constitution. But with the aesthetically perfect we do not require as much truth as with the logically perfect. With the aesthetic, something may be true only *tolerabiliter*. In this way it is aesthetically true that Milton represents the angels

[o] "Namen Geographie."

[p] Reading "groß" for "gewiß."

in the paradise lost as quarreling, and caught up in battle, for who knows whether this cannot occur. A good fable must in all cases contain aesthetic truth. There is such truth, e.g., in Aesop's fable of the wolf, when he says of the sheep and the wolf by the river that the patient lamb replied gently to the wolf's malicious complaint, and that he made an effort to calm its wrath, but that the bloodthirsty, unjust wolf answered, or at least that with his vile answer he meant: In short, I am hungry now, I have to eat you –.

§ 28

Distinctness, furthermore, is a perfection of cognition, and it has the peculiarity of belonging to logical as well as to aesthetic perfection as a necessary property. An extensive distinctness, which one encounters in the beautiful understanding, is an aesthetically pure one[;] intensive distinctness, however,[q] which one finds in the deep understanding, belongs to logical perfection. The poet describes the spring for me with extensive distinctness. He piles marks one upon another. The philosopher, however, describes the same thing with intensive distinctness[;] he looks, namely, not to the multitude of the marks, but rather he seeks to represent really clearly and distinctly only a few marks, indeed, where possible, only a single one. 57

Beauty of the understanding rests on the fact that one has many marks of a thing. Depth of the understanding, however, requires only that some marks be known clearly, and at the same time distinctly, and that it is easy to have insight into them.

§ 29

The author explains certainty here "as the consciousness of the truth of a cognition." For the time being this explanation is good enough, and sufficient. We will discuss this along with other things later on. Certainty belongs to logical and to aesthetic perfection. The uncertain, the wavering, always displeases. For aesthetic certainty authority is often sufficient enough. I.e., it is enough when in such a case one rests on the prestige of great men, who believed, e.g., in the immortality of the soul, or in a future world,[;] in this way one will be convinced enough aesthetically, although this does not constitute a logical certainty. What great men say, who are highly regarded in the learned world, is a ground for aesthetic certainty, but never for logical certainty.

If a cognition is to be aesthetically true, then in this cognition much needs to be heaped up, one thing on another, and a multitude of represen-

[q] Reading "intensive Deutlichkeit" for "intensive, Deutlichkeit."

tations need to be put forth all at once. If I want to prove, e.g., the shamefulness of this or that deed, then I will not indicate and prove the shameful according to morals, but rather I will ramble, so to speak; I will show, e.g., how the fields, the trees, etc., etc., shudder at this deed, how everything quakes, how the heavens wrap themselves in gloomy clouds so as not to be witness to this deed, which is so abominable. He who attains this cognition and one like it must also be blinded by the confusion of it. Thus it happens, too, that the judgments of other people are adequate for the certainty of the it.

58

§ 30

A cognition that has an influence on our will and *per consequentiam* on our actions (those to be controlled by the will) we call a practical cognition.

From the consideration of all the perfections of cognition we see that the principal capacities of our cognition are properly the following: (1.) *understanding*, (2.) *feeling*, and (3.) *desire*.

If (1.) I *make* my cognition perfect in *regard* to my *understanding*, then, it is *logically perfect*. If 2nd I make my cognition perfect in regard to my *feeling*, then it is *aesthetically perfect*.

Finally, if 3rd I make my cognition perfect in regard to my *desires*, then it is *practically*, or *morally*, *perfect*.

Moral perfection rests on *logical* and on *aesthetic* perfection taken together. Logical perfection includes the following three things:

1st *distinctness*
2nd *truth* and
3rd *certainty*.

But *distinctness* is the first and the foremost property, on which things particularly depend in the case of logical perfection.

Truth, as well as *certainty*, help little if they are not *distinct*.

The 3 principal *caractères*[r] of aesthetic perfection, however, are

1st *truth*
2nd *certainty* and especially
3rd *extensiveness*.

For in the case of aesthetic perfection, the cognition is not distinct but rather confused. Nonetheless, because of what is confused and heaped-up in the cognition, truth cannot even be found to a high degree in aesthetic perfection. For it does not properly occupy my will but rather only my taste, and just so is it with certainty, too. Not every sensible

59 certainty is aesthetically perfect, but properly only that which excites our feeling and flatters it. One can have, e.g., the greatest cognition[s] of geogra-

[r] French: characteristics, marks.
[s] "Kenntniß."

phy, etc., which, although it is perfect, is nonetheless not aesthetic, and just because it does not excite our feeling.

§ 31

The author draws everything together here and says that we ought to make our cognition at once logically and aesthetically perfect. The whole of the cognition that we possess ought to have all possible kinds of perfections. But who can achieve[t] this? In each part of our cognition such a thing can very often fail to occur. If I want, e.g., to make a book logically perfect, then I do not have to produce everywhere at the same time the aesthetic and practical, nor can I. And if, on the other hand, I want to make a book aesthetically or practically perfect, then I cannot always, in doing so, think about the production of the logically perfect. –

Many theological propositions do not bind[u] our faculty of choice immediately. Thus we can leave aside much logical and aesthetic perfection without thereby harming man. Just as a wise teacher conceals much that he knows that is beautiful, disclosing it when he knows that the minds of his listeners are so constituted that they want to become accustomed to speculations and to be turned away from the practical[;] and just so too, in certain cases, must one often abstract from the practical in one thing or another. Many things can be true and yet still harmful to man. Not all truth is useful. It is also certain, meanwhile, that all the harmfulness that a truth can perhaps sometimes have is in every case only accidental. Thus there are certainly recommendations for cognitions and judgments that can finally develop into bribery, and again there are negative recommendations,[v] disdain, complaints concerning other cognitions or judgments, but without investigating how, after all, these cognitions are constituted. To avoid these two-sided errors, let us, in every investigation of a cognition, take it completely alone[,] separated from all foreign questions of use or harm, and in particular when we ourselves have an interest in this use or harm[;] for otherwise partisanship at once states its judgment and deadens 60 all cold reflections of the understanding.

Opining has always been the fruitful source of all errors of the human understanding.

§ 32

All of men's actions occur because of the drive toward perfection. This is achieved, however, when our feeling is excited by pleasure and displea-

[t] "prästiren."
[u] "verbinden."
[v] "Miß-Empfehlungen."

sure. If a rational cognition presupposes feeling,[w] then it is a rational pleasure and feeling.

But if it follows only from a confused cognition, then it is a sensible pleasure and feeling. We have to make our cognition perfect according to both kinds of feeling.

What excites our rational feeling is *logically perfect*. E.g., when I delight in thorough instruction. But what excites our sensible feeling is aesthetically perfect.

In general, the horizon of our cognition practically determined is far narrower than the horizon of our cognition logically determined.

§ 33

Here the author shows how logical perfections can be combined with aesthetic ones. E.g., one finds logical perfections in Wolff and in other writings, but no aesthetic perfections. In beautiful books, however, one finds again fewer logical perfections, and on the other hand many more aesthetic perfections. But the *autores* of such books have the lowest position. Everything that stimulates and excites us serves to disadvantage our power of judgment.

Aesthetic perfection, especially excitement and stimulation, are in many respects opposed to logical perfection, since the former concerns sensibility, the latter on the other hand the abstract. But in many respects, however, it is required in accordance with logical perfection, namely for what belongs to sensible aesthetic intuition.

He who wants truly and lastingly to convince himself of the truth of his propositions must refrain from all sensation, impression, stimulation, and sought-after beauty. So that the reader will not believe that he wanted merely to persuade him, deceive him, and flatter him. So that he will give his propositions approval, because he is not in a position to prove them to him.

61

§ 34

All the cognition that we possess ought to be logical and aesthetic. If, therefore, we want to increase the logical perfections, we must not destroy the aesthetic ones. Furthermore, if we want to promote the beautiful in our cognition, then we must not wholly ruin the logical. If one wants to cultivate his understanding and at the same time his taste, therefore, one should read not merely comedies, novels, gallant tales, etc., and other such books, where there are beautiful and aesthetic cognitions, to be sure, but where no logical perfections at all are to be found. Feeling is of course

[w] Reading "das Gefühl" for "dem Gefühl."

excited by this and taste refined, but it is also certain that the understanding is harmed[;] in this way it becomes duller and unusable. With children one should begin with the sensible. Geography could be expounded for them in such a way that they always sense and are excited. Thus instead of having them commit names to memory *verbose*[x] one could tell them instead about the noteworthy features of the sea, particular customs of foreign nations and peoples, etc., and not just show them on the map – that is Paris, that London, etc. – without commenting on anything, as commonly happens. From history, again, one could expound for them, in the liveliest and most exciting way, the events that have happened, so that their feeling and desires would thereby be improved. With the more mature ages one could also start various exercises for the understanding with them. One could read them suitable, selected poems and good speeches and get them to reflect on them.

But one must not force them, often before they can even think, to an oratory which in any case is later of no use to them, except that they forget it, as commonly happens in school; for what one has had to learn unwillingly, or even by means of force, one soon forgets by oneself. Dry cognitions, which become so popular, like reciting the names of places, emperors, dates, etc., ruin the youth to the highest degree. A child learns them with ill humor, and he does not retain them but instead, out of fear of punishment, seeks only to recite his lessons perfectly, etc. It is not at all his intention that what he has once learned should always remain in his memory. Even if one says to him that he cannot be or become happy otherwise, he pays this no heed, he is fully disinterested, and satisfied simply with his present pleasure. Detests everything that will lessen it for him, then. Hence he will naturally retain, and seek to retain, only what pleases him and stirs his feeling. If now everything is expounded in such a way, then he would gladly learn everything and with pleasure be able to retain it.

62

To be *truthful* is the greatest virtue in the world, on which all the remaining ones are grounded, and without truthfulness all the remaining virtues are in fact nothing but pretenses. This virtue, therefore, should be expounded for children first of all, and at the same time they should always be accustomed to it, if not through words, then at least through mien.

One should strive above all things to implant in children a strong loathing toward each and every untruth, whatever the pretext under which one might be able to excuse it, as, e.g., toward a maggot or other vermin. They will learn afterward in their lives gradually to accustom themselves to lie just as little as they pick up maggots. They will always be honest and will hate all possible pretense.

[x] verbosely (reading "verbose" for "verbosus," with Hinske, KI, lxxiii).

Every man has furthermore a natural and for him, as it were, innate drive toward benevolence. Just as we are glad when we can make another laugh with our flashes of wit, we are still more glad when we ourselves have made others happy, or have simply given them joy, pleasure, etc. (Only a few malicious souls, who wish for, or even promote, the unhappiness of their fellow men, are excepted from this.) This, too, one would have to know how to sustain in a child. One should, e.g., give a child something to give to other children who are poorer, but not only after they ask for it like beggars, since they are miserable. For by this means one accustoms them merely to sympathy, which is very different from true charity[;] one should have the child pass something on to others merely in order to give it, because it is beautiful and praiseworthy to pass on what one has left over; because they deserve it, although they do not ask for it or do not have the heart [to do so].

If now one has taught the child this much through sensation, then this will certainly improve his moral character. And he will take pleasure in moral tales.

63 If one has accomplished this, then one can teach the child to read[;] then he will himself see how the skill of being able to read helps him. He will himself get the desire for it, he will make an effort to acquire skill, and the sooner the better, since this reading puts him in a position himself to read letters, poems, moral tales,[y] and other beautiful books, and furthermore not to need to ask others to tell him something. Now when this has happened, then one should seek to further his historical cognition. Because this has to provide the ground for rational cognition. One should not load him down with a terrible multitude of names[;] he naturally sees no use in this and consequently has no desire for it.

If one presents stories morally, then he will take pleasure in this, and will consider the names just as something secondary, but nevertheless retain them.

One should seek, finally, to broaden his rational cognition, too, and to further it. One should tell him the grounds when he asks the causes of something, but not load him down with distant grounds. If he asks why no grain grows in this or that field one should tell him, because it is sandy, etc., but not give him any extensive explanation of fruitfulness[;] this serves no purpose except to confuse his understanding.

§ 35

In this § the author says that one must let the small perfections go if greater ones are hindered by them. Greater logical perfections must be

[y] "Moralische Begebenheiten."

put ahead of small aesthetic ones, and greater aesthetic perfections, again, ahead of smaller logical ones.

If one follows this rule, one will write logically, also aesthetically beautifully, and will be able to express himself in an exposition.

§ 36

The opposite of each perfection is in all cases of two kinds, namely, either the *contradictory opposite*, if the perfection is merely lacking, or secondly the *real opposite*, which abolishes completely the perfection which might exist based on some other ground. An example of the first would be, e.g., those *medicamenta* that do not help at all but also do no harm[;] these can often be prescribed[; this] is appropriately compared with the contradictory opposite of healing[;] but those medicines which not only have no use but also do harm have the real opposite of healing. So too is it in cognitions. 64

The imperfection that is the contradictory opposite is called a *lack*[,] and the imperfection that is the *real* opposite of the perfect is called *a mistake*. Thus, e.g., ignorance of the immortality of the human soul is the contradictory opposite, but the mistake, where one even believes the human soul is not immortal, is the real opposite of the cognition of immortality of soul. Ignorance lacks only grounds[;] hence it can easily be helped. With error, however, there are real grounds that are opposed as opposing grounds to the true cognition.

A mistake[z] must therefore be much more avoided than a lack.[a] It is much worse if I have to remove what has actually been proved from other grounds than if I do not yet know anything; because in the last case I can more readily be taught than in the first. E.g., he who does not define something at all can get by with his common cognition, whereas if he makes false *definitiones* and afterward applies them, there arises from this a far greater, more important harm, which could not have arisen in the case of a lack. In the case of *vitia*, however, cognition is not only not increased but rather diminished, and that which is already there is actually removed.

§ 37

Common and historical cognition can be much more perfect than learned cognition. They are to be regarded as *heterogenea*, but they can also be considered in relation to a *focus imaginarius*,[b] e.g., whether they are lively, fruitful, and so forth. By historical cognition we do not understand aes-

[z] "Die Fehler: vitia."

[a] "Mangel, Defectus."

[b] point at which an image is focused, e.g., behind a mirror (reading "Focum Imaginarium" for "Focum Perfectionis").

thetical, but rather merely dry cognition. But this dry cognition in the case of a man, e.g., regarding the conditions and events of his life, can be much more fruitful and extensive than learned cognition.

A *mathematicus*, who otherwise possesses much cognition, will not get 65 as far in *praxis*$_L$ with his science of engineering as another who has not studied the theory but has acquired for himself a merely historical cognition of *praxis*$_L$.

Machiavelli, e.g., had a great, learned cognition of how to place a whole army in battle order, but when he was once actually commissioned to command an army, instead of putting it in order he put the whole army in disorder, because he had no historical cognition of the secondary circumstances.

In many respects the learned man with his solid cognition actually does not accomplish nearly as much as someone else whose cognition is historical, because the first is not as universally useful as the other.

§ 38 et 39

Rousseau is of the opinion that the sciences have brought more harm than good. We have capacities that are far greater than is necessary for this life. Our theoretical capacities are in us much stronger than the practical ones. We can improve the former more than the latter, and thus [arises] a disproportion, a monster, in which the head is too large *en regard* to the other parts of the body. If we did not have another life to expect, then learnedness would certainly be more harmful for us than useful. For here we often fail to have enough advantages for the troubles we give ourselves. But in the meantime, learnedness has also provided us with many advantages here. Navigation, the art of ruling, etc., would surely have remained very obscure and imperfect without it. How useful it is that by it alone as by a light the darkness of superstition has been destroyed, and that superstition so fortunately rooted out. Many old women can now grow older with honor and conclude their lives in peace than previously, since they quite often came under suspicion and had to lose their lives in a miserable way.

Learned cognition considers the universal and therefore gives occasion for discoveries and improvements.

§ 40

If learned cognition is at the same time beautiful, then it is most useful,[c] especially in *praxis*$_L$. We know the cognition of the scholastics, these dry 66 philosophers who bind themselves to a very constrained method, [we

[c] "die nützlichste und brauchbareste."

know] how it destroyed, as it were, the moral properties and capacities of men and lowered them to superstition. An irreplaceable loss! But of course all of this could not be otherwise, and it all came about because their cognition, and consequently also their expositions of morals, etc., were merely learned and not at the same time beautiful, but rather were completely dry. Thus a cognition that is beautiful but not learned, and one that is learned but dry, is harmful.

THE SECOND SECTION

Of the extensiveness of learned cognition

§ 41 et 42

The extensiveness of learned cognition is opposed to its *poverty*. This concerns either the *material* or the *formal*. If someone lacks historical cognition, then he is in complete ignorance. Thus, e.g., the ancients were in complete ignorance of the existence of the new world[;] they had no historical cognition of it. The common man is still wholly ignorant in regard to many things. But one can also be in ignorance in regard to the grounds of a thing: 1. in that it is completely unknown to us, so that one has no historical cognition concerning it. E.g., when one does not know at all whence thunderstorms, rain, snow, etc. arise.

2. When one does not comprehend the *nexus*$_L$ of things with their grounds, although the grounds are now known to someone. E.g., when I know the ebb and flood have the moon as their cause, but do not yet understand, and have insight, how it happens that the ebb and flood proceed from the attraction of the moon.

§ 43

As for what concerns ignorance, this can be divided into

1. *a necessary ignorance, and on the other hand*
2. *a voluntary one.*

Where no data are given to us for settling something, ignorance is necessary. E.g., to settle where the human soul will be after death. *Item*$_L$ concerning the power of reproduction for animals and men. 67

Third, the position we have in the world makes ignorance necessary for us. But when because of certain moving grounds we dismiss some things from our minds, so that we try industriously not to know them when we see that something is too hard for us, or is useless, then this is logical ignorance.

Logic is more a doctrine of skill, which belongs to the youth, but the doctrine of wisdom belongs to the man.

§ 44

That circle within which we can see things is called our horizon. The complex of things that man can cognize in a learned fashion without detriment to his remaining cognitions is the horizon of his learned cognition. What lies beyond the horizon can be seen in the geographical sense. But here it ought to mean such things as one cannot cognize even if one wanted to, ignorance of which is necessary. We are ignorant about many things even in historical cognition[,] e.g., about the joys of heaven, about mysteries, because they perhaps cannot be expressed by our words[;] we are often in ignorance about a few things because of our weak capacities, but about other things in regard to circumstances, the time, the place.

We determine the horizon of our cognition

1. *logically* merely by the faculty, by the measure of our powers
2. *practically* in accordance with ends.

People believe it is always good to know more than they may, and that it is better to know too much than too little. But all effort to an excessive degree toward a purpose is superfluous, and is badly applied. It is necessary, then, that all our efforts be adequate to the ends we have set before ourselves, otherwise man squanders the capital of his powers, which is very limited; we say something goes beyond our horizon when it goes beyond the capacities of our cognition.

Many more things are beyond the learned horizon than are beyond the historical one. The former is thus much smaller than the latter. Much 68 that I cognize historically I can never cognize learnedly and beautifully. E.g., I have a historical but not a learned cognition of the *commercium animae et corporis*.[d] We must not get ourselves involved with all objects, therefore, but always think about the fact that we have a horizon in cognition. Thus it is also not necessary to get ourselves involved in investigation concerning the condition of the soul after death, either, which is beyond our horizon.

It is very hard to determine what is really beyond our horizon. If it frequently appears to me as if something were beyond my horizon, so that I hold it to be an impossibility, such a thing can still in time come within my horizon due to investigation and industry. It is the true philosophy of the lazy when one maintains of all things that they are beyond our horizon.

But if someone says: I can of course cognize something, but I do not need to, it is superfluous for me, or is even harmful to me, I ought not to

[d] intercourse between soul and body.

cognize it, this is as much as to say: it is beyond my horizon. One determines his horizon according to taste

1. According to the taste of the man.
2. According to the taste of the age.

But if it is true that most men draw the horizon of their cognition only according to taste, this is only a superficial cognition, in order to seem learned to all, to be able to be judged learned by all. But this is, as it were, only the foam of cognition, which even involves a certain impudence.

Our age is almost one like this. But the harm from this is also unavoidable. Namely, that all sciences are finally treated only superficially.

The more a science is restricted to a single purpose, the greater the degree of the perfection it can attain. In our times one would almost think that everything would be refined and learned. Instead of doing rough housework, as before, women now read fine writings. That is called *being well read*, and in this they seek an excellence. But this great extension causes science to lose its worth. The logical horizon of our capacities is

1. *historical*[,] which is and must be the most extensive.
2. *rational*, but this is very narrow.

The *historical horizon* is to be cultivated particularly in our youth. Yet the purpose must also be known, in accordance with which I acquire historical cognition. 69

He who has all historical cognition of all possible sciences is the polyhistor.

Philosophy is the field of all historical cognition, of the theologian, the *physicus*[.]

A polyhistor possesses the materials for a science, his head is a true *bibliotheca*[;] polyhistory also involves philology in particular, the science of the tools of learnedness.

The more perfect a science is to become in its kind, the narrower it becomes. Those who have all historical cognition and all cognition of reason are the great, universal minds, of whom there are only very few.

Every one must think that according to his capacities, be they great or small, he has a certain determinate horizon suited to himself. E.g., he who knows something of geometry, assuming too that it is still not much, must and can well think that finding out how to square the circle is beyond his horizon.

The horizon of our cognition changes with time. What is now beyond it finally comes finally within it, if I gain more capacities and cultivate these properly and better.

A beginner commonly thinks that nothing is beyond, but rather everything is within, his horizon, that he is perfectly well in a position to cognize, and to settle, everything. But with time one sees the illusion and knows how to limit his horizon, or else falls into the thought that everything is hard for us, or beyond our horizon.

How many are there among the so-called philosophers in name only who are concerned only about their external glitter, and completely conceited, who in fact think they are in a position to be the teacher of a philosophy. Yet such a thing is far beyond their horizon.

§ 46

Things are lowered beneath the horizon of learned cognition when they 70 are unworthy of our learned cognition. A few absurd opinions of the ancient philosophers are not even worthy of our historical cognition, of our acquainting ourselves with them.

By nature, however, not even the least thing is unworthy of our historical cognition, unless one should want to apply oneself very much to it, so that one neglects more important things.

Foolishness and methods have also put a lot beneath the horizon of our cognition. E.g., because of the foolishness of man the investigation of urine is now considered to be almost indecent, although it quite often serves to distinguish diseases.

§ 47

Things are outside the horizon of our learned cognition which are excluded from it because they make us neglect more important things. Nothing can be outside the horizon of an unlimited understanding[;] this occurs rather only with a limited understanding.

We must use our capacities economically, so that we can apply them to important things.

What does not belong to that science that we have really[,] honestly chosen to cultivate is therefore outside our horizon, unless it is beyond or beneath it.

To occupy oneself principally with foreign things, and to the neglect of more important ones, is actually to overstep one's horizon. One can make the historical horizon as broad as possible. Very seldom is a thing outside the historical horizon, but rather outside the learned horizon.

As the understanding grows, more and more objects come beneath its horizon, and this is gradually broadened.

Rousseau says, completely correctly, that all those who have written about education, and thus most parents also, want to make of children perfect men, whereas they ought first to make[e] a perfect child of them.

[e] "bilden."

They place beneath the horizon of the child what actually belongs beneath the horizon of the man.

§ 48

That which is not beneath, or beyond, or outside our horizon is within our horizon.

The determination of the learned horizon is too difficult for a youth to be able to make it.

People of insight, who by themselves have in their way failed, can best determine the horizon. They will indicate to the student what is necessary, what unnecessary, and how one can easily fail here.

It is better if one first seeks to gain insight into very many things than if one tries to learn only a few things, and these completely thoroughly, because this is easier for a youth and more stimulating. One should seek first to form an overriding concept[f] of many sciences, then one should take up one science after the other thoroughly. This would have the value that when one had planned to treat this or that individual science quite thoroughly, one could comprehend the *nexus*$_L$ with other sciences, and with each one could provide an elucidation with the others. It is quite wrong, then, when parents want to determine the horizon and the manner of life for children still in the cradle. When, e.g., they want to conclude, from the fact that it has a serious expression, and that it can cry and scold well, that it will be well suited for the pulpit[;] and because another in his youth would happily investigate all things, and analyze them and take them apart, they surmise that someday he must become a skilled *anatomus*.

§ 50

Ignorance is always an imperfection and can therefore certainly never be praiseworthy, but it can well be beyond blame, when one renounces certain objects in order not to neglect, on their account, more important cognitions.

Leibniz could have had a blameless ignorance in many things. E.g., in chemistry, in antiquities, and in general in very many other things, which overload a great genius far too much.

§ 52

Ignorance can be divided into *common* and *learned* ignorance. For a learned man to comprehend properly that he knows nothing, great learnedness is required.

[f] "Haupt-Begriff."

72 *Quantum est quod nescimus!*[g] But no one has cleverer thoughts than a beginner. For he does not yet understand at all what it means to know something, that is, [to know] little or much or nothing. Also, he does not himself know whether he knows something or not. But with time one learns to appraise one's insights, and to see that they still have very great shortcomings and imperfections.

Socrates held it to be his greatest learnedness that he saw that he knew nothing. – A beginner believes he can define and demonstrate everything, but he does not see at all that so many materials are a labyrinth for him[;] but he comes to cognize this when he possesses more learnedness. The learned man is in many things just as ignorant as the common man. He is in a position, however, to philosophize concerning this ignorance himself, and to be able to indicate its ground and its degree.

When one has undertaken many investigations, has learned much, has inquired into much, only then does one first come to cognize his ignorance. Who represents to himself that we know only a mere external determination concerning substances, and no other? The only one who knows this and is in a position to see how small, how defective and imperfect, all his cognitions are, is one who has walked enough through the fields of learnedness.

§ 53

A cognition which is extensively great, or which comprehends within itself very many objects, the author calls polyhistory. Those who study for the sake of gallantry commonly apply themselves to this polyhistory. Their cognition is like a great land, which contains many white places,[17] and which for a long time has not been able to be as fruitful as that land which, though admittedly smaller, is on the other hand better cultivated.

§ 55

A cognition becomes full and complete when it is sufficient for a certain end. It is exact when it contains nothing more than is required for the end that this cognition has.

Many a preacher can have cognition sufficient, e.g., for the schoolmaster's office, although not for that of the preacher. He would surely have 73 become an excellent teacher, but now he is a miserable preacher. On the other hand, many a schoolteacher, who at the moment can manage his office only badly, would have become a better preacher than he now is a schoolmaster.

[g] How much is that of which we are ignorant!

§ 56

He who simply skims over learnedness, who only acquaints himself with everything historically, so that he can talk about everything in society, has only meager learnedness and, as it were, only a skeleton of it.

Such a one is worthy of contempt to the same degree as one who makes a great show with his clothes, but who, because of a shriveled stomach or some other disease, and of miserable circumstances, feels the greatest agony.

He who possesses a meager cognition can never satisfy himself, and sees that it is only a delusion.[h] He cannot be satisfied and pleased with himself. He is not in a position to enjoy himself. He has to seek out others, go among others, and he takes pleasure in the fact that at least others, though ignorant, consider him learned.

§ 57

One must always strive to broaden his learned cognition. If we do not go forward, then we are sure to fall behind once and for all.

One must have an immediate inclination toward learnedness if one wants constantly to increase it and never to let it fall into decline. But commonly one acquires thereby only as much as one needs to get bread and to be able to live.

§ 58

We would surely not overload our heads with learnedness and do ourselves harm if we observed this properly and took the easy before the hard.

It would be better if one might expound all the sciences first in a very easy way; so that one would not need for this much beyond the common use of the understanding. Once one had thus expounded the sciences, one could then expound them in their complete perfection and acuity, which commonly occurs at the beginning, even though this perfection is not needed by all, and much harm frequently arises from it. 74

Many would be satisfied with a provisional exposition of the sciences in the beginning, e.g., in accordance with Gesner's *Isagoge*,[18] rather than with a more extensive exposition of them, which on that account becomes obscure and difficult.

[h] "ein Blendnuß."

§ 59

Hippocrates wisely says: *ars longa, vita brevis.*[i] Indolent people commonly complain about the length of the time they have left to live. But the time that they have spent being completely inactive and dreaming seems to them to have been fleeting and appears very short, because they did nothing in it and consequently can remember nothing at all important that happened then.

Many sciences are of such a kind that, with the passage of time, human capacities will be overstepped by their extent.

Thus history, e.g., is already very extensive[;] with time and its duration, more and more is always happening. More and more events are always occurring in the world. These all add to history, and this science finally will thus become extensive and grow, so that our memory will finally be far too small. For it is already quite hard now.

Perhaps it will go similarly with mathematics. For what it contains now is already quite large enough for our capacities. Perhaps with the duration of time it will thus become so great that our successors will not dare to venture upon it.

Perhaps in time mathematical writings will stand like the Egyptian pyramids, which no one imitates, but which only recall those who passed away in an earlier time.

But although learnedness is so extensive, our life is still long enough for us to see properly what all is around us, if we wanted to apply all our time to it.

To earn bread is an ignoble, unworthy end for learnedness. Great insights are not at all useful for earning bread. A small measure of learnedness, *hardiesse*,[j] the art of disputation, the shamelessness of advancing oneself and of diminishing other great minds, are best suited for earning bread: anyone can attain office except the worthy.

75

§ 61

To guard against forgetfulness, the author says, one must learn much, so that one will still know something, even if one has with time forgotten something – so that one will not just be stripped of all knowledge.

But it is probably best if one has attained the skill of being able to philosophize concerning objects by oneself, and of being able to cultivate the sciences. He who has this, is like a *musicus* who has forgotten all the pieces he had learned but can play whatever is set before him and can himself compose.

[i] Art lasts long, life is short.

[j] French: boldness, impudence.

§ 65

A learned man who brings his science to bear in company is called a pedant, but to be this, someone must really possess a skill, which he seeks to bring to bear everywhere, even given that it frequently does not fit. He must not be completely dumb and ignorant, however. In all conditions of life there can be, besides learned people, also pedants. Among the nobility, e.g., there are pedants of the hunt, who talk of nothing but their hunt, dogs[,] foxes who have played pranks on them, hares[,] roe, stags, etc.

Thus there are pedants of finery, who cannot be angry enough, and who know and can find no end of complaining, if a *manchette*,[k] or a lock, or a ribbon, is damaged or tangled. In society one is called a pedant if, in his conversations, he brings to bear unnecessary investigations, and distinctions, which would be more suitable for the podium than for a society for entertainment.

In learnedness one becomes a pedant when one always wants to define and to make unnecessary qualifications. The methods used today to instruct women are ways of making them pedants.

Charlatanism involves thinking oneself great and acting proudly and setting oneself above others, when one has little insight. 76

The mathematical method with which in earlier times people boasted and tried to be thorough was nothing but a kind of charlatanism. To play or to show off with one's demonstrations, or with one's wit, is also charlatanism.

To avoid this properly let one acquire thorough learnedness. If this has happened, one will thus at once become aware of and have insight into how much we lack, and how little we have cause to boast of our modest sciences and cognitions, but instead how much cause we have to call out with humility: *quantum est, quod nescimus.*[l]

THE THIRD SECTION

Of the quantity of learned cognition

§ 66–91

In the foregoing Second Section we spoke of the extensiveness of learned cognition, but this actually pertains to the quantity of cognition. Thus the author has done wrong in dealing with the extensiveness of cognition as well as with its quantity in separate sections.

In the previous section we actually considered what is extensive in

[k] French: cuff.

[l] How much is that of which we are ignorant.

cognition, and now it remains to consider what is *intensive* in it. In this, however, the author draws a completely unnecessary distinction.

The degree of dignity with which we have insight into things depends especially and first of all on our choosing the right things. To this pertains correct taste, and good feeling, by virtue of which one is able to choose important objects, which have many or few consequences, but important ones.

The concepts of politeness and impropriety[m] do not have great consequences in common life, to be sure, but they do have many, and are therefore of great importance.

77 What is lacking in importance in one or some consequences is often made up for quite well by the multitude of the consequences.

The correction of error, of conscience, on the other hand, has few, but great, consequences.

Furthermore, it pertains to the dignity of our insights that we not apply too much effort to a thing, and withdraw our industry from other objects, when this is actually not so necessary. The art of correctly estimating the importance of cognitions involves especially good feeling and true correctness of imagination. I can easily show someone else the consequences, but one cannot teach him to feel the magnitude of these consequences.

Concerning *metaphysica*, I can say to him that he will receive clarified concepts of his soul, of providence, of the highest being, of the world. But if he is without feeling in regard to this great gain, then no description will help him at all.

A cognition is great insofar as it has a universal use, but all these cognitions are disadvantaged in that although their use is great and one cognizes many things by means of them, one cognizes all that much less in these many things themselves.

I think little about many objects.

But there is another cognition, by means of which one cognizes much in few things. The previous mistake arises in most cases from the fact that one thinks always *in abstracto*, and from this many other [mistakes] arise. Baumgarten says: beauty is *perfectio phaenomenon*, perfection in appearance. But can one from this explanation actually observe beauty in objects, in cognitions? By comprising much under itself, a cognition comprises that much less in itself. The lack of a cognition is not always blameworthy, if only the lack does not contradict a given purpose. But as soon as this is so, then from this *lack* arises an *error*. From this by itself it follows that those who promise to give a definition of a thing run the risk that one will immediately fault[n] them for the slightest missing characteristic, which one would not have done if they had indicated that they did not intend to

[m] Reading "Unanständigkeit" for "Unbeständigkeit."

[n] "imputiret."

develop the matter completely but only to explain it in a way appropriate to a certain consideration. It is likewise with demonstrations and proofs. 78

The limits we set for our desire for knowledge are so necessary that without them we can scarcely cognize another science properly. To get to the point where we are in a position to cognize a cognition completely, then, we must voluntarily impose on ourselves, as it were, an arbitrary lack in regard to other cognitions that are perhaps opposed to this cognition, i.e., a kind of ignorance of them, so that we can turn all our energy to this, and comprehend it quite perfectly.

Lacks[o] are nothing other than limits of a thing that ought to begin there. They are its *termini*, restrictions, and the lack actually subsists quite well with the perfection of a beginning.

The evaluation of cognitions does not involve any acuity but only feeling. *Mathematici* can be very acute but nonetheless have no taste for *metaphysica* or some other logical, or moral, investigation.

Cognitions frequently seem to us to be dry and of no value. Afterward, when we once wander through them and penetrate into their interior, their advantages are soon revealed. Thus, e.g., electricity was nothing but a fine toy; afterwards, however, it showed itself to have the use that it now may help to cure some diseases. Perhaps with time we will even be able, with the help of electricity, to drive away thunderstorms.

Euclid thereby discovered many properties of the circle, and only with time were the extensive advantages of this seen. Many things have come to be despised and contemptible only on account of misuse. E.g., the Wolffians have spoken so long and so much of monads that they are ridiculed by comic poets.

The expressions monad, best world, sufficient and insufficient ground, are so dishonored by the learned crowd that now one actually hesitates to avail oneself of them. Much that is in fact possible and good can also quickly be made ridiculous and represented as absurd.

Thus, e.g., Voltaire ridiculed Maupertuis's thought when the latter holds that the Egyptians should have dug holes[p] in the earth rather than pyramids in order to make an immortal name for themselves,[19] so that he comes to be completely ridiculous, although he was perhaps one of the greatest men of his time. 79

Meanwhile, no one wishes to apply his learnedness to useless objects, nor to take it along in common society, as has happened, e.g., with the doctrine of the best world, which was finally applied to everything possible.

Finally, it is to be noted that much is taken to be useless cavilling

[o] "Die *Mängel Defectus*."

[p] Reading "Löcher" for "Bücher."

because one is too weak for it and is not in a position to be able to have insight into it and to cognize it.

"As one often despises a beautiful woman because he has not won her in accordance with his pleasure, and as the fox proclaims the grapes to be unripe when he cannot snatch them. – "

One can never, or very seldomly, have insight into, and know in advance, every use of this or that cognition.

Did Euclid ever think, when he discovered his propositions, that from these propositions one would discover the distance of the heavenly bodies?

The author says that lesser truths[q] must not be neglected, since they are frequently useful in connection with principal truths. Because a cognition is hard, it is not just for that reason to be valued highly.

Because something is imposing, it sometimes pleases even though it has no use. This includes, e.g., the sophistical fragments of the scholastics, the fallacies, the 4 figures of the syllogism. One of the scholastic learned men is supposed to have made himself so thin by studying the sophistical proposition called the liar that he finally had to wear lead soles, so that he would at least have some weight, and a strong wind would not knock him down and hurl him off the bridge.

When many details come together they finally constitute a great cognition.

A cognition can be great on account of its many consequences, even if these consequences are not great and important. Thus is it, e.g., with calculation.

What is great for one is small for another. The Latin language, like metaphysical questions and investigations are important and great for learned men.

80 For women, however, these are unnecessary. For noble people too[,] princes, etc., not all cognitions are necessary[;] rather, in many sciences and on many matters they can rely on the learned, as one who does not understand this or that craft relies on the craftsman when he commissions him to make a thing. For such gentlemen as princes, etc., it would be unnecessary to go far into *metaphysica* and its investigations.

Instead one should instill in them true learnedness, which is necessary for them, that is, one should teach them first and foremost justice, the worth of man, of their subjects, hatred of flatterers and flattery, true care of the citizens of their land, and to distinguish the true from the false interests of the state, and one should properly imprint the cognition of all this in them; then some of those monarchs who are now of evil sentiments will be full of noble magnanimity, and of sublime sentiments worthy of their position. We will have happy princes, subjects, and countries. In

[q] "Zwischenwahrheiten."

accordance with its feeling, a great mind does not occupy itself with small matters[;] he comprehends what is important and chooses it as his object.

THE FOURTH SECTION

Of the truth of learned cognition

§ 92 et § 93

The universal highest question of someone who wants to learn *logica* is quite naturally, What is truth?

Now to answer this question, which is so appropriate to the understanding of man, and in particular of a beginner, will cause more difficulties than one would think, and there have been people who have seen that we are actually not able to give any distinct, complete, precise concept of it.

It has always been so[;] none of the ancient Roman jurists, e.g., was really able to say *what is right* and not *right*[r] (*quid sit jus*), and nonetheless the concept that we have of it is complete enough for use and sufficiently good enough. 81

But to see the difficulties that can arise with the concept of truth, we observe the following: First, if a mark[s] of truth is to be given, then a judgment[,] a rule[,] will have to be given. Thus the highest criterion cannot be given.

If a cognition does not agree with the character of the thing that we want to represent and to cognize, then it is false, in that it cannot subsist with truth. If on the other hand a cognition is in conformity with the character of the thing that we represent, then it is true.

The skeptic, on the other hand, said: Something is true if it agrees with the object, but I cannot have insight into this unless I first consider and cognize the object. Hence this amounts to nothing but the fact that the cognition of the object agrees with the cognition of the object. But this is *identitas[,] idem per idem*[t] – nothing, the skeptics said[; it] is a circle in the explanation of truth. This argument is called a diallelon, and since the skeptics concluded thus, they drew the main conclusion that any distinction between the true and the false is nothing.

In the case of false cognition, I do not cognize or grasp the thing itself, which I want to represent, but instead another. E.g., if I represent the polyp as a worm, then I have a false cognition of a polyp.

False learned cognitions are ones that ought to be learned, or ones that seem to be learned, but are in fact not so. This always happens, however,

[r] "*was recht*, und nicht *recht* sey."

[s] "Merckmahl Criterium."

[t] identity[,] the same through the same.

when one clothes indistinct, common cognitions in *termini occulti*, through which one really does not get a correct concept of the thing at all, however, but merely an explanation *idem per idem*. E.g., if one were to ask about the cause of the propagation and the increase of human and animal understanding, and if one wanted to have a distinct concept of how this comes to pass, then the ancients said with an affected, learned mien: the cause of the propagation of men and animals is the *vis plastica*, the power of propagation.

One imagines that one has given an actual ground of the thing, then, 82 but in fact says nothing more than what one actually asked and wants to know, although in other words.

One clothes the concept of such a thing somewhat differently, puts a plume on it, so to speak, and then values it excessively highly.

In the writings of the ancient philosophers we quite frequently find such *qualitates occultas*, and in the writings of Crusius they are as frequent as they ever could have been among the ancients. He says, e.g.: something is true because no one regards it as, or can hold it to be, other than true.

The one says just as much as the other, thus it is a *qualitas occulta*.

Now if we do not want to be asked further[u] about the cause of this or that, then we often state a ground which, however, is not one. E.g., if I ask why this [man] yawns [when he] looks at that [man yawning], the ancients said somberly, the ground of this is sympathy.[v] But this word indicates nothing other than shared feeling.[w] Thus they said nothing except that it happens because the one must share feeling with the other. But how is this brought about in the case of yawning? Hence they thereby explained nothing.

With the truth of learned cognition it is also a matter of the formal. The cognition itself must actually not be a common, but instead a learned cognition.

The material in a cognition can quite frequently be true, the cognition can be in conformity with the thing, and thus as a common cognition have truth.

But if the same cognition is supposed to be learned, though actually it is not so, then it will thereby become a false learned cognition.

To extend *qualitates occultae* is the death of philosophy. One believes, then, that one possesses an actual learned cognition, although in fact it is nothing but a common cognition.

What Crusius says of probability in his writings[20] is quite pleasing to very many. But in fact it is nothing but what we already know through

[u] Reading "Wenn man sich nun" instead of "Wenn man nun," with Hinske (KI, lxxi).

[v] "die Sympathie."

[w] "ein Mitleiden."

merely common cognition. Only it is expounded with a certain pomp, which is aways very characteristic of Crusius.

Thus it follows naturally that it carries the illusion but not the essence of learnedness and of a learned cognition.

The *first thing* in every thing, cognition, science, art, etc., causes great difficulty. 83

Truth and *error* are never found in concepts but only in judgments. He who never judges will also never err, then, but he will never speak a truth, either.

The concept is always the *datum*$_L$, regarding which I am to judge. Concepts are the materials for judging.

There are methods for avoiding all errors, but these are so simple that just for that reason one does not pay attention to them. However, they consist briefly in this: do not *judge* so much, do not decide often, indeed quite seldomly, except in certain cases where it is also necessary. Do not always settle whether something is true or whether it is false; rather,[x] do so seldomly.

There is a certain moderation in thinking and in judging, then, and it is needed in order to avoid error.

But how many philosophers of our times like always to decide.

To this impudent maintaining of accepted or even of concocted opinions, to these deciding judgments[y] concerning propositions of reason, which were already familiar to the ancients, Pyrrho responded: "*non liquet*."[z] – Many authors entwine themselves in doubtful circumstances of this sort by means of deciding judgments and secondary thoughts,[a] which are often understood as errors.

A *home-made remedy*[b] against errors is to distinguish nothing, to judge little, and thus it happens that one finds that a village full of farmers has fewer errors by far than an academy of sciences[;] thoughtlessness protects them against errors.

But then if we want to avoid all errors, we will have to decide to leave many [things] unconsidered.

This tells us, and just indicates, what the restrictions on our judgments are, and one has to judge concerning just these restrictions. If one had extremely important ends, however, so that every error, even the smallest, would be dangerous, then it is of course better to stay in one place, and merely to judge regarding what concerns our opportunities[;] thus it is, e.g., in morals.

[x] Reading "immer, sondern" for "immer, und," with Hinske (KI, lxxiii).

[y] "entscheidenden urtheilen."

[z] It is not clear.

[a] "Neben Gedancken."

[b] Ak, "Hauptmittel"; MS, "Haußmittel" (KI, lxviii).

Ignorance is an empty space in our head and on account of this it does not hinder any true cognition,[c] [even] if it does not extend it.

So long as our cognitions are only speculations, we can still probably 84 dare to err, but as soon as an error becomes harmful, and this happens as soon as it enters the practical, then it is very dangerous to retain it.

Judgments are actions of the understanding and of reason.

But the senses do not judge[.] Not all concepts arise out of the understanding, but some from the senses[;] all judgments, however, come merely from the understanding.

Often men hold a certain judgment of their understanding to be a sensation, and representation of the senses, although in fact it is anything but that.

There is no disputing about sensation. It is a *datum*$_L$, and not yet an error. But often such a sensation is actually the judgment of the understanding on the occasion of such sensations.

Appeals to such feelings and sensations are nowadays very fashionable[;] often some people want to feel and to sense right and wrong authoritatively,[d] and in fact by means of an inner moral feeling peculiar to themselves alone. Ridiculous. The understanding must necessarily be at work in this.

Truth is nothing but the agreement of a cognition with the laws of the understanding and of reason[,] and on the other hand the opposition of a cognition to the laws of the understanding and of reason is falsehood.

No power in nature deviates in its actions[e] from its laws or conditions, under which alone it can function[;] thus the understanding taken alone cannot possibly err.

All judgments agree with the laws of the understanding[;] all judgments of the understanding are thus true. Even in our erroneous judgments the understanding must always have done something, and in this, then, it cannot be that everything is false, but rather something must always be true.

It is completely impossible for a man to err completely when he judges.

In error, then, there is still truth. But we judge then in a mixed way, and run together the effects of the remaining powers of the mind, and from this arises the erroneous, which is so contrary to the understanding, and about which we nonetheless think falsely, and often believe with complete certainty, that it is an effect of the understanding. Although it is in fact nothing but, as it were, a bastard of sensibility and the understanding.

85 Now since, as we have shown, no judgment occurs without an *ingrediens* of truth, it follows necessarily from this that we will have to moderate our

[c] "Kenntniß."

[d] "meisterlich."

[e] Reading "in ihren Handlungen" for "nach ihren Handlungen," with Hinske (KI, lxxiii).

judgment concerning the *critica* of truth, and concerning the judgments and also errors of others. For it is a certain *principium*: We can never arrive at truth when we are always disputing, when one is always contradicting the other.

Every discovery of an error that is in fact crude and obvious is very sad. One would prefer not to make such sad discoveries, then, [but instead] to help one another mutually and in friendship, to support each other, and not always to act against the other.

Thus instead of contradicting a thing, one will have simply to investigate whether there isn't actually a truth to be found in it, [and] what needs to be supplied [; one will have to] act in every case in a social way, and then to make comprehensible to the one who errs, in a way that is least biting and is instead loving, how it is not surprising that he was able to err so very easily.

This lazy way of judging, this good-heartedness of sentiment that is so fitting, is just as necessary for the attainment of honest[f] cognition as it ever may be in common life.

But naturally, therefore, there is no total error. Otherwise the understanding would have to contradict and act against itself and its precepts.

Errors, however great and important they seem, are always only particular.[g]

One cannot instruct anyone except through what remains of the understanding that is still in him. One cannot improve a person except through what remains of the good that is still in him.

In instructing the understanding and improving the will I must of course always presuppose something true and something good.

Any other man's judgment is always a judgment of one of those men whose judgment, taken altogether, is my judge and is the greatest judge[h] of the products of my understanding.

A contradiction is of course nothing but an occasion where one says yes, but the other, in contrast, says no.

It follows that this must naturally to a certain extent disturb any rational man. But it is a universal duty of a philosopher in such a case always to aid humanity universally and to think generously: these opinions, seemingly so bizarre and absurd, are perhaps not as badly thought, not as absurd, as it may seem. 86

Everything that unifies men and makes them sociable[i] actually contributes much toward furthering the perfection of the whole of the human race. Conflict, however, produces nothing. It holds everywhere, and so in the whole world, among the learned:

[f] "rechtschaffener."

[g] "particulär."

[h] "Beurtheiler."

[i] "verträglich."

Concordia res parvae crescunt[,] discordia dilabuntur[.][j]

Furthermore, the restrictions, i.e., the narrow limits in which the human understanding is enclosed, are not to be regarded in the least as sources of errors, as so many supposed philosophers hold; they are in fact causes of man's ignorance on many matters, to be sure, but not of error[;] but as soon as one combines with this ignorance a self-conceit[,] an audacity[,] a learned pride in judging more than one knows and is in any position to know, error can arise from this.

The only cause of error, then, is the unsuitable arrogance of overstepping the restrictions, and limits, of one's own understanding.

The understanding alone does not err. The senses alone do not err either[;] they are passive and do not judge at all.

Only the human understanding judges.

Hence there must also exist certain materials[k] for judging.

The understanding must necessarily combine with sensibility in order to be able to judge, and this does not depend in the least on the faculty of choice[.]

Naturally, too, there are subjective conditions of our understanding and our thinking. And all of these we account to sensibility.

Sometimes the understanding is, as it were, in a certain way perplexed. Its horizon is completely foggy, but since concepts must always be furnished[l] for the understanding and laid out for its selection, we see quite well that sensibility must always assist the understanding[,] but often this just does not happen enough.

87

All distinguishing of the true from the false involves the cognition of inner sense[,] i.e., I must be and become conscious what really lies in my concept, and what I think.

Inner sense is often dull, and its horizon shrouded in fog, and it does not give us enough help.

Meanwhile, though, inner sense also belongs to sensibility, but without it the understanding cannot judge, so the understanding must judge with the help of sensibility[;] and just this connection and mixing together of the understanding with sensibility is the source of all errors, namely, the effects of the understanding are taken for effects of sensibility.

As we see, then, the understanding and sensibility cannot err alone. So we see how an error is possible.

All errors are, so to speak, crooked lines, which we determine while being driven from the one side by the understanding, from the other side by sensibility.[m]

[j] Through concord small things grow, through discord they fall apart.

[k] "Materialia, Stoffe."

[l] "fourniret."

[m] Reading "von der Sinnlichkeit" for "vom Irrthume."

We see before us the play of things in the world, but we do not have, on this account, any complete concept of their movement.

The senses do not judge. Inner sense, which alone teaches us, through which we become aware whether we have all the *requisita* of cognition or not, does not always serve us properly, and from this arises a semblance, as though the objects themselves lack something for their cognition.

One can have, e.g., correct rules for calculation, and for all that still go wrong in carrying them out. Here there is commonly an error of inner sense[;] this happens due to oversight.

The only means of avoiding error, then, will be for me to discover certain criteria by which, in every judgment, I can properly distinguish what comes from the understanding from what outer or inner sense supplies[n] us.

But the understanding, abandoned by inner sense, judges at once, no matter what comes of it, if inner sense offers it either something wrong or nothing at all.

All criteria of truth are either

A. *internal* or
B. *external.*

The former *are objective* criteria, which contain the ground for why something is really true or false. The others, however, [are] *subjective* criteria[,] which contain certain circumstances, by means of which one is in a position to make a supposition about the truth or the falsehood in a thing. 88

§ 94

That by which true cognitions are distinguished from false ones is the mark of truth.

The principle of identity is the formal mark of truth in affirmative judgments, the *principium contradictionis* in negative ones.

Material marks are the *notae intermediae*, by which I prove a judgment, the *principia materialia*.

In a completely simple[o] idea neither truth nor falsehood is to be met with, naturally. Instead this occurs only where there is comparison.

When I attribute to the thing a mark that either contradicts it or is even completely contrary to it, or when I deny of it a mark that is identical with it.

That by which I cognize that the comparison with the thing is or is not correct is called the *nota intermedia* (*principium materiale*)[.] E.g., if I want to prove that a body is divisible, then I assume a *nota intermedia*, that it is

[n] "Suppeditiren."
[o] "einfachen, und gantz Simplen."

composite, and infer in the following way: everything that is composite is divisible, *atqui*[p] every body is composite, *ergo*$_L$ every body is divisible.

Some propositions are so constituted that they have in themselves no material mark of truth at all but instead bear only the formal mark. These are actually the immediate judgments that we have of a thing and can prove and derive from nothing more. E.g., that a body is composite.

Simple concepts have in themselves the mark that they are always true. E.g., if I represent the moon as round, this is a true concept because I actually think it thus.

But if I compare this representation of the moon with the representation of other planets, if I doubt whether the moon is round or oval, then in this I can easily err, and my cognition can as well be true as false.

89

§ 95

Among all the marks of truth the first internal sign, or principal mark of it, is internal *possibility*.

We are instructed by experience concerning the possibility of many things, which one otherwise would actually not have held to be possible.

Nevertheless, possibility is far from being a sufficient ground of truth: because something is possible, and we can represent it to ourselves and think it through our reason, it is not therefore actually true.

But *possibility* is at least a ground of probability[;] if something is possible, and can be thought by us, then we at least believe and hope that it can be true, assuming that we are not also in a position to maintain it with certainty.

Impossiblity, however, is on the contrary always a sufficient[q] ground for the infallible proof of the untruth or falsehood of a thing.

When we have insight that something is completely impossible, then commonly we immediately hold it to be false, too.

But in this regard it is to be noted, too, that in both cases we can err. Quite frequently we hold something to be useful and *per consequentiam* also to be true and correct, which, however, when we investigate it more closely, is actually wholly impossible and false. And on the contrary, again, we hold something to be impossible and false which is actually possible, and at the same time true, or where not true at least useful.

§ 96 et 97

If the consequences of cognition are true, then the cognitions themselves are also true. E.g. It is true and settled for all that there are fire-spewing

[p] but.

[q] "zureichender, und Sufficienter."

mountains, warm baths, etc. As this is true, it can also be true that there is a central fire in the earth.

To be sure, we can with some ground infer from this the central fire in the earth, for these fire-spewing mountains, warm baths, etc., can with much confidence, indeed, even with probability, be regarded as conse- 90 quences of such a central fire, and from the consequences one can quite frequently correctly infer the ground.

If all the consequences of all of a cognition are true without exception, then the cognition is certainly true too. For if any falsehood at all were to be met with in the cognition, then there would have to be falsehood in the consequences as well. But if this is not so, then nothing in the cognition can be false.

If, e.g., we are informed in the newspapers of a successful battle, and of the victory of a hero; if this is even published from the pulpit, if we encounter festive events and if festivals of thanksgiving are held, in short, if all its consequences are true, then the battle itself must also be true.

Sometimes, however, we cannot cognize all the consequences of a thing, and then sometimes a few false ones may have mingled in with them and be present. Although we take the cognition itself to be true. E.g., if we assume the central fire situated in the earth, then from this it will follow again, that the layers of the earth which are not far removed from this central fire would be completely withered and destroyed by this much too great and violent heat, and that they would finally have to collapse.

But since, as one quite well sees, this consequence is false, it is quite easy to observe that the central fire cannot be taken to be completely, undoubtedly certain and cannot be reliably maintained.

If a cognition is to be possible in connection, then it must have correct grounds and consequences that are important as well as true.

§ 98 to 99

Cognition of the possibility of a thing arises out of experience[;] reason can contribute nothing to it. E.g., that the magnet attracts iron.

We can comprehend the possibility of composite bodies through reason, if we are convinced of the possibility of simple effects.

But the first possibility of causes and effects becomes evident only through the senses from experience. Therefore reason also yields no 91 objection to the impossibility of a thing into whose possibility or real existence we have clear insight through experience. Through the actuality of a thing, experience instructs us naturally of its possibility.

Reason, however, can derive from these examples of experience certain laws of the possibility of this or that thing[;] the first[r] *principia data* and

[r] Reading "ersten" for "ersteren," with Hinske (KI, lxxiii).

materialia[s] of possibility, however, must necessarily be given from experience and must arise out of it.

We must not take something to be impossible, however, because we cannot think it or represent it through the senses: e.g., one who was born blind cannot, through reason, provide himself with any representation of colors, because experience has deprived him of the *data* for this[;] nonetheless, he cannot and may not infer their impossibility. If we accept that, then all philosophy is abolished.

There are *logical truths*. They are those that relate merely to the understanding and reason.

From another side, we can think of an *aesthetic* and a *practical* truth. The former relates namely to the condition[t] of taste, the latter on the contrary to the rules of the free will.

Logical truth, however, is not always aesthetically true, and it does not always bring with it practical perfection.

Every truth is always, in itself, a logical perfection, or a perfect cognition, according to the rules of the understanding and of reason.

Much can be aesthetically true without being logically true[;] it may only stimulate and please. Thus it is, e.g., with novels.

Even practical truth need not always be grounded on the understanding and on reason either. E.g., if I slander someone to someone else, I can in this way arouse his affects, and in this way his will, although this slander is not logically true.

Logical truth is distinguished from aesthetical truth in the fact that when something delights and excites me, I can neglect something concerning its truth. Thus logical truth can frequently give way to aesthetic truth.

92 Frequently the truth does not please us most of all, but rather even lies do. We are happier with fables than with logical truths. He who takes nature as his basis in painting, e.g., is not always in accord with delight and stimulation and pleasure. Fiction frequently excites us more.

Our wishes often belong to *fictiones*. They often tend toward something better than nature actually offers. Thus, e.g., we are pleased by enthusiasm in friendship, are stirred by the earthy shepherd's life. It is true, of course, that even in aesthetic truth there must always be a certain logical truth, but the more we look to the aesthetically true, the less logical truth there can be in the subject that we want to represent. Thus, e.g., it is aesthetically true that man will not rise again when he is dead. Although this runs directly contrary to the logical (and to say nothing of the practical) truth.

What all men say is true according to the rules of taste, and thus it is aesthetically true. For a universal consensus is sufficient for this. How-

[s] principles that are given [and] material.

[t] "Verhaltniß."

ever, what is true according to the rules of taste is quite frequently false according to the rules of reason.

Men often think of what they hope or at least wish for as possible, and actual, because they would like to have it.

All fables contain an aesthetic truth, but seldom a logical truth. E.g., animals talking. Here there must of course really be something true; but aesthetic truth takes precedence over the logically true. In it one represents something possible. It does not involve any absurdity, either, that animals should be able to talk.

Under a certain *hypothesis*$_{L}$, which can be made up, a certain degree of logical truth can prevail even in a fable.

But no learned man has yet been able to determine exactly the degree of truth that has to obtain in this case, and the greatest aestheticians have not yet succeeded in indicating this. Objective marks will often not be sufficient for us. Here one can only rely on the agreement of our cognitions either among themselves or with the cognitions of others[;] thus it happens, e.g., in calculation.

We always test a proposition on the reason of others, or on our own [reason] at various times and occasions, and in various situations of our reason. But very often we also rely on illusion, i.e., on the way it first appears to us. We only want to attain the approval of others. 93

We gladly publicize our judgments when thereby we derive merit, or believe that we can attain it.

The human understanding, since it has a natural law to extend its cognitions just as much as possible, must not be forbidden the means by which alone it can distinguish the true from the false, and by which it can not just enrich but also correct its cognitions.

Thus one must not set up any obstacles to making judgments public, that is, to putting them forth, for the insight of all. That is, indeed, the universal right of every man, and the only certain way of attaining truth.

Even mathematics derives propositions, and the triumphant, invincible certainty of its apodeictic proofs and convictions, not from objective criteria of truth, but rather from subjective ones, because in this science there is something that agrees with everyone's reason.

Where, however, cognitions rise up but are soon thrown even further down, there the suspicion is very great that the universal approval that accompanied them in the beginning and once, was grounded only on the particular minds, and hence cannot be enduring.

§ 100

A cognition is either wholly true, or either partly true or partly false.

A cognition can never be utterly false, however, although it can frequently be wholly true.

Every judgment arises out of the understanding, therefore it must to some extent agree with the laws of the understanding and of reason.

It is therefore impossible that a man should make a completely false judgment, and even accept it as completely true.

For otherwise the judgment would have to contradict the laws of the understanding.

94 Thus a cognition that is presented as thoroughly false will nevertheless always be only in part false and will always contain a certain degree of truth. Indeed, even in the judgments of a madman (however peculiar this remark may seem), on closer investigation there will always be at least a partial truth that can be found.

If we were to suppose that some judgments could be utterly false, it would have to be possible for the understanding to deviate from all laws, and in this way[,] under this supposition[,] all the prestige of our doctrine of reason would fall and disappear[;] on the contrary, we would be able to trust it very little.

If someone else were able to judge completely falsely, then in just the same way it would be as possible for us as for him. In all use of our understanding and our reason, then, we would never be anything but quite uncertain.

Thus when we believe we have found falsehood in someone else's judgment, we must be convinced by this very means that some partial truth or other must prevail therein, however hidden it is.

In this principle, however, much fairness actually prevails. Such a way of thinking is moral and sympathetic,[u] so that one does not deny all truth whatsoever to others in their cognitions.

But as[v] exclusive self-love allows only its own welfare to be promoted, without in the least caring for or contributing anything to the well-being of others, so too is exclusive judgment,[w] where one ascribes to oneself alone the possession of all true cognitions, and on the other hand denies them completely to all others and attributes to them only false ones[;] nothing but a ruinous conceit, since one esteems only himself alone and despises all those around him.

Such minds, infatuated with this self-conceit, think themselves in their own understanding a Goshen,[21] and that everything else is veiled in Egyptian darkness.

Many judgments and concepts are true in regard to their essential features, but false in regard to their accidental features.

We can frequently judge falsely in theory. Regardless of this, however, our judgments in *praxis*$_L$ can nevertheless be true.

[u] "theilnehmend."

[v] Reading "So wie aber" for "So aber," with Hinske (KI, lxxiii).

[w] "das Ausschließende Urtheil."

95 Even in natural theology there can actually be many erroneous ideas and *speculationes*, which are still true in *praxis*$_L$. E.g., with the omnipresence of God, one can represent and think this as nothing, or as an extension through the whole of space.

This latter concept is false, of course, but regardless of that, it is true in regard to *praxis*$_L$. God may be omnipresent in whatever way he will, in any case, he really is so[;] and we must therefore fear his omnipresence, let it consist in what it may.

When a speculation is actually erroneous, but this error does not on that account have any influence on *praxis*$_L$, i.e., on the morality of morals,[x] then it is indifferent in regard to morals and not as detestable as if it also ruined morals.

Thus when our judgments are in conflict with the judgments of others, in order to be able to compare these judgments with and against one another we must observe the following rules: A cognition[y] of truth is when our judgments agree with the judgments of others who can have science concerning it[,] or what is all the same, when they are universally valid.

When, therefore, there is something to be found in my judgment thus contrary to the judgments of others, then in respect of the truth of my judgment I am not very certain, and I must first of all be occupied with searching for an agreement of my judgment with the judgment of others, one that is posited and also hidden and far-removed, and at least in most cases this agreement will actually be very easy to find. For in our non-agreeing[z] judgments there is really more agreement present than we suppose.

Only it is necessary that we understand the judgment of others and not misinterpret it.

There is also no *systema* of universal truths of reason that is completely and utterly true except for mathematics, just as no cognition can be completely false.

A cognition can be true *partialiter*, in that it is wholly true but does not concern the whole object but only a part of it. Nonetheless such cognitions are always certain.

96 Thus he who confidently gives the approval of truth to someone else's complete philosophical *systema*, all at once and without thinking much about it, concerning him we can always correctly infer that he does not yet understand it and is not in a position to distinguish correctly the true from the false. For it is certain: no *systema* can be wholly true, there is always a falsehood posited in it, even if it does not concern what is essential in the

[x] "die Moralität der Sitten"

[y] "Kenntniß."

[z] Reading "nicht übereinstimmenden" for "übereinstimmenden."

system. With philosophical truths, errors and mistakes are always so mixed together with the truth that one always finds something there to improve.

§ 102

A cognition that contains enough truth as is required just for the attainment of the principal end is exact[;] but it is rough, on the other hand, when one cannot attain the principal end with it. (Exactness is a cognition, but it cannot suitably be opposed to roughness, but rather the roughness of cognition must be opposed to its unity.)

Precision, meticulousness, is when I do not point out anything more that is true in a cognition than is necessary for insight into it. The transgression of this rule is a great error. That in a cognition for which only a little attention is required is called *rough*[;] that for whose clarity greater attention is required is called *subtle*.

Very often it is necessary to be *subtle*. Because from the neglect of subtlety such great confusions arise. Although subtlety is often blamed, since it requires far too much attention.

In regard to practical cognitions, one can appeal to and rely on the healthy understanding.

A *rule* for testing oneself and one's science concerning any cognition is this: if I understand and have insight into a thing perfectly, then I must be able to communicate and represent it so clearly to another man that he will have insight into it just as perfectly as I, if only he has a healthy understanding. If I cannot do this, however, it is a certain sign that I do not yet understand it rightly myself.

97 Every cognition is subject to partial untruth. But this untruth concerns merely the more or less exact. And nevertheless it can always be exact enough to attain its purpose. E.g., if I measure a mountain, I will never be able to measure so exactly and infallibly that I might not err in the least, even if it were only a very few inches[;] regardless of that, however, the quantity that emerges by means of my survey is sufficient and exact enough to determine the complete height of the mountain. Many of our judgments of reason are made merely by visual estimate and of course they can therefore, in accordance with more refined reason and learnedness, not be exact enough[;] but regardless of that, they are exact enough for their purpose.

The highest and most tiresome exactitude, which may be reached only with much accuracy and learnedness, but is of no use in regard to its principal end, is called *pedantry*. In mathematics it is quite otherwise. Here there must always be exactitude. Nothing must be left out.

§ 103

If a cognition, considered historically, is correct, it can nonetheless be incorrect, considered *formaliter*. E.g., the soul is immortal[;] this proposition is true *materialiter* and correct. When one represents this, however, the form can often be completely false.

A cognition is true *materialiter*, however, when we have a material science of it. [It is] true *formaliter*, however, when the grounds for proving and deriving it are correct.

Much that is undoubtedly certain in regard to *praxis*$_L$ is false in regard to reason. E.g., a part is smaller than the whole, or, the world must have a beginning.

Thus a cognition can be true *materialiter* and false *formaliter*, but not conversely[;] then it is a formal error[.] This occurs more frequently in philosophy than is believed.

Thus there is no material, but rather a formal error in those *qualitates occultae* which are given as a ground for the cause of a thing, and which answer[a] the given question with the question itself.

All definitions that explain *idem per idem* are formally erroneous. 98

These formal errors [are ones] where one grants the philosopher the proof in a cognition, since one is already prepossessed in favor of the cognition *anticipando* and holds the proof to be dispensable.

Where my healthy understanding precedes the cognition of the truth I am not in the least fussy about investigating the acuteness[b] of the proof, and I need not be so. This acuteness that one metes out to certain propositions often comes from the fact that they have to be regarded not only as very true but also as very necessary.

Thus it is with the two articles of faith of natural religion

1. There is a God.
2. There is another world.

Those who want to investigate such shallow proofs of necessary propositions of this sort and to make a few fine *distinctiones* immediately acquire a bad reputation, because it is believed that they could well be enemies of the propositions themselves.

These are the *piae fraudes*,[c] which are so suited, so peculiar, to man.

One thinks and believes he has a right to this when one believes that he does not deceive someone if he communicates to him something good by means of all kinds of pretense, dissimulation, etc.[;] indeed, one often

[a] Reading "und die gegebene Frage . . . beantworten" for "und die gegegebe Frage beantwortet."
[b] "Schärfe."
[c] pious deceptions.

seeks credit, without looking to the moral in this deception – which deception always remains – to see if it is in itself reprehensible; the recommendation of virtue must be virtuous. –

Many things are often cognized as true without any marks. Such truths, irrefutable in themselves, are called *unprovable*, i.e., because one cannot doubt them. Besides, it is not necessary to prove them in particular.

A cognition whose consequences are all true is true, too. But if just one consequence is false, then the cognition is false, too.

From a false cognition nothing true can arise. For a false cognition is the true *nothing*. But the consequences of a cognition that is partly true, partly false, can be true.

In the investigation of a cognition one will thus need to look not so much to its true as to its false consequences.

99 It is admittedly true in general that so-called apagogical proofs, or the *demonstrationes ad absurdum contrarium*,[d] where in order to establish and support his opinion, one makes it clear and shows how ridiculous and completely absurd it would be if one were to suppose its opposite [– it is true] that these proofs are very easy, but they do not give me enough light in regard to the sources of a cognition.

The connection of cognitions with their grounds is thus the surest and best mark of the truth of a cognition.

§ 104

Historical cognitions are distinguished from *rational* ones according to the form of reason in the cognition.

A cognition is *historical* if it does not agree with the form of reason, *rational* if it does agree with it, and in fact without regard to the object. But here we also have to reflect on the object if we want to establish the distinction between dogmatic and historical cognition.

1st *Dogmatic* cognition is one that is universal and that arises *a priori* from reason.

2nd *Historical* cognition, however, is not always universal, and it rests on the assertions of things that have happened, on the assertion of others[;] thus it arises *a posteriori*.

All of morals is dogmatic[;] one does not teach, blame, and point out there what is commonly detested by men, but rather what ought to be blamed.

But *physica* is not dogmatic. One of its parts would be pure physics, where from universal rules and concepts of bodies we derive their properties.

[d] demonstrations to the absurdity of the contrary.

The weight of bodies pertains to experience, however, and is a historical cognition *a posteriori*.

All *dogmata* should rightly be grounded first on reason, but they can frequently be historical, too.

The objects of *dogmata* are not individual things but rather universal properties and characters of things. The objects of history are individual things, however.

But although *dogmata* have universal properties as their object, they can often still be cognized historically, although they are rational by their nature. 100

All *dogmata* are by their nature *objective*$_L$ rational, though they can be *subjective*$_L$ historical.

Now we must also speak of systems. The author restricts the meaning of this word far too much by applying it merely and solely to dogmatic truth.

A better definition of a system will thus be the following:

A *system* is a multitude or manifold of many simple cognitions and truths combined together, such that taken together these constitute a whole. Every system must thus bring with it a unity, but this unity can have as its ground either coordination, as with historical cognitions, or subordination.

A *systema* is, however,

A. historical
B. rational.

The form of a system will in most cases be regarded as arbitrary.

The understanding varies among men[;] he who likes to deal with the parts is *subtle*. He who deals with the whole is the *great* man.

A legitimate system must be built by a single individual. It cannot possibly be a patchwork, to which one adds this, another that.

This capacity to form a system is so advantageous because it is so rare and has at the same time so great a value.

One must always have a kind of *systema*, for each of our cognitions must have a logical place.

The first *systemata*, naturally, are astonishingly defective. Gradually they become larger and more complete.

§ 106

We have already established the distinction between logical and aesthetic truths above.

Much can be logically true without on that account containing an aesthetic truth, and much can be aesthetically true, on the other hand, without on that account containing logical truth.

101 This includes all *fictiones*.

This includes all aesthetic truths, which are true according to the rules of taste.

In these cognitions there prevails a kind of fashion, actually. This includes, e.g., proverbs, which actually are subject to a kind of fashion; although they actually are not always propositions such as are in accordance with taste.

All that is in conformity with the rules of taste and agrees with the rules of appearance is aesthetically true.

Poets, who merely want to write aesthetically truly, are not tested on the balance of logic[;] one does them a great wrong thereby. They are writers, not moralists and logicians, and they retain always their worth.

To be aesthetically true, there can frequently be a certain degree of untruth. Which nonetheless must not be completely opposed to the truth. E.g., if a philosopher were to call out: My dear friends, there are no friends[;] this is aesthetically true and a good thought, because good friends are very rare, and a complete agreement of minds is very rare.

§ 109

Now we come to a very important doctrine for all of logic, namely, the doctrine of the *origin of error*. Does error arise from the lack of reason?

Answer: No. From the lack of reason nothing arises but ignorance. But ignorance is quite distinct from error.

He who knows little can still judge completely correctly about this little.

The second question is:

Does error not arise also from the *lack* of reason combined with the desire to judge?

Answer: He who knows certainly that he is ignorant will not presume to judge about something that he does not understand.

But assuming that he did not feel himself unable, and that he thought 102 he knew much and thus wanted to judge about much, then nothing more would arise from this, his efforts to judge would be in vain.

But how can it happen that the understanding seems to have insight only with difficulty? That the understanding in judging deviates from its laws?

No power can of itself conflict with its own laws. E.g., if a body is left to its weight, then according to the laws of gravity it falls downward, and one is actually in a position to figure out the velocity of its fall.

With our judgments through the understanding, then, if there were no power active, if no power interfered, we would actually never err, but would only be frequently ignorant.

Thus no error arises from the understanding properly, but rather there must be another power active in the understanding at the same time if an error is to arise. The powers of nature deviate from their laws only when foreign laws mingle with the given laws.

Thus if we had nothing but understanding, we would judge only little, to be sure, but we would judge all of this little truly.

If we had a wholly pure will, furthermore, then granted, we would do only a little good, but we would never be able to sin.

Deviation from the rules of the pure will constitutes the morally evil, and this arises only when and because other effects of other powers mingle with the otherwise pure laws of the will. E.g.: The inclinations and affects. Just in this way, when foreign powers mingle with the correct laws of the understanding, a mixed effect arises, and error arises from the conflict of [this with] our judgments based on the laws of the understanding and of reason.

Every error is a *phaenomenon*, a puzzle in regard to the concept of its own possibility.

It is, as it were, a wholly unusual, unnatural appearance, which contradicts the laws of nature.

What is contrary to the laws of nature is not an object of investigation for us, but that which occurs seldom and is contrary to the laws of nature is an object of investigation.

Error does occur frequently, to be sure, but it conflicts with the laws of the understanding and of reason, and thus it is worthy of being an object of our investigation.

Error proceeds merely from the understanding and from reason, because foreign powers interfere, but never from the senses or from imagination. 103

Since our understanding and reason judge *objective*$_{L}$, there are other subjective grounds of our judgment, which, however, do not agree with the understanding and reason.

All error arises when we hold subjective grounds of our judgment to be objective ones.

The whole business about ghosts is grounded, not on the judgment of the understanding, but in the imagination, which, in the observation of an object, joins to it other similar objects, although they do not exist.

The understanding combines concepts with a thing in conformity with its laws and in conformity with the thing, the object, itself.

The imagination, however, brings in other images, which relate not to the object but to the subject.

From this mingling of the imagination with the understanding arise effects that do not agree perfectly with the rules of the understanding and of reason.

Many errors arise from custom, others merely because a change has occurred in the subject. E.g., when we make a mark on the wall.

Many errors arise because one constantly renews in one's mind the images one once had, and therefore regards everything similar as the thing itself. E.g., when a young man is treated sharply by his teacher, so that he hates him, and when he later sees a man who resembles him, he is often inclined to hate him, too, merely on account of the similarity with his disciplinarian.

One can often reject something through the understanding and accept it again through the effect of another power. All of this arises merely from the mingling of powers, which, if they are not contrary to one another, are nevertheless of different kinds.

We cognize the quantity of things only by judging in respect of distance, e.g., the difference between a fly and an elephant.

We readily notice a fly nearby, but we notice an elephant in the distance, too, and thus we just infer that the latter must be larger than the former.

104 The imagination can alter these judgments very much, however, and can bring about in our soul other impressions, other representations of the thing than we should produce of it if we [were to] have insight into its true properties.

Therefore if we remove from man his imagination, his sensible wit, the judgment of the understanding will always be true.

The understanding mingled with powers of another sort errs, and this error we must comprehend again through the understanding. From this it becomes clear that we have to comprehend and cognize errors through the very power whose errors we want to note.

No error can arise from the understanding or from reason alone, for no power can act against its own laws.

§ 110

That ignorance in itself cannot in the least be an origin of error has already been shown in the previous paragraph in several ways.

§ 111

Error is either *avoidable* or *unavoidable.*

If we do not judge at all, we can of course avoid all errors. He who does not judge does not err. An error through ignorance can also be prevented. This ignorance consists, however, not in the ignorance of lack, but rather in the ignorance of intention,[e] and this latter is really a kind of wise ignorance. Many *speculationes* are nothing but a pathway to the greatest errors. Many errors can be avoided, however, if we have the intention not to settle anything, to decide anything. Many things are such that they

[e] "des Vorsatzes."

cannot possibly remain undecided, however. E.g., when a judge is supposed to settle disputes, given that he also errs on these points and in these cases, then error is unavoidable in respect to him.

One can opine something, and with grounds, without erring, but when one states this same mere opinion and defective supposition as a certain truth, then one frequently errs.

The inclination to decide is thus the most certain path to error and is a certain dogmatic pride (customary in some so-called philosophers)[;] but if one does not trust the marks of truth that one has cognized thus far, and thus does not pass judgment but often reserves it instead, then one actually avoids many errors. 105

§ 113

A cognition is

1. *obviously* or
2. *covertly false.*

This division of false cognition is relative

We have a kind of average understanding, which is derived from the understanding of all men, and is, as it were, a measuring stick, i.e., an ideal.

Now if we take an error that can subsist with this average degree of understanding, then the error is still bearable. But if it cannot exist with it, then it is not to be endured, and it is an absurdity.

Absurdity presupposes, namely, not only a false cognition, but also that the common understanding (*le sens commun*) can see this as false.

Any covert false cognition can be made obviously false, and then the cognition is reduced *ad absurdum*, so that he who previously had this cognition, though he is not absurd, would be manifestly absurd and would act contrary to all reason if he were to hold it to be true after all the grounds that have been laid before him for the falsehood of his cognition.

It is foolish, then, when learned men call each other absurd and yet thereafter want to dispute with one another as to whether what they wrote is true or false. For by calling each other absurd, one thus denies to the other all true cognition whatsoever[;] and if I suppose that someone does not possess and is unable to possess any cognition at all, then how can he see my grounds for the falsehood of his cognition, or pride himself on a true cognition and believe himself to possess it? But then how am I in a position to dispute? 106

In the 114th paragraph the author treats of the necessary and of the contingent, and of contingent truths, concerning which we have nothing more to note.

THE FIFTH SECTION

Of the clarity of learned cognition

§ 115

All grounds of cognition are either *internal* or *external*. The former are determinations in the thing itself, by which it can be cognized without comparison with other things. Through the latter, however, I only acquire a cognition of a thing insofar as I compare it with other things. And these external grounds of cognition are called *marks* or *characteristics*.

Internal cognitions cannot even appropriately be called *marks* or *characteristics* of a thing, however.

In the comparison of one thing with another we can always represent two sorts of things, either sameness, identity, or difference, diversity. E.g., marks of sameness in men and animals are that they both have a perishable body. Marks of difference, however, are that the former have been given a rational soul, while the latter have no reason at all.

In most cases one needs marks of identity, but in many, too, marks of diversity.

All *genera*$_{L}$ and *species*$_{L}$, e.g., arise from marks of identity but not of difference.

If one wants, e.g., to distinguish the metals from one another, then one must again have *notae diversitatis*, e.g., that gold is heavier than all metals, etc. For this is the foremost distinguishing mark of gold from silver, copper, etc., and the remaining metals.

107 A mark is thus not merely a *ratio disjunctionis*,[f] as some have defined it, but also a *ratio identitatis*.[g]

A mark is called in general a *nota*.

All marks in general are either

1. *internal*
2. *external*.

Sunt vel externae, vel internae omnes notae.[h]

1. The marks that I cognize of a thing are *internal* if I consider the thing alone merely in itself[.]
2. The marks that I have of a thing are external if I compare the thing with other things, and such marks are called *characteres*$_{F}$, distinguishing marks, characteristics in the proper sense.

[f] ground of difference.
[g] ground of identity.
[h] All marks are either external or internal.

The use of all marks will thus naturally be able to be likewise

1. *internal*
2. *external.*

If I cognize the internal marks, which taken together constitute the complete concept, then these marks are *complete*, and sufficient, all that there is to cognize in a thing, what can be cognized in it *absolute*$_{L}$.

The absolute cognitions[i] of things are far harder than the cognitions that one acquires through comparisons. For these latter are far easier and for us more natural, because it lies, as it were, in our nature that in the comparison of things with others we far more easily become aware of, and are able to observe, the agreement or difference in objects. Thus, e.g., ugliness, *en comparaison* with beauty, and with true beauty, strikes the eyes when it occurs among many ugly persons[;] and when he sets out to pass judgment on himself, man himself in most cases asks, not how good he is and how much he still lacks, but rather whether he is not as good as, or even better than, others. Thus it happens that Herr von Wolff, and even our author[,] take marks and characteristics to be one and the same.

In the beginning, in most cases, most things are held to be only very slightly different, if not wholly of the same sort[;] but with time, then, differences are gradually discovered, and after one attends to the things more and more, more and more of their marks are found. But this gradual searching out of the marks of a thing involves as much fineness of the understanding as being able to find a certain similarity, a oneness, and agreement, among things where there appear to be, or even actually are, the greatest differences. 108

§ 116

In this § the author speaks of *mediate* and *immediate* marks. If a thing can be cognized through a certain mark without the mediation of a mark different from this mark, then such a mark is *immediate.* A *mediate* mark, on the other hand, is a mark of a mark: e.g. Perishability is a mark of man. But an *immediate* one, for perishability is a mark of a mortal being, i.e., of a body[;] man is mortal, however, and has a body.

There are degrees, then, of remote marks, and thus there are degrees of mediate marks. The first degree is when a thing can be cognized only through a *nota intermedia.* But among all marks, one of which is the mark of the other, a relation of subordination is always to be found. But there is also a relation of coordination, and this occurs among immediate marks, where every particular mark is a new ground of cognition of the thing.

[i] "Kenntnißen."

Through experience we can become aware of nothing but marks that are coordinated, i.e., placed next to one another. Reason, however, is only in a position to provide[j] subordinate marks of a thing, i.e., to portray for us series of marks.

In the subordination of marks I have no more than a single immediate mark, and the remaining *notae* are marks of marks. But in the *coordinatio notarum*[k] all marks are immediate.

In the series of subordinate marks, i.e., of marks ordered beneath one another, there is always a *first*[,] i.e, the concepts are restricted.

In coordination, however, there is no restriction.

109 There are uncountably many marks that belong to a thing immediately, and our understanding is not in a position to have insight into all properties and to determine them exactly.

In subordination, the immediate mark is called *nota infima*, and the last mark of all marks is called *nota summa*.

Through the subordination of marks I attain a deep, i.e., intensive quantity. But through the coordination of marks[,] of *notae*[,] one achieves an extensive quantity[;] i.e., cognition that is worked out according to the ground and is extensive.

The series of marks that are coordinated with one another is, as it were, a line without limits, which is infinite; for it is always possible[;] indeed, it is to be assumed that posterity, with time, will be able to discover more and more immediate marks of a thing.

The series of marks that are subordinated to one another is limited, however, and has its restrictions, and often, in fact, quite soon, when no further mark of a mark can be stated therein.

Metaphysica is that science by means of which we search for the *terminus a priori* of subordinate marks. Through it we attain simple, irreducible concepts.

Too much beauty is also harmful and actually arouses suspicion. Beautiful simplicity occurs frequently by nature. The greatest art consists, however, in hiding the art that has been applied somewhere, so that it is not at all noticeable, but instead seems to be mere nature.

Profundity is in a certain way contrary to beauty[;] cognition becomes dry, the more that is abstracted in it. I cannot have full insight into mere abstract cognitions in general unless I can portray and have insight into a case *in concreto*. The dry often degenerates into the comical,[l] however, and this often involves art: thus, e.g., in the case of remarks[m] made in society, and this is usually called *simplicity*.

In all description one seeks more to understand the thing than to have

[j] "suppeditiren."
[k] coordination of marks.
[l] "ins Poßierliche."
[m] "Einfälle."

insight into it. In all explanation, however, one seeks again on the contrary more to have insight into the thing than to understand it.

Experience increases the multitude of marks coordinated with one another.

The extensive quantity of a cognition is, as it were, its volume, while its intensive quantity is its density. In certain cases the extensive quantity of cognition is more valuable, but in others the intensive. In morals, e.g., the intensive quantity of a cognition is more necessary, but in physics and medicine the extensive quantity of cognition is quite frequently more indispensable. 110

Dry cognitions are not at all adequate for sensibility and hence not for beauty, either. Thorough, deep, solid cognitions can and must be dry, however, without complaint. One replaces this dryness when one considers the abstract *in concreto* in a certain case. (*Analysis* proceeds *ascendendo*, but *synthesis* proceeds *descendendo*.)

§ 117

Through negative marks of a thing I think of something that is not actually to be found in the thing. Through affirmative marks, however, I think of what is in fact present in the thing. Negative marks, however, are possible only through the fact that one previously thinks of the marks opposed to them, thus affirming. Thus, e.g., I cannot know what darkness is unless I previously have a clear *idea*$_L$ of light.

Negative marks only serve to avoid errors, however. E.g., animals do not have rational souls. But affirmative marks serve to attain an extensive, undeveloped cognition of a thing. E.g., God is omniscient, etc. Gold loses nothing of its *massa* and weight in fire, is ductile.

Besides ignorance, there is another, still more dangerous evil for the understanding, and this is *error*. Through affirmative marks we avoid ignorance, but through negative marks we avoid error. These are the ends for the two sorts of marks. Through negative marks one acquires no new cognition, of course. They are still very necessary, nonetheless, and important, for through them one guards against erroneous cognitions.

The fewer the means we have available for attaining true cognitions, the more we need to have negative marks, in order not to err in cognition of the thing. Thus, e.g., in no science is there a greater multitude of negative marks than in the rational doctrine of God,[n] in natural *theologia*. For in this we do not have available any means at all for attaining extensive cognitions. Thus every second we are inclined, e.g., to err in the concept, idea, and representation of the divine being and in general of God himself, because we would like to compare Him sensibly with 111

[n] "in der vernünftigen Gottes-Gelahrtheit."

the things of which we become aware on earth, but these cannot be a measuring-stick for God. God cannot be cognized by us through the senses, and consequently the whole of our cognition of him can only be very restricted.

If, therefore, we consider God in *theologia naturalis*, and remove all negative marks through which we speak of him, then nothing further remains for us but the *idea* of the most all-sufficient, most all-perfect being.

Negative judgments are actually frequently foolish, because what is denied is often already impossible in itself. E.g.: man has reason, therefore he is not a stone. It is true, this is a settled truth, which no one will doubt. But because it is also obvious that no one will venture in earnest to hold a man to be a stone, this judgment is idle.

§ 118

Every mark is a ground of cognition, which is appraised through its consequences. Accordingly as the consequences are of worth, with respect to reason or to our perfection and happiness, the marks will also be of worth as grounds of cognition.

The logical worth of the marks is to be derived from the former consequences, their practical worth from the latter ones.

If many consequences can be derived from one ground, then it is fruitful, or it has extensive quantity[;] e.g., from the sun flow many consequences in respect of the earth. Thus the rules of morals are very fruitful in that they have an influence on our life, i.e., on our conduct,[o] that is very great.

A mark is great *extensive*$_L$ if I can cognize many consequences of a thing, 112 but a mark is great *intensive*$_L$ when I can cognize not so much many consequences of a thing as great and important ones. The former mark is called *fruitful*, but the latter *correct*.

Empty speculations have a logical worth. They often have many consequences in respect of reason, although they admittedly have no influence on the happiness of man[;] e.g., that the moon is inhabited, etc. This proposition has no influence on the will, on the state, etc. No one becomes more perfect, happier, or better through this cognition, in respect of his external understanding, although he becomes somewhat more perfect in respect of his reason.

Other cognitions are aesthetically correct because they excite our taste and pleasure, e.g., poetry delights, because it is in conformity with our

[o] "Wandel."

taste. All the importance of cognition exists only when it is considered by itself alone, without comparison with other cognitions.

§ 119

Marks either suffice for our ends, and then they are *comparative sufficientes*.[p] Or [they suffice] for distinguishing a thing from all others, hence for all logical ends, and then they are *notae absolute sufficientes*.[q]

All experiences have only a relative *sufficientia*. E.g., if I consider closely a pear tree, then I can easily distinguish its leaves from the leaves of all other trees in the forest. This cognition is thus sufficient in relation to other cognitions.

The *sufficientia relativa* or *comparativa* suffices to distinguish a thing from things that we are familiar with up until now, but not from all things that are possible, that might exist sometime. E.g., gold differs from all other metals through its weight, but a metal has also been discovered, named *platina*, that is white in color but has the same weight as gold. Consequently this mark, this distinguishing ground of gold from all remaining metals, is not sufficient enough.

Things that strike our senses can only be cognized and distinguished through marks that are relatively sufficient, but not by means of such marks as suffice absolutely. 113

The *sufficienta notarum*,[r] however, is:

1. *externa*
2. *interna*.

The former consists in the fact that the marks of a thing are sufficient to distinguish it from other things through comparison. But the latter consists in the fact that a mark of a thing suffices for the derivation from it of all its remaining determinations. From this *sufficienta* arises the division of grounds of cognition into

A. *internal* and
B. *external*.

In the case of the latter, one cannot derive anything from them, e.g., gold has a yellow color, man is an animal that laughs. The former are fruitful, however, so that much flows from them.

External grounds of cognition can frequently be quite important in themselves, but in respect of their inner sufficiency can be unfruitful and useless.

[p] sufficient comparatively.
[q] marks that are sufficient absolutely.
[r] sufficiency of marks.

§ 120

Necessary marks are such as are *ad essentiam pertinentia*,[s] without which the thing cannot be thought at all. *Pertinent autem ad essentiam*

1. *vel solum ut causae*

aut 2. *ut causata*[t]

Omnia autem ad essentiam pertinentia A. *essentialia*, e.g., extension[.]
B. *attributa.*[u] E.g., the divisibility of bodies.

Contingent marks are *extra essentialia*, however, marks without which the thing can nonetheless be thought, e.g., learnedness in the case of a man.

If the *essentialia* are marks then they are not subordinate but instead are coordinate[;] the *attributa* are not coordinate with the *essentialia*, however, but instead are subordinate[,] since they follow from one another.

§ 121

Marks *extra essentialia* are either

A. *internal* or
B. *external.*

114 The latter are also called relations. The internal ones, however, are again

1. *necessary*
2. *contingent.*

The former are again

1. *complete*, or marks that are sufficient for the derivation of everything that is contained in the thing or
2. *incomplete.* If the marks do not suffice for the derivation and cognition of everything that belongs to the thing.

The internal contingent relations are called *modi*$_L$. The modification of external relations does not modify man himself, although among the things of nature an alteration of relation seems in most cases to be bound up at the same time with an alteration of the modification.

Summer and winter are actually not changes in the sun itself but only altered relations[v] of the sun to our earth.

[s] pertaining to the essence.

[t] They pertain to the essence, however, (1.) either solely as causes or (2.) as things caused.

[u] All things that pertain to the essence, however, are (A.) essential [marks] . . . [or] (B.) attributes.

[v] "relationes, und Verhältniße."

Modi$_L$ are nothing but inner determinations and alterations that can be thought in a thing.

Relationes, however, are alterations that occur in a thing in relation to others and in relation to other things.

Now we pose the question, whether there cannot also be precision in the case of the *completudo notarum, necessaria interna*,[w] so that no superfluous marks[x] are found, which are no longer necessary to distinguish the thing from all others and to derive all the determinations belonging to it, so that everything is omitted which is such that even if it is lacking, the concepts will nonetheless be complete even without it.

Responsio[:] yes. It occurs frequently. The *notae rei necessariae internae sufficientes*[y] constitute precision.

If the marks contain no less than is required for distinguishing the thing, then this is *precision.*

If, finally, the marks of a thing are completely appropriate to it, then they are *notae adequatae.*

The adequate concept of a thing insofar as it cannot be derived from any other is the concept of the essence[,] *essentia.* 115

The essence of a thing is the first sufficient basic concept, which suffices for the derivation of everything that belongs to the thing.

The *notae necessariae* are

A. *primitivae* or
B. *derivativae*

The former constitute the *essentialia*, but the latter the *attributa.* E.g., in the case of the triangle the 3 angles are just as necessary and indispensable as the 3 sides. But we derive the former from the latter, and they are hence *attributa*[;] but the sides themselves are basic concepts[,] *essentialia.*

In order to cognize the essential in a thing, the following is necessary: To cognize the *attributa* I have to cognize the internal necessary marks, which, however, are accompanied by others. But to cognize the *essentia* itself I have to see that the marks cannot be derived from any other[;] in order to cognize the *essentia* itself, I have to know that the marks and *essentialia* are complete, and taken together are sufficient for cognition of the whole.

The coordination of marks that is complete constitutes *completudo.*

The basic concept of everything that is necessary to a thing is its essence. To investigate the essence of things is the business and the end of philosophy.

The marks which, taken together, constitute the essence of a thing are

[w] completeness of marks that are internal and necessary.

[x] Reading “keine überflüßigen Merckmahle” for “überflüßige Merckmahle.”

[y] marks of the thing that are necessary, internal, and sufficient.

the *essentialia*. The consequences from the essence, the *rationata sive consectaria*,[z] these are the *attributa*. *Modi* are *notae internae, quarum possibilitas tantum per essentiam determinatur*.[a]

The *modi* are thus not *rationata essentiae*[b] in regard to their truth, but only in regard to their possibility. *Modi* are thus nothing but contingent marks.

Modi as well as *relationes* do not belong to the essence at all, *ad essentiam non pertinent*, either as *constitutiva* or as *attributa*.

All the marks of a thing belong either to the essence of a thing, *essentialia*[,] or they are not *essentialia*: *Ad essentiam pertinentia sunt vel essen-*
116 *tialia, vel attributa. Extraessentialia autem sunt vel notae, sive notae internae, vel relationes, sive notae externae, quarum possibilitas tantum per essentiam determinatur.*[c]

Essence is divided into

1. the logical
2. the real essence.

The complete basic concept of a thing is in general its essence.

The first ground of everything that I think in the concept of the thing, however, is the *logical* essence. The first basic concept of everything that really and in fact belongs to the thing, however, is the *real essence*.

From this it naturally becomes clear that the *logical* and the *real* essence must necessarily be quite distinct from one another.

When I utter words and combine a certain concept with them, then that which I think of[d] in connection with this word and expression is *the logical essence*. E.g., if I utter the word matter, then everything that is inseparable from the concept that I combine with the expression matter is the logical essence of matter. One can always represent and think the logical essence by itself. Thus, e.g., with matter, I always think of an extension, an impenetrability, a certain constant inertia, and lifelessness, so that it is not in a position to alter its position or to move by itself but only through the assistance of another, foreign power.

These all are the *essentialia* of the word *matter*, and consequently taken together they constitute the logical essence of it.

The subjective basic concept is what is contained in an internal concept of the thing. But this does not yet prove that still more marks cannot exist

[z] things grounded, or consequences.

[a] internal marks whose possibility is determined only by the essence.

[b] things grounded in the essence.

[c] Things that pertain to the essence are either essential things or attributes. Extra-essential things, however, are either marks (or internal marks) or relations (or external marks) whose possibility is determined solely by the essence.

[d] Ak, "hier dencke"; MS, "mir dencke" (KI, lxviii).

in the object.[e] Instead I combine with the thing only what I represent. Thus, e.g. in the case of the word matter, several other properties can still occur.

The logical essence is the subjective basic concept. This concept holds only for me, however, and not for others. Someone else can represent more or fewer marks with the thing.

The essence of our concept is not always the essence of the thing itself, indeed, it seldom is.

The logical essence is far smaller than the real essence. The logical essence is a concentrated basic concept of a thing. It only comprehends what we represent in the thing.

This joining, combining, of concepts is really very suited to the human understanding, and quite necessary. It has to proceed economically with its powers; such a *compendium*$_{L}$ is just as good as an extended concept of the thing, however. 117

The real essence comprehends everything that can ever actually belong to a thing. This eduction is the only means for making our concepts really distinct.

Distinctness is one of the most essential logical perfections, however. Through it my cognition becomes far more suitable for use, but through the real essence my cognition becomes far more extended.

The logical essence must not be mixed up with the real essence, however. For in my concept that I have of the thing I do not yet think of everything that lies in the thing and belongs to it, or that can lie in it or belong to it. E.g., if we take the concept of matter, modern *philosophi* have discovered that in the essence of matter lies also the power of attraction; I would certainly never have thought of this property immediately with the word matter, and there can perhaps be other marks belonging to matter which are not yet discovered and which only a philosopher will cognize.

From this it becomes clear that infinitely more is contained in the real essence than in the logical essence.

We cannot actually cognize the real or objective essence of a single object of experience or of the senses. At the most it is possible for us properly to have insight into its logical or subjective essence.

What we think in connection with the word for a thing is very small, and scant, indeed, often only very little[;] but everything that really belongs to a thing *revera*[f] is frequently immeasurable and cannot be determined at all.

To search for the real essence of empirical concepts and objects is thus a completely vain effort[;] one can, however, represent the logical essence of concepts of reason, and clarify it suitably.

Our empirical concepts are very changeable, because our experience is

[e] Reading "nicht daseyn können" for "daseyn können."

[f] actually, in truth.

extended more and more each day. The logical essence is therefore also very alterable and changeable, because with time we think more and more
118 determinations in the concept of a thing. All moral concepts are pure concepts of the understanding, however.

There are, namely, such pure concepts of the understanding[,] which have their origin not from experience but merely from pure reason. He who wants to find the real essence must be acquainted with all the marks that belong to the thing constantly. Then he must search further for the ground of these, and must endeavor to investigate them, and this is the real essence, then. E.g., a body that grows through internal development belongs to the logical essence of a plant. The basic concept of its constant determination is the real essence, however, to which it can also belong that plants beget their like.

The concept that water is a fluid element, without odor or taste, 14 times lighter than quicksilver, etc., is the logical essence of water[;] for if I have mastered physical cognitions about something, then I think of all this as soon as I mention the word water. From this, of course, I cannot at all derive all the remaining properties which are determined for water, and which belong to it or can belong to it, and perhaps are not yet all discovered, although we do not always think them in this connection[;] consequently it is not the real essence.

We can never state the real essence of individual things, but we can do so for their *genera*$_L$, e.g., for body in general.

Nevertheless, we are not acquainted with all concepts and [with all the] determinations of all things that belong to them constantly; and then we are not always in a position, either, immediately to state the true ground of all these determinations[;] consequently only seldom can we indicate their real essence.

§ 124

Clear and obscure concepts are spoken of herein. The author first treated of confused and distinct concepts in the first section of the *logica*, without first thinking about clear and obscure cognition. How does it happen, then, that he now begins to speak of these?

Responsio[.] At the beginning of logic, the concept of clear and obscure cognition is something that can be accepted without proof, and must thus
119 be presupposed and taken as a ground. But here one can derive it from what was dealt with before.

Here, then, it is just the reverse. *A representation* is obscure (to return to our material), however, of which one is not conscious[g] *immediately*. Namely, one can become mediately conscious of this cognition by means of reason,

[g] Reading "nicht bewust" instead of "bewust," with Hinske (KI, lxxi).

and thus a way remains to make an otherwise obscure cognition clear, distinct, and thus to make insight into it easier. E.g., if I see the Milky Way with the naked eye, I see nothing but a white band, but if I make use of a *tubus*, then I at once become aware of the individual parts as individual stars, and then judge at once by means of reason that these must be the stars that I saw with the naked eye merely as a white band. I am conscious of this representation mediately, then, but not immediately; hence in the beginning it is only obscure, but afterwards it is distinct *mediate*$_L$, or clear.

§ 125

A cognition is either obscure in itself, so that it simply cannot become clear regardless of any effort that is applied. Or it is obscure relatively, so that it can become clear under certain circumstances, but not under others.

The former cognition, obscure in itself, is completely impossible according to its description, however[;] for everything can become clear, however hard it may seem to us, and what seems to us most obscure is always obscure only relatively when we investigate it.

Logic prescribes for us the rules that we ought to apply in order to know how we ought to proceed with cognitions of which we are conscious that we actually possess them.

All clarity is the right way to attain distinctness. Clarity itself is not yet a logical perfection, which distinctness, however, is. Logic presupposes clarity, then[;] it supposes[h] it and does not produce it itself[;] it has to do with cognitions and representations already made clear.

Distinctness, too, is then not the proper object with which it is occupied. Distinctness, *disjunctio*, is of course to be distinguished from perspicuousness.[i] Insofar as there is clarity of marks in a cognition, to that extent is the cognition *distinct*. 120

A cognition is brought *in perspicuum*, however,[j] only when it is so lucid and clear that the humblest understanding has insight into it[;] on the other hand, a cognition is *imperspicua* or *non perspicua* when it is too great for the whole horizon of the whole human race, when it can be called *incomprehensible*. *Perspicuousness*,[k] on the other hand, means nothing but *comprehensibility*.

Often a cognition ceases to be comprehensible to the degree that it ought to become really distinct. But this simply cannot be avoided, unless we simply do not speak of the thing.

[h] "Supponiret."

[i] "Augenscheinlichkeit Dispicuitaet."

[j] Reading "aber wird eine Erkenntniß gebracht, erst" for "aber eine Erkenntniß gebracht, geschieht erst," with Hinske (KI, lxxiii).

[k] "Perspicuitaet."

If we go back now to the distinction between clear and obscure cognition, we have further to remark that all obscure cognitions can be obscure, however,

A. *objective*$_L$
B. *subjective*$_L$;

but if we are to say it properly, then the former does not occur, but only the latter.

But when the relation of a thing to the boundaries of human cognition is such that it cannot be cognized clearly enough, but always remains obscure, then in most cases we do not ascribe all responsibility to him who does not cognize the thing clearly enough, but rather to the thing itself, or to him who expounds it. Although it frequently lies with the former rather than with the latter. We call this cognition, into which [man] does not and cannot have insight, *obscure objective*$_L$. A cognition is *obscure subjective*$_L$ when the responsibility for the thing's remaining obscure, regardless of all the effort applied, lies not with the thing and the cognition itself but with the one who wants to cognize something, namely, because he either possesses great ignorance, and thus naturally is not in a position to cognize the thing, or also because he simply did not apply enough of the requisite industry to it.

This latter obscurity, however, is really not grounded at all in the nature of the cognition itself or even, as some hold, of all men and their understanding. For if this were to be, then the cognition simply cannot be cognized clearly by a single man; rather, it lies simply either in the incapability and ignorance or in the negligence of this or that individual subject.

121

Thus it happens, then, that the same cognition that is clear to one subject can be obscure to another, and, on the contrary, the very cognition that is obscure to one subject can be clear to another.

Few men ever have a proper concept of what it means to have a proper, clear concept, or cognition, of a thing.

No man can, so to speak, understand himself better[;] he judges everything he says to be fully clear to himself, and just for this reason it happens that he is deterred from properly investigating whether he really understands himself properly or not.

Metaphysica and morals[,] these 2 pure sciences of philosophy, are of such a kind[l] that in them man is never in a position to represent the slightest concept distinctly unless he can previously attain for himself a complete[m] concept of the whole, i.e., of the whole science.

Either someone who wants to study *metaphysica* has a very pure, very

[l] "von der Art, und also beschaffen."
[m] "einen Completten, und vollständigen."

distinct concept of it, or he knows nothing at all of it. These are the only two ways. There is simply no mean in this.

On the other hand, someone can be quite comprehensible, especially if he does not know anything yet, or at least knows no errors, and he who hears him goes away exactly as clever as he came[;] this is very easy, and such an exposition, which does not damage but also does no good[,] can be easily comprehensible.[n]

Thus it is not possible in some cases to combine easy comprehensibility with complete distinctness[;] and they certainly judge wrongly who hold the easiest exposition to be the best, and who evaluate a somewhat more difficult, less childlike exposition, which is meant for reflection, as obscure, not understandable, even exaggerated.

It is so hard to make the obscure clear that no man has yet discovered a universally valid means for it.

Exhaustiveness is the sufficiency of a cognition for a certain purpose. When it serves to comply with the purpose and to pass judgment on it, the *consequence* is called the *end*.

With all *completudo*, then, we compare the cognition with a certain purpose. But this *completudo* is 122

A. *externa*, which appears in the comparison of the cognition with others.
B. *interna* which exists in itself, and lies in the cognition itself.

Completudo comparativa, however, can often be so very useful to us that we simply do not have need beyond that for *completudo absoluta*, or *interna[,]* and we can do without it. Exhaustiveness, however, rests solely and only on the multitude of the coordinate or juxtaposed marks.

Philosophia has the purpose of instructing us how we are to learn to understand ourselves better and better.

All new cognitions that deviate much from the usual way of judging are wholly obscure in the beginning and are not understood by the best mind[;] and this frequently happens, not because the cognitions are obscure in themselves, but because it is commonly very difficult to deviate from the usual way of judging, and to observe this or that thing from another side. He who, e.g., has learned dancing from a bad teacher, and who is later supposed to start learning it from one with skill, finds it really very hard to forget the accustomed old steps and movements of the feet again, and to follow the newer, better method. So is it, too, with cognition[;] everything that deviates from the old, already introduced kind of cognition, of exposition, of writing-style, etc., is difficult to understand and obscure.

All those who discover new methods in any of the sciences are obscure in the beginning, then[;] indeed, they are often disdained for just this

[n] "faßlich und Begreiflich."

reason, because we love the old far too much and do not want to depart from it; until, with time, we have become comfortable with this new method; since we find that it is often better than the old one.

Locke and *Newton* experienced the fate that in the beginning their writings were utterly obscure and not understandable, or at least they seemed to be, until one subsequently considered them more closely and discovered their merits.

123

§ 131

The doctrine of obscure cognitions is not at all logical but only metaphysical. *Logica* is not a science concerning the nature of the subject, of the human soul, for cognizing what really lies hidden within it. Instead it presupposes clear concepts and treats of the use of our understanding and of our reason.

In our soul all cognitions actually lie hidden, and all that is necessary is just to develop these cognitions, and to bring them into a brighter light.

Rational philosophy teaches us nothing new but only seeks to make distinct what we already know and to bring us to consciousness of it.

But empirical philosophy, on the other hand, is occupied with bringing us to new cognitions, which thus far we did not know.

§ 132

In this paragraph the author speaks of exhaustive clarity.

Completudo, however, is

1. *externa*
2. *interna.*

The former consists in the fact that the marks that are attributed to a thing suffice to distinguish it from all other things.

The latter, however, consists in the fact that the marks of a thing are sufficient to derive therefrom all its possible remaining determinations.

Completudo externa always presupposes *completudo interna.* Where the latter is not, the former certainly is not either[;] and again the former, namely, *completudo externa*, is attained by means of *completudo interna.* I cannot know immediately that a thing and its marks are sufficient enough to distinguish the thing from all remaining things[;] this must occur rather through *completudo interna.*

124

Internal *completudo* is not only a means to external exhaustiveness, then; rather, the latter cannot even be attained and acquired without the former.

No empirical concept can be internally complete, then. Thus internal exhaustiveness does not occur in the case of objects of experience. From this it follows at the same time that external exhaustiveness is also not to be met with in the *objecta* of experience. For internal exhaustiveness is always the ground of the external. E.g., in the case of metals, herbs, plants, etc., I cannot cognize the thing according to all determinations, consequently cannot yet distinguish it in every case from all other things.

In many books that treat of physics one finds *definitiones* of objects of experience. But it is a certain proposition that these never are, nor can be, correct and sufficient. For every *definitio* must be complete.

No one can attain a complete concept of objects of experience, then, which would serve to distinguish them from all remaining things, merely possible and real.

Therefore Locke made an effort to show that no one, however learned he may be, could be in a position to state a correct definition of man. From this it becomes clear, however, that none of our concepts of objects of experience can ever be complete *absolute*$_{\text{L}}$[;] but a *completudo comparativa* can exist in their case, namely, when the marks of a thing suffice to distinguish the thing from everything that we have cognized in experience until now.

Pure concepts of reason can be both *internally*
and *externally* complete.

In the case of empirical concepts, the things outside us, about which we judge,[o] are the *exemplaria*,[p] and our concepts are the *exemplata*.[q] In the case of pure concepts, however, the concepts themselves are the *exemplaria*, and those things of which we have the concepts are the *exemplata*, as, e.g., the concept of virtue, of right and wrong, of goodness, of legality and illegality, of actions, of the simple and the composite, and of the contingent and the necessary.

These concepts do not arise at all from objects[;] therefore I cannot represent their determination just in part; rather, they are arbitrary. 125

Reason is the creator of these concepts, and consequently the thing has no other determination than what reason has attached to it.

Mathematica is of this kind[;] it has nothing but pure concepts of reason, which can therefore be fully complete internally and externally. E.g., the mathematicians think of a *conus*, a cone, or a right-angled triangle that revolves around its *cathetum*[r] or one of its sides. Here he thinks everything that suffices to distinguish the thing from all others, for the sphere is not a thing outside him, which he has cognized in part according to certain determinations, but rather a thing in his pure reason, which he thinks of arbitrarily and in conformity with which he attaches certain determinations, whereby he intends that the thing should be capable of being differentiated from all other things.

[o] Reading "von denen wir urtheilen" for "die Urtheile."
[p] patterns.
[q] copies.
[r] leg.

Only pure concepts of reason are exhaustive, then, but not *objecta* of experience, which is distinctly clear from what was put forth previously.

No one should venture to define empirical concepts, then, but one can well have correct *definitiones* of pure concepts of reason.

§ 133

The author speaks herein of cognition that is wholly or in part clear, wholly or in part distinct.

Representations are wholly clear when the thing that I think of is composed of no more determinations than the ones I thereby represent. Representations are in part clear, however, when I do not think of each and every determination, but only of some of its determinations.

Some of the ancient philosophers thus distinguished concepts into *rationes archetypas*[s] and ἔκτυπα [or] *ektypas*.[t] The former are to be regarded as archetypes and *originaria*, the latter as copies and *exemplata*.[u]

The former include pure concepts of reason, the latter on the other 126 hand empirical concepts. The former can be wholly clear, but the latter, on the contrary, are never wholly clear, but always only in part. If, e.g., I see a house before me, and cannot go around it, then the house is only in part clear for me, namely, in regard to the side that I have seen; the rest is wholly obscure.

In the case of empirical concepts I always cognize only those determinations of the thing that excite our senses, and in fact in such a way that we are conscious of them.

§ 135

Liveliness and *strength* of cognition are not *opposita*, but rather both are combined with one another. Liveliness is an aesthetic perfection. Distinctness, however, *rationabilitas*,[v] or rather deep distinctness, is a logical perfection. The deeper the distinctness of a cognition is, the fainter its liveliness becomes. The livelier a cognition is, on the other hand, the shallower it is.

Liveliness in a cognition is attained with the help of much combination.[w] One attains distinctness in a cognition, however, when one seeks to produce it by means of much abstraction.[x]

Through coordinate marks we make a cognition lively, but through

[s] Ak, "Archetypos"; MS, "Archtypas" (KI, lxviii).

[t] Reading "Ektypas" instead of "ektypos," with Hinske (KI, lxxi).

[u] Reading "exemplata" instead of "exemplares," with Hinske (KI, lxxi).

[v] accessibility to reason.

[w] "einer großen Verbindung."

[x] "einer großen Absonderung."

subordinate marks deeply distinct. Extensive distinctness is bound up with the liveliness of a cognition, the deep distinctness of a cognition, on the other hand, with its dryness. E.g., in a description of spring I represent it in a lively way through a multitude of marks coordinate with one another. The poet does it thus. He shows, e.g., the budding flowers, the new green of the forests, the cavorting herds, the renewed rays of the sun, the lovely, charming air[,] the revival of the whole of nature.

In all oratory and poetry one seeks to put forth marks that are coordinate with one another, of which one is immediately aware in the thing to be described, in order to make the concept of the thing lively.

By this means one reaches aesthetic perfection in a cognition. The philosopher, however, who represents a thing with a deep distinctness, emphasizes only one mark of the thing and omits the remaining ones, but seeks out marks, and the grounds for the marks he thinks of in the thing. His reason is occupied first and foremost with this, then. 127

When one represents the thing through subordinate marks, then, the form of the cognition is wholly different from when one represents the same thing through coordinate marks. Aesthetics is occupied only with painting things, and with making them distinct through coordinate marks. Reason, however, climbs from one mark to another and thus omits many coordinate marks[;] but in this way cognition becomes dry.

The poet and the orator cognize much in few things. The philosopher, on the other hand, considers many objects and cognizes little in many objects. His cognitions are thus universal, they do not concern merely individual *objecta*, but rather whole genera of them. He represents only a few marks, to be sure, but with a deep distinctness.

Distinctness of reason is a distinctness *a priori*, which I cognize through marks *a priori*.

We cognize *objecta* by means of extensive distinctness without needing the use of reason, without engaging in reasoning.[y] But for deep distinctness reason is necessarily required.

For lively cognition sensibility is required. Sensibility is the perfection of cognition when we represent a thing like objects of the senses.

Rationabilitas belongs to things insofar as we think of them through general concepts. But sensibility, on the other hand, insofar as we represent a thing through individual concepts.

All sensibility brings about liveliness. Suitability to reason,[z] however, produces dryness. Our concepts of reason attain sensibility when we represent universal judgments *in concreto*. This happens, e.g., through examples and *similia*.

The sensibility of a cognition is not in any way an imperfection of it. In

[y] "vernünfteln."

[z] "Vernunftmäßigkeit."

sensibility we think of the universal – into which we already have insight in abstract cognitions – *in concreto* in those cases in which it really occurs.

Extensive clarity of cognition, bound up with sensibility, produces liveliness.

128 Our understanding always vacillates here, as it were, between 2 hazards. If we seek to cognize something aesthetically perfectly, then we soon lack the correct grounds, that which is solid in cognition, and we end up in shallowness. But on the other hand, if we cognize something through logical perfection, then we very easily lack aesthetic liveliness, etc., and we fall into dryness. Indeed, it is actually quite hard to hit the right mean between the two dangerous wrong tracks.

Nevertheless, it is also possible to unite both perfections with one another to a high degree.

Clarity of cognition, like completeness, *completudo*, is

A. *extensiva*
B. *intensiva.*

Claritas extensiva rests on a multitude of coordinate marks, which are cognized in a thing immediately.

It is the right path to liveliness, in that it brings with it much sensibility, for the latter just consists in *coordinatio* of its marks.

The completion of the perfections of all our cognitions is finally to give them sensibility, so that one represents the universal in particular circumstances and cases and thinks of the *abstractum in concreto* in a single, individual sensible case. E.g., if I think of friendship, true love, and the mutual helpfulness that flows from these, in the case of Damon and Pythias.[22] Here, then, I think the universal in individual cases. But in this way my cognition becomes lively[,] e.g., when I think of patriotism in Cato.

Without sensibility our pure cognition of reason is just very impoverished.

Extensive clarity and liveliness require only understanding, because with coordinate marks I do nothing but judge.

Claritas intensiva, however, rests on subordinate marks[,] and reason is necessarily required for this, because in this case we infer and derive one mark from the other.

Claritas extensiva serves for the description of an object. *Claritas* 129 *intensiva*, however, investigates the grounds of the thing. From one mark belonging to the thing, it seeks [to infer] that another mark must also belong to the thing. It seeks to find out the cause of things, then, and always asks for the why. Why this, and why that, indeed, why is it not otherwise?

The senses give us lively but not fully distinct cognition.

He who can narrate everything that he has ever seen, completely and in order, possesses much liveliness of cognition[;] indeed, by this narration he can often bring about a lively cognition in others.

Sensible clarity is nothing other than liveliness[;] in intuition there is clarity, but sensible clarity. Clarity through universal concepts is a logical clarity.

Mathematics is the only science that is in a position to judge according to its concepts.

He who is able to combine in his cognition both liveliness and deep distinctness has in fact already reached the highest degree of perfection of human cognition[;] but this is so hard that it seems to be almost impossible for everybody.

Through sensibility perfection of reason is not lost at all; rather, it only attains greater liveliness.

From this we see completely distinctly, then, that sensibility does not conflict at all with rational perfection, but rather it furthers this latter in certain cases[;] indeed, it often brings about for it a greater correctness, in that we frequently omit, and have to omit, *in abstracto* marks which actually belong to the nature of the thing, but which can be restored when one considers the thing *in concreto*. Orators and poets can frequently be very helpful to the philosopher, therefore.

This is a most universal rule of good, and especially of learned exposition: Combine sensibility with an exposition and give it to your instruction.

Logical clarity, however, rests on subordination[;] sensible clarity, on the other hand, rests on coordination of marks.

In just this way, we can also have A. a *sensible* distinctness according to aesthetic laws. 130
and B. a *logical* distinctness according to logical laws.

We must often abstract, but this is actually very hard for us, too.

1st Sensible distinctness according to laws of aesthetics is nothing other than *distinctness of intuition*.

2nd *Logical distinctness*, on the other hand, according to laws of the understanding and of reason, or of logic, is nothing other than the *distinctness of reflection*.

Something can be very lively, but all the less distinct[;] again, something can be appropriate, many-colored, and lively, but at the same time still not very distinct, and confused.

§ 139

It is false that our cognition becomes distinct only through analysis, as the author maintains.

Our cognition can be made distinct in two ways

A. *per synthesin*
B. *per analysin.*

But here we must distinguish well between the science of making a distinct cognition and the science of making distinct a cognition that was previously obscure. Namely, we either make a distinct concept, and this happens *per synthesin*, or we make distinct a concept that was previously confused, and this happens *per analysin.*

In *synthesis* we produce and create a concept, as it were, which simply was not there before, [one that is] completely new both *quoad materiam*[a] and also *quoad formam*[;][b] and at the same time we make it distinct.

All the concepts of the mathematicians are of this kind, e.g., the concepts of triangle, square, circle, etc.

All concepts fabricated[c] by reason are at the same time distinct, but only 131 *per synthesin.* If a concept is made distinct *per analysin* then it must already be given[;] thus we are occupied with making clear and distinct what is confused and obscure in this given concept, with developing, with explicating, and thus with illuminating it. This includes, e.g., each and every concept of metaphysics.

With these one is supposed to become conscious solely and simply of the marks that belong to the thing[,] e.g., with the concepts of virtue, of vice[;] and we therefore need do nothing but analyze and explicate,[d] make the confused concepts distinct.

The matter is already there, then, we are only supposed to give the thing a form. By means of analytical distinctness we do not cognize any more in a thing than we have already thought in it previously; instead we only cognize better, i.e., more distinctly, more clearly, and with more consciousness, what we already actually knew. E.g., with the concept of perfection I will first direct someone to the cases in which he makes use of the expression perfection, in order thereby to instruct him what he really understands by perfection[,] what sort of concept he makes of it, and what he thinks when he utters the word perfection and ascribes it to a thing. Here he will find, naturally, that he calls many things perfect that are really very imperfect, or are even quite vicious. E.g., the libertine takes his *vaga libido*[e] to be the greatest possible perfection. For if this did not exist, it would be impossible for him to indulge it so strongly, and to find in it a pleasure so very great, which obscures everything else for him. Analysis,

[a] as to matter.
[b] as to form.
[c] "fingirte."
[d] "zu Analysiren, aus einander zu setzen, und zu zergliedern."
[e] restless desire.

then, really amounts to making the confused distinct. The composition of cognition,[f] however, or synthesis, is helpful and useful simply and solely to produce something new and at the very same time, all at once, to make it distinct.

In general, all concepts of the human understanding are either

1st *conceptus dati* or
2nd *conceptus facti.*

A *conceptus datus*[,] a given concept[,] is one that is produced either through the nature of our understanding or through experience.

Conceptus facti[,] concepts that are made, are such as are created by us arbitrarily, or fabricated, without previously having been given. 132

All these fabricated concepts are produced simultaneously with their distinctness.

Here, namely, one fabricates something arbitrarily, and in fact simultaneously with the consciousness of it.

There are many such *conceptus facti* in aesthetics and in mathematics. In *philosophia*, on the other hand, there are *conceptus dati*.

A cognition does not become distinct through analysis alone, for the action whereby a cognition becomes distinct is one and the same with that through which its marks become clear.

A cognition can acquire distinctness of reason *per analysin*, but also distinctness of the understanding *per analysin*.

Through analysis I merely bring the marks of a cognition under more universal marks, into which I previously had insight *per analysin a priori*. But *per synthesin* I learn in addition new marks of a cognition *a posteriori*[,] e.g., with the concept of the essence of gold.

The latter is *empirical distinctness*; the former, however, is distinctness of the understanding, which has its origin in my reason and occurs by means of analysis. E.g., morals is nothing more than the exposition of our ethical representations, of virtue, of the good, of evil. Socrates said: I am the midwife of my listeners' thoughts.

To make a cognition is *to fabricate*[.]

We now want briefly to indicate the degrees of the representations of all cognitions.

1. "in general, *to represent* something[g] is the most universal and most usual[,] also the easiest cognition of a thing. But *representing* something, where *consciousness* is combined with it, is distinct from simply *representing*, where we are frequently not even conscious to what these representations are actually related."

[f] "Die Zusammensetzung der Erkenntniß."
[g] "sich etwas *vorstellen*."

Sibi aliquid repraesentare id est cognoscere, repraesentatio.[h]

133 But when there is combined with such representation the capacity of bringing what I represent under a universal concept, and thus of being able to know to what my representation actually is related, then this is the

2nd degree, namely, *to be acquainted*,[i] "then I am acquainted with what I represent."

3. "the following degree is *to understand*[j] something, i.e., to be acquainted with something through the understanding, or to be acquainted with something distinctly through a distinct concept."

Nature provides us with many things that we are able *to be acquainted* with but not really *to understand*. Furthermore,

4. *To have insight.*[k] Much "that exists in nature we do understand, but we do not have insight into it. E.g., the growth of plants."
To have insight is to cognize something through and by means of reason, that is, *a priori*. "Here, then, the thing need not even be given to me. Men frequently believe that they already have insight into something when they are only in a position to give an explanation of it."

To make[,] *facere*[,] a cognition is to fabricate it[,] *fingere*.

A *conceptus factitius* is thus at the same time a *conceptus fictitius*. To make a cognition arbitrarily and *with consciousness* is thus to make a distinct cognition.

All mathematical *definitiones*, e.g., are merely fabricated and are thus nothing but concepts of the thing that are made, arbitrary, [and] distinct.

5. "*To comprehend*[l] something is finally the last and highest degree[,] namely: it is *to have insight into* something through reason, but in such a way that it is sufficient for a certain purpose, that is, *to have insight comparative*$_L$."

But if I have insight into something sufficiently for any and every purpose, this is just *comprehending absolute*$_L$.[m]

Much that I really understand, am acquainted with, and have insight into, I still do not on that account comprehend. And on the other hand, what I *comprehend comparative*$_L$, I do not yet therefore comprehend *absolute*.

134 In the whole of nature there is nothing at all into which we have insight *absolute*$_L$, that is[,] sufficient for every purpose.

[h] To represent something is to cognize, is representation.

[i] "*kennen*."

[j] "*verstehen*."

[k] "*Einsehen*."

[l] "*begreifen*."

[m] "so ist dieses das *Absolute* schlechthin *begreifen*."

Sufficientia notarum rei est completudo, et est[n]

A. *externa*, i.e., when the marks that I have of a thing are complete and sufficient enough to distinguish this thing from all others. Thus the whole concept of it must be known.

Always, then, an externally sufficient concept is always internally sufficient, too. Furthermore, conversely, an internally sufficient concept is always externally sufficient, too. And a concept that is not internally sufficient is not externally sufficient either, and one that is not externally sufficient is again not internally sufficient either.

Philosophia est vel pura, vel applicata[o]

In *philosophia pura* each and every concept is given through the understanding and through reason. E.g., the concepts of the *possible*, and again of the *impossible*, of the *necessary*, and of the *contingent*.

Omnes conceptus sunt vel[p]

1. *pure rationales*
2. *empirici.*

All concepts are made distinct through analysis, that is *per analysin*, where previously they were obscure and confused. By this means one learns, namely, to have insight into the partial concepts of a complete concept.

A distinct concept arises, however, *per synthesin.*

With *analysis*$_{\mathrm{L}}$ the concept either becomes completely distinct, or it does not.

All my concepts of reason can become completely distinct, but empirical concepts are excluded from this and always remain incompletely distinct.

§ 140

Here in this *paragraphus* the author speaks of the *comprehensible* and the *incomprehensible*. To acquire a better *idea* of this, we intend first to represent the degrees of human cognition once more. This cannot be further described, nor defined.

The 1st degree is *to know*[q] something, that is, to represent something with consciousness. 135

The 2nd degree is *to be acquainted*[r] with something, i.e., to be able to

[n] Sufficiency of the marks of a thing is completeness, and it is . . .
[o] Philosophy is either pure or applied.
[p] All concepts are either . . .
[q] "*wißen.*"
[r] "*kennen.*"

cognize something in distinction from other things through comparison with those things.

The 3rd degree is *to understand*[s] something[,] i.e., to cognize something distinctly through the understanding.

The 4th degree, finally, is *to have insight*[t] into something, or to cognize something through reason.

When I have insight into something, I cognize it through mediate marks, I infer, then, and thus search for a *nota notae*, a mark of the mark.

If I am to understand something, the understanding must be occupied with it[;] I must cognize a thing through immediate marks, but in doing so I must also judge.

To understand something is far easier than to have insight into something, for in the first case it is only necessary that I coordinate the marks of a thing, but in the other case I must subordinate them. To understand what gold is I need nothing more than to know the properties of this metal, that it is, e.g., ductile, yellow, heavier than others, etc., that it does not rust. But to have insight into what gold is I must investigate one of its marks in particular and abstract from it its ground. E.g., why it does not rust, why is it ductile, heavier than others.

The fifth and highest degree of our cognition, finally, is *to comprehend*[u] something, that is, to have insight into something sufficiently, or to the degree that is necessary for a certain insight.

One can comprehend something either *absolute*$_{\text{L}}$, or *wholly*,[v] or else *partialiter*, i.e., *relative*$_{\text{L}}$.

I comprehend something *relative*$_{\text{L}}$[w] when I have insight into it in such a way as is required for this or that end.

We never comprehend something *totaliter* or *absolute*$_{\text{L}}$. Even the most learned among us cannot boast that he has insight into something in such a way that it serves for all purposes. With respect to religion the common man, if only he has a healthy understanding, always comprehends as much as the greatest *theologus*, as much as it is necessary for him to know in order to live righteously and to be able to arrange all of his actions according to God's laws.

136 Nevertheless, this will never be sufficient for all his ends.

In regard to the practical perfection of cognition, we all have equal insights, then, although we differ as to our insights with respect to logical perfection[;] however, even he who has greater insights and more extensive cognitions comprehends nothing *absolute*$_{\text{L}}$.

[s] "*verstehen*."
[t] "*einsehen*."
[u] "*begreifen*."
[v] "Totaliter gäntzlich."
[w] Reading "Relative" for "Absolute."

The author wrongly translates the word to *comprehend*[x] by *concipere*, although *concipere* really means nothing other than *to have insight.*[y]

The 6 degrees of our cognition, of which we have spoken more extensively above, are rather

1.	*repraesentare*	*to represent*
2.	*scire*	*to know*
3.	*noscere*	*to be acquainted with*
4.	*intelligere*	*to understand*
5.	*concipere*	*to have insight*
6.	*comprehendere*	*to comprehend*

Frequently something that is comprehensible to one man is incomprehensible to another.

In the beginning something is not comprehensible to us, which, in the course of time, can be comprehended by us very easily. Nevertheless, we can frequently err in that we believe and fully hold that others will comprehend what we ourselves do not comprehend, *et vice versa*, if we take it to be the case that what we do not comprehend is incomprehensible to others.

If I am to make distinct the concepts of a thing, then my representation of it must first be clear. Then I must attend to the various marks of the thing; after that I must consider many marks in a thing together, or compare them, hold them up to one another and compare them with one another. In this comparison there occurs not only a mere collection[z] of its marks, but rather a placing next to one another[,][a] a coordination of them.

Finally, however, comes *abstractio notarum*, or that action in which, in making distinct its representation, I ignore all such marks of a thing as could hinder and disturb me, or are not of use to me and thus are superfluous. 137

§ 144

In this § the author shows the distinction of distinct cognition into *cognitio totaliter* or *partialiter distincta.*[b]

Frequently one cognizes an object distinctly as to one part, but indistinctly as to another.

In experience much is hidden from us, but in logic more distinctness is to be found.

Indistinctness really arises from lack of attention to the parts of a whole concept.

[x] "*begreifen.*"
[y] "*Einsehen.*"
[z] "Collection oder Samlung."
[a] "eine Nebeneinander stellung."
[b] cognition that is totally [or] partially distinct.

One usually ascribes the responsibility for this indistinctness either to the thing itself, of which one has indistinct[c] cognition, or to the person and the subject in which the indistinctness of the cognition exists. When a thing has far too many marks, so that one is not in a position to survey them all at once, then the responsibility for the indistinctness of it necessarily lies in the thing itself.

With empirical concepts there is always more confusion than with the concepts of reason.

Concepts of experience spring up through the excitement of our senses, but these latter cannot have insight into all the determinations of the things, but rather many of them still remain hidden from us and unknown.

§ 147

Our cognitions are either

1. *adequate*[,] *i.e., complete* or
2. *incomplete* and not *adequate.*

Following Baumgarten, and Baumgarten in turn following Wolff, the author in this *paragraphus* has named a certain kind of distinct cognition complete.

If the marks of a thing are cognized fully distinctly, then this is intensive clarity of cognition of the first degree; but if I cognize the immediate marks of a thing distinctly, but derive from these other, mediate marks, 138 then this distinctness of cognition is intensive clarity of the 2nd degree, and in Wolff's expression, [it is] the completeness of cognition[.] E.g., when I say: vice is a readiness[d] to sin.

Now *readiness* is ease in acting.[e] To sin, however, is nothing other than to live contrary to moral rules and laws. *Vice* is thus a readiness to perform actions[f] that are contrary to the moral laws.

This 2nd degree of intensive distinctness of cognition cannot possibly be completeness, however, for otherwise the third degree of distinctness would have to be more complete. And this would go further and further. Here all comparison ceases, and if something is already complete *absolute*$_{\mathrm{L}}$, then there can be nothing to be found that would be more complete.

The author has, in an improper way, called a complete cognition an *adaequata cognitio*, and again incomplete cognitions *cognitiones inadaequatae.*

Completeness itself, however, consists in nothing other than *completudo*, and precision.

[c] Reading "undeutliche" for "deutliche."
[d] "Fertigkeit."
[e] "eine Leichtigkeit zu handelen."
[f] "Handlungen zu ediren."

A cognition is complete (*cognitio rei adaequata*[g]), then, when the representation of a thing is really in conformity with and is adequate to it,[h] so the cognition contains nothing more, but also nothing less, than really lies in the thing: *Si repraesentatio rei de re quadam nec supra, nec infra rem est.*[i]

All distinctness through subordination of marks is of various degrees, and hence one cannot call a cognition complete until its marks are no longer subordinated to any other concept.

§ 149–151

Completudo, or exhaustiveness, we have already considered above, and we will speak more of precision afterward in what follows.

Completudo consists in nothing other than the sufficiency[j] of a distinct concept of a thing for the derivation therefrom of all of the thing's remaining marks.

Omnis cognitio sufficiens est[k]

A. *extensiva*, that is[,] *exhaustiveness*
B. *intensiva*[,] that is[,] *thoroughness*.

For thoroughness, then, profundity[l] is required[;] thus it includes proof, and is attained by ascent to the highest mark of many marks subordinated to one another. 139

Some complete thoroughness is required in regard to *morals*.

Nevertheless, we quite frequently err here too. Thus it is, e.g., with a certain *casus necessitatis*,[m] like a necessary lie, a Christian deception, etc.

Exhaustiveness properly consists in nothing other than the fact that nothing is lacking, that the concept can be whole.

Nevertheless, even in the case of this exhaustiveness an error can occur, namely, if my concept contains too much, [more] than it should contain in order, accordingly, to be complete.

There is yet another perfection, which comes to this, that neither more nor less than is necessary is contained therein. And this perfection is called *precision*.[n]

A cognition is precise, then, when it has not too many marks and not too few.

[g] a cognition adequate to the thing.
[h] "derselben recht gemäß, und angemeßen."
[i] If the representation of a thing is, concerning the thing itself, neither above nor below the thing.
[j] "Sufficienz, oder Zureichung."
[k] All sufficient cognition is . . .
[l] "Tiefsinnigkeit."
[m] case of necessity.
[n] "*die Abgemeßenheit, die Praecision.*"

Cognitio est praecisa, quando non abundat notis.[o]

But precision is the determinate degree of marks, then, in accordance with which they do not contain more than is necessary in order to derive from them all remaining determinations of the thing.

It requires more effort to make a cognition precise than to bring it to superfluous thoroughness, i.e., more than to make it complete.

Precision is actually a great and difficult art[;] one sees this more easily in all cases, even by means of experience; thus even the mathematician, who is otherwise so precise, nevertheless finds no precision in the squaring of the circle. The calculations that have previously occurred for this are all such that the number arrived at was either too great or too small, and it has not yet been possible to hit it correctly.

But to be in a position to be able to observe such precision in regard to philosophical concepts, this certainly involves far more art and skill. A complete and precise concept, taken together, is *adequate* to the thing, and then such a concept is called a *conceptus adaequatus. Cognitio rei adaequata.*[p]

140 The situation here with marks is like that with a measure. A measure is adequate to the thing when it contains neither more nor less than is necessary for quantity to be measured. A mark is also adequate to the thing of which it is to be the mark when it contains neither more nor less than lies in the concept of the thing.

With *completudo* I take care that there is not too little in the cognition, but with precision I see to it that there is not too much in it. *Completudo*, as is easy to see, is always much more necessary than *praecisio*, for although superfluity in cognition is a mistake, which one makes an effort to avoid as far as possible[,] we can better and more easily bear that than a lack in cognition.

Precision is properly a perfection only relatively, because it helps one to deal with his cognitions[q] economically, and not to use his powers on a thing superfluously and thus, as it were, to squander them where it is not necessary, so that one afterward has no faculty for other, more useful cognitions. *Precision* is thus nothing other than a rule of economy, which just for that reason has a certain internal beauty; it is to be found especially in mathematics, geometry, and mechanics.

The *superfluous*[r] in a concept comes about, then, just when one concept already lies in the other, and this superfluity is always a consequence of lack in *praecisio*.

One says in many words, and more than are required, what one could have expressed and said in a few. Just as when in arithmetic one expresses

[o] Cognition is precise when the marks are not superfluous.
[p] Cognition is adequate to the thing.
[q] "Kenntnißen."
[r] "Das Überflüßige, das Abundans."

a fraction in very large, lengthy[s] numerals, which one would have been able to express just as well and correctly in a few small numbers.

There is a certain kind of precision in proofs, too, in accordance with which there is not a single proposition more or less than serves for conviction. One finds such exceptional precision likewise in *mathematica*. This beautiful science, as we see, is thus a model in many respects, and there has always been an effort to establish its properties, and among them in particular precision, in philosophy. 141

In the case of systematic exposition and cognition, precision is a principal perfection.

With beautiful[,] i.e., aesthetic cognitions, on the other hand, precision is a dispensable perfection.

In oratory and poetry, one is not miserly with expressions, but frequently rather far too wasteful. One frequently says a thing more than once, but nevertheless only with other expressions and in other images. Precision is thus merely a rule of economy and of cleverness, but not at all of taste and of aesthetics. Precision is only a rule of cleverness[;] it is thus hard to attain, and that precision where one is precise and economical in his expressions, so that someone else thereby attains a certain degree of clarity of concept, is a particular talent, and thus also a work of genius, very difficult, indeed, almost impossible to attain through mere art. Each and every aphorism is of this kind, all proverbs have a certain kind of precision or adequacy. By means of these one says something complete and wise with few expressions. Precision thus belongs merely to logical perfection.

In the 151st *paragraphus* the author calls precision of cognition a determinate cognition. This expression is wholly wrong, however.

Indeterminate marks are such as contain too little, and our author says again that indeterminate marks are such marks as contain too much, or more. Something can be complete without containing any precision at all. Now we will speak somewhat more of profound cognition. Intensive distinctness in a cognition has various degrees, as we heard earlier.

A greater degree of distinctness of cognition through *subordinate marks* is *deep distinctness*. A *higher degree* of distinctness of cognition through *coordinate marks*, on the other hand, is *extensive distinctness*. I cannot attain depth of cognition unless I go from one mark to the other, and in this way cognize one mark of the thing mediately through another.

Profundity is nothing but the faculty for profound distinctness, or for a long series of marks by means of, or mediately through, ascent. Here I ascend from experiences that I have had to their first grounds, or from the first grounds to the first experiences. 142

The first, from which I here begin, can be either the first, or also, if I end there, the last.

[s] "weitläuftigen."

§ 154

In this *paragraphus* the author teaches us nothing more than a mere name. He does not show us here how one can and should make concepts lucid and clear, but merely acquaints us with the name of a thinker who has clear concepts.

Some men are of such a kind that they foolishly fancy that only in their own minds are things lucid. While on the other hand they think that other people have nothing but obscure and confused concepts. "In their minds alone is there a Goshen,[23] while everything else, in contrast, is hidden in Egyptian darkness."

A learned man, however, must strive above all to attain clear and distinct concepts of the things that are or can be objects of his considerations[.]

THE SIXTH SECTION

Of the certainty of learned cognition

§ 155

Certainty is nothing but subjective necessity in the quality of judgments. The opposite of judgments is the denial of what is affirmed in the judgments, or also the affirmation of what is denied in the judgment.

Many judgments are so constituted that their opposite appears to me to have to be completely impossible, and it is thereby necessary *subjective*$_{\mathrm{L}}$.

143 Everything that is true is just for this reason at the same time certain *subjective*$_{\mathrm{L}}$.

Objective necessity is thus really truth.

In a multitude of cases we find that we judge much to be true that we always find *subjective*$_{\mathrm{L}}$ in certain cases to be uncertain, indeed, whose opposite we even find to be possible.

It is clear, then, that the uncertainty of a cognition rests merely on its objective falsehood, while the certainty of a cognition, on the other hand, rests on its objective truth.

If something is true, then it is at the same time certain[;] if something is false, it is always at the same time without doubt uncertain.

The true cannot be false *objective*$_{\mathrm{L}}$, that is, based on the constitution of a thing, or on a true property[;] it cannot be uncertain whether it is true or false.

All uncertainty is thus grounded in the subject and is subjective, i.e., it is grounded in him who is not in a position to have insight and to cognize something as true or as false.

Every ground of truth is a ground of holding-to-be-true[;] every ground of cognition, even supposing that it is insufficient, is nevertheless a ground for holding-to-be-true.

All holding-to-be-true based on grounds concerning which we do not investigate whether they contain a large or a small degree of *truth* is *plausibility*. If the degree of *truth* is greater than the degree of the grounds of the opposite, then the cognition is probable. Here, then, there does not exist in the slightest any settled truth.

With probability, there really is sufficient ground, but yet this ground of truth is greater than the grounds of the opposite[; it] outweighs them.[t]

Holding-to-be-true on account of the illusion of cognition is called *persuasion*.

Here one accepts any degree of truth in order to be able to approve a cognition, without investigating whether the grounds of the opposite have a greater degree of truth or not. Judgment according to the measure of probability is not persuasion[;] instead, judgment from mere plausibility is. Persuasion is really a kind of delusion; for one always considers only the one side, without in the least reflecting on the opposite side, which is most detrimental, however. 144

Consciousness of a cognition, however, through the sufficient ground of its truth, is called *conviction*. This arises solely from reason's *consciousness* of the necessary in the cognition. Where there is a contingent cognition, which can be thus but can also be other than it really is, there is no conviction. One can suitably represent conviction as composed of many moments or elements, i.e., of small degrees of *persuasion* and of *holding-to-be-true*, and can accept all the moments or degrees of holding-to-be-true and of persuasion as being of the same kind.

When the moments of holding-to-be-true constitute exactly half of the sufficient ground, then a cognition is uncertain, doubtful[;] *ambigua ejus modi cognitio*.[u] Here the mind always remains undecided, then[;] it swings, as it were, between fear and hope. There are on the one side exactly as many grounds as on the other, which balance one another.

But if there is even one more degree of truth on the side of the insufficient ground than there is on the side of the opposite, then the cognition is no longer *ambigua*[v] but rather probable.

But if on the other hand there is a lesser degree of truth on the side of the insufficient ground than there is on the side of its opposite, then the cognition is not only uncertain, not probable, either, but even improbable. Nevertheless, the cognition still remains plausible. Hence it cannot simply be rejected, for plausibility requires merely the slightest degree of truth.

All certainty is to be regarded as a unity, and as a complete whole, and

[t] Reading "dieselben" for "dieselbe."

[u] Cognition of this mode is uncertain.

[v] uncertain.

thus is the measure of all the rest of our holding-to-be-true, and of each and every one of its degrees.

Certainty, however, arises from nothing but the relation of equality between the grounds of cognition that I have and the whole sufficient ground itself.

If the grounds of cognition that I have are not equal to the whole sufficient ground, then my cognition is *uncertain*. It is true that there is a certain dissimilarity in objects and concepts, but concepts can nonetheless become homogeneous if one brings the manifold under a universal concept.

145

This production of similarity arises merely from comparison. One compares, or holds up the ground of truth against the grounds of falsehood[;] then sees whether the grounds of truth contain a greater degree of truth than the grounds of the opposite[;] and then, after more mature reflection, makes a judgment that is more correct and more fitting concerning the probability and improbability of a cognition.

If we had no cognition of the sufficient ground of certainty, we would not be able to make any judgment whatsoever concerning the probability or improbability of a thing. All of these arise, namely, from the relation of our grounds of cognition to certainty. One is accustomed, however, always to assent at first to that of which one has several convincing grounds of truth, and which one sees by oneself.

The mere sufficient ground is sufficient *objective*$_{\mathrm{L}}$, but the insufficient ground *subjective*$_{\mathrm{L}}$. The former determines in the thing what ought to be held concerning it, but the latter, on the other hand, is very doubtful[;] for it is quite easy to see that today one can have more, but tomorrow once again fewer grounds of truth concerning a cognition.

The *sufficient ground*, however, is the one whose opposite cannot possibly be thought or represented as true.

Naturally, then, it actually contains everything that exists in the thing.

The *insufficient grounds*, on the other hand, include[w] only what we think and represent of the thing, and what we cognize of it.

As we have just said, then, certainty and the sufficient ground are the measuring stick. All judgments are plausible, not probable, when no relation of the grounds of cognition to certainty exists in them.

This plausibility can change very much, however.

Probability and *improbability* are *objective grounds*. *Plausibility*, however, is a *subjective ground*[;] that is, *probability* and *improbability* lie in the object itself, in the thing that is to be cognized; *plausibility*, on the other hand, lies in him who has no cognition of a thing.

146

In a subject, is the condition the same whether the cognition it has is only a persuasion or a certain truth, a conviction, or not? It is not thereby altered externally at all, not even in the least.

[w] "enumeriren."

But it is simply not possible at all to state an infallible, certain, and universal mark of conviction, for distinction from persuasion.

Now since it is impossible to state really and with certainty which grounds of judgment and of persuasion lie in the object and which in the subject, we accordingly make the following important general remark, namely, "every error properly arises only because we confound the causes of approval that lie in the object itself with those grounds that lie in the subject."

To investigate, however, whether something that we accept is actually a merely plausible and invalid persuasion or an actual, certain conviction, one first of all weighs the grounds of the opposite in particular.

If I find now that I meet with grounds for the opposite of my cognition as numerous and as important as for that to which I have actually assented, then from this I easily see that my whole cognition must have been not a conviction at all but rather merely a persuasion[,] a *phaenomenon* of conviction.

All of our representations together are such phenomena[.] E.g., in the case of the rainbow it seems as if it were supported by the earth; it is a mere appearance, therefore[;] on closer investigation, namely, we see that this is not so.

Experience teaches us that the strength of our persuasion of a thing can be and is just as great as our conviction of its opposite is afterwards.

A means for sensing what is really necessary and required for true conviction, then, is the following: to study industriously such sciences as open the most certain path, i.e., which actually convince us of certain truths. E.g., mathematics[.] Furthermore, let one devote himself to such sciences as confirm the grounds of reason through experience, as, e.g., experimental *physica*.

Since we lack a universally sufficient mark, then, for correctly and infallibly distinguishing the subjective grounds of holding-to-be-true from the objective ones, the phenomenon of conviction based on true certainty and conviction, we have to be satisfied with striving to convince ourselves in individual cases of the certainty of this thing or that, so that at least we can always be in a position to distinguish the false from the true. But in order to be able carefully to avoid error in this or that cognition, one must take note of, and observe, the following: 147

1st "One must compare his cognition of this or that object with the cognitions of other people concerning one and the same object[x] and carefully hold them up against one another, since it is not to be supposed that every man should have one and the same grounds moving him to hold one and the same thing to be true[;] instead there is the greatest probability that what one person considers from one side, someone else, who thinks something

[x] "über ein, und eben dasselbige Object, über ein, und eben denselben Gegenstand."

else and who conceives the whole thing differently, will be opposed from the other side."

2nd "One must accept and suppose the opposite of the cognition that one has[;] one must place oneself, as it were, in the position of his opponent and of one who disputes the truth of my cognition, and then look to see whether it may be thought as true or at least as probable. Even if this occurs only to some extent, one still has cause to put some distrust in the truth of the cognition he has. If this does not in the least occur, and if I can impartially see and also maintain that the opposite of the cognition that I have would be absurd, impossible, and that it would be foolish to want to accept it, then from this it becomes clear that my cognition must be true and correct."

Etc., etc., etc. In respect of *certainty*, however, there are three various kinds or degrees of holding-to-be-true

1. *knowing*
2. *opining*
3. *believing.*

148 1st *To know* is to judge something and hold it to be true with certainty. To know something, then, involves a great deal. I can never say that I know that there are inhabitants on the moon[;] I have not been there, I have not seen them.

2nd *To opine* is to judge something incompletely, and this occurs when the grounds that we have for taking something to be true are insufficient and do not outweigh the opposite, and this is then an opinion.[y]

In these *opinions*, however, the grounds, and thereby also the degrees of holding-to-be-true, can grow and increase; but it is to be noted that in the case of *opining* one always remains undecided

To opine something practically, however, involves

3. *believing.* Here I am always decided, without however finding it necessary for me to be decided.

Opinions are thus nothing but subjectively incomplete grounds for taking-to-be-true.

Man always opines.

To accept something without a subjective necessity according to logical concepts is *to believe.*

A logical necessity, however, is nothing but the necessity of holding-to-be-true according to logical laws of the understanding and of reason.

The necessity, however, of accepting something according to practical laws is always subjective. To believe is thus nothing but to accept something of which I am not yet logically certain.

Belief, furthermore, is also a practically sufficient holding-to-be-true.

Certainty, on the other hand, is a holding-to-be-true that is also theoretically sufficient.

[y] "eine Opinion."

In the case of *believing*, I am not at all inclined to listen to my opponent's grounds. For my grounds for holding-to-be-true are in this case always practically sufficient. In the case of believing there is also a certain direction of our judgment through the will.

If I accept something, then I do not yet consider it to be certain, and thus, when I concede something, then I do not at all hold it to be true.

A *practical certainty* would be firm belief, and both as to its conviction and as to its power to destroy all doubts this will be as strong as belief in accordance with logical laws ever can be. Indeed, this belief is frequently stronger than many an apodeictic certainty concerning its cognition. This occurs, however, only in the case of universal cognitions[z]

149

A. of reason
B. of experience.

We can also *believe* something without thereby attaining a practical certainty of it, but merely at the most a greater degree of holding-to-be-true.

There is also practical holding-to-be-true, and certain believing, whose suspension would suspend and nullify all universal and necessary laws of the practical will, of the whole of morals, ethical doctrine, theology, religion, etc., and [nullify] what can only be thought sublime[;] and all of this is firm belief, then.

Of such propositions we have 2:

1. There is a *God.*
2. There is *another world.*

These 2 propositions are the only ground of all religion, morality, etc. These 2 propositions are the true *conditio sine qua non.*

Belief in these 2 propositions is not historical but rather rational, derived from practical rules of reason.

This belief is not an opinion but a certainty, which is so constituted, however, that although it is not actually apodeictic nor irrefutable according to the laws of logic, it still nonetheless outweighs by far all holding-to-be-true that is based on logical grounds, and is superior to these.

When it comes to deciding about all our well-being, our happiness and unhappiness, apodeictic *certainty*, which comes and arises merely from the understanding, does not have the inner force to compel the subject to hold to it, however convincing it otherwise is.

So is it even with mathematical propositions and demonstrations, which otherwise have the greatest and surest certainty. However certain it is that a circle has 360°, however apodeictic the Platonic theorems in geometry are, still no one would want to die for their infallibility and irrefutability.

Belief in accordance with practical, and in particular in accordance with

[z] "Kenntnißen."

moral laws, however, has full power to strengthen the subject who has it
150 with full confidence, and to bring that subject to the point that it will hold to it[a] in spite of all dangers and unhappiness[,] even when it concerns[b] the decision concerning everything that affects the subject's weal and woe.

People have been seen to die for moral propositions, after all.

The resolve not to allow oneself to be diverted by anything is more a resolve of practical and moral belief, then, than an effect of apodeictic certainty, and it is far more unshakeable, indeed, it in fact always carries with it a certain kind of merit.

A cognition is certain *objective*$_{\text{L}}$ when it contains those grounds in accordance with which all men, in respect of it, must agree. A cognition is certain *subjectively*, however, when it contains the manner in which all men actually agree in respect of it.

Perspicuousness is the intuitive[c] in certainty, *evidence*.[d] Thus, e.g., mathematical propositions are evident. But we are certain of many things without their having evidence.

We have 2 methods for grounds of holding-to-be-true. The *agreement* of other men with our opinions, and the testing of our thought according to other men's sentiments, is really a most outstanding logical test of our understanding by the understanding of others. Man needs this communication[e] of his cognitions very much in order to be able to pass judgment on them rightly.

Men have a natural inclination to communicate to others the judgments that their understanding has made, and merely from this arises the writing of books, whose cause has otherwise been set down to vanity, to ambition, by other critics of the human race, who would happily interpret everything most unfavorably.

Men who separate themselves from all human society necessarily find in the end, when they begin to investigate their condition and the causes of their misanthropy, that they do not themselves have enough means to distinguish the true from the false.

The freedom to communicate one's thoughts, judgments, [and] cognitions[f] is certainly the only[,] most certain means to test one's cognitions[g] properly, however, and to verify[h] them. And he who takes away this free-
151 dom is to be regarded as the worst enemy of the extension of human cognition, indeed, of men themselves. For just by this means he takes

[a] Reading "anhängt" for "anzuhangen," with Hinske (KI, lxxiii).
[b] "angeht, betrift."
[c] "das Intuitive, das Anschauende."
[d] "die *Evidenz*."
[e] "diese Mittheilung, diese Communication."
[f] "Kenntniße."
[g] "Kenntniße."
[h] "verificiren."

away from men the one true means they still possess for ever uncovering, becoming aware of, and correcting the frequent deception of their own understanding and its false steps.

Theft of the right to think without constraint and to bring one's thoughts to light, is really theft of the first rights and of[i] the greatest advantages, of the human race, and especially of the human understanding.

Men have, as it were, a calling to use their reason socially and to make use of it. Just so too the temporal goods of this life.

From this it follows naturally that everyone who has the *principium* of conceit, that the judgments of others are for him utterly dispensable in the use of his own reason and for the cognition of truth, thinks in a very bad and blameworthy way.

This is actually logical egoism, however, which of course could not and would not require that one communicate his own judgments to others, too. This so-called logical *egoism* consists, then, in nothing but the presumed but often false self-sufficiency of our understanding, existing for itself and, so to say, isolated, where one believes he knows enough by himself, and believes he is infallibly correct and incorrigible in all his judgments.[j] And we easily see that this conceited mode of thought[k] is not only completely ridiculous but is even most contrary to real humanity.

§ 157

Sensible certainty is to be distinguished by us from *certainty of the senses.*

Through observations, experiments, and frequent, oft-repeated experience we attain certainty of the senses.

The *sensible certainty* of a cognition does not really arise, however, through the actual intuition of objects by means of our senses, but rather merely through the fact that we make cognitions distinct, convincing, and capable of insight more easily or with less effort.

A cognition can properly be called rational in two ways, namely, 152

1st "insofar as one can have insight into it through reason and it also agrees with reason[;] all true[,] well-grounded, provable propositions are of this kind. Or"

2nd "insofar as it arises merely from reason[;] in most cases all logical cognitions are of this kind, and on this account they can also be called precise and, in the most proper sense, *cognitions of reason.*"

In the case of the certainty of a cognition, one can look either to its logical certainty and certainty of reason or to its aesthetic and sensible certainty.

[i] Reading "Rechte und der" for "Rechte der," with Hinske (KI, lxxiii).

[j] Reading "in allen seinen Urtheilen" for "alle seine Urtheile," with Hinske (KI, lxxiii).

[k] "diese Einbilderische Denckungs Art."

The latter cognition is admittedly subject to many errors, but on the other hand it is also quite easy to have insight into it.

§ 158

A cognition that is perfect according to the rules of coordinate concepts is called, in the common manner of speaking, *complete*. Although one could rather and more correctly call it an extensive cognition, because coordinate concepts are put forth simultaneously, and are thus, so to speak, as it were, extended over the object.

§ 159

Those grounds to which other grounds are subordinate are really not at all the complements of these latter with respect to the sufficient ground; rather, they are their origin. In the series of grounds coordinate with one another, however, one concept is of course frequently a *complementum* of another.

In the case of the highest degree of certainty of reason I look to the series of marks subordinate to one another, in order to get to the first ground. In this way I seek to discover intensive clarity of conviction. In the case of the highest degree of sensible certainty, however, I always look to the series of marks coordinate with one another, in order to be able to produce a certain strict and accurate completeness according to the rules of extensive clarity.

153

§ 161

A cognition can always be certain, however,

1. *mathematically* but also
2. *philosophically*.

The peculiar thing about mathematical certainty is that although it arises from reason, just as the philosophical does, one nonetheless [proceeds] synthetically in it, that is, in the series of marks subordinate to one another one ascends from the lowest and simplest to the highest.

In philosophical certainty, on the other hand, one goes through the series of concepts that are subordinate[l] to one another, to be sure, but this does not take place synthetically but rather analytically.[m] And one descends from the composite and highest concept to the simplest and lowest.

The mathematical certainty of cognition is always very distinct and

[l] "subordinirten d.i. untergeordneten."

[m] "Analytisch, d.i. vermittlest der Zergliederung."

intuitive, so that one can have insight into it very easily. But this arises because all mathematical concepts are synthetic and arise through arbitrary composition. For one can most easily be conscious of that which one has oneself invented. In philosophy, on the other hand, all concepts are analytic, they are not arbitrary, as in mathematics, so that one can accept and establish something according to one's own liking[;] instead they are already given confusedly, and only through philosophy are they to be made distinct and easy.

Since the concepts in philosophy are already given, then, the philosopher cannot so easily be certain that he has touched on all the marks that belong to a thing, and that he has insight into these completely perfectly. Instead, many *notae* may still belong to the thing, of which he knows nothing.

None of the marks of a thing can escape or slip away from the mathematician, however, nothing can evade his sharp eye. For he has himself arbitrarily assumed them, if not invented them, and has arbitrarily ascribed them to it[;] consequently he must of course be perfectly conscious of them all.

§ 167

154

The author speaks in this *paragraphus* of shallow cognitions.

In our language, and with our expressions, we quite frequently draw upon analogies.

We make use, namely, of certain images, in order, by their means, to give sensibility to cognitions that are in themselves abstract.

In just the same way, here in logic we also call certain cognitions (as well as modes of understanding, expositions, etc., etc.) shallow, *ad analogiam* with water.

According to physical principles, a body of water is called *shallow*, as is known, when its depths are to be found not far beneath the surface.

A cognition is shallow *ad analogiam*, then, when it is grounded on mere experiences and not on any investigation.

Thoroughness of cognition is opposed to, or contradistinguished from, its shallowness[;] the former is, namely, the *terminus*$_L$ of certainty.

A cognition is *superficiel*$_F$, however, when one contents oneself with mere illusion, i.e., when one is content and satisfied with the cognition that one has acquired with the very first glance at it. With a superficial cognition, then, one cognizes nothing more than what strikes one's eyes at once[,] immediately. Thus one has, e.g., a superficial cognition of geography when one is able to do nothing more than to enumerate the names of the countries, cities, rivers, etc. Thus one has a superficial cognition of history, if one knows a few striking historical facts about states, without looking to their origin.

Through and by means of a superficial cognition one sees, so to speak, the debris[n] swimming on the surface of the water, but one is not aware of the pearls that lie at the bottom of the sea.

Superficial cognitions, which are concerned only with the surface of a thing and with cognitions of [that surface], are most closely related to shallowness.

A cognition is *thorough*, on the other hand, when one gets to its ground, i.e., when one goes just as far as one can go in order to attain complete certainty.

155 A cognition must be deep to be thorough. If the series of grounds subordinate to one another is very long before one reaches complete certainty, then the cognition is profound.

All cognitions, the empirical as well as the rational, can become thorough.

Thorough empirical cognitions, cognitions of experience, however, are not the kind that can become profound, only the rational ones are. The ground of this is that with empirical cognitions, there is not a series of subordinate, but only of coordinate, grounds.

Empirical cognitions are thorough, however, when they contain as many coordinate concepts as are necessary for distinctness.

One has a thorough historical cognition, e.g., when one goes back to the *autores* who first wrote about a thing.

A cognition can be thorough even if it is very limited in respect of extensiveness.[o] But thorough cognitions must always be preferred to extensive[p] cognition.

Extensiveness, namely, without profundity is nothing but an empty shadow[;] it is like a naught, or zero, a cipher, in which there is no real being.

§ 168

Here the author speaks of three different kinds of actions that we must undertake in order to be certain of a cognition or to reject it. These 3 actions are, namely, nothing but our different procedures in regard to the approval that we believe we owe or do not owe to those cognitions, as there is

1st the *giving* of approval
2nd the *withdrawal* of approval, and
3rd the *withholding* of approval.

[n] "die Stoppeln."
[o] "Weitläuftigkeit, und Ausbreitung."
[p] "ausgebreiteten, und weitläuftigen."

The *first* is *a positive* action,
the *second* a *privative*
the *third*, however, is no action at all.
In the *first case*, namely, I take something *to be true*
In the *second case* I accept something *to be false* 156
In the *third case*, however, I do not *judge* at all, but rather I suspend[q] my *judicium*.

With every cognition we can think either of a
plus
or of a *minus*, or of a
zero.

Affirmative judgments increase our cognitions, and thus are a *plus*[.]

Negative judgments do not increase our cognition, and thus are a *minus*. For they only seek to lessen the false in our cognitions, to put us in a position not to accept anything but what is true[;] in short, they only serve to avoid error[.]

But when in any cognition, finally, we neither affirm something nor deny it, then this is the condition of zero.

Just as in respect of our external humor[r] we are in the condition of *plus* when we are pleased, in the condition of *minus* when we are sad, and in the condition of zero when we are completely indifferent or insensible.

The *withdrawal* of approval adds nothing to our cognitions, of course, but it nonetheless restrains us from error.

When we *give* a cognition our approval, however, then our *knowledge* receives an *accrementum*[.][s]

The *withholding* of approval, however, brings about uncertainty. Although it can be rather useful in many cases. But here we must necessarily discuss the following questions. Namely, whether our free choice has an influence on whether we *give* our approval to a cognition, or *withdraw* it from it, or whether we even *withhold* it.

Answer[.] In most cases, such a procedure of giving our approval, or withdrawing it, or holding it back[,] does not rest at all on our free choice, but rather is necessitated through and by the laws of our understanding and our reason.

Thus it happens in *mathematica*, for example. A businessman, e.g., who 157 sees from his bills that he owes much, and more than he has to hope for and possesses, will of course not be able to withdraw his approval[t] from this cognition, which is so evident, however much he might like to[;] even assuming he does not regard [the cognition] especially *positive*$_{L}$, he will

[q] "Suspendire."
[r] "unseres äußeren Humeurs."
[s] accretion, growth.
[t] "Beyfall, und Consens."

nonetheless not be able to to regard the sum of the debt *negative*$_L$[,] as available, existing capital, since he is too much and too evidently convinced of the correctness of the arithmetic in this matter, and the account of the debts contains far too much evidence.

This much is certain, if we were in a position and if we were disposed to give our approval, now to accept something at will, arbitrarily, or also now to reject it, then we would thus be placed in a position to further, to produce, and to increase our pleasure, our comfort, indeed, even our happiness.

On the other hand, we would also be capable, to just that degree, of removing arbitrarily whatever could bring us sadness and cause us irritation. But then, with such arbitrary cognitions, either there would have to be no sufficient grounds to maintain their opposite, or, assuming these were present, then we would have to be under no necessity of reflecting on them. In this way the debtor would easily be able to consider himself a creditor, someone who has been dismissed would be able to consider himself his prince's darling, etc., he who receives the saddest news would be able to consider himself happy, or at least to remain *in suspenso* (although, considered from another side, suspension between fear and hope is far more difficult and more terrifying, even more unbearable, than the consciousness of his misfortune)[;] and even when the complete ruin of his position, his honor, etc., and of all his means lay before him inescapably and in the near future, nevertheless [he would] always be in a position, with his soul content and his mind undisturbed or excited, to be able to sleep well and peacefully, and to eat and drink well.

This free *arbitrium* in regard to approval might perhaps be included among the happinesses of the ancient poets, however. It disappears entirely, and in the presence of certain degrees of the grounds it is always very hard, if not utterly impossible, to withhold one's approval.

158

Hence in very many cases one can not only count on the approval that someone must give to someone else, but one can even demand it, that is, one can wring and force it from him.

The mathematician, whose propositions display themselves with sufficient grounds and are proved, can always speak authoritatively[;] he can with right demand of me my approval for his propositions[;] and he who in spite of this wishes to remain *in suspenso* and always to doubt whether he should accept these propositions, etc., or on the other hand reject them, will always make himself ridiculous and show that he does not know at all what mathematics and its properties are.

In spite of this, however, although approval does not depend[u] *immediate*$_L$ on men's choice, it nevertheless often does depend on it *indirecte*,

[u] "abhängt, oder dependiret."

mediately,[v] since it is according to one's free wish[w] that he seeks out those grounds that could in any way bring about approval for this or that cognition, which cannot demand the *consensus aliorum debitum*.[x]

If approval does not arise immediately through the nature of the human understanding and of human reason, then it still requires closer direction of choice, will, wish, or in general of our free will, toward the grounds of proof.

It is certain, of course, that in the human soul there occurs an arbitrary direction of the powers of the mind toward what we would like to see and what we wish for.

We give our approval at once to a cognition that is agreeable and pleasant to us, without even taking the trouble to investigate more closely the proper, true grounds for taking it to be true.

If something is very weighty for us and of very great importance, so that a great part, indeed, even the greatest part of our peace of mind and of our external well-being and happiness depends upon it, then in this case the mind is just not free enough to consider the matter indifferently and impartially from both sides, to weigh grounds for it on one side and the grounds for its opposite on the other side, to hold the importance of all these various grounds up against one another properly, and to pronounce on their advantage; instead the mind, and often even our understanding, are chained, as it were, and restricted, so that we immediately and readily approve what is advantageous to us and grant it our approval. And, on the other hand, [we] soon reject and disapprove what could cause us harm or sickness.

159

In the *suspensio judicii*, finally, that is, in the withholding of our approval, one really undertakes no action whatsoever, as we mentioned above.

A judgment is dogmatic when one either in fact accepts or affirms a cognition that has been put forth, or on the other side rejects and denies it. But when, on the contrary, one does not make a judgment, but rather withholds it, and hence neither affirms something nor denies something, then this judgment is *skeptical*.

The skeptical in judging, where one does not make any decision[,] does not settle anything, but instead leaves everything unsettled, and entertains doubts about everything concerning which one cannot maintain anything with certainty, until one has suitable grounds of proof either for accepting it or for rejecting it. This cautious[y] and careful procedure in judging, where one is very much on one's guard against affirming something of which one is not wholly reliably convinced, and against denying anything

[v] "*mittelbahr*, mediate."
[w] "nach seinem freyen Belieben."
[x] agreement of others that is owed.
[y] "caute."

into whose impossibility or not being one does not have fully distinct insight – this procedure is actually most adequate and most advantageous for distinct truth. Provided only that one does not have the constant resolve to doubt everything forever, and to leave everything undecided. Thus it happens that a true philosopher is quite inclined not to waste his approval unnecessarily on just anything, but rather always to withhold it until he has enough and fully sufficient grounds of truth. But just as soon as he has sufficient grounds for the truth of a cognition, and apprehends their validity himself, he asks nothing more, but rather his custom is to subscribe to the cognition at once, and to cognize it as true, indeed, to maintain it.

The insatiable desire that prevails among many so-called philosophers or dogmatists to decide every cognition – that is, to accept or to reject – 160 immediately[,] at first glance[,] without the slightest investigation[,] has seduced some and is always the surest way to infinite errors.

One of the most outstanding causes, however, that very frequently misleads man into making a false judgment, or even into an error, is the *affects*.[z]

These perverters[a] of man, which in common life produce so much disorder, are in no less a position to confuse man's understanding and to lead it into errors. Now these affects of man direct the grounds of certainty concerning a thing solely to one side, and they do not allow him to consider the other side as well. Thus we can of course blame someone who has given approval to a false cognition, namely, when the responsibility actually lies with him for rejecting those grounds that could have convinced him of the object of the cognition he has, and could have freed him from his error.

Only mathematics and pure and immediate experience are of such a kind that they leave us no grounds for their opposite.

All of our other cognitions, on the other hand, are of such a kind that they quite frequently offer us grounds of proof for maintaining the opposite of a thing that are just as great as the grounds of proofs for accepting the thing. It is certainly really prudent, therefore, to know how to withhold one's approval in most cases, until one has enough grounds for the thing.

Deception is universal in almost all things, therefore this is in fact an actually certain path, indeed, in many cases an infallible one, for avoiding many illusions of reason and for dispensing with error. Nevertheless, this withholding of approval must of course not be such that one is inclined at the same time never to let himself be convinced of the thing and always to refuse it his approval[;] for in this way we never decide anything, so we remain ignorant in all things.

[z] "die *affecten*."
[a] "verkehrer."

The withholding of approval, namely, with the mentioned inclination never to decide anything, is really nothing but a lazy doubt, a lazy addiction to doubt,[b] or at least the path thereto.

Suspensio should only help [one] not to accept something until one has enough grounds, but not on this account to reject every hope at all of being able to attain full certainty concerning a thing or a cognition. 161

Reflecting is distinct from *investigating* and *investigation*.

To reflect is to compare something with the laws of the understanding. *To investigate*, however, is actually to reflect mediately. Concerning many things we can quite well cognize without investigation what is true, what false. But *reflection*, on the other hand, is always necessary for any judgment, and for the distinction of the true from the false, even if it be in general, or in a [particular] cognition, etc., in all cases indispensable.

§ 169

The word ***praejudicium*** has a double or twofold meaning, namely,

1st it means a provisional judgment, which is, however, not an actual prejudice at all.

2nd It means an actual judgment. E.g., if one prizes one man's writings much higher than another's, before one has even seen them, then this is not a real prejudice but rather only a provisional judgment, since reason infers something from certain grounds.

Here reason does not really decide anything, then, but rather it only judges from those few grounds that it has of the thing[;] it thinks in accordance with these grounds, represents something.

This judgment is not at all dogmatic, then; rather, it is just always combined with a certain postponement.

This provisional judgment is not a ground, namely, for taking something to be certain, not even in the least. In the meantime, however, this much is certain, that in the present condition more grounds are available for the acceptance of the thing than for its rejection and for maintaining the opposite of this thing. Therefore one readily praises a book that is supposed to come from a learned, famous, and well-known man, even before one has read it oneself, merely because one represents to oneself that in accordance with his reputation, a very famous man has to write worthy things, hence this book will also be well written. 162

There has never been an inventor in the world, and there has never been anyone who invented something, who did not at the same time make a provisional judgment concerning his invention and the invented thing. He was not certain of the thing, but the judgment cleared the path for him to try, and to experiment. E.g., miners judge from strata in the earth where

[b] "eine faule Zweifelsucht."

they are to find metals, and they make suppositions until they have gotten certain cognitions[c] concerning the mines, cognitions which no longer deceive them and in consequence of which they reach[d] their end.

Cognitions arise in us, however, either through cognition of the object or through and by means of properties that belong to the subject, that is[,] subjective grounds of cognition.

A subjective ground of holding-to-be-true prior to all reflection, as the ground of the action of the understanding that is necessary for this and, moreover, useful, can be called *prejudice.*

Inclination is a disposition of the mind to love something and to be taken with it.

The inclinations are very seductive; to overpower them constantly is certainly the greatest art, indeed, is almost impossible, and so is it in logic, too, with the *argumentis ab utili*[e] and with the *argumentis ab odio.*[f] And this happens especially, of course, when this or that thing gets entangled with an interest of men, close or wide-ranging, universal or particular, and thus has a special involvement with that interest.

The prejudices that arise from inclination are various.

A further subjective ground of holding-to-be-true is *imitation*, too, toward which man is accordingly by nature quite inclined[;] and the judgments that arise from this stretch out across man's whole life.

Of all the things that can only harm and be opposed to the philosophical spirit, the *spirit of imitation* is always actually the worst. *Imitation* is the cultivation of one's understanding, his will, indeed, of his choice, according to the example[g] of others; if, namely, one is not skilled in thinking for oneself, then one takes refuge in others and copies from them completely

163

faithfully, as the painter copies the original, except that this portrayal is frequently quite unfitting, indeed, comical.

One thing, then, is quite often opposed to that spirit of holding cognitions to be true that does not want to err, [namely,] *custom*, which often opposes the understanding, but is difficult to destroy once it has taken root.

Those people who blindly mix up a provisional judgment with a decisive judgment are in far too much a hurry. Thus a certain *suspensio judicii* is very necessary and useful here, so that one does not hurry too much. This *suspensio* teaches us, namely, how we ought to regard grounds that are plausible but by no means sufficient, ones that we do not at all take to be convincing[;] and consequently in many cases it keeps us from many wrong turns and errors in cognitions.

[c] "Kenntniße."

[d] Reading "erreichen" instead of "nicht erreichen," with Hinske (KI, lxxi).

[e] argument based on usefulness.

[f] argument based on hatred.

[g] "nach dem Beyspiel, und Exempel."

The very dangerous enemy of men, of which we spoke above, is one of the greatest causes of *over-excitement*.[h] A calm man who is not disturbed, confused, excited, etc., by any strong movement of the mind will not hurry at once, and not as easily as one who has an affect[i] and is unstoppably driven on by it.

Reflection is, however, an important[,] very great and certain path, if not for extinguishing the affects, nevertheless for quieting them, for hindering their dangerous consequences, and thus for avoiding errors. By reflecting one allows and takes time to investigate, and in fact to inquire, whether something is true or false or not, whether one can accept the opposite of it or not. And by this path, where one reflects on the thing peacefully, one is even soon convinced of the truth of a thing or cognition.

Philosophy likewise strives to restrain the affects as much as possible and to root them out. Hence really learned people, and philosophers, can keep a tight rein on their affects, so that they are not easily taken by a thing without first having sufficient grounds.

Instead they weigh everything that they take as *objectum* of their considerations cold-bloodedly, that is, with calm mind[;] furthermore, they carefully consider in everything one side as well as the other, and in this way they arrive best, most easily, and most certainly at a proper cognition of the true.

By means of provisional judgments we seek to assist ourselves toward closer investigation[;][j] we judge, however, before we have considered and cognized the thing more closely. 164

One does not hit upon the truth without seeking it, but even without seeking it one must make judgments concerning the path by which he thinks he will hit upon it.

We do not attain complete certainty except by means of investigation; but any investigation must still be preceded by a provisional judgment.

Between a provisional judgment and prejudice only a small distinction appears to exist and to be actual, in that both judgments are judgments that always precede the investigation of a thing or of a cognition.

Provisional judgment, however, as a means to investigation, connected with consciousness and with the resolve thereby to hit upon the path to investigation, is not only most highly suited for our understanding, but is also a certain, indeed, infallible path for attaining the truth of a cognition.

No important invention, none of weight, has actually occurred without this.

But when one judges and accepts something before investigation, with the resolve not to undertake any closer investigation concerning the whole

[h] "*überhitzung*."

[i] "im Affect ist."

[j] Reading "Untersuchung" for "Ueberzeugung."

thing, but rather to rest completely content with it, then this is in fact a punishable prejudice, which not only does not further the cognition of truth but even actually hinders and harms it.

The former judgment, namely, a cautious,[k] provisional judgment, but with the resolve to investigate the cognition more closely in order to attain the truth, is thus actually useful to truth, and subsequently it directs investigation, too, which one then undertakes concerning the cognition. The essential thing in all prejudices, however, is that they are universal rules for judging.

It is not a prejudice, however, when one accepts a proposition without extensive investigation[;] rather, one accepts this proposition through a prejudice. Hence we have two conditions and special properties of the human understanding:

165 1st *To have a prejudice*, or to be occupied with one, and then
2nd *not to have a prejudice*, but rather to accept something through prejudice.

Almost everyone, be he who he may, esteems the fashions and customs of his country or his fatherland as the best and most proper. Among us, e.g., we bare our heads, but not so among the Turks[;] therefore we consider them crude, although it is not yet settled whether it is crudeness to cover one's head or to bare it. The Turks, again, perhaps consider us impolite. But this is actually not a prejudice, but rather only something that is accepted through prejudice.

Prejudices are not grounded on reflection. They lack this, for otherwise they would be actual judgments of the understanding.

Reflection, of which we have already spoken above, is nothing but the comparison of a cognition with the laws of the understanding and of reason. We are not directed merely by the laws of the understanding and of reason, however, but quite frequently also by the inclinations, or by our taste. In the case of the inclinations, no reflection at all occurs.

Prejudices, however, have very many sources, and varied ones.

Custom is likewise one of the causes and grounds of judging without reflection. Without having an inclination to something, one nevertheless quite often takes it to be true merely out of custom. Hence if one wants to cleanse someone of his errors, one must not only convince him of the opposite of what he believes, but also slowly and bit by bit[,] with time[,] accustom him to it, and give him time to accept the truth. Even with the most convincing, most evident, and most certain proofs, he who had long been suspended in error and had been taken with doubt will not be capable of being won over immediately and all at once, and thus convinced, and completely overcome by the irrefutability of the proofs, so that he immediately dismisses all doubt and would decide and be disposed to

[k] "cautes."

accept the truth at once without resistance[;] rather, this quite frequently requires a long time.

There are the following 3 sources of prejudices, however, which are the most common and the greatest[:]

1. *imitation* 166
2. *custom*
3. *inclination.*

In youth one does not yet have any skill in judging, hence one allows oneself to be driven by imitation, and one quickly accepts as certain and undoubted what is maintained by others, in whom we either place a particular trust or who have particular prestige with us, or what the universal *votum* of many prescribes for us.

Now if in addition to this imitation we add the custom of judging thus and not otherwise, then this prejudice becomes all the stronger and gains ever more power.

A child, e.g., certainly always accepts as the greatest and most important truths the first impressions that occur to its mind, in most cases quite easily[;] indeed, it also even retains these the longest.

In accordance with the given rules[,] the laws of the imagination, such prejudices are of course not easy to dislodge from the soul once they have taken root in it.

No reflection at all really occurs here, then, but rather one accepts at once what others have maintained before us, without oneself reflecting on whether or not it is rational to accept it.

Thus it happens that when children in their tender youth are taught false concepts, images, representations, etc., these latter cannot be uprooted from their imagination[;][l] and thus one has great cause to proceed very carefully and to take care that one does not prematurely spoil children's understanding, and in a certain way render it useless.

Furthermore, custom is, as it were, a very fertile source of many ruinous prejudices. When one has frequently performed an action, has had good experience with it and thus has accustomed himself to it, there finally arises from this in the course of time a certain kind of necessity to act thus and, indeed, not to proceed otherwise.

To clothe oneself fashionably (but according to one's social position, nonetheless) is laudable and good, for it is more acceptable and better to be a fool in fashion than out of it. But to judge, to infer, to think, to write, 167 as it were, in accordance with the fashion, is always silly and a proof of no reflection at all. Ceremonies, modes of dressing, compliments may be brought under fashion, but not the understanding.

Inclination is also a cause and ground of some judgments, furthermore,

[l] "Imagination, oder Einbildungskraft."

and in this case, to be sure, one judges and infers that something is good, acceptable, and perfect because it excites us, because it stimulates us and suits our taste.

Still more, *inclination* occasions us always to undertake examinations and investigations only from one side, and of course only from the side where we wish that it were so and not otherwise, and thus it occasions us to leave the other side, which might perhaps provide us with grounds for the opposite, completely uninvestigated. We even seek to find grounds with whose help we can refute[m] the opposite of what we wish. Here, likewise, the laws of the understanding and of reason are, as it were, absent and not at home[;] there is simply no reflection, and instead certain sensations simply occur.

All prejudices arise from imitation, custom, or inclination, and without these three sources no prejudices, which are very frequently such obstacles to truth, would ever occur in the world.

Everything that is immediately certain needs no investigation. All cognitions must be reflected upon, that is, they must be compared with the laws of the understanding and of reason and held up against one another. But not all cognitions need to be investigated, for *to investigate* is nothing other than to compare something mediately with the laws of the understanding and of reason.

All cognitions whose agreement with the laws of our understanding and reason occurs immediately are indemonstrable; these can be accepted without investigation, they need not be proved, indeed, one cannot even undertake an investigation of them.

In the proper sense, one is not in a position to do this. A prejudice, however, is nothing but a certain universal ground for judging without any reflection.

But a cognition that is accepted merely by means of a prejudice is not at all a prejudice itself; if we want to speak properly, we must understand 168 that there are actually only a few prejudices, but on the other hand infinitely many errors arising from these existing prejudices.

A prejudice always arises when one judges without reflection, i.e., when one judges concerning a thing or its cognition without previously having compared this cognition with the laws of the understanding or of reason. Prejudices cannot properly lie in defects or mistakes of our understanding and our reason, then, but must arise instead from other powers.

The understanding and reason themselves, left to themselves, never err[;] this much is settled without doubt and is certain, for this would be an evident *contradictio in adjecto*, as we[n] have already remarked above[;] they would have to be in opposition to their own powers, and yet no power

[m] Reading "widerlegen" for "darthun."

[n] Reading "wie wir" for "wir wir."

can oppose itself[;] rather, it comes from the fact that other, foreign powers mingle with the powers and laws of our understanding and of reason, from which arises a mixed effect[;] and thence an error naturally arises.

First of all, prejudice cannot possibly arise, and cannot correct itself, based on the laws of the understanding, for it is a judgment without reflection. That which is accepted by means of a prejudice, however, is not yet on that account always false as to its matter.

But prejudices, furthermore, are just not wholly necessary sources of errors[;] but this much is still certain, that every cognition that is accepted through a prejudice is always false in itself as to form.

Frequently a certain intended end can of course be attained through a cognition, but the method of attaining this end may often not be the genuine or proper one. And thus it happens quite frequently with the actions of men.

Any man at all, if only he wants, can revenge himself on one who has insulted him too much,[o] that is, on his enemy, and make him pay for the injustice he has done[;] but the way of revenging oneself, and the form of avenging oneself, are unjust and not allowed: One ought not to be one's own judge. He on whom one revenges oneself cannot complain in the least, no injustice at all has happened to him, but rather one has merely paid him in like coin.

169

But this is just not the suitable manner of avenging oneself on someone. From this there would only arise such great disorder that finally it would almost be irremediable. Instead, divine and human laws prescribe for us the legitimate way to attain compensation for our injury, our honor, etc., without having to shame ourselves by the way in which we attain it.

It happens thus with prejudice, too. That judgment and the cognition can very often be quite true in respect of the object, but not in respect of form.

One must therefore take good care not to reject immediately all prejudices whatever, but instead one must test them first and investigate well whether there may not yet be something good to be found in them. Again, one can actually find a kind of prejudice against prejudices, namely, when one immediately rejects everything that has arisen through prejudices.

In this way one can quite frequently reject the greatest and most important truths, and innocently rob oneself of those that are capable of[p] and ripe for investigation and research. As, e.g., when one accepts what all men say and always takes this to be completely certain, this is a prejudice. But now it is really the case that very many truths rest merely on what men

[o] "der ihn beleidiget, oder zuviel gebotten hat."

[p] Reading "welche der Untersuchung" for "welche nicht der Untersuchung," with Hinske (KI, lxxiii).

say,[q] and that they have and can have no other ground, but nevertheless on closer investigation they really are certain truths.

Now if one wanted to reject all these truths straight away, many men who do not have enough capacity and enough strength of mind to investigate everything according to the laws of the understanding and of reason and to examine it with proper reflection would thereby be robbed of very good cognitions.

There are some men who are of the kind that their mind is an enemy of what is true, and that such prejudices thus take root among them first of all and most easily, men who seek to cast suspicion on every truth that is assured and firmly and earnestly maintained by others.

Without any doubt, a great many useless prejudices are to be found[.] But is our procedure reasonable and legitimate if, merely on account of 170 the fact that a prejudice is perhaps useful, beneficial, or just not harmful to someone else, we therefore do not merely fail to smother the prejudice in him, but instead generate, produce, maintain, and multiply it? This is another and completely different question. This is really a kind of deceit and a breach of faith and honesty to generate and to sustain prejudices in others because they are useful in this or that case.

A prejudice considered by itself can in itself provide something useful, of course, but in spite of this such methods, which one applies in order to provide, or to try to produce, something useful by their means, are not right, not allowed.

Nonetheless, however, it still remains true that it would be an obvious impertinence if one wished to rob someone – who has a prejudice that is either not completely harmful to him, or is even in certain respects useful and advantageous – of that prejudice by a manner of deceit and thus put him in distress and confusion.

But to strengthen a prejudice in someone is just as objectionable[;] as, e.g., when one proceeds irresponsibly in instruction in morals, it is just like this when one makes use of an often superstitious error in order to restrain man from one or another vice, in order to restrain him from it and to frighten him off. That is the so-called *fraus pia*.[r]

Everything true, however, that is produced by means of one or another prejudice, is false *formaliter*, although it can be and is correct *materialiter*. How miserable is the education that seeks to ground true moral rules in youths through prejudices and errors.

Many prejudices are such and of the kind that if one dared to attack them, to extinguish them, to try to clear them away, they would nonetheless make the mind of man all the more embittered, indeed, would deafen

[q] "auf der *Sage* der Menschen."

[r] pious deception.

man to listening and attending to true doctrines and important *dogmata*$_L$, which have great consequences for them.

There actually are quite comfortable prejudices, with which man is quite at ease, and it would therefore be great folly to deprive someone else of such prejudices, which would be, and often actually are, in a position to contribute so very much to his well-being. 171

The case is otherwise, however, with harmful prejudices, which can frequently have influence not just on an individual case or man but even on the welfare of a whole republic. These one can and must always strive to root out as much as possible with the greatest industry, because one is thus not[s] harmful to him who has this prejudice, and helps and is useful to others, indeed, a great multitude of people.

Thus we must not be suspicious of other men, even when they are quite filled with prejudices, be it with or without their responsibility.

The common man has and preserves very many prejudices, to which he very often holds quite stubbornly; but it is also just as certain that the learned man, even the greatest, has just as many of them, and far more dangerous ones. This latter sometimes holds to his *canones* just as much as any other, and he does not leave them, as the common man does not leave the proverbs he has inherited from his forefathers and has confirmed through long experience. Only there is this difference, that in the case of a learned man the prejudices are disguised under the name of *canones*, but with the latter[,] with the common man[,] they are disguised under the name of proverbs.

§ 170

The author here distinguishes prejudices from one another. He calls some prejudices *logical*. Just as if he had it in mind to indicate thereby that there are other kinds of prejudices that are not *logical*.

Usually it is the *aesthetical* that is contradistinguished from the *logical*, and therefore prejudices will be and be able to be divided into

1. logical, and
2. aesthetic prejudices.

The former consist in the fact that, and occur when, our cognitions are contrary to the rules of the understanding and of reason[;] the latter, on the other hand, consist in the fact that our cognitions are contrary to the rules of taste.

Fashion is actually nothing but a prejudice of taste, in accordance with which, through a prejudice, one takes something to be beautiful or ugly. Fashion is thus the source of aesthetic prejudices. Fashions make one 172

[s] Reading "nicht schädlich" for "schädlich."

represent to himself that some inner beauty or other resides in this or that kind of clothing or of dress[;] thus one thinks and also judges according to the rules of taste.

Imitation and *custom* are the greatest sources of aesthetic prejudices. Frequent approval of one or another object makes, as it were, an archetype in the soul, with which one is in no position to compare other things that look otherwise than this original which has been established and which, as a model, is incapable of improvement.

If everyone wanted to clothe himself according to his own pleasure and taste, we would finally have the most splendid kinds of clothing[;] now, however, proper taste in clothing is really lacking, and just for the reason that in this matter fashion reigns, which everyone follows incessantly and constantly.

All fashion in general is harmful rather than useful, for it is opposed to the rules of pure reason as well as to the rules of taste. And he who is or wants to be fashionable in his judgments of taste, or even of reason, certainly has no reason. He thereby shows his very poor talents and his complete lack of all taste. Nevertheless, it is more acceptable to be fashionable in taste than to be fashionable in thinking, judging, and in *sentiments*$_F$; to be fashionable in clothing is acceptable and often good. But to be fashionable in *sentiments*$_F$ is *actual, logical prejudice*. Prejudice of taste reigns not only in clothing but also even in style.

Almost every century has a style or form of its own[.]

In writing style, what prevails is sometimes a great pomp of inflated words. Sometimes timid contortions of wit prevail, sometimes again a completely shallow writing style prevails, which people like to call *natural* because it is easy, costs little or no effort, and can be produced without art. 173 Sometimes, again, people love in all things a writing style such as one had been accustomed to use in letters. Sometimes, again, people love above all a heavy, dark, puzzling, enigmatic writing style, which they prefer to a light, complete, distinct style, which is supposed to reveal a certain profundity and the author's deep-thinking learnedness because one must ponder over it a long time and one has, as it were, a puzzle to solve before one comes to figure out what the author meant by this, to be able to discover the author's real sense and meaning, and to find what the author thought.

Taste is quite ruined by imitation, a fertile source[t] of all prejudices, since one borrows everything, thinks nothing of a beauty that one might be able to invent and come up with oneself, as [compared to] what others have already thought up and have previously cognized, and what is considered beauty by these people.

If, therefore, everyone wanted to try, not so much always to imitate, but

[t] Reading "Nachahmung, eine ergiebige Quelle" for "Nachahmung einer ergiebigen Quelle," with Hinske (KI, lxxiii).

rather to be an original himself, then we would certainly soon see the greatest geniuses, who would be sublime and great in judgments of taste.

Just in the same way, again, there are various kinds of prejudices in various fine arts and belles lettres,[u] as, e.g., in music, in poetry, in painting, in statuary, etc. Everywhere[,] in every taste[,] prejudices always prevail, even, indeed, in moral taste.

Custom and *examples* make this happen and are therefore the causes of the fact that in these things so many prejudices, so many fashions, reign.

It has been noted that the English nation has more numerous and greater originals than the French and other nations. This actually derives, however, from the freer and less constrained form of government. For there almost every one is his own master, at least of his own genius. In most cases he naturally thinks, judges, and acts without being moved by examples, or at least without directing himself according to them, following them, imitating them. Everyone thinks, then, and judges the same thing according to his taste, and therefore there are so few copies there.

On the other hand, though, countries, states, in which a monarchical form of government is introduced and prevails are not in a position to produce any such *originalia*, or at least not nearly as many, for here people are commonly guided very much by examples, which often become norms in thinking, in action, and in judging[;] and in fact customarily the magnates of the empire, those who are great in the empire and at court, are in most cases the *originalia*, the models, according to which men usually seek to shape themselves, and to imitate them. 174

Here the author divides prejudices further into prejudices (1.) *of excessive trust*, and (2.) *of excessive mistrust*[;] but both kinds of prejudices are in fact the same and are inseparably bound up with one another and united.

The cause of prejudices of excessive trust, however, is really nothing but the desire to extend one's cognitions, but without discernment and true judgment of that with which one wants to enrich them[.] And industrious observation teaches, to be sure, how this happens in most cases among the youth, while age, on the other hand, as that which has more experience and more cognitions than youth and has also suffered more delusions, frequently reflects more and examines whether it is worthwhile, and whether it is worth the effort, to strive for the attainment of this or that cognition, and whether this is correct or not. And due to these fluctuations[v] and this frequently repeated doubt, [age] frequently falls prey to the prejudice of excessive mistrust[;] and in most cases it also comes about that the older we gradually become, the more faint-hearted and mistrustful we become then, too.

[u] "in verschiedenen schönen Künsten und Wißenschaften."

[v] "dieses hin und herdenckens."

In the prejudice of excessive trust,[w] however, we give to a few persons a certain superiority over ourselves, [and] we must therefore attribute to them more cleverness, more learnedness, etc., than to ourselves[;] and we choose them as originals, in accordance with which we strive to form ourselves.[x]

People of high rank are in most cases of the kind that one is influenced by very many prejudices toward them in respect of their skills and attributes. One constantly takes them to be clever, learned, sublime, noble-minded, etc. Even clothing often makes [one] learned and clever; even a person in uniform awakens respect[;] he appears at once to possess more understanding than others, although he very frequently sits in the greatest shadows of darkness.

175 What a man of high rank says is frequently noticed, rather than what a common or poor man produces. Although the latter is quite often cleverer than the former. Furthermore, there is a *prejudice of excessive multitude*,[y] where one accepts, and persuades oneself, that many persons are more in a position, and in a better position, to pass judgment on something than few are. This is the common and lowest prejudice of prestige.

Therefore some are frightened when for the first time they are supposed to give a public speech, lecture, etc., before a large assembly. The same person would perhaps not be frightened to speak before 2 or 3 persons, but before a few 1000 one is afraid. One judges, namely, that what finds approval among all is true and must actually be so in the *objectum* itself, although this is frequently quite false.

The prejudice of excessive multitude arises in most cases out of the prejudice of imitation. A great number of men, who give their attention only to me, carefully observe only me, must necessarily be a source of awe to me.

With respect to morality, however, the prejudice of the multitude is very harmful, disadvantageous, in fact shameful[;] thus it happens, too, that man likes to follow the great crowd, even in his actions which have an influence on morals; he hopes, as it were, to hide himself among the crowd when he does something evil, and thus to be able to escape unseen the eye of the eternal, heavenly judge.

A like judgment can easily be produced by a great multitude; no one has the spirit of imitation as much as a great multitude.

Thus when something is such that it acquires the universal approval of the people at once, just as soon as it appears and at first glance, then it is always quite often to be feared that it is not good for much; and a rational man who acquires universal and thoroughgoing approval all at once must

[w] Reading "Zutrauens" for "Mißtrauens."

[x] "uns selbst zu bilden."

[y] "*Vorurtheil der gar zu großen Menge.*"

not only actually not rejoice, but must rather be dispirited. Books that are praised[z] just as as soon as they have come to light from the press are certainly in most cases very shallow.

What is good and in fact excellent, what produces correct but new truths, commonly finds very great opposition in the beginning, and this lasts until, after closer examination and investigation[,] after research and discovery of the real properties and of its difference from other cognitions, one discovers its beauties, and what makes it particularly superior to other writings, and until one begins to prize these highly. 176

All prejudice of excessive prestige can appropriately be divided into three kinds, however. – – –
namely,

1st the judgment of excessive prestige that others have with us.
2nd the prejudice of excessive prestige that we have with ourselves.
3rd the prejudice of excessive prestige that a cognition has with us on account of a few perfections that it brings with it, and from which one infers that still more perfections must be found in it.

As for what concerns the *first* kind of prejudice, we are in most cases inclined to ascribe more to others than to ourselves, and to trust them more. We believe that someone else will know better something that we do not know. This prejudice arises not only from the consciousness of our own weaknesses, for this is no ground for attributing to others more than to ourselves, but rather from a certain respect that we have for the whole human race, since we judge that what we lack will be found in others.

A different prejudice arises from a certain laziness.

Nothing is more comfortable than to imitate and to draw one's cognitions from others. From this prejudice arise the various and sundry citations in books, where one cites the judgments of others and their opinions of this or that thing, and presents these *citationes* as proofs.

There is actually a kind of laboriousness involved in this, a diligence, but no difficulty. One has to work long, although without a certain exertion of one's powers. This prejudice of the excessive prestige that others have with us caters to the desire for comfort. One need not think oneself, but instead can rely wholly on the genius, on the understanding of another, and merely imitate others.

Yet another kind of prejudice of prestige toward others arises from vanity. In this way one actually, as it were, subjects himself to others[;] one makes himself the slave of someone great, and of someone else's understanding and power of judgment. But frequently this happens only in order to be able to command others, in order to have great mastery over others, who are still less than we are. 177

[z] Reading "Bücher, die gelobt werden, sobald" for "Bücher, die sobald."

Nowhere, however, is there greater pomposity, nowhere greater pride, than in *polyhistory*. Here, namely, out of ambition and vanity, one elevates great learned men in order, under this pretence, to be elevated oneself, to be able to elevate oneself, and, as it were, to elevate oneself far above the so-called learned crowd. One presents a great, famous learned man to the eye of the learned world and seeks to persuade all others firmly that they will always act in vain, irrespective of all the possible industry, work, and effort they can apply, since they could never be in a position to be equal to this great man, or to come near to him[;] indeed, since one regards the sayings of this great archetype as incontrovertible and unimprovable *oracula*, one simply rejects all their opinions, merely because they contradict, or seem to contradict, the judgment of the great man. One is afraid oneself, or seeks to make all others afraid, to try to strive ever to become equal to this learned man, just as if it would be a vain undertaking to strive after this.

Just so does it happen, e.g., that most proud people, who do not like to be subjected to or to obey others, or who envy their fellow citizens one or another power, most like to have the unrestricted government of a monarch in a state, and they help to promote this, in order to be equal with one another and not to need to be afraid of any of their fellow citizens[;] and this is in fact the true origin of all monarchies. There is actually nothing more harmful for the human race, however, than always to represent others as unattainable examples, and to take them, as it were, as models for imitation. One thereby copies more the errors than the good properties of the original that is set up, because everything in the world is

178 imperfect, and thus even these models cannot be fully excluded from this. The Scriptures themselves say that we ought never to choose as our model anyone but God, this being that is completely perfect in all respects. Always to direct and form[a] oneself according to others, and so according to highly imperfect men like us, brings about more harm than good.

Such prejudices of prestige and of imitation are much supported by bad upbringing and inept instruction, namely, when, for confirmation of his judgments of the understanding, one quotes, cites, and refers to[b] the judgments and opinions of others, not one's own reflection or experience. And although this method, whether in oral or in written expositions, is very pleasant and is witness to wide reading, nonetheless, it frequently just grounds the prejudice of prestige.

We have already spoken above of the prejudice of the prestige that a great multitude of people has with us. We may suppose that what all people accept is universally valid. There lies in our nature a certain

[a] "bilden."

[b] "allegiret."

inclination to communicate our opinion to others, as we indicated above, so that if someone were in the desert and had to stay there without any human society, all his judgments would seem to him to be for nothing and in vain.

This inclination does not arise from vanity at all but rather from human reason's particular and excellent disposition to communicate.[c] If one judges alone, namely, and for oneself, then one is never really certain whether the judgment does not spring from a certain delusion that could somehow take us in. We therefore desire to test it on the understanding of other men and to investigate. Here one makes, as it were, an experiment and checks whether what we think is universal, whether others accept it, or whether it is not in agreement with reason. Thus one, so to speak, as it were, polishes those judgments that one has, i.e., those of which one is the discoverer, on the sure touchstone of the understanding, and on other men's insights.

Opposed to this inclination of human reason to communicate its judgment is *logical egoism*, of which we also said something above. Where one believes, namely, and fully persuades oneself, that one simply does not need the help of the judgment of others in a judgment of the understanding. It is true, of course, that in matters of the understanding the judgment 179 of others judges nothing. But it is still not on this account superfluous, nor yet dispensable. By instinct, man's understanding is *communicatio*. If it is communicative,[d] then, it must really be sympathetic,[e] too, and it must be concerned with what others judge of it.

The prejudice of the prestige which other people have with us is, furthermore, the *prejudice of antiquity*, or the *prejudice of modernity*, on which the liveliness of wit depends. *The prejudice of antiquity* is grounded on esteem toward the *old*. What survives of the old into our times always contains the illusion of being good, for one infers that it would be hard for it to have survived and to have come down to us if it were not good and were of no value. Just as we also take those buildings to be good which, if they are old, nevertheless still stand, without having gone to ruin, while on the other hand others have gone to ruin due to the length of time.

No judgment is more universal than that the world is gradually deteriorating.[f] Everything in the world deteriorates:[g] animals, horses, etc., become worse when they have lived long[;] bodies, e.g., clocks, become worse with time. And one makes this very judgment of the whole world, of the whole of nature in general, that it is gradually deteriorating more and

[c] "mittheilenden Beschaffenheit."
[d] "mittheilend."
[e] "theilnehmend."
[f] "veralte."
[g] "deterioriret sich."

more.[h] Thus one wonders at people who are old and still healthy, robust, and says, Where do we find one such as this among us today? So is it, too, with the books that survive among thousands of others that are lost[;] on this account we take them, not without some ground, to be exceptionally good, because they have retained prestige in spite of the usual decay that commonly befalls such writings.

Young people are in most cases inclined to the *prejudice of modernity. Age*, on the other hand, [is inclined] to the *prejudice of antiquity*. "Just as youth is usually generous, but age stingy." Nevertheless, it is also true, of course, that the cause of prejudices can frequently be alteration of temperament.

To *age* belongs *industry* and *diligence.*

To the *new*, however, [belong] genius, liveliness, and constantly changing wit.[i] Of course we see the individuals of nature decay and perish[;] all works of art perish. Rome itself falls. Cliffs split apart, etc. – Man perishes and dies at every age. Half of mankind perishes by the age of 15 years[;] in the 16 ½ th year, none[;] in the 50th year, one in 100. It is held, furthermore, that in all things, the perfections of the world are themselves gradually declining. Horace says: "our descendants will produce still worse brood than we are."

180

But this prejudice is completely incorrect. Only in more recent times have people considered this thing more and better than in ancient times.

What nature produces has such persistence that nothing, no time, no age, can alter it. If we exclude the time before the Flood, then after that everything in the world is equally good, equally strong, the propagation and power of propagation are just as good, just as possible, although one nation here can have some advantage or other over others, of course, to which the special circumstances of climate, of food supplies, etc., must of course contribute something.

With many books one can see in the first moment when they appear in the world that they will not long be prized or esteemed. These books are like those *papillons*[j] that appear with all splendor, are admired by everyone, but do not last longer than the summer and are soon thereafter forgotten. Other writings, however, which contain much thoroughness, are of such a kind that they are carried forth from one age to the next and always retain their authority.

From this it flows naturally that one reserves a kind of esteem for these, and holds them to be valuable.

If one considers how in the sciences time reveals everything bad, one can well ask, How will it turn out with our current learnedness?

A living language always changes, but a dead one never does[;] all

[h] "sie deterioriret sich mehr und mehr, sie veralte allmählig."

[i] "Witz ohne Stätigkeit."

[j] French: butterflies.

autores are inexhaustible sources for it. Current German poets will certainly seem bad after 100 years. Dead languages have the advantage that they remain eternally beautiful and independent.

Our current languages may well never become dead ones, for only the Scriptures and religion make a language dead. Thus the theologians are the proper guardians of learnedness, and with them many languages would come to a complete and utter end. 181

The *corpus juris*[k] is certainly the greatest and most certain proof of human profundity. The discovery of the pandects[24] in Naples in the 11th *saeculum*, however, is the best find among books that men have ever attained. In general, however, the ancients are always inimitable models for writing style.

When one considers the ancient world as a whole, and all its individual creatures, one easily sees that the longer the series of copies that are subordinated to one another, the greater the divergence from the *originalis*.

The first creatures were quite perfect, but through their reproduction and distribution they became more and more dissimilar, at least to one another. Regardless of this, however, one nevertheless finds that no change has occurred in the kinds and *genera*$_L$ of creatures; instead, everything is still as it was at the creation of the world and of all things. It is always a prejudice, then, if one prizes the old so excessively.

Moreover, the esteem we have for the ancients arises from a certain kind of illusion of our understanding and our reason.

We always prize learnedness highly[;] even in our own case, we always feel a certain esteem[l] for ourselves if we are learned.

Learning the ancient involves and requires learnedness. This is a further ground for the prejudice of antiquity. Cognition of the ancient frequently involves great learnedness[;] therefore it happens that we think highly of the ancient, just because we are able to have insight into it only through learnedness. This esteem for the ancient frequently falls on the ancient *autores*, because they wrote something, the understanding of which requires learnedness. This is a genus of inner deception. One esteems the *ancient*, and *per consequentiam* also the *ancients*.

The language of the ancients is itself already a [matter of] learnedness[;] from this it follows, then, that what is written in such a language already acquires a certain kind of esteem, because for the science of the language alone a certain learnedness is required, without which one is not in a position to understand it. 182

In the case of the ancients,[m] so much proves useful that one simply does not notice their errors, indeed, one is not even in a position to cognize

[k] body of law.

[l] "eine gewiße Hochachtung, eine Estime."

[m] Reading "bei denen Alten" for "denen Alten."

whether there are errors in an ancient writing or not. It seems to be wholly reasonable, however, to prize the ancients highly, with thankfulness, because we are only their pupils, after all. Indeed, we ourselves hope that someday we will also be known among our descendants as *the beloved ancients*, and we promise ourselves the same esteem and thanks from them that we now render to the ancients. The ancients are for us the original itself, who are beyond all judging, beyond all critique. What a prejudice, when an author is such that one no longer criticizes or passes judgment on his language but instead accepts it as perfectly beautiful and beyond improvement.

If one meets with contorted modes of speech in a Cicero, Horatius, etc., and others of that sort, who have been accepted as *autores classici*, beyond improvement, then one will not say that Cicero, etc., should not have spoken thus, that he could have avoided an error if he had expressed it somewhat differently, etc. Instead one approves of it; and we are allowed to speak thus too, merely because Cicero, etc., has done so so perversely. Just so do all the ancient poets, in all their mistakes, have the *licentia poetica*. Here we see which prejudices arise from the prestige that antiquity has with us. Hence there are so many advocates of antiquity who, as soon as something is invented in modern times, show at once that the ancients already knew all of that. That there is nothing properly new, then, but only what is sought out from the writings of the ancients and somewhat brought to light.

But here we must *ask* whether we do not have cause to make into a prejudice a certain *provisional* judgment in favor of antiquity and the ancients concerning their cognitions and insights.

Answer. Of course; the ancients quite certainly had the advantage over us that they at least had no established models, no *originalia*, which they could have followed and should have copied. They themselves had to provide and become their own originals, whether they wanted to or not, because they had no other guidance but nature and their reason.

183 Today, however, due to the excessive multitude of *originalia*, nothing but copies are produced, and many potential new originals are stifled.

The ancients had another advantage in regard to their thinking in the fact that their realms were in most cases divided into small[,] very numerous countries and *republiques*, which were all quite free and did not need to groan under the burden of a monarchical and strict sovereignty (for freedom in thought originates from a free form of government, as we have already had occasion to remark above)[.] This free condition, so advantageous for the development of the arts and sciences, was found above all in ancient Greece. Here one knew nothing of any monarchy, and instead everything followed its own inclination and ruled itself.

This mode of life, this form of state and of government, naturally brought it about that such great, inimitable, outstanding geniuses and minds were found among them and showed themselves to the world, especially in the fine arts, and in particular in painting an Apelles, etc., in oratory a Demosthenes, in poetry [. . .].

Even today we still find that in those countries where the spirit of freedom reigns, much, and much more, is discovered, many more *originalia* arise, and far fewer copies appear, than where a despotic, monarchical form of government is introduced.

England provides us with an example of this[;] here one finds even today the most and the best *archetypes* and models. There everyone thinks for himself, speaks, writes for himself, etc., without choosing a model and imitating it, trying to follow it everywhere.

On the other hand, countries where monarchs and individual princes rule despotically, and one has command over all, produce nothing but copies and seldom *originalia*. Here the court is in most cases the original, and everyone strives to imitate what goes on at court. The writing style of the court is the writing style of all others (just as one likes to wear the clothes that are customarily worn at court). One sees this today, e.g., in France[;] there one seldom meets with an original, but instead in most cases with mere copies. Everything there is modish, both in clothes and in judgments and writings.

184

The writing style of the English authors can thus be quite easily distinguished from all others. The one always says something different from what the other has said. The French, on the other hand, always write in one and the same writing style[;] the one makes use of almost the same modes of speech as the other. Hence it happens, too, that one French author cannot easily be distinguished from another, and among them one seldom meets with anything special[,] exceptional, new[,] or unusual.

Now we come to the *prejudice of modernity*. This is grounded partly on the provisional judgment that we make in most cases in favor of, and to the advantage of, the new. We have cause to make favorable judgments toward the ancient, but also toward the modern.

All those sciences that presuppose an extensive, historical, correct cognition, become ever more perfect in modern times, for it is known that modern learned men strive more and more to extend historical cognitions. In empirical cognitions, the modern always has an unassailable advantage over the ancient. In sciences, on the other hand, for which persistent industry, everlasting effort, is required, the modern has likewise a more favorable judgment over the ancient, and not because it contradicts the ancient, but because it frequently adds more to it. If one prizes the modern highly because it contradicts the ancient, however, then this is really a very harmful prejudice. But in part the prejudice of modernity is also grounded on a certain illusion of our understanding, our reason, and our imagination. The old man loves the old, but a young man the new. Age makes man much inclined to defend antiquity, youth on the other hand to speak in favor of modernity. If youth owes all its cognition and all science to the ancients, and has merely learned these things from the ancients but not discovered them by itself, then it has no merit of its own, and thus it is also quite inclined to invent new sciences and to add more to the ancient ones.

Whole nations are frequently much inclined toward the ancient, others again toward the modern. The Spaniard and the Portuguese love the ancient, the Frenchman, on the other hand, the modern. Inert, slow, melancholic, and reflective minds love the ancient very much. Lively, vigorous ones, on the other hand, love the modern. The former are 185 enemies of new fashions, the latter friends. The Frenchman is stylish in clothes, in systems, in medicines, etc. The Frenchman is the first originator and founder of each and every fashion, and the only one who will always remain so. He alone has the fickleness and facility necessary[,] requisite for this. The French are thus too much given to the prejudice of modernity, which arises

1. from the fact that the modern contradicts the ancient or
2. from loving the modern, first because it preserves the ancient, but also because it adds something new to it.

Inclination is also a great source of favorable prejudice. This includes the insinuation, e.g., of the external control of mien, of name, e.g., with books the title. "A good title sells the book," and in accordance with current fashion an easy,[n] impertinent, French title, e.g., when Beaumelle publishes a book with the title, *Mes pensées*, etc.[25] Should we not esteem the ancient inhabitants of Greece, since in this favorable climate all learnedness arose[,] as we said above?

But a kind of recommendation that stimulates respect toward someone originates from the fact that,[o] when we have disdained someone, if we discover and become aware of something unexpectedly great, a beautiful insight, a genius that surpasses all our expectation, we then prize him all the more highly[;] we admire him all the more, because we disdained him previously. Thus it is when we hear a woman, of whose insights and skill we have only a negative view, speaking with great insight, wit, etc.[;] we admire her all the more, and our disdain or contempt thus changes quickly into veneration. Just in this way, e.g., do we learn to esteem, and revere, etc., the great wise man Epicurus, of whom we perhaps had a negative view in the beginning, when we investigate more closely his behavior, his speeches, his judgments, cognitions.[p] He who strives to consider everything from the worst side, and who prefers to seek out

[n] "Leichter, legairer."
[o] Reading "daher, daß wir, wenn" for "daher, wenn," with Hinske (KI, lxxiii).
[p] "Kenntniße."

errors everywhere rather than good attributes, certainly has a very malicious heart.

It is always with discontent and reluctance that one reads books where the fame and the honor of the human race[,] along with its good attributes[,] are subverted. It is characteristic of human nature that is not spoiled by a bad heart always, in every writing, in every action, to assume and to suppose the best[;] and actually one always gains thereby, too, rather than being harmed. 186

Some time ago a quarrel arose among some learned Frenchmen[;] some elevated and defended the ancient, others, on the other hand, the modern. The former held the ancient to be an original, and the modern only frequently spoiled copies[.] The latter, among whom Fontenelle[26] was also prominent, maintained that the modern could frequently surpass the ancient, even greatly. The ancients can frequently be in a position to produce products superior to modern ones, but frequently the modern can also surpass the ancient by far.

In oratory, poetry, statuary, in painting, in all the fine arts and sciences, then, the ancients have surpassed us. But couldn't modern times also produce better products than the ancients produced? This is a wholly different question. Oratory, e.g., was so much cultivated among the ancients because everyone was allowed to appear before a people that was free, and he actually did appear frequently and speak.

Here, then, everyone who was disposed to make a public exposition before such a public convocation necessarily had to apply all his industry and effort to achieve his end of moving the people and of attaining the approval of his listeners.

Question[.] Would it ever be possible to destroy and root out each and every prejudice in man?

Answer. It almost seems to be impossible. Man is accustomed to have motives[q] in his soul which he cannot resist, and which rush on ahead of the judgments of the understanding, and in this way form a prejudice.

To be sure, man can learn to distinguish what arises from motives, what from the understanding[;] that is actually a great deal, and then he cannot be deluded and deceived any more, and not as frequently as previously, although the inclination toward this is still there at each moment, of course[;] but to rid oneself of this completely and fully, to get free of it, this seems to be impossible and would never happen. Both in common life in morals and here in logic, nonetheless, each and every pious deception in the application of the powers of the understanding is unforgivable; i.e., philosophy always tries to destroy[r] the intention and the effort to want to produce something true with the help of prejudices. 187

[q] "Triebfedern."

[r] "verfolgt."

A *proposition* is not a prejudice, be it as false as we wish. For a prejudice is nothing other than the mere desire to want to judge, yet without the proper acuity or reflection.

How, then, do our prejudices arise?

The inclination of the mind to judge in accordance with authority, inclination, custom, fashion, this is prejudice. Proverbs are in most cases false, for many of them are of such a kind that one can use them no matter what.

In most cases, children learn Latin in school with difficulty. Why is that? Because one demands and wants of them that they should be able to speak pure Latin, when they are scarcely aware of the principles of this language and its first grammatical rules. All the prejudices of which we have previously spoken arise, then, either

1. from bad education, or
2. from examples and imitation of them[.]

The prejudice of excessive trust placed in oneself is nothing other than *egoism*. Egoism, however, is *vel cosmologicus*, when one holds that there is no other thinking being, no world outside me, *vel logicus*,[s] when one holds that he alone judges rationally, that no one else is in a position to judge something or better to be able to have insight into it. This latter[,] namely, *egoismus logicus*[,] seems initially actually to be allowed. One has no need to consult other judgments, of course, when one cognizes something correctly oneself[;] one need not seek to bring about an agreement of others with the cognition that one has oneself. But on closer investigation we find that one cannot be certain whether one has judged rightly or not if one has not compared his judgments with the judgments of others and tested them on the understanding of others. For a cognition is not correct when it agrees with my private understanding but when it agrees with the universal laws of the understanding of all men. Therefore, as we have already shown above, 188 every man has an inclination to communicate[t] his judgments to others. This is the true friendship of sentiment. The logical egoist thus robs himself of a great, extremely important, necessary advantage, very conducive to the enrichment and improvement of his understanding, the ability to distinguish correctly the true from the false *per communicationem judiciorum, et mutuam dijudicationem eorum invicem.*[u] Sometimes, however, *logical egoism* also arises from a certain kind of meekness and faintheartedness, since one trusts himself and his insights far too little and believes that his judgments would not be worth being known by others in the whole learned world.

Logical egoism is opposed, however, to another prejudice, namely,

[s] either *cosmological* . . . or *logical*.
[t] "zu communiciren, und mitzutheilen."
[u] through the communication of judgments and the mutual adjudication of these from both sides.

where one builds all his judgments on the reason of others, judges nothing himself, but merely imitates, in that one elevates others above oneself and trusts nothing to oneself. To speak briefly, these are the prejudices of the lazy.

There are also certain arts and sciences, however, which are of such a kind that they can be learned, indeed, must be, through mere imitation. These include, e.g., all crafts,[v] likewise mathematics, in which one may expound to someone certain propositions, and demonstrate and prove them properly, propositions which he commits to memory and thereby in fact is in a position to become an actual *mathematicus*. But other sciences, on the other hand, are again of such a kind that they cannot be learned at all by imitation, but instead genius is required to learn them. These include, e.g., the whole of philosophy. We are certain that no one will ever be able to become a true philosopher, provided that one does nothing more than imitate the philosophers of earlier times, that one leafs through, or reads through, their writings now and again, and that one accepts as true what they have said, and in so doing completely forgets oneself, so to speak. If one does not trust oneself in the least, then, and makes no judgments at all oneself, either, but swears *in verba magistri*.[w]

Nothing is more harmful in philosophy than to imitate. Nothing is more unfortunate and ruinous for the understanding, e.g., than to pick up a Wolffius, or a Crusius, or others, to commit his *definitiones* to memory, to impress them there, *strictissime*[x] and word for word, and to prize them as stars of the first magnitude, but to value oneself at nothing[;] instead, one must learn to think for oneself, to judge for oneself, to reflect on objects oneself, and, in order to be able to become and to be a philosopher, to learn to philosophize. Philosophy cannot in the least be learned from books, but only through one's own reflection and one's own meditation. 189

We have two sorts of prejudices that relate to learnedness, however. Namely, a prejudice[y] *for* learnedness, and again a prejudice *against* it and for the common, healthy understanding.

Learned people, and also other[,] common people have a prejudice for learnedness. They often accept everything that is said and also taught by learned people. Moralists, on the other hand, have a prejudice for the common and healthy understanding, which *praejudicium* is also characteristic of many common people. This latter prejudice comes about because no one denies that he has healthy understanding. There has never been a man, namely, who believed he had no *sens commun*, *sensus communis*, common, healthy understanding. One admits readily and willingly that one has a bad[,] deficient memory. Again, someone else admits that he has no quick-

[v] Reading "Handwercke" for "Handwercker."

[w] in the words of the master.

[x] as strictly as possible.

[y] Reading "Vorurtheil" for "Urtheil."

ness in conceiving, no wit, no witty observations, no genius for this or that individual science, no taste in poetry. But everyone believes himself to possess *sensus communis*. No man will so readily deny this of himself.

Now since, of those who have a healthy understanding, the fewest are learned people, and since it is a known but true proverb: *ut ars non habeat osorem, nisi imperitum*,[z] then of course we must not wonder if from this it quite easily arises that be it out of ignorance, be it out of envy, learnedness is scarcely respected by many, if it is not disdained, and on the other hand that the common[,] healthy understanding is elevated infinitely.

Here the author also brings up the prejudice of the accepted system. In almost all parts of learnedness the prejudice of unity occurs.

A system is distinguished by nothing other than the fact that there is a unity in it. The human understanding, however, is such that it approves everything in which a unity can be found, and from this arises the prejudice for unity, of course.

190

We always believe we have made everything perfect, or as perfect as possible, when we have been able to bring it to the point where we have reduced it to a unity.

Just so is unity in a certain way ingratiating and pleasing, in that it seems to contain in itself economy with the powers of our understanding.

Further, where unity can be found, there one necessarily finds order, too.

Also, many beginners have a certain prejudice for the excellence and the advantage of a thing that they have learned with much industry and work, and which has cost them much effort, much sweat. (So to speak[.] E.g.[,] someone has had dreadfully much work, and has had to make an effort, in learning the French language. But he was serious about learning it and finally accomplished his end, too, so he has a great prejudice for the internal worth of the thing.)

The prejudice of lazy trust arises from a certain kind of crude ignorance and inertia in attaining this or that cognition, and from a quite ill-placed, contemptible contempt toward cognition that arises from this, merely because one cannot share in it. Thus, e.g., as the fox in the fable disdains the grapes that he cannot snatch, in spite of his leaps and effort, and scorns them as sour.

In almost all parts of learnedness the prejudice of unity probably occurs[.]

When very many properties and determinations of a thing can be derived from one ground, we are commonly accustomed in most cases to make the provisional judgment, and to have the supposition, that we will of course be able to derive from it all the remaining determinations of the same thing, and that this one ground that we have concerning this thing

[z] that art has no enemy but ignorance.

will thus be almost the true and fully sufficient ground of this whole thing. We sometimes accept a ground, namely, and infer from its consequences that this is the only true ground, regardless of the fact that such a thing is very seldom fully certain.

E.g., if we entertain one or another supposition that this or that man is a thief, then we frequently infer merely from the consequences whether this supposition can be true or not true but rather false. If we find, e.g., that this or that man stands in connection with us, that he at first had and possessed nothing at all, but later suddenly squandered very much money, and that this happens at that the same time that this or that money of mine disappeared and presumably was stolen, then we surely believe that he must be the thief who stole our money. Although this presumption can very frequently be false and incorrect, indeed, even insulting and sinful. From this provisional judgment the prejudice of unity arises, namely, when one finds a ground for a thing that has very many consequences and determinations, then one derives all further consequences and determinations from it. Thus it happened, e.g., with electricity in the beginning, in order to give an example. At that time, namely, one explained everything that was the least bit remarkable by means of it[;] indeed, there were even some refined minds who went so far as to want to maintain that electricity had an influence on religion, namely, in that they wanted to exert themselves to explain, e.g., even Christ's healing of the bleeding woman[27] by means of the powers of electricity.

191

Anyone who finds, or at least believes he finds, the source of all wisdom and cognition in one ground, is always much inclined to ascribe to it even more than can really be found in it. Someone else believes he has healthy understanding but will nevertheless amuse and please himself; but he is far more inclined to satisfy his inclinations as much as possible, rather than to choose the path of reflection and of work[;] and in this way one often falsely holds an understanding that is neither exercised[a] nor cultivated to be the common understanding. For one can rightfully and in a proper sense call this understanding a *plain*[b] *understanding*. For although we now combine with this expression a negative view and an unfavorable meaning, it is known that the beloved ancients had the proverb: *Plain and right and thus good.*[c] And here they took the word *plain*[d] in a very good sense.

All the prejudices of the kind of which we have previously spoken can be divided into

"1) *prejudices of pride*
2) *prejudices of meekness and of excessive fearfulness.*"

[a] "Exercirt."
[b] "einen *schlechten Verstand.*" ("Schlecht" also means "bad," as the lines following suggest.)
[c] "*schlecht und recht, und damit gut.*"
[d] "*schlecht.*"

192 *The former, the prejudices of pride*[,] arise when one imputes far too much to his insights, cognitions, and judgments.

The prejudices of meekness and fearfulness arise, however, from the fact that one attributes far too little to his judgments generally, or to his powers of understanding.

Often there arises in us even a prejudice *toward* but also *against* a whole science, and this because the science has perhaps often erred, and we have noted its mistakes closely and given attention to them. Thus it happened, e.g., with *metaphysica*, and when it happens thus with many sciences that they often err, then there arises from this a kind of skepticism, addiction to doubt, which can often extend itself to all the sciences. This comes from a weak understanding, however, which does not want to be laughed at, although it is not in a position to pass judgment on cognitions[e] and sciences itself. Such people commonly believe little or nothing at all. And this prejudice of mistrust, which originates in experience, unfortunately arises only too often among men.

Fashions are nothing but stimulants of vanity or encouragements for the application of a certain vanity,[f] and thus they arise through the choice of prestigious, great men, men of high rank. Thus it happens in most cases, e.g., in style, in *musique*, in architecture.

That which does not rest on true honor but instead merely on the effort to please, i.e., on fashion, is a matter of vanity.

Much, e.g., that now is actually accounted as lastingly beautiful in our writing style is nonetheless nothing but the fashion of our time. Very many learned men and beautiful minds[g] are actually often more harmful than useful to the learned world.

A *Young*,[28] a *Klopstock*,[29] a *Gleim*,[30] etc., have, e.g., really spoiled a multitude of weak minds.

The ignorant in most cases imitate the errors, but not the beauties, of the original that they have before them, only in order to try to become equal to a person who, due to this or that book, poem, etc., is in a position to get much attention. Thus it would be, e.g., if some man or woman seeks to imitate the lisping of a beautiful person,[h] thus becoming ridiculous.

193 Sometimes a mistake helps a man's wit, talents, etc., which otherwise are not very considerable, to shine forth and to glitter.

Fashion introduces clothes, manners, indeed, often even morals, and in a certain way it is almost good to follow fashion, if only its customs are not opposed to the eternal and unchangeable laws of morality, for with its help men are in a certain way better united and made to agree.

The prejudice of shallowness, furthermore, is the same prejudice of

[e] "Kenntniße."
[f] "Empfehlungen des Gebrauchs einer gewißen Eitelkeit."
[g] "Schöndenkende Geister."
[h] "einer schönen Person."

which we have already spoken above, namely, the prejudice *for* the healthy understanding. For this latter is shallow in objects of learnedness.

Voltaire is certainly one of the greatest defenders of shallowness. He seeks, namely, to derive almost everything from the healthy understanding, and his judgment sometimes has no sufficient ground.

Healthy reason is not to be rejected as much as one thinks[;] often it is actually the source of many cognitions.

Thus it is of course a prejudice, again, if one rejects the *sensus communis*.

There is also, furthermore, a certain prejudice *against* healthy human reason, and also a prejudice *for* healthy human reason. In the former prejudice, namely, one believes that we cannot have insight into anything at all by means of human reason, but in the other case, on the other hand, one believes one can have insight into everything by this means. In the former case, then, we trust, healthy human reason too little, but in the other case we trust healthy reason too much and ascribe too much to it.

One must not despise the human race, take all its prejudices to be worth nothing and want to despise them, but instead grant it the advantages it has. It is true that one cannot have insight into much through reason (namely, through common healthy human reason), but nonetheless it is not on this account to be rejected, but rather always has its worth.

Until the end of this *paragraphus* the author speaks of the prejudice against antiquity, and also of the prejudice against modernity. But we have spoken of both these prejudices above.

The prejudice *against* the *ancient* is always combined and inseparably united with the prejudice *for* the *modern*, and again every prejudice *against* the *modern* is always combined on the contrary with a prejudice *for* the *ancient*; and the one kind of prejudice cannot be thought without the other. For he who loves the ancient much cannot esteem the modern *et vice versa*. 194

§ 171

"Every cognition from merely insufficient grounds is uncertain." When a cognition from merely insufficient grounds of truth is cognized in such a way that I have insight into far more grounds *for* than against the thing, then it is *plausible*. If finally, however, there are many more grounds for than against the cognitions, or when more than half of the grounds, at least, are for the cognitions (whether I have insight into these grounds or not), then it is probable.

Plausibility rests merely on the subject[.]

Probability [rests] on the object, in such a way that I thereby actually cognize more grounds for the thing than there possibly are for maintaining the opposite of the thing. With *plausibility* an error can actually be met with, and that in form, since one is not conscious of the insufficient grounds. The first rule is thus: with all cognitions, even true ones, seek first of all to become conscious of the uncertainty that arises and ever could arise from insufficient grounds[;] one should place himself, as it were, in the position of the opponent, of the doubter, who believe themselves to have sufficient grounds for maintaining the opposite of this cognition; for otherwise one will almost always, in most cases, err and deceive oneself.

One can never know whether one cognizes more grounds for than against the thing, and one cannot gain insight into this until one has a cognition from a sufficient ground.

Hence with all cognitions one must seek first of all to acquaint oneself with the sufficient ground, or to know and to cognize how many grounds are properly required for full certainty of a thing, so that one can distinguish suitably whether something is plausible or probable in the first place.

195 When one does not cognize the sufficient ground of a thing, then neither can one determine how many grounds for its truth are necessary in order first to make the cognition probable.

If I subtract the grounds for holding-to-be-true from all the possible grounds that are necessary and required for certainty, and if I compare these directly with one another and consider them, then the remaining ones are grounds for the opposite. Then I can quite easily see which grounds are predominant, whether they be grounds for or grounds against the cognition. Plausibility can alter greatly, for its certainty[i] is grounded in the subject, but probability always remains unchanged[,] the same, and this merely because it is grounded in the object.

Writing style is naturally very changeable, especially because today one can cognize more grounds *for* this thing but tomorrow, on the other hand, more grounds *against* it[,] [a]ccordingly as one directs his thoughts to the thing in various ways, and as one further investigates and reflects upon this or that and strives to seek it out. The ground of approval is always at least the beginning of the sufficient ground.

It is, however, *a ground*, even if it is not complete. It is wholly wrong, indeed, even erroneous, to hold an insufficient ground to be no ground at all[;] it is at least matter for further investigation and inquiry. An ounce is always a ground for lifting a pound, although it is not yet sufficient, for several ounces taken together make up a pound.

All our conviction and assurance concerning any cognition must necessarily go through all the same elements. First we only suppose that something is true. In all things, be they what they will, incompleteness makes

[i] Reading "Gewißheit" for "Wichtigkeit."

the beginning. By investigating, and by untiring attention, we make something complete.

True sagacity is always, as it were, a spying out[,] a scent, of the truth in advance. It is one of the most outstanding talents of good minds and contemplation. Thus it happens, e.g., with discoveries of [new] worlds.

Grounds of supposition have often in these same cases been causes of inquiry and causes of discoveries. In this way the new world, etc., was discovered, and in this way much more can still be discovered. If we have a few such insufficient grounds of truth before us, then we either have plausibility (and this is only the least degree), *verisimilitudo*, or we have probability, *probabilitas*, as a greater degree.[j] The sufficient ground of holding-to-be-true, unity, is that whereby a thing is posited. 196

No ground can be more than sufficient, for otherwise it is not a ground at all, just as nothing can be more than true, more than false, more than good, more than bad, for otherwise it is nothing.

The sufficient ground comprehends everything in itself, but the concept of *everything* contains also at the same time a unity. But I can never say more than everything about a thing. Nothing is more than true.[k] Nothing is all-too-true. Nothing is too certain. Nothing is more than sufficient, as we often wrongly express ourselves in common life. The insufficient ground of holding-to-be-true produces plausibility.

Probability is a fraction, where the sufficient ground of truth is the *denominator*, the insufficient grounds that I have for taking-to-be-true are the *numerator*.

One can actually calculate mathematically the degree of probability or the degree of improbability of one or another empirical thing. Thus, e.g., in all games, lotteries, in the death of human beings according to their years, and many other augmentative phenomena,[l] as changes in the world.

With our philosophical truths we cognize nothing other than a plausibility, of this thing or that.

We have certain grounds for the truth of the thing, and we cognize fewer for the opposite of the thing, since there is no one who is in a position to teach us more grounds against the truth of the thing than for it[;] our cognition is thus nothing more than plausible.

People earlier held the moon to be a small, luminous body, which was there solely and simply for the sake of our earth. Later, however, people gradually began to measure the magnitude of the moon, and then they found that it was smaller than our earth, that mountains and valleys exist on it. Again, some *astronomi* even conjectured that it has inhabitants, but others, on the other hand, that it does not.

[j] Reading "die Verisimilitudinem . . . die Probabilitatem" for "die Probabilitas . . . die Verisimilitudinem," with Hinske (KI, lxxiii).

[k] Reading "wahr" for "zu wahr."

[l] "Augmenten."

This cognition of the moon was thus quite changeable, and just on that 197 account not probable, but instead only plausible[;] for the other, that which is probable, cannot be changeable at all, but instead remains always one and the same. Since all probability is not subjective but rather objective.

All plausible judgments, on the other hand, alter daily, accordingly as one cognizes more or fewer grounds for or against the thing. What is probable, on the other hand, is probable, so to speak, for eternity. For the grounds of probability are still insufficient, of course, but nonetheless still greater than the *possible grounds* for the opposite.

To know, however, whether the grounds for the truth of the thing are greater than the grounds for the opposite, or whether the grounds for the cognition constitute more than half of the sufficient ground, one must first strive to attain a solid and honest cognition of the sufficient ground, as was recalled above. Mathematics alone is the science which is of such a kind that we can thereby cognize the sufficient ground of a thing. In philosophy, however, that does not hold at all[;] thus it happens, too, that all our cognitions in philosophy, which are not undoubtedly certain, can never be probable, but always only plausible. With probability, namely, we do not judge what is actual, but only what is possible under certain conditions.

This possibility always remains unchangeable, however, under one and the same circumstances.

By means of probability, then, we really cognize degrees of possibility; if these degrees are great, then there is a large probability, but if they are small, then there is a small probability.

A cognition is doubtful, taken *subjective*$_{L}$, when the grounds for the thing that I cognize are equal to the grounds against the thing, i.e., the grounds of its opposite. Something is doubtful *objective*$_{L}$, on the other hand, when the grounds for the possibility of a thing, or of a matter that I cognize, are completely equal to the grounds for the opposite of this thing, and hence there are just as many grounds for the thing as against it.

Something can be practically certain *subjective*$_{L}$, although *objective*$_{L}$ only very little contributes to its sufficient ground.

198

§ 175

As for what concerns certainty, there are three particular and completely different genera of it, namely,

1st logical
2nd practical
3rd aesthetic certainy.

Logical certainty is certainty according to the rules of the understanding and of reason and hence is an objective certainty that is grounded in the thing itself.

Aesthetic certainty is certainty according to the rules of taste.

Practical certainty is certainty according to the rules of free will.

Someone is *practically certain* when the grounds he has for holding a cognition to be true are sufficient to determine him to actions; nonetheless, if he does not will to act, then these grounds are not at all sufficient enough to make him logically certain. In many cases, practical certainty actually involves very little cognition, but in many cases, again, much more is required for moral or practical certainty than for logical certainty. E.g., when it comes to damning someone, to condemning someone to death, etc.

Someone can be aesthetically certain if he holds the opposite of a thing or cognition that he has to be impossible merely because it does not please him. Thus, e.g., if his cognition is to believe in a divine being, eternal government, a future world, reward for good actions, punishment for bad ones, etc. Certainty here rests merely on feeling[;] as something gives someone pleasure or displeasure, so accordingly does he accept it or reject it.

In this way the human mind is actually subjected to very many illusions and deceptions[;] frequently we take something to be certain merely because it pleases us, and we take something to be uncertain merely because it displeases or annoys us. This certainty or uncertainty is not objective, however, but instead subjective. Frequently it can even keep us from properly seeking for, or investigating, the opposite of a thing and the grounds for that opposite.

Often we find more comfort in holding something to be true because we would have to inconvenience ourselves if we were to give ourselves the trouble of investigating the *contrarium* of the thing. We take the opposite to be impossible merely because we have no desire to try to investigate it. 199

Practical certainty, finally, is a certainty according to the rules of *prudence* and of *morality*. The latter is a moral certainty, however. There have been a few who believed that the moral is much less than the practical. Thus one says, e.g., that it is morally certain that there are inhabitants on the moon, etc. But this does not have the least connection with my actions. However, when something is practically certain, then it is often not on that account morally certain at all, and when likewise something is morally certain, then frequently it is not yet on that account logically certain. The possibility of a thing can produce in us a practical certainty[;] e.g, if someone only believes that it is possible that there is a God, then this thought must nonetheless have an influence on his life, just as if he were completely certain and convinced of this cognition.

The plausibility of a thing can likewise produce a greater degree of certainty.

Something can be completely certain in the practical sense although in the logical sense it is only plausible or at most probable.

The poet cannot be more than merely morally certain about one thing or another. Stories are of such a kind that they can only be practically certain. Logical certainty is quite often lacking and one can easily manage to find grounds for the opposite and to contradict historical reports.

One can easily prove that the *historicus* has told not true stories, really, but instead only fables and *fictiones*. Actually, too, there are many such people, who occupy themselves with weakening the full certainty of history, which requires no art, either, but instead is easy, because what is necessary and sufficient for practical certainty is not sufficient for speculation and for logical certainty. Practical certainty is one that in respect of certain actions brings about just the same thing as full certainty. E.g., if 200 something of value in my house disappears and at just the same time my servant disappears, then my practical certainty is that the missing servant has stolen what I am missing. Although no logical certainty exists, and the servant can have gone away and disappeared for completely different causes and in another way.

Practical certainty, however, is twofold

1. pragmatic and
2. moral certainty.

When a cognition that is probable in itself is just as certain a ground for actions according to the rules of prudence as if it were fully certain, then such a thing is *pragmatic certainty*.

When, however, a cognition that is probable in itself is just as certain a ground for actions according to the rules of morality as if it were completely certain, then such a thing is *moral certainty*.[m]

Even what is logically improbable can nonetheless be morally certain, e.g., when I demand money from someone and do not know whether I have already received it or not, and the other[,] my presumed debtor[,] knows just as little whether he has paid it to me or not, then according to morals I cannot demand any more of him, although it is logically uncertain whether he has paid something or not. Logical certainty of the existence of God can also be attained, although such a thing is very hard. All men, however, can attain moral certainty, even without great logical *speculationes*. If only we sharpen someone's moral judgments, we can thereby easily bring him to conviction of the existence of God.

Logical certainty of a future life is very hard to attain, but one can well attain moral certainty of it if one considers that here on earth happiness is not always a consequence of good behavior, hence another world is to be hoped for in which this will occur.

Moral certainty and uncertainty must be spoken of and treated along with other things in morals proper.

[m] Reading "*Gewisheit*" for "*Weisheit*."

Most, almost all *autores* are completely unaquainted with moral certainty, and instead they take it in each case to be probability[.] E.g. It is uncertain whether there are inhabitants on the moon, but nevertheless is still probable. A few accept this as a moral judgment, but this is not the case, for such a *judicium* has no influence at all on behavior. It is a logical probability and a mere speculation. 201

Nothing is a moral judgment except what has a relation to my actions. If someone is supposed to act, then, and must, and his grounds are merely probable, then the grounds that have the greatest probability constitute practical certainty.

§ 176

Every ground of the opposite of a thing, of which one is conscious, is called *a doubt*. Every obstacle to holding-to-be-true is a logical difficulty, and this is

1st *objective*, i.e., a doubt.
2nd *subjective*, i.e., a scruple.

The latter, that is, subjective difficulty, is really incomprehensibility, where I do not reject a cognition but instead notice that I cannot come to terms with it. This subjective obstacle of the understanding is fine work for a philosopher who wants to study mankind. The study of scruples is of great importance.

The study of doubt is somewhat easier[.] To find a scruple in ourselves before we can say that we cannot comprehend a cognition is very hard. Scruples hinder man from holding-to-be-true and cannot be resolved either by the man who has them or by someone else.

Scruples can become doubts, however, namely, when one becomes conscious of them, and this is also most necessary.

One transforms a scruple into a doubt by considering the cognition with which the scruple is accompanied in all manner of various relations and in various conditions, since then one will find out and notice at once, without any effort, which is the side on which we cannot yet be fully decided, and which, on the other hand, is the side where no further scruple remains.

In themselves, then, scruples are not at all to be despised, or immediately to be reproved and rejected.

There are scruples subjectively, however, that lie in the man who has one or another cognition, and these one must not heed. Objective scruples, however, which lie in the cognition itself, one must seek to make clear. If someone expounds for me nothing but plausible propositions, then I have a scruple and do not yet give him my approval. E.g., I consider the proposition that all moral judgments should rest on a particular feeling and sensation, I give it approval, but a certain scruple still remains in me 202 nonetheless[;] I cannot refute the proposition, but nonetheless I cannot trust the cognition.

If I consider the scruple more closely and reflect on the thing better, then there arises from this a doubt. I see that if I accept this proposition as true, it necessarily follows from this that someone who does not have this feeling and this sensation would be in no position to make any moral judgments, which seldom, or even never, happens.

From this doubt, however, something else again must necessarily arise, namely, I will make various objections against the truth of the proposition; and these objections finally eventuate in a complete refutation based on certain grounds, which otherwise is called simply a reply.

If I reject the doubt based on grounds that only one man holds and accepts as correctly sufficient,[n] then these grounds, as well as this reply, hold merely for an individual subject[;] hence it is then a so-called *responsio, et refutatio ad hominem.*

This occurs with a kind of reluctance[o] and occurs merely in order to get the opponent off one's back as quickly as possible. If, on the contrary, I refute the doubt on grounds that hold for everyone, hence are universally valid, but are convincing and assuring in such a way that no one else is in a position to object against this, then this is really a categorical refutation, *refutatio categorica*[;] and this occurs for the sake of really bringing the truth to the light of day and clearing away false cognitions as much as possible.

Often scruples always remain in a cognition and cannot be cleared away.

The development of scruples is a very beautiful science.[p] By its means a 203 scruple is, as it were, pulled out of the darkness, and then, after it is properly placed in the light, it has to be refuted as a significant objection.

No more miserable condition for man can be thought, however, than the condition that leaves us undecided. The condition of undecidedness, particularly, however, when it affects our interest. This condition of undecidedness is far more troublesome than the condition of speculation.

Everything that holds us up and makes us inactive, leaves us in a certain kind of inaction, is quite opposed to the essential determinations of the soul. Man even prefers to know a future misfortune in advance rather than remain uncertain in the supposition of it, suspended between fear and hope.

Doctors are often themselves responsible for the cowardice of their patients[;] they feed them in most cases with empty words and conditions, fancies.

[n] "hinlänglich, und zu reichend."

[o] "Wiederwillen."

[p] "eine sehr schöne Wißenschaft."

Young people, in particular, are in most cases such that they do not at all like to be *in suspenso*, for they are such that they always want to go further. In all this uncertainty, however, a certain kind of certainty can nonetheless occur, namely, the certainty that all our cognition is very restricted and limited, and consequently only quite imperfect and lacking.

Namely, we can always cognize the grounds of uncertainty with certainty and reliability[;] that is a certainty of subjective philosophy.

§ 177

Settled truths are those truths against which no further objection can be made.

These include, e.g., the *res judicatae*,[q] that is, things settled *in foro*[r] by a legally binding judgment[.] Thus after a completed legal action it is, e.g., a settled matter that when the judge issues his verdict, this or that man, e.g., must accordingly pay a certain designated sum of money to that man or this.

All new truths whatsoever always find in the beginning very many opponents, very much resistance[;] there must be a certain time necessary and required for settling them, after one has investigated them better. Thus it happened, e.g., in the beginning with the writings of Cartesius. In the beginning they found very much opposition, and 30 years and more went by without their truth being settled. 204

Through this settling of truth no new cognition is actually added to it, but instead what happens is just that all other men cease judging concerning it, and subscribe to it. As long as there is controversy concerning a thing, then, as long as disputes are exchanged by this side or the other, the thing is not yet settled at all.

§ 178

Frequently we can have complete certainty of this or that thing, but the grounds of the certainty are frequently such that one still notices much uncertainty in the mode of inferring. E.g. The soul is immortal; this is completely certain. But philosophy's grounds for it are not so evident that one should be completely convinced by them. The philosophical form thereof is still quite uncertain.

Every uncertainty is a ground for a legitimate doubt, since I still find it possible to search for grounds for the opposite of the cognition.

The consciousness of the insufficiency of a ground for truth is at least helpful toward accepting that it is still possible that there are still grounds

[q] things adjudicated.
[r] in court.

for the opposite of the thing. Doubt in the proper sense is not yet present in the uncertainty of a cognition.

The uncertainty of one thing or another makes doubt completely possible, however, in such a way that one has grounds for the opposite. Often, from one's having seen and noticed that reason is very often erroneous[,] there arises a kind of hatred of reason, misology, approximately of the same kind as misanthropy[,] hatred of man, which arises from distrust of the whole human race, which one draws from the observation of how little men act rightly.

"The author[s] who teaches in his writings what will hold for perhaps over a hundred years deserves, without doubt, the greatest thanks," says Terrasson.[31] The world is still always moved by its prejudices, which that author wanted to root out, until the world finally starts to reflect on this correctly 205 and, with the passage of time, gradually calms down and grants this.

We cannot always investigate the grounds of conflict, of discourse. It is not good or advisable to argue over this or that thing with people who have themselves written great books and works about it; for we might infer that it will not be so easy to bring them to the point where they will so readily think lightly of their own work of many years, etc., esteem it little, or themselves refute it.

In an internal proof one is immediately conscious to himself of the uncertainty in a cognition. An external proof, however, is the[t] consciousness of the uncertainty of a cognition, not immediately, but instead mediately, in accordance with the judgments of others. In some *quaestiones* of reason such a plausibility can be met with and found that I simply cannot withdraw my approval from it[;] but if I expound it to others, they nevertheless often have just the opposite opinion, and then I become aware for the first time that according to the minds and insights of others, my cognition is not yet completely, undoubtedly certain.

In common speech the word doubt means any uncertainty, and in this respect and this sense doubt is either *dogmatic* or *skeptical*. The former is a doubt of decision, but the latter a doubt of retardation, of postponement. From the former certainty arises, but from the latter closer investigation and inquiry, in order to attain proper and undoubted certainty of cognition.

In dogmatic doubt we reject all inquiry and do not accept something toward which we have, or believe ourselves to have, a grounded doubt. We decide, in short, and say: In this matter there is no question of attaining any certainty. Thus dogmatic doubt regards very many cognitions as if nothing at all could be established or settled concerning them. A philosopher who makes the judgment concerning universal truths of reason that one can bring them to complete certainty and reliability, but who will have

[s] "Verfasser, und Autor."

[t] Reading "aber ist das" for "aber, das ist, das," with Hinske (KI, lxxiii).

nothing at all to do with the consideration of such truths of reason as are or can be open to one or another doubt, is called a *dogmaticus*. The *mathematicus*, e.g., is like this; all his proofs are at once decisive[;] he expounds a proposition positively, even proves it to be so *decisive*$_{L}$, [so] that it is completely impossible for judgment not to occur. 206

The *methodus dogmatica philosophiae*[u] will thus consist in our attaining full, sure certainty in all judgments, in not being satisfied with indecision, and in leaving nothing undecided. By this dogmatic method, however, one will never fully settle the actual certainty of a thing[;] one will not teach truths in this way, but instead will quite often propagate errors instead by seating oneself, as it were, on the judge's bench of human reason and issuing the verdict that no certainty at all can be attained concerning this or that cognition, that all inquiry will hence in every case be undertaken in vain[;] and in this way, as it were, one sets limits and restrictions to the human understanding.

All reflection, all efforts to provide oneself with true certainty concerning something and to attain conviction, are thereby completely removed, and what can arise from this except ignorance, indeed, probably error?

The dogmatic spirit in philosophy is thus the proud language of the ignorant, who like to decide everything and do not like to investigate anything at all, whereas our understanding is quite inclined to examine everything first and to investigate it exactly before it accepts and maintains anything, also to look around well first, without blindly rejecting something that occurs to us. The dogmatists could be opposed to the dialecticians.

Cognitions are 1st those whose certainty can be cognized apodeictically. These are cognitions *a priori*, into which we have insight through mere reason. We will never be able to attain an apodeictic certainty with testimony. Apodeictic judgments are judgments *a priori*, and cognitions of this sort are *dogmata*$_{L}$[;] mathematics, e.g., is of this sort.

There can be no apodeictic certainty at all in cognitions of experience. It is not a pure impossibility that all those who talk to us much of *praxis*$_{L}$ in thinking, acting, judging, inferring, nevertheless deceive us, without on that account having to have bad intentions, however. Everything that is apodeictically certain is capable of a dogmatic mode of cognition, but everything else really only of a dialectical one. 207

The ancients divided their philosophers into *dogmatists* and *skeptics*, searchers, investigators, *speculatores* of truth, who always sought but never could find it.

Furthermore, there were intellectual philosophers[,] among whom Plato said:

"everything that we want to cognize well and have proper insight into must occur *a priori* merely and solely through reason. The senses contain nothing but deception."

[u] dogmatic method of philosophy.

The sensuous philosophers,[v] on the other hand, among whom we reckon Epicurus as the foremost, said on the contrary:

"Everything that we are in a position to cognize *a priori* through reason is nothing but a chimera. Only the senses give real, true certainty."

These were joined, however, by a third, who made peace between these 2 heated, quarreling parties by shouting out: "I believe both equally little, or not at all."[w]

Neither the intellectual nor the sensitive has certainty. In the human understanding there is nothing but confusion. And[x] from this arose then formal skepticism,[y] which seems to originate from so famous and highly esteemed a man as Socrates. When, namely, the dogmatists either wrangled among themselves or maintained one or another proposition with all gravity and certainty, he listened to them in the beginning in complete humility[;] but soon he began to ask them for advice, as a listener desirous of learning, as it were, and as a pupil of the heated and pathetic dogmatists, since they disputed with one another[;] and he could thereby catch them with their own words, and he knew how to confuse them in such a way that in the end they completely contradicted themselves, and were often made ridiculous before whole assemblies. He did this so often and at such propitious moments that the enemies of the proud dogmatists rejoiced in advance when Socrates visited their auditoria, and these dogmatists were in fear of him when he began to ask questions, as they had to answer him, since he knew how to act like a pupil desirous of knowledge. From this there finally arose among his followers a ruinous inclination to doubt completely any and every dogmatic cognition and its certainty. *Pyrrho*, however, can with right be regarded as the real founder and 208 disseminator of the skeptical sect. His *non liquet*,[z] which he uttered with equal validity against the proud claims of the dogmatists, thus at least often making them hesitate a great deal, as well as his careful and tireless[a] efforts to investigate carefully all the propositions of the dogmatists, are known to all.

If we reflect on the matter properly, however, philosophy has nonetheless gained far more from the *sceptici* than from the proud dogmatists: although it is true, of course, that the former, through misuse, finally degenerated into bitter sarcasm. *Skepticism*, however, or the method of skeptical doubt, where one establishes a distrust in oneself, considers the grounds for and against the cognition that one has, and in this way strives

[v] "Sensual Philosophen."
[w] Ak, "nichts"; MS, "nicht."
[x] Ak, "Verwirrung, und"; MS, "Verwirrung. Und" (KI, lxxi).
[y] "der förmliche Scepticismus."
[z] It is not clear.
[a] Ak, "unermüdende"; MS, "unermüdete" (KI, lxxi).

to come to complete certainty concerning it, this is the *kathartikon*, reason's best means of purgation. This skepticism hinders errors as much as possible, leads man to more inquiry, and is the path to the truth of the matter (although not all at once and suddenly, of course, but instead slowly and gradually through more and closer examination).

The doubt of postponement is thus actually a certain mark of the maturity of reason and of experience in the truth of cognition.

But if we were to ask in this connection which method of philosophizing will be the most appropriate and the best in academies, and which will please the most, the dogmatic or the skeptical?

Then we would necessarily have to answer: the dogmatic.

If a learned man steps up here and establishes something dogmatically concerning this or that cognition, then nothing can be easier for the listener[;] he need not examine anything, investigate anything, but instead only fix in his memory the little that the teacher says and expounds to him. In this way he remains completely at rest and in comfort[;] he need only memorize; whereas doubt about cognitions is far less comfortable, but instead is far more unsettling, and requires one's own reflection and investigation.

Doubt can thus be divided into

A. academic
B. skeptical doubt.

The school of Plato, the great *dogmaticus*, was called the *Academy*. Academic doubt is quite distinct from skeptical doubt. 209

1. "The academic doubter proved and demonstrated *per definitionem* that nothing could properly be proved, nothing defined, which was, however, a *contradictio in adjecto*,[b] and this was dogmatic, seeming doubt."[c]
2. The Pyrrhonic, i.e., skeptical doubter says, on the other hand, that to each and every one of our judgments, or at least to most, another judgment may always be opposed[d] which maintains exactly the opposite of what is contained in the former judgment; this was actually to be regarded more as a kind of very fine and outstanding observation than[e] as a reprehensible doubt. And it would actually have been desirable for one to employ this observation correctly and carefully; very advantageous consequences would certainly have arisen from this for the whole of human cognition.

But how? Is it not a *contradictio*, to establish something in the case of an error, and to be a dogmatic doubter?

Answer. Both can quite well co-exist. Dogmatic doubt is always com-

[b] Ak, "adjecto"; MS, "objecto" (KI, lxix).
[c] Reading "der Dogmatische, scheinende Zweifel" for "der Dogmatisch scheinende Zweifel."
[d] "entgegen setzen, und opponiren."
[e] Reading "Beobachtung, denn als" for "Beobachtung, als," with Hinske (KI, lxxiii).

bined with persuasion of the certainty that nothing at all can be established or maintained concerning this or that cognition.

Hence dogmatic doubt consists in nothing but judging that one can never attain complete certainty with a cognition, and that all inquiry, furthermore, is thus always conducted in vain and for nothing.

Skeptical doubt, on the other hand, consists in being conscious of the uncertainty with a cognition and thus in being compelled to inquire into it more and more, so that finally one may nonetheless attain certainty with the help of careful investigations. The former, then, the dogmatist, rejects certainty completely and altogether. The latter, the skeptic, however, searches for it little by little. The origin of the expression skepticism is properly as follows[:] σκέπτεσθαι.[f] This word means in Greek: *to inquire, scrutari, investigare, indagare.*[g] Thus the *scepticus* constantly inquires, he examines and investigates, he distrusts everything, but never without a

210 ground. In this he resembles a judge, who weighs the grounds for something as well as against it, and who listens to the plaintiff as well as the defendant, prior to and before deciding the matter and passing judgment. He postpones his final judgment quite long before he dares to settle something fully. These were the ancient and pure attributes of *scepticismus* and of an unadulterated skeptic.

Skepticism in the beginning was actually very rational, but its followers spoiled it and earned it a bad reputation.

These latter were so subtle[h] that they even went so far as to say that everything is uncertain, even that it is uncertain that everything is uncertain. That was actually a kind of purgative of human reason, which was such that after it cleansed our understanding completely of all impurities, i.e., of all false delusion, prejudices, incorrect judgments, it disposed of itself in turn.

In fact, nothing is more harmful to the learned world than universal rest and agreement and peace, however; at least this always hinders improvement and increase of learnedness[;] here it is almost approximately just as with the English, who, when the court stands in agreement with its subjects and is fully at one with itself, immediately think there is danger and believe they have lost all their freedom.

A universal resolve to doubt everything is of no use whatsoever; it is wholly absurd[;] but there are few men, or we could probably even say none, who would be inclined to such a childish and harmful addiction to doubt.

True skepticism, at all events, is a thing of great usefulness, and as such it is nothing other than an exact, careful investigation of all *dogmata* that are put forth as apodeictic, which, insofar as they actually are so and stand

[f] Reading "σκέπτεσθαι" instead of "σκέπτομαι," with Hinske (KI, lxxii).

[g] to examine, to investigate, to search out.

[h] "Subtil."

the test, shine forth and strike the eye in all their *valeur*,[i] in all their strength, only after this test.

Skeptical method is a true investigating of truth by means of postponement, in that one does not accept[j] or reject anything at once, but instead first lets there be dispute about it. We are really not at all inclined by our nature to postponement. In our times people called skeptics are in part such as do not in the least deserve the name of philosopher (e.g., a Voltaire)[,] in part such as are not real *academici* but instead merely display a skeptical method in itself and, as it were, affect it, e.g., a Hume. Among 211 the modern skeptics, however, we can reckon Bayle,[32] etc.

Among us, then, the name of the skeptic is in most cases now regarded as something hateful[;] one thinks, namely, of one who does nothing, who devotes himself to nothing but striving to overthrow the most undeniable and most certain truths; someone is held to be a dogmatic doubter, then, who believes that he is not in a position to judge about anything, and that there is no matter on which one can attain complete certainty, which nothing can topple. Previously, however, an honest skeptic was nothing but someone who postpones his judgment until he has had opportunity and time to take this or that matter under consideration, and who only then ventures to infer whether a cognition is to be taken as true or is rather to be rejected as false. The skeptical method is directly opposed to the dogmatic.

The method of judging, however, where one doubts, namely, more than one decides, where one thus believes that our cognitions can be false instead of true, is *suspensio*, or that kind of distrust toward the cognition we have where we likewise do not actually settle anything, but where we nevertheless judge and first investigate whether the grounds for the cognition or those against it have the upper hand.

With this method we collect the grounds of approval or of rejection, but we do not settle anything, we do not decide at all. This kind of suspension is thus directly opposed to dogmatic pride. The *dogmaticus* asks: is something true or not? He decides immediately, then[;] but the one who suspends his judgment, who does not trust himself much at all, he always inquires, examines, investigates everything beforehand, in order to discover by this means the path to truth and to attain genuine true insight.

Human nature is actually far more inclined to decide than always to examine, and to settle rather than always to investigate. For we are not at all satisfied when we have to leave something uncompleted, especially in our cognition, but instead we want to settle everything, so that in case the need occurs we can recur to a completely certain and reliable cognition. 212

Our understanding is actually more satisfied by decision[;][k] we believe,

[i] French: value, worth.

[j] Reading "annehmet" for "nennet."

[k] "Decision, und Entscheidung."

namely, that we have at least gained something thereby, with which we can settle several cognitions.

The dogmatic mode of philosophizing is thus directly opposed to and contradistinguished from the problematic mode of philosophizing.

In the former, one settles everything, but in the latter one does not decide at all, but instead one postpones his judgments until one has properly sought out the grounds and the opposing grounds, and then one can make a judgment.

In physics above all one must philosophize problematically, and every cautious learned man will without doubt make use of this mode of philosophizing. The doubt in the problematic mode of philosophizing, however, is either a skeptical doubt, an inquiring, investigating, examining one, or a dogmatic, settling, deciding doubt.

The history of philosophy, when it comes to this point, namely, to the point of the origin of the sect of skeptics, always refers in most cases to Socrates. The sophists, who in ancient times, out of vain ambition and fancied science, believed themselves to have the right to decide everything, and who defended a thing from whatever side simply pleased them, were hateful to Socrates, since he held, and publicly maintained, that they were merely seeming wise men[l] (which is really all they were, too).

He judged that there were many things we do not need to know[;] hence he also had the motto, which was sufficient testimony of his philosophy: "*quod supra nos, nihil ad nos.*"[m] Thus he established that our best cognition is to come to know ourselves, that man is the proper object of all philosophy. Hence he accepted nothing but what he had examined. He did not give his approval blindly to any cognition, but instead inquired and examined.

When someone was inclined, therefore, to decide something immediately, he showed him the opposing grounds and difficulties that would make it necessary for him to suspend his judgment. This inclination to decide nothing without examination did not derive in his case from any 213 pride, but instead from a high degree of modesty, since he did not place too much trust in himself but instead actually had a kind of distrust toward all his cognitions. And he also impressed this modesty above all on all his followers, although it did not stay with them long, for his immediate pupil Plato soon began to become somewhat more dogmatic[;] and from him arose and originated the Academic sect, which was opposed to the skeptical sect.

These latter endeavored to philosophize problematically, but the former, the dogmatists, decided everything[;] their whole philosophy consisted in deciding.

[l] "Scheinweisen."

[m] What is beyond us is nothing to us.

Pyrrho was the first to bring the skeptical sect into favor, and his followers were therefore called Pyrrhonists, too.

This sect did not really doubt all truths, but instead it lengthened investigation and postponed decision. Thus they proved through doubt that the grounds for decision were not yet complete, and thus they led the dogmatists, who wanted to decide everything, to the path of caution.

The skeptics, however, are also called *zetetici*,[n] seekers, and investigators, and this because they sought and inquired. With all propositions, then, they will neither doubt them decisively nor decisively take something to be true and accept it.

Thus the *zeteticus* is not one who has the maxim to reject everything whatsoever and to decide *positive*$_{\text{L}}$ concerning everything at all, or to maintain it blindly, but instead is one who reflects on his cognitions and examines them.

Pyrrho had a certain motto for his sect: *non liquet*.[o]

To anyone who maintained his propositions with the greatest and most settled gravity he shouted out in opposition, *Non liquet*, It is not yet settled, and then he began to expound his speech against it.

A skilled and learned way of humbling some proud dogmatist and of showing his weak side. This is a certain motto for every pure reason. One must not accept anything at once, but instead examine, and investigate the objects, and consider. This sect of Pyrrhonists, however, departed so far from their founder that it was later accepted that Pyrrho himself had completely denied the certainty of any and every *dogmatum*.

That Pyrrho denied many *dogmata* and that he established a just and well-considered mistrust, that further he rejected in particular many rational judgments, is indisputable and not to be denied[;] but that he denied each and every *dogma*$_{\text{L}}$, that is utterly false. One who accepts no *dogmata*$_{\text{L}}$ cannot teach any morality. In any case, there are certain, so to speak, eternal principles of our reason, which cannot be disputed at all. But Pyrrho was also accused in addition of doubting all empirical judgments and not trusting them. But this is nothing but a fabrication, which has no ground. Pyrrho was a very wise man[;] he would have been a fool, however, if he had wanted to reject all empirical judgments, whichever they might be; in the beginning, then, a Pyrrhonist did nothing but moderate his judgment, but afterward the skeptics admittedly sought to place everything in uncertainty[;] they strove to show that in all our cognitions there can be no certainty at all. And thus there arose *scepticismus problematicus et dogmaticus*.[p] The former doubted, to be sure, but first it investigated, and by means of this investigation it wanted to attain certainty. The

214

[n] From the Greek, ζητητικός, disposed to search or inquire.

[o] It is not clear.

[p] problematic skepticism and dogmatic skepticism.

latter decided, on the other hand, and accepted that a complete certainty was not to be attained in any matter.

This inclination to want to take nothing as certain arises actually from nothing other than a desire for completion. He who saw that in many matters we cannot attain certainty, who doubts the truth of many things and *dogmata*$_L$ and did not accept them until an examination had occurred, saw it as better to doubt everything and to dispute the truth of each and every principle by putting forth opposing grounds.

We actually have no writings remaining from Pyrrho himself, except that Diogenes Laertius puts forth something from them. In the meantime, this much is certain: that one imputes[q] to him, as to Epicurus, far more than he actually did. It is said of him, e.g., that he denied the certainty of all experiences, that he therefore walked directly into swamps and morasses, that he feared neither the running of horses nor deep chasms or ditches[;] and add to these disparaging reports that he is said to have lived to be 90 years old, as an obvious proof that all such charges as had been invented about him must be false[;] for with such boldness he would certainly have lost his life earlier.

215 Carneades, the founder of the last academic school[,] deviated from Pyrrho's doctrines very much and actually maintained that one could not attain a proper certainty, or come to certain truth, in any matter.

Skepticism, however, is either *logicus*, *logical*. This includes, e.g., the diallelon that truth is supposed to consist in the agreement of a cognition with itself.

Many of the arguments of the skeptics had and received their names often from the *terminus medius* of the *syllogismus*. Thus one of their arguments, e.g., is called the liar, which ran thus: if you say you lie, and in saying this you speak the truth, then you speak the truth by lying, *atqui*[r] you say you lie, and by saying this you then speak the truth by lying. But the right conclusion should be: *ergo*$_L$ you speak the truth by saying you lie.

Or skepticism is also *physicus*, *physical*, where one casts doubt on the certainty of all physical laws, e.g., the possibility of movement. Thus the ancient *sceptici* had a certain argument, which they named, also on account of the *medius terminus*, the Achilles. They inferred namely thus: if the running Achilles were to have a race with a tortoise with a mile's head-start, and even if Achilles were in a position to run a hundred times faster than the tortoise, he would still never be able to overtake the tortoise.

The grounds that skepticism used in defense of this argument were: that all numbers were divisible *in infinitum*, that however fast Achilles ran, therefore, there would still always be a *spatium*, although very small, between him and the tortoise.

[q] "imputiret, und aufredet."

[r] but.

They inferred here merely through reason, without recurring to experience, for then they would have found that Achilles must necessarily overtake the tortoise in 1 ¼ miles, provided only that he could run 1000 times faster than the tortoise. Furthermore, skepticism was *vel moralis*,[s] and this consisted in maintaining that all the rules of virtue are fashions, or customs and practices in actions that men undertake. Thus, e.g., close marriages were not forbidden at all in Egypt as they now are among us[;] furthermore, e.g., among some Negroes the greatest, most outstanding, and final service of love that children who love their parents dearly can show them is that they will put them to death when they become old. Among the Spartans, e.g., thievery was not punished, provided only that it could take place in such a way as not to be publicly noticeable, and stealing was even allowed, provided only that it took place in secret. 216

Skepticism, furthermore, was *vel historicus*,[t] *historical*, which consisted in believing that all stories and reports, even tales of ancient times, have to be held to be uncertain[,] fabricated, and mythical.[u]

Skeptics of still another kind had the custom of always talking much and conversing about the uncertainty of the senses. They denied straight away the certainty of each and every experience. Thus there was, e.g., a skeptic who, after he had frequently, on many grounds, maintained that one could not trust the senses at all, wanted to persuade his friend of this quite certainly and undeniably by saying to him: Every day I have in my larder many supplies, but when I go there, count the supplies, and return the next day, the supplies are always fewer than they were yesterday, a certain and incontrovertible proof that the senses must deceive. His friend, who well saw what must lie behind this, advised him to guard the key to his larder as much as possible, most carefully. The skeptic's servant, however, who was very sly, soon learned how to get hold of the key, and under this pretence continued depleting his master's supplies, until one time his master nonetheless caught him in the act and recommended the rightful punishment for him for his thievery, but had to learn in this matter that one can, indeed, trust the senses.

Skepticism of this sort could well be called *dogmaticus*, for the *skeptici* were themselves dogmatists, in that they doubted things, etc., but nevertheless believed they had a right that every man should give approval to their proofs and accept their doubts. Thus they contradicted themselves, for they said that everything is uncertain, without distinction, and nonetheless they maintained their propositions and attributed to them an infallible certainty. They had, e.g., the proposition: Everything is uncertain, and in such a way that it is even uncertain that everything is uncertain[.]

[s] *either moral.*

[t] *or historical.*

[u] Reading "Fabelhaft halten zu müßen glaubet" for "Fabelhaft zu seyn glaubet," with Hinske (KI, lxxiii).

217 As for what concerns modern times in respect of *scepticismus*, the dogmatic method was very common at the beginning of the Reformation. At that time philosophy was held and considered to be a necessary support for religion[;] hence not many doubts or opposing grounds were lodged against the certainty of philosophical propositions, but instead these were taught and established. After a free mode of thought had later slipped in in many nations, however, people began, with more and greater resoluteness and certainty, to doubt the truth of many previously unassailed propositions, and not just to believe and to accept everything at once. Soon people strove to resist the proud dogmatists in something and to show the groundlessness[v] of many of their propositions. In most recent times, *David Hume* is especially known as a *scepticus* who had an overwhelming, indeed, a somewhat extravagant inclination to doubt. His writings, which appeared before the learned world under the title, "Philosophical Inquiries," and were also called "Miscellaneous Writings,"[33] contained political articles, essays on literature, moral and also metaphysical articles[;] but they all tended toward to skepticism. In these writings of Hume is to be found a gentle, calm, unprejudiced examination. In them he considers, namely, first of all one side of a thing; he searches for all possible grounds for it, and expounds them in the best oratorical style. Then he takes up the other side, presents it for examination, as it were, completely without partisanship, expounds again all the opposing grounds with just the same eloquence, but at the end and in conclusion he appears in his true form as a real skeptic[;] he complains about the uncertainty of all our cognition whatsoever, shows how little these can be trusted, and finally he doubts instead of inferring and settling which of the two cognitions is true and which false. He would, however, certainly be one of the best authors, and one of those most worthy of being read, if only he did not have the preponderant inclination to doubt everything, but instead wanted to seek to attain a true certainty by means of the examination and investigation of cognitions.

Cardanus, in his book *De vanitate scientarium*,[34] also expresses *scepticismus* and maintains, as it were, that everything is uncertain.

Voltaire is the *scepticus* of the modern skeptics of our times. His 218 *scepticismus*, however, is far more harmful than it is useful. He expounds neither grounds *for* nor grounds *against* the matter. He inquires and tests nothing at all, but instead doubts without any proof that a cognition is not to be trusted. His grounds are thus nothing but illusory grounds, which can deceive a simple man, to be sure, but never an acute and reflective learned man. And just for this reason Voltaire is especially dangerous for the great horde and for the common man. For he provides the common man with wholly false grounds for doubting this or that thing. But if one

[v] "den Ungrund."

wants closer instruction in the *scepticismus* of modern times, then one can read with great profit the writing that Haller published under the title: *Examination of the sect that doubts everything.*[35] Also, the writings of Hume mentioned above are actually, in a certain way, to be recommended too.

§ 181

In this *paragraphus* the author speaks of *opinion in general.* It is contradistinguished from persuasion, however. In both there are uncertain cognitions, but in persuasion one holds these to be certain. In opinion, on the other hand, one does not hold them to be certain. Therefore we must strive above all to distinguish *persuasion* from *conviction.* Someone who holds something to be an opinion cannot also hold it to be a persuasion, and actually errs as soon as he does so. Persuasion is thus always reprehensible, since in this case one takes something to be true on insufficient grounds.

The distinction between persuasion and conviction is, however, rather difficult, and hence is very seldom determined rightly. This is because one has perhaps never experienced a true conviction, but only the illusion of it.

Opinion, however, is really not a mistake, but only an imperfect cognition, a lack, since something in our judgment does not have sufficient grounds.

We can always put forth many opinions without thereby erring, if only we do not hold them to be convictions. The crowd does this quite often. Although a cognition is completely false, opinion about it can nevertheless be completely certain, and can agree with the rules of the understanding and of reason. E.g., if someone in common life selects a servant who is of good parents and has a good upbringing, then he is of the opinion that he is good, that one can trust in him. Here reason is present and applied, although the opposite thereof can very often occur and my cognition can be false. Wolff was of the completely reasonable opinion that there are inhabitants on the moon, for at that time discoveries were not as numerous as now, when it has been seen that the moon has no atmosphere.

219

Opinion can often be false as to matter, although it is true as to form, and conversely, it can be true as to matter but false as to form[;] in the first case it is false, but in the second always true.

If my cognition agrees with the constitution of the thing itself, then *it is true.* But if it is contrary to the constitution of the thing, then *it is false.* An opinion can, however, be quite true as to form, reasonable and thorough, even though it does not agree as to matter with the constitution of the thing.

An opinion is never a certainty, the opposite can always occur[;] nonetheless it can also quite often be reasonable and right.

One obtains an opinion for something from certain grounds that one cognizes. The outcome of the thing, however, teaches us whether our opinion was true or false as to matter. Whether the form of our opinion was right, however, this the *eventus*[w] of the thing cannot really show us.

The principal mistake in our cognitions consists in what is formal and not in what is material in the cognitions. One can hold something to be true in accordance with every form of reason, and have a grounded opinion for something, when the data that one now has for the thing outweigh the grounds for the opposite, although the outcome of the thing first actually teaches one whether the opinion was true as to matter and whether the *eventus* was other than one opined.

Each and every opinion is quite changeable. Today one can have more grounds *for* the opinion, tomorrow more *against* it, whereupon one must change one's opinion at once and accept another, often one opposed to it, which cannot in fact be at all detrimental for a true philosopher.

220 *Hypotheses* are a completely special kind of philosophical opinion. Not all philosophical opinions are hypotheses, however, but only a few. They do not serve to explain the appearances of the world, but instead only to explain something in general, which may arise from reason, or from experience, or from appearance.

A *hypothesis* is an opinion concerning the truth of a ground based on its sufficiency for the consequence. If, namely, I hold something to be true *a priori* on account of its grounds, then this is nothing other than an opinion. But if, on the other hand, I cognize the ground from the sufficiency of the consequences for the ground, then this is also an opinion, but not *a priori*, but instead *a posteriori*, and thus a *hypothesis*. A hypothesis is, as it were, a presupposition. Thus a doctor makes hypotheses when he cures the sick[;] he has to subsume everything under hypotheses, and see whether the consequences that he now has before his eyes follow therefrom.

If all the consequences that follow from an assumed *hypothesis*$_{\mathrm{L}}$ are true and agree with what is given, then it is not an opinion anymore but instead a certainty.

It is a demonstrated truth, furthermore[;] but since we are not in a position, or very seldom, to draw out each and every consequence, then in most cases they are only pure opinions[;] hence we must say that if all the consequences that we have been able to draw from a *hypothesis*$_{\mathrm{L}}$ are true, then I have great cause to conclude that the hypothesis itself is certain and true. If a *hypothesis* is *strengthened* by other things of which we are assured besides its sufficiency for its consequences, then it is *confirmed*. A *hypothesis subsidiaria* is a *hypothesis* that presupposes a new hypothesis. But the more I must assume in it, the less steadfast it is. The more unity there is in the *hypothesis*, the better it is, for otherwise in most cases fabrication gets added. And in this way there arises a philosophical novel. A novel of reason,

[w] outcome.

as, e.g., of Cartesius, etc., etc. A world-system based on pure phantoms of the brain. But let us note the *rule*: I can of course invent things in order to philosophize, but in philosophizing itself I cannot invent.

Every presupposition has infinite consequences, however. But something is certain in a relative way when the grounds for approval exceed all grounds for the opposite[;] this is then a comparative certainty. Something 221 is certain *absolute*$_{\text{L}}$, however, of which the opposite is impossible or absurd. Two presuppositions are one and the same representation, and not at all different, if they are such that from the one the very same consequences flow as from the other.

Thus the *Copernican system* is a *hypothesis*. One can still represent the opposite as possible, however hard that is, and as easy as this system is, and as much as it accords with reason and agrees with all the phenomena of the heavens. –

With all hypotheses one must necessarily secure acceptance and certainty for them in such a way that they can be confirmed and derived not merely *a posteriori* through relation to their consequences, but also *a priori* through the *nexus*$_{\text{L}}$, that is, through relation to their grounds.

From the sufficiency of a ground for a given consequence it can never be inferred with full truth that this is the true ground of the consequence, for this is only an *opinion*. There is a ground of possibility here, but not of certainty, for a consequence can often arise from several grounds, and can originate from more than one ground. The more sufficient a ground is, however, the more will one infer that it is the ground of the consequence. For all *hypotheses* are posited *arbitrarily*. Namely, I assume something and see whether something is sufficient for deriving therefrom a certain consequence or not.

If a ground suffices for all the determinations that are contained in a certain given consequence, no more, but also no fewer[;] if it is adequate, then, so that from it can be inferred neither fewer determinations (and thus it is *complete*) nor more (and thus it is *precise*), then it is the true ground, since it is such as it ought to be.

It is impossible for there to be more grounds than are adequate for a consequence. Grounds that are distinct from one another cannot also agree with one another in all cases. Grounds that agree in all consequences, however, are not different grounds but one and the same ground.

If a ground suffices for *some* of what is contained in the consequence, then according to logical rules there is an opinion that the ground is true. If the ground suffices for several determinations of the consequence, then the opinion is that much *more probable*.

Until finally, when the ground suffices for *all* the determinations but 222 also *not* for more determinations than are contained in the consequence, then there is a true ground, and then *hypothesis* ceases. The ground becomes a *theory*. A certainty.

If a consequence is given to me and I am supposed to find its ground, then this is a *hypothesis*. If a ground is given to me, however, and I am supposed to derive its consequences, then this is an opinion, to be sure, but not a hypothesis. With a *hypothesis* the consequences are given but the ground is invented.

One of the most famous hypotheses is the *Copernican*. Copernicus assumed that the sun stands still and the planets move about it, and saw whether from this all the appearances of the heavenly bodies can be explained; later, however, his hypothesis becomes a true opinion and a complete system, which deserves to be approved by all. If it is asked why all bodies have just this inclination to fall toward the earth, then here the consequence is present, and the ground has to be found.

Cartesius assumed that bodies made certain vortices[;] others assumed that these vortices crossed each other, and from this they thus sought to explain that bodies fall, and always toward the center of the earth.

In *metaphysica* there are many hypotheses. The proof of the existence of God is at first an hypothesis. One assumes a being that is the most perfect among all others and then investigates whether grounds of explanations can be derived from this for that of which nature, experience, and the creatures here on earth teach us.

Plato and Malebranche assumed it as a hypothesis that man stands in a wholly special connection with the deity and saw whether they would be able to explain from this the consequences into which they had insight.

Hypotheses actually have very great value, however, and can never be fully banned from human cognition. All judges make hypotheses, which they often reject again on better investigation. Hypotheses are the path toward theory, and frequently toward a truth completely opposed to it.

By means of hypotheses one does not always find what one intends, but instead frequently something else[;] one tries, one tests, assumes something, and investigates whether from it one can explain the known consequences or not; if the first occurs, then one accepts the *hypothesis*$_{L}$,[x] if the latter occurs, one rejects it.

223

Since from the sufficiency of a ground for the consequence the truth of the ground can be inferred, and this ground is fabricated, it follows from this: The more that is fabricated in a ground, the more that follows from it *licite*,[y] and the newer it is. And the more the hypotheses that must be accepted in order to explain something, the more fabrication takes place.

In the case of some inferences one must fabricate many *hypotheses subsidiariae*. If we have consequences and fabricate the ground for them, then it can frequently be that we have still more consequences than the ground suffices for.

[x] Ak, "an. findet"; MS, "an, findet" (KI, lxix).

[y] permissibly, legitimately.

Thus we must fabricate new grounds, and these new grounds are nothing but *hypotheses subsidiariae.*

These are actually opposed to true philosophy, however, and they show *effrenis fingendi licentia.*[z] If I am to invent everything, then I want to explain everything. Unity is therefore a principal attribute of hypotheses, namely, that one assumes a ground which suffices for explaining all determinations and consequences of the thing that we cognize, without, however, needing to help oneself to *hypotheses subsidiariae* and the assumption of these.

The unity of hypotheses is a major ground [for establishing] that the ground is the true one, and that there can be no other from which one could explain just as many consequences.

It is also a principal ground of the truth of a hypothesis if one shows that the ground that one has fabricated for the sake of the sufficiency of the consequences deserves to be accepted on the basis of other causes. Here one shows from other grounds, namely, that what was fabricated must be accepted[;] thus one confirms the truth of the hypothesis.

All holding-to-be-true derives from a double combination, namely, either because the ground is sufficient for the derivation of all consequences, or because it agrees and is, so to speak, *aequivoce*[a] with other grounds that have a certain similarity to it. With all hypotheses, therefore, we will first show the *sufficiency of the fictio historica*[b] for their consequences, and also the agreement of the fiction with other grounds, so that there are still other grounds from which consequences can be derived. Hypotheses must first, as inferences, be probable, but at the same time it must also be possible to confirm them through other grounds. E.g., he who wants to explain a thunderstorm assumes an electrical kind of matter in the air and shows afterward from other grounds that there actually must be a sulphurous and electrical matter in the air. On the one hand, hypotheses have something really quite detrimental to philosophy, insofar as they give allowance to fabrication. But on the other hand, they are also very beneficial, namely, if the *fictiones* are heuristic or have as their purpose the fabrication of something. 224

In philosophy, hypothesis is thus actually a wholly indispensable method of reason and of our understanding[;] all hypotheses must be assumed wholly problematically[;] consequently one must not be obstinate about any *hypothesis*$_{L}$ and hold fast to it, so that one cannot quickly let it go when one sees its falsity or uncertainty. Many attempts at fabrication are often completely in vain, in that one does not discover any truth thereby. Thus hypotheses also have the disadvantage that if they are artfully devised and if

z unbridled license to fabricate (reading "effrenis" instead of "effrunua," with Hinske, KI, lxxii).

a the same in meaning.

b historical fiction (reading "Fictionis" instead of "Fictiones," with Hinske, KI, lxxii).

one has noted in addition their agreement with many consequences, they take root in our understanding[;] and if one immediately thereafter has insight into their falsity, it is nevertheless not so easy to be rid of them[.] Thus, e.g., if this or that hypothesis were sufficient for new and correct consequences, and if it is only one, e.g., the hundredth, that contradicts the ground, then one rejects this one, although it is evidently true, rather than getting rid of the hypothesis that seems so good. It is therefore quite sad if an age is dominated by nothing but hypotheses which, however, are false, and which thus do not suffice to discover the true ground. Such hypotheses do more harm than good, for they do not suffice to explain everything, and if in addition one assumes them as true, one acquires only false cognitions and representations instead of true ones. He who will not get rid of false hypotheses, because he has contrived them and they seem so probable to him, is like a man who has raised a child with much effort and care and who afterward does not want to reject it, so as not to lose all his work, effort, and expense.

Nevertheless, such hypotheses, in which nothing but false hypotheses are fused together, serve to get true hypotheses fabricated in subsequent ages, for one who is familiar with all possible false paths cannot possibly fail to find the right path at last. The remaining propositions which our author puts forth in

225

§ 182 et 183

are for the most part tautological and hence do not deserve closer investigation or explanation (the author frequently proceeds thus). When he says in the 7th rule, § 183, that when one has not fabricated far too many opinions, we can observe further that there is much that can be a perfection as to quality, but not a perfection as to quantity, namely, if it exceeds a certain degree, which constitutes perfection.

But this degree is hard, indeed, almost impossible to determine[.] It requires us to say, e.g., that one ought not to be too candid[;] the art consists in determining quite exactly the degree of candor and of reticence that one must not exceed, provided one wants to be not too candid and not too reticent.

There are innumerable deceptions in morals[;] rules are given that say nothing more than what one has long known[;] this is nothing new for our understanding, then.

Certainty is either

A. *comparative* or also
B. *apodeictic.*

Comparative certainty is the relation of the grounds of the holding-to-be-true to the grounds of the opposite.

Apodeictic certainty, however, is absolute and consists in the relation of the grounds of the holding-to-be-true to the sufficient ground.

History is certain merely *comparative*$_L$, never apodeictically. Morals, however, and therein the *jus naturale* in particular, contains many apodeictic certainties.

Also distinct from apodeictic certainty is mathematical certainty in intuition, which is evident. Mathematics expounds its propositions

1. discursively
2. intuitively.

Neither moral, physical, nor even metaphysical propositions can be mathematically certain.

Even though they are apodeictically certain, evidence is in all cases certainly lacking. The term arbitrary truths amounts to nothing, for can truth also be false? What a contradictory expression! 226

A proposition is, however

1. true
2. false
3. arbitrary.

and then it is not settled whether it is the latter or the former; that is, it can be true, but also false. I cannot form[c] the object arbitrarily, but I can arbitrarily dispose[d] the subject as is most comfortable for me[;] I can cognize the object, and make the object comprehensible by me in the most comfortable[e] way.

Everything that is mediately certain is provable. What is immediately certain is unprovably certain, i.e., it is so undeniable that it needs no means for certainty or for proof.

Proof, as a means to apodeictic certainty, is *demonstration*. Proof, as a means to comparative certainty, is *probation*.[f]

A mathematical demonstration, however, is also *intuitive*, evident. It speaks of the universal *in individuo*. Who can comprehend that? Just as little as we can comprehend that we can see everything with our eyes, although they are so small. We always see objects that strike our eyes, without however in the least wondering, how does that happen?

§ 184

In this *paragraphus* the author says one should guard against each and every false cognition, one should avoid illusory conviction or illusory persuasion.

[c] "bilden."
[d] "disponiren."
[e] "Commodeste, und Bequemlichste."
[f] "*Probation*."

But everyone knows this already[;] he would have said something excellent if he had put forth the marks by which persuasion can be distinguished from conviction.

Persuasion does not consist in material falsehood but instead in false form, since one holds an opinion to be a complete certainty. The matter itself can always be true, but this is not the manner, the way, to attain truth.

In the case of persuasion one need not err as to the object, but one errs 227 as to form. Since one holds the grounds for opinion[,] for holding-to-be-true based on insufficient grounds, to be grounds for certainty based on sufficient grounds.

In fact, however, we always have only a theory of morals, a speculation concerning the moral behavior[g] of men, and not an actual, practical morals. Therefore no one can demand, either, that one should put forward the *notae* in which false persuasion is distinct from conviction in the true sense. This is still to be discovered. We have likewise only a theoretical logic, and not at all a practical one.

Some persuasion arises from logical grounds, some from aesthetic grounds that do not derive from the understanding or from reason but instead arise out of a certain inclination. Often we are not indifferent about finding a matter true or false, and then there is a strong ground that we will be persuaded of a cognition. Man in general is subject to very many illusions[;] they play with him as with a ball. The one who can most easily be persuaded, however, is one who is very easily inclined to be moved to one or another affect.

The great horde, the crowd, the common man is thus in most cases persuaded quite easily, and most easily, by someone who understands the art of taking people in. He who can be easily persuaded, however, can also be easily moved to an affect. The two are thus combined with one another almost inseparably.

§ 185

Science (which really does not belong here, and whose consideration the author has brought in here wrongly and in a certain way inappropriately) can be opposed to supposition and also to opinions. *To believe something*, or *to opine*, is quite distinct from *to know*. For *to know* means to hold something to be true with sufficient certainty and grounds, so that no doubt remains or can remain.

As for what concerns the degrees of holding-to-be-true, they are the following:

[g] "das moralische Sittliche verhalten."

1. *to opine*, or holding-to-be-true based on any insufficient ground, which nevertheless has more importance than the ground of the opposite, which I cognize and into which I have insight.
2. *to believe*, or to hold something to be true to such a degree that it is sufficient for action and for deciding to act. 228
3. *to know*, or to cognize the truth sufficiently.

The [German] word [for] *to know*[h] is the origin or root of [the German word for] certainty.[i] But certainty we have already explained above. A science, however, is nothing other than a cognition, through which we know something. The [German] word [for] science[j] is contradistinguished from art[;] hence in common life we also commonly say, this is not a science but an art, and conversely. E.g., this happens with riddles[;] one cries out, this is not science but instead an art (a great distinction).

There are actions for which a certain art, and on the other hand again there are certain actions for which science, is required and necessary. But something is called *an art* (to separate these concepts) for which a specific perfection of *praxis*$_L$ is required. Something is called a *science*, however, for which a specific perfection of theory is necessary. Every art involves a practical skill in acting. The practical skill that one has in art cannot be attained, however, merely by rules and by particular, certain precepts, but instead one must also have a particular skill. Furthermore, science is opposed to critique. Every theoretical cognition is either a doctrine or a critique. Critique, however, is in fact nothing other than a species of theoretical (hence not practical) cognition concerning any product that there is, which shows us the rules according to which this product is developed.[k] *Doctrine*, however, is that theoretical cognition in which one comes across the grounds for how a matter can be developed,[l] or states the rules according to which a good product can be produced.

A critique is actually not a science, for otherwise we might be able to produce good products ourselves at once. But with critique this happens only after a long time, when one gradually learns to apply the cognized rules to oneself. In common usage, the word science is often used falsely, and one involves other concepts with it than this word actually contains.

§ 189

229

In the case of certainty it is not the truth of the thing we cognize that is necessary, but rather the holding-to-be-true. The greater the probability

[h] "*wißen*."
[i] "Gewißheit."
[j] "Wissenschaft."
[k] "ausgeübt."
[l] "ausgeübt."

of a thing, the more the understanding is necessitated to take it to be true. This necessity of accepting the thing does not lie in the *objectum* itself, however, but instead in the subject, because the grounds of the opposite fall short of those that I cognize for the truth of the thing. This subjective necessity to accept something is quite deceptive and changeable, because it is not grounded in the *objectum*.

The author speaks here also of mathematical certainty of the first and second degree. The former rests on reason, the latter on experience, and the two certainties are thus distinguished in the *data*$_L$. All mathematical certainty includes a sufficient ground, a precision, and a certain intuiting[m] of the cognition, the *intuitive*.[n] Mathematical certainty carries with it a certain sensibility,[o] for this always occurs only with quantities, but never with qualities.

In philosophy there are no intuitive cognitions, but only in mathematics, which has to do with quantities. In mathematical certainty, as in philosophical, there is distinctness and sufficiency[;] precision and evidence are to be found only and exclusively in the former, however. *Historical certainty* cannot possibly ever become apodeictically certain. The grounds for historical certainty are, however

1. *purity of insight*
2. *correctness of the power of judgment*
3. *truthfulness*, furthermore
4. *the inclination toward truth or toward speaking the truth*, and finally
5. *honesty*.

For the last two grounds are the causes of the third ground, namely, of the truthfulness of him who maintains it. But now from the consequences nothing can be apodeictically inferred, because there can be far more than one consequence of one and the same thing. Certain historical cognitions will have grounds for holding-to-be-true such that they are sufficient for practical, though not of course for theoretical certainty. Consequently apodeictic certainty is actually distinguished from practical certainty not *in gradu*[p] but instead *in specie*,[q] even if some wish to maintain the former.

230

§ 190

In this *paragraphus* the author calls hypotheses arbitrary truths. An arbitrary proposition makes something be true, only the proposition must not contradict itself. Such an arbitrary proposition is called a *positio*. Some-

[m] "ein gewisses anschauen."
[n] "das *intuitive*."
[o] "eine gewisse Sinnlichkeit."
[p] in degree.
[q] in kind.

thing that is objective can never be assumed arbitrarily, but instead only the subjective is established through the faculty of choice. All arbitrary propositions concern what one ought to do[,] the practical, and thus they never teach what the thing is. A *positio* occurs only in regard to *praxis*$_{L}$, and thus it is distinguished from hypothesis. Arbitrary *positiones*, which concern actions, occur notably in mathematics, e.g., with the circle, that one divides it into 360 degrees, with logarithms, with the relation of arithmetical to geometrical number, proportions, progressions.

The word hypothesis therefore does not mean an arbitrary proposition at all but rather an opinion based on certain grounds *a posteriori*, which are sufficient for these consequences or those.

In the case of positing I do not actually establish anything at all that lies in the object, but only what I arbitrarily wish and want to have in it. Mathematical quantity rests on the arbitrary[r] repetition of unity. What holds here of a certain kind of triangle, circle, etc., holds at the same time of all triangles, circles, etc., of this kind. One triangle, circle, quadrilateral, etc., takes the place of all other possible ones. Any triangle at all contains, e.g., 180 degrees[;] this holds of all other possible triangles. Any square has four equal sides and four right angles[;] this holds of each and every possible square, etc. Here the universal is always seen and considered in a particular case, then.

§ 191

Any certain proposition is either unprovably or immediately certain, or it is mediately or provably certain. That cognition which contains in itself the ground of truth of another cognition is the ground of proof, and the connection of the cognitions with their truth is the *proof*. There are actually three things to be found here, then, namely 231

1. *the ground of proof, or the material*
2. *the proof, or the consequentia, or the form*
3. *and finally the conclusion, which follows from the consequentia.*[s]

In every proof, what one investigates is actually not the proposition to be proved but rather the *ratio probandi*.[t] The *materia* of the proof is the *medius terminus*, and its form is the *consequentia*. Some proofs are *empirical*, other proofs are *rational*. And the latter are either *mathematical*, and then they are called *demonstrationes*, or they are *philosophical*, and imperfect *probationes*. If convincing proofs lack evidence, the intuitive, or precision, then they are not yet *demonstrationes*.

Even granting that they are sufficient, rational proofs are still not *demon-*

[r] "Willkührlichen und beliebigen."

[s] Reading "der Consequenz" for "dem consequens."

[t] ground of proof.

strationes, therefore, and still less are empirical proofs *demonstrationes*. Empirical proofs can frequently be quite sufficient and evident, but regardless of that they are not *demonstrationes*, for they are not rational. The word unprovable means here, as we mentioned above, those certain cognitions whose certainty and truth one need not and cannot doubt.

Provable cognition is not clear through itself, but instead is held to be true only by means of other cognitions[,] as a consequence. Thus if one holds a provable cognition to be unprovable, one errs in form. The proofs of God's existence, of his properties, of his effects are not unprovable but instead provable. With unprovably certain cognitions I postulate,[u] I demand approval, as it were. With provably certain cognitions, however, I beg and ask, as it were, the approval[v] of others. All immediate experiences are unprovably certain and also cannot be proven. E.g., there is a sun in the heavens, the barometer has fallen or risen, this is all immediately certain and thus unprovable.

If, however, I establish universal judgments based on experience, or propositions of experience, then these are always provable. All rational and 232 unprovable cognitions are *axiomata*, and they are either *synthetic* or *analytic*. In every judgment one conceives[w] the subject as a mark of a thing, with which I can otherwise be unacquainted. One knows merely the mark, then; with this I am acquainted. E.g., the proposition, A body is divisible, is analytic, for to the subject to which a body belongs, divisibility also belongs, and to that to which divisibility belongs, to that subject belongs a body as well. But a body has an attractive force, this proposition is synthetic, for separated from all experience, attractive force does not lie in the concept of a body.

All analytic propositions, where the predicate lies in the notion of the subject, belong under the law of identity.[x] Synthetic propositions, however, whose predicate does not lie in the notion of the subject but in a mark that is distinct from the subject, do not belong under the *principium identitatis* and *contradictionis*.[y] This *principium* relates only to analytic propositions[.] In the case of synthetic propositions a predicate is added to the notion of the subject that is not contained in it. And all the propositions that are thus constituted can be cognized only intuitively, not through reason. One cannot cognize any coordination at all through reason, for reason only subordinates. All synthetic propositions are either immediate propositions of experience or intuitive propositions that are produced through the understanding and do not lie in the notion of the subject. Analytic propositions, however, can be drawn out of the concept of the

[u] "postulire."

[v] Reading "Beyfall" for "Begriff."

[w] "concipiret man sich."

[x] Ak, "in der Identitaet"; MS, "der Identitaet."

[y] principle of identity [and] of contradiction.

subject *per analysin*. For they are contained in the notion of the subject and subordinated to it. Here reason can busy itself and analyze the subordinate concepts and separate them from one another. E.g., gold does not rust. This is a synthetic proposition, this is illuminated merely from immediate experience, and it really cannot be derived from the notion of gold *per analysin*[;] if something is postulated, it must be such that it convinces everyone absolutely. In a proof, falsehood as to matter is only accidental, but falsehood according to form is essential. False matter can be corrected, but false form is completely *incorrigible*$_F$. Furthermore, falsehood of form is far more extensive and more universal than falsehood of matter. The *proton pseudos*,[z] where someone infers absurdly or also accepts false propositions, likewise lies in form; for it is peculiar to form that it be subjected not only to many errors but also to uncorrectible ones. 233

§ 196

To prove something *directe* means to prove something in connection with its grounds. That is an ostensive proof; that through which one proves that that which is the opposite is false is an apagogical proof, then.[a]

To prove something *indirecte*, on the other hand, is to prove something in connection with its consequences. This latter, however, can never occur except *negative*$_L$ or by denial. We never cognize all the consequences of a thing, however, but instead we are unacquainted with many of them. Thus it happens that indirect proof can never become demonstration, but it can become philosophical probation.

If we want to prove that a cognition is false, this can actually occur. To have drawn the opposite of such a false cognition already proves the partial falsehood of the cognition[;] thus it happens that apagogical inference is so popular, because it is the only one that can give apodeictic certainty. Since direct inference is not in a position to give anything but comparative certainty. Apagogical proof, however, is also the one that comes closest to evidence. Thus it is much easier than direct proof, too, since it brings the opposite *ad absurdum*[;] and it is settled that absurdity always strikes the eye more strongly than any truth whatsoever, just as the cessation of the greatest pleasure is not nearly as sensible to me as the opposed pain, and a pleasure is increased by the pain that precedes it. Truth, e.g., contains the striking, the *frappante*, far less than does the representation of the absurdity of the opposite. The mistake in this proof, however, is that it can prove that the opposite of the proposition is false, but it cannot prove it by itself. On this point direct

[z] transliteration of Greek πρῶτον ψεῦδος: first, or basic, falsehood.

[a] Reading "beweis; das, wobey man zeigt, . . . ist also" for "beweis, dabey man zeigt, . . . also."

proof, genetic proof, is far better than the former[;] namely, the latter discovers not only truth but also at the same time its *genesis*$_L$, its generative source.

However popular it may be, then, one makes use of apagogical 234 proof only *ad interim*, etc. Proper, true insight is actually attained only through direct, genetic proof. A cognition is proved *directe* when its truth can be shown from the relation to the grounds. But *indirecte*, on the other hand, when its truth flows from the relation to the consequences. Direct proofs are actually genetic and are developed *per rationes essendi, non vero cognoscendi.*[b] Indirect proofs, however, are developed *per rationes cognoscendi, non essendi.*[c] To infer affirmatively from the consequences to the grounds is wrong, but instead this must always happen negatively[.]

§ 197

If I am to say that something is demonstrated, the proof must be such that it convinces everyone, that is, the proof must hold not for me alone but also for others. For demonstration requires evidence, so that the cognition and the proof of it are such that one cannot possibly postpone his approval. From this it becomes clear, then, that we must use the word demonstration sparingly. Much can be a philosophical probation but not a demonstration. Mathematical proofs are of such a kind that they are all *demonstrationes*. Thus something cannot be put forward as a demonstration until experience has taught that it is impossible to withhold one's approval and to oppose it, or until other men agree that it is no longer possible to doubt the cognition.

In philosophy, then, *demonstrationes* can only seldom be found. No aesthetic proof can be a demonstration, then, for an aesthetic probation arises merely out of the agreement of cognitions with our feeling and our taste[;] thus it is nothing but persuasion.

I can prove something to someone aesthetically as soon as I am acquainted with his passions and his feeling and am in a position to excite them. This probation is not universally valid, however, and is therefore wrongly called a demonstration by our *autor*.

§ 199

Everyone has an inclination to demonstrate[;] evidence pleases everyone[;] what is sad is only that it is so hard and can very seldom be attained.

[b] through grounds of being, not through grounds of true knowledge.

[c] through grounds of knowledge, not of being.

§ 200

235

Excessive inclination to demonstrate, says our author, is addiction to demonstration.[d] Charlatans do not actually have any addiction to demonstrating themselves, but instead they deceive those who lie sick with the addiction to demonstrating. The addiction to demonstrating due to pedantry is the true addiction to demonstration, however, and it actually consists in the fact that one has an inclination either to demonstrate everything or to accept nothing that is not demonstrated and proven undoubtedly. Thus pedantry in demonstrating believes trustingly that in the whole of human cognition one simply cannot make progress without demonstration. But regardless of that, this pedantry can nonetheless quite often be combined with a sharp critique of cognition. It is really not ignorance, then, and not error either, but instead one perhaps does not demonstrate at all, because something cannot be demonstrated, and [one] prefers not to accept those cognitions that cannot be demonstrated. One can nourish this addiction to demonstration if one knows how to conceal the weak side of demonstrations. But one gets rid of it if one knows and has insight that in many things nothing can be demonstrated at all; and if one cognizes, then, that much is cognized as a demonstration that is not proven at all, or is only a probation.

What prevails in our current age is not an addiction to demonstrating but instead a certain shallowness, a kind of gallantry even in learned cognitions. But the latter is nonetheless always more bearable than the former. For shallowness only needs an addition to become thorough[;] hence it is completely capable of improvement. The addiction to demonstrating, on the other hand, is *incorrigible*$_F$[;] with it, one quite often takes false cognitions to be true and is even proud of this falsehood and not at all desirous of being taught, and correctly convinced, concerning its opposite.

§ 201

Sensation is the representation of our present condition insofar as it originates from the presence of a certain object. Sometimes representations arise in us of which we ourselves are the originator, but whose presence we derive from the existence of a thing. And then it happens that we often confuse fictions with sensations, and in this way we commit an error. We can often invent something for ourselves, but this is not a sensation. Thus, e.g., the fear of an impending pain is distinct from the pain that is present. The fear of pain itself, namely, is a fiction. On the other hand, the pain itself is a sensation. About sensations one cannot

236

[d] "die Demonstrations-Sucht."

speak or engage in reasoning[e] any further, for they are the *principium materiale*[f] of all our representations.

A representation of sensation[g] simply cannot be invented by us but instead must be given to us by means of the senses. *Experience* and *sensation* are distinct as to form and as to degree. As to matter, the two are the same, but in experience there is a form as well, reason. Experience is nothing but reflected sensation, or sensation that is expressed through a judgment.

Experiences, namely, are not mere concepts and representations but also judgments[;] e.g., the representations of warmth or of cold are concepts of experience. They are universal characters of things, but we cannot have insight into these merely through the senses, but actually only through[h] judgment. Non-rational animals have no experience, then, but instead only sensations. Anyone who can describe the objects of his experience has experience, for description involves not merely sensation but also a judgment.

Mere sensations, without judging about them, cannot be described. Every experience is actually immediate, and according to our *autor* mediate experiences are *contradictiones in adjecto.*[i] The judgment that is made immediately on the occasion of sensations is the judgment of experience.

§ 203–204

All judgment is either *empirical* or *rational.* Some can be empirical as to matter but rational as to form. But some can be rational both as to matter and as to form. The form of all our experiences is rational. All experiences have the form of reason, and without this they will not be experiences.

237 With experiences we must be active through reason[.] With sensations, however, we are merely passive. The proofs of certain cognitions are always rational as to form, but as to matter they can arise either from experience or from reason. A proof without the form of reason is no proof at all[.] If we want to prove something, we must infer from certain *data*$_{L}$[,] granted that the matter arises from the senses, or is a sensation[.] And hence every proof is rational. Regardless of this, however, it is called empirical if its matter is a sensation, or if the ground of proof originates from experience. When one has an empirical proof, the ground of proof is immediate[;] thus a sensation always originates in accordance with experience from sensation. Immediate sensations cannot be proved.

[e] "raisoniren d.i. vernünfteln."

[f] material principle.

[g] "Eine Empfindungs-Vorstellung."

[h] Reading "nur durch" for "durch."

[i] terms where the adjective contradicts the noun (Ak, "objecto"; MS, "adjecto," KI, lxix).

We must learn to distinguish inferences based on experiences from *judicia discursiva* about the experiences.

Nothing is more deceptive than for one to infer secretly from certain examples, but without knowing that one is inferring, and thus for one to put forward an inference from experience as an immediate experience. Immediate experience shows us only what is in our senses, without our thereby inferring anything.

The judgment that expresses appearance is an immediate judgment of experience. Now if we mix up the judgment that expresses the appearance with those judgments that express the causes of the appearances, then we confuse the *judicium discursivum* with the *judicium intuitivum*. The *judicium discursivum* is thus the one that expresses the cause of the appearances, the *intuitivum* the one that expresses the appearance itself.

Care in not mixing up *judicia discursiva* with *judicia intuitiva* is of particularly great importance, and it is unavoidably necessary to exercise it properly so that one does not fall into various errors. All proofs occur from reason, and the verifying of a cognition from an immediate experience is not a proof but instead a *factum*, an *inspectio ocularis*,[j] as it were.

A proof from reason, however, of which the author speaks in the 204th *paragraphus*, is a proof which arises from reason in respect of the ground of proof, or as to matter, as well as[k] in respect of the formal, and which thus has no need of experience. Proofs from reason have as grounds of proof such propositions as arise from reason, but in part these propositions arise from experience as to their first origin. A proof from reason is thus not always a proof of pure reason[,] without application of experience. A proof through pure reason, however, can only be developed from such cognitions as simply are not objects of the senses. If cognitions are even in part objects of the senses, then they have to be derived, as to their[l] first *principia*, from experience. Proofs of pure reason find a place therefore only in mathematics and metaphysics. That which can be demonstrated through pure reason not only does not require a proof from experience, but does not even permit one. There have been a few who have endeavored to invent an experimental geometry, but all their efforts amounted to nothing but child's play.

238

Experiences do not permit any universal judgments at all, except of possibility. Experience simply cannot teach me with apodeictic certainty that all men must die, e.g., but only that all men who have previously lived have died. A proof from pure reason proves universal propositions, however, and thus cannot be supported through proofs from experience, for these do not prove any universal propositions. A demonstration from pure

[j] inspection by eye.
[k] Reading "als auch in Absicht" for "oder in Absicht."
[l] Reading "ihren" for "ihrer," with Hinske (KI, lxxiii).

reason is so distinct from a proof from experience that if the two were to be combined with one another,[m] a bastard would necessarily arise from this. Proofs from pure reason are like a light, while all proofs from experience, on the other hand, disappear, just as the light of the moon is dispensable and disappears once the sun's rays make the day. That which can be proved through pure reason attains no new proof through experience, but instead only a mere illustration and elucidation. To have the idea of a thing is very hard.

One can get much value from a science, indeed, can get solid cognitions from it, yet without having an idea of it. Obviously it happens thus, e.g., with logic, with jurisprudence.

239 Logic is a science that sets forth the actions that arise according to form. All *conceptus* are (1.) *empirici*, which are concepts arising from experience[,] (2.) *intellectuales*, from the understanding[,] (3.) *arbitrarii*, from the faculty of choice. There are intuitions in concepts, i.e., *perceptiones communes*[,] universally valid or common representations. All *perceptiones*, however, are

1. *intuitive*[n]
2. *reflexive*[,] requiring reflection.

Reflexive *perceptiones*, however, are again

A. *communes*
B. *singulares.*

In logic, however, all *perceptiones* must be *communes*. If they are applied abstractly,[o] then they acquire the name of *particular concepts.*[p] No cognitions can arise through logical abstraction.[q] Through a *conceptus communis* I can consider an object

A. *in abstracto* or also
B. *in concreto.*

The word *conceptus abstractus* is, however, a bad expression. For what purpose might the art of the human understanding be able to form common concepts?[r] They serve to indicate the place for each concept, and they are, as it were, the representatives of a multitude of things[;] hence they serve particularly for elucidation. The common[s] concept contains many [concepts] under itself[;] but these concepts that it contains under itself contain it in themselves[;] it is contained in them.

[m] "mit einander combiniret und zusammen verbunden."
[n] "*intuitive anschauend.*"
[o] "absonderlich."
[p] "*besonderer Begrife.*"
[q] "Absonderung."
[r] "gemeingültige Begrife conceptus communes."
[s] Reading "gemeingültige" for "gemeinschaftliche."

A wonderful reciprocal relation[.][t] E.g., humanity applies to all men, and in all men lies humanity. The multitude of things, however, that I can think under the *conceptus communis* constitute the *sphaera conceptus*. The more things a mark belongs to, the greater a concept is in its extension, i.e., in its capacity,[u] but the less it contains in itself, on the other hand.

The concept of something holds of everything and contains nothing in itself, and so is it always. But every *conceptus communis* can be considered as a *conceptus superior*[,] a higher concept; nonetheless we name it thus particularly insofar as it contains other *conceptus communes* under[v] itself. E.g., man contains the male [under itself]. Thus there is a subordination of our concepts. A *conceptus communis* is called genus[w] in regard to the concepts that are contained under it, but *species*$_L$ in regard to the concepts under which[x] it is contained. Thus, e.g., man is genus in regard to males, etc.[;] but in regard to a rational being, man is again species. The limit of concepts subordinated to one another is the *conceptus summus*, i.e., that concept that is a genus but not a species. The *conceptus infimus*, on the other hand, will be a species that is[y] no longer a genus. A *conceptus singularis* has no *sphaera*, however. The *genus summum*, then, and the *individuum*, are the two limits of logically subordinated concepts. Every concept has an extension of those concepts to which it applies, the *sphaera notionis*, and the proposition is familiar: *quo major est sphaera conceptus, eo minus in illo est contentum, et vice versa.*[z] That *conceptus* whose *sphaera* is only a part of the *sphaera* of another *conceptus* is called a *conceptus angustior.*[a]

240

A *conceptus singularis* has no extension at all, and hence no *sphaera*.

§ 205

Cognitio a priori is cognition, and *probatio a priori* is proof[,] from above. *Cognitio a posteriori*, however, is cognition, and *probatio a posteriori* is proof[,] from below. These expressions are far more suitable than the expressions of the *autor*, from afterward and from beforehand[.] Proofs *a posteriori* are proofs from experience. On the other hand, proofs *a priori* are proofs from reason.

When one proves something from pure reason, no experience occurs. If one shows something from experience, however, then the proofs from pure reason are omitted; nonetheless, some proofs can be given *partim a*

[t] "Gegenverhältniß."
[u] "Capacitaet."
[v] Reading "unter sich" for "in sich."
[w] "das Genus, die Gattung."
[x] Reading "unter denen" for "in denen."
[y] Reading "ist" for "hat."
[z] The greater the sphere of a concept, the less is contained in it, and vice versa.
[a] narrower concept.

priori, partim a posteriori,[b] when experience is the origin of the proofs of reason. Reason and experience are connected, however, either through coordination or through subordination. With subordination I posit an experience as ground and infer from it by means of reason.

241 In the case of coordination, however, I first prove from reason completely alone, and then from experience completely alone, so that the proof from experience serves the proof from reason as a proof *ad evidentiam.*[c] In this way the *connubium rationis et experientiae*[d] is produced. Experience has no need at all of proof from reason, and on the contrary proof from reason does not require proof from experience. Neither is subordinated to the other[;] the two constitute not one proof, but rather two. For in the proofs there is merely a coordination. But one can be much deceived in this. If the proof from reason is a demonstration, or a complete proof, then proof from experience does not serve to strengthen it at all, but for illustration; and if the proof from experience is a complete proof then proof from reason does not help it at all either. Proofs from experience and from reason do not make a coordination, and still less, if they are already coordinated, a distinctness. Many insufficient proofs coordinated with one another never yield a demonstration, but instead they are merely *probationes* and cannot bring about any apodeictic certainty. Proofs from experience and from reason cannot possibly possess their evidence, then, unless they are subordinated[e] to one another. Where we find very many proofs of a thing we can also conclude that we will never attain apodeictic certainty; a single proof from sufficient[f] grounds is far better than 1000 insufficient proofs that are subordinated to one another, because through these one is not in a position to attain complete certainty. It frequently happens, to be sure, both in mathematics and in other sciences, that more than one sufficient proof of one and the same thing is given, but this happens in most cases to show one's art in demonstrating, not because several more proofs for the evidence of the thing are demanded. But even if several proofs coordinate with one another are put forth, these do not serve for greater distinctness and certainty; instead, the thing remains unsettled, as before.

§ 206

One can opine something without believing, namely, if one has more grounds for the cognition than against it. Here I hold something to be true
242 without its having an influence on our actions. To know something, how-

[b] in part a priori, in part a posteriori.
[c] for the sake of evidence.
[d] marriage of reason and experience.
[e] "Subordiniret und untergeordnet."
[f] Reading "zureichenden," with Ak, although MS has "unzureichenden" (KI, lxix).

ever, is nothing other than to cognize it with certainty. In the case of believing, on the other hand, there is a great degree of holding-to-be-true, so that one might bet on the fact that something is true.

Belief is either belief in things or in a person. One can immediately hold a thing to be true merely because one has grounds for the thing, and that is called believing a thing. On the contrary, however, one can also believe a thing immediately because a person puts it forward as true, though otherwise, in itself, one would not have held it to be true[;] and then one believes in a person. But this belief that relates to a certain kind of person is of two kinds. Sometimes we believe just anyone, be he who he will, merely because he says something, without attending to his person, or to his *caractère* or social position. E.g., when someone says it snowed in his area, or many ships arrived, then we simply believe this without investigating much; in these cases we do not judge about the credibility of the witnesses, then. But in certain matters, again, we do not believe just anyone, but rather we demand a particular credibility of him who puts something forward as true before we accept such a thing and hold it to be true. Belief toward a person, however, is either *moral* or *historical*. The former consists in trusting the honesty of the other, although he has not given any statement or[g] story. The other consists, however, in the holding-to-be-true of what the other asserts, merely because he has affirmed it. For historical belief there need not be any particular morality in the other, but instead we hold something to be true because he relates something that has happened. Moral belief, however, requires that one have a particular trust toward a person, trust that he is good and honest. If, e.g., in the absence of his master, a faithful servant faced with impending danger abandons his own things and saves his master's things, in the hope that he will reward him well for this service, then this is moral belief. Historical belief is required only in theology for holding something to be true on account of an assertion. But anyone at all, even the most wicked, can have this belief. Without fidelity and belief[h] no *republique*, no public affairs,[i] would be able to exist, and no *pacta* would be able to exist either. Fidelity is always required in regard to him who promises something, so that he keeps to what was promised[;] belief, however, is required in regard to him to whom something is promised, namely, so that he accepts as true that the other will keep his promise. The two must be combined with each other. For if everyone were faithful, but no one believed it, then no agreements, etc., would be able to occur, just as little as if all people believed, but no one were faithful. Belief is thus much needed in common life[;] if no one would give credit, then things would often look really very

243

[g] Reading "oder" for "der," with Hinske (KI, lxxiii).

[h] "Treue, und Glaube."

[i] "gemeines Wesen."

bad, for one cannot always pay cash immediately. It also indicates a very bad mode of thought if one never trusts anyone in anything, but instead one wants to see everything that is promised and pledged to him present and fulfilled. The Greeks were of this sort[;] they believed no one but instead wanted to have everything paid at once in cash. Thus did the saying arise: *Graeca fide mercari.*[j]

Theological belief trusts someone merely based on his assertion and holds this to be true. With historical belief the object of belief is always something that has happened, someone else's experience, but not a judgment of reason[;] hence, e.g., if someone were to say to me with confidence, Believe me, there are inhabitants on the moon, I will naturally be able to answer him, Have you been there? Have you seen them? I cannot believe what you have produced merely through reason. Hence judgments where someone else engages in reasoning[k] are not objects of historical belief. Theological belief is thus merely historical. Religious belief, however, is not merely historical but moral, since one holds something to be true on account of a promise, and on account of this undertakes certain actions in the hope of reaping good consequences sometime in the future. Through this belief one must hope that there will be a future world and future rewards and punishments of these actions. In all virtues there is natural, moral belief, since one believes that good actions will be rewarded for themselves, in spite of the fact that one did not see any particular promise for oneself. Such a virtuous person is to be compared with a *creditor*$_{\text{L}}$[;] he hopes to get a future good,[l] granted that he does not yet have a trace of it. Here we are not speaking of this moral belief, however, regardless of the fact that it is the one most worthy of consideration and 244 most excellent, since one attains credit and trusts not only to the present but to the future, since one does not will to be paid for everything in this world but instead to be paid for something in a future life.

Dogmata permit no ground of holding-to-be-true other than either one's own experience, or that one makes observations of reason, engages in reasoning, concerning it. The experience of others also occurs here. It follows, then, that it cannot be cognized through belief either.

The subject, however, who asserts something, and whom I am to believe, must have three attributes above all: 1st) *capacity* to obtain an experience. The subject must therefore have rational reflection. 2nd) It must have the capacity to preserve faithfully the experience obtained[,] or have a good memory. 3rd) It must be able to declare[m] the experience obtained, to expound it, and to acquaint everyone with it. The moral character of

[j] To trade with Greek trust [i.e., without credit].

[k] "vernünftelt."

[l] Reading "hofet das künftige Gute zu bekommen" for "hofet das künftige Gute."

[m] "declariren."

the subject, however, is that it also have the mental constitution[n] to represent faithfully, not otherwise, and to declare the experiences as they were obtained by him[;] and the pragmatic principle for believing the subject, finally, is that it have no grounds for expecting advantages if it asserts the opposite of the experience as it has obtained it.

What can we accept on the basis of belief? We cannot accept dogmatic cognitions that someone else asserts *on the basis of belief,*[o] then, but can only accept experience. We cannot accept universal cognitions of reason on faith, because with them one can very easily err. Assertions of *dogmata* are thus not testimony[;] instead, assertions of empirical cognitions, experiences, are *testimony*. A *witness* is thus actually one who asserts an experience. One who asserts universal judgments of reason as true is not a witness, and the best historical belief is not concerned with *dogmata* (insofar as they are divine *dogmata*), but rather only with experiences. But the conditions under which a subject who has obtained experiences is to be believed are grounded partly in the subject's own attributes, partly in its condition. The subject's attributes are partly *logical*, since it is capable of having, of obtaining, experiences, of knowing, and of asserting. They are partly *moral*, since the subject also has the will to assert the true, or to declare the experiences as they were. As for credibility in respect of condition, one must also divide the condition into 245

A. the logical condition and
B. the practical condition[.]

The most honest man can now and then get into situations where his honesty succumbs. E.g., when he is kept from saying the truth by threats or promises[;] hence one must pay heed to his condition too.

A large part of our cognitions arises through belief, and without belief we would have to do without very many historical cognitions. We would have no greater cognitions than those, at most, of the place where we live and of the time in which we live.

It is thus a great aid to historical cognitions to adopt the experiences of others[;] by this means we can experience what happened 1000 years before us and 1000 miles away from us.

If there were extensive deception of the senses, we would not be able to trust the experiences that others have obtained[;] if those who obtained the experiences had such a defective memory, furthermore, that they could not remember them and their imagination brought forth other images[;] if, finally, our language had such flaws that we could not express ourselves and communicate our experiences rightly; then communication of the experiences of others would be wholly impossible. But even if it is

[n] "die Gemüths-Verfaßung habe, seu ut animum habeat."
[o] "*auf glauben.*"

presupposed, as really is true, too, (1.) that we have the capacity to obtain experiences and (2.) that our memory is also faithful enough to maintain and to preserve the experiences we have had, without their being destroyed by imagination, (3.) that in our language we are also capable of making others acquainted with experiences obtained, then for the credibility of these persons or those, who have obtained experiences, it is still required that they be honorable and have an inclination toward truth. But this inclination toward truth often arises more from love of honor than from honorableness. Just because the whole of men's *commercium* would be removed if no one asserted the truth, since then no one would trust anyone else; because a lie is something harmful, too, and asserting the truth is the most certain path for avoiding disdain. E.g., geography, phys-
246 ics, history, and other sciences always presuppose the experiences of others. In common life one must not believe the common man in regard to such cognitions as do not affect the interest of all men, but are rather indifferent. For in such cases it is all the same to him whether something is thus or otherwise, since he does not have insight into the importance of the cognition. The learned man, however, has far more credibility in this kind of cognition, for to him even the slightest matters in all cognition will be important[;] he will also be more inclined, from love of honor, to assert everything precisely as he has experienced it, since otherwise he would lose his credit.

As for other things that concern the credibility and honorability of witnesses who make assertions about experiences they have obtained, everyone is taken to be honorable and upright until the opposite has been proved, namely, that he deviates from the truth. According to the well-known rule of fairness:

quilibet praesumitur bonus,
donec probetur contrarium.[p]

To attain proper cognition of the truth, however, it is required in any case that one also investigate whether someone speaks the truth or lies.

§ 208

An *eyewitness* [q] is one who has obtained experiences himself, or has seen something, hence is fully convinced of a cognition.[r]

A *hearsay witness*,[s] however, is one who has heard, i.e., received from an eyewitness, or who is a witness to the testimony of the eyewitness. Due to

[p] Everyone is presumed good until the opposite is proved (reading "praesumitur" for "prosumitur").

[q] "*Augen Zeuge.*"

[r] "Kenntniß."

[s] "*Hören Zeuge.*"

one of the greatest human errors, when they are hearsay witnesses of a matter, they are inclined to want to be eyewitnesses. They tell a thing with as much certainty and confidence as if they had seen it themselves, although they have only received it from others. But what kind of distinction is there between the credibility of eyewitnesses and of hearsay witnesses? The hearsay witness has, as it were, only half as much credibility as the eyewitness, for with him I have to investigate first his own credibility, and then also that of the one who saw the thing.

In a series of witnesses who are subordinated to one another credibility decreases. In a series of witnesses coordinated with one another, however, the truthfulness and credibility of the testimony always increases. E.g., if someone describes the history of a learned man or of a king, but his successor does not hand down the history itself but instead clothes it in his style, and this happens thus again and again *continuo*, then its credibility becomes less and less[;] but if, at the same time, many assert one and the same thing, then its credibility is all the greater, particularly if these are honor-loving people. 247

§ 210

A series of witnesses coordinated with one another is called a public report *sive rumor.*[t] A series of assertions subordinated to one another is called an *oral tradition.*[u] If, however, in a series of witnesses, coordinated as well as subordinated, the first originator, i.e., the eyewitness, is unknown, then this is merely a common saying, *sive rumor sine capite.*[v] And such an assertion is to be trusted little or not at all[;] little belief is to be accorded to it. There are certain assertions, however, regarding which one need not investigate the credibility of the witness at all, but which one rejects before any investigation.

This seems at first glance to be very obstinate, but it is also certain. Cognitions that are completely and utterly and obviously false do not need any investigation at all and in fact deserve complete disdain. Of this sort are the assertions about the divining rod[;] these deserve no investigation, one can reject them at once[;] they deserve no refutation, for they are false in and of themselves.

There are grounds for rejecting testimony, then, that are not historical or derived from the character of the witness, but rather are rational and lie in the character of the thing itself. But one has to be very cautious in this and not just reject a cognition at once, until it is apparent that the thing is obviously false. Much seems at first glance to be completely false, but on

[t] or general opinion.
[u] "mündliche Üeberlieferung, *traditio oralis.*"
[v] or general opinion without a source.

closer investigation one finds its opposite. Empirical judgments about the possibility or impossibility of an *eventus* still do not justify us in rejecting 248 the cognition at once, without investigating the credibility of the witness. Someone testifies to something that is quite improbable and contradicts the ordinary occurrences in nature[;] then he cannot demand that we ought to believe him at once, merely on his assertion; instead, if he wants to have this, he must give proof. Thus, e.g., when Pontoppidans[36] writes that in certain seas there is an extremely large fish which looks like a piece of land and which he calls an octopus,[w] then because such an animal has never been seen, he must prove this. But if someone testifies to something that quite obviously agrees with experience and reason, then one believes him without proof. If, however, the credibility of the witness simply cannot be shaken, but the story or the testimony that he gives contradicts reason and experience in the highest degree, then the question arises, do we have to give approval to his assertion in this case and, as it were, deny our reason, or not?

Answer: The best thing is neither to reject the cognition nor to accept it as true but instead to postpone one's approval until one has more grounds for or against it. Now and then there are persons who assert something, whose credibility one cannot in the least doubt, concerning whom one also cannot accept that they have the intention[x] to deceive others, but whom one still need not trust. The mistake in their assertion, however, lies in most cases only in the experience that was not obtained, or in a *vitium*[y] of memory, which does not preserve the experience faithfully enough. Thus it also happens that people have put forth something very probable and have maintained that it is true, but when someone asks them whether they could swear to their assertion they doubt and have to be quite evasive. Then they commonly say that they could perhaps have forgotten something since that time. In any case, imagination can also reproduce for them images other than the experiences which they had.

§ 213

Unbelief[z] can be taken in the moral sense, when one lacks all trust in the moral character of a witness. He who has such moral unbelief holds all 249 men to be liars, he trusts no man, he believes no promises, but instead always doubts the uprightness of other people. Moral unbelief is opposed to the moral foundation of all human society. Without fidelity and belief, as indicated above, no state can exist. It is commonly to be found, how-

[w] "Crac."
[x] "den animum, oder Vorsatz."
[y] error.
[z] Reading "Unglaube" for "Glaube."

ever, among those who themselves possess a moral depravity, so that one cannot accord them much belief.

These people pass judgment on other people according to themselves. Moral belief, on the other hand, trusts everyone, even without any promises. The belief in a future world is of this kind. Incredulity,[a] however, is distinct from unbelief.[b] It consists in the fact that one does not want to give approval to the logical grounds of testimony. This incredulity can also be called logical unbelief,[c] and thus it is quite different from moral unbelief.

This logical unbelief does not lie in a certain lack of heart, but instead of cognition, in a certain lack of experience, since one is not acquainted with someone else's grounds and does not have insight into their importance. It is found principally among those who do not have a proper familiarity with literature[;] to them, everything seems paradoxical and ridiculous, although it is true and worthy of belief. One has to be very cautious about having to do with such people, because one is simply not in a position to convince them.

§ 214

Seeing belief[d] is belief that is combined with examination of the witness and rests on this. Blind belief, however, is belief that accepts testimony without examination or investigation of its credibility. The former leads to truth, but the other is the path toward error, thus harmful, but the former is useful.

§ 215

The unification of all three of these sources of cognition rests on the fact that they have as a ground not one proof, but rather many. Belief always requires a *connubium*[e] of other sources of cognitions, namely, of reason and of experience, so that it will be evident and convincing. When a source of cognition is not able to give a sufficient proof of the truth of a thing, then one has to make use of the remaining *fontes cognitionis*,[f] and from this try to produce greater evidence. If a source of cognition is sufficient to give a complete proof of a thing, however, then one does not need the others. If something can be shown completely and evidently

250

[a] "Ungläubigkeit."
[b] "Unglaube."
[c] Reading "Unglaube" for "Glaube."
[d] "Ein sehender Glaube."
[e] marriage.
[f] sources of cognition.

through reason, then one does not need experience in order to make the proof still more complete. If experience is sufficient to give a complete proof of a thing, then one need not consult reason.

THE SEVENTH SECTION

Of practical learned cognition

§ 216–248

If a cognition contains in itself moving grounds for actions, then it is practical. All practical cognition is either cognition of ends or of means[;] the latter must be distinguished from the former. Practical geometry teaches no ends, no moving grounds for actions, but only means for attaining certain ends. It shows the conditions under which an end can be attained with respect to measurement.

Every doctrine of skill is a practical cognition of means. Every doctrine of morality is a practical cognition of ends, however, as is also the doctrine of prudence. Our author speaks in general in this whole section of cognition, how it relates to free will. In logic, however, the relation of cognition to will is simply not considered; instead, this belongs to morals. The relation of free will [to cognition] is not an *objectum domesticum* of logic. The practical science of skill gives us no moving grounds for actions. For any science that shows only means and not ends contains no moving grounds[.] All moving grounds, namely, must be derived from the end. A cognition is called practical insofar as it is contradistin-251 guished from theoretical cognition, or from mere contemplation and speculation. A cognition is practical, however, *vel explicite vel implicite*. *Explicite*, if it shows the rules themselves for actions. *Implicite*, if it presents the moving grounds or represents truths from which certain practical rules for actions can be derived. E.g., the proposition, Thou shalt not lie, thou shalt be faithful and honest, is practical *explicite*. But the proposition, There is a God, consequently one is bound to arrange his actions in such a way as accords with the holy will of this divine being, is practical *implicite*. In metaphysics there are in most cases pure *speculationes*, not practical but rather theoretical, which have no influence on the free will, then. Such *speculationes* are neither harmful nor useful. For they contain no moving grounds of action. Many of the subtleties and errors devised by men are nothing other than pure speculations[;] hence we pass over this section, because it is placed here inappropriately and belongs more to morals than to logic, and no advantage is to be hoped for from the treatment of it in logic, for this is occupied likewise with speculative cognitions.

THE EIGHTH SECTION

Of learned concepts

§ 249

Not every representation is a *concept*. A representation through the senses is, e.g., a *sensation* A representation through the understanding is an *appearance*. A representation through reason is a *concept*. The senses sense, the understanding coordinates, but reason subordinates. Universal representations are concepts, and concepts are universal representations. Sensations, on the other hand, are only singular representations, appearances likewise, but concepts are universal and arise through reason. As long as I cannot subordinate a thing to a universal representation I do not yet have a concept of it. On many points we have learned cognition, but no proper concept.

§ 250

252

In the case of learned and unlearned concepts there is really no specific difference to be noted. The distinction between common and learned concepts is better. A concept is just not a simple representation. The concept that results from many representations can be very rich, pregnant, beautiful, and learned, and lively. A concept that possesses much liveliness is an aesthetic concept. An aesthetic concept arises through a multitude and a combination of coordinated representations. A proper concept of reason arises, however, through a multitude of subordinated representations. The matter of an aesthetic concept consists of its relation to our taste and feeling; its form, however, consists in a multitude of representations coordinated with one another to produce the proper liveliness. Poets and orators especially make use of such aesthetic concepts[;] e.g., when they want to describe summer or spring, they do not show its causes, but instead they picture only the various changes that take place at these times of year in the fields, among the animals, in the forests, in the air, in the country, and in the city. There are many things of which we have sensations, to be sure, but no concepts. We meet with concepts only in certain cases, where reason subordinates representations to one another.

§ 254

This division in this §*phus* is not in any way correct. We do not attain any representations through abstraction, rather, representations must be given prior to abstraction, and through it they only become clear. All our cognitions are either given, or made and invented. *Omnes conceptus sunt vel dati, vel facti, sive ficti.*[g]

Many cognitions are given to us through experience, and the matter of all cognitions arises through sensation, through the senses. But often one fabricates cognitions through imagination[;] we form our own world for ourselves, as it were.

Conceptus dati sunt porro dati a priori through pure reason, *vel dati a posteriori*[h] through experiences. All *conceptus a posteriori dati*[i] are abstracted *ab experientia.*[j] Others, however, do not arise through experiences but

253 instead are drawn from the laws of pure reason[,] e.g., the concept of the possible and the impossible. A *conceptus abstractus*, however, means in particular a representation that is abstracted from experience, and not a representation abstracted from reason.

Conceptus dati are thus *vel abstracti* from experience, *vel rationales.*[k]

The concept of every species and genera of things that strikes our senses is a *conceptus abstractus*[,] e.g., of horses[,] sheep, etc.: if I say *a horse*, then this is a concept given *per experientiam.*[l] But the universality of the representations arose through abstraction. The universality of all concepts through experience arises through abstraction from individual concepts and images[;] the representation itself arises through experience, however. Here the matter itself lies in experience, but the form of universality lies in abstraction. Through abstraction not the least cognition arises; rather, universality arises through abstraction. The first origin of our cognition is thus experience. Concepts of experience are thus ones that were given through experience and became universal through abstraction. Therefore all concepts of experience are abstracted concepts. Pure concepts of reason, however, are not given through experience by means of abstraction, but instead through pure reason, and in this way they differ from concepts of experience. The concept of right and wrong is in this way a pure concept of reason. These concepts remain constant even granted that no experience occurs. If the world were ever so godless, everyone would still have the concept of right and wrong. Concepts of experience simply do not exist without experience, however. If there were no horse, then no one would be in a position to fabricate a horse, either.

Fabricated concepts are ones that were made, insofar as they are not given. These fabricated concepts are called *idea prototypa.* Abstracted concepts, however, are *ektypa.* The former are original. The latter con-

[g] *All concepts are either given or they are made (or fabricated).*

[h] Concepts that are given, furthermore, are given a priori [through pure reason] or given a posteriori.

[i] concepts that are given a posteriori.

[j] from experience.

[k] Concepts that are given [are thus] either abstracted [from experience] or are rational

[l] through experience.

cepts are copies, however. He who made the beautiful fables made nothing but *prototypa*, for such a thing simply does not exist.

The stoical philosopher, on the other hand, is such a *prototypon*, ἀρχέτυπον.[m] All mathematicians' definitions are nothing but *ideas prototypas*. E.g., the concept of the octagon is not borrowed from experience; 254 instead, the mathematician thinks such a thing through his pure reason. He represents a figure that has 8 lines and is enclosed by them.

Every inventor must fabricate,[n] and all inventions are fabrications, although not all fabrications are inventions. Fabrication produces archetypes[,] abstraction produces imitations through arbitrary combination or through arbitrary separation.

By leaving out and by adding in one makes *fictiones*. All fabrication, furthermore, is arbitrary or non-arbitrary.[o] Fabrication that is non-arbitrary is a chimera.

Hypochondriacs are very much subject to non-arbitrary fabrication. This is now properly the place to speak of arbitrary fabrications, which are combined with consciousness and the will to have it. If man can subject everything to choice, then he is the most perfect of all beings, and hence arbitrary fabrication will often be very useful to him, too.

All concepts that do not arise through attention, through the senses, which also are not given but instead are arbitrarily fabricated, are pure concepts of reason. Of this kind are the concepts of the necessary and the contingent, of causes and effects. Concepts that arise through the senses, however, and are abstracted from experiences, are concepts of experience.

§ 255

We must principally endeavor to distinguish concepts of experience from concepts of reason. What does not strike the senses has nothing to do with experience. From the mixing of concepts of experience and of reason arises the *vitium subreptionis*,[p] which is spoken of in metaphysics. Right and wrong are not concepts of experience but of pure concepts of reason, but they would be concepts of experience if the wrong were what is not customary, what men do not do.

But this is never so. Much is right, which no one does, and wrong, which everyone does. In the case of the concept of cause and effect, many commit the *vitium subreptionis*, in that they want to derive it from experience, although it is a pure concept of reason. Concepts of experience all 255 relate to space and time. Concepts of reason, however, are the foundation of cause and effect. We have no experience of possibility and impossibility,

[m] archetype.

[n] "dichten, und fingiren."

[o] "Unwillkührlich."

[p] error of subreption.

but only of actuality. We also have experiences only of affirmative, but not of negative representations[;] what[q] cannot be, cannot become sensation. E.g., when we have read a book, we cannot experience immediately that this or that passage is not contained in it, but instead we must find this out by inferences.

§ 257

Here we really have nothing to observe[;] metaphysics, namely, speaks of it more extensively. The only question still remaining for us is: how, out of many experiences, does one make concepts? This is not as easy as it perhaps seems at first glance. One can have obtained many experiences, yet not have abstracted from them any concepts of experience.

To obtain concepts of experience involves instruction. Anyone who has good *organa sensoria* can experience, but to abstract from individual experiences universal concepts of experience, under which the *experientiae singulae* may be subordinated, requires a skill in seeing what is common to many experiences.

§ 259

One cannot make any money by stealing it from someone, and in the same way one cannot make any concepts by abstraction. Through abstraction our representations are only made universal, as already indicated above. If we have no representations of things, then no abstraction will be able to make concepts for us. In logical abstraction we compare many concepts with one another, we see what these contain in common, or wherein they agree, and through this our representations become concepts.

If many concepts have a mark in common, then this mark is contained in them. The things are contained under the concept that is abstracted from them. This concept is a common ground for cognition. It is contained in all things, and all things from which it is abstracted are under it.

256 A concept can be abstracted from experience and also from the laws of pure reason. The latter are not abstracted from things but instead are called rational.

By abstracted concepts we always understand concepts of experience, however.

§ 260

First we wish to speak of fabricated concepts. Every concept that is not given through experience, i.e., the sensation of things, nor through rea-

[q] Reading "was" for "das."

son, is a fabricated concept. This concept, however, is either made so that in respect of matter an experience does provide its ground after all, or so that the matter is not taken from experience at all, but instead both the matter and the form as well are fabricated. But the latter is impossible. All fabrication arises, however, by means of arbitrary combination or by means of separation. By means of combination, when I join together what is never combined in experience or unified with one another. Through separation, however, when I separate from a thing what in experience is never separated from it. With fabricated concepts, arbitrary combination and arbitrary separation are in most cases combined. The novelist claims for his hero all the praiseworthy attributes he still lacks, in order to present a really perfect person, and if he only observes a few flaws in him, then he abstracts from them at once, he abstracts all of them from the hero[;] or if this is often difficult, or simply will not work, then he at least strives to make the hero praiseworthy even in his misdeeds, and thus to be able so to paint his failings, or to give them such an appearance, that they lose the ugliness that is peculiar to them and that strikes the eye, or that they even seem to be so many virtues.

The Arcadian shepherds' life, which was so famous among the ancients and was so much painted by the poets of the time, is of this kind[;] it is one of the most pleasant representations that one can ever have or can represent. Everything beautiful, gracious, and exciting is thought in it[;] the greatest abundance in everything that can stimulate is combined with it[;] on the other hand, all adversities, displeasures, all lack, which after all has often and commonly occurred and does occur in the shepherds' life, is abstracted and removed, so that by this means a fully perfect ideal of bliss can be sketched out. 257

All *conceptus* are either

A. *conceptus singulares* or
B. *conceptus communes.*

In the former I think only one thing, but through the latter I go further, namely, I think that which is common to many things.

Thus the former concepts consider something individual. Thus, e.g., Rome, Bucephalus, etc. This is a *conceptus singularis*. The latter, on the other hand, are concerned with a *complexus* of many individual things, thus, e.g., a city, a 4-footed animal, etc. A man, that is a *conceptus communis*. The representations of immediate experience are all *conceptus singulares*, for they represent individual things. Mediate concepts of experience, however, which are abstracted from many experiences, are *conceptus communes*; so, too, are all our concepts of reason. The concept of God, to be sure, only belongs to one being, to which alone it is to be ascribed, but without settling whether only one God is possible or more, one can make out several concepts of God. But afterwards a proof must be added that the concept of God is a *conceptus singularis*. Every *conceptus communis* contains under itself all concepts to which it is common. E.g., the concept of mortality contains under itself all men and animals, because it is common to them. But such a *conceptus communis* is contained in all the things that it contains under itself. The *conceptus communis* is the ground of cognition, or the mark of all those things that are under it.[r] But it is also at the same time a partial concept of those things that it contains under itself. For it is abstracted from those things that are contained under it.

Marks are always coordinated with a thing and as parts constitute together the whole concept of a thing[;] but the thing is subordinated to the marks that are given of it and is contained in them. The *sphaera notionis*[s] means actually the multitude of things that are comprehended under a concept as a *nota communis*.[t] Through a *nota communis* I can think many things, then. The *sphaera conceptus communis*[u] can be large, however, or can be small: the very same concept under which many things are comprehended is contained in the things that are under it.

258

The larger the *sphaera* that a *conceptus communis* has, and the more it contains under itself, the less is contained in it. A concept that contains much under itself arises through the fact that what is common to many things is abstracted. It is thus a mark of a mark; thus it has much under itself, to be sure, but little in itself. For a mark of a mark contains still much less than the first mark, of which it is a mark. If I think something of many things, then that which I think of these many things is very little. But the less a concept contains under itself, the more it contains in itself, and an individual concept contains the most in itself, for here I cognize only one object, to be sure, but very much concerning it. The more I think in my concept, the less I think through the concept. A *conceptus communis* arises only through the fact that what is common to many objects is considered. That which varies in them is left aside, however, and not considered. This *conceptus* contains little in itself, to be sure, but it is a concept of a large *sphaera*[.] E.g. The concept of body has a large *sphaera* but contains little in itself. A concept can never come to be of a larger extension, so that it contains more under itself, except by containing less in itself. This consideration teaches us in particular to evaluate the worth of our cognition. Through reason we cognize nothing but *notae communes*, hence little of many things[;] much is contained under, but little in, cognitions of reason. By means of experience we cognize few objects, but very much concerning them. Concepts of experience have[v] *minores sphaerae*[,][w]

[r] Reading "ihm" for "ihnen."
[s] sphere of a notion.
[t] common mark.
[u] sphere of a common concept.
[v] Reading "haben" for "sind."
[w] smaller spheres.

but they contain much in themselves. A mark of a mark always has a larger *sphaera* than a closer mark, or always contains under itself more than does a *nota proprior*.[x] The *nota* of a thing in general is the *nota remotissima*[y] of a thing. Later comes the *nota remotior*, *remota*,[z] and only then come the closer marks. The *nota remotissima* contains the most under itself, however. If several concepts stand in such a relation that one is contained under the other, then the one that contains the other under itself is a *conceptus superior*,[a] and the concept that is contained under the other is called the *conceptus inferior*.[b] One and the same concept can, however, according to various relations, be now a *conceptus superior*, now a *conceptus inferior*, accordingly, namely, as it contains other concepts under itself or stands under another. 259
E.g., I say men. Then I compare man with non-rational animals and say *animals*[;] then the concept of man contains very much under itself. E.g., white men, Negroes, and various nations[,] etc., and in this respect it is thus a *conceptus superior*. But it is a *conceptus inferior* insofar as it is contained under the concept animal. The *conceptus nullo inferior*[c] is, however, the *conceptus summus*.[d] This includes the concept of a thing, or of a possible thing. This *conceptus summus* is *superior*$_{\mathrm{L}}$ not merely *relative*$_{\mathrm{L}}$ but *absolute*$_{\mathrm{L}}$. The *conceptus infimus*,[e] however, is that which is *inferior*$_{\mathrm{L}}$ not just *relative*$_{\mathrm{L}}$ but instead *absolute*$_{\mathrm{L}}$. *Conceptus singulares* are *infimi*. *Conceptus universales*, however, are *summi*, and between these *conceptus infimi* and *summi* there is a *longa series* of *conceptus inferiores* and *superiores*.

§ 261

Every mark is a ground of cognition of things[;] through reason we cognize all things only by means of marks. The further a concept is removed from the immediate mark of a thing, the higher it is and the more it contains under itself. The very same *conceptus communis*, in respect of the *conceptus communes* that it contains under itself, is called, relatively, a *genus*$_{\mathrm{L}}$[;] but in respect of the *conceptus communes* under which it is contained it is called, relatively, a *species*$_{\mathrm{L}}$. E.g., learned[f] persons are a genus in respect of the particular kinds of learned persons, philosophers, doctors, etc., jurists. They are a species in respect of the concept of a man in general, however. A *conceptus communis* is called *species*$_{\mathrm{L}}$ because it (1.) is contained under another

[x] a mark that is closer, more specific.
[y] most remote mark.
[z] a mark that is more remote, [and one that is] remote.
[a] higher concept.
[b] lower concept.
[c] concept that is lower than none.
[d] highest concept.
[e] lowest concept.
[f] Reading "gelährte" for "ungelährte."

communis superior conceptus, but also (2.) because it is itself a *conceptus communis*. For a *conceptus singularis*, even if it is immediately subordinated to another *conceptus communis*, is not a *species*$_L$. E.g., if, under the learned, I think of Herr von Wolff, this is no longer a *species*$_L$, but instead an *individuum*. Every *species*$_L$ is *infima* insofar as under it are contained no *conceptus communes*, but merely *singulares*. *Species infima est, quae tantum individua sub se continet.*[g] Otherwise one can always think a *species*$_L$ in turn as a *genus*$_L$, and subordinate other concepts to it. E.g., a philosopher is a species of learned 260 man. But this becomes a *genus*$_L$ if I think under it in particular the Wolffians, the Crusians, etc. All *genera*$_L$ that are contained under higher *genera*$_L$ are, in respect of these *genera*$_L$, *species*$_L$, to be regarded as *species*$_L$. The *genus summum*, however, is what can no longer be a *species*$_L$. The *species infima*, however, can no longer be a *genus*$_L$. In the second case it is subordinated to another, but in the first case others are subordinated to it.[h] Just for this reason the very same concept can, in different respects, be *genus*$_L$ as well as *species*$_L$. The subordination of concepts, however, can occur both *logice* and *realiter*. Logical subordination consists in the fact that I take that which is common to many concepts and thereby form for myself a universal concept, under which I can subordinate the individual representations. In this way I make for myself various *genera*$_L$ and I subordinate the *species*$_L$ and *individua* to them. Real subordination, however, consists in the fact that I actually combine concepts with one another, so that not only is one contained under the other, but instead they also cohere[i] as causes and effects.

Now we come to the *sphaera notionum*.[j] The more abstracted a concept is, the larger is its *sphaera*. The larger the *sphaera notionis*[k] is, the more the things of which I can judge, but the less I can cognize.[l] The senses cognize much with respect to a few things, but reason cognizes little in many things. Reason and experience must thus be united as much as possible, in order to be able to replace what is lacking in the one ground of cognition through the other ground of cognition.

§ 262

The concept that contains another under itself is a *conceptus latior*,[m] but the concept that is contained under another is a *conceptus angustior*.[n] Thus the

[g] A species is lowest which contains only individuals under itself.

[h] Reading "im zweiten Fall . . . . im ersteren Fall" for "im ersteren Fall . . . . im zweiten Fall."

[i] "cohaeriren."

[j] sphere of notions.

[k] sphere of a notion.

[l] Reading "desto weniger" for "von desto weniger Dingen."

[m] broader concept.

[n] narrower concept.

concept of man is a *conceptus latior* in respect to the learned. But the concept of the jurist, etc., philosophers, [is] a *conceptus angustior* in regard to the concept of the learned [man]. The first concept is thus the one that contains under itself only a single thing, and through which I can cognize only a single thing.

The *conceptus latissimus*,[o] however, is the one through which I can cognize the most things, or to which the most things are subordinated, and are contained under it.

261

A convertible concept[p] is one that contains just as much under and in itself as another concept[,] which can thus suitably be exchanged with it, and of which one can take the place of the other completely. A universal or common[q] concept is one under which many are contained. Every *conceptus communis* is thus at the same time a *conceptus universalis* in respect of those concepts that are contained under it.

A concept can be contained under another concept only in part. *Quare conceptus inferior semper est particularis, ratione conceptus superioris, quare conceptus superior vero semper est universalis, ratione conceptus inferioris*[.][r] Abstract cognition, namely, is the most universal cognition in respect of the concepts that are contained under it, that is, [it is] the cognition which contains *conceptus summi* under itself and descends to all *conceptus inferiores* that are contained under it. Metaphysics is the science that contains under itself such *conceptus summi*[;] hence it cognizes the most universal character of things.

§ 263

We can properly pass over this *paragraphus*, for here the talk is not of inferences, but instead only of learned concepts. The place to speak of it will be in the doctrine of inferences, *quare hoc non tractare volumus anticipando.*[s]

§ 264

Here the author speaks of the value of abstract cognition. This is very great, but it is not very necessary to bring this up and to go through it, because the largest part of all our cognitions rests on this.

[o] broadest concept.

[p] "Wechsel-Begrif."

[q] "gemeinschaftlicher."

[r] Hence the lower concept is always particular in relation to the higher concept, and the higher concept is always universal in relation to the lower concept.

[s] Hence we do not want to treat it here by way of anticipation.

§ 266

The author now speaks of concepts through arbitrary combination. All *conceptus ficti*, however, are made *vel per combinationem, vel per separationem arbitrariam.*[t] It is to be noted in general, however, that in all our fabricated concepts only the form is and will be fabricated.

The matter will never be able to be fabricated[;] he who has no sight 262 cannot fabricate any color, he who has no hearing cannot fabricate any sound. But all form is fabricated in accordance with the relation of space and of time and in accordance with the universal nature of our reason. All concepts are either empirical or transcendental concepts of reason. The latter concepts include the representations of the possible and the impossible, of the necessary and the accidental[;] these latter do not spring in any way from experience and are not abstracted from it, but instead they are produced through pure reason. Concepts are thus either given or made. They are given either through experience or through pure reason. They are made if they are not given either through experience or through pure reason. These concepts that are made, however, are always fabricated only as to form. Through abstraction I think of a part of the concept, but by means of separation I negate something from my concept. Abstraction,[u] separation[v] are thus distinct from one another. Through separation only fabricated concepts arise, but never through abstraction. A *fictio separando facta*[w] involves a removal[x] of what otherwise is usually combined with a concept. We fabricate much *separando*[y][;] all novels arise by means of this kind of fiction. Also, we must fabricate the idea of God in just this way, in that one separates from it all imperfection and thus attains the concept of the highest being. Through combination, however, we fabricate something when we put much together that in experience is never connected. In this way, as already indicated above, novels arise. The stoic wise man arises by means of this fiction[;] one gives to him more power than is proper to man. Fabrications are either *fictiones aestheticae* or *heuristicae*. The former contribute to pleasure, the latter to fabricating.

Mathematics and physics have many *fictiones heuristicae*[;] hypotheses are of this kind[;] *fictiones* occur either as to quality or as to quantity, furthermore. *Fictiones aestheticae* as to quality are the best[;] those according to quantity are not the best, however. For these do not require great art, except merely in description, in order to acquire a lively concept thereby. If only I have an object, then I can soon attribute to it a colossal

[t] either through arbitrary combination or through arbitrary separation.

[u] "Absonderung, Abstraction."

[v] "Trennung, Separation."

[w] fiction made by separating.

[x] "eine remotion."

[y] by separating.

magnitude, which can cause wonder, of course, but no excitement. But there are also nonarbitrary fabrications, or nonarbitrary fabricated concepts of reason. E.g., of spirits. These concepts did not arise and were not given by means of experience, nor by means of reason. One comes to these nonarbitrary concepts by means of an unnoticed fabrication, and by means of secret inferences of which one often is not aware. 263

§ 268

The distinctness of a concept is a property of a logical perfection. The act of making distinct[z] occurs through analysis. But if I make a concept distinct which, e.g., contains many marks, then I will have to try to avoid tautology among these marks[;] thus will I promote precision of marks. I.e., I will restrict the quantity of marks, without however being detrimental to quality. The totality of the distinct representation of a thing is also sought, and often I need this totality very much. In all distinctness of concepts I can be satisfied with partial distinctness,[a] but if my marks are sufficient for the whole concept of the thing, then I have a totality. But if precision is also sought, then I have a complete, precise concept of a thing, and that is a definition. Definition, and the action of our soul therein, can be perfectly compared with the reduction of fractions *ad minimos terminos* in arithmetic, e.g., $4/2\ 3/6\ 2/3\ 1/3 = 4/12$.[37] And this is also the purpose of defining. We want to have (1.) a *distinct*[,] (2.) a *complete*[,] and then (3.) a *precise* concept of a thing. In order to find out whether a definition is correct, then, we always ask (1.) whether the definition offered, as a proposition, is true[;] and thus we can use many *definitiones* as true propositions, in which many otherwise imperceptible marks occur. False *definitiones* can sometimes even serve as true propositions, indeed, one can often do without the complete definition due to the usefulness of such a true proposition. Granted that it does not fulfill what it promised, it can nonetheless be useful[;] it can be of use, although it does not achieve its intention.

(2.) Let one ask whether the definition, as a concept, is distinct, whether I can cognize it clearly. For any distinctness, however, it is required that a mark be a clear ground of cognition of the thing. All tautology in definitions is thus a lack of distinctness, and such a definition is not only not a definition, but is also not a distinct concept. All empty propositions are tautological. E.g., the soul in an animal is a dominant monad[;] this proposition is not empty, but in it a *comparative*$_L$ *obscurum* is explained *per aeque obscurum*.[b] But here the uselessness of this proposition can still be removed. With a tautology, however, this does not hold. 264

z "Die Deutlichmachung."

a "mit der Partialitaet."

b a comparatively obscure thing [is explained] by an equally obscure thing.

(3.) Let one ask whether the definition, as a distinct concept, is exhaustive, i.e., distinct. *Nam definire est fines conceptus alicuius ponere.*[c] I.e., the definition is a determination of everything that just belongs to the thing. (4.) The question arises whether this distinct and exhaustive concept is also precise,[d] namely, [so] that the marks of the definition do not flow from one another, and are not subordinate to one other, but instead are coordinate with one another. The marks must stand with one another as *compartes* in a whole, but not next to one another as terms of a series. If everything without which a concept can nonetheless remain distinct and complete were omitted, then such a concept is called *conceptus rem adaequans.*[e] The *completudo*, then, and the precision of a concept together constitute its adequation. An *adaequatum*, then, allows no *comparativum*. Wolff says: A concept is adequate when the marks of a concept, and again the marks of the marks, are distinct. *Definitio autem adaequat conceptum.*[f]

This includes precision[;] the latter consists in the fact, namely, that not even one mark in the definition is already contained in the other, or what is the same thing, that no repetition should occur therein. E.g., if I were to say, A body is *extended, divisible matter*, this would be to act contrary to precision, for the mark of divisibility already lies within the mark of matter, and consequently the mark of divisibility is merely repeated; for it lies already in the one mark of body, namely, in the concept of *matter*. In short, the most correct and the best definition of precision is this:

Praecisio is a *reductio* of a definition *ad minimos terminos.*[g] Just as in *arithmetica*, e.g., one usually brings fractions *ad minimos terminos*. Definition, accordingly, is nothing but the relation of equality of two concepts, namely, so that one can always be substituted for the other.

265 Now let us ask, however, if the concept in the definition is completely equal to the concept of the *definitum*. And here we must note: *materialiter id est quoad objectum*[;][h] if these concepts are in fact always equal, simply so far as their form is concerned, then they are not and must not be completely equal to one another. So far as the matter is concerned, I always think the same object, not always in the same way, however, but instead in a different way[;] namely, I represent distinctly in the definition what I previously represented *confuse*$_{L}$ in the *definitum*[;] and every definition must accordingly be distinct. For distinctness in general, however, and hence also in the case of the distinctness of definitions, marks are required[;] but *in the first place*, these marks have to be clear concepts[;] they also have to be clearer than the concept of the *definitum*, and from

[c] For to define is to posit the limits of a certain concept.
[d] "abgemeßen, das ist Praecis."
[e] a concept adequate to the thing.
[f] A definition, moreover, is adequate to the concept.
[g] to minimal terms.
[h] *materially, that is, as to the object.*

this flows the canon: *ne definiatur obscurum per aeque*[i] *obscurum.*[j] E.g., if, to someone who does not know what a *monas*[k] is, I wished to say that the soul is a thinking monad in the body, this would be offending against this rule. *Secondly*, these marks must also be *clear grounds of cognition*. For as a ground of cognition it is supposed to be distinct from the consequence[;] consequently it must be thought differently, and far more clearly, than in the *definitum*[;] for what merely says the same thing names no ground for me. And from this flows then this rule: *ne notae in definitione sint tautologicae.*[l] This is otherwise called defining *per circulum*. The *circulus vitiosus in definiendo*[m] is either *implicitus* (hidden) or *explicitus*, namely, when the marks are one and the same even in their expression. An example of the first is, e.g., the definition, A ground is that *by reason of which* something is cognized[;][n] here the *by reason of which*[o] means just the same as *quâ ratione*,[p] and consequently a *tautologia* is hidden[q] herein[;] and therefore the form in the definition must always be different from the form of the *definitum*. This was the first *requisitum* of a good definition, then, namely, that it be distinct.

The 2nd *requisitum* of a proper definition is now this, that it be adequate, or that it take in neither more nor less than is contained in the *definitum*. One can also properly call it *completudo* or *exhaustiveness* and *sufficiency*. Now the *completudo* of a definition includes that (1.) the marks are sufficient for distinction of the *definitum*[r] from all other things. (2.) [that they are] also sufficient for cognition of its identity with other things[;] or in short, that the definition be neither *latior*[s] nor *angustior*[.][t] But what does that mean? In the comparison of the thing with others, every ground of cognition is to be used in two ways. 266

1st thereby to distinguish its identity or
2nd its diversity from all others.

Thus definition is complete if the marks are sufficient to cognize thereby

1. the difference of the concept from all others that do not stand under the universal concept of it, and
2. the sameness of it with other concepts that stand together under a universal

[i] Ak, "aequum"; MS, "aeque" (KI, lxix).
[j] The obscure is not to be defined by the equally obscure.
[k] monad, or unity.
[l] Marks in a definition should not be tautological.
[m] vicious circle in defining.
[n] "*warum* etwas erkannt wird."
[o] "das *Warum*."
[p] as ground.
[q] "implicita verstecket."
[r] Reading "zur Unterscheidung des Definiti" for "des Definiti."
[s] broader.
[t] narrower.

concept[;] the former is *sufficiency* for *distinction*, but the latter *sufficiency* for *cognition.*[u]

Now we can note that the more marks a concept contains, the less is it the same as others[;] hence if there are too many marks in the definition, then this can very well contribute to distinction, but not at all to cognition[v] of the concept[.] Hence we can also say: the *definitium* is *angustior* if it does not suffice for the cognition of identity, and *latior* if it does not suffice for the cognition of diversity. Or if there are too few marks, then the definition is *latior*, but if there are too many marks, then the definition is *angustior.* It is certainly curious that the means for cognizing identity are exactly opposed to those I make use of in order to have insight into its diversity from others. For the more I wish to cognize difference, the more must I heap up marks, but the more I wish to have insight into identity, the more I must reduce the number of marks. Now we can observe this, too: *quo maior conceptus determinatus est, eo angustior est quoque definitio.*[w] In addition, concerning persons too we can then say: People who have much wit commonly make *definitiones latiores*. E.g., they will quickly say: living beings are those that grow and beget. But one experience, e.g., begets another, yet it does not for this reason beget a living being. This definition is thus *latior*. It does not serve for the investigation of all things and for the distinction of the thing from others, but instead for cognition of the sameness of the thing with others[;] and from this we also see, then, that the *latitudo* of a definition belongs to the cognition of identity. But as far as the caviller is concerned, he often makes *definitiones angustiores*. He seeks to find distinctions where none are to be met with, and that is the so-called *argutatio inanis.*[x]

267 From all that is said follows the logical rule, and the 3rd canon: *Ne definitio nec latior nec angustior suo*[y] *definito sit,*[z] or with one expresssion: *definitio et definitum sint conceptus reciproci.*[a]

That is the 3rd *requisitum* of a good definition, and it appears as if with this demand on definition all remaining provisions are at an end. But because in various expressions a mark that has already appeared in the definition can occur in it once again, a certain precision is nonetheless necessary in the definition in order to guard against this[;] and accordingly, it is required that one concept or one mark must not already be present in the other.

As far as tautology is concerned, we already understood it above as a

[u] "*Agnition.*"
[v] "Agnition."
[w] The more broadly a concept is determined, the narrower is its definition.
[x] inane, empty argument.
[y] Ak, "sub;" MS, "suo" (KI, lxix).
[z] A definition should be neither broader nor narrower than the thing defined.
[a] The definition and the defined should be convertible concepts.

great error, for in tautology the marks adduced are not grounds of cognition, and thus the definition is mixed up with the *conceptus definiti.*[b] But as for this, namely, if the *notae* in a definition are the same and differ from one another merely in expression, then this is not such a great mistake, and distinctness can occur in this case. One errs in this case only in that one expresses his own thought all too luxuriantly. Now in order to get rid of this in definition a certain precision is quite necessary. As said, however, this serves more the neatness of the definition than its essence itself, but still this is always desired in definition. It is just the same here as it is with clothing[;] it renders me just the same service if it is made large as if it is made the right size, but for the sake of neatness we reject the former and choose the other.

Now as for what concerns precision, it is violated, e.g., by the well-known and customary definition of the circular line. One says, namely, the circular line is a *curved line*, whose individual points are equally far removed from the *centrum*. But the word *curved line* is completely unnecessary here and lies contained already in the concept of what follows. For every line whose parts are equally far removed from the *centrum* must necessarily be curved. Hence in a definition one must not coordinate that which is already contained in the same concepts.

Now description is distinguished from definition, for the former is a distinct concept, which, however, is complete merely *comparative*$_{L}$. Its exhaustiveness is sufficient merely for my purpose, although this can be completely contrary to the purposes of all others. Description is thus not absolutely complete, then, like definition, i.e., it does not serve for every purpose, but only for my private purpose[;] but it is not on that account to be rejected. 268

Now we can note: All *definitiones* are either *nominales* or *reales definitiones. Nominales definitiones* are ones that contain everything that is equal to the whole concept that we make for ourselves of the thing[;] *reales definitiones*, however, are ones that contain everything that belongs to the thing in itself.

Or

Those definitiones *are nominal* whose marks, taken together, are adequate to the whole concept that we think with the expression of the *definitum*. E.g., if I think and say, Salt is that which is dissolved in water. I do think that in the concept of salt, to be sure, but that is not all the possible characteristics of salt itself. Real *definitiones*, however, are ones whose marks constitute the whole possible concept[c] of the thing. Now

1. all *definitiones* of arbitrary concepts,
2. all *definitiones* of concepts of reason, and 3.) all *definitiones* of arbitrary inven-

[b] concept of the thing defined.

[c] Reading "den ganzen möglichen Begrif" for "den ganzen ähnlichen Begrif" (cf. *Logik Philippi*, 24:456, l. 21).

> tions are real *definitiones*. But why, we ask, are *definitiones* of arbitrary concepts always real *definitiones*? Just because it lies solely with me to make up the concept and to establish it as it pleases me, and the whole concept has thus no other reality than merely what my fabrication wants[;] consequently I can always put all the parts that I name into a thing[,] and these must then constitute the complete, possible concept of the thing, for the whole thing is actual only by means of my will.

Secondly, however, the *definitiones* of such things as are arbitrary inventions are also *reales definitiones*, consequently the *definitiones* of all works of art, too, for they are always established only through an arbitrary concept.

Now we wish to mention that all mathematical *definitiones* are *definitiones* of arbitrary concepts. Mathematicians also have a few given concepts which, however, they cannot define, and the mathematician must 269 not do this either, for otherwise he philosophizes, and that is then a great error for a mathematician, into which error Wolffius himself fell. The mathematician is simply not concerned at all with what others think under a concept, but instead he says: I wish to name this thus, and so it shall be called, too. As soon as the mathematician represents the concept in the definition as given, he philosophizes, and only then can one argue with him, but not before[;] and then he infringes against the philosopher, who can then make a claim against him[;] and it is due to this ground that a mathematician cannot define a place, a direction, a straight line, etc., for these are all given concepts.

As for what else is relevant to this, many arbitrary concepts and also heuristic *definitiones* are to be met with in philosophy, but they are not philosophical *definitiones*.

We can also say, then: All *definitiones* of arbitrary concepts are

(1.) *real*[;] (2.) each of them is free of all error[;] (3.) each of them is a *complete definition*. Arbitrary *definitiones* simply cannot be false, for since he says, I will that this shall be called thus, it is called thus, too, and he cannot commit any error, even if he tries with force to commit it. Only in regard to precision can he make a mistake here[;] but this is not an error, but merely a mistake, and from this we see again what a great advantage a mathematician has. Namely, all of his concepts are true, and he can make a mistake only with respect to precision, though one can also say that he has offended against the common use of words. E.g., if he calls the circumference of a sphere or of a polygon the periphery, although it should be called the perimeter. Furthermore, the names of things that arise in art are also always true[;] their inventor is always right, for they are arbitrary concepts. Only when we wish to define *others'* works of art do we have to listen to what the others wish to understand thereby. These *definitiones* of arbitrary concepts are all synthetic and they arise only *per synthesin*, for no concept can arise *per analysin*, rather, it is only distinctness that can thereby be given to it. Only among arbitrary concepts is the concept supposed to *arise*, and therefore all arbitrary *definitiones* are made only *per synthesin*. A definition arises *per analysin* only insofar as when the *definitum* is given to us confusedly, and then I can make it distinct *per analysin*. *Per synthesin*, however, I make the concept together with its distinctness[;] in respect of given concepts we can therefore note that all given concepts are either given by means of reason or by means of experience. Those given by means of reason are made *per analysin*, and those given by means of experience are made *realiter per synthesin*. Now concepts of reason can all be defined by means of *definitiones reales*. For because the concept is given to me by means of reason, I may think in it only that which reason shows me in the thing, and in this way I then have a real definition[;] and therefore we can also say, all metaphysical and moral *definitiones* can all be real and occur only *per analysin*, for the concept is already given by means of reason, and I am merely supposed to make it distinct, which happens only *per analysin*, however. E.g., the concept of honesty, etc., is constituted thus. But then how is it, 2ndly, with concepts of experience in respect of their definition? Here we have to note that *definitiones* of concepts of experience are never other than nominal *per analysin*[;] *secondly*, concepts of experience are never *real* except *per synthesin*. With an empirical concept I always ask, what is given? And with it I can then make a definition in two ways, *nempe vel definio conceptum datum. Vel definiendum est definitum ipsum*[;][d] with all concepts the former is always a nominal, and the other a real definition. For *my* concept contains only what I think in the thing, not, however, what belongs to it by nature[;] if I want to attain the latter, then I must make a real definition, and these occur in the case of empirical concepts only *per synthesin*, as, on the other side, I cannot get nominal definition in this case except merely *per analysin*.

270

Now we ask: In the case of empirical concepts, is a definition possible? Oh, no[.] With all empirical concepts there is only a description. At the most it seems that only nominal definitions would be possible. For to define *realiter* is to indicate all the marks which, taken together, constitute the whole. And a real definition is thus the *completudo* of the marks that belong only to the thing itself. But in the case of empirical concepts I do not define the object but instead only the concept that one thinks in the case of the thing. Marks of experience are thus changeable, and serve only for nominal definition.

271

Because the concept is already given by means of experience, then, and I am to make it distinct, I need only enumerate all the marks that I think in connection with the expression of the *definitum*, and thus it seems, in fact, as if there could still be a nominal definition. But even this is not possible

[d] namely, either *I define a given concept. Or the thing to be defined is the defined itself* [i.e., the object].

in this case. For even in the naming of empirical concepts we do not all have the same opinions. For one has a completely different experience of the thing than the other, and in the case of empirical concepts, therefore, we can think only of a description, which I can consider merely in relation to my purpose, but not to all purposes.

What kind of purpose do we have here, then, we ask.

The purpose in this case is not to elicit cognition of the *definitum* by means of its analysis, but instead merely to give a meaning to the *definitum*. The final end in this case is thus merely an indication of meaning,[e] namely, so that this will not be lost from language. For in the Hartz Mountains, e.g., spruces are called firs and again firs are called spruces. I define an empirical concept in order to add something to it afterward *per synthesin*. But I do not define a concept of experience so that I can become familiar with the object by means of analysis. I do not define any concept of experience, e.g., gold, in order to infer something therefrom and to draw consequences from this definition[,] but instead only in order to establish the word-meaning of the *definitum*[.] In this connection we note this: the *definitiones* of morals are analytic, and they serve the purpose that I can draw from this concept all possible consequences. The *definitiones* of morals are all real, and therefore I only need to analyze them[;] thus it is actually *curieux* that one can infer from the use of definitions to their particular kind. Empirical definitions are concerned only with the understanding, but not at all with reason (for I have insight into meaning only by means of the understanding)[;] hence they also have no philosophical use at all. From this it follows, then, that *definitiones* of empirical concepts are wholly unnecessary, for even if there could actually be a few, they would still be merely nominal *definitiones*. For by means of them I do not say that taken altogether, this constitutes the complete concept of the thing, but 272 only that this is all that I think in the case of the concept of the thing. All empirical concepts are capable only of description[;] all arbitrary concepts are synthetic, and their definition real. Finally, because they are given, all concepts of reason are analytic, and their *definitiones* are likewise real. Now we make these remarks: In the case of all given concepts of reason, definition is not the first thing, but rather the confused concept of the *definitum* is. For in the case of given concepts of reason, I am only supposed to make the confused concept distinct by means of the definition, and thus the confused concept of the *definitum* must precede all definition[;] only in the case of arbitrary concepts does the definition always precede, for this in fact gives the concepts their *esse*. Now all distinctness of definitions can be attained only through reason *per analysin*, and a concept of reason becomes complete only *successive*$_L$. Namely, when I consider one clear mark after another[;] and since every cognition, if it has

[e] "Vorbedeutung."

clear marks, is a judgment, all *definitiones* are at the same time judgments. Analytical definitions are preceded by many *judicia elementaria*, which expound the marks that are contained in the concept of the *definitum*.[f] Sometimes it is to my purpose to prove something on assumption,[g] where only a mark is necessary and the whole definition is often superfluous[.] E.g., if I say: the soul of man is incorporeal, then I do not need the whole definition, but instead I take out only the one mark, namely, divisibility, and say: every body is divisible, but the soul is simple, consequently it cannot be corporeal.

In philosophy one must never infer the definition too early[;] then it must be the case that I can cognize the whole thing from one mark[;] for this blocks the path toward cognition of the thing. Before I infer the definition, I have to analyze the concept for a long time and postpone my judgment, so that with time I will perhaps attain a still more thorough cognition of the object.

As for what concerns Wolff's mistake, it consists in the fact that Wolff wanted to apply the procedure of mathematics in philosophy[;] all concepts in *mathesis* are arbitrary concepts, and must not be given at all.

§ 285

The particular is cognized from the universal. In the case of universal concepts I have

1. to look to the lower concepts, which are contained in the universal, 273
2. but also to the distinction of these lower concepts, and all this happens in logical division. The synthetic method consists, namely, in the fact that I compare the *sphaera* of the concept with all its lower concepts, but in such a way that I also attend to their proper distinction.

A correct division involves

1. that it is complete. I.e., that the *membra dividentia* (those are just the lower concepts), taken together, exactly constitute the universal concept.
2. But the *membra dividentia* must really be opposed to one another, so that I can say with truth *either, or*. There must always be an actual distinction, too, e.g., I will not divide thus: all men are either virtuous or vicious or philosophers. This concept lies in man, to be sure, but it is not represented *in oppositione*. Division can be codivision as well as subdivision. Subdivision, however, is where the *membrum dividens* is again subdivided.[h]

The rules that the author puts forth herein do not serve any purpose at all[;] through them I merely learn to express, to represent *in abstracto*

[f] Reading "die der Begrif des Definiti in sich enthält" for "die den Begrif des Definit in sich enthalten."
[g] "annehmlich."
[h] Reading "subdividiert" for "subordiniert."

everything that I already know, which I already actually employ *in concreto* if only I follow my healthy reason.

THE NINTH SECTION

Of learned judgments

§ 292

From the previous section we are already acquainted with judgments, actually, because we dealt with distinct concepts, which can only arise by means of a judgment[;] for to cognize distinctly is *to cognize everything by means of a clear mark.* But to cognize something by means of a clear mark is also just to judge. Thus we can also say that distinct concepts are ones that are cognized by means of a judgment. Now the 2 concepts that are 274 compared with one another, and in such a way that one contains the marks and the other the clarity, constitute the material of the judgment. That concept, now, that is to be made distinct through comparison with its mark, is called *the subject.* On the other hand, that concept that is added to the mark as a ground of distinctness is called the predicate.

Comparison is of two sorts, for I can compare two concepts either through the relation of connection[i] or through the relation of opposition between themselves. A judgment, now, in which the predicate is thought in connection with the subject, is called an *affirmative judgment.* A judgment, however, where the predicate is thought in opposition to the *subjectum* is called a *negative judgment.* The form of judgment is the relation. The sign that indicates this relation, or the form, is the copula *est,*[j] and because every relation is either affirmative or negative, the copula is accompanied with *yes* (*id est,*[k] or merely with *est*), but if it is negative with an *id est non.*[l] The negation *no*, or the *non*, does not affect the matter at all, but instead only the form of the judgment[.] It must be posited, then, not with the subject or with the predicate but instead with the copula, e.g., *anima non est mortalis,*[m] but not *anima est non mortalis.*[n] For otherwise the negation of the judgment of reason does not affect the form but instead the matter of the judgment, and consequently it is then not a negative, but instead a so-called *judicium infinitum.*[o]

[i] "Verknüpfung."
[j] is.
[k] it is.
[l] it is not.
[m] the soul is not mortal.
[n] the soul is non-mortal.
[o] infinite judgment.

In every judgment there occurs

1. the matter of the judgment, that is, subject and predicate. The matter of judgment, now, is called the *termini* of the judgment, and based on grounds that we will hear later, we call the subject the *terminus minor*,[p] and the predicate is called the *terminus major*[q] and is always regarded as a universal concept, under which the *conceptus subjecti*[r] is contained. All judgments have the end of distinctness, but in a judgment one represents the predicate as the ground of the distinctness of the subject. Because the ground of distinctness is in a mark, now, we see that the subject must always be contained under the predicate as a mark. The

2nd thing in each judgment is its form. The copula *est* always expresses this[.] This copula is posited *simpliciter*, now, if it indicates the relation of two concepts in their connection[;] but if it expresses the relation in the opposition of these concepts, then it is accompanied with the word *non*. This *non* expresses the negation of the judgment, now, but N.B.: only when it affects the form of the judgment, i.e., the copula. 275

§ 297

Where the author says that all true judgments have a ground, the ground of truth is the condition of judgments[;] unprovable judgments have no particular ground of cognition, but instead they are themselves the grounds of cognition, and consequently they cannot contain any grounds of truth[,] as the author nonetheless says here[.] Such, e.g., is the judgment, Every body is extended, for this judgment cannot be derived from anything else. But now if the condition of truth is merely added to a judgment, the judgment is then determined. Now every judgment is determined, and I simply cannot represent to myself how there can still be people, among whom our author is included, who say that certain judgments are undetermined[;] one should really say unrestricted, for what is not determined is also never a judgment.

§ 301

All judgments are either *universal* or *particular*. It is universal if the *nota* of the subject is contained in the *sphaera* of the predicate either completely or not at all, and in the first case it is a *universal affirmative judgment*, but in the other case, namely, if the *nota* of the subject is completely outside the *sphaera* of the predicate, it is a *universal negative judgment*. A particular judgment, however, is one where the *nota* of the subject is contained, or

[p] minor term.

[q] major term.

[r] concept of the subject.

not contained, only partly under the *sphaera* of the predicate[;] in the first case it is a *particular affirmative judgment*, and in the other a *particular negative one*.

Several judgments *quoad quantitatem*[s] do not exist, for as regards singular judgments (*judicia singularia*), or those where the subject is an *individuum*, these are included among universal judgments. But concerning them, one can observe this further: a singular judgment must be either *wholly affirmative* or *wholly negative*. Nothing more occurs in this case, for 276 it is included in the universal judgment, and thus every singular judgment is universal. Now this was the division of judgments *quoad quantitatem*, namely, into universal judgments and particular ones. In regard to quality, now, all judgments are either *affirmative* or *negative*, and in fact either *universal* affirmative or *universal* negative or *particular* affirmative or *particular* negative. Logicians express the first by *A*, the second by *E*, the 3rd by *I*, and the 4th by *O*. This whole designation is mere pedantry (Barbara[,] Celarent[, etc.]), and what is more, all of syllogistic is mere pedantry[;] and I will show hereafter that inferences of reason outside the first figure are not simple, as is falsely held, but instead are composed of a *consequentia immediata*[t] and a *ratiocinium*.[u] Now although syllogistic is unnecessary, one must still know it.

The following remark is to be noted well: *Omnia judicia sunt vel problematica, vel assertoria*[v] (*decisive*). A *problematic* judgment is one in which I *only consider* the relation of two concepts *undetermined*, but do not *posit* it[;] in this judgment I consider something as given for investigation, i.e., I establish no relation in the judgment, but instead I only see what would follow from this were it really so. Regardless of this, they have great use. For by means of the relation of two such judgments one can nonetheless learn to use a certain caution in judging, and to make our judgments useful.

§ 305–307

Every relation in judgments is either a relation of connection or a relation of opposition. That judgment by means of which the relation of connection of two judgments with one another is indicated is called a *hypothetical* judgment. That judgment, however, in which the relation of opposition of two judgments is indicated is called a *disjunctive* judgment. Those judgments where one thinks the relation of two judgments with one another are called, in fact, judgments of relation[w] (*relative*$_{L}$)[;] now these judg-

[s] as to quantity.
[t] immediate inference.
[u] inference of reason.
[v] All judgments are either problematic or assertoric.
[w] "Verhaltniß Urtheile."

ments consider the relation of one judgment to the other, either as to connection, and then they are *hypothetical* judgments, or as to *opposition*, and then they are *disjunctive judgments*. In the case of the former, one always finds the relation of ground to consequences. Now in conditioned judgments, that which contains the ground is called *antecedens* or also *prius*. That which contains the consequences, however, is called in these judgments *consequens* or *posterius*. As for what concerns disjunctive judgments, in them the relation of opposition is again of two kinds[;] either it is a relation of two, or of more judgments, which contradict one another[;] but we will show that a true disjunctive judgment occurs only with two and not with several judgments, for a true and pure contradiction cannot occur except with two concepts that stand exactly in opposition to each other. *Then it is called a bimembris propositio*, and since disjunctive judgments contain the relation of a true contradiction, they can only include 2 judgments. If we judge merely rationally, then the *propositio disjunctiva* must be in the judgment *bimembris*, but those disjunctive judgments whose *propositio disjunctiva* is not *bimembris* have all arisen out of induction[;] for how else do I know that I have correctly enumerated the cases except from experience, and thus *per inductionem*. A disjunctive judgment, if it is to become certain without induction, must be *bimembris*. A disjunctive judgment is nothing more than a representation of a logical division, or *representatio divisionis logicae*.

277

§ 310

An exponible judgment is one that actually in a hidden way has 2 judgments, not in such a way that it has 2 subjects or predicates, but rather in such a way that the judgments in it are of two kinds as to quantity, also as to quality[;] for they are *affirmative*, but also *negative*. Now logic has the duty that it must explicate[x] exponible judgments. What is meant by the questions *quae? qualis? quanta?* (1.) The question *Qualis est propositio?*[y] aims at quality, namely, whether the judgment was affirmative or negative. (2.) *Quanta est propositio?*[z] contains the question, whether it was a universal or a particular judgment? (3.) *Quae est propositio?*[a] is the question, whether the *judicium* is *purum* or *modale*. A judgment is called modal, however, which carries a condition of judgment with the *praedicatum*[.] These questions must be answered according to the character of the judgment. Therefore if an empty judgment appeared, people used to say: *quae? qualis? quanta?* I.e., there is nothing in the judgment.

278

[x] "exprimiren."
[y] Of what sort is the proposition?
[z] Of what quantity is the proposition?
[a] What is the proposition?

§ 312

A judgment is expressed practically if it enunciates a possibly necessary action. This probably seems to be contradictory, that *something is possibly necessary*. But here it is completely correct, for the action is always necessary, to be sure, namely, if I want to bring the thing about[;] but the case is not necessary, but merely possible. It is very good that one does not posit the *imperativum* with this kind, but instead only the *infinitivum*, and that one expresses them with *if*, etc.

§ 313

Provably certain means nothing other than a *mediately* certain judgment. But a judgment is absolutely *unprovable*, on the other hand, if it is *immediately* certain. And such judgments must also be found in the human understanding[;] for even though we have ever so many deductions, and we can cognize these from their grounds as from their marks[,] still we must finally come to a ground that is not a consequence of another ground but instead is the very first ground of all of the consequences themselves[;] and this is then *immediately certain*, or an unprovably *certain judgment*. But now whether there is just one such absolutely first ground or many of them, this is treated in metaphysics.

All unprovable judgments, insofar as they are the ground of all judgments, are called *principles*[,] and they are either *theoretical* or *practical*. A proposition that is *unprovable practically* is called a *postulatum*. All these *principia* are either *material*, namely, insofar as they have a *medius terminus*, or *formal*, which have no *medius terminus*. These latter have no determinate *predicate*, but instead they are concerned merely with the *relation* of predicates to subjects in general. These include the *principium contradictionis* and the *principium identitatis*. For these there is, namely, no determinate subject or predicate, or no determinate case[;] instead, it can be applied to any subject and predicate. Now in our judgments we have two 279 forms, namely, *synthetic* and *analytic* form[;] the *principium contradictionis*, now, is only analytic.

§ 318

Here the author gives an instruction for demonstration. We have such a thing as tautological *definitiones*, hence also tautological *resolutiones*, namely, where one answers the very same thing that was asked. And that is what our author does here. When there is a question, let us attend quite well to whether the proffered reply and resolution of the question is not merely an analysis of the question itself. But then through this I have not taught the other to resolve the question, but instead have only made him familiar, by means of analysis, with what was in it. Thus I have not done anything more than make him understand better that which he asked me. This is what the author does many times, too. It is *curieux*; he merely shows me that I should do that about which I asked him, and he does not show me how I should do it. In my recent disputation *De mundi sensibilis et intelligibilis forma et principiis*[38] I also had to clear up various *quaestiones*, but I did not merely analyze the *quaestiones*, but instead in fact also indicated marks of the thing that were completely correct and complete. E.g., p. 30, § 25 (*vid. Dict. Metaph.*,[39] in which this disputation is bound)[.] There,[40] namely, this infallible mark of sensibility is put forth: *si de conceptu quocunque intellectuali generaliter quicquam praedicatur, quod pertinet ad respectus spatii atque temporis: objective non est enuntiandum et non denotat nisi conditionem, sine qua conceptus datus sensitive cognoscibilis non est.*[b] *vid. ibid.*

§ 319

Where the author speaks of intuitive judgments.[c] An intuitive judgment is actually a singular judgment insofar as it is cognized immediately, but a *judicium discursivum* is an inferred judgment.[d] All immediate judgments, however, are intuitive only because they are cognized immediately, insofar as their form is sensitive[;][e] for otherwise, if the form is rational, then immediate judgments are nonetheless not intuitive judgments[;] it is only discursive judgments that can be contradistinguished from intuitive ones, and the ancients called universal judgments *discursiva*, but the singular ones *intuitiva*, and that is how we will take it here, too. Now this was concerning intuitive judgments or judgments of experience. Now it belongs to metaphysics to investigate whether a judgment is a judgment of experience or not. Logic does not consider judgments insofar as they are given[,] as metaphysics does, but instead insofar as it is to compare them. Logic only shows whether judgments are universal or particular, and thus it is occupied only with opposition and identity. All propositions are either *theoretical* or *practical*. The former are such as merely show the relation of concepts to other concepts, but the others indicate the *relation* of action to concepts. Both propositions are *provable* or *unprovable*. Propositions that are provable *theoretically*, if they arise by means of a *ratiocinium polysyllogisticum*, are called *theoremata*. Every provable proposition, however, that is only monosyllogistic is called a *corollarium*. A proposition that is provable practically is a *problema*[,] but a proposition that is unprovable

280

[b] If anything that pertains to an aspect of space or of time is predicated of any intellectual concept in general, then it is not to be said objectively, and it denotes only the condition without which the given concept cannot be cognized sensibly.

[c] "von den Anschauenden Urtheilen."

[d] "ein geschloßen Urtheil."

[e] "Sensitiv."

practically is called a *postulatum*. In the case of all propositions that are provable theoretically, the proposition itself is the *theorema*, but the proof of the proposition the *demonstration*; the action that is to be done in this case is called the *quaestio*[.] The propositions in accordance with which it is cognized, its *resolution*. A *lemma* is a proposition that is in fact provable, not in this discipline, however, but in another, from which it is taken. With this one must take great care, so that one does not assume something and put it forth as something proved in another science, although it is not proved there at all[;] indeed, one often finds in authors something that they assume at the beginning, which they promise to prove at the end, but the proof is forgotten. *Scholia* are propositions that are added to a system not as *essentialia* but instead only as *accidentalia*.

§ 341–346

Every inference in general is a judgment, only with this difference: if the judgment is *mediate*, then it is an *inference of reason*, or a *mediate inference*. But if the judgment is *immediate*, then the inference is only an *inference of the understanding*, namely, one is judged from the other *absque medio termino*[;][f] then the judgment, or also the *conclusio*, is *immediata*[.] Or 281 one is inferred from the other *per medium terminum*,[g] and then the inference is *mediate*$_L$, or also an *inference of reason*. We will now consider only immediate[h] inferences. As for what concerns their mode of origination, this is fivefold, for they can arise either

1. *per judicia aequipollentia*[i] or
2. *per judicia subalternata*,[j] or
3. *per judicia opposita*[k] or
4. *per conversionem logicam*[l] or
5. *per contrapositionem*.[m]

Now[n] as for what concerns the *consequentia per judicia aequipollentia*, because both judgments in it are completely the same as one another, this is really not a *consequentia*[o] at all, and hence the so-called inference *per judicia aequipollentia* is not an inference at all. The *consequentia per judicia subalternata* occurs without any alteration of the positions of the *termini*,

f without a middle term.
g through a middle term.
h Reading "unmittelbahre" for "mittelbahre."
i through equivalent judgments.
j through subalternate judgments.
k through opposed judgments.
l through logical conversion.
m through contraposition.
n Inserting a paragraph break after "per contrapositionem."
o Reading "Consequenz" for "Consequens."

the quality also remains the same, only the quantity is altered therein. In the *consequentia per conversionem logicam* the quality must likewise never be altered but only the quantity. In the *conversio logica*, however, both the position of the *termini* and also the quality must be altered. With the *oppositio judiciorum*[p] logicians have hit upon the following division:

1. 2 judgments are set against one another *contradictorie* when a particular negative judgment is opposed to a universal affirmative[q] judgment (or conversely). E.g., all men are mortal, but some are not mortal.
2. judgments are *subcontraria* when in 2 particular judgments that have the same subject and predicate one is affirmative and the other negative.
3. there is also a *contrarietas judicii*[;][r] this occurs when in 2 judgments the one is *universal* affirmative and the other *universal* negative. *Judicia subcontraria* contain less than is required, or not enough, for proper opposition[;] *judicia contraria* contain more than enough for proper opposition, and *judicia contradictoria* exactly enough. And we therefore can say that *judicia subcontraria*, because they do not contain enough, can (1.) both be true, but they (2.) cannot both be false.

Secondly, *judicia contraria* can both be false, for in the two there is too much, and just in their too much they can also be false. Of 2 pure oppositions the following must constantly be able to hold good: *posito uno tollitur alterum.*[s] *Et vice versa*[.] In all logical conversion (*vid. ant.* § 346) of judgments the judgment that is to be converted is called *conversum*, the judgment that is to arise from this conversion the *convertens*. A *conversio* in which the quantity[t] of the judgment is not restricted[u] is called *simplex*, but where it is restricted,[v] a *conversio per accidens*. Universal affirmative judgments may be converted *per accidens*, but all negative judgments can be converted *simpliciter*[;] that is the only rule of *logical conversion*. The rule of *contraposition* is this: *only universal affirmative* judgments may *be contraposed*. 282

THE TENTH SECTION

Of learned inferences of reason

§ 354

Inferences of reason are judgments that occur *mediately* by means of a *medius terminus*. As previously said, there are also certain judgments and

[p] opposition of judgments.
[q] Reading "einem allgemein bejahenden" for "einem bejahenden."
[r] contrariety of judgments.
[s] through the positing of one the other is denied.
[t] Reading "Quantitaet" for "Qualitaet."
[u] "gehindert."
[v] "gehindert."

consequences, which we have named *immediati*[;] these were indemonstrable. Unprovable consequences of one judgment from other judgments we also called, not an inference of reason, but rather an inference of the understanding. On the other hand, however, there are also certain *consequentiae* from other mediate judgments, and these are always *provable*. There are uncertain illusory inferences,[w] which are not inferences of reason but only mere *themata* to these, and of this sort are the so-called *ratiocinia disjunctiva* and *hypothetica*, or also *speciosa*. Here we will not treat these inferences, which are only *themata* to inferences of reason, but instead will treat only inferences of reason themselves.

If two concepts are put together and the one is the mark of the other, then in these concepts a certain relation is posited. Now this relation can be represented immediately, and then it is a *judicium*. But if it occurs *per notam intermediam*, then it is a *ratiocinium*. Or the inference of 283 reason is nothing other than the comparison of a *nota remota* with the thing itself by means of a *nota intermedia*. The *mediate relation* of a *nota remota* with the given concept is always *remota* in respect of the thing, but this is also a *nota proxima* of the *nota intermedia*, and hence a *nota rei ipsius*[;][x] this is a *judicium medium*, or a *ratiocinium*.

An adequate inference consists in an inference of reason whose rule is this: *nota notae rei est nota rei ipsius*[,][y] and this is also the basic rule[z] of all *syllogistic*, and at the same time the whole distinction between a judgment and an inference of reason. A *judicium*, namely, involves an *immediate* clear mark, but a *ratiocinium* involves a *mediate clear mark*. Consequently a *ratiocinium* is the relation of the *nota remota* by means of a *nota mediata, vel intermediata*[a] to a certain given concept of a thing. In a *ratiocinium*, then, these 3 actions occur: 1st the *nota proxima* or *intermedia* is compared with the *nota remota*, 2nd the *nota proxima* is compared with the thing, *et* 3rd the *nota remota* is compared with the thing itself. The *nota intermedia* is also called the *medius terminus*. Now because in every judgment the predicate constitutes the *major terminus*, we can say: in every inference of reason there are 3 *termini*. (1.) the proposition that I am to cognize by means of the *nota intermedia*, (2.) the *nota remota* and (3.) the *terminus medius*, or the *nota intermedia*, which contains the ground of the relation of the thing to the *nota remota*. And these constitute the 3 *termini*, namely, *major, minor et conclusio*. In every inference of reason (1.) the *terminus major* is compared with[b] the *terminus*

[w] "Scheinschlüße."
[x] mark of the thing itself.
[y] A mark of a mark of a thing is a mark of the thing itself.
[z] "die Grundregel."
[a] a mark that is mediate or intermediate.
[b] Reading "mit" for "in."

medius, or the *nota proxima* with the *nota remota*[;] (2.) the *terminus medius* with the *minor* or the *subject*[;] and finally (3.) the *minor* with the *major* or the *predicate.*

To infer, then, requires only the synthetic mode of reason[;] now this requires always that one descend from the universal to the particular[;] if one turns this around, it's contrary to reason and then a leap is made. And therefore the *major propositio*, or the predicate of conclusion, must always come first, or I must first go *per notam remotam* to the *nota proxima*[;] then I have to go again from the *nota proxima* to the thing, and finally from the thing to the *nota remota*. That is the synthesis of reason, 284 and if one loses sight of this, then one does not observe the order. In every inference of reason there are certain *termini*, then, of which there must be no more than 3, and in every proper inference of reason there are not more than 3 *judicia*, either. The first 2 are called the *premises*, while the 3rd judgment is called the *conclusion*. Now the premises constitute the matter of inferences of reason, but the conclusion the form[;] and hence the correct form of an inference of reason will rest solely on the correct consequence of the conclusion. Now in both inferences the *medius terminus* or the *nota intermedia* always occurs (but not at all in the *consequens* itself). *Every inference of reason* is nothing but a representation of a mark by means of a *terminus medius*. An inference of reason involves one mark being subordinated to another mark of the thing as a *notae nota*.[c] In an inference of reason I thus compare the *nota remota* with the *nota proxima*, then the thing with the *nota proxima*, and finally also the *nota remota* with the thing itself. All form of inferences of reason is only *of two kinds*, and there are not more, either, for the judgment is either *immediate* or *mediate*[.]

The basic rules of all affirmative inferences are these:

1. *Nota notae rei est nota rei ipsius*[.]

The only basic rule, however,

2. of all *negative* inferences will thus be:
   Repugnans nota notae rei, repugnat rei ipsi[.][d]

This is now the basic rule of all inferences of reason.

Logicians have a certain *dictum de omni et nullo*, which they take to be the very first ground of all *ratiocinia*. But these basic rules that have been presented precede even this.

Among logicians, the *dictum de omni et nullo* runs thus: what belongs to a universal concept belongs also to all concepts that are contained under it.

[c] mark of a mark.

[d] If a mark conflicts with the mark of a thing, it conflicts with the thing itself.

§ 392–395

When, in an inference of reason, the relation of two *judgments* (not of two concepts) is considered, then that is called a *ratiocinium extraordinarium*[;] or when an inference of reason is accepted, where the *major propositio* is not a *judicium ordinarium* but rather a *judicium extraordinarium*, then it is also called a *ratiocinium extraordinarium*. 285 All *ratiocinia extraordinaria* are either *hypothetica* or *disjunctiva*. For in them either the relation of connection or the relation of opposition is indicated; if it is the first, then it is called a *hypothetical* inference of reason, but in the other case a *disjunctive* one. Now the *judicium hypotheticum* consists only of 2 propositions and hence no *judicium hypotheticum* can produce a *ratiocinium*. In the *judicium hypotheticum* only the *consequentia*[e] needs to be proved, for in this judgment nothing is enunciated or maintained. But with *judicia categorica* not only the *consequentia*[f] but also the assertion itself must be proved from correct grounds. The conditioned inference is not an inference of reason but instead only the *substratum* for the inference of reason, for it must first be proved *per ratiocinium*. Hence it is only the question itself, and the *datum*$_{L}$ that is to be proved[;] hence nothing is actually proved thereby, but instead a ground is merely stated, of which one affirms at the same time that its consequence is correct[;] but how it is correct, that I do not see at all by this means[;] it is, so to speak, only the ground of proof, not the proof[;][g] that is to say, by this means merely the matter of the proof is given, not the form. This analysis is certainly not unnecessary, and [is] completely correct. For in the *judicium conditionale* no subject is connected with a predicate by means of a mediate mark, and in such an inference there is simply no *major propositio*, and hence they are not ordinary inferences of reason at all, but instead only *substrata* for these[;] one does not really infer in accordance with them, but instead one only says the very thing that one wants to infer. Every proof concerns either the truth of the *antecedens* or of the *consequens*. Every *syllogismus hypotheticus* has 2 *modi*, namely, a *modus ponens*, where an affirmation is inferred in the conclusion, and the *modus tollens* where, namely, a denial is inferred. An affirmation is inferred here according to the rule: *atqui verum est prius, ergo quoque posterius*.[h] The denial, however, is from the falsehood of the *consequens* to the falsehood of the *antecedens*, but not[i] according to the rule: *atqui*

[e] Reading "Consequenz" for "consequens."

[f] Reading "Consequenz" for "consequens."

[g] Reading "der Beweißgrund, nicht der Beweis" for "der Beweißgrund, nicht das Beweißthum."

[h] but the former is true, hence the latter is too.

[i] Reading "und zwar nicht nach" for "und zwar nach," with Hinske (KI, lxxiii).

falsum est prius, ergo quoque posterius. Remoto[j] *antecedente non tollitur consequens sed sublata consequentia tollitur antecedens.*[k] Here, then, I can never infer *a negatione antecedentis*[l] to the *negatio consequentis,*[m] but of course I can infer conversely.

As far as disjunctive inferences are concerned, these are inferences in which the *major propositio* is disjunctive. A disjunctive inference is a logical division[;] in it I represent to myself a divided concept and all the *membra* that are equal with the *divisum*. In it the subject of the *major propositio* is the *divisum*, and the predicate is all the *membra dividentia*. Consequently the correctness of a disjunctive inference rests on the correctness of a logical *division*[;] all things, that is, must stand in true disjunction and opposition to each other, and besides they must all be complete. 286

§ 397

A dilemma is actually a *ratiocinium hypotheticum*, whose *consequentia* is *disjunctive*. Let one proceed in this case according to the rules of the hypothetical as well as those of the disjunctive mode of inference. *Atqui falsum est prius, ergo etiam posterius.*[n] One never has a dilemma as a *modus ponens*, but always as a *modus tollens*. By means of a dilemma we do not seek to prove a proposition properly, but instead only to convince someone of its falsehood. The dilemma is also called a *cornutus*,[o] because by means of it one refutes another and also at the same time cuts off all paths[;] he may take whichever he will, still he is caught. And therefore this dilemma is much used in dialectic[.] On account of this the *sceptici* like to use it.

§ 398

Here the author speaks of immediate inferences, but it is not appropriate, for they are not inferences of reason but rather inferences of the understanding. For they have no *medius terminus*.

§ 399

Inferences of reason are either formal or *ratiocinia cryptica*.[p] *Ratiocinia cryptica* are those where I only enunciate 2 judgments, but think the 3rd

[j] Reading "posterius. remoto" for "posterius remoto," with Hinske (KI, lxxiv).

[k] But the first is false, therefore the latter is also. When the antecedent is removed the consequent is not denied, but when the consequent is denied the antecedent is denied.

[l] from the negation of the antecedent.

[m] negation of the consequent.

[n] But the former is false, hence the latter is also.

[o] horned one.

[p] hidden inferences.

while doing so. In such a *syllogismus* one always says less than one actually[q] thinks, and this is the so-called concealing,[r] which often is quite healthy and fair. But pretending[s] is when one speaks otherwise than as one thinks. And is of course to be rejected as unfair.

287 *Enthymema*[.] This is an inference in which only 2 judgments, a *praemissa* and the *conclusio* are posited. These also include the *ratiocinia contracta*. These are *syllogismi* where not 2 propositions but only one proposition and the *medius terminus* is present. Also included here is *induction*, which is particularly noteworthy. The rule of reason in the case of apodeictic certainty in inferences always goes from the *universal* to the *particular*. There are inferences, nonetheless, where we infer from the particular to the universal. The former is the *ratiocinatio rigida*. But the latter is the *ratiocinatio laxa*. Now this last includes (1.) *inductio*. (2.) *analogy*. *Inductio* is the inference where I take to be true, as if it belonged to all, what belongs to many things under a universal inference and concept. I infer thus: what belongs to as many things as I have ever cognized must also belong to all things that are of this species and genus. This kind of inference is completely opposed to logical rule, to be sure, but we cannot do without it, and along with it most of our cognitions would have to be abolished at the same time.

2ndly, as for what concerns inference according to an analogy, this is nothing other than an induction, only an induction in respect of the predicate. When, namely, 2 things have come together in respect of all attributes that I have been able to cognize in them, then they will also come together in the remaining attributes, which I have not cognized in them, and thus runs the inference in regard to *analogy*. Analogy and induction are merely crutches for our understanding. For in universal propositions of truth we will always be able to proceed according to logical strictness, but in the use of our cognition (*a posteriori*) we often have to make do with the probable too.

There is a *complete induction*, also an *incomplete* one. *Complete*, when its *membra* are equal to the given concept, or when everything can be derived from a particular concept.

§ 402–405

Every inference false in form is a *paralogismus*. But every inference that is supposed to be a means for producing error in another is called a *sophisma*. There are various *sophismata*, which can be covered by many 288 names, which is not at all necessary, however. In addition there are also

[q] Reading "wirklich" for "willkührlich."

[r] "dissimuliren."

[s] "simuliren."

some *sophismata* that deserve a place in *logica*, for some of them can be truer than the others. In addition the author is thinking here of the *sophisma ignorationis elenchi*. For us, however, only this needs to be noted: He who, in a dispute, forgets the disputed question, commits a *sophisma ignorationis elenchi*.

§ 406–407

If inferences of reason are coordinated with one another, there arises from this a *ratiocinium compositum*, also *polysyllogisticum*. A *ratiocinium* is called *polysyllogisticum*[t] when the *conclusio* of one inference of reason is the *praemissa* of the other. That *syllogismus*, now, whose *conclusio* is the premise of the other is called a *prosyllogismus*. But that *syllogismus* whose *praemissa* is a conclusion of the former is called *episyllogismus*. Or more briefly: the *prosyllogismus* contains the ground, but the *Episyllogismus* the consequence of an inference of reason. *Vid. auct*:[u] §406–408: There is a *sorites per syllogismos hypoth.*: and then it is called *sorites hypotheticus*[;] or the *sorites* can arise *per syllogismos categoricos*, and then it is also called *categoricus*.

The *formalia ratiocinia* are used only in disputation but not in books and the like, for otherwise this would become too troublesome. And as for what otherwise concerns the many inferences of reason, these make things more indistinct than distinct. They are only expressed because reason actually thinks them.[v]

§ 410

Where the author speaks of a leap in proof, *legitimate* as well as *illegitimate*, we observe only this: *nullus saltus in intellectu est possibilis, et non aliter saltus possibilis est, quam in enunciando.*[w] The immediate connection of a distant ground with the consequence is, namely, a *leap*. In thoughts, now, such a leap is completely impossible, but it can well occur in enunciation, and in this case it can of course sometimes be *legitimus*, namely, if I believe the other will unfailingly know what was left out and thus supply it in his thoughts.

§ 411

289

The actual omission of a proposition that deserves a proof is called *petitio principii*. This comes from *peto*[,] *I beg*. In the case of this kind

[t] Reading "Polysyllogisticum" for "Der Polysyllogisticus," with Hinske (KI, lxxiv).

[u] See the author.

[v] Reading "weil sie die Vernunft würcklich dencket" for "wie die Vernunft würcklich dencket."

[w] No leap in thought is possible, and no other leap is possible except in enunciation.

of conviction, namely, I have to beg the other, as it were, for his approval, and from this we see, then, that this cannot be called a proof.

The *circulus in demonstrando* is the mistake where one accepts the conclusion of a proof as its own premise. This happens:

1. when one wants to prove what is unprovably true or immediately certain
2. when one wants to prove unprovably false propositions[;] in both these cases the circle in proof is always necessary. Above all, however, it arises
3. when before any proof one is certain of the truth of a proposition that is unprovable, then one grants the other the proof, and therefore a circle in proof can always creep in.

§ 412

A proof proves *too little* when it proves only a part of the proposition. It proves *too much* when it proves more than can be proved. A proof that proves *too little* can be true, but one that proves *too much* is always false. For when it is said that the proof proves *too much*, then this amounts to the fact that it proves more than is true, but this is nothing other than the fact that it is false.

§ 413

Finally, the author speaks some about the value of inferences of reason, which seems to be almost unnecessary, for who will not take the use of reason to be valuable?

The second principal part
Of the method of learned cognition

§ 414

Method[x] is nothing other than the form of a whole of cognitions, insofar as it is arranged according to the rules of logical perfection. Now because logical perfection is of two kinds, however, namely, either logical perfection according to healthy reason or logical perfection according to learnedness and science, method will be able to be divided in the same way. For the rules of healthy reason are distinct from the rules of science. In all sciences and learnedness the method of healthy reason must reign, to be sure, but everything that occurs in learnedness need not also, conversely, occur in healthy reason. In all sciences I look not to how something appears in employment, but instead to how it can be judged before any employment. I look to how something can be thought *in abstracto*, too[;] but if, on the contrary, I proceed according to the rules of healthy reason, then I must show everything *in concreto*. The second kind is a cognition that brings with it a certain life. The first, however, serves only for speculation and curiosity. Now the methods of the learned are various:

290

1. *quoad objectum.*[y] I.e., as to the matter that they comprehend under themselves, or on which they are erected. For the object can be either
A. historical cognition, or
B. rational cognition. The latter includes, e.g., *mathematica*, and *philosophy*, the former geography and the proper history of history.[z]
2. Also, as to the subject. For there is
A. a method for the instruction of women, and a separate method for men.
B. a method for the instruction of children, and another for adults.
C. a completely separate method of instruction for people who are determined to a low social position, and another again for people determined to a higher social position[,] etc. Our method must be arranged completely differently for a farmer than it will be brought to bear only on a person of average position.

[x] "Die Lehrart."
[y] as to the object.
[z] "die eigentliche Geschichte von der Historie."

3. These differences can also be concerned with the powers of cognition. For there can be either
(1.) a method merely of healthy reason, or
(2.) method can be scientific, or there can also be
291 (3.) a difference of method itself in the[a] subject, but
(4.) the distinction in respect of the 2nd method is of course this: method can be either
A. *analytic*
B. *synthetic.*
Analysis and synthesis are either as to coordination or as to subordination.
α the *synthesis* of coordination is the combination of the parts with the whole.
β the *analysis* of coordination is the resolution of the whole into its part.
γ the *synthesis* of subordination is the combination of grounds with consequences.
δ the *analysis* of subordination, however, is the derivation of the consequence from its grounds.

In all historical cognitions there is the connection of coordination, but in all rational cognitions only the connection of subordination occurs. In history, namely, I enumerate one thing after another, be it as to space or as to time. But in rational cognitions and sciences we always derive one thing from another. In analytic coordination, namely, I go *from the whole* to its parts, but in synthetic coordination from the parts to the whole.

In historical cognitions the analytic method is most advisable. First, that is, I have to form for myself an idea of the whole, and then I make an idea and concepts of the parts contained thereunder. In all rational cognitions there is the form of subordination, and this, now, is either *synthetic* or *analytic.* In the former I go from ground to consequence, in the latter from consequence to ground.

§ 427

Artificial method is contradistinguished from natural method, just as a distinction is to be drawn between a rational cognition, i.e., one that does not contradict reason, and a cognition of reason,[b] where one understands 292 by this one that arises out of reason. Thus a cognition is also called natural in two senses, namely[,] (1.) when it agrees with the nature of the object and of the subject, and then (2.) when it arises from nature. Method[c] has to be not only subjectively but also objectively natural, i.e., adequate to the object.

[a] Reading "in dem Subjekt" for "in deßen Subjekt."
[b] Reading "Vernunft-Erkenntniß" for "Vernünftigen Erkenntniß."
[c] Ak, "Erkenntniß"; MS, "Lehrart" (KI, lxx).

§ 428

Methodus tabellaris,[d] i.e., to understand and to outline a whole science in tables, is very beautiful. It requires insight, however, not to make too many divisions or useless ones. The method of taking apart[e] a system is no method[;] the manner of composition of the parts constitutes the system.

§ 429

An unnatural art is called *affectatio*[;] everything by means of which one seeks to appear artful is called affected. Thus it is affected when one does not give his art, but rather hints at an artful investigation. The affected is commonly combined with pedantry. It becomes particularly conspicuous when one applies a single method to everything, whether it is suitable or not.

§ 430

Socratic method occurs by means of conversations, where one extracts everything from the pupil by means of well-arranged questions and leads him to answers. It has great value. It is a genus of catechistic method, but it is very tiring.[f]

Platonic method consisted in a free speech where one is aware of no[g] system.

§ 432

In historical sciences[h] one has 2 methods, the *chronological* and the *geographical*. The two can be combined with each other. The last is better than the first. In all cognitions that hang together one must first take into consideration the whole rather than its parts, and of the parts the large ones rather than the small ones, the higher division rather than the lower.

§ 434 293

The author says of history that it belongs to no doctrine, but it is just as much a doctrine as dogmatic truths. We must distinguish:

[d] Tabular method.
[e] "der Zertheilung."
[f] Ak, "erinnerend"; MS, "ermüdend" (KI, lxxii).
[g] Reading "kein System" for "ein System," with Hinske (KI, lxxiv).
[h] Reading "In Historischen Wißenschaften hat man" instead of "Die Historische Wißenschaft hat," with Hinske (KI, lxxii).

A. *doctrine*[,] i.e., a connection of various cognitions and doctrines.
B. *discipline*[,] when a connection is brought into a method.
C. *science*, when cognition is completely developed according to such a method.

Science is a complete discipline. With doctrine I direct my attention only to what is taught, with discipline I look to the method. Doctrine and discipline occur in historical cognitions as well as in dogmatic ones, then. With sciences there must always be doctrine.

§ 435

One thinks tumultuously[i] when one thinks without method.

§ 436

To meditate is not to remember cognitions that one had but rather to produce new ones that one did not yet[j] have. Methodical meditation prevents one from not getting enough[k] materials for meditating. In the beginning one meditates tumultuously[;] one has to write down what occurs to us, as thoughts occur to us that we otherwise do not have. Let one first write down all thoughts as they come, without order[;] afterward let one begin to coordinate and then to subordinate. In every development, 3 tasks must precede

1. One writes down all thoughts without order.
2. One makes a universal plan.
3. One develops all the parts[.]

In reflection, one practices doubting, but also[l] the endeavor to get proper insight into[m] everyone's opinion, to put ourselves in the position of that opinion. It is good if one alternates meditation with other sciences that are relaxing.

[i] "Tumultuarisch."
[j] Reading "noch nicht" instead of "nicht," with Hinske (KI, lxxii).
[k] Ak, "genug seine"; MS, "genugsame" (KI, lxx).
[l] Reading "Nachdencken, aber auch" instead of "Nachdencken auch," with Hinske (KI, lxxii).
[m] Reading "einsehen" instead of "ansehen," with Hinske (KI, lxxii).

The third principal part
Of learned expositions

THE FIRST SECTION

294

Of the use of words

The character of words is an object worthy of the philosopher's[n] consideration. Their right use is to signify a thought exactly.

§ 449

A *terminus inanis*[o] is one whose meaning we believe we understand but do not in fact understand. An expression is deceptive[p] where we believe that something is possible and yet it is impossible.

§ 450

A *terminus familiaris* is that expression whose sense has never been investigated because it has never been heeded.[q] Every language has such terms. I say, e.g., *addicted*[.] On closer investigation such terms are often deceptive.

§ 452–454 et 457

The phrase *learned merchandising*[r] is a deceptive business, since one puts forth words as things[;] what is more common than this expression and deceit! An expression that can be understood is called understandable. Something can be understandable without being distinct. When 2 expressions have one meaning, or where their meanings are at least not very different, then they are called *synonymous expressions*. If an expression has

[n] Ak, "der Philosophen"; MS, "des Philosophen" (KI, lxx).

[o] empty term.

[p] "betrügerisch (deceptrix)" (reading "deceptrix" instead of "déceptif," with Hinske, KI, lxxii).

[q] Reading "beachtet" instead of "gebraucht," with Hinske (KI, lxxii).

[r] "*Krämerey* der *Gelahrten*."

more than one meaning then it is called *terminus vagus ambiguus anceps.*[s]

THE SECOND SECTION

Of the learned style of writing

Style[t] actually means a carver's tool. Here it means the character in which one expresses one's thoughts. Everyone has his own particular style, just 295 as everyone writes his own particular hand. Style is to be considered (1.) insofar as it is adequate to its *object.* (2.) To the person (subject) and the person's social position. (3.) To those for whom one writes. For everyone a particular style is suitable, and everyone cannot bring his thoughts into someone else's form.

§ 473 et 475

Appropriateness of writing style consists in the fact that it is such that the style is not too great for the thing but instead is fitting. Euphony in writing style is something that belongs among the chimeras rather than to what is true. The English say that Virgil's poems sound good, but when one hears an Englishman recite the verse, this would be insufferable to our ears. *Sonorum*[u] consists in the mass of the syllables. Congruence consists in the fact that the style is suited to the thing. This can only be learned by experience.

THE THIRD SECTION

Of a learned speech

Concerning the *donum didacticum*[v] and the requirements of a teacher. In the case of a teacher there must in general be 2 things. He must possess (1.) the ability to descend[w] toward the lower[x] capacities and (2.) an ability to ascend[y] toward the higher capacities.

1. Every teacher must know how to put himself in the place of his listeners[;] I can teach another only by means of his own understanding, hence I have

[s] a term that is vague, ambiguous, equivocal.
[t] "Styl"; from the Latin "stilus," a sharp instrument used to carve waxen tablets.
[u] Sonority.
[v] didactic gift.
[w] "eine Condescendenz."
[x] Reading "schlechtern" instead of "Schlechten," with Hinske (KI, lxxii).
[y] "eine Coadescendenz."

material to work on[z] that already lies in the mind of the other. This is called *the ability to descend*[.][a] It presupposes[b] that one knows how put oneself in the place of those one teaches. Only very few teachers of religion, and others, can do this.

2. The 2nd *requisitum* of a teacher is the ability to ascend,[c] namely, that one rises to the talents that are elevated above the average. He who knows little certainly cannot do it. The best is to choose a middle degree. How must one[d] act in public lectures, where one does not cognize the capacity of the *auditores*?[e]

§ 493

We must distinguish imparting[f] an opinion to someone and refuting someone's opinion. In the first case the subject is empty, but in the second I have to empty the subject. Before all instruction I must first have the *data*$_L$ in which the other errs. Every error is to be regarded as a phenomenon that is worthy of an explanation. First I have to have insight as to how he could have come to the error. Then I also have to track down the part that is true in his error.

296

§ 501–504–509–512

Verbal dispute is when various persons believe they are disputing various opinions, yet are at odds only in words, and are at one concerning the thing itself. Concerning predestination, some thought that it is more a verbal dispute than a real dispute.[g] An *argumentum ad hominem* is an argument that obviously is not true for everyone, but still serves to reduce someone to silence. E.g., when I get something *ex concessis*[h] and from the particular propositions that someone else has. These are good means for getting someone off one's back and for ending the dispute, but not for finding truth. *Retorsiones*[i] and *reprehensiones*[j] are personal controversies[;] *distinctions* serve quite well for getting out of the trouble. An *instantia* is when something is said[k] universally and I show that it is not

[z] Reading "bearbeiten" instead of "Arbeiten," with Hinske (KI, lxxii).

[a] "die *Condescendenz*."

[b] Reading "setzt voraus" instead of "sagt voraus," with Hinske (KI, lxxii).

[c] "die Coadescendenz."

[d] Reading "erwähle. Wie muß man sich" instead of "erwähle, man muß sich," with Hinske (KI, lxxii).

[e] listeners.

[f] Reading "beybringen" instead of "zubringen," with Hinske (KI, lxxii).

[g] "Sachen Streit."

[h] from what is conceded.

[i] retorts.

[j] reprehensions, or rebukes.

[k] Reading "gesagt" for "gebraucht."

universal. A defense that is concerned with the person is called an *apology*[;] if it is concerned with the judgments of others, it is called a *refutatio*.

§ 514

A *formal* disputation[l] is the action where, in the presence of learned people, one advances a few propositions to defend them against all objections. Disputation could yield great value, if it were not a *certamen personarum*."[m] And if one were to seek truth by means of agreement, not by means of dispute.

THE FOURTH SECTION

Of learned writings

All learned writings are either *historical* or *dogmatic*. A writing can be historical both as to its material, if it is something that really happened or 297 cognition of the *individuum*, and as to its form. That form which is not rational, where I do not derive by means of universal cognition of the grounds, is called historical.

A cognition is called historically dogmatical as to form when the data are *dogmata*$_L$ but they are expounded historically. As to matter, however, when some things are historical but others are dogmatic. Everything that happens is considered in connection with space and time. When one considers what happens insofar as it is at different times, however, this is called *history*,"[n] but insofar as it is at the same time it belongs to the field of *geography*. There are various kinds of geography and history.

§ 519

The distinction that the author draws, in which he divides history into political history, church[o] history, learned history, and private history, is determined by various objects of historical cognitions. There could also be a moral history, which considers the morals of common life and also moral *data*$_L$. Biography is the life of a single subject. All history, of whichever kind it may be, should have the end of extending reason[;] it should provide the material for the use of reason.

[l] "Eine Formelle Disputation."
[m] conflict among persons.
[n] "Historie."
[o] Reading "politische, Kirchen-" instead of "politische Kirchen," with Hinske (KI, lxxii).

§ 520

That history which becomes useful through universal rules is called pragmatic; this can have a relation either to speculation or to practical reason. If one learns merely the names of the sovereigns and knows their reigns, then this provides little material for the use of reason, i.e., for speculation, or for practical rules. In the beginning, nonetheless, one must abstract from the use of reason and equip oneself optimistically with many historical cognitions. Learned history becomes pragmatic when one considers learnedness in relation to human reason, if one looks to its growth or to the causes by which it is held back. There are 2 methods of composing dogmatic writings, either *tumultuously* or *methodically*. The latter method brings about a system. A system is a whole. Systematic writings differ from tumultuous writings in that they constitute a whole that fits together. Excerpts[p] are actually systems. The *principia* of dogmatists have to be expounded in dogmatic writings, then pulled together and considered *in concreto*. And one must mix with this something historical, in order to provide evidence.[q] 298

§ 525

The method where one does not draw a cognition from one's own sources but instead takes from those who have drawn from the source, is called compilation. History is compiled if I have assembled it not from primary sources but instead from later ones. One can also compile philosophy, where one gathers together what others[r] have thought by means of reason. One proves his skill, however, if, with clever selection, one pulls together the *most important* things from authors who possess great acuity, from the most thorough histories. The *compilator* is distinct from the *plagiarius*, of course. This last pretends to have drawn from the primary learned sources, although he only exhibits someone else's product.

§ 526

The French, especially, are of such a *caractère* that among them the sciences grow more *extensive*$_L$ than *intensive*$_L$. *Epitoma* require much understanding, to be able to select the most important and most comprehensible.

[p] "Auszüge, Epitomen" (reading "Epitomen" instead of "Epitome," with Hinske, KI, lxxii).

[q] "Evidenz."

[r] Reading "was anderen" instead of "was wir," with Hinske (KI, lxxii).

The fourth principal part
Of the character of a learned man

The character of a learned man is of two kinds: the character of his head and of his heart. The first is concerned with cognition, the latter with inclination. The character of the heart has a strong connection with the character of the head, if learnedness is to be furthered. The character of the heart has a great influence on the direction of the understanding, and it is therefore not unimportant even in the case of speculative sciences.

299

§ 530

The character of the head concerns understanding, reason, and taste. The faculty of imitation is exactly opposed to the faculty of genius. Those who possess the capacity of genius sometimes do not have the spirit of imitation, which, on the other hand, is common to the highest degree among those who show no genius. The Russians are supposed to have the flaw that they lack genius and just for this reason are not able to teach it. Hence science always dies out among them. Philosophy requires genius, likewise *belles lettres*[;][s] useful sciences,[t] however, require the spirit of imitation. Mathematics only requires imitation. Learnedness and good taste are distinct from one another.

§ 533

Native wit[u] is the natural capacity of the healthy understanding and healthy reason. This cannot be learned[;] what is subsequently learned is called schooled wit.[v] All instruction presupposes certain cognitions, or at least the capacity for them. It is more acceptable to lack schooled wit than to have that without native wit. That which is learned is beautiful in man, but he himself is absurd in its application. Pedantry arises thus, and by means of schooled wit one becomes still more ridiculous than ever[,]

[s] "zu schönen Wißenschaften."
[t] "zu nützlichen Wißenschaften."
[u] "Mutterwitz."
[v] "Schulwitz."

because one then has more materials. Schooled wit is a completion of native wit.

§ 540

Particular learned exercises include

1. learning. This occurs by means of oral exposition or by means of the reading of books. One learns either by producing a cognition or by reproducing cognitions that one possesses. To teach is actually to get cognitions to be produced by others. The one who learns is purely passive in this matter, but he must also be active. He must have receptivity, i.e., the capacity of understanding, and must also apply it. Oral exposition has a great advantage over written, for oral exposition is not as artificial as the written. It is also more comprehensible, for there is one less action of the mind than in reading. In reading, namely, I also have to hear in my thoughts.

§ 541

300

2. The reading of learned writings. Much depends on order[,] how one reads[,] and on the choice of writings[,] where one begins. There is a question as to whether *compendia* or great works[w] should be read first. One should not begin with *compendia* that contain much thought in little space, but instead with ones that contain few thoughts in a large space. In mathematics and in history one must first acquaint oneself with the universal. First of all one must proceed in accordance with the main thing.[x] Historical books that one selects for reading must first of all concern not so much the precise facts as rather the universal ones. One must proceed according to a certain order, and in the morning and evening read books of speculation, at midday historical books. One must read much and, so to speak, digest what is read, and the field must not be altered very much. One has to read every book at least 2 times, once quickly, where one marks the places that require clarification. Some books are of great importance and require considerable inquiry[;] these one must read often. E.g., Hume, Rousseau, Locke, who can be regarded as a grammar for the understanding, and Montesquieu, concerning the spirit of the laws[.]

§ 544

Excessive repetition is just as harmful as excessive inactivity. § 546: Imitation in matters of style is not advisable. § 548: no rule can be given for the

[w] Reading "Compendia oder große Wercke" instead of "Compendia der großen Wercke," with Hinske (KI, lxxii).

[x] "hauptsächlich."

discovery of new truths. § 549[:] An *autodidactus* is one who makes himself learned by means of meditation and reading. This is always a great genius. An oral exposition is always to be preferred, meantime. One can make more *reflexiones*.

§ 553

Learned industry[y] means the strength of the effort that one applies in order to learn something. Man is by nature idle, and laziness is itself the final end of his industry.[z] Future rest is the spur that moves men to activity. The quantity and worth of objects can excite industry greatly. Learned industry, if it continues, is called constant industry. Distinct from
301 this is vehement industry, which consists in excessively strong effort. The mind suffers in the case of vehement industry[;] representations die out.

§ 554

One who is studying must first weigh carefully his end and the extent of his powers[.] It is bad for others to prescribe for us our end, and for one not to be acquainted with himself when one begins to study. One must never study with vehement industry, but one must never stop learning. One only knows how to judge what one has to learn when one is close to the end. It also belongs to the character of a learned man that he is a person without title, estate, or civic rank. Principally, that he be a man of all estates, and that his cognition be universally useful and not be suited merely for the form of the school[.] The final end of learnedness ought to be to give the human race its true form, to free it of prejudices, to refine its morals, and to elevate the powers of the soul[;] then it is a good thing for the human race[;] but if it is used merely for operation,[a] then it is to be regarded only as a kind of *luxus*.

End of the logic

[y] "Der Gelährte Fleiß."

[z] Reading "der Endzweck seines Fleißes" instead of "der Fleiß," with Hinske (KI, lxxii).

[a] "zur operation."

PART II

The Vienna logic and The Hechsel logic

The Vienna logic

Kant's
lectures on logic written
by a society of auditors

Prolegomena

Everything in the world happens according to rules[;] as we perceive this in the corporeal world, so do we find it even in the employment of our own powers, although we are not immediately conscious of the rules at all. We attain this employment through mere attempts, and from these very attempts, e.g., teaching someone to speak or to walk, we can derive the multitude of rules. In this way we can learn many rules by ourselves. Grammar consists of endless rules. On this aaccount a few have held language to be a divine inspiration, too. This much is certain, however, that all languages, in accordance with their first principles, can be reduced to a grammar. Moreover, grammar is a doctrine of the understanding, of course. For as our soul combines concepts, so must words also be combined. It is too abstract to be taught in school. Let us take only the abstract rules of the *genere substantivo*, etc. Let us investigate more closely these rules according to which our powers work. The understanding is the faculty of rules itself, and only the understanding can test these rules. By what rule does it do so? This is hard to discover, because if it errs itself, the understanding cannot indicate the correctness of the rules according to which it proceeds.

All rules for the use of our powers are either *absolutely* necessary or *conditionally* necessary. Without the former no use of the understanding occurs at all[;] without the contingent rules, the use of the understanding for a certain purpose will come to an end. The necessary ones must be such that they hold of the understanding without distinction among objects. They must concern only the form of the understanding.

Note. In all thought there is matter and form. Matter concerns the object and form the mode of treatment. Thus physiology and psychology are distinct as to matter. As to form, if they are treated empirically, they can be alike. Our senses give the matter of cognition.[a] Intuition lies in the understanding. Words are the matter of language, but grammar the form. Thus a science that is occupied with the form of the understanding is called logic.

791

Our understanding has various objects of cognition and of science, such as history, mathematics – but universal logic abstracts from all this content, from all variety of cognition, and considers in everything only the

[a] Reading "die Materie der Erkenntniß" for "der Materie die Erkenntniß."

form of concepts, judgments, and inferences. In short, it is one of the sciences that prepare us for others.

Προπαιδευτική[b] (*propositiones*). Every man observes the rules before he can reduce them to formulas. Gradually, however, he attends to what he does. The complex of all these rules is called *logica naturalis*. The science that expounds these rules systematically [is called *logica*] *artificialis*. It is an affectation to label this natural inclination with the name of science. In this way one could have a natural optics, mechanics. As said above, logic is divided into *naturalis* and *artificialis*. This division is bad because logic is held to be the complex of rules of the understanding that we employ without being conscious. Since we do not know these rules, however, there cannot be a science. Consequently this is a contradiction. *Logica naturalis* is cognition[c] of the rules of the understanding *in concreto*, *logica artificialis* [is such cognition] *in abstracto*.

For us, then, only *logica artificialis* is ever called logic. We can divide[d] the laws of our understanding in the following way[:]

1. Rules for how we think.
2. Rules for how we ought to think.

Sometimes we think completely wrongheadedly. This use can never agree with the rules. This is the misuse of the understanding and is excluded here. Logic teaches this last, namely, how to use the objective rules of our understanding. Logic has the peculiarity that the subjective laws are also objective rules, because the universal rules are the sole condition of our thought. Sometimes we give approval to a thing out of habit or inclination. This is not a universal law. Consequently the subjective laws of willing cannot be objective laws of the understanding. Some logicians presuppose psychology in their logic. Since this is an empirical science, there would arise from this a science of how we think under various hindrances, not of how we ought to think. There would be nothing but contingent and natural laws. But that is not what we are asking about. Logical rules must be derived from the necessary use of the understanding. In a grammar we consider the universal rules without which no language[e] at all can exist.

792

There are two kinds of cognition. An *a priori* one, which is independent of experience; and an *a posteriori* one, which is grounded on empirical principles. Now since experience teaches us nothing but contingent things, but universal logic abstracts from all content and consequently rests on *principia a priori*, it is counted among the *scientiae rationales*. Logic is called this, however, based on a twofold ground:

[b] Propaedeutic.
[c] "Kenntniß."
[d] Reading "eintheilen" for "mittheilen."
[e] Reading "Sprache" for "Sache."

1. It is drawn from reason.
2. It has reason as its object.

What belongs in the definition, however, is really only that it is rational as to its object.

With any science the end is either to extend or to elucidate our cognitions. Logic only elucidates, because it considers form, which cannot be extended. A universal precept that rests on grounds *a priori* is called a canon. Logic is called such because it rests on rules *a priori*. It is a canon of all thought, morals a canon of all willing. – Logic is a rational science, a canon for the understanding. Just as grammar is for passing judgment on language as to form. Words are the matter. A science that extends our cognitions[f] is called an organon. Logic cannot be called such because it abstracts from all content. Just as little can it be an art, since this is an organon of a cognition.[g] A few insist [that it is] the art of making definitions. But these must always be closely tested, and taste, by which to judge according to laws of the senses, has no canon, because it arises *a posteriori*. Thus logic and aesthetics are distinguished by the difference of their objects.

Definition. Logica est scientia regularum universalium usus intellectus.[h] Now if logic is to be a science of the universal laws of the understanding, then these must be necessary rules, because they are to have relation to everything without distinction among objects, and without them nothing at all can be thought. All necessary rules must be derived *a priori*. Rules of experience are *a posteriori*. Gravity is to be found throughout the world. I will never be able to have insight that all bodies are subject to gravity[i] unless I have insight into the necessity of gravity *a priori*. A science that rests on *principia a priori* is called a demonstrated science. Experience cannot be demonstrated because we first have to prove its necessity.

793

Logic is thus a demonstrated science. A science that can be taught from *principia a priori* is called a *doctrina*, consequently logic is one too. When the rules of judgment precede the passing of judgment, then it is called a *doctrina*. When the passing of judgment precedes, [it is called] critique. For once I have the rules of experience, then I can pass judgment on them. Now we ask, What is logic, a critique or a doctrine? Because it is to be a touchstone and is to precede our understanding it is a doctrine. Passing of judgment critically always presupposes a doctrine. Logic is not a critique at all, then. It can be used for that purpose, however.

[f] "Kenntniße."
[g] "Kenntniß."
[h] Logic is the science of the universal rules for the use of the intellect.
[i] "daß alle Körper schwer sind."

Logic is divided into 2 parts.

1. Analytic.
2. Dialectic.

1. *Analytic*, or logic as critique of cognition in regard to truth, is that part which, through the analysis of our understanding, presents the universal rules[j] of the form of our understanding, hence the necessary rules of all truth. It is consequently the mere canon for passing judgment on the understanding.

2. *Dialectic* is the misuse of this canon, when we make it into an organon and try to cognize truth therefrom. Analytic is the art of separating in regard to our judgments. There is a great illusion that we can cognize truth through the canon for passing judgment on the understanding, since [cognition] is correct as to form. Since analytic abstracts from all content, however, and considers nothing beyond form, it cannot be an organon of new truths. Among the ancients, the dialecticians were those who disputed *pro et contra*. They were sophists, and sought to deceive. They assumed false propositions, accommodated everything according to the formal laws of the understanding, and consequently provided themselves with a great illusion of truth. It is possible to speak in logical form of a thing of which one understands nothing, namely, by heaping inference upon inference, etc. – and the listener is thereby deceived. Thus logic is misused as an art, and it becomes an organon, but not of truth. As long as this art flourished, logic was nothing but a cultivation of dialectic as an art. 794 A century ago it was still the case that the professor who expounded dialectic as an art was the best one. What we call dialectic is a means by which one can cognize that something is opposed to the formal laws of the understanding. Consequently it is only a purgative. In our judgments, inferences, etc., we are subject to illusion through the senses. Furthermore, there are certain means of truth, which one can imitate without otherwise having anything in common with truth. E.g., an author who imitates the form of thoroughness, but who otherwise expounds untruths. We are often deceived by these skills when we are unfamiliar with the content. Agreement with logical rules is the *conditio sine qua non*, of course. But this is not sufficient for finding truth. How dialectic arises one can see in the schools. A school essay[k] is full of words without content.

Our author believes that dialectic is the logic of probability. But probability is a judgment concerning truth according to correct but insufficient grounds. If its grounds are correct, however, then it belongs to analytic. Dialectic is the logic of illusion, where this is accepted as empty. The application of logic can only be to objects. Universal logic proceeds,

[j] Reading "allgemeinen Regeln" for "allgemeine Regel."
[k] "Schul-Chrie."

however, without distinction among objects. Consequently the canon must be theoretical. On this account, however, universal logic cannot be applied, either, because practical logic presupposes cognitions[l] and sciences, but universal logic cannot presuppose any sciences because it is a *propaedeutic.*

For there is no practical part in logic, as our author opines. Otherwise dialectic would be a pure illusion. For there cannot be a practical logic, such as the art of education. For this already presupposes study of universal logic. All sciences are the *praxis*$_L$ of logic, however, because without logic nothing can go forward. Logic must not be divided into the theoretical and the practical part, then, but into the dogmatic and the technical part. The dogmatic part is the canon; the technical part is the prescription of rules for the school. Universal logic ought to consider the form of the understanding. Therefore it abstracts from all speculation and considers the logic of universal human reason. Here it departs from the sciences. Like all sciences that have their concepts *a priori*, logic is divided into the logical doctrine of elements and the logical doctrine of method. The doctrine of elements is the *dialectica* or the analytic of reason (or theoretical logic). For it is *propaedeutic.* The doctrine of method is the logic of the form of a system of cognitions. We can sketch a special doctrine of method for one science or another. And this is then technical logic, or an organon. This organon can only appear at the end of a science, because only then am I acquainted with the nature of the science. It is the completion of the rules for its perfection, which contains all the *termini technici* whereby we distinguish logical directives in critique. It is [in logic] what the chapter on metaphor, metonymy, etc., is in oratory. It considers not just the form of the understanding, but rather the form of systems, and is to a great extent of dialectical content. It speaks only of various kinds of form in systems. In art one needs manner, in science method. In the former I act according to examples, in the latter according to grounds. It contains the complex of all formal rules for the use of the understanding.

795

We have a logic of common reason and a logic of speculative reason. We can have the faculty of cognizing rules *in concreto* but not all of them *in abstracto*. The faculty of cognition of rules *in concreto* is the common understanding[;] insofar as it is correct, the healthy understanding. The cognition of rules *in concreto*, or when we judge according to an experience, according to an example, is the walker for those who cannot act on their own behalf.[m] It is necessary to know rules *in abstracto* and to cognize how far these rules extend. The healthy understanding serves for thinking healthily and correctly. If it will just limit itself to what is grounded on experience, then it will never become presumptuous. But if one wants to

[l] "Kenntniße."

[m] "der Gängelwagen der Unmündigen."

have an understanding that is not only healthy but perfect, then one must possess a speculative understanding. For there is a great multitude of concepts that are too high for the healthy understanding, but which it nonetheless needs. The logic of speculative reason is thus the faculty for having insight into rules *in abstracto*.

Exposition in a science looks not just to the understandability of the object but rather to the activity of the subject. In logic, exposition can be of two kinds.

1. *Scholastic*. When it is congruent[n] with the desire for cultivation of those[o] who wish to treat this cognition[p] as science.

2. *Popular*, for the sake of those who do not wish to make a science of it 796 but only wish thereby to put their understanding in order[;] this is quite beneficial for the common world[q] but requires much genius, because popular logic belongs to those cognitions that involve the ability to descend.[r] The ancients had more popularity in their exposition because they spoke before the people. Among the moderns, the French have advanced furthest. Scholastic presentation is the foundation of the popular, however, since it is the foundation of all the sciences, and the latter is only, as it were, an ornament of the sciences.

[n] "angemeßen."
[o] Reading "derer" for "denen," in accordance with Lehmann's correction (24:1102).
[p] "Kenntniß."
[q] "das gemeine Wesen."
[r] "mit zu den descendenten Kenntnißen gehört."

History of Logic

[The word] logic comes from λόγος (*sermo*)[s] and has the meaning of reason. Epicurus called it a canon[,] a science of the cautious and correct use of the understanding. Aristotle can be regarded as the father of logic. But his logic is too scholastic, full of subtleties, and fundamentally has not been of much value to the human understanding. It is a dialectic and an organon for the art of disputation. There is much acuity in his organon. All our logical terminology is from him. Otherwise it tends to mythology and subtlety and is banned from the schools. Still, the principal ideas from it have been preserved, and this is because logic is not occupied with any object and hence it can be quickly exhausted. His logic flourished for many centuries in all schools, until Petrus Ramus first wrote a logic in 2 parts,[1] treating

1. *de inventione,*[t]
2. *de iudicio.*[u]

Through his refutations of Aristotle he became the object of deadly hatred. After them come Malebranche and Locke. This last wrote a treatise *de intellectu humano*. But both writings deal not only with the form of the understanding but with content. They are preparatory exercises for metaphysics. Among the moderns, Leibniz and Wolff are to be noted. The logic of Wolffius is the best to be found. It was subsequently condensed by Baumgarten,[2] and he was again extended by Meier. After them, Reusch[3] and Knutzen[4] wrote logics. Reusch is a philosopher in Jena. At just this time the *Récherches de la vérité*[5] came out. The logic of Crusius[6] is crammed full of things that are drawn from other sciences, and it contains metaphysical and theological principles. Lambert[7] wrote an organon of pure reason. It is remarkable that one cannot give a precise definition of a science even when it has come almost to its perfection. The cause is that 797 our reason cannot develop its ends until late, on account of their truth. But in the end a science thereby acquires its proper perfection. Since logic is a propaedeutic to all philosophical sciences, the concept of philosophy must be established here – cognitions of reason from concepts are

[s] Both words mean "discourse."
[t] concerning invention.
[u] concerning judgment.

philosophical cognitions. Cognitions of reason from the construction of concepts are mathematical cognitions. The system of the former is called philosophy, of the latter mathematics. Cognition of reason is opposed to historical cognition. A cognition is historical as to form when it is a cognition *ex datis*. Cognition of reason is a cognition *ex principiis*, which has been drawn from grounds *a priori*.

A cognition can have arisen from reason. But the way I cognize it is nonetheless historical if, namely, I only acquire it as it was given to me. E.g., the polyhistor who studies the philosophy of the ancients. Here the cognition is *objective*$_{L}$ a cognition of reason, but *subjective*$_{L}$ historical. To learn philosophy and to learn to philosophize are two different things. One of the greatest mistakes in instruction is when one has an author's system[v] of philosophy memorized but does not have the author judged. Hence it is necessary to use more reason in the method of reason. Many philosophers boast of nothing but the imitation of someone else's reason.

It is commonly believed that mathematics and philosophy have two different objects, that philosophy is a cognition of quality, and mathematics a cognition of quantity. We maintain that philosophy and mathematics[,] in particular the first[,] are concerned with all objects. Quantities are spoken of in philosophy as well as in mathematics. The specific difference between these two sciences is that philosophy is a cognition of reason from concepts, mathematics a cognition of reason from the construction of concepts. Construction of concepts is when I exhibit a concept *a priori* in intuition. Through philosophy[,] from concepts[,] one cannot have insight into anything in mathematics. Only with intuition does one have insight into the construction of this or that proposition *ex principiis*. Mathematics has a great advantage over philosophy, then, since all its cognitions 798 are intuitive, while those of philosophy are discursive. The cause of the fact that in mathematics we only consider quantities is that only quantities can be constructed. Qualities cannot be constructed but can only be cognized from concepts. The distinction of mathematics rests, then, not only on the objects but on form. Philosophy is the system of philosophical cognition. Here I omit [the word] speculative, for cognition of reason within a system must be speculative throughout. For a system is from *principia a priori*. This is philosophy in the scholastic sense. We also have a philosophy according to a *conceptus cosmicus*, and then it is a science of the ultimate final ends of human reason. Speculative cognition of reason differs from the common through the fact that the former is cognition of reason according to rules *in abstracto*, the latter according to rules *in concreto*. Cognition of reason according to rules *in concreto* is the popular kind of exposition, which is suited for the common man. If it is correct, then that is healthy reason. Philosophical cognition is speculative cogni-

[v] Reading "das System" for "Systeme."

tion from concepts. Mathematical cognitions are cognitions of reason from the construction of concepts. I can provide evidence for a concept,[w] that is, I can give an intuition of a true concept, if I provide evidence for it *a posteriori*. But the mathematician provides evidence for his concepts *a priori*. E.g., if I have a circle that is not really correct, I can nonetheless demonstrate. For the representation already lies in me. Scholastic philosophy is instruction aimed at skill, true philosophy a doctrine aimed at wisdom, which must be the highest good for our striving. It is the legislation of reason. We can distinguish artistry of reason[x] from its legislation. The artist of reason or philodox, as Socrates calls him, is one who equips reason for any end one might wish. The mathematician is an artist of reason, likewise the logician and the physicist. But in the end one sees that philosophy as a doctrine of reason is necessary. Philosophy, then, is an idea of the most perfect legislation of the human understanding, and the philosopher is the legal expert of human reason. Now since this title is so sublime, no one can rightly allow himself to be called a philosopher. The cause of the fact that we esteem highly someone who arranges his actions according to the strictest laws of morality, and who never departs from the straight path, is perhaps that morals is in fact always the end toward which all speculations tend. Morals constitutes a unity of all cognition of reason, and only he who follows its rules can be called a philosopher. Whence comes the word philosophy? It has been attributed to Pythagoras first of all. Not as teacher of wisdom, but [due to] the high concept he had of the wisdom of the sublime god.

799

Philosophy *in sensu scholastico* involves two things. (1.) A sufficient supply of cognitions of reason. (2.) A correct connection of these, or a system. For a system is the connection of many cognitions in accordance with an idea. Our historical cognitions[y] only serve for this when[z] our reason can make use of them according to its ends. Since ends are subordinated to one another, there must be higher ends, and thus there arises among these ends a unity, or a system of ends. The true worth of our use of reason can only be determined through the connection that this cognition has with the final ends. There is therefore a science of wisdom. If we call the inner *principium* of the choice of various ends a maxim,[a] then we can say that philosophy *in sensu cosmico* is a science of the highest maxims of the use of our reason. And here the philosopher distinguishes himself more through the maxims of his mode of thought than through the connection of his cognitions. Philosophy in the scholastic sense (philodoxy) is an

[w] "Einen Begriff kann ich belegen."

[x] "Vernunft-Künsteleyen."

[y] "Kenntniße."

[z] Reading "nützen nur dazu, wenn" for "nützen dazu, daß," following a suggestion by Hinske.

[a] Reading "Maxime" for "Maximen."

organon of skill, and the philodox is related to the philosopher as the businessman is to the legislator in the state. If the philosopher is to cognize the connection of all cognitions of reason with the final ends, he must determine

1. the sources of human knowledge,
2. the beginning of the use [of those cognitions],
3. their limits. This is one of the hardest, but also most sublime things in philosophy, which presently only a few have attained.

And on this account philosophy *in sensu cosmico* is also called philosophy *in sensu eminenti*. Philosophy cannot be learned, because every philosopher erects his own building on the ruins of another, and if a system were actually given to me that was so clear that it contained only irrefutable propositions, I would still not be a philosopher if I memorized all its propositions. I would not learn to philosophize then, but would only

800 possess a historical cognition, without knowing the sources from which it was drawn. One can also say here just what one can say in jurisprudence: The *legis peritus*[b] in the highest laws of reason is the true philosopher. The *leguleii*[c] in the highest laws of reason are the sophists and the dialecticians, who provide themselves with a certain illusion of wisdom, and with this seek to accomplish certain ends by force.

Man needs two things in philosophy:

1. A cultivation of our skill. This is necessary because for all ends we need a skill in the use of all means to these ends. One can just as little be a philosopher without cognitions[d] as one can become a philosopher through mere cognitions.[e] The best principles of our mode of thought have no lastingness unless the science of wisdom secures them. Innocence is amiable, but not secure against seduction[;] instruction about all that can tempt, and about the origin of errors into which [innocence] can mislead us, must also be added. He who has hatred toward all the sciences, and who pretends that wisdom alone is to be esteemed, is called a misologist. Epicurus is criticized for wanting to produce a doctrine of wisdom whereby all the sciences would be given up and misology would be introduced. Misology commonly arises from the fact that someone feels himself empty of all skills. There is also a misology, however, among those who have extensive cognitions,[f] and here it arises from the fact that these cognitions[g] were unable to satisfy them. Only philosophy can provide this

[b] legal expert.
[c] pettifogging lawyers.
[d] "Kenntnisse."
[e] "Kenntniße."
[f] "Kenntniße."
[g] "Kenntniße."

inner satisfaction. It closes the circle, and then it sees how all cognitions[h] fit together in an edifice, in rule-governed ways, for such ends as are suited to humanity.

2. In considering philosophy as skill we will look more to its method than to the purpose toward which it is directed. Of course we will also turn our view toward the highest maxims. Since we are directed by the method how we are to learn to philosophize, however, and since philosophy consequently places the human spirit in the greatest freedom, it deserves the greatest attention. No people on earth began to philosophize earlier than the Greeks, since no people thought through concepts, but instead all thought through images. They first began to study rules *in abstracto*. Which people investigated the concepts of virtue, of the highest good? The Egyptian wisdom is nothing but child's play compared to the Greek, and modern authors have proved that the Egyptians did have surveyors, to be sure, who measured fields according to a certain accepted standard, but they did not understand anything about mathematics. The Greeks were the founders of mathematics, who demonstrated it from first grounds and elements. They are the core of the human race and its benefactors. In Greek history it is obscure where philosophy arose. The Thracians seem to be the most insightful and the earliest. The fragmentists among them are Orpheus and Musaeus. The wise men in Greece had nothing but sentences and moral sayings, which had long been known among the people. Sentences are thoughts condensed into a familiar expression, in order to inscribe them in memory more easily. One among them is noteworthy, and from him all philosophy proceeds[:] Thales, who, on account of his acquaintance with natural science is also called *physicus*. He is the founder of the Ionian school. His followers are Anaximander and Anaximenes. It is remarkable that the language of the poets was the first one in which things that are objects of reason were expressed, so that philosophy is greatly hindered by poetry. Pherecydes was the first philosopher to write in prose, and soon after him Heraclitus. Their writings seemed to everyone quite obscure, because at that time philosophy was wholly new. The language of the poets is astonishingly rich in ideas. The works of Homer, Hesiod prove that. But at that time the ideas had not yet been made free of corporeal secondary meanings. These were followed by the Eleatic sect. Its founder was Xenophanes, and after him Parmenides. They taught that in the senses there is nothing but deception, and only in the understanding is there truth. Here philosophy becomes much enlightened and breaks away wholly from the poets. Zeno, a man of great acuity, belongs to this sect. – What was understood under the name of dialectic at that time was the pure use of the understanding. Hence there are great encomia for dialectic among the ancients. The

801

[h] "Kenntniße."

doctrine of the highest good was reckoned to it, [and also] that concerning that being in us which thinks, etc. When the understanding breaks away from the guiding thread of the senses, it runs the risk of losing itself in labyrinths. Hence it is comprehensible how such a use of the understanding could have fallen into mere subtleties. From these arose the current name of dialectic, which pedants know well how to use. About the time of 802 the Ionian sect, Pythagoras founded the Italian school in *Magna Graecia*. He is the only one among all the philosophers who had something peculiar. He was a great mathematician, and he knew how to bring music under mathematical laws. He founded a society of philosophers, who were bound to one another through secrecy. He expounded geometrical doctrines only to his friends. This philosophy spread throughout the land. Its essential points, which they taught, were to provide much more moderate concepts of the gods than the people had, and somehow to oppose the machinations of the princes. It was in fact a kind of free-masonry. Finally they acquired such a reputation that all the cities wanted their regents to come from among the pupils of Pythagoras, who lived in Crotona. – He believed in the transmigration of souls, but one cannot say much about this, because he had nothing but secrets. – [He] played with numbers. At about this time a man appeared in Greece who opened a new pathway among speculative minds, [asking] how one is to attain the highest good[:] Socrates, whom Xenophon describes as someone who comes closest to the idea of a wise man. He possessed a great skill for cornering the dialecticians by means of questions and answers[;] this is called Socratic irony. His follower was Plato, and the latter's follower was Aristotle. The former cultivated the practical part of the Socratic philosophy, and the latter brought speculative philosophy to greater perfection. Now follow the moral philosophers. The Epicureans founded all virtue on an ever joyful heart. The Stoics founded virtue on a renunciation of all pleasure of life, and in the elevation of the soul. Although the Epicureans taught many things that were erroneous, they were nonetheless the best natural philosophers among all the Greeks.

The foremost schools* of the Greeks had special names. – Plato's Academy was not an individual building but rather an open place under the open sky among the most outstanding buildings. It is divided into 3 parts.

803 1. The Academy of Speusippus, who still remained a faithful follower of Plato and who taught completely dogmatically.

* *Note 1*. The opinions of individual men were called schools.

2. The cognitions were not regarded as objects to be learned by youths, rather, old people also occupied themselves with them.

3. The philosophers at that time had an influence on the public and on the constitution of the state.

4. If they were moral philosophers, people demanded of them not only their doctrines, but also the confirmation of those doctrines through their own examples.

2. __________ of Arcesilaus. He was a mere doubter. Thus it happens that the *academici* are also called *sceptici*. Plato expounded his doctrines dialogically, and in such a way that he did not decide, but rather let there be dispute on both sides. Now the method that suspends the matter and makes it probable that it could be otherwise easily finds approval.
3. __________ of Carneades, who was likewise an extremely subtle and dialectical doubter.

The *lyceum* or *gymnasium* was Aristotle's school, and because he commonly walked in the square with his followers they were also called *peripatetici*. He had no famous followers. Theophrastus and Demetrius Phaleraeus wrote no books, and they also did not extend Aristotle at all. A *porticus* was a covered walkway, a picture gallery, and the school of Stoic sect. In speculative philosophy these latter were mostly dialectical, but in morals quite practical. Their founder was Zeno of Citium. His most famous followers are Cleanthes and Chrysippus. They laid the ground for the most magnanimous principles in the world, although their doctrines are idealistic and too high for realization.[i]

Horti,[j] the school of the Epicureans. These latter did battle with the Stoics and in the end were pushed aside by them, because everyone esteemed such high principles. Lucretius's book *De rerum natura* is the only one that was written according to their principles. Besides the *sceptici academici*, the skepticism of Pyrrho is also noteworthy. The *dogmatici* maintained that truth can be proved exactly. Pyrrho maintained that philosophy lies in the balance of our judgment and in the skill of being able to uncover all false illusion, without otherwise being able to prove anything decisive. But since men are more timid than eager to tear things down, this sect found little approval. Sextus Empiricus is noteworthy because he collected all these doubts.

When the philosophy of the Greeks came to the Romans, it did not increase in the least. Cicero follows Plato in speculative philosophy, the *porticus* in moral philosophy. In natural philosophy only Plinius Secundus accomplished anything excellent.

When the Roman Empire was overrun by the barbarians all culture disappeared until the Arabs, in the 10th *seculum*, spread through the Occident and began to cultivate the sciences. All philosophy was taken 804 from Aristotle, who was followed in a slavish way. In the 10th *seculum* the scholastic school arose, which produced nothing but commentaries on Aristotle. Since Aristotle, as is known, had worked on nothing but speculative reason, people dealt only with astounding subtleties in logic and metaphysics. About the time of the Reformation, the remaining scholastics were swept away. Immediately after the scholastics the *sceptici* rose to

[i] "Ausübung."
[j] Gardens.

prominence: Huetius,[8] Bayle,[9] Hume, who were called *antilogici*. Then came the *eclectici*, i.e., philosophers who did not cling to any sect particularly. This improvement is not to be attributed to any circumstance more than to the *studium* of nature, which was combined with mathematics. Order in thought was thereby furthered. The Lord Chancellor Baco de Verulam[10] contributed to this in his organon for the sciences, in that he called attention to the method in physics, namely, to observations and experiments. Cartesius was the first to take this path. Leibniz in Germany and Locke in England gave direction to speculative reason, in that they sought to purge it of all scholasticism and to bring everything to distinct concepts. – No philosopher has ever had such extensive skill for philosophizing dogmatically as Leibniz. It is dangerous because there is much that is false in our dogmatic propositions on account of the illusion of experience. Thus it is better to criticize the truth. – Locke treats philosophy psychologically, i.e., as someone who analyzes the human powers of cognition. Since his time, people in our own country have begun to study the human soul. In our times natural philosophy is flourishing to the highest degree. In morals we are still not much further than the ancients. Some base morals in willing, others in self-love, etc., etc., as with the ancients. As for what concerns metaphysics, after we have gone through all the parts we hesitate, and because of the great difficulties one finds among us a kind of indifferentism toward this study. *Status anceps*.[k] This is the age of critique for this study, and the time is near when its building will be torn down and a wholly new one will be built on the ruins of the old. In other respects, only metaphysics is true philosophy, and in it lie the real sources from which the understanding derives its use of reason.

[k] A condition of uncertainty.

Tractatio Logices[l]

805

OF COGNITION

All our cognitions can be considered in two relations.

1. In relation to the object. This is representation.
2. In relation to the subject. This is consciousness of the representation.

Representation cannot be defined because for that one always needs new representations. All representation is either sensation or cognition. It is something that has a relation to something in us. Sensations do affect, but they quickly vanish, too, because they are not cognitions. For when I sense, I cognize nothing. Cognition is of two kinds, either intuition or concept. The former is singular, the latter universal. For a concept belongs to all.

In all cognition matter and form are distinct. Matter means the object, form the way of cognizing the object. With form, it depends on consciousness. A cognition of which I am conscious is called clear. If I am not conscious of it, it is called obscure. Consciousness is the standard condition for all logical form in our cognitions. Hence obscure cognitions are not objects of logic, because no logical rule that is obscure to us can help us.

All our clear representations can be distinguished logically into distinct and indistinct representations. Indistinct representation is the consciousness of a representation as a whole, but without distinguishing the manifold that is contained in the whole. Distinctness is clarity that also extends to the parts. All the Wolffians call an indistinct representation confused. – But the opposite of confusion is not distinctness but rather order. Indistinctness is of course an effect of confusion, not confusion itself. There are also indistinct cognitions that are indistinct not through confusion but rather through lack of representation. The concept of something is completely simple. Here neither order nor confusion can be brought in. There are two kinds of distinctness of cognitions[:]

1. A sensible distinctness in intuition, when we are conscious of the manifold that is contained in the intuition.
2. A distinctness of the understanding in concepts. When a cognition is devel-

806

l Ak., "*Tractatio Logices*"; MS, "Tractatio Logices."

oped not as to content but as to form and the various parts of the representation that lie in the understanding are developed.

All our cognitions are either intuitions or concepts. The faculty of intuition is sensibility. The faculty of concepts is the understanding, and to cognize something through concepts is to think. Intuition, however, is only concerned with something individual, concepts with something that several things have in common. From another side, sensibility is so defined[m] that it is a receptivity, a capacity to be affected by objects. The understanding [is defined] as a spontaneity, a faculty of representing things as they are, not as they affect us. Sensibility is consequently the lower faculty of cognition, because sensibility gives me the material for thought, but the understanding disposes over this material. There are two kinds of perfection of cognition[:]

1. Perfection according to the laws of sensibility, aesthetic perfection.
2. Perfection according to the laws of the understanding, logical perfection.

One of the aesthetic perfections in exposition is that a case *in concreto* gives intuition to the rules *in abstracto* and makes them sensible, but it must not be put in place of the understanding, for then the understanding would be ruined[;] rather, intuition must be its companion. Concepts without sensibility have no object at all. The condition of all our concepts lies finally always in the senses. Intuition is therefore a very necessary thing. And although it sometimes misleads the understanding, the understanding is itself culpable for not investigating it better. A cognition is perfect according to the laws of sensibility if it is new, easy, lively, perfect according to the laws of the understanding if it is thorough.

Logical perfection rests on the agreement of cognition with the object, aesthetic perfection on agreement with the subject. The rules of agreement of cognition with the object must be necessary and must hold for all cognition and for every understanding, for because my cognition is to agree with the object, it must also agree with that of others. Aesthetic perfection rests on the particular laws of human sensibility, and it is thus 807 not universal for all creatures. But since objects are represented not only through concepts but also through intuition, there must also be necessary and universal laws of sensibility. Herein lies the concept of the beautiful. The ground of sensible satisfaction is subjective, to be sure, but subjective with respect to all of humanity. E.g. Music. Symmetry. What agrees with the laws of the understanding, however, holds not merely for men but for all thinking beings. But logically perfect cognitions can at the same time have an aesthetic perfection, too. For certain philosophical expositions are called beautiful.

Among all the properties of aesthetic perfection, none is more congru-

[m] "erklärt."

ent with logical perfection or more essential to aesthetic perfection than intuition. It is the form of sensibility, whereas sensation, stimulation, never give universal laws in this way. – Beauty, distinctness, and universality are 3 essential parts of logical perfection. He who wants to convince his listeners must not waken their sensations but must instead present the matter to their intuition.

Sensations, e.g., stimulation, excitement, are the matter of sensibility, intuition is its form. Imagination also holds only for the form of sensibility, but not for its matter. The essential aesthetic perfection is the opposite of the logical[;] distinctness of intuition is nothing more than liveliness in aesthetic truth; the principal thing is not that cognition agree with the object, if only it agrees with our laws of sensibility. The poetically true is not what is logically true, but instead what accords with illusion. Common prejudices have aesthetic truth.

The universality of concepts is the opposite of that which aesthetic perfection involves. In the latter case things are supposed to be represented universally *in concreto*, in the former universally *in abstracto*. Aesthetic perfection contains the essentially beautiful if it is beneficial to logical perfection, the non-essentially beautiful if it is detrimental to it. What belongs to sensation and not to intuition contributes nothing to concepts. What someone senses he can never tell, unless the other senses it too[;] hence this belongs to the non-essentially beautiful. The pleasant involves stimulation, which is often mixed in with the judgment of taste[;] hence we love women on account of their delicate design, which, however, compared to the strong design of men, is an imperfection according to the universal rules of taste. The sublime involves excitement, but this is quite deceptive. Thus the church orator must seek to achieve the end of his sermon not through this but through distinctness, truth, and universality. For sensations are always opposed to logical perfection. If the thing excites, then it hinders thorough inquiry, and the judge can be corrupted by tears. Disturbances of the mind do injury, in that they often promote the opposite of the intended end. Hence the preacher must make use of intuition, and must speak in images and likenesses, when an object is presented to us but no consciousness of the alterations of our condition is united with it. Logical perfection is the *conditio sine qua non* and the basis of all thought. Aesthetic perfection cannot exist by itself, but is only the ornamentation of already correct logical perfection. Now one can, to be sure, leave something out of logical perfection. But one must not mutilate it. One can also, as it were, ignore some of the truth, since one cannot make it wholly universal, yet without in the least causing any lack in logical perfection. Poetry is reckoned first of all under aesthetic perfection. In it logical perfection is somewhat less in degree than aesthetic perfection, and aesthetic perfection always struggles with logical perfection for a place. But the needs of human nature require that sensibility and under-

808

standing go as a pair, and the greatest learned man cannot break away from all sensibility. From this arises popularity, or the ability of the understanding to descend, when it departs somewhat from scholastically correct cognition in order to become more comprehensible. Only one must take care with aesthetic sensations that our attention not be led from the object to the subject. Gentle excitement can give occasion for further reflection, to be sure. But it is not sufficient for conviction.

Our intuition is enriched through history, which gives us cases where that which the concept says *in abstracto* can be expounded *in concreto*. Through observations from common life, moreover, for which good instruction is given in Spalding's sermons,[11] if only they are not shouted

809 down by sensations. – A short while ago much was said of sensations. He who speaks much about feeling cannot think, however, but everyone can feel.

From what has been set forth there arises a unification of the aesthetic and the logical in cognitions. For a cognition can be thorough and logically perfect, but at the same time dry[;] it can be beautiful but at the same time shallow. Cognitions[n] that have the end of instructing, and which in this case have to be thorough, can be dry. Others are only supposed to entertain, hence they may always be shallow. Some ought to contain both. To contrive this requires much genius. For the understanding requires insight, sensibility requires easiness. Hence there is a kind of conflict between the two, where one must make the choice as to which is closest to the end, which satisfies most[;] e.g., mathematics can attain the tasteful only late, because everything must be expounded convincingly.

The perfection of cognitions in general is

1. logical.
2. aesthetic.
3. practical perfection.

Logical perfection is concerned with the understanding and is the cognition of objects through it. Aesthetic perfection is concerned with feeling and with the condition of our subject, namely, how we are affected by the object. For through the beauty of cognition I do not seek cognition[o] of the object but of the subject. Practical perfection is concerned with our desires, through which activity is effected.

The perfection of a cognition rests on 4 principal points.

1. On the quantity of the cognition, in that a cognition is universal. A cognition that serves as a rule must be more perfect than one that holds only in particular cases.

[n] "Kenntniße."
[o] "Kenntniß."

Logical perfection as to quantity or in regard to the judgment is *universality*. That of aesthetic perfection is *common validity*.[p]

2. .... quality, distinctness of the cognition. Contains the *quo modo*.[q] Logical perfection as to quality is *distinctness*, [that] of aesthetic [perfection is] *liveliness*.
3. .... relation, truth of the cognition. Truth is the relation of cognition to the object. If a cognition passes over into moving the mind,[r] then the truth is concerned only with my subject and is aesthetic truth. Logical perfection as to relation is *objective truth*. [That] of aesthetic [perfection is] *subjective truth*. 810
4. .... modality, insofar as it is a certain and necessary cognition. Logical perfection as to modality is the *necessity of cognitions according to the understanding*. [That] of aesthetic [perfection is] *empirical necessity* – –

With aesthetic perfection one can think of

1. subjective truth. This is the agreement of cognition with the subject's mode of thought. Appearances of ghosts, etc., are aesthetically true. The sun, etc., has aesthetic truth[;] logical truth is not at all demanded here. The poet needs only aesthetic [truth], how it appears to our senses and seems to be. The sun sinks into the water, says the poet. If he were to say that the earth turns on its axis, then he would assimilate to logical truth and not be a poet.
2. Subjective distinctness (*relatione*) in intuition, when I fix the rules of objects through examples[;] portrayal. If I wish to cognize something according to aesthetic perfection in regard to liveliness of intuition, then it has to be quite lively. If, e.g., someone wishes to cognize spring logically, then he judges as to quality and has everything distinct through a single mark. The poet speaks here of a multitude of things, of the twittering of birds, etc. It is quite lively, however.
3. Aesthetic universality, i.e., popularity, that a cognition is suited for the *sens commun*. I must presuppose the way I judge, the way everyone else can judge. Here, then, there is subjective universality.[s]
4. Necessity and certainty of aesthetic perfection, that a cognition of the senses is necessary, i.e., that the experience and voices of all men confirm it. Subjective necessity is custom.

Manifoldness and unity constitute every perfection. Our power of cognition strives very much for manifoldness. But it has the need that it must have unity. Otherwise it would not satisfy us, because cognition without unity, when one thing is not connected with the other, does not increase our cognitions.[t] In the case of aesthetic perfection, e.g., the painter must know how to group the manifoldness of the figures so that a unity

[p] "*Gemeingültigkeit*."
[q] in what way.
[r] "Geht eine Erkenntniß zu Gemüthsbewegungen über."
[s] Reading "Allgemeinheit" instead of "Deutlichkeit," which is Lehmann's suggested rendering of a series of dashes in the MS.
[t] "Kenntniße."

811 emerges, if his painting is to please. Truth is the pre-eminent ground of unity and the most necessary and pre-eminent thing. Without truth there is no cognition. In logical perfection it is the positive, greatest condition, With aesthetic perfection it is the *conditio sine qua non* and the foremost negative condition, since here it is not the principal end, which consists in pleasantness and agreement of sensibility. Because, however, no satisfaction can arise where the understanding does not join in and uncover errors, with aesthetic perfection there can be no contradictions. No man, accordingly, can make progress in things of taste unless he has made logical perfection his basis. Most of what is produced by those who fashion taste[u] in Germany is extremely disgusting, if one reads [by comparison] the products of foreign peoples who have not studied the *belles lettres*.[v] True aesthetic perfection is found in [the] Spectateur,[12] Sulzer,[13] Wieland,[14] in whom one notes that they have their heads full of ideas and that they add all the contrivances in order to persuade the mind, in order to accommodate themselves to the comfort of taste. Certain books have nothing attractive about them, although they are quite thorough, namely, because their authors never thought about giving their exposition verve, about enlivening them. – Logical perfection is the skeleton of our cognitions. He who has learned something thorough,[w] therefore, can easily relax logical strictness and add beauty. – Novels and phantasies, which go beyond the [normal] course of things and make the heart faint. History, geography, reading the ancients, which unite both perfections, anthropology [too], must be our instructors and must make the spirit more alert. No science can be beautiful. For science contains universal rules, which precede their employment. Feelings can be combined with the beautiful, they can please and excite us, but they contribute nothing to the play of our representations as powers of cognition, though they do as sensations, of course. They are not as universally communicable as intuitions[x] and concepts. Stimulation and feelings belong to the essentially beautiful, approximately as a golden frame belongs to a beautiful picture.

One must pass judgment on the beautiful more from its effect on sensibility than from the understanding, however, since beauty is agreement with sensibility, but the understanding alone is the faculty of rules. 812 Taste cannot be reduced to laws, then. For a law serves not just for passing judgment but for action that follows it.[y] The rules of taste are empirical, but these do not make our judgment true; rather, they only serve to bring our judgment under certain concepts when it is cultivated through much practice. Taste, accordingly, cannot in any way be treated

[u] "Geschmackskünstler."

[v] "*schöne Wissenschaften*."

[w] "etwas Tüchtiges."

[x] Reading "Anschauungen" for "Vorstellung."

[y] "zur Befolgung."

as a science. Hence, too, there are no beautiful sciences.[z] Fine arts[a] are arts that occur, not according to logical rules, but through empirical attempts. For only the effect distinguishes the rules of sensibility, which recognizes[b] no rule of the understanding, and on this account, too, we have no rules of taste. Aesthetics[c] cannot be a canon, then; rather, the attempts of the fine arts always precede, and then the rules follow, which serve, however, only for criticizing art. Thus one must acquaint oneself with models of beauty, in order to acquire taste thereby. For in taste, man is subject to fashion and is inclined to complaisance. Someone has taste if what pleases him pleases all. And thus the social inclination of all has produced and modified taste. Now the ancients have withstood the critique of many *secula* and thereby retain their prestige, and he who reads them and on whom they leave an impression, acquires taste, only he must not try to imitate them. Taste is an effect of the power of judgment. This power comes later than wit, and even later than understanding. It shows how we can make use of the judgment of sensibility[;] in order to choose, consequently, one must have collected a multitude of cognitions.[d] Our cognition has need of a certain means, and this is language. This means, however, is subject to many alterations. Hence one must write in a dead language. Affectation and straining for beauty are displeasing to the highest degree.[e] The natural understanding, in its simplicity, is better. We can occupy ourselves in two ways[:]

1. *per otium* 2. *per negotium*.[f]

All occupation with taste is play. Occupation with the understanding is true business. Considered as play, the former deserves all approval. But if the play seems to be business, then it is exaggerated. E.g., if in a speech someone tries to be witty, then his play becomes business. In no language are there two words that are actually *synonyma*. Least of all are philosophy and learned cognition synonymous, as our author holds; rather, they are vastly different. A science is a system. It is thereby distinct from universal cognition, whatever this may be as to its object[.] Naturalists in the field of the learned are those who lack the systematic, and who possess nothing but a rhapsody. One can comprehend a system better in oral exposition than from books, since in the former one does not engage in as much reasoning as in the latter, but instead a certain thread is followed.

813

[z] "schöne Wissenschaften."

[a] "Schöne Künste."

[b] "erkennet."

[c] Reading "Aesthetik" for "Aesthetisch."

[d] "Kenntnißen."

[e] "Der gesuchte Zwang und Grimaße des Schönen mißfällt im höchsten Grade."

[f] 1. through leisure 2. through labor.

A science can be:

1. A science of reason, which can be cognized only according to universal principles of reason. E.g., mathematics.
2. A science of learnedness, which one can learn historically. Such as history, languages, philology, acquaintance with all the tools of learnedness, literature.

A philosopher is not a learned man; rather, he looks at what the value of learnedness finally is. He must possess learnedness, however, in order to be able to make use of philosophy. He is not an artist of reason, then, but rather one who studies the laws of reason. To become learned is to imitate someone else in what he knows; consequently the pupil can never become more learned than his teacher. Mathematics can be learned. But many new things can be found through it, too. Philosophy, however, cannot be learned, but philosophizing [can], since we expound more the judgment about the thing than the thing itself. He who begins to memorize philosophy removes himself further and further from it. For in man there lie judgments which, if they are not contaminated by adopted propositions, are plain and pure.

Our author divides imperfection into *defectus*[g] and *vitia*.[h]

In metaphysics we have[:]

1. *defectio privative dicta*[i] (*defectus*)[, which] is to be reproved to a slight extent, namely, when dryness, but also thoroughness, reigns in a work. Lack is the non-being of a cognition. – Ignorance is lack of cognition.
2. *Defectio contrarie dicta*[j] (*vitia*), when, e.g., *vitia grammaticalia* and affectations appear in a letter. There are logically essential *vitia* and logically non-essential ones. In our language some contradictions prevail. I go out *alone* with *someone else*. The English call that a *bull*. Such a mistake belongs to the essential *vitia*.

814 An error is a *vitium* of judgment. Since logic expounds universal formal rules and abstracts from all objects, aesthetic and practical perfections cannot really belong to it; rather, these are regarded as digressions[k] and as things not proper to logic. Practical cognition actually influences our will. But it is taken up here so that we can cognize logical perfection all the better, and distinguish it from other cognitions. Practical perfection is determination of the ends of human actions. Aesthetic perfection is popularity. The *horizon* is the congruence of the limits of our cognition with the ends of mankind and of men. Thus it is a complex of cognitions[l] which, taken together, are adequate to our ends. Now we can consider either the ends of all mankind, i.e., the absolute horizon, as well as the particular

g defects, lacks.
h errors.
i imperfection in the privative sense.
j imperfection in the sense of a contrary.
k "episodisch."
l "Kenntniße."

horizon, i.e., the horizon of one man, which is consequently a horizon that is determined relatively. As for what concerns the particular horizon, the horizon of an uncultivated man is different from the horizon of an expert. The former learns sciences without setting before himself a certain end. At the most, in order to be able to speak in society[;] the latter, in order thereby to become useful to others. The horizon of a religion is a catechism, i.e., a complex of cognitions[m] that are necessary to man as man. It presupposes a cultivated understanding, however, to determine the cognitions[n] of all persons and the *nexus*$_L$ of all useful cognitions[o] among one another[;] moreover, [it presupposes] a power of judgment that has [been] matured by years and by experience. – To determine the horizon of universal human cognition logically is not possible everywhere. In metaphysics one can, on some matters, see the limits of human cognition. In natural science, however, this cannot be done, due to the great extent of this study. It is possible that it could sometime happen, though. In the case of the aesthetic determination of the universal horizon it depends on how the aesthetic horizon is situated relative to the logical. If it is to be universally useful, logical [perfection] requires distinct truth and certainty, which need not be found so exactly in aesthetic [perfection]. We must look more to logical perfection, however, and at least the ratio between the two must be exactly determined. Some things I cannot know. These are over my horizon. Other things I need not know. These are outside my horizon. E.g., the *medicus* as *medicus* need not know all the legal procedures. What is it useful to know, however, and what can I do without? Gesner[15] expresses himself about this in his writings and lectures about his Isagoge, in that he lingers over the amusing question of those who ask, about everything, What is the use of that? What is the use of being acquainted with the dress of the Hebrews? Thus: *quaerit delirus, quod non respondet Homerus.*[p] What is not useful now can be useful sometime. E.g. When, by experiment, a new law is given in nature. If only you have really extended and justified your cognitions,[q] acquaintance with their use will come afterward. This answer is sufficient for the determination of the universal horizon of men. For even he who collects the absurdities of men, and who, among all human endeavors, is of the least use, since he only establishes, as it were, a catalogue of the rubbish in the world, can still be of some little use in regard to history.

815

The horizon is the concept of our cognitions,[r] which cognitions, taken together with the ends we have, are adequate. It is

1. *logical.* In relation to our faculty of cognition, how far we can go and

[m] "Kenntniße."
[n] "Kenntniße."
[o] "Kenntniße."
[p] a madman asks but Homer does not respond.
[q] "Kenntniße."
[r] "Kenntniße."

how far we must go. Everything must be aimed at perfection. Hence we can go as far as we get.

2. The horizon in relation to taste is *aesthetic.* This is popularity. One seeks to win the approval either of the public or of experts. In the first case one seeks current learnedness, which is suited for everyone and is pleasing. But in this way one ends up with shallowness, as is the case among the French.

3. *Practical*[,] in relation to use. But in regard to particular ends, one must always ask for the higher purpose, and have a universal and determined ground for doing this or that. E.g. If the theologian wants to play the role of a learned man, then theological learnedness is the most important thing of all. He must study natural theology, in order to oppose the free-thinkers, and also physico-theology, because of the difficult *eventus*[s] in the holy scriptures,[t] mathematics, *theologia sacra*, etc., etc. But as preacher and as teacher of his parish he need only have clear ideas of the truths that he expounds, in order to find their importance. The expression *over the horizon* is not really adequate to the thing. For what is on the 816 horizon of the sky I can see. We see quite well that we should represent what lies outside the surface on which all our possible cognitions[u] are contained. Historically, human cognition[v] has no limits. For human experience extends it continuously. The limits of mathematics cannot be determined, since new things are constantly added. But the horizon of the cognitions of physics in general is quite restricted, because it is occupied merely with objects of sensibility. As for the extent to which our reason can depart from all experience, no horizon can be indicated. That which we ought not to know is *beneath our horizon*. This can be said *relative*$_{L}$. E.g. When someone brings religious disputes to the pulpit, then the public gets things into its head that it ought not to know. The most important use of this doctrine concerning the horizon is the relative use. I can always say, relatively, that something is beyond this man's horizon, if he becomes cultivated. But one can err in this, too, if one does not set about it properly. In the extension of his horizon man stands, as it were, on a mountain, and describes a greater *radius*$_{L}$ for his circle. But be cautious that you do not endlessly change your horizon and take another center-point. For all connection of your cognitions will thereby disappear. Hence we must have a certain center-point, on which all our cognitions come together. And this must occur in the first years of study. And one must enrich his understanding with historical cognitions, to be sure, if one wishes to collect a supply for the whole of life. For only at this time is the memory capable of taking in things that do not die out perpetually. But

[s] events, occurrences.

[t] "in den h. Büchern."

[u] "Kenntniße."

[v] "Kenntniß."

with the growth of judgment the acuity of memory comes to an end. Moreover, we must know how to determine the horizon of our cognitions properly at the beginning. But commonly men attain this insight too late, when they see where the horizon should have been determined. And this stems more from the negligence and the amusements of youth than from ignorance. The horizon of other men can be determined according to the variety of [their] cognitions. In instruction, exposition must be arranged according to what my pupil, in these years, takes an interest in; subsequently, as a youth, he will have yet another interest, and thus I must always comprehend the horizon of my student. I must not make it too narrow, and, e.g., in the pulpit I must not place too little confidence in the comprehension of common people. Sciences have a horizon. That is the *territorium* of the science[;] hence some things do not belong in the *territorium* of the science, which nonetheless need to be known in the science. 817

The imperfection of our cognition is

1. ignorance, the imperfection of lack, which thus constitutes an empty space.
2. Error, an imperfection of enrichment,[w] when I have collected ideas that conflict with the truth.

The fate of someone who errs is worse, then, than that of someone who is ignorant, for error hinders the entry of truth. To remove it one must first reduce the man to ignorance. Thus it is a double imperfection. For it is not only a negative lack of truth, but also a cause for resisting perfection. With all science there is risk. But irrespective of this, we must run the risk of error, because otherwise one could never make progress. Two things bring about error: ignorance, and the desire to know, which actually produces it. Ignorance is not a great reproach if the opportunity to know certain things has been lacking. The name of idiot is supposed to mean someone ignorant, in the way that the ancient sophists distinguish wise men and idiots.[x] But the pride with which an idiot regards himself is ill-advised.[y] The name is appropriate, not for one who is ignorant, but for one who presumes to judge of all things, although he knows nothing. In common life the remark is made that it is quite useful that a man should not do the whole of a thing. An ignorant man is one who does not have as many cognitions[z] as he needs in regard to this or that end. E.g. In the production of a needle more than 4 to 10 people cooperate. This division makes everything perfect, and everything easy. It is like this in cognitions,[a]

[w] "der Bereicherungen."

[x] "idioten Dummköpfe."

[y] Reading "womit sich ein Idiot betrachtet, ist übel beraten" for "womit man einen Idiot betrachtet, ist übel berichtet."

[z] "Kenntniße."

[a] "Kenntniße."

too. One man finds pleasure in rummaging through archives, another holds this to be empty. Ignorance is not a reproach, accordingly, because in part we men do not need to know, and in part we are not able to know. Cognition[b] of one's own ignorance is a science, which involves a cognition[c] of empty space, in which possible knowledge can be found. The common man is ignorant with respect to astronomy. But he does not know his ignorance. It is quite necessary, then, to uncover for man the chasm of his 818 ignorance, and this can be done only by those who have extended their knowledge and hence have insight into how little of it there is. Helvétius says now one knows everything except what Socrates knew, namely, nothing.[16] Opposed to this ignorance, on the other hand, is great knowledge.[d]

1. Historical *polyhistoria*, learnedness extended without[e] determinate limits.
2. Knowledge of reason extended without determinate limits, *polymathia*. The two together can be called *pansophia*.

In the sciences, then, there is a difference between those that can be drawn from reason and those that must not be taught based on reason, such as geography, etc. In the previous *seculum* the inclination of most men ran toward *polyhistoria*. This requires also philology, i.e., cognition[f] of the tools for the study of the ancients,[g] in which the models of historical cognition have been brought down to us. Philology, under which are comprehended the *linguist* and the *humanist*, and also the literator, constitute polyhistory. The philologist must be a literator, he must be a humanist, i.e., he must cultivate his taste and be able to communicate to others. Now for the cultivation of taste he takes the classical authors, i.e., [ones] who are models and exemplary. A linguist is one who studies ancient languages with critique, and if he chooses them as models of taste, then he is a *humanist*. Only the ancients will always remain models of genuine taste, because their languages are dead languages. Now the literator is one who can name many books of the ancients, as to their editions, their authors. He who is acquainted with many books is a literator. He who is acquainted with many languages is a linguist, and taken together these constitute the great learned man. This is great knowledge,[h] of which Paul says that it inflates. For if the polyhistor is acquainted with so many books, he believes he knows just as much as those who wrote them, although he is acquainted with them only historically. Philosophy can tear down pride and make evident one's true ends. Learnedness without philosophy is

[b] "Kenntniß."
[c] "Kenntniß."
[d] "das Vielwissen."
[e] Reading "ohne" for "nach."
[f] "Kenntniß."
[g] Reading "zum Studium der alten" for "der alten," following a suggestion by Hinske.
[h] "Vielwissen."

cyclopic learnedness. Philosophy is the second eye, and it sees how all the cognitions[i] of the one eye agree with reference to a common end. One part of philosophy is called the *humaniora.* The character of humanity consists in sociability. The *humaniora* are liberal arts.[j] A liberal art is merely play, a bread-winning art[k] is work. What belongs to fine art, however, is not yet wholly liberal,[l] for the painter, etc., is still mechanical. The poetic art and oratory are more liberal. A humanist is one who treats beautiful things and cultivates his spirit in the study of the ancients, in order to drive out its wildness. There arises thereby that urbanity that we are aware of in the ancients, and historical cognition is of importance in this respect, that it drives out rusticity. 819

All these cognitions[m] can be drawn together into a main science and are regarded as means to that science. So, too, even the bread-winning science that people study. It is customary among men to prefer to do something out of inclination rather than due to the compulsion of duty. Some are often failed by their inclinations, which do not advance them. This is a man's hobby-horse, and he would rather ride it than ride the cart-horse of his office. Since duty, then, is something from which you like to be free, learn something with which you can play with your reason. E.g., the study of botany, of geography, etc.

These secondary sciences must be reflected on in accordance with the plan of our knowledge. Often they are the necessary means in a science. E.g., a *medicus* must have natural science as an aid, and philology, moreover, because being well read provides a multitude of experiences. Often, however, they are only a play of entertainment, and are set out for anyone's liking. There is difference of scientists between bread-winning art and free art. And thus learned people are either members of learned guilds or are independent of guilds.[n]

A learned man is often opposed to those who practice mechanical arts. The learned man is thus accepted as one who does no manual labor. Thus the learned men in Siena let the nails on their hands grow, as proof that they do no manual labor. A science is a bread-winning art when it is a means of livelihood[;] if it should interest only the spirit, and civilize the talents, then it is a liberal art. Bread-winning arts are thus major moving springs of activity, but the sciences are greatly restricted by these bread-winning arts, since in them one must direct himself according to universal delusion[;] for if truths are not immediately of any use, one must nonetheless expound them, because the public has gotten used to that. Thus some things that are

[i] "Kenntniße."
[j] "freye Künste."
[k] "Brotkunst."
[l] "frey."
[m] "Kenntniße."
[n] "entweder Zunftgelehrte, oder zunftfreye Gelehrte."

received and that appear in *examina* could be struck from logic. In short, members of learned guilds are bound to their métier. – Liberal art has 820 many advantages here, since it is not restricted to the conditions of the trade, and what is sought is not at all the delusion of the multitude but rather the inner worth of the sciences. Yet on the other hand, liberal art does not have enough motive power to compel men enough to apply themselves to it with great effort. Gallantry and pedantry are mistakes in the use of our knowledge. The word pedant is Italian and has its origin from *magister pedarius*,[o] who was placed in charge of a young man and followed him at every step. He had to instruct the young man in sciences and in scholastic learnedness, but was never admitted to his father's society[;] hence he did not learn to make any use of his knowledge in intercourse with other men.

In the use of our cognition, it can be suited either more to the school or more to the world. The school contains precepts and methods, i.e., means for teaching and learning. A cognition is scholastically correct, then, when it contains all the forms according to which one is supposed to teach. Every science has 2 perfections, a scholastic one and a popular one.

Scholastic perfection consists, then, in didactic form, which serves to make cognition easier for a beginner. It constitutes the essence and the ground, it is agreement of the use for our reason, and is the meticulousness of logical rules. It is the exposition, then, that can be either scholastically correct or popular. Popularity consists in the accommodation of a science to the power of comprehension and the taste of the common world.[p] Such a cognition is not just for the school but also for the world. –

Scholastic method gets accustomed to a certain fussiness, e.g., *termini technici*, demonstrations, definitions – which are not suited for a dilettante. Nonetheless, the scholastic style is the greatest perfection, and always the first thing, in that it contains the certain rules of our procedure, and without them all thoroughness would vanish. Scholastic perfection must precede, then popularity follow, for to start with popularity is quite absurd. But if we dedicate our cognitions to human society, then we must put these rules aside and yet retain as much science as is congruent with the power of comprehension and the inclination of others. Popularity requires familiarity with the world and intercourse with men, and he 821 understands his subject best, certainly, who can make it comprehensible and clear to someone else who is not learned. But with popularity one must not abandon thoroughness, since it is nothing but an alteration of the exposition. – Now pedantry is restricted capacity in the use of cognition, when one is restricted merely to the scholastic use. It is considered pedantry when, in abstract concepts, someone begins with Adam. It indicates a certain thoroughness, however. Pedantry is fussiness in the formal,

[o] a teacher who goes on foot (i.e., one of little repute).

[p] "des gemeinen Wesens."

micrology, trading in trivialities. The pedant is a bad copy of the methodical mind, who establishes the right end for his knowledge, and who also knows how to attain it. A pedant, however, with his great learnedness, never gets to his end. There are pedants in all positions, e.g., pedants of the hunt, pedants of war, pedants of finery and of politeness, who always talk about their own thing and are occupied with it. The learned pedant is the most bearable. For in his case the objection is only lack of familiarity with the world, although one can otherwise learn from him, even if one finds no pleasantness in doing so. In the other areas, however, pedants are empty-headed. Besides pedantry, gallantry can also join with cognition. Someone is gallant if he grants superiority to someone based on the care with which he has refined himself, superiority that he does not claim for himself. Among the ancients the concept of gallantry was wholly unknown. Horace, *Carmina*, Book II, Ode 16, To Grosphus, when he praises his patron, ascribes to him superiority in possessions, [but] to himself superiority of spirit, and thus obviously gives himself the advantage. In general, one does not find among them the least delicacy about indulging others. – No people has more gallantry in writing style than France. Most books there are accommodated to the taste of the fair sex, and hence women are also the judges of scientific objects. In social intercourse they must set the tone of conduct, of course, but to water down whole sciences on their account, until the sciences are congruent[q] with their capacity, causes shallowness, and scholastic perfection loses its worth in the process. The Germans fail miserably, and they show something embarrassing[r] in their character when they try to equal the French in gallantry. This gallantry is dangerous because it is so stimulating and seductive that, because the entire public shouts its approval, we value this more highly than the reproach of learned men.

The quantity of learned cognition is extensive according to the multitude of the cognition, or intensive according to its importance, i.e., in regard to its consequences and effects. We can consider this importance 822

1. in a logical respect, where it is that which contains logical perfection, namely, that through which cognitions become more thorough, more distinct, and more certain[;]
2. its practical importance consists in the usefulness of the cognition. This[s] cannot be foreseen and must therefore be developed. Logical perfection teaches practical perfection, since usefulness thereby becomes more determinate. Thus it is the first perfection. But a cognition can have[t] logical perfection *respective*$_{\mathrm{L}}$.

q "angemessen."
r "etwas genirtes."
s Ak, "Dieser"; MS, "Diese."
t Reading "haben" for "ganz haben."

Fruitfulness of cognition is concerned with the quantity and multitude of the cognition. The content of cognition lies in the manifold and indicates its parts. The perfection of cognition requires that it be true. Truth is agreement of cognition with the object. But this is really only a nominal definition[;] this is one of the strangest phenomena in a science, when one cannot answer a question that constitutes the essence of the science. Such a question has long been posed in logic, namely, What is truth? Pilate was the first to raise this question. Here [logic] appears to run aground,[u] although it tries to give rules of truth to the understanding. The definition above is not suitable. For the object is not in us,[v] only the cognition of it is. Hence we cannot compare our cognition of it with the object, but only with our cognition. Since, then, no cognition is true except that which agrees with the object, no cognition of the object is true except [that] which agrees with our cognition of the object. The ancients called this a diallelon,[w] a fallacy. E.g., when, to prove his sincerity, someone appeals to the sincerity of someone else. Thus Lavater[17] maintained many things based on endless inferences, and spoke of the character of the future life, which has not the least semblance of incorrectness or opposition about it. But does this cognition have an object that agrees with it? Such cognitions are then called empty. Thus cognition is true if it agrees with itself. But in this way all lies can be true, if they need no other confirmation than the agreement of ognition with itself. – Is there, now, a universal *criterium*$_{L}$ of truth? A rule, by which universal truth may be distinguished? It is impossible. For it is supposed to be a universal *criterium*$_{L}$ of truth, without distinction among objects. If it were a *criterium*$_{L}$ for certain objects only, then it would not be universal. But since it must abstract from all distinction among objects[;] and since all truth is agreement of cognition with the object, in which case the cognition of one object is distinguished from another[;] and since the cognition of universality has no characteristic mark whereby an object is distinguished[;] a material *criterium*$_{L}$ of truth is therefore impossible. The matter of all cognition is the object, the form the mode of treatment. Logic is concerned with form, truth with the object. Hence it is impossible, in the first place, and contradicts itself, to give a universal material *criterium*$_{L}$ of truth. Since logic abstracts from all content, however, there can only be formal critieria of truth. Truth requires two things[:]

823

1. Agreement of cognition with the object.
2. Agreement with itself.

[u] Reading "zu scheitern" for "beym Namen zu scheitern" (MS, "beym Hafen zu scheitern').
[v] "bey uns."
[w] Reading "diallele" for "dialectic," in accordance with Lehmann's correction (24:1102).

Agreement of cognition with itself, regardless of the objects, is a formal *criterium*$_{L}$ of truth. For this makes a cognition possible as cognition. Without this no cognition at all is possible. Hence it is always indispensable, although it is not sufficient for a material *criterium*$_{L}$. It is a *conditio sine qua non*, e.g., the principle of contradiction is a formal *criterium*$_{L}$ of truth. For someone who expounds a logic so fine that it agrees with itself, however, this *criterium*$_{L}$ does not suffice. Thus the answer to the question, What is truth? would be the agreement of a cognition with itself, and this is a partial ground for holding it to be true. A universally sufficient material *criterium*$_{L}$ cannot be demanded. – If I abstract from all the different objects, then I retain only a concept of an object. A universal *criterium*$_{L}$ of truth deals only with the form of thought, which is agreement of the cognition not with the object, but with itself.

The rules for agreement with itself are[:]

1. A cognition must not contradict itself. This is the *conditio sine qua non.*
2. *Affirmatio*, if cognitions as grounds fit together with their consequences. If, e.g., as the ground for the dampness of the west wind, I cite the fact that it comes over the sea, then that is a partial ground of truth. The inner *criterium*$_{L}$ of truth requires that a cognition be grounded. A *criterium*$_{L}$ that rests on the *principium* of sufficient reason must always infer from the ground to the consequence.
3. Among various cognitions there ought to be unity, i.e., the relation of many cognitions to one.

824

Opposed to truth is falsehood. When falsehood is held to be truth it is error.

1. Falsehood, i.e., a lack of agreement with the object.
2. Illusion of truth.

Is truth possible? In logic, truth is an agreement of cognition with the laws of the understanding[;] since the understanding acts here according to its own laws, there is nothing here to make it absurd that truth should be possible. Is error possible? I.e., to what extent is the form of thought contrary to the understanding possible? It is hard to comprehend how a power can deviate from its own laws, since it acts only according to certain laws. If these laws are essential, then the power cannot deviate from them[;] if, then, among the formal laws of the understanding that logic expounds an essential one is possible, then the understanding cannot deviate from it. E.g., a heavy body cannot cease falling. – If we had no sources of cognition other than the understanding, we would opine that the understanding would always judge simply according to its laws, even if it sometimes judged restrictedly[;] but through the understanding we have no object, since it contains merely form. Sensibility, i.e., the faculty of intuition and of sensation, provides the material for thought, and it is the other source of cognition. Now if a cognition is to be related to the object, then the two work together[;] sensibility gives intuition and the understanding the concept. When a body is affected by 2 powers, there arises a third movement, where it does not remain on the track either of the one or of the other, i.e., the diagonal force. E.g., a ball that would have gone directly into the center of the target goes somewhat toward the edge of the target when it is pushed sideways by the wind, and it was pushed there neither by the power of the [gun]powder nor of the wind. Now sensibility 825 influences the actions of the understanding, and from this arises the understanding's diagonal direction, where it sometimes attains truth, sometimes illusion. The cause of illusion is sensibility, then, and the understanding, insofar as it passes judgment concerning this. Sensibility is not in itself a source of errors, however, for insofar as it relates to its objects, there is an agreement with the laws of this power of cognition. The ground for the fact that the senses do not judge erroneously is that they cannot judge at all. For only the understanding judges. Error is neither in the understanding alone, then, nor in the senses alone; instead, it always lies in the influence of the senses on the understanding, when we do not distinguish well the influence of sensibility on the understanding.

Logic, since it abstracts from all content, cannot say more of the influence of sensibility than that it presents the subjective ground of our judgment. The understanding is the objective ground of our judgment. But when something subjective, which in fact belongs to sensibility, flows into our judgment, then sensibility has mixed itself in, and this is the source of errors. From this mixing arises *cognitio hybrida*, a bastard cognition, which is composed of 2 parts. Here sensibility does not serve the understanding but instead confuses it, and from this arises the diagonal direction of the understanding. E.g., someone who adheres to an opinion holds the opinion to be something probable. Probability is an objective ground. But subjective adherence brings the effect that is taken to be objective. – Because the understanding is in fact active in every error, men always bring out truth when they judge at the risk of error. Those who make many errors always have something true, too, for they have used their understanding and cultivated their powers.

With regard to error, we cannot complain about the restrictions on our understanding, either. Then we indict nature. For the restrictions on the understanding are the cause of ignorance, but not of errors. For when in ignorance, I need simply not judge. Hence we are ourselves responsible for every error, when our inclination draws us out of our limits. In all our judgments there is always something true. A man can never err completely and utterly. For in accordance with what he perhaps presupposes, he can always have some truth, even if only partial. A total error would be a complete opposition to the laws of the understanding. But then it could 826 not arise from the understanding, which can produce nothing that conflicts with its nature. What is deviant from its laws is the influence of sensibility. In every error there is always still a true judgment, but much from sensibility is also insinuated, so there is falsehood in it, but it is only partial.

Since we abstract from all relation to the object, and consider only the rules for the agreement of the understanding with itself, the *criterium*$_L$ of truth in logic can only be the agreement of the laws of cognition with themselves. The rule of agreement of cognition with itself is the principle of contradiction and the principle of sufficient reason, which are not sufficient *materialiter*, but are sufficient to judge of a thing *formaliter*, whether it agrees with itself. The principle of contradiction is a negative proposition. A cognition is false if it contradicts itself. But a cognition that does not contradict itself is not therefore true. The principle of contradiction is such, in fact, that nothing can be opposed to it, but as a positive *principium* for cognizing truth it is not sufficient. It is positive insofar as through it I can have insight into the necessity of the truth in a necessary cognition. – The principle of sufficient reason is when a cognition fits together with a ground, or when nothing but true consequences can be inferred from a cognition. Both propositions, then, press for unity. – If a cognition does not contradict itself, but instead its opposite would contradict itself, then it is true. If a proposition does not contradict itself it is possible, but from the *principium contradictionis* not all the unity of a cognition can be inferred. E.g., that my thoughts penetrate into the souls of other men is possible, but not on that account true. When one cognition is the ground of others, then there is a connection of the two cognitions. When the ground is true, so also is the consequence true. If all the consequences are true, then the ground must be true too. The principle of contradiction is treated diligently in metaphysics, and that the *criterium*$_L$ of truth is the *principium rationis*.[x]

1. *A priori*[,] the connection of a cognition with its ground.
2. *A posteriori*[,] the connection of a ground with its consequences.

A cognition without a ground is groundless but still not false, e.g., that plants have souls[;] but that a cognition be true, this requires grounds, and that the cognition be connected *a priori*. We infer from the consequences to the truth of the cognition 827

1. *negatively*[.] [I]f even a single consequence is false, then the whole cognition is false. For if the cognition were true, then this consequence would also have to be true. Among false consequences people also include dangers. But dangers are often only relative dangers, and often they rest only on external circumstances, if, e.g., the times are so bad that even truth brings danger. What is relevant here, then, is not the dangerousness

[x] principle of the ground.

of the proposition, but its falsehood. Those who start [talking about] dangers are looking for tricks to defeat someone before he can use reason.

2. *positive*$_L$. In cognizing the truth of a proposition it is not possible for me to infer from the truth of a few consequences to the truth of a cognition. The cognition can have some truth, and from this the truth of a few consequences arises. The remainder can be false, however. Hence I cannot infer the truth of the cognition based on such a ground. If all the consequences whatsoever are false, then there is nothing true and nothing healthy in the cognition. The positive inference is thus the *onus probandi*,[y] where I must show the truth of all the consequences. In the case of the negative inference, however, I need only show the falsehood of a few consequences, and hence this is a sufficient *criterium*$_L$. Only it is difficult, however, indeed, it simply cannot happen that I could know all the consequences. For if I knew them, my cognition would be certain. But we need this, and so we make this probable inference. If most of the consequences are true, then they are all true. For if a cognition does not contradict itself, then I search for its ground, and I examine the consequences of that ground. If many consequences can be discovered, but not all, then I accept it as an incomplete cognition, in that I infer from the truth of various consequences to the truth of the proposition. For since it is impossible to show the truth of all the consequences, it follows that we also do not have any strict, sufficient usefulness of the criterion, but can only use it as a ground of probability. Here the principle of sufficient reason is treated not as in metaphysics, where it holds of the object, but rather as a logical proposition. For since the principle of contradiction is not yet a sufficient *criterium*$_L$ of truth, the connection of the cognition must nonetheless be investigated through it. The principle of contradiction is the principle of the co-existing and of agreement,[z] the principle of sufficient reason is the principle of connection.[a]

828

A cognition is totally false or partially false. A cognition can always be false and yet one can discover partial truths in it; e.g., there is more truth in polytheism than in atheism. – In disputations there are certain subtle fallacies for confusing others. E.g., one who says, All Moors are men. The respondent is a man. Therefore he is a Moor. The respondent is a man, to be sure, but not a black man, and hence he does not speak completely falsely. It is often good to search out this truth and not immediately to throw away everything that contains an error. We can argue in 2 ways, either because we have different interests, and then we argue as enemies, or we have a common interest but do not agree about the way to promote it, and then we argue as friends. All men have a common interest in the

[y] burden of proof.

[z] "der Satz des zusammen bestehenden, und der Einstimmung."

[a] "der Satz des Zusammenhanges."

investigation of truth, and hence we must be participants in such argument, in that we do not dwell on showing where the other has erred, but rather on where he is right. Now this sympathetic sentiment[b] is moral, to be sure, and does not properly belong to logic. But logic prescribes its rules as correct maxims. If we believe that a proposition is wholly false, then we must simply recall our proposition from above, p. 85,[18] that no proposition can be wholly false. One can invent a total falsehood, of course, that no one will hold to be true. But this is not an error, then. If the thing is so false that there simply is no interest in seeking out any degree of truth in it, and hence it is beneath all observation, then it is *absurd*. Thus if the falsehood is clear to the universal understanding, the cognition is absurd. The distinction between total and partial falsehood concerns either the object or the cognition. The lack in a cognition is the partial falsehood of the cognition (*vitium*), or the cognition is wholly true but does not touch the whole truth of the object (*defectus*). With partial falsehood, it is a matter of a lack of the totality of the truth of the cognition, not of the totality of the truth of the object; if this incorrectness does not constitute the essential end of the cognition, then it is true *tolerabiliter*. E.g., prejudices in religion, which one must seek to tolerate and to correct. – – We have noted that a cognition is such that not everything is true in it as cognition, or that the whole cognition is true, but the whole truth of the object is not present. E.g., he who tells a story and hides a part of it does not on that account lie. For he only makes use of cunning here, and it is sometimes necessary and unavoidable, too, to keep a part secret. One conceals when one merely hides something, and if the whole of the object is not contained therein, the cognition in this case is true. – This examination of how many errors are found in a cognition, and whether on this acount this or that cognition has to be attacked, is of great importance and presupposes much prudence, which has to be grounded on a power developed through experience. – With regard to exact and crude cognition, a distinction is drawn between them. Exactness has to do with the relation of the cognition to the object, with whether the object is cognized wholly or in part. E.g., the determination of breadth by steps is sufficient and exact for the determination of a journey, but not for the determination of the boundaries of an estate. With numbers, fractions can be left off if it is exact enough for payment. But a businessman closing his books may not leave off 1/10, because then the balance, which is the proof of the correctness of the account, is not exact. Thus a cognition can be exact for one purpose but can be called a crude estimate for another purpose. Exactness often looks like pedantry, when it is exact *objective*$_L$ in matters where this is not required at all for my purpose. E.g., with fortifications the ancients always determined how many cubic inches would have to be carted out to

829

[b] "Diese theilnehmende Gesinnung."

complete a moat. Scrupulous exactness is distinct from *exactitudo* or precise exactness, in that precise exactness is appropriate to the end, and just on this account receives the name *exactitudo*. In the sciences that rest on principles *a priori*, exactness is extraordinarily important. E.g., in mathematics. Most modes of thought are almost never concerned with the exact, and there are few thorough minds who observe exactness in all things, though this exactness has its great worth and must never be neglected, since it elevates the power of judgment even if it is not immediately appropriate to the end, and if it also requires only a little effort.

There are judgments *en gros* and *en detail*. Madame Geoffrin[19] was a great Maecenas[20] to learned men, although she herself was not a great genius, in that she encouraged accomplishments, and said that one must judge of every man *en gros*, because he would lose much if one were to pass judgment on him *en detail*. But anyone can pass judgment *en gros*. E.g., the book pleases me, it is beautiful. But not [everyone can say] what is in the book, find fault with it and praise it *en detail*. Our modern, great, so-called geniuses learn sciences *en gros*, and hence all their judgments and cognitions are *en gros* and never *en detail*. From this arises superficiality in cognition. On this account it can never become exact. Exact cognition is distinct from subtle, scrupulous cognition, i.e., exactness that is concerned with parts, skill in noting something that more easily escapes common attention, which is also called the microscopic in passing judgments. A cognition is micrological when one clings to small things and cannot see the big things on account of the small ones. Subtle exactness is on this account not micrological. For the subtle mind can nonetheless be extended by concepts in regard to cognition. For we must distinguish objects not only at great distances but also on small points. But some restrict all their cognition to small things, and a subtle mind is commonly micrological. What is diametrically opposed to subtle cognition is crude cognition. Diametrically opposed, if one falls out of one mistake into the one opposed to it. Both are open to reproach. For he who clings much to subtleties is blind with respect to the whole. It seems that more can be expected from crude cognition, however, which is concerned with large things and with the whole. – Crude cognition is not crude error, which contradicts the common laws of the understanding; rather, it is crude insofar as it is not extended, and is still rough, and contains marks of a merely common understanding. Our author says that all truth is dogmatic. – All our cognitions are either historical or rational. Cognitions are historical if they are communicated to us from elsewhere[; they are] subjectively rational insofar as they are drawn from principles of reason. [They are] objectively rational insofar as the cognitions lie in reason as to their true sources. Objective[ly] historical cognition is possible only by means of the senses and of communication and instruction. Philosophy is in some people historical *subjective*$_{L}$[;][c] objectively, all philosophy is cognition of reason. – All rational cognition is at the same time apodeictic, i.e., it carries with it the proof of necessity. Only through experience can I cognize contingent things[,] but through reason, on the other hand, [I can have] necessary cognition, too. Philosophy and mathematics, accordingly, are apodeictic cognitions. That the stone is heavy I cognize through experience, to be sure. But only reason gives me proof of the necessity of heaviness. Apodeictic propositions are of two kinds[,] mathematical insofar as they belong to mathematics, dogmatic insofar as they belong to philosophy. Accordingly, all cognition of reason from concepts is *dogma*$_{L}$, all cognition of reason from construction of concepts is *mathema*. If I say that every body is divisible[;] this is an apodeictically certain proposition. – In revealed religion propositions that contain doctrines which reason cannot cognize are called *dogmata*$_{L}$. This is an improper expression. Only if our reason were extended would it have this cognition, and then they would be *dogmata*$_{L}$, although now they are only historical cognitions.

831

Our author calls a complex of dogmatic truths a system. – But the object of systematic and of common cognition does not make any difference; instead, the two are distinct only as to form. A system is where everything is subordinate to an idea that is concerned with the whole, and that has to determine the parts. E.g. Someone can know many histories without having a science thereof. For he does not have the form. He did not make himself a sketch of the whole, and did not order everything according to an idea. This idea, then, makes systematic form. We can think the system as an aggregate or whole of cognition. Totality, now, is the determination of the whole, and this lies in the idea. With an aggregate, however, nothing is determined. For I do not know what is still to be added. With a system, however, everything is already determined. – A cognition can be rhapsodic, and nevertheless not be tumultuous. For what is opposed to the tumultuous is the methodical, and without method a cognition is tumultuous. But a cognition that is produced methodically, but without system, is rhapsodic. E.g., when we guide ourselves in accordance with the power of comprehension of the subject who is to be instructed.

Some have expounded their subject through aphorisms, without representing the articulation of the whole, in that this is always there but cannot be seen by one who does not have the idea of the whole. It is necessary, then, to treat things systematically in order to get a concept of completeness and to have a touchstone for how the different parts agree with the

[c] Reading "Die philosophie ist bey Manchen historisch subjective" for "Die subjective philosophie ist bey Manchen historisch."

832 whole. With sciences one must always have their skeleton before one's eyes in order to pass judgment, in accordance with this, as to whether this or that belongs to the science. – Aesthetic truths are ones that are suited for universal comprehensibility[;] logical truths are scholastic, or as our author says, learned.

A false cognition and an error are distinct. If I propound and examine a false judgment, there is not yet any error[;] error is the holding-to-be-true of falsehood. Thus illusion must be added, and, to be sure, logical illusion. With optical illusion, the senses are deceived. Moral illusion is when that which serves our best interest seems to arise from duty. Logical illusion arises from the pure form of the understanding. Now our cognition can well be in accordance with the understanding as to form. For I can easily imitate form without having internal correctness of the propositions, and thus logical form itself gives an illusion of truth, of which sophists often make use. No error is unavoidable in itself, because one simply need not judge about things of which one understands nothing. Ignorance can well be unavoidable. For this does not always rest on our will, but often on the restrictions of our nature. With error, however, we are ourselves always culpable, in that we are not cautious enough in venturing a judgment, for which we do not have enough cognition.[d] There are cases, however, where something must simply be judged, and here it happens that someone falls into an error that was in this relation unavoidable. E.g., a man wishes to cross a river that is frozen. By accident, however, the ice at one place is thinner, and he drowns. If he could have judged this beforehand, he would not have gone over. Error is always something positive[;] not being true, however, is something negative, for the positive thing in an error is that it is nonetheless thought. Illusion is the subjective ground of an error. An incorrectness and a falsehood is obvious if it is clear to the common human understanding. If the incorrectness is not clear to every understanding, then it is hidden, but it can be made obvious, and all refutations aim at this. In the case of refutations, it is a duty first to show whence this or that incorrectness of human cognition has come, i.e., I must discover the source of the error, i.e., the illusion, and afterward I can prove to him the falsehood. For if I do not do the former, and do not make distinct enough for him the means by which 833 he has been misled into holding this or that to be true, then I leave him still in uncertainty and doubt. Hence I must also not call someone absurd immediately. For he would certainly not have accepted this or that cognition if he had not been led by this or that hidden illusion to hold it to be true. Such a man, who immediately calls someone else absurd, insults the other very much and fails to recognize the interest of universal human reason. That which contains an obvious falsehood is an absurdity. But one

[d] "Kenntniß."

cannot prove an obvious incorrectness to anyone. For through some misunderstanding or other it is not obvious to him. The expression absurd, stupid, has to do first of all with the error itself[;] secondly, it has relation to the person who has the error. For I thereby declare it to be unworthy of being accepted in the class of the universal human understanding. If I have declared my refutation of the judge whom I hold to be stupid, then I cannot have the purpose of instructing him. For by denying him common human understanding, I have declared him unworthy of instruction, and I would act stupidly myself. My refutation would have to be directed to others, then. But others who have healthy human understanding will see the absurdity by themselves. Hence it is not good to use these expressions. One must instead let an absurdity go, unless it carries with it something hateful that I have to remove from it.

He who merely senses and does not judge does not err. Thus every error lies in judgment. Judgments are actions of the understanding and of reason. One can say *generaliter* that objectively, truth is agreement with the object; subjective truth is agreement with the laws of the understanding and of reason. The understanding agrees, then, with its own laws or laws of the understanding. We have a faculty of the necessary and the contingent[;] thus we have employments[e] of the pure understanding. This part is called transcendental philosophy. Our understanding is of a special kind, in that it is not capable of any intuition. For only the senses can do that. Now a second power comes into play, namely, sensibility. We have spoken of the understanding in regard to error in judgment. We have cultivated our understanding so much, now, that it does not err by itself. The senses also do not err by themselves. Why? Because they do not judge at all. In our sensibility there is something that is related merely to the object, and that is intuition, and something that is related to the subject, and that is sensation. Clarity of cognition involves marks.[f] A mark is a ground of cognition, principally, too, in the comparison of things. In comparison, I look to the identity or diversity of things. We need marks not merely to distinguish things, as our author holds, but also to discover their agreement. E.g. I do not want merely to distinguish a sheep from a goat, but I also want to know wherein it agrees with another sheep. – Marks can be regarded as a positive representation of the whole representation of the thing. A cognition is distinct, accordingly, when we are conscious of its partial concepts and represent these to ourselves clearly. Now if these partial concepts are divided again, then I get marks of marks. These parts of marks are called subordinate marks, through which our cognitions climb to universal and higher marks, which are common to most things. E.g., what is virtue? A mastery over the inclinations. What is mastery? The

834

[e] "Beschäftigungen."

[f] "Merkmahle notae."

power that one has over another. What is power? etc. Through these subordinate marks arises deep distinctness, where one penetrates further and further. – We can have marks through coordination, in that two marks are *compartes*.[g] E.g., a body is an impenetrable whole. (1.) a whole (2.) impenetrable. The latter does not apply to the whole; rather, both are applied to the concept of body, which, as *complementum*, they comprise. The series of coordinate marks can go on to infinity. E.g. Gold is heavy, extensible, refractory, does not rust, etc., etc. There is still not completeness here. For one could discover 1000 more such marks. A cognition becomes distinct, then, through clear marks. Now a cognition can become distinct through an aggregate of coordinate marks, and then it grows extensively with the addition of each new mark. I take many new marks until they seem to constitute the whole aggregate. One proceeds this way with definitions. In a certain respect they can have limits, namely, for this or that end. Cognition also grows through the series of subordinate marks, however, in that one analyzes marks and pulls out of them new marks, 835 which already lay within the cognition, to be sure, but which were not yet clearly represented. It is more pleasant to extend one's cognition through coordination than subordination. The latter is hard, since one must attend to a concept whose marks become subtler and subtler, until they are finally not capable of any more division. Nevertheless, this division has limits. This is intensive quantity of distinctness, which makes the understanding do more, to be sure, but which extends cognition more and makes it exceptionally correct. Here marks are not added, but instead I only decompose[h] the concept, since I do not join mark to mark, and hence do not add anything, but instead break into parts. This way of continuing[i] the series of marks involves a progress that is limited, for I finally come to partial concepts that are irresolvable, and I come to the concept of the simple. A cognition is distinct when the marks themselves are clear. If I can set forth clear marks, then I can explicate my concept of a thing.[j] If I cannot set forth any marks, then I cannot explain to another person what he does not understand, but instead must make do with examples. The quantity of distinctness through coordinate marks is extensive distinctness.[k] The quantity through subordinate marks is deep (intensive) distinctness. – Poets want to exhibit everything distinctly in intuition, and on account of this purpose they coordinate marks in a thing in order to make the distinctness extensive. The poet is distinguished from the philosopher through the fact that the latter works for the understanding, the former for sensibility. To be sure, the poet must observe logical correctness to the

[g] equals.

[h] "decomponire."

[i] "prosequiren."

[j] "so kann ich mir über ein Ding expliciren."

[k] "die ausgebreitete Deutlichkeit (extensive)."

extent of having unity. But his proper end has to do with pleasing sensibility. The reading of poetry has great value, then, in that it provides our understanding with the faculty of extensive distinctness, which is the easiest and most entertaining distinctness of all, because it is acquired historically. Deep distinctness is a matter for philosophy, and it depends on the fact that I pull out one mark in addition to another, and continue this until they become microscopic. Cognition is not extended by this; rather, we descend to the depths. It is used most of all in metaphysical investigations, where I always seek for the ground of the ground, without adding new ones. It is intensive distinctness, which makes our cognition very dry, to be sure, but thorough. For if we always stay with the whole and never disturb the depths, then we only swim on the surface and have superficial cognitions.[l] Marks serve either as internal or as external grounds of cognition. A cognition serves an internal use insofar as it helps us to see the manifold in the object. It serves an external use when one wants to distinguish the object from others, or to see its agreement with others. A few marks, which are of little importance for internal use, can nonetheless suffice quite well for external use. The marks for the sake of internal use are of greater importance. For if I cognize[m] the thing from within, then these marks will certainly suffice for external use, although this latter does not suffice for internal use. 836

1. Negative and affirmative concepts.
2. Negative and affirmative marks of concepts.

If the object itself is a lack, then I can only have a negative concept. E.g., freedom is that the will not stand under the compulsion of men. In logic, which abstracts from all content, we can only treat negative or affirmative marks, and the way to make concepts distinct likewise occurs through affirmation or negations. Through negation I have not extended the concept and cannot thereby have more distinct insight into the concept. An affirmative concept must be added, and deeper distinctness must be provided. Through the latter we have insight into cognition, as to its content, more distinctly and with greater clarity. A negative mark is not used to increase our insight, then; rather, it serves only to exclude a concept from other things, in order to guard against errors. All affirmative marks serve to ground and to produce a cognition. – The understanding is actually concerned with furthering the perfection of cognition. But it is the understanding's accomplishment if errors do not enter in. Negative marks are here the *conditio sine qua non*. For since we are in danger of getting into falsehood, they must serve to ward off errors, and they are one of the outstanding means for making our cognition perfect. Negative

[l] "Kenntniße."
[m] "kenne."

marks that ward off one of the errors into which no man has fallen have no 837 value. For they are useful only when they ward off a possible error. There are certain sciences that contain established, negative marks. It would be desirable if we could erect a wall of negative marks around every science, without leaving a door open here or there, where error can slip in. Theologians begin to speculate with reason about things that God says in creation, to raise questions about the situation and character of this or that revealed doctrine, and this is the source of many errors in theology. Negative marks ward off errors in this way. Ignorance in things is not harmful. But not only do errors not increase cognition, they hinder it. It was mentioned above that we are ignorant in many things, that we also cannot always ask about use; rather, as much as possible, we ought without hesitation to pursue everything worthy of being known. Ignorance is different from arbitrary ignoring, when one does not take notice of some circumstances that contribute nothing to the purpose of the thing. What is outside our end we do not need to know. In conversations and with things, we ignore, i.e., abstract from some things that are known, but are put aside because they do not pertain to the end. In the exposition of religion, then, ignoring requires much prudence. One should ignore the errors of the common crowd, for if one disturbs the rubble that glows beneath the ashes, then it blazes up. But what one ignores must not be detrimental to the principal end. But to occasion errors oneself is true deception[;] that is the *peccatum philosophicum*[n] of the Jesuits, who, if they had a good purpose, also believed it good to act with bad actions. To ignore is something completely different than to forget,[o] then, in that it brings the thing with it. Importance has to do with the relation to use and to the end. A cognition is important if it is an important ground in use, or serves for several ends. Importance is always relative, however. E.g. Politics is a matter of great importance for the minister[;] for someone else it is unimportant. Few place importance on serious and important things, but rather on secondary things. Some hold it to be unimportant to speak about the most important objects of religion and morality, and they act honestly on the basis of mores, or based on an intention,[p] etc. To inform someone of the importance of a thing is very hard. I can speak about the importance of the 838 end, of course. But the importance of the means is hard. E.g., to educate a courtier I can recommend speaking French, being widely read, etc., etc. But I ignore the importance of the means. Logic, however, abstracts from the importance of the content and speaks of relative, formal importance. A cognition is logically important when it is a ground of major consequences. If a cognition is the ground of many and numerous consequences, this is

[n] philosophical sin.

[o] Reading "vergessen" for "vorstellen."

[p] "aus Sitten, oder aus Vorsatz."

fruitfulness of cognition. E.g., what constitutes the cultivation of our senses is unimportant, yet just as frequently it is useful and fruitful. Virtue is more than *conduite*[q] and pertains therefore to importance. Cognitions are sufficient for internal use when everything that is pertinent can be understood from these marks; they are sufficient in external use when they serve, in comparison, to see how things agree with others or are different[;] no mark is absolutely sufficient, but rather always sufficient in this or that respect. E.g., marks are sufficient for *praxis*$_L$ but not for speculation.

Necessary marks cannot be separated at all from the concept of a thing; rather, they belong *ad esse*. *Contingent* marks are not constituent parts of the thing but rather are *accessoria*. E.g., reason is necessary in the case of man. Learnedness is contingent. – Marks that do not belong to the thing as *constitutiva* are extra-essential[;] essential marks are *constitutiva* of the thing. Extension *ad essentiam corporis pertinens est.*[r] Movement is extra-essential and an *accessio* to the concept of body. Hence we can divide all *praedicata* into *ad essentiam pertinentia et extraessentialia.*[s]

The essence is the *complexus notarum necessariam interne sufficientium.*[t] In logic the talk is of the essence of concepts, not of things. The necessary marks of a thing are distinguished. Some belong to the thing as consequences[u] of other marks of the very same thing, *aliae notae conceptus alieni non nisi ut rationes competunt.*[v] E.g., that man has a language is an internal mark, but it derives from other marks, namely, that he has reason, a tongue, etc., etc.[;] that he is an animal, however, I cannot judge from anything else. *Ideae conceptus quia sunt rationes, minime derivatae sunt essentiales,*[21] i.e., those[22] that lie in the concept not as consequences but as ground, those that *ad essentiam ut rationata pertinent*[w] are *attributa*[;] these latter must be derived from essential marks[;] *essentia ipsa est complexus essentialium*[;][x] attributes also belong to the essence, but as consequences, and not as constituent parts of the essence. 839

Extraessentialia are of two kinds, first *interna*: *modi* or contingent character[s], (2.) external relations.[y] All relations are contingent[;] internal marks, on the other hand, can sometimes be *essentialia*. E.g., learnedness is extra-essential, but with some it is nonetheless an internal determination[;] to be a master or servant, on the other hand, are relations.[z] For on a

[q] French: conduct.
[r] is pertinent to the essence of body.
[s] those that pertain to the essence and those that are extra-essential.
[t] complex of necessary marks that are internally sufficient.
[u] "ut rationata, als Folgen."
[v] other marks of a concept belong only as grounds (omitting "alieni," for which I can find no suitable meaning).
[w] pertain to the essence as things grounded.
[x] the essence itself is the complex of essential marks.
[y] "externae relationes äußere Verhältniße."
[z] "relationes Verhältnißbegriffe."

desert island one is neither master nor servant[;] all the external marks are therefore external or internal to things.

We speak of the essence of things according to the concept that we have of things, according to the logical concept. But we can also ask about the essence of the thing in and of itself. This is what constitutes the essence and belongs to it necessarily, even if it is not contained in our concept, in short, the basis[a] of a body.

This is the real essence. The other is the logical essence. People complain that the essence of things is unknown to us, namely, the ground of all that really belongs to things. Nevertheless, we can cognize the logical essence quite easily. The logical essence means nothing more than the complex of all marks that first constitute a certain concept. *Complexus omnium notarum conceptum aliquem primitive constituentium.*[b] *Complexus omnium notarum,*[c] i.e., a concept, which is complete with regard to the marks which, taken together, constitute the concept. The logical essence involves the totality of marks, then. They are supposed to be primitive marks, i.e., ones that belong to the concept not as consequences but as *constitutiva*. E.g., if I want to know the logical essence of bodies, I find many marks. Among these, a few belong to the essence as consequences, others are constituent parts, the *essentialia*[d] of a concept, which is called the *complexus essentialium.*[e] Extension, impenetrability,[f] figure are primitive, while divisibility, etc., etc., are attributes. It is possible to give the logical essence of all things. For we must have concepts of all the things about which we speak, of course, and these we must explain in order to find their *essentialia* and *rationata*,[g] and that which belongs to the essence *primitive*$_{\mathrm{L}}$ and *derivative*$_{\mathrm{L}}$.

To have insight into the real essence exceeds human understanding. 840 We cannot provide a complete ground for a single thing. This requires a universal, complete experience, and to obtain all possible experience concerning an object is impossible; we cannot explain any thing in nature *a priori* and without any experience, because the understanding cannot speculate about that with which it is not acquainted. The real essence is also called the nature. If I distinguish essence and nature, then I distinguish the logical from the real essence. When we abstract the marks of our concept, we have the logical essence. But if we investigate the innermost ground of a body, then I will cognize its nature, i.e., its real essence.

The matter of distinct and clear cognitions does not belong to logic.

[a] "das erste Grundstück."
[b] The complex of all marks that constitute a certain concept primitively.
[c] The complex of all marks.
[d] essential [marks].
[e] complex of essential [marks] (reading "essentialium" for "eßentiae").
[f] Reading "Undurchdringlichkeit" for "Durchdringlichkeit."
[g] essential things [and] things grounded.

Logic is supposed to teach the rules of the understanding for representations that are found in us. We must be conscious of representations, then, in order to cognize the rules with their combinations. If we are not conscious of them, however, then we also cannot proceed thus with them. Logic requires clarity, then, where I am conscious of my representation, but it is not capable of making obscure representations clear. What concerns logic, then, is not that we assume obscure representations in the soul, but rather how clarity is brought to distinctness, and this to exhaustiveness, how many clear representations are to be made universal and compared, etc. Obscure concepts are discussed in psychology. Representations are called obscure in comparison with ones that have[h] the degree of clarity that is demanded. When a representation distinguishes the thing from a few but only a few things, when the matter is adequate for some but not for all comprehension. There is also a logical obscurity, then, which is distinct from psychological obscurity, of which one is not at all conscious. Logical distinctness is comparative distinctness, the latter is absolute. E.g., the concept of instinct is an obscure concept. One knows, of course, that it is a drive to act, but that does not exhaust everything. – One can have comparative obscurity in a situation. In a situation where it is sufficient for distinction, it is clear[;] in another situation, where it does not suffice for this, it is obscure. E.g., when a cognition ascends[i] in relation to certain subjects, it must be the case that it transcends the capacity of others. This simply cannot be avoided. One must be very attentive in this, however. A teacher can speak very distinctly, even if he knows nothing at all, by accommodating himself to his listeners' power of comprehension, usurping their terminology, and on account of this he is for them distinctly obscure. One must always speak relatively obscurely when one wants to ascend to a clarity that is to some extent universal. The teacher must draw people to him through obscurity, so that they thereby learn with universal distinctness, [but he must] not lower himself to them completely. Distinctness is relative in regard to the man[;] it must be accommodated to the speculative understanding and not to the common human understanding. Our object must be such that we can comprehend concepts through abstraction. If one cannot do this, then one must let it be and not complain about obscurity. One must study what is appropriate to our power of comprehension and not find absolute sciences blameworthy even if others can go deeper. Concerning total and partial obscurity, it is to be noted that a cognition cannot be wholly clear, *sed obscurae quaedam notae in conceptu claro universali notae singulares possunt esse obscurae univeralis autem clarae.*[j] E.g., a flash of light does not illuminate, but many of them make

841

[h] Reading "den Grad . . . haben" for "nicht den Grad . . . haben," in accordance with Lehmann's correction (24:1102).

[i] "conscendirt."

[j] but certain obscure marks in a clear universal concept can be individually obscure, yet [be marks] of a universal that is clear.

things bright. So too with concepts. A representation that is clear on the whole but not in respect of the parts is an indistinct representation. E.g. Blue and yellow make green, but with the green color we are not always conscious of these parts that lie within it[;] so too with concepts. E.g., the concept of justice. It is supposed to signify that which is done straight and without deviation or cunning, but it is not the way it is with a straight line. For everyone seeks[k] his own advantage, without also harming others. In short, there is much involved in explicating all the manifold in a concept, and in afterward being able again to develop parts of parts, and we have numerous concepts that we can cognize only in the whole. It is a part of philosophy to provide the deep distinctness of the parts of parts. In the end, however, we always come to partial concepts that are simple and can only become clear to us. E.g., reality, mathematical point. When we ourselves arbitrarily put together a concept, it can be wholly distinct. For because we have made it ourselves, we also know what we have brought to it and we are conscious of the partial concepts. If it is given to us, however, then we cannot always have distinct insight.

Clarity can be understood either subjectively or objectively. Through objective clarity the object becomes clear[;] it is the logical[ly] greater perfection, whose first degree is that we are conscious of [the cognition], 842 and whose second degree is clarity in the parts, i.e., distinctness. Cognition grows subjectively through the quantity of logical clarity, when the representations in the subject excite more attention in relation to the rest of the cognition and occupy the power of the mind more strongly. When a representation obscures others in the mind instead of being obscured by them, this is the clarity that excites a greater alteration of condition in the mind. We often need to affect our condition through a representation and to tighten the mind's moving springs. This subjectively greater clarity is called liveliness. Liveliness of cognition belongs, accordingly, to aesthetic cognition and to sensibility. Here one must attend to exactly how liveliness can be brought in where there is obscurity. A certain degree of liveliness can be used everywhere without detriment to obscurity. E.g., a fitting expression. Yes, that is good, for without any liveliness no attention would be excited. – In a sermon distinctness and correct explication must come first, and then liveliness must also be given to the exposition, in order to excite attention and to move the soul. This liveliness has its degrees. The intensive degree is the strength of the cognition. The extensive degree depends on intuition, not on feeling, where the thing is placed before the eyes through examples from common life and cases *in concreto*. The more we produce marks here in order, through intuition, to free the thing from the pure idea, the more we bring about subjective clarity that is greater *extensive*$_{L}$. This is the most necessary thing: that concepts thereby become

[k] Reading "sucht" for "sieht."

more adequate to our understanding and more distinct. For through sensibility the understanding must direct in accordance with ends. – Intensive liveliness rests on feeling, not on intuition but rather on the strength of the cognition. Feeling requires that it depict beauties and produce excitement, i.e., movement of the mind. These are astonishment, fear, admiration, etc. Through these we are transposed into a condition most unsuitable for judging. If intuition is already there, feeling can be added. For then we are already convinced, and we could not easily lose the intuition due to stupefying feeling. Everything one does must occur from principles. Otherwise it is ambiguous, so that the same excitement leads me to good actions today, to bad ones tomorrow. Feeling excites tears, but nothing in the world dries more quickly than tears. When a judgment has penetrated deep into the soul, sensations can also be taken in, but as secondary causes and, as it were, as parts. The majesty of religion is too great, however, for one to play with feelings in the pulpit. They must not be the nourishment of the soul but only its companion, so that when our soul is illuminated by cognition, a moderate excitement arises and brightens the soul. But this excitement must not drown out intuition. This is the excitement that the aesthetic has as to form. In the case of [cognition] that is concerned with intuition, we must not produce much excitement. For this excitement affects only the understanding that does not heed this. To learn exactly how this intuition and sensation must be combined – how, namely, one can give intuition to all conviction, and yet also allow sensation to be added – one should read Sulzer, and above all his theory of the fine arts, or his preparatory exercises.[23] Let one strive for cognitions[l] in history. Rousseau likewise shows much understanding in his writings, but he lets himself be carried away too much by his enthusiasm[;] nonetheless, he has so much that is well-intentioned and true that it must be left to each to distinguish this from his enthusiasms. One can also use Hume in this respect.

843

The greatest logical perfection as to clarity is distinctness. In Wolffian logics it is always only the analytic mode of distinctness that is considered. There is a far more extensive mode, however, namely, the synthetic production of distinctness. Analytic production does not nourish cognition, it only analyzes cognition that is given to me, so that I learn to distinguish better what was already contained beforehand in the cognition. It does not grow as to content, then; instead, I only cognize it with more consciousness. Philosophy, most of all, occupies itself with this mode[;] e.g., through morals I do not nourish my cognition but only place it in better light. Socrates said he was the midwife to his listeners, i.e., he made them reflect better concerning that which they already knew, and become better conscious of it. If we always knew what we know, namely, in the use of

[l] "Kenntniße."

certain words and concepts that are so subtle in application, we would be astonished at the wealth of our cognitions. E.g., philosophers and jurists have not yet been able to develop and to explicate the concepts of justice 844 and fairness. But we need only give one of them a case *in concreto* and he will quickly say to what extent it is just, and to what extent it is fair. In my concept of fairness, then, something must lie hidden that is distinct from that of justice[;] and I make use of this mark, which is clothed in obscurity, *casu*.[m] One of the greatest skills of the learned man who is not merely scholastically correct but who also possesses popularity is that when he speaks with people who cannot bring their concepts to the light of day, he can draw everything out of them, and he says to them what they think. The preacher, e.g., thereby satisfies his listeners in the most pleasant way. When one would like to say, I did not in fact teach this[.] – Indeed, were you not properly conscious of everything that you knew? – This act of making a concept distinct[n] occurs above all through definitions. But if this is completed, then it is also necessary to extend one's concept, and then distinctness grows synthetically, in that new marks are added. *Platonic* or Socratic questions are of such a kind that they drag out of the other man's cognitions what lay within them, in that one brings the other to consciousness of what he actually thought. They are quite distinct, then, from catechistic questions, where what is asked for is only what lies in memory. – Definitions have the highest degree of analytic distinctness, they are the final purpose of all our concepts.

The healthy understanding has the peculiarity that it anticipates speculations so strongly that we have already advanced matters a good bit before we begin to speculate about them, e.g., in the concepts of fortune, fairness, etc. If someone makes an incorrect use of the concepts he had, then we are not simply to hold the concept to be deceptive[o] and blameworthy[;] for our concepts always contain a great deal of reason in them, but when we do not develop them rightly, then we can sometimes stray from the proper path. To make a distinct concept is the synthetic method, to make a concept distinct is the analytic one. When a distinct concept is to be made, one must first introduce marks[;] e.g., a certain object has impenetrability, heaviness, etc., and I will call it a body. I invent for myself a concept, accordingly, e.g., a republic without punishment, where everyone acts well for his own best interest. Such a fiction is a distinct concept that I have made myself. 845 Mathematical distinctness is wholly synthetic. The mathematician says that whatever people may have represented by a circle, I think only that it is to be where a straight line moves around a fixed point. Here I have not made the concept of a circle distinct, but rather have made a distinct concept. A few

[m] in the case.

[n] "Diese Deutlichmachung des Begriffes."

[o] "chicanisch."

say that in the case of distinctness as to logical form, i.e., in the case of analytic distinctness, the energy of cognition dwindles, and that aesthetic perfection loses its *pondus*[p] if I always make someone cognize distinctly what he thought confusedly. In the case of illusion, e.g., in that of beauty, this may be true, but when the talk is of truth, the analysis of cognition cannot in this respect be a hindrance, but instead is helpful. The analysis must not go on so long, however, that the object itself is finally lost to the eyes of those who are not conscious of it. For by concerning myself with *minutissima*, I often lose the representation of the whole. With analytic cognition I make a given concept distinct. Synthetic cognition gives me the concept simultaneously with distinctness. The *mathematicus* makes concepts with distinctness. The philosopher makes concepts distinct. Since the former[,] the mathematician[,] gives the concept, he indicates at the same time all the partial marks of which it consists. From this it becomes clear that the act of making objects distinct[q] occurs synthetically, the act of making concepts distinct[r] occurs analytically. In the synthetic [act] I add new marks to the concept of an object through experience. It arises in such a way that the parts of the cognition precede the whole cognition. In the analytic [act] the whole precedes the parts. E.g., I cannot explain virtue synthetically. For I am supposed to say what we all think under the concept of virtue, not what I perhaps understand under this concept in accordance with my own caprice.

To comprehend, i.e., to cognize through concepts, is what the author calls *concipere*. This is not very good, however. For we have no expression in German for *comprehendere*, i.e., to cognize through intuition. The degrees of distinctness are[:]

1. The lowest degree is to represent something. When I cognize that which relates to the object, I represent the object.

2. To cognize, *percipere*, is to represent something in comparison with others and to have insight into its identity or diversity from them. To cognize something with consciousness, then. For animals also cognize their master, but they are not conscious of this. 846

3. To understand something, *intelligere*, to cognize something in the understanding, not merely with consciousness. The understanding is the faculty of concepts.

To cognize something through concepts, then, is to understand something, *concipere*.

4. To have insight into something, to cognize something with reason, not merely to understand, but [to cognize it] in accordance with concepts that are universal as to their determination. E.g., not merely what a house is, but also the usefulness, the furnishings, etc., of the house. – How few

p weight, importance.

q "die Deutlichmachung der Objecte."

r "die Deutlichmachung der Begriffe."

there are who have insight into something even if they understand it. E.g., the manufacturer of gunpowder knows that it has a driving force, that it has come about in such and such a way. Many attain understanding. This makes them have certain rules of the understanding. But they do not have insight, *non perspiciunt*.

5. To comprehend,[s] to have sufficient insight, insofar as something serves a certain purpose. To comprehend[t] absolutely means, if I cognize from reason, that it is sufficient for all purposes. But we cannot cognize anything in this way. The *mathematicus* has insight into the properties of the thing for many purposes, but not their absolute sufficiency. One can have this *relative*$_{L}$, nonetheless. – This comprehending is something very tricky. Men must really comprehend what they learn, at least for the purpose for which it is comprehensible. E.g. In matters of religion, secrets of nature, morals. For if he does not have insight into these sufficient to his purpose, he can make no use of them. Hence one must not talk at once of incomprehensib[ility], even if something cannot possibly be cognized in a speculative respect. There is in us a particular use of reason, where it seems to be sufficient for us to have insight into something once the thing is there, so that we persuade ourselves that we could also have had insight into it through reason[;] but if we ask ourselves whether we really could have cognized this *a priori*, then it seems as if we could not have. This includes all experiments – in natural science. [Reason] is quite sufficient to comprehend what I have determined *a priori*. E.g., I can comprehend the eclipse of the moon, because I know the moon's path. But if I did not know that saltpeter has such a driving force, would I be able to know beforehand that the powder would explode in this way, even if I could 847 explain the powder ever so well, or could manufacture it? In the end it becomes plain, if one goes into the matter, that we can only say of few things that we have insight into them sufficiently. Many can explain the concept. But most are quite far removed from comprehending. – People have tried to demonstrate what lies in experience. E.g., the properties of the lever are demonstrated quite well in mechanics. But these cognitions always display something faulty, from which it becomes clear that if experience had not given us this, we would never have hit upon it. What I cannot determine *a priori*, then, I cannot comprehend or have full insight into. E.g., the refraction of light rays in water can now be explained, and reason can make things in experience quite comprehensible, but it is false to flatter ourselves that we would have been able to have insight into this *a priori*.

A concept whose marks are clear is distinct. Marks are subordinate or coordinate. Subordinate marks constitute a series, and if we progress in

[s] "Comprehendere, begreiffen."
[t] Reading "Begreifen" for "Begriff."

the series of subordinate marks then this is *profunditas*, thoroughness. Here we ask first of all what the immediate mark of body is. Extension. What is extension? etc., until we finally come to marks that constitute basic concepts. Profundity is progress in the series of subordinate marks until we come to their limits. In coordination, or with the aggregate of the marks of a concept, there is no determinate limit, unless the concept is to be defined analytically.[u] E.g., virtue is a readiness in lawful actions, a readiness in actions that is adequate to the idea of the highest good[;] moreover, it is domination of the inclinations, and so on, and so on.

A distinct concept that contains all the marks which, taken together, constitute the whole concept, is an exhaustive concept[;] and this perfection, which contains all the marks taken together, is called *completudo*. With all cognition, consequently, we demand[v] an exhaustiveness, namely, that all the marks be present that constitute the whole concept. – If a distinct concept lacks no mark, something may nonetheless have been neglected with the concept, namely, that there are one or several marks too many[;] with a cognition, however, in accordance with which my understanding is to be moved to its proper activity, one wants to have all the marks, but not too many. It is an unnecessary waste of the understand- 848 ing's attention. This perfection, insofar as the concept does not overflow with marks, is precision. The author calls only the determinate precise, or, as it were, cut back. For the sake of precision, mathematics is most excellent. – The perfection that arises from *completudo* and precision unified is adequate perfection[;] *quando adaequatur objecto*,[w] when it contains neither less nor more than is contained in the object, the cognition is adequate. Precision in a concept could be called logical elegance. Precision is actually only a negative perfection, in that I take away that which is excessive in the marks of a concept. Wolff calls a concept adequate insofar as it has profundity and intensive distinctness, and insofar as it is distinct through subordinate marks, whose marks are in turn clear. We say, *notae simul sumtae adaequant conceptus*,[x] and we mean correct ones. For [the Wolffians], that is adequate in which marks of marks are clear, although this is not sufficient because I can make the marks of the marks clear once again. Here, then, the Wolffian school has a precarious concept. Precision is a perfection for assessing our cognitions and for becoming certain that in them there is not too much, not too little. This exactness serves as a guarantee. For he who says less than he should here will say more than he should there. The lack of precision rests on tautologies, that I posit a mark twice, or in various ways. E.g., God is a being that is omnipotent, infinite, etc. Here omnipotence already lies in the infinite. There are cases where

[u] Reading "analytisch erklärt werden soll" for "analytisch werden soll."
[v] Reading "verlangen" for "erlangen."
[w] when it is made adequate to the object.
[x] the marks taken together are adequate to the concept.

precision cannot appropriately be sought, and where it causes indistinctness, although it provides all the more distinctness for a capable mind. E.g. In the catechism one can say a thing twice. For of two words that mean the same thing, one is often easier than the other. – The complex of marks that are exhaustive and precise in a given concept are adequate[y] to the concept. Among experts[z] lack of precision is a great mistake. He who disregards the demands of experts, however, and only wishes to teach the ignorant, can deviate somewhat from precision. – The author now deals with the lucid mind. Many can reflect thoroughly on things but cannot give them lucidity, i.e., popularity. Scholastically correct perfection con-

849 sists in the agreement of cognition with the previously mentioned rules, namely, that it be adequate to the concept. This is logical or scholastic perfection, which is determined, namely, by rules of the understanding. Popular distinctness is aesthetic distinctness, and something becomes aesthetically distinct through examples, in that it is exhibited through intuition. The more that I can combine my concepts of abstraction with representations *in concreto*, the more popular does my cognition become. Popularity, then, is when cognition *in abstracto* is combined with cognition *in concreto*, and thus understanding and sensibility are combined with each other. Scholastic perfection, however, is always the principal thing. There are authors who are popular, but when logical perfection is lacking, they are unreliable, although they are attractive. – What is understandable even to the most common man has the greatest degree of perfection that is aesthetic. What is clear to the most common man is also clear, certainly, to the speculative man. This highest degree of popularity must be present in religion and morals. At the same time, however, logical perfection must not be neglected in any way. For it is the foundation through which a cognition exists as a cognition and is suited to be adopted by the understanding. For some purposes only a certain degree of logical perfection is needed, and the lowest degree of logical perfection is the highest degree of popularity. The moralist must not neglect the distinctness of concepts, but he must also have examples at hand and, as a good anthropologist, must represent human nature and show the agreement of his doctrines with that nature. – When both these perfections combined can be comprehended even by the most common understanding, this is the highest degree of lucidity, which for many men is impossible. Some can know the rules *in abstracto* but do not have the ease of wit and strength of imagination to select the deepest examples to help others see things. Of the certainty of cognition. There are three degrees of holding-to-be-true. Holding-to-be-true and truth are distinct subjectively and objectively. If the holding-to-be-true is subjectively incomplete, it is called persuasion.

[y] "angemessen, adaequat."

[z] "Kunstverständigen."

But a subjectively complete holding-to-be-true is conviction, the state of mind where I give approval to a cognition, the holding-to-be-true. This is the phenomenon of the human soul about which we are engaged in reasoning here,[a] and not whether the cognition is objectively true.

The 3 degrees of holding-to-be-true are opining, believing, and knowing. 850

Opining is not yet conviction, for otherwise it would have to be at least subjectively sufficient, for me in the condition of mind in which I find myself. With opining, our judgment is problematic, i.e., I settle nothing; rather, I only have a degree of holding-to-be-true, although this degree is not sufficient. Opining has nothing harmful about it, as long as I am conscious of the insufficiency of my holding-to-be-true.

Opining is a holding-to-be-true based on a ground of cognition that is neither objectively nor subjectively sufficient. When I hold something to be true, e.g, that there is a passage through the Arctic Ocean, I am conscious, nonetheless, that my cognition of the thing is still precarious, and is insufficient with respect to the object; hence it is an opinion. Where this [opinion] does not satisfy[b] me, and I would not like to wager anything on it, it is also subjectively insufficient. Locke says that man is an animal[;] the philosopher[,] a man who holds his opinion to be true, opines this. Opinions make up the greatest part of our cognition. The first thing in a cognition is always a will,[c] an obscure foreseeing, which produces a holding-to-be-true in us. In some sciences opining is not allowed at all. E.g., in the case of duties one must not opine but instead know. One cannot risk doing anything on the basis of pure opining.

In speculations, one can perhaps opine something. In metaphysics, opinions are discussed insofar as they can be brought to the touchstone of experience. E.g., [opinions] about pure spirits. Here it is shown that because there would be no end of opinion here, opining is not allowed. One must not opine about possibilities[;] they have to be certain. If one says how we live after death. Can I opine here? No, I have to know or to believe. Here nothing can be settled by experience, nor, unfortunately, *a priori*. One must not opine, but instead know, that which can be proved *a priori*. In general, I must either know or believe what can be settled with reason. Opining counts for nothing here. – When I say I opine, I have to make a claim to knowledge. In opining I always take a step toward knowledge. For there is an insufficient ground, to which complements still must be added in order to make it perfect. Here I think a complement to the whole.[d] If a cognition is of such a kind that knowlege is impossible for it, 851 then opinion is so too. E.g. Based on the needs of my reason I see that

[a] "worüber hier raissonirt wird."
[b] "satisfacirt."
[c] "ein Wille."
[d] "ein complementum ad totum, ein Ergänzungsstück zum Ganzen."

men must be created by a rational being, for men are born of their parents, etc. But someone must have been the first, who was not born of any man. This is only a belief. For here there are subjective grounds. Why do I assume this? Because my reason needs it. No knowledge is possible here, hence no opinion, either. Thus it is impossible for man to know *a posteriori* the continued existence of his soul after death. Here there is belief, again, namely, that since everything in nature is in accordance with ends, but man has speculative reason among his needs, through which he is distinct from other animals, so that he asks about the first cause of movement, about the sun, etc. Here he cannot with reason trace the first seeds of life to their final development. For life is too short, and in old age reason does not have its proper strength, either. There must be another place, then, where human reason can attain its proper development. Thus runs the belief.

In the case of belief we judge assertorically, i.e., we declare ourselves for the truth, although it is only sufficient subjectively for us, and we cannot convince everyone else of it. I can have a subjective ground for holding something to be true, and in such a way that this is steadfast, but is not sufficient for me at every time, but instead is restricted only to the condition in which I find myself[;] for I can advance to better insight. This is only relative, then. But there is also a belief in connection with which I cannot alter my holding-to-be-true at all, which one cannot call theoretical belief[;] instead, this is a practical belief. Hence it is fully as strong as conviction and as the greatest apodeictic certainty. This practical belief is moral belief. This is when, based on my moral sentiment, I accept something that is necessarily connected with this, which is regarded as[e] wholly unalterable. E.g., I can see, based on the conformity to ends and the order in the world, that there is a God. Yet some things seem contrary to ends. For this, such speculative grounds are not sufficient; only morality is. If I am to make someone convinced of my belief, however, then it is presupposed that he has just such moral sentiments. Theoretical belief is alter-

852 able,[f] to be sure, if it is not supported by moral belief. For I can advance to better insight, and find something contrary in nature, and then my holding-to-be-true comes to an end. – It is permissible to accept propositions of reason on belief only for a single kind [of proposition,] namely, in mathematics, because here, on account of its evidence, one cannot err very easily, and one sees the error at once. In philosophical sciences, however, it is absurd to accept propositions that are maintained without proof. In history I can also have knowledge, if it is such that it can be communicated to everyman. E.g., that London lies in England, because

[e] Reading "das als" for "das."

[f] Reading "wandelbar" for "nicht wandelbar."

we all have days when mail arrives, and we hear the very same thing from so many people who agree.

Believing is a subjectively sufficient but objectively insufficient holding-to-be-true. Sense is always subjective. Knowing is an objective holding-to-be-true, with consciousness. He who undertakes something must risk something in accordance with his opinion. This belief can be a wholly rational belief, and *subjective*$_L$ I can have such a sufficient ground for holding something to be true that I can make my decision about cognition[g] accordingly. E.g., sowing, setting out to sea, etc., is grounded on this. One believes that the grain will come up, that the east wind will blow, and then the west wind. Nonetheless, we cannot be certain about all these things, and we have only subjective grounds for holding-to-be-true. Now if I can hold something to be true on my own account, however, even if it is not very certain *objective*$_L$, I can never have a subjective ground for holding-to-be-true in morals; instead, objective truth must always reign in this field. The judge cannot condemn anyone to death unless he deserved it according to someone's charge and there is no opposition.[h] That someone has been found with blood on him is subjectively sufficient for holding-to-be-true, but not objectively. Someone can hold something to be true in accordance with a quite rational ground, yet also not be able to say, of the very same thing, that he knows it. – With knowledge, what is important is not the ground of the holding-to-be-true. For one who believes something may hold it to be true with more tenacity than one who knows it[;] instead, what is important is the proper mode of holding-to-be-true. Some hold to practical truths with great zeal even if there is no logical truth in them. – A bet is a trial through which one tests whether someone else knows what he believes, and holds it to be true with firm belief. Someone who will not bet wants to maintain something boldly, without 853 this costing him anything. Often one will only bet a ducat. Two ducats frighten some people away from the bet. He who wagers life and limb is fully convinced subjectively. And there are such cases. E.g. He who renounces certain advantages of life, and who lives in a holy way because he knows he will be rewarded, has a strong belief. He who believes so strongly that he gives his life, for it is as good as the greatest certainty. But one cannot say that he knows this, but only that he believes it. E.g., religious secrets. In mathematics there is no belief. Here there must be knowledge. For it would be ridiculous if someone said, I believe a triangle is a figure that consists of 3 sides and 3 enclosed angles. Belief in the truth is firm only practically, and its ground is only subjective. He attains knowledge through his conviction of the understanding with the most disinterested understanding, whereby he becomes capable of making what he

[g] "Erkenntnißentschließung."

[h] "ehe er ihn nach Jemandes Ausspruch verdient hat, und kein Gegentheil ist."

knows distinct and certain for others, too. In the case of the very firmest conviction, accordingly, knowledge is not needed. But one knows only when one can give the very same certainty even to the most disinterested understanding. In short, we can capture the distinction between belief and knowledge thus: *Opining* is a holding-to-be-true that is insufficient both subjectively and *objective*$_{L}$. *Believing* is a holding-to-be-true that is subjectively sufficient but objectively insufficient. Hence believing is the opposite of opining[;] knowing is a holding-to-be-true that is sufficient both objectively and subjectively.

When a holding-to-be-true is concerned merely with the subjective, without looking to the objective, in which case someone else could also be convinced, then I say that I am persuaded. I cannot give any account of my subjective grounds for holding-to-be-true[;] they hold only for me and not for anyone else. When I say that I cannot persuade myself of the thing, then this holds only for me[;] I see quite well that someone else, who is not as well acquainted with the thing and cannot distinguish as well, might well persuade himself. – Every language has marks of sincerity, based on which an honest man believes at once that the thing is meant thus in the heart. I cannot express to someone else, however, how truthfulness in tone and in words affects me, and what moves me to holding-to-be-true[;] I [merely] say that I am persuaded of it. – When I say that I am convinced, this is still a subjective ground, too. For it is concerned only with the 854 subject. But there is also a subjective necessity here, hence a ground must lie in the object. Otherwise the condition in me could well change. Something lies in my holding-to-be-true that lets me believe[;] I will never deviate from this[;] I believe I find a ground in the object, even if I cannot immediately make it distinct. – Who is persuaded most easily? Children. For their judgments are merely subjective. They believe what they wish. Their cognition seeks to extend itself, and thus their inexperience makes them accept what pleases them, and not even inquire into what the understanding requires. People who are predisposed[i] concerning something can also be persuaded, however, i.e., an opinion gets a footing in the man, and other opinions then find the place no longer empty. Men are usually quite predisposed. For the judgments of our youth come first, and later ones find no place, therefore. For the understanding cannot clear it out again, since it is hard to arrive at something free from all impressions,[j] as in law the *prior occupans* is always the most fortunate. Predisposition includes predilection, when one is strongly inclined toward someone by love, when that which our patrons, friends, etc., have maintained influences our judgments as well, so that we hold these judgments to be objective. When a man gives approval to such a judgment, he does not know what actually

[i] "praeoccupirt."

[j] Reading "frey von allen Eindrücken" for "von allen Eindrücken."

determines him, whether understanding, or idea, or sensibility. Now[k] sensibility together with the understanding can yield a mixed effect. If only we could always distinguish what sensibility and understanding do, then the influence of sensibility would not be harmful. But if judgment rests on predisposition, then these influences are hard to note. In the case of holding-to-be-true, then, the hardest question is, Whence did it arise? [I]f sensibility has much effect, the thing is not therefore to be rejected. For the understanding also has a part in this, and cognizes[l] enough grounds as to the object. When our approval has for the most part objective grounds, however, then we nonetheless have to be distrustful, above all when men are divided concerning the matter[;] and then we have to investigate which of the two opinions has subjective grounds. How can one distinguish conviction and persuasion, then? We distinguish the two even through feeling. One says, I am persuaded that this did not happen thus[;] insofar as I can judge from the course of things, I have to declare myself against this story. I am convinced when the thing is so logically perfect that I can communicate it to someone else[;] when I represent to myself that I would hold the thing to be true no matter what the risks[;] if I were to waver, then I would not really be convinced. But if I believe I am not risking anything when I put up all my interests as security, then I am convinced.

855

When we *opine*, this is a cognition that does not even have subjective grounds, then[;] it is the beginning of holding-to-be-true. Belief already means a subjectively sufficient holding-to-be-true, which does not seem to be objectively sufficient but nonetheless has various grounds, which are determined in the understanding. Belief always presupposes conviction. For in it there is something firm. When someone says, I believe that could happen, he only opines, and this is only a confusion of words. For he would willingly let himself be shown otherwise. The cause of belief, e.g., in the case of the hope for another world, is when someone cannot prove to us the opposite and its impossibility, and one has here a ground in the understanding. E.g., the unequal distribution of good and evil. The subjective ground, however, which is grounded on morality, cannot be counted as an objective ground. Belief is firm, then, when it leads a rational man to neglect the advantages of his life for his belief. He who is moved by duty and hope combined to renounce all these advantages believes and is convinced. In regard to its effect on the subject, this holding-to-be-true will not yield to the highest certainty, and practical conviction is the strongest possible. This practical conviction can fall on certain propositions, and these are then morally certain propositions. These are the ground of all morality, and they agree with our greatest conscientiousness, if we live according to them and thus subordinate our actions to them.

[k] Reading "nun" for "nur."

[l] Ak, "er kennt"; MS, "erkennt."

Everyone can see that no one will rob him of the belief that the apparent disharmony between good and evil will come to an end[;] and on this account I ask, Do I have ground enough to accept it? Yes, a practical ground, but not a logical one. It fits together so firmly with reason, however. For the greatest mathematician could not do anything here if I were not willing to be robbed of the belief even at the cost of my life.

If this conviction does not immediately serve for speculative but only for practical conviction. E.g., the concept of God is not given for speculative 856 employment, but instead for practical employment. If, then, with certain propositions that men treat as belonging to a science, one reduces them so much that one allows them only practical but not theoretical conviction, then one has not taken anything from them; instead, one has taken from men the conceit that they can have insight into these propositions on speculative grounds. Practical grounds thereby appear in a brighter light, since men are led back to their interest. Sensible certainty is divided into certainty of the senses and empirical certainty. The senses alone still do not make experience; rather, experience is the judgment of the understanding concerning the combination of our sensible representations. Sensible certainty, accordingly, is nothing but the certainty of the cognized connection[m] of the senses. – The senses and understanding constitute all our cognitions.[n] The senses give appearance. The understanding connects it, and this makes experience[;] and experience, then, is the cognized connection or unity of appearances. Men must combine intuitions *objective*$_{L}$, then, in order to be able to say anything about them. There are logicians who talk only about the certainty of the senses, whether our sensible representations in themselves are true, i.e., whether they have objects, or whether they are for the most part only a great illusion,[o] which corresponds to the object. E.g. We dream. We hold this to be just as true as when we are awake[;] now whether, as to the object, such representations are real or ideal, whether they are such as they present themselves to us, or whether they merely give us the way in which the senses are affected, or whether they are only deceptions of our imagination, this question does not belong to logic but rather to metaphysics, where the origin of illusion and of truthfulness from the senses is discussed. – In the end it comes to this, that there is neither truth nor falsehood in the senses, and that both lie only in the use that our understanding makes of sensible representations. For the senses do not judge at all, and on this account they do not contain errors, not because they never judge falsely, but because they do not judge at all. – Here, then, the question can only be about the certainty of empirical cognition. This is a

[m] Reading "der erkannten Verknüpfung" for "des erkannten Verhältniß."

[n] "Kenntniße."

[o] Reading "Schein" for "Sinn."

cognition of objects through the understanding, insofar as they are presented to the understanding. All empirical certainty concerns only the relation of sensible representations, how certain representations can be compared with one another. We distinguish this sensible certainty from rational cognition. This latter can be expressed distinctly in two ways.

1. A cognition of reason,[p] if its object is a mere object of reason. 857
2. A rational cognition[q] concerns the form in which I cognize an object through the senses, be its object empirical or rational.

Some cognitions are merely objects of reason, e.g., morals[;] these are material rational cognitions. Metaphysics deals with the character of rational cognition as to the object. Logic deals with the second thing, namely, with the formal. Our cognition can comprehend objects of experience, and our certainty can be either empirical or rational. E.g., the principle of force[r] by means of the lever has empirical certainty, but also rational certainty. For even if experience taught us nothing about this force, I would already be able to cognize it through reason. That certain things are not alike, experience can say. That they necessarily have to be so, however, reason teaches. It elevates the certainty, then, in that it presents the cognition as necessary. – Sometimes we can have no rational certainty. Then we must content ourselves with empirical certainty. This is so above all in natural science. That cognition of which we can acquire rational certainty is superior, however. – With things that we would never have hit upon had we not learned them from experience, certainty of experience is best. But if we cognize grounds that are necessary, and through which we could also have foreseen it, then rational certainty takes precedence. All our cognition is either from concepts or from the construction of concepts. The first is called discursive, the second intuitive, and hence all our rational certainty [is] discursive or intuitive, too. Rational certainty, insofar as it is intuitive, is mathematical certainty[;] insofar as it is discursive, it is philosophical certainty. Mathematical certainty differs from philosophical certainty, then[;] they are both certain, are cognized through reason, but the one certainty is discursive, the other intuitive.

Both moral and mathematical propositions are apodeictically certain, i.e., are combined with the consciousness of necessity, in contrast to empirical ones, which are only assertoric. Both can convince completely, accordingly, even if they are distinguished by being discursive and intuitive. Mathematical certainty is thus called evident,[s] i.e., so that the objects are not exhibited *in abstracto* through concepts, but in an individ- 858

[p] "Eine Vernunft-Erkenntniß."
[q] "Eine vernünftige Erkenntniß."
[r] "der Satz von der Potenz."
[s] "evident."

ual intuition. If the question is about the degree of certainty, however, one cannot change philosophical propositions into mathematical ones. Some come very close to intuition, but still they are different. Wolff made the mistake of trying to judge discursively in mathematics. E.g., the definition of similarity for triangles. The proposition, Do what is right, need not be constructed. For it is aleady clear. In contrast, one would not extract the proof that 2+2=4 from any concept. Hence philosophical and mathematical certainty cannot be mixed up. Our author speaks now of the *modi judicii veritatis et falsitatis*,[t] or of the *modi* of holding-to-be-true.

1. A cognition is said to be widely accepted, i.e., if it finds approval with all, although in itself it is not certain. This is a merely external mark, then, from which certainty cannot yet be inferred.
2. A cognition is settled, i.e., it is accepted as a universally cognized truth.
3. A cognition is undeniable, indisputable, it is impossible to doubt the proposition's truth.

A proposition is settled in two senses. For one thing, if it is objectively certain, i.e., indisputable, or also *subjective*$_L$, if one has accepted that a cognition is cognized as certain. In natural science there are many settled propositions, but also a multitude of accepted propositions. Undoubted propositions are not called settled, namely, because they cannot be disputed any more. E.g., mathematical propositions. Objections can still be found to many physical problems[;] if cognition of nature is only contingent, one may not maintain apodeictic necessity in his judgment, either. Cognition is called thorough when it is adequate to the nature of that cognition in general.

Thorough cognitions differ according to differences of their nature. A moral exposition is thorough in a different way than a physical one is. Thoroughness is not a logical perfection, or perfection of certainty, but only the perfection that is adequate to the nature of this cognition. Someone can be a very thorough teacher of his parish if he adapts[u] truths to his 859 listeners' power of comprehension, and this very exposition could be less thorough for *doctores theologiae*, if it is to be an essay, where one looks to those *principia* that have to be put at the basis of a cognition in accordance with its nature.

Shallow cognitions indicate something different from superficial ones. Shallowness indicates a lack of depth of cognition, that one does not go to the depths[v] with his cognition, but instead stays on the shore, and does not follow up his cognition to its first grounds. Certain cognitions swim like

[t] the modes of judgment of truth and of falsity.

[u] "aptirt."

[v] Reading "die Tiefe" for "die Höhe."

debris on the top,"[w] but are comprehensible to the common understanding and adequate to the end[;] these are shallow cognitions. If one wishes to have a cognition that goes beyond the limits of the common understanding, e.g., if one wishes to be instructed concerning meticulous subtleties, which reason has to have in metaphysics, this would be superficial if it were adequate only for the common understanding. If I wanted to teach him only the first concepts of metaphysics – there is a God, an immortal soul – then I would give him a shallow cognition, but one adequate to the end. A cognition is also called superficial when one knows the titles of books, without oneself understanding anything of the science.

OF APPROVAL AND THE WITHHOLDING OF APPROVAL

We can see from our expressions, I accept that, I concede that, or I withhold my approval, that there must be something in our approval that is arbitrary, where we ourselves have to determine whether we will hold the cognition to be true or not. We will investigate, therefore, to what extent our judgment depends on the will here. The understanding cannot subject itself to the will on any other ground except to the extent that it is put to use. Otherwise its conviction rests on grounds, not on decisions. Now because the will is a major cause through which certain convictions arise, the will does have an influence *indirecte* on this understanding. If we could convince ourselves immediately of what we wished were so, everyone would make for himself, through the understanding, the happiest chimeras he can – namely, if these chimeras, which are produced by the will, did not have to give way to refutation by the understanding. – Certain cognitions are such that even if we find nothing mistaken in the moving grounds, we are nonetheless distrustful with our judgment, on account of the similarity of this cognition to others in which we have often erred[;] this is the *suspensio judicii*,[x] the intention not to let a provisional judgment become a determining one. There are admittedly grounds here for holding-to-be-true, which are more certain than the grounds for the opposite. We can have grounds, but hold them not to be determinate, and thus we distinguish provisional from determinate judgment. We can divide[y] this withheld approval in two. *Suspensio judicii indagatoria*[z] is when one still intends to seek out the grounds for the determinate judgment. This is actually a postponement of judgment, in order to inquire more about this in time[;] or [there is] *renunciatio judicii*,[a] in that we renounce

860

[w] "wie die Stoppeln oben."
[x] suspension of judgment.
[y] Reading "eintheilen" for "mittheilen."
[z] Investigative suspension of judgment.
[a] renunciation of judgment.

our judgment and give up all hope of determining anything. Skepticism renounces all judgments in regard to various things. E.g., whether the soul is corporeal. The philosopher holds this to be not yet decided, and suspends his judgment.

To withhold one's approval is a faculty of a practiced power of judgment, and it is not found in beginners or in youths, but only with increasing age. For our faculty of cognition is so desirous of extending itself that it tries with the greatest impatience to extend itself as soon as an opportunity offers itself. In young minds this inclination to accept the seeming as true is so great that they find it very hard to withhold their judgment. When they see, however, how one can be misled into making a judgment that one has to retract, i.e., when they are made more clever by much experience, then they suspend [judgment] more. – It is a hard action, even for one who has a strong power of judgment, to maintain oneself for long in the condition of withholding one's judgment. For man has an inclination always to accept one of two propositions as true. [The power of judgment] is almost never so perfect in man that he could be wholly indifferent, and even if he withholds it, he always has more inclination toward one side than toward the other. – One often withholds one's judgment so that one will not subsequently need to retract his judgment, the more so as one makes a claim to the dignity of a grounded insight, insofar as one might lose something of his reputation in doing so. The greater the authors, the more cautious they are in their expressions concerning things that are still controversial, and they expound 861 their propositions problematically, not assertorically[.] This reservation[b] is always a reservation[c] that one might wrongly place trust in his judgments, however well grounded.[d] – The *suspensio judicii* is distinct from when I do not deal with a matter at all, [when] I leave something *in dubio*, since my purpose simply does not require decision concerning it. This is *judicium anceps*,[e] and it is childlike, while *suspensio judicii*, on the other hand, is manly, and occurs in a man of experience. – Opposed to *judicium anceps* is *judicium praeceps*,[f] which is still worse. This is something different again from suspending.[g] When I suspend, I do not have grounds enough for a determinate judgment. I leave it *in dubio*, if it is not at all relevant to my end whether it is true or not true. Provisional cognitions constitute such a major science that it could be a very useful chapter for logic if it were not too deep to decide, e.g., how provisional judgments can be made into determinate ones. This requires the most

[b] "Zurückhalten."
[c] "Zurückhaltung."
[d] "daß man ein Mißtrauen in seine noch so gegründete Urtheile setzt."
[e] undecided judgment.
[f] precipitous judgment.
[g] "das suspendirende."

exact cognition[h] of the objects themselves. Hence logic cannot speak sufficiently of the nature, value, limits, requisites, and condition[s] of provisional judgments. That would instead become an organon for philosophy, which we presently do not yet have. – Every man judges provisionally in that which he judges first, e.g., based on a face. The first appearance, the bearing, the clothing that one has in society, must pass judgment on him, although that is not sufficient. Provisional judgment, just because it is first, commonly has such a strong influence on man that afterward determinate judgments cannot eradicate provisional ones even through the strongest grounds. We judge of a book provisionally according to its title. Provisional judgments can gradually have a greater approximation to determinate judgments, however. In meditating, provisional judgments must come first. I take this along, and I believe it fits into the connection. Afterward, with an overview of the whole, the determinate judgments perhaps turn out completely differently. Our understanding notes provisionally something of what it ought first to discover by itself. We accept the truth, and we have a scent of the key to our cognition. Our understanding is directed by this, then, in that it gives us the means to attain the end of cognition.

That which is for us sufficient for approval is determinate. A provisional judgment must not be held to be determinate. In refutation, the opponent can have made a good provisional judgment. Then one must lead him, through modesty, to the point where he suspends his judgment. 862

We can always judge, if only we are conscious that it is a provisional judgment. *Praevia judicia*, i.e., provisional judgments, are of great importance, since with them one has certain maxims for provisional investigation of a thing. In all things one must always judge something beforehand. E.g., in searching for metal in mines I must already have a provisional ground for digging in this particular mine. In meditating we must judge provisionally where the truth might well lie. The logic that would set forth the maxims for provisional judgments would be of great importance[;] it would actually be a *heuristic*$_L$ for new truths, but it is not yet discovered. One judges provisionally when, before one judges determinately, one has certain grounds for directing his investigation more toward one object than toward another. Faced with the prospect of objects in which I seek a future cognition, I judge something, so that afterwards I can undertake experiments concerning this. Before all discovery investigation must be undertaken. For one finds nothing by pure luck, without investigating, and without guidance. – As soon as one meditates about something, one already makes plans, whose execution is preceded by a certain half-judgment[i] about the properties that are still to be discovered. If all this were illustrated by examples of discoverers, of how,

[h] "Kenntniß."

[i] "ein gewißes halbirtes Urtheil."

through provisional judgments, they had arrived at this and that, this would give guidance for attaining the discovery of more cognitions. The judge in criminal law could make use of this as a thing of great importance. Provisional judgments are also called *anticipationes*, where one suspends his determinate judgment. One has not yet decided on determining judgments. Thus one anticipates these to a certain extent. Epicurus called the concepts of our understanding, which the understanding presupposes prior to experience, *anticipationes*.[j] Prejudices are quite distinct from these provisional judgments, and are the exact opposite of them. For [in prejudices] one determines without, or instead of, judging provisionally. – We must distinguish investigating from reflecting. Many a proposition can be accepted without investigation[,] e.g., [w]hether the whole is greater than its parts. Although we do not need to investigate[k] here, it is necessary, nonetheless, that we reflect, i.e., that we seek out the connection of a cognition with our power of cognition from which it is supposed to arise. Our faculty of cognition is manifold, and all its powers are in play. They run through one another, and each operates in the case of the object that is suited for it[;] and we always seek for the faculty of cognition that is proper for [an object], without that being difficult for us. E.g., the proposition that between two points there can only be one straight line is laid before the understanding for reflection, and intuition tests whether we can only draw the one line here. We must always do this, even with cognitions that do not seem to need to be investigated. For when a cognition arises from the influence of a power of cognition that has no validity in regard to this object, then the cognition must either be turned away or be suspended. I have to see whether the senses or the understanding or the imagination is in play here. For all errors rest on the fact that sensibility influences the understanding. When one believes that one has this through understanding, and sensibility has a secret influence in the matter, then errors arise. – It is customarily said that nothing comes from nothing. We must have a material out of which we make cognitions. We cannot produce this matter ourselves. Hence everything must come from experience, and yet nothing is ever evident unless reason alone has made it.[24] If you wish to be convinced through the understanding alone, whence will you take it? – The reflection[l] mentioned is needed even where investigation seems to be impossible. E.g., with mathematical propositions. We accept some judgments without reflection[m] and without attention to the power of cognition that has an influence on the judgment, and from this prejudices arise. Prejudice is the mechanization of reason in principles. A prejudice is a *principium* for judging based on subjective causes that are regarded as objective. Subjective causes all lie in

863

[j] Reading "anticipationes" for "anticipation."

[k] Reading "untersuchen" for "unterscheiden."

[l] Reading "Ueberlegung" for "Ueberzeugung."

[m] Reading "Ueberlegung" for "Ueberzeugung."

sensibility. Objective grounds lie in the understanding. Accordingly[,] because sensibility has influence, the judgment cannot be true. – A prejudice, accordingly, is a *principium* of judgments, of reason in principles. I cannot say, e.g., that what this man says of his son is a prejudice – that he himself has a good mind but that he has been seduced by others – if the son himself is a bad man[;] instead, the judgment arises from a prejudice. Erroneous judgments based on prejudices are not themselves prejudices[;] hence actual prejudices are a source of many false judgments in the principle[n] of these judgments. In the example given, the proposition is taken from a *principium*, and has in fact the effect of a *principium*. With a prejudice, one must always reflect on where it comes from. E.g., The apple does not fall far from the tree[; this] could be called a prejudice, because it is a universal proposition and hence a *principium*. But one could also say that it has arisen from earlier prejudices, which children have from their parents. – All prejudices are *principia* for judging. From them a judgment must arise, then. Someone has found a proposition such-and-such maintained by Leibniz. Now he holds [Leibniz] to be thorough, although he does not have any insight into the proof. This is not a prejudice, but rather inclination based on a prejudice. The prejudices of well-known merits give strong presumption that everything that is said, e.g., by Wolff, Leibniz, etc., will be meritorious. – Prejudice is a *principium* for judging, not from objective grounds[;] but if all the grounds of the judgment are drawn not from the object but from the subject, then they are drawn from such sources. Hence I may only say to myself that it seems to me thus, and not that the object is so. All grounds must actually be objective, then. Objective grounds are opposed to subjective ones. With grounds, I think only of something universal, and with subjective causes a certain condition operates in man. – Custom easily makes propositions to which we have long adhered become quite necessary for us, so that we finally make of them a ground for judging[;] and in this way one can make *principia* for judgments out of pure customs. E.g., it is a custom to have a superstitious respect for someone, namely, because this man has always been such in earlier times[;] thus there arises from this a principle for judging, i.e., an inclination, which has become our own through frequent exercise. From this it becomes clear how a *principium* arises out of subjective causes. – One judges the maxims of others critically, and holds his own to be good. Here is the prejudice *suum cuique pulchrum*,[o] whose subjective cause is self-love. In the manners of others there is often nothing improper, even if[p] we hold it to be so.

864

Here the understanding is just misled and holds these to be objective grounds, and this then causes us to judge through the admixture of

865

[n] "im Grundsatz und principium."

[o] to each his own beauty.

[p] Reading "auch wenn" for "wenn."

sensibility. The principal sources of prejudices are subjective causes, accordingly, which are falsely held to be objective grounds. They serve, as it were, in place of principles, because prejudices must be principles. The principal sources of prejudices are above all imitation, custom, and inclination.

[The] idea of [prejudice] is a ground for judging based on subjective causes, and each prejudice holds as a *principium* for judging, i.e., it is of universal influence. Thus

1. *Imitation.* The human understanding seeks to extend itself, and in the case of the ignorance that one finds in children and in the common man, it extends itself by the example of others, in that it imitates the thought of others. Imitation is thus a ground for holding to be true something that someone else has said. E.g., what all men maintain must be true. This includes all proverbs.
2. *Custom* is the second source of prejudices. It operates most strongly among the old, just as imitation occurs more among the young than among the old. Young people have not yet lived long enough to allow custom to become so important in them. If one is old, however, then he cannot easily take on another form. Indeed, custom operates among old people so strongly that one cannot remove them from it, above all if it has arisen, in addition, out of imitation. Then the man is wholly incurable. For imitation makes all reflection by oneself impossible. When, e.g., an author wants to expound a new system of a science, custom makes him have many difficulties in the beginning. For time must first pass before such a cognition stops the stream of customs and gradually brings it to a standstill, and then gives it the opposite direction. Thus prejudices based on custom can only be removed by the passage of time.
3. *Inclination* or *Disinclination.* Predilection or inclination is when, before one investigates a thing, one is already predisposed toward it beforehand.

Imitation is most contrary to the free use of our reason, because here we accustom ourselves early to making use of the judgments of others instead of our own. The free use of reason can be divided into the active 866 use and the passive, and judgments of imitation are *habitus* of a passive use. I make use of my reason actively when I derive something myself from the laws of nature. It is harmful to represent certain men to youths as masters, so that they have to imitate their language or expressions mechanically. For from that comes a passive use of reason, and this is a *contradictio in adjecto.* For all reason, as to its nature, is a self-active *principium* of thought, and even when I take experience as the ground in thinking, reason nonetheless makes universal rules of experience. The use of reason consists in self-activity, then, but the laziness of men makes them prefer to proceed passively, rather than raising their power of cognition so far as to make use of their own powers. Accordingly, they have merely subjective and historical cognitions, because they merely imitate. Such a procedure is fruitful soil for rapidly proliferating prejudices, and it hinders all improvement and progress in a thing[;] and yet it is so universally widespread, because it is so suited to the human inclination to comfort. There is nothing more harmful, then, than when one accustoms pupils to imitate authors, or rather to ape them.

Sentences and proverbs are a principle of imitation. Proverbs are expressions taken from common life and from the language of the crowd. The first source[s] of proverbs are commonly prejudices. E.g. The apple falls not far from the tree, etc. Sentences are aphorisms that indicate wide reading, and since they therefore belong to a certain extent to learnedness, they are used by those who want to put on airs and to show their learnedness. – A formula is a rule whose expression serves as a model for application. We have them only[q] to come to the aid of memory thereby[.] Thus we have formulas in algebra, grammar, law, etc., etc. Even the greatest learned man makes use of such formulas[;] if in the beginning he has reflected on the rules, he then makes formulas for himself, in order later to proceed more easily in application, so that if he knows the formulas, he knows immediately all the *actus* that he has to observe. They are of great importance, accordingly, but mere imitation of formulas does not bring about such good things. – A saying is a proposition whose expression has a certain precision in indicating its sense. When an expression is pregnant, then, and in this full content a certain precision of expression nonetheless prevails, so that it seems that one could not provide such a comprehensive exposition in fewer words, that is a saying.[r] Sayings serve as laws. Hence passages in the holy scripture[s] are called *dicta*$_L$.[t] One cannot give *dicta*$_L$ from philosophers, then, as did the followers of Pythagoras, the *acusmatici*, in saying αὐτός ἔφα.[u]

867

Mechanization in matters of the understanding very much helps the understanding in some respects, if I have first thought this through myself. But to accept such things without reflection[v] is also a fruitful source of errors. Such mechanization prevails in formulas, i.e., universal propositions clothed in quite precise, determinate words. Of this kind are[:]

1. Proverbs, *formulae vulgares*, which hold for the common man's understanding. To accept these without testing, however, is not advisable.
2. Sentences, aesthetic formalities, *prescriptive formulas*, in which a rule of conduct is contained. One finds such things in poets, such as Horace.
3. *Canones*, *formulas of science*. We have such things in all the sciences, and they serve to make it possible to expound the thing more easily.
4. *Dicta. Formulas of belief* in theological matters, where the words themselves are held to be holy, and hence are accepted without any modification.

[q] Reading "Man hat sie nur um . . ." for "Man hat nur . . ."

[r] Reading "ist das ein Spruch" for "ist – das – ein Spruch."

[s] "der h. Schrift."

[t] sayings.

[u] he himself said it.

[v] Reading "Ueberlegung" for "Ueberzeugung."

All of these, now, if they have taken root in me without mature reflection, are a root for unspeakable errors.

Sayings must always be derived from someone else, then. – A sentence is not always a *dictum*$_L$, but it has a certain similarity in that it recommends itself by the impressiveness of the thoughts. A sentence is when that which accords with reason recommends itself with impressive words to the *sens commun*. A saying is when something seems to be drawn from the common understanding, but nonetheless expresses something precise with words appropriate thereto. *Bons mots* are universal sentences that are recommended more by wit than by a rich power of judgment. –

A sentence has much to recommend it. For it serves as foundation and is entertaining for the mind, in that much is thought with little content, and this little content is suited for the reason of everyone.

868 *Canones* are rules[w] that look more to the content of the expression. They are universal propositions that serve as foundations in the sciences. A *canon*$_L$ can also be expressed by means of sentences, and then it pleases all the more. Proverbs, mottoes, are the most commonly used expressions in popular judgments of the understanding and of reason. Something can be an expression of the healthy understanding and yet not be popular. Then it is a sentence, but not a proverb. Proverbs contain the current wit of the people, but expressed in a concise way, so that it differs from customary figures of speech. They make known the common understanding of the people, and always have something provincial about them. For they are commonly expressed in national images. They are *canones* for the most common crowd. For they are the rules that took root in the first equipping [of the mind], and hence they hold universally. Thus we find, too, that they do not occur among people of refined upbringing. When someone presents a *canon*$_L$ in the more refined world, however, e.g., from an *autor classicus*, then this is readily accepted. Prejudices are severely tested when one tries to ground wisdom in sentences and proverbs, because one always looks around to see what others have said. From this there always arises partiality toward the opinions of this or that famous man or philosopher. These were the prejudices of imitation. Custom shows its effect when one has had a single mode of thought for a long time and now is supposed to depart from it all at once.

He who wishes to expound something new in religion, metaphysics, etc., has to struggle with many difficulties. But time makes a proposition with grounds of proof eventually strike the eye so clearly that people have to wonder how it was that they were not able to have insight into it before. The first judgment on a thing that is new always occurs according to the very prejudices that one wanted to root out from the matter. When one struggles against a prejudice, it defends itself, as it were. For one cannot

[w] "Lehrsprüche."

immediately be dissuaded from the inclination to a certain verdict, and then one has to do, not with reason, but with this inclination. For with reason, things would progress more easily. This lasts until finally the inclination becomes more universal. Then it is accepted by all. – The question arises, Is it necessary for a teacher, and advisable, to leave prejudices untouched, or even to encourage them so that they gradually take deeper root in the minds of the listeners[?] [This] amounts to asking if it is permitted to deceive people for a good purpose. The purpose may be as good as it will, but the means is still worse than the best purpose one can have. 869

One could well leave them untouched, because one can content oneself with letting an error persist if only one does not strengthen it[;] one would only draw man from his old custom, and one could not very quickly accustom him to the new one.[x] – It is advisable, nonetheless, to uncover all errors and prejudices, if one is perfectly convinced of the correctness of his insight. For subsequently people will see that one is right. One must investigate men's procedure everywhere, then, and expose for them what they do based on prejudices. The disadvantage that one suffers initially from this opposition will be richly repaid. We have a calling, too, not to hide the universal commandments of reason but instead to promulgate them, and if we remain silent, then it seems, as it were, as if we did not hold people to be worthy of knowing this. – Some men do not have need for insight in certain things[,] e.g., in speculative matters, without which they can quite well get along with their conscience, and which do not have the least influence on their actions. If their prejudices are practically detrimental, however, then expound what you know better than this man does, and believe that the harm that you can have in the beginning is smaller than the benefit to the others. Now we come to positive and negative prejudices. We can take them both at once, however. For with negative prejudice one quickly understands positive prejudice as well. They are prejudices of prestige, of trust in the multitude, in the age of a people. In all these matters prejudices can prevail, i.e., where the senses run ahead of the understanding. Hence the understanding, which is already prepared for this, shows a propensity in its judgment to have respect for the learnedness of a man, perhaps, or conversely, to place greater trust in the common understanding than in learnedness. This matter will be treated in detail below. These prejudices are grounded on a propensity to agree with the opinion of others. All the prejudices through which we imitate others by grounding our prejudice on the prestige of other men can be called servile prejudices. Yet there is also an egotistical prejudice, where one regards the works of his own spirit with predilection, and finds the offspring of his understanding to be free of mistake. 870

[x] Reading "an die neuen gewöhnen" for "gewöhnen."

Prejudices of the prestige of a person are servile prejudices. – In historical matters, the prestige of other persons is necessary throughout and constitutes the foundation of our prejudices in many cases. For things that rest on testimony[y] I cannot find out by myself, because my use of my understanding is not sufficient to determine the truth of history, which rests on experience. Here I can, without prejudice, build on the reports of others[;] indeed, in this case it is necessary, for because I cannot attain them through my own experience, they must come from persons who have such prestige with us that we believe them. This acceptance of what someone else says is not grounded on a prejudice, but instead is a condition that is sufficiently valid for our understanding to give him approval. When cognition has its ground of proof in nothing but reason, however, but does not take it from experience, then the testimony of others cannot be a ground of conduct[;] and this very judgment, which runs ahead of our understanding and produces a propensity in us to hold something to be true without any testing, is the prejudice of prestige[;] if, e.g., I would like to believe in the immortality of the soul because Plato said this. Insofar as it rests on reason, truth holds anonymously, i.e., one must not ask who said this, but what he said. It does not matter here to what family the cognition belongs, and whether he who said it was of great merit; instead, it matters what he said. – People complain about the fact that matters of state and religion have produced so many anonymous writings, through which people grind their axes over the matter. Of course if the man is himself malicious, it is all the worse if he acts anonymously[;] but as for what concerns the thing itself, this must hold anonymously, the man may conduct himself as badly, or as well, as he will. If a noble and honest man says something bad, it is no less bad because he is honest. – The respect of a nation for a certain man is on this account harmful, because it leads men to the laziness of not establishing things themselves in their cognition, but rather letting others rule over those things. Concerning this, 871 Locke says that the prestige of great men fosters disputes, often *ad verecundiam*,[z] when people try to make others be quiet because a great man has said it. This inclination toward the prestige of great men arises from the custom of imitating that which is prescribed to us as certain, and out of a lack of insight, in that we always seek for an authority on whom we can rely, and who, as it were, has understanding *for us*, and to whom we can always appeal. – Thus the prejudice of the prestige of the person causes something special in our inclinations, because it serves to flatter our vanity *indirecte*. For as the subjects of a mighty despot are proud, even if they live in the lowest conditions, namely, because they are all nothing in comparison to him, and the one can become as great tomorrow as the

[y] Reading "auf Zeugnißen" for "auf zwey Zeugnißen."

[z] [through arguments] directed to modesty (i.e., ones based on authority).

other is today, so too, if a man is raised to the level of a great learned man, this often happens only so that he who prizes him will be held to be the equal of all other learned men. For because, in accordance with this elevated praise, all others are nothing in comparison with the great man, the small difference among the others is negligible. It is envy toward other men, then, that leads one to make a single man great. We no longer envy the person who is prized, but we also do not allow others to try to make themselves equal to him. – Citations of learned and famous men cannot be regarded as grounds of proof. For the real question is always how much of a ground the claim has in reason, and not *who* said it. Regardless of this, however, the inclination toward citations of other authors carries a certain weight with it to strengthen our approval toward a thing[;] consequently it is an external *criterium*$_{\mathrm{L}}$ of truth, i.e., the agreement of the universal human understanding is a ground for the supposition that I will have judged correctly. It is a kind of testing of judgment[a] on more than one understanding. But in metaphysics, e.g., it often happens that men all have the same deception. There is a science that has the property that it simply cannot dispense with citations, namely, law. Here we see how uncertain all juridical judgments must be. An original justice could actually be introduced, however, without citation. Now just observe from experience the disadvantage of this or that law. For the multitude of cases that can occasion the direction of the will each time can never be completely determinately expressed in a law. One must take help from other eyes, then, because no one is so acute that he can investigate every case exactly. If you have paid attention to the varied results of legal processes, then you will be in a better position to be able to decide. – Citations always have something pleasant, namely, where whole passages are brought in from other authors. It is indisputably the entertaining thing, which occasions their pleasing us. Regardless of this, they must not serve as grounds of proof, because this is only an external *criterium*$_{\mathrm{L}}$ of truth. 872

Prejudice based on the prestige of the multitude is a prejudice either of the healthy understanding or of learned men, toward which principally the crowd has an inclination, since with the crowd the judgment of the multitude holds good. The crowd is not in a position to estimate the worth of an individual person, hence it holds to the multitude, but NB, not to just any multitude. – Proverbs already constitute a prejudice accepted by the multitude, since one presupposes that what all men say must of course be true. This is only a historical judgment, however. But in matters of religion, because the crowd does not trust itself to judge of such things, it trusts to learned men who hold for us as models, as it were, in religion. This holds true with all written religions. Here everyone believes his learned men, his missionaries, who study these books and give information about such reli-

[a] "eine Art der Experience des Urtheiles."

gions, so that it is difficult, just on this account, to make converts here. Here the prejudice is grounded on a multitude of persons, then. In this connection it is to be observed, however, that what I accept out of prejudice can also, accidentally, be true. It is false and logically objectionable for me to accept it as a prejudice, however. Hence the cognition is not blameworthy as if it were false, but because I have accepted it out of prejudice. In regard to cognitions, prejudices of the great man prevail for the learned world. But even the learned man has, in turn, a prejudice for the common condition. It is easy to find that the great crowd always has a favorable prejudice for the learned man, and they have good grounds for this, too. For [learned men] have to investigate cognition and make it their principal business, but [the crowd] comes upon such things only occasionally. – Among learned men there is a prejudice for the common understanding, and a distrust of the learned understanding. This arises in the learned man who desires knowledge, when he sees that all his efforts will not satisfy him. He believes he has

873 not taken the right path, and on this account he returns to the common understanding, because here he believes he finds the proper key to a cognition that is obscure to him. This happens when he has virtually run through the circle of the sciences, and above all in those sciences that he cannot make sensible without concepts, e.g., metaphysics, law. In natural science he does not at all have a more favorable prejudice for the common understanding than for the learned understanding, because he sees that one can accomplish more here through experiments. But as for what concerns judgments about the existence of a highest being, or the nature of our soul, when the learned man has there used up all his art and still gets no satisfaction, and when he finds so much that is customary in himself and other learned men, then he believes that the key lies somewhere, and he seeks it in the common understanding. But this belief is very deceptive. For how will these unpracticed eyes accomplish more than if they were cultivated? And how can concepts of another world be brought to concepts? Although there are certain cognitions that can be exhibited *in concreto*. E.g., all moral questions can be given *in concreto*. Here the common use of the understanding judges more correctly than the speculative use of the understanding, because it has the matters before it in experience. Here, then, in the speculative use of the understanding one must often call on the common understanding for help on account of the particular propositions that arise in the end from the purely speculative ones. There are certain sciences, then, where speculative reason alone, without the assent[b] of the common understanding, is not assured, and where a certain provisional opinion of the speculative understanding must probably lead the assurance of the common understanding astray. E.g., the proposition of the jurists, *damnum*

[b] Reading "Beistimmung" for "Bestimmung."

patitur dominus,[c] investigated by the common understanding, is most highly unfair. Hence the learned man cannot take refuge in the common understanding in such cases. But this is not a prejudice among the learned, then, but rather only a method of putting its speculation to the test. For there are so many cases in the practical sciences, all of which one cannot possibly survey in speculation[;] hence one must also take cases *in concreto*.

Opposed to the prejudices of prestige is logical egoism, i.e., the prejudice in accordance with which we hold the agreement of our understanding with the reason of others to be unnecessary[d] as a *criterium*$_L$ of wisdom. There are sciences in which we actually often have to rely on our own reason, and without needing this external *criterium*$_L$, [yet] without committing the mistake of egoism. E.g. In mathematics the evidence is so great that no one can resist it, if only he follows the proofs set forth. Otherwise, though, this historical *criterium*$_L$ of the agreement of others cannot be completely dispensed with. For although it is not a sole *criterium*$_L$, it is a joint *criterium*$_L$. For in discursive cognitions of reason, where we present everything through concepts, one can never hold the agreement of others to be dispensable, the cause being that mistakes that are not possible in an intuitive representation are so easy here. The mistake that I committed arose out of an illusion, which arose from the condition of how I cognized the cognition[;] hence I cannot hold the judgment of others to be dispensable. For they can correct my judgment, e.g., when I see something in the distance I say that it is a horse, the other that it is a tree. Perhaps I have only deeply imprinted the thought of a horse beforehand, and it is only through this illusion that I believe that I see a horse in the distance. Egoism, accordingly, is the mistake where one believes that when the question is about the *criterium*$_L$ of truth, one does not need others to pass judgment.

874

Logical egoism is either *indifference*[e] toward the judgments of others, in that I hold the judgments of others to be unnecessary for passing judgment on my own judgment, or it is *conceit* and arrogance, where one allots it to himself alone to make a correct judgment about a thing for all others.

Providence has directed, however, that we expound our judgments to universal reason, and has placed in us the drive to do this. Many believe that this is nothing more than the motive of vanity. That could be, but the purpose of providence is nonetheless achieved, and we actually do exert ourselves better, too. If it does not happen that we lay our thoughts before universal human reason, then we have cause to call into question the validity of our judgments, because we do not wish to follow nature's wise precept that we test our truth on the judgments of others. It is wrong,

[c] the master suffers the punishment.

[d] Reading "unnöthig" for "unmöglich."

[e] "Indifferentism oder *Gleichgültigkeit*."

accordingly, for the state to forbid men to write books and to judge, e.g., about matters of religion. For then they are deprived of the only means that nature has given them, namely, testing their judgment on the reason of others. The freedom to think in silence is given by the people who 875 tyrannize so despotically. But that is only because[f] they cannot prevent[g] anyone from doing it. I can always think what I will. But as for what concerns logical egoism, it has to be conceded that since human nature depends on using this external *criterium*$_{L}$, I also have a right to expound my thoughts publicly. The prejudice of antiquity is one of the most detrimental prejudices. It is quite natural that an old man has it most of all. For since he can no longer shape himself into a new form, he defends the old as much as he can, and he defends himself, as it were, in what he possesses. Young people are more for the new, because they are still brave enough to acquire new cognitions. – There is also something universal in this prejudice, however[;] there is a certain opinion that lies at its basis[;] namely, men believe through and through that everything in the world becomes worse, and that everything in the world deteriorates. Now this is to a certain extent true, of course. But our lifetime is far too short to observe how everything gradually deteriorates. There is one thing in nature that is wholly unalterable, and that is the species, even if every individual deteriorates. In such a way people come to imagine that the species is gradually degraded, and that men will gradually become nothing but skilled oxen, that the old German honesty may come to an end. Certainly, however, men were not larger, more virtuous, [and] wiser before than they are now, and a man who has not ruined his body by bad conduct will still produce just as healthy a son as Adam did. The hereditary factors are the same as before. Hence we are not in a position, in deviation from this, to find exceptional and remarkable things. The prejudice of antiquity rises and falls from time to time. Now it seems to be climbing high again. Earlier, modernity rose higher. In the case of the ancient, if one contents oneself with combining historical cognition[h] of the ancients with his other cognitions,[i] then it is useful and good. If we believe that we can find wisdom in them, however, then we err badly, and we would bring down all the sciences if we tried to go back to the learnedness of another age, and to add to our practiced judgment what the ancients collected as children. They can quite well form our taste, however.

Prejudices often arise from opposed causes. For accordingly as a mind is 876 disposed, it falls into a prejudice from an opposed cause. The prejudice in favor of the ancients arises from a detrimental judgment against the old, just like the prejudice in favor of the learnedness of women, because one has an

[f] Reading "deswegen, weil" for "das Schlimmste, daß."

[g] Reading "verwehren" for "wehren."

[h] "eine historische Kenntniß."

[i] "Kenntnißen."

unfavorable prejudice toward the capacity[j] of the sex. If one has an unfavorable view of the ancients one can nonetheless form a favorable representation of the ancients, because one confuses admiration with astonishment. For if one has an unfavorable prejudice concerning a thing, and yet finds something there that surpasses our expectation, one is astonished. Admiration, however, is the pleasant sensation when we find something very great. E.g. We are astonished if a child, whom we did not think capable of it, can speak quite cleverly. But in the end this astonishment can degenerate into admiration. Astonishment is the condition of the soul in intuiting the new and the unexpected, admiration [is that of intuiting] the unexpected good[;] e.g., if a woman begins to speak like a book, then one is astonished and believes that she is smarter than she actually is. – The ancients did not have nearly the advantages[k] in the sciences that we have. We should not suppose, then, that they had the same cognitions as we. Hence we are astonished when we see that they thought as we do. This brings about astonishment toward one of the ancients, because he, in the age in which he lived, said something so clever, and the astonishment finally degenerates into admiration, since we find more merit in him than he actually has. E.g., when someone cites a passage from Plato, this would certainly be badly said if a modern tried to say it thus; but it is a lot, we think, that the man was able to make out so much even then[;] and in the end we admire the proposition, and no longer [just] the man. It is from this that the prejudice arises. For it is unjust that we admire the proposition instead of the man, whom we have good cause to admire.

The second cause of prejudices in favor of antiquity is that all the cognitions[l] that we have of antiquity are themselves, for us, learnedness. Although the sciences of the ancients concerning which we now have reports contain little, or even no learnedness. Even cognition of the language of the ancients is learnedness and always wins respect. Accordingly, cognition[m] of the accomplishments of the ancients wins respect, and here it happens again through an illusion that their insights themselves win respect, although only the cognition of the man who knows something demands respect. A proposition produces a reflected favorable light because[n] the learned among the ancients also had insight into the proposition. For learnedness deserves favor, even if the proposition contains nothing useful. For it is always a pleasant thing to hear that Cicero said that, because it indicates the author's wide reading in the ancients[;] just by accepting the exposition with favor I accept the proposition with favor, even if it does not belong to learnedness. Because the proposition is

877

[j] Reading "capacitaet" for "capricitaet."

[k] Reading "Vortheile" for "Vorurtheile."

[l] "Kenntniße."

[m] "Kenntniß."

[n] Reading "weil" for "daß."

expounded in such a *vehiculum*, then, and the proposition thereby gets prestige, because it has come to us from a distant place and time, this brings about the prejudice for believing that it is said better than in modern times. We have cause to make favorable judgments about antiquity, without a prejudice needing to lie hidden in this. This ground suffices, however, only for measured respect. But when we have the ground we often go beyond its restrictions, and bestow upon them unmeasured respect. Time sifts all things[;] what is famous today is disdained and rejected tomorrow. But what has not declined over a long time, there we may suppose that it has an inner worth. The writings of antiquity have been sifted thus, because only in this way have they been preserved, so that they differ from other writings. Hence we have cause to judge favorably of these writings. But this is no proof that the writings of antiquity have an absolute great worth[;] rather, they have a great worth only in relation to other writings, and if one makes this relative worth into an absolute one, a prejudice arises from this. If, then, we take the bad and the good books of the ancients, and from this make a judgment of the general cognition[o] of the ancients, how astonishing will this judgment be? If, e.g., our descendants were to get in their hands the rubbish heap of books, where it would be desirable that these did not exist at all, they would probably not be able to comprehend how, at a time when the true course of the sun was discovered, such nonsense could also be thought. But if all the bad books were left out, then they would hold us all to be giants in judgment. Thus it is with the ancients, too. If we accept the opinion of the ancients, and trust ourselves to them in such a way that in the process we 878 give up our use of our own understanding, then it is a prejudice that arises here. Prejudices have the peculiarity that they completely hinder the individual use of the understanding.

Another cause for judging in favor of the ancients is gratitude. We are their pupils. For one generation is always the teacher of the next. Gratitude seems to demand that we give honor to the ancients, and then we believe that we must prize excessively those to whom we owe thanks. Indeed, we also think that we will become the ancients[;] and as we disdain someone who ridicules an old man, because he will himself become old, we would be subject to disdain if we wished to ridicule the ancients[;] and so that the injustice will be righted, esteem for the ancients is exaggerated. For we hold it to be virtuous to exaggerate our gratitude, too. For people did do something there that redounds to their honor. Judgments in favor of the ancients also arises from envy of contemporaries. If a man has always studied the ancients, he has neglected the modern, and hence he admires only the ancients because he understands only them. Now because he cannot surpass the moderns, he does this: he

[o] "von der durchgängigen Kenntniß."

always praises the ancients. One no longer envies the dead, but those who are still living are an object of envy. When someone has studied the ancients industriously, then, he prizes them highly, in order not to give the moderns precedence over himself. – No knowledge inflates more than philological knowledge does, or than that which is called polyhistory, which occurs when one has a kind of universality in regard to cognitions[p] of the ancients, although this is not sufficient, but is rather historical. The *literati* always find everything in the ancients, and they do not allow that the moderns have found this. When the magnetic needle was discovered, a word was immediately discovered in Terence that already indicated this. Philolaus supposedly already had Copernicus's world system. Philosophy strikes down all pride and brings about a certain misology toward that which is science. For it reveals the chasm of our ignorance to such a degree that we guard ourselves against proceeding further on the path. But all of philology cannot extend our understanding by one degree; instead, it only makes us not lose the combination and the cognition[q] of the connection of our cognitions[r] with the ancients.

The prejudice of modernity. The modern itself is never an advantage.[s] The ancients have provided something as a basis. We hope, however, that the modern will be better. This produces much vanity, as the prejudice of antiquity produces much pedantry. 879

The prejudice based on an accepted system does not actually belong to the universal prejudices. A system is a unity in cognition that can be derived from a *principium*. In the end we get a certain predilection toward this *principium*, in that we judge that everything that appears in the system deserves great respect, and this makes us often close an eye when mistakes in the system appear. This is actually only a private prejudice of self-love.

The prejudice of distrust in antiquity. All the negative prejudices can be cognized from the foregoing, for it is easy to cognize that a distrust in antiquity arises from an excessive love toward myself, etc.

Prejudices are actually not part of logic at all. For logic has to do with the objective grounds of the understanding, and not with its subjective grounds. The subjective causes are explanations of the actual appearances, of how it happens that men cultivate themselves, the one in this way, the other in that way, according to their understanding. This actually belongs to anthropology. Logic considers only the objective, universal grounds of reason, without seeing whether the understanding is corrupted or not. Prejudice is a mere fact.[t] All explanation of fact belongs to psychol-

[p] "Kenntniße."
[q] "Kenntniß."
[r] "Kenntniße."
[s] Reading "Vortheil" for "Vorurtheil."
[t] "eine bloße Gegebenheit."

ogy. We can include it here, however, because it can possibly exist in the use of logical instruction, and one must pay heed to the causes that can lead us from the proper use of [logic].

OF PROBABLE COGNITION

Everyone makes the mistake, and so does our author, too, that instead of saying that the cognition is probable, they talk of the object, insofar as I hold the object to be probable, although my cognition can be true and certain. My cognition is probable when those of the cases that determine the thing are more than those that determine the opposite. If we have this before our eyes, then we can say that a cognition is probable[;] but the logic of the probable is not a pure logic. It would be a science that had as its object objects for which the causes are possible, where we then see how 880 many causes there are for the effect and how many for the opposite. Thus it can be supposed, based on a ground, that that for which there are more grounds is probable, although this is not sufficient. All probability is a fraction, whose denominator is the number of all the possible cases, and whose numerator contains the number of winning cases. E.g., if someone is to roll 8 with 2 dice, he has 6 winners[25] and 36 possible cases. The fraction is $6/36$, then, of which the opponent has 30 cases and he has 6. *Probability* of the object rests on the relation that the grounds of an occurrence[u] have to full certainty. One cannot have proper insight into probability, then, unless one knows what full certainty involves. For since, for probability, one must have a general measure,[v] and since the measure for every insufficient ground is the sufficient ground, the measure for probability is certainty. – Here mathematics can provide a certain measure whereby it compares quantities, because quantities contain nothing but what is homogeneous. But in philosophy this does not work, because here the grounds of the possible winning cases are all non-homogeneous. If I take all possible cases and say that the winning cases must also be contained in these, then the relation of the grounds of holding-to-be-true is non-homogeneous. E.g., there is much testimony for an accused. (1.) The deed was done while he was not at home. He actually was not at home, either. This is a *res facti*.[w] (2.) Someone else had seen him at the time. Here the credibility of the other man is the ground. The grounds in philosophy are always different as to quality, nonetheless, and they cannot be enumerated, but only weighed. Often in philosophy the quantity of probability cannot become very determinate, because the grounds are not

[u] Reading "welches die Gründe einer Begebenheit" for "welche Gründe eine Begebenheit."

[v] "ein großes Maß."

[w] matter of fact.

homogeneous. But in the cognition, what is regarded as probable is not the cognition but rather the object. The cognition can be true in itself.

As for what concerns the probability of cognition, this is grounds for holding-to-be-true before any investigation. If I find no contradiction in the cognition, but rather connection with other things, then I do not say that the object is true. The probability of cognition does not mean much; what matters is rather whether the object is true. – Men often think, when they predict something probable, that they have achieved a real triumph, even if they had no grounds for holding it to be true, it came by chance although the judgment was ungrounded[;] hence the cognition was not probable, even if it was cognition of a probable object. We must not always follow probable cognition. It is only the beginning of the beginning of testing, and it can lead us to inquire further concerning the truth. A cognition is doubtful when there are grounds for and against it.[x] No doubt can be raised against it, because it maintains the opposite just as well.[26] This indifference in logic is just that which is indifferent in the practical, then, where the understanding is wholly indifferent in regard to the cognition. A cognition is doubted when one has already declared for it, but, on the other hand, opposing grounds are brought against it. A doubt is a mere obstacle to holding-to-be-true. It is the condition of the mind when there is something that hinders us from approving. One can consider it objectively and subjectively. If the doubt is objectively distinct, then it is an objection. If it is objectively indistinct and obscure, then it is a scruple. In common speech *dubitatio*, subjective doubt, and *dubium*, objective doubt, are confused with one another. One says, I have many doubts about that[;] if these are not objective grounds then one could well doubt for himself. But one cannot expound that to someone else as grounds, in order to move him to doubt too. The grounds of subjective holding-to-be-true are to be located in education, in that one cannot quite accustom his mind to accepting a different opinion yet. – One has a scruple against a cognition when one cannot take away the obstacle to the holding-to-be-true. This scruple can also be subjective. It is what frightens us in cognitions, so that we do not wish to approve the cognition with all our soul, because something in us is opposed to full approval. – Scruples are not to be disdained. For in the beginning all our cognitions are obscure, and so in the beginning, of course, some things are expounded for us with scruples, since there are grounds that conflict with the object. If a scruple becomes clear, then it becomes an objection, and before it is made clear, the scruple must not be rejected, then. It indicates great talent when one can make his scruples clear to someone else. Objections presuppose that cognitions are already taken to be true. Doubts do not presuppose that; instead, we can always proceed problematically there. – Objections do not yet refute;

881

[x] Reading "dieselben" for "dieselbe."

rather, they ought only to weaken the cognition. In all holding-to-be-true, 882 they have the value, therefore, that the certainty of the cognition comes to greater perfection. Hence a thing cannot be attacked any more, because the opponent has put forth all the grounds for the opposite. Law and religion need objections, consequently, because they arrive thereby at greater certainty. Doubts can be provided with an answer. Objections are refuted. Every doubt must not only be replied to, for then it is only turned aside, but it must be resolved, in that I must show how it was possible for it to arise. If this does not happen, then the obstacle to holding-to-be-true is not yet fully removed, and the ground for new doubts remains. From this it follows that refutation of objections must take place in a friendly way, so that instead of merely driving the other back, one must also inquire by what means an otherwise good understanding could have been brought to such objections, i.e., through what illusion the objections arose. If we find confusion, then we must explain this to him and thus *nodum resolvere, non secare.*[y] *Probabilitas* is probability, *verisimilitudo* is plausibility. A cognition as cognition can be called a plausibility, but the thing that I hold to be true or probable is not on that account *verisimilis*,[z] but rather probable or improbable. The distinction rests on this. In the case of probability, I compare the grounds of the holding-to-be-true to certainty. If the holding-to-be-true is greater than half the sufficient ground, then the cognition is probable. If it is less than half, then the cognition is improbable. For if I have more than half the ground, then I have more grounds than are even possible for the opposite, and these are[a] necessarily also more than all the grounds that are possible on the other side. In mathematics, in the case of probability, one can determine the sufficient ground of the holding-to-be-true with numbers, because the things are homogeneous in their grounds of possibility[;] and when things are only of one kind, then they need only be counted up [to determine] whether my grounds constitute more than half. But in philosophical cognitions I can only determine the grounds of truth discursively. For by virtue of the fact that the grounds here are not homogeneous, it happens that I cannot say that here is half the sufficient ground. For one cannot indicate how a ground is related to the sufficient ground, because no equal ratio[b] can be 883 indicated between non-homogeneous things. Laws and examples from nature, without the testimony of others, are grounds of this kind. Where can the half-way point be found here? Hence a logic of probability is an *impossible* undertaking. If one understands thereby the part of logic where the concepts of the probable, the doubtful, etc., are made understandable,

[y] untie the knot, not cut it.
[z] Reading "verisimilis" for "verisimile."
[a] Reading "diese sind" for "diese."
[b] "kein gleiches Verhältniß."

then this can properly occur. But if degrees are to be indicated, in order to pass judgment on whether it is probable or not, then it is impossible, because in the case of certainty one does not achieve insight into the grounds for certainty until one has actually attained certainty[;] and since in philosophy the grounds of holding-to-be-true are non-homogeneous, we can only weigh them, i.e., try to measure the grounds by our approval. We cannot measure them, however; instead, the art of measurement of probability concerns mathematics. – In the usual logics one always has rules according to which the understanding is to be used in the case of probability. But the rules are understood even more obscurely than if one wished to make use of them. They do not help us in use, either; rather, this requires merely reflection. – Understanding is the faculty of rules. The power of judgment is the faculty for deciding whether a rule ought to be used at this place, hence it is the faculty for subsuming under a rule. I cannot give this faculty mere rules that are set over it. In the investigation of probability in philosophy, then, where the power of judgment also reaches, there are no precepts for probability. There is a mathematics of probability, and this is used, too. E.g., in the schools, in calculation, instructions are given for the best way of finding out probability, in relation to the mistakes of other methods. E.g., I calculate the elevation of a star 20 times. One time I get 10 degrees, 13 minutes[;] the other time I get 13 degrees, 11 minutes. I figure all this total together and divide it by 20, and then I have the probable elevation. Thus mathematics determines certain rules, in accordance with which the object can be cognized probably. In philosophy, however, this is impossible. You can give examples, of course, in order to exercise your faculty of judgment. But you will never be able to give rules as to how far something is probable or not. Probability is concerned with things. Plausibility is concerned with whether, in the cognition, there are more grounds for the thing than against it. For if I compare the grounds for holding-to-be-true with the sufficient ground and have no grounds for the opposite, then plausibility emerges. E.g. Someone alleges that the *thinking being*, the soul[,] will not come to an end even in death, because in life it did not depend on the body, and I would object, perhaps, the contingency of reproduction[;] then I ask, Is this probable? The objection amounts to nothing, consequently the cognition is plausible. In the case of a ground for holding something to be true, when no ground for the opposite is present, the cognition is plausible. If I know a ground that says the very opposite, however, then it is doubtful. If I compare the thing with the sufficient ground of truth, however, then it is probable. For all probability consists in the approximation of holding-to-be-true to certainty. Objective doubts are the ground that makes a cognition false. Subjective doubt is the condition of the mind where we have just as many grounds for as against the things. Man is in doubt[,] subjective[;] he has doubts[,] objective. Principles of doubt are (1.) the principle

884

of maintaining.[c] The maxim, All cognition is to be treated with the purpose of thereby maintaining something, is called the dogmatic principle. A dogmatic cognition is one through which all the things that are opined are maintained. The maxim to treat a cognition with the purpose of gaining insight into how to attain full uncertainty and the impossibility of certainty is (2.) the *skeptical maxim*[; this is] the mode of philosophizing where one renounces all affirmative cognition and regards all the grounds of his judgment in such a way that one opposes them with equally strong opposing grounds. We treat something dogmatically when we decide the matter with full certainty, we treat it skeptically when we seek to show complete uncertainty. Both, taken universally, are mistaken. For some cognitions are impossible, although dogmatism seeks to make them certain. E.g., concerning the change of weather. From the view of the universal character of things one cannot settle dogmatically whether there is a simple being. Here we must often take another path in order to settle something. Proceeding skeptically nullifies all our effort, and it is an anti-logical principle, an [antilogical] attempt to drive off ignorance. For if I bring cognition to the point that it finally nullifies itself, then it is as if we were to regard all men's cognitions as nothing. Regardless of the fact that skepti- 885 cism is so harmful, this does not hinder philosophical method from being good for treating something that is uncertain, in that I endeavor to push the uncertainty to the highest degree, in the hope that through this procedure I will finally discover traces of the truth. This is the suspension of judgment in order to attain certainty. This method, then, where we do not merely doubt everything, but also investigate the cause of the conflict of the understanding with the understanding itself, in order thereby to illuminate the truth, is the critical method. We have, accordingly, a dogmatic, a skeptical, and a critical method. –

To proceed dogmatically with all cognitions, i.e., to hope for decided certainty without taking into consideration the grounds of the opposite, produces an insufficient illusion. For if I believe that nothing more can be sought out against the truth, then I stop investigating at once. But then the matter also has little foundation. One can well investigate[d] something dogmatically, but not proceed dogmatically. With the dogmatic method one must also proceed skeptically, i.e., when I test whether I cannot say something in the matter on the side of an opponent. Skepticism, then, is where something is maintained dogmatically on both sides. One can do this by oneself, but then which of the two can decide better? Now comes the critical method, i.e., I investigate the sources of the dogmatic and the skeptical methods, and then I begin to see on which grounds a claim rests and on which grounds its opposite rests. Critical method is thus the intermediate

[c] "der Grundsatz des Behauptens."

[d] Reading "untersuchen" for "versuchen."

method[e] through which a cognition can attain certainty. It guards against the dogmatic method because it opposes dogmatism with skepticism[;] and since it has thereby weighed the grounds of both, it alone can decide how many grounds I have for holding-to-be-true. Skepticism is a dismissal of all instruction of reason, and it contradicts itself. It treats everything as illusion, and nonetheless it distinguishes illusion from truth, because it warns us not to accept anything as truth[;] thus it must have a mark by which it can cognize truth, and since it indicates the ground for why one should doubt everything, the opposite must of course also be possible. It can be refuted by itself, then. The doubters of ancient times were remarkable. Pyrrho is the first doubter. He lived at the time of Socrates, and he doubted all things, which he expressed thus: *non liquet*.[f] This is Pyrrhonic doubt. But academic doubt is also remarkable. For after Plato's death Speusippus continued his school, [and] after him Arcesilaus[;] Carneades [led] the third school. Plato had Socrates' method in his dialogues, but he was not a skeptic at all; instead, he did that only in order, by long suspension [of judgment], finally to bring the truth to light.[g] Speusippus remained true to him and taught as dogmatically as Plato. But Arcesilaus set up a skeptical school. This is academic skepticism. He said that everything is so uncertain that it is even uncertain whether this is uncertain[;] this was called a real purgative of reason, so that by seeking to purge reason, he also got rid of reason itself. The third school of Carneades consisted of disgusting sophists and dialecticians[;] what they maintained today, they denied tomorrow. A hypothesis, the author defines, is an opinion, and an opinion of philosophers, since they explain the world from the appearances. But he still does not explain opinion sufficiently. 886

The distinction between opinion and hypothesis is this. An opinion is an incomplete holding-to-be-true based on insufficient grounds, from which I derive nothing. A hypothesis, however, means judgment about truth based on grounds that are sufficient. When something is accepted as a ground from which I can have insight into the sufficient ground of given consequences, then this is a hypothesis. Accordingly, it is the holding-to-be-true of a presupposition, not of a cognition insofar as it itself is derived from grounds, but instead because it is mediately certain. Experience and axioms are *immediate*, certain propositions. An axiom is when I accept a cognition as certain because it can be cognized *a priori* based on the nature of the thing. Cognitions of experience are shown based on sense.

One cognition is deduced from another *mediately*, or it is held to be true based on a ground, and this is a hypothesis. When I hold a cognition to be true because it is a good ground for other grounds, then it is a hypothesis.

[e] "die Zwischenmethode."
[f] it is not clear.
[g] "die Wahrheit zu eruiren."

I assume something, and then I see what other kinds of cognitions[h] can be derived from this. I assume it, then, not on account of the ground from which it is derived; rather, I hold it to be true on account of the consequences[i] that can be derived from it. It is somewhat turned around,[j] then, in comparison with other cognitions. The holding-to-be-true is grounded 887 on this. I assume the cognition arbitrarily as a ground, but by assuming it I can indicate the grounds of other cognitions that are certainly true, and insofar as it is connected with truth, accordingly, it is called a hypothesis. All holding-to-be-true of a hypothesis is grounded on the fact that through it as a ground other cognitions are to be explained as consequences. I actually infer, then, from the truth of the consequences to the ground, and thus I infer the truth of the cognition from the consequences. E.g., I say that there is a central fire in the earth, because fire-spewing mountains, earthquakes, and other phenomena prove that. Inferring from the consequences to the ground is also a *criterium*$_L$ of truth[,] p. 88[,][27] namely, if true consequences are derived from [a cognition], then I infer its truth. Although it is a partial *criterium*$_L$ of truth, it is not nearly sufficient[;] instead, the cognition is true only if all the consequences of the cognition are true. But since we cannot possibly derive all the consequences from the cognition, this path *a posteriori* actually yields an uncertain inference that the ground is the true ground. From a false ground some true consequences can be drawn, because there is truth in it in part. A hypothesis always remains a hypothesis, then, i.e., it does not become a complete certainty. For I cognize only the sufficiency of the cognition for *some* consequences, and only the sufficiency of the cognition for all possible consequences would produce apodeictic certainty. The derivation of many consequences still does not affect the certainty of a cognition at all. For the very same cognition can be drawn from other grounds. It does make a ground of probability, then, but not of certainty. Some sciences do not tolerate any hypotheses. E.g., mathematics. In natural science, however, they are indispensable. When, however, as many consequences as we can ever find can all be derived from an assumed ground, then the hypothesis always grows in probability, so much so, in fact, that although it can never be apodeictically certain, an analogue to certainty comes about, i.e., one yields to the hypothesis as to full certainty. E.g., in the case of the Copernican system, no one has hit upon a single observation that cannot be derived from it. Here, then, there is an analogue to certainty. It is not apodeictically certain, however. It is quite possible that the creator made a different arrangement of the planets, as the hypothesis of Tycho de Brahe 888 shows.[28] Our conviction, however, is grounded on the fact that however

[h] "Kenntniße."

[i] Reading "Folgen" for "Gründe."

[j] "etwas umgekehrtes."

many consequences are found, they can all be derived from Copernicus's system. We approximate to apodeictic certainty, accordingly, and it is combined with this *comparative*$_{L}$.

A hypothesis is not a cognition that is completely held to be true, but something in the cognition must be fully certain, namely,

1. the possibility of a presupposition must be fully certain[;] if an assumed ground is possible, the thing nevertheless remains uncertain. For there can also be another ground with which the cognition fits. But the possibility in the hypothesis must be fully certain. E.g., I would like to assume the *commercium pneumaticum*,[k] i.e., the power through which man can affect other minds. This hypothesis may not be assumed at all; rather, it is a pure fabrication. For the possibility of this presupposition is not even certain yet. If we have no cognition[l] of the possibility of certain powers, then we must not ground anything on them as hypotheses. The use of hypotheses need only approximate to certainty, but their possibility must be certain.

2. The *consequentia* must be fully certain, i.e., if I hold something to be certain, then the consequences that I infer from it must be fully certain. Otherwise it will be held to be a pure chimera. – E.g., if, in a burglary, one wants to identify the perpetrators, one makes a hypothesis, and then it must

1. be possible that these people were able to do it. If that is so, then
2. the action[m] of those who stole must be comprehended completely, i.e., it must follow certainly that they were able to do it.

3. The hypothesis requires unity. Not more than one presupposition is needed in order to explain a multiplicity of consequences. As soon as we make many presuppositions, all the hypotheses lose some of their probability. In the case of unity, I infer that because many consequences fit with one ground, it is all the more probable that the true ground is true and is the right one. When, however, some consequences can be derived from the hypothesis, but not many, and new hypotheses must constantly be made in order to support it, then there is little probability there. – A *hypothesis subsidiaria*, an assisting hypothesis, is when something is assumed in order to come to the aid of a hypothesis that could not be 889 sustained without a new hypothesis. In this case a hypothesis loses all its credibility. –

Tycho de Brahe's explanation to explain the fact that the planets stand still was of this kind. He made *cycli*, and in order to explain these deviating *cycli* he assumed *cycli* in the *cycli*, and so on, and so on[;] and here one sees that it goes on without end. In philosophy, everything that is said by the

[k] intercourse between spirits.

[l] "Kenntniß."

[m] "die Vollziehung."

hypothesis is explained distinctly, and often quite true and correct consequences are derived from hypotheses. Every man who makes experiments first makes hypotheses, in that he believes that this or that experiment will have these consequences. If the investigation fails, he need not let his spirits sink, just as the alchemist always keeps working on the hypothesis of making gold.

In philosophy, above all in natural science, they cannot be dispensed with, since that which can occur as the proper cause of things we hold to be such. In accordance with the analogy of things, we accept one and all other causes. Thus, e.g., it is a hypothesis that rock crystals form prismatically. There are sciences, however, where no hypotheses at all occur, and this is so in metaphysics, in fact. E.g., that the soul of man can have an effect in the world even without the body, in which case it can be granted that it can appear after death and have effects on the souls of other men. It is not permitted to add such hypotheses, because I cannot prove the possibility of such affection. Possibility must always be given through experience. Similarity to this power must at least be shown, so that I have some cause for assuming the proposition. *Persuasion.* One could say that holding-to-be-true on the basis of grounds of which one does not oneself know whether they are subjective or objective is *persuasion.* We are attracted by something and we call this persuasion, because we cannot give account of our holding-to-be-true, and cannot say whether the cause of the holding-to-be-true lies in our sense and touches our inclination, or whether the understanding has gotten it from cognition[n] of the object. If this is not the case, then we are conscious that it is pure persuasion. Persuasion often precedes conviction. This seldom happens, however, with someone who has insight into much and has learned much in order

890 to attain certainty, because he can quite well distinguish persuasion from conviction. Furthermore, he who has often been deceived and taught a lesson is not so easy to persuade. Nonetheless, there are some people who feed themselves with hope. This is not good, however. For the mind must be ready for anything. It indicates a shallow mode of thought when a man lets himself be persuaded so easily, or easily persuades himself of something. This is a major cause of the fact that men find no difficulty in accepting this or that proposition in religion. They persuade themselves easily, although they cannot indicate a ground for this. Many a man cannot do this, but instead he must have something that satisfies him, and he does not immediately give grounds if he does not know whether those grounds are subjective or objective. We see quite well, then, that we must not blame any man because he will not give approval to a thing immediately. For men are quite different in this way. One man can persuade himself easily, another wishes a hundred times that the thing might be so,

[n] "Kenntniß."

and yet his understanding will not immediately applaud, namely, because it demands objective grounds. – There is something on which approval rests, which is a mixture of inclination and understanding. Now some men do not seek to analyze this properly, in such a way that they investigate which of the two produces their approval. – Many men call conviction what is actually persuasion. Persuasion is not always false. It is just that *this man* has the thing based on persuasion, not on conviction. The man can cognize some grounds concerning the object through the understanding. But many subjective grounds are added in. E.g. From the example of famous men, who, as one says, were no fools, from the antiquity of the thing, and other such things. All this is mixed together and produces the effect called persuasion. Through persuasion one can accept certain things, but also uncertain[o] ones. When someone will not accept certain things, then, this is not a matter of the heart but of the head. E.g., parents are easily persuaded that their children are innocent, and that they are led astray by the neighbors' children[;] whence does this inclination arise? They are merely imagining this, however, if a stranger sees at once that the boy himself is a ne'er-do-well. The inclination is so important that they content themselves with subjective and actually half-formed grounds. Someone else demands suitable grounds and does not allow himself to be put off so easily. If others will not accept at once what seems to us so clear, this will make us careful; for our grounds cannot be set forth as the first principles of custom. 891

Science. A complex of cognition. Is divided into aggregate and system. An aggregate is a common cognition. A system is a science. A system rests on the unity of the idea, namely, how the manifold of a cognition is juxtaposed.[p] It presupposes the idea of the whole, then, in which the science is contained. With an aggregate one also intends to get to the whole by constantly adding parts. With an aggregate the parts precede the whole, then; with a system, the whole precedes the parts. This distinction is very important. All of metaphysics is nothing but an aggregate and a rhapsody, because we have never yet had the idea of the whole, [of] how far man can go beyond reason, and on what sort of means he builds what he says. Hence metaphysics is a constant rhapsody. The metaphysician tracks down everything, based on what he believes, so that everything stands in combination with the whole. But he still does not have a concept of the whole, and the whole is unknown to him. –

Sciences are historical sciences or sciences of reason. It is not good that the author understands by science only a cognition of reason. For a system can be given for historical things, too, namely, by my setting up an idea, in accordance with which the manifold in history is to be ordered. Unfortu-

[o] Reading "ungewiße" for "unwichtige."

[p] "neben einander gerichtet."

nately, however, the *historici* are commonly rhapsodists. The idea could be this. Human actions derive from human nature, in order to fulfill completely its determination[;] if I take as my idea how human nature has developed in various ages, and how it has gradually gotten closer to its determination, i.e., to the completion of all the purposes that are prescribed for humanity on earth, then I bring a system to mind, in accordance with which I can order history. Certainty is either

1. empirical certainty. This rests either on one's own experience or that of others, when I hold the thing to be certain on account of their testimony. It is also called historical certainty. It is just as good empirically as my own experience, however. For often I must not trust my observations as much as those of some other man, of whom I know that he is an attentive man, and that I am probably overlooking something in the matter.

892 The certainty is all the stronger. For there are some things that I do not attend to as much as another man does.

2. Certainty of reason is always apodeictic certainty, i.e., that something cannot be thus, but must rather necessarily be thus. Empirical certainty is never apodeictic. Mathematical certainty is intuitively apodeictic, philosophical certainty is discursively apodeictic.

Arbitrary truth. It seems strange that the author speaks of arbitrary truth. For because I say it, something is not yet true; instead, truth must lie in the object. It is better for us to say *arbitrary propositions*, then. These are propositions where I will that something be so, propositions that actually rest on my will, then. They are commands of my reason, where the cognitions depend on the arbitrariness of my cognition. I order, for example, that the circle shall be divided into 360 parts, that we shall count with 9 numerals and 0. These are arbitrary propositions. For one can also count with 4 numerals, as Leibniz did. – Proof is divided into acroamatic proof, which is discursive, and mathematical proof, which is intuitive. The first is conducted from concepts, the second from the construction of concepts. We do not speak of empirical proofs here at all. One must not immediately exult in the certainty of his propositions, then, for no proposition in philosophy can have mathematical certainty. For I cannot exhibit to anyone, e.g., a whole world in intuition. In every proof there is

1. the *proposition* that is to be proved
2. the *ground of proof*, and
3. the *consequence* of the proof, namely, how the cognition follows from the ground of proof. The ground of proof is called an argument. Sometimes the conclusion is also called an argument. In philosophy one must always investigate whether the ground of proof is possible in the case of the cognition.

Such investigations are quite necessary[:] whether a ground of proof can be accepted here or there, whether a cognition is related to experience, or whether we partake of it through reason. Whether we will attain consequences through the ground of proof is what matters in metaphysics, which examines the consequences themselves. Those cognitions of logic that are certain without being granted are *unprovable*, says the author. Otherwise, unprovable also means a thing that requires a proof but has none. A cognition whose falsehood cannot be proven is unprovably false. 893 An *indemonstrable proposition* is a proposition that is immediately certain. What is certain without any ground of proof is immediately certain. No matter how much is mediately certain in a cognition, one thing is always immediately certain. Not only will we have[q] indemonstrable propositions in all sciences, then, which do not need proof[,] as the author holds, but in philosophy every proposition is indemonstrable as soon as it is immediately certain. A proof is direct, i.e., positive proof, or it is apagogical, i.e., negative. Direct proof shows that the proposition is true, apagogical proof that the opposite is not true. It merely refutes the opposite. In mathematics [apagogical proof] is quite illuminating, but in philosophy one must use it very sparingly. For apagogical proof does not do as much as direct proof. The latter goes back to the sources from which a proposition derives. Apagogical proof only shows a mistake, however, and that I would come upon an absurdity if I did not accept the proposition. I have proved the proposition by this means, but not comprehended it. They are also not to be adopted in philosophy because I can often refute my opponent, since we both, on that account, judge falsely. We are both wrong, and if I have refuted the other, he can just as well refute me *apagogice* without any contradiction, and neither can thereby prove his proposition.

Historical belief. Our author relates belief merely to testimony. We distinguish, however, between *believing something* and *believing someone*. We can *believe something* without someone's having said it to us. We can believe someone if we have accepted something on someone's testimony. Proofs from experience can well show that the thing is, but not the absolute necessity of the thing. For experience gives only something contingent. Proofs *a priori* give apodeictic certainty, however, whether they come from concepts or from the construction of concepts. If I do not cognize an object from mere concepts, but rather *a priori* in intuition that corresponds to the concept, then I construct the concept, and this is a demonstration. This proof has evidence in it, i.e., the proof is intuitive. This is mathematical proof. Philosophical proof is never intuitive but always discursive, i.e., it is always conducted with words. Since philosophical proof is not cognized in intuition, it cannot be called demonstration, either. Both 894 proofs are apodeictic, but with the difference that the one is in intuition, the other in pure concepts. Hence we must never use the word demonstration of philosophical proofs.

[q] Reading "Also werden wir nicht nur . . . die den Beweis nicht nöthig haben" for "Also werden wir . . . die nicht nur den Beweis nicht nötig haben."

It is commonplace to speak of demonstrations in the case of apodeictic proofs that have nothing at all intuitive in them. Demonstration derives from *monstrare*, to display, to lay before the eyes. Hence it can actually only be used of proofs where the object is exhibited in intuition, and where the truth is cognized not merely discursively but also intuitively. We will put restrictions on philosophy here, then, and never call its proofs demonstrations, however apodeictic they may be. In mathematics one makes no progress at all if one tries to prove everything from concepts alone; instead, they must necessarily be constructed. – The Greeks are the first to have discovered demonstrations. No people knew what it was to demonstrate before this emerged among the Greeks. It is said that the Greeks learned their wisdom from the Egyptians. But the Egyptians are children compared to the Greeks. They did have various cognitions, but not sciences. The Greeks first enlightened the human understanding. Many stories are presented in the authors about those who demonstrated this or that proposition.[r] If they had merely learned them from the Egyptians, then they would not have needed to demonstrate them anymore at all. The Egyptians had merely empirical surveyors, who were able to measure well according to certain rules, without proofs. No people knows what demonstrations are except those who have learned it from the Greeks. All those who did not learn it from them hold it to be folderol, and yet demonstrations are the sure step that extended insight has made into mathematics. Without this, all its attempts would be deceptive, like all philosophical attempts, in which human reason often deceives itself. In the case of belief there is often a distinction to be made between believing something and believing someone else. Believing something relates merely to the cognition and to the ground of the holding-to-be-true. A cognition can be from reason, and yet the ground of the holding-to-be-true, although it is logically insufficient, be fully sufficient practically[;] i.e., although the ground of the holding-to-be-true in this cognition is not fully correct logically[,] before the pure under-
895 standing[,] the cognition can yet be taken to be true practically. This is *belief of reason*,[s] which is fully distinct from knowledge and means logically insufficient holding-to-be-true that is, however, practically sufficient, and in both cases based on grounds. E.g., in mathematics it is said initially that the diameter is to the periphery as 100 to 314. Only later, in trigonometry, is this proved. Here the holding-to-be-true is grounded merely on the fact that famous men have discovered it, then[;] because it is already known that no error can easily conceal itself in mathematics, one has good cause to believe firmly that it is true, but he cannot say, I know it. – Where cognitions rest wholly on reason, to believe something on the

[r] Reading "über diejenigen, die die demonstration . . . geführt haben" for "die auf die demonstration . . . geführt haben."

[s] "der *Vernunft-Glauben*."

testimony of others[t] is a complete misuse of reason, for the testimony of others must rest only on experience. Because errors that conceal themselves cannot so easily persist in mathematics, however, I can surely rely on the fact that the diameter is to the periphery as 100 to 314, although I only believe it and cannot say, I know it. We can also accept certain propositions of reason on belief. Great mathematicians accept propositions in mathematics, perhaps without having gone through the demonstration. In philosophy one cannot do this, however, because errors so easily conceal themselves there. Historical belief, where we hold something to be true because we believe someone else, can become certainty. – Belief is thus belief of reason or historical belief. Belief of reason is that which is sufficient based on the ground of reason, not logically, to be sure, but practically. Historical belief is where I hold something to be true merely on the testimony of someone else, in any event without grounds. A belief of reason is one that is just accepted, although we have no certainty at all about the thing, but it has practical grounds[;] e.g., that the soul is immortal can move me to better conduct of my life. This practical ground can never rise to a ground that is called *knowledge*. For knowledge means that the holding-to-be-true is sufficient logically, too. It can be a holding-to-be-true that is so strong, however, that is just as unshakeable as the greatest certainty. He who wishes to speculate, however, must have cognitions that are sufficient according to logical grounds, too.

Historical belief can be actual knowledge. Accordingly, *belief based on testimony* must not be distinguished from knowledge, although belief of reason must always be distinguished from knowledge. We can see that historical belief can also be knowledge if I ask someone, What is the capital of Spain? and if he would say, *I believe* it is Madrid[;] then I would say, You have to *know* this, not believe it. If one wanted to say that one cannot know it unless one has been there oneself, then I can answer, If I am there myself, I cannot learn it except from what the residents there tell me, and hence I accept it on the testimony of others. The fact that it is testimony does not hinder there being certainty in this matter. For we can just as well accept something on the testimony of others as on our own experience. For there is just as much that is deceptive in our experience as in the testimony of others. Our *thought* in the holding-to-be-true of an experience is subject to many risks. To be sure, the testimony that we accept from others is subject to just as many risks as our own experience is subject to errors. But we can just as well have certainty through the testimony of others as through our own experience. Believing is thus the same kind of thing as knowing. If we contradistinguish believing from knowing, then this is only practically sufficient holding-to-be-true. What

896

[t] "Anderen Zeugnißen etwas glauben."

we cognize through reason we cannot always *know*. What we cognize through historical belief we can know. – What can I interrogate a witness about? I can hold something to be true when the other man has infallible reason or his experience tells him to say it. I can hold something to be true by means of a witness of *infallible reason* in truths of reason, or on account of that which he has from his own experiences. Since there are not as many errors to be found in the case of experience as in that of speculations, it is easier to believe what experience presents than what the other has cognized from reason, because reason is not as infallible. Mathematics involves infallible reason. Hence as soon as a proposition is maintained by mathematics it is infallible. – Since the concept of the infallibility of reason belongs to the highest perfection, we cannot accept any testimony as infallibly true except divine testimony itself. People object here, But can a man not testify to divine oracles? *Resp.* he cannot testify to anything except through an experience of inspiration that he has had, and in this

897 case it is always possible that the man can err. Here grounds cannot be believed *subjective*$_{L}$, then, but instead all grounds must be examined exactly. – And thus in the case of testimony by someone else I also believe much that he presents as his own experience based on the testimony of third parties.[u] E.g., when someone tells what he has read, then he gives testimony to his own experience out of a book, Here I rely, then, (1.) on the statement of someone else, and (2.) on the experience itself that the third[v] party had.

One science, namely, jurisprudence, is of such a kind that although it rests on reason, one nonetheless makes much use of testimony in it. In philosophy, it is not a matter of what testimony one produces, but which grounds[;] and it deserves closer attention that although *jus* is of such a kind that it rests on reason, one still accepts the judgment of others also. The cause is perhaps that because *jus* rests on laws, and these contain a great manifoldness of cases, a special determination is needed where errors are possible, in that one holds to be universal what admits of exception. Now if one wishes to have a law fully valid and usable, one believes that others will not very easily have overlooked something. Hence those learned in law are also called *juris periti*,[w] although it is a science of reason. It is a deplorable situation when it happens thus, however. For even if men are ever so practiced in giving heed to all cases, it is nonetheless possible that they have still overlooked some. – All citations, if they are to provide grounds of proof, contain historical belief[;] if I did not intend to hold something to be true on the testimony of someone else, I would not cite him, i.e., call him as a witness. I can of course tell some-

[u] "Anderer."

[v] "der Andere."

[w] ones experienced in law.

thing, e.g., that Plato claimed this and that, and quote the passage, but then I am not citing Plato. – In regard to science of reason, citation is a *heterogeneum*. The two do not fit together. It is a great weakness, consequently, when one sees oneself compelled to add historical belief to the grounds of reason. – In all empirical cognitions historical belief is indispensable. What we cannot know or experience ourselves, we must cognize through the experience of others, and historical belief by its nature applies merely to the experience of others. In matters that concern reason, I cannot call anyone as a witness; rather, in the case of what others have experienced, their declaration of their experience, on account of which I hold the thing to be true, is the testimony that produces historical belief. 898 The credibility of a witness requires[:]

1. The competence of a witness consists in the fact that he was *able* to say the truth. This requires

a. that he have sufficient skill to obtain experience. It is not so easy, in all cases, to obtain experience, and this involves practice. And in experience there is much deception of the senses. The common man is not a suitable witness. For he cannot obtain experiences properly. For when he is overcome by fear, he sees one thing for another and overlooks some things.
b. that he was in circumstances in which he was able to obtain experience. Above all, the common man cannot do this in all the inner circumstances. E.g., he is often sleepy, fearful, distracted, etc.
c. that he also has the skill to declare his experiences, so that one can understand his sense well. This is not so easy. Some men tell things quite meticulously. Others can give only a light silhouette of their experience, and cannot give an account of all its circumstances.

2. The sincerity of the witness, that he *wanted* to tell the truth. The common man is too crude to place great value on the truth. A mouth full of lies, he believes, does no harm, if one has some interest in the matter. They always report evils in a magnified way, so that everything is exaggerated and becomes shocking. One has to make them attentive by threats with the oath. Then they begin to hesitate and become quite doubtful. – The same thing holds for ancient times. Not a single historian among the ancients restricts himself very meticulously to the truth; rather, they always consider how to write beautifully. They accept all sorts of rumors without investigating them. E.g., Herodotus has many old wives' tales. But they also do not consider it very important to tell the truth. E.g., Livy seeks to write in a flowery style, and he has general speeches made that never were made. – We in our times are more compelled to speak the truth by circumstances, above all by experimental physics, and by the fact that one seeks to determine the appearances exactly through observations and experiments, in order to see into the laws of nature with more certainty. Only at the beginning of the previous *saeculum* did people begin to see that it is necessary to tell the truth completely, and then everyone had 899

to be quite exact in his reports, and if someone deviated from the truth only a bit in his writings, he was ridiculed and dishonored. On this account, we usually make use in all cases of more cautious expressions. E.g., Jurin[29] always says to what extent this is true, etc. This exactness in the reporting of experience later spread from natural science to history. For people saw that it is necessary not to injure the truth on the least point. Now we have things that make it easier to learn the truth. Printing presses, and further, gazettes, show at once where there is a mistake in one's writing[;] historical fables[x] cannot be told anymore, as they were in Rome. For while earlier it took someone 3 years to get from one country to another, now, due to the establishment of postal service, news comes from one place to another in a few days. E.g., all the tales of Apollonius Tyanaeus and Alexander of Paphlagonia came to Rome, having grown along the way. In Rome they found approval and were believed, as Philostratus then wrote of them, too.[30] Now, however, due to postal service, the gigantic increase in rumors has been stopped. In ancient times, however, it was not the case that the truth was determined so exactly. There are many honest people. But they often did not hold it to be necessary to be very meticulous, if untruth carried no penalty, or it brought amusement, or even if they even believe[d] that it was a report of great value. The latter is the so-called *pia fraus*,[y] if this is not a contradiction. – From all this it becomes clear that historical belief carries with it astonishing credibility, because the witness must have so many properties in order to speak the truth. – Thus every man has his own different interest, on which we cannot always pass judgment. Many a man seeks merely to embellish a matter in his tale, etc. Since, then, without such critical grounds we cannot, in passing judgment on testimony, believe a witness, historical belief rests in important cases on such a doubtful basis that it has to be examined closely. For in how many ways is the human will disposed? If this belief does not have the required properties, then, it is better to put it wholly aside, if one cannot figure out why men speak thus and not otherwise. Nonetheless, certainty can be grounded on the testimony of other men, as history and geography are grounded thereon.

900 A hearsay witness testifies to his experience of the testimony of someone else's experience of a thing. An eyewitness testifies to his own experience of the thing. He who relates a report that he read somewhere is a hearsay witness[;] he who expounds something that he, the listener, could not cognize from his own experience is a hearsay witness. In the case of common tales, and tradition or rumors, one cannot determine the witness himself. The witness is a multitude of persons, where it is believed that

[x] "Histörchen."

[y] pious deception.

the multitude will have credibility. There is tradition insofar as one man has conveyed his testimony to another orally. Tradition is a series of subordinate pieces of testimony, then.

If the concept *unbelieving*, which also appears in theology, is to mean a reproof, then it cannot consist in the difficulty of extending belief to testimony, for this is not a difficulty; rather, as soon as it is a reproof, the ground has to be moral. The former can redound to his honor if he is disbelieving or unbelieving. E.g. In the case of a universal rumor, this cannot redound to his moral detriment. With all tales, it is good and praiseworthy to be unbelieving, and one must proceed critically here, if this is possible. Belief can be divided into two, theoretical belief and practical belief. In the case of theoretical belief, one can be unbelieving. In the case of moral belief, he is called unbelieving who has no moral interest in accepting something as true, while he sees, however, how important this or that proposition is. Moral belief can be presupposed in every man, and moral unbelief is consequently quite reproachable. He who rejects the proof of the existence of God according to mere reason can also be called unbelieving[;] and he who no longer believes in virtue, if he does nothing out of a moral interest but everything out of hypocrisy, can also be so called. Here man gives up all intention to be virtuous, since he does not believe in virtue.

Of *practical cognition*. Here a twofold division is to be noted, whereby we defend against an ambiguity that can be occasioned by the words. A cognition is called practical as opposed to theoretical cognition, but also in contradistinction to speculative cognitions. – When a proposition is a proposition that commands, an *imperativus*, and says that something *ought* to happen, then it is a practical proposition[;] it says which free actions would be good for a certain purpose. An *imperativus* is a proposition, then, that impels to a possible free action, insofar as this would be good and necessary for a certain purpose. All practical propositions, if they are opposed to theoretical ones, are *imperativi*. These are various: in sciences that are nothing but science or skill one takes certain optional purposes, in accordance with which one presupposes what ought to happen. E.g., in geometry, when I say, To measure a straight line take . . . , etc. [T]heoretical propositions, on the other hand, do not say how it ought to happen, but rather how the thing is. E.g. A straight line is the shortest path, etc. These can be distinguished from practical propositions in an instant, because practical propositions are always *imperativi*, and [theoretical propositions] are easily distinguished from propositions that testify to the properties of action. – Secondly, however, practical propositions are also opposed to speculative ones. Cognitions can be theoretical and yet be either practical or speculative. For although they do not say what ought to happen, because they are theoretical, practical propositions can nonetheless be derived from them, and they are to this extent opposed to specula-

901

tive propositions. E.g. That there is a God is a theoretical proposition, but it is *practical in potentia*[;] you must just act as if there is a highest legislator for your actions. Thus although they are in themselves theoretical, [such] cognitions are not distinct from other practical cognitions, namely, because they are practical *in potentia*. – Speculative propositions are all those from which no rules or *imperativi* for our actions flow[;] in natural theology, propositions are merely speculative. E.g., whether God's omnipresence occupies space or consists merely in an influence on his creatures. This has no influence on our actions and thus is mere speculation. But whether the divine will is also a holy will, this is a proposition of practical importance, from which rules for our conduct can be derived. Theoretical propositions, accordingly, are either speculative or objectively practical propositions, i.e., ones that are practical *in potentia*. One could also say that all cognition is practical or theoretical. Cognition is practical where imperative propositions[z] are expressed, in that they indicate the necessity of a free action. Theoretical cognitions contain the cognition of an object, what it is, but the use of the cognition is always a speculative or a practical use. And this distinction is not[a] a distinction among cognitions, but rather among uses of cognition. We have many a cognition only for speculative use, many for practical use and for rules of our conduct. The use of moral propositions can be a speculative use. Those who engage in reasoning concerning the principles of virtue make a merely speculative use of them. The ancient philosophers who philosophized about the highest good never applied this in practical use. Not all cognitions can be applied to practical use. – Who can make practical use, e.g., of mathematics or natural science? We want to apply our cognitions to practical use, however. For through practical use our cognitions acquire more and more truth, and the final end of all our cognitions seems to rest on the fact that they ought to contain a rule about what agrees with our highest ends[;] and if no consequences for conduct flow from a cognition, then it seems to be without value. Hence, too, all speculation looks toward the practical, although one cannot have insight into this right away. He who drew the first mathematical figure thought, in fact, that a use could sometime be made of it. Otherwise it would only have been an occupation to while away the time. But supposing that through mathematics we only wanted to cultivate our reason, that would be as good as a practical use. For reason can prescribe rules for our conduct, and this pertains to practical use. Thus the prestige of our cognition is grounded above all on its practical use. For we cultivate cognition in the expectation of its practical use. We can sometimes consider this worth of cognition as a mediate worth, as a means to other ends, or as an immediate worth, and this is then called

902

[z] "die Sätze des imperativi."

[a] Reading "ist nicht ein" for "ist nicht so wohl als ein."

dignity. Nothing in the world has dignity. It is the final end, for the sake of which the world has this arrangement. Some things in the perfection of man have a mediate worth, e.g., some of his properties. But one thing has an immediate worth in man, and that is his dignity. Mathematics has many uses, [e.g.,] that calendars can be made according to it, or fields measured, etc. This is its mediate use and its market value. But in these respects it is not to be preferred to many other means, since everything that is only a means is without worth. Plato already says, however, that this mediate value is by far not the highest end of mathematics. For the propositions have in themselves their internal excellence, which exceeds by far all the fields that can be measured. Longinus[31] says that that, disdain for which is sublime, is not sublime. E.g., wealth is not sublime. For disdain for wealth is sublime. By virtue of the fact that mathematics determines fields and wealth, then, it is not sublime[;] but it has an internal worth, and in mathematics there is a splendor, and something that elevates our reason, and in connection with which we feel our reason in all its strength. Through the thoroughness of its proofs and its method it has a sublime worth. Again, however, if we weigh this rightly, then we see that this is still not genuine dignity, and that what constitutes *true dignity* is only that the will is good. For what would be the use of skill if man were to use it deceitfully? The true worth of the will is its use of this skill. All the cognitions that contribute to the dignity of man are far from constituting his highest worth; instead, his worth is in using all his talents well. The true dignity of man rests on *morality*, then. What serves to improve our will, then, is also called practical[;] and on this account philosophical morals is also called practical philosophy, because practical matters come up in this science. – If cognitions are such that nothing practical can be drawn from them, and that no actions at all flow from them, then such cognition has a merely speculative use. –

903

The whole doctrine of practical use, with which the author deals, simply does not belong to logic. For nothing belongs to logic except the logical form of all cognitions, i.e., the form of thought, without regard to the content. It can only contain propositions that can be demonstrated, then. Experiences of things, in connection with which empirical principles must be taken as a basis, do not belong to logic, because they cannot be demonstrated. Practical cognition is distinct from speculative cognition as to content, however. Hence logic can have to do with practical cognition. – The author deals with desires and abhorrence. But in logic one must think as if one had no will, otherwise[b] it would become a practical science[;] thus we have the science of thinking, and not of willing. –

He speaks further of living and dead cognitions, dead, i.e., which can move the will because they are practical, and yet do not move it and hence

904

[b] Reading "sonst" for "es."

are mere speculation. – It immediately strikes the eye, however, that none of this belongs to logic. He speaks of indifference,[c] when something is indifferent,[d] etc.

OF CONCEPTS

Until now we have spoken of cognition in general, to what extent cognition is distinct or clear, certain or uncertain. We have dealt with the mode of proofs and of holding-to-be-true, with belief and knowledge, etc. Now the author takes cognition apart into its elements, which should have occurred right at the beginning. Logically, all origins[e] in thought are divided thus:

1. The cognition is a simple cognition, a *concept.*
2. The cognitions are combined in a *judgment.*
3. That judgments are combined and that *inferences* arise therefrom. The ancients said, *Quot sunt operationes mentis? Resp. tres. apprehensio simplex, judicium, et ratiocinium.*[f] Now as for what concerns *concepts*, we wish to begin with that which is simplest of all in our cognitions, namely, that the cognition is a representation.[g] A representation with consciousness is *perceptio.* I have a hallucination and think that I am conscious of it. Insofar as I also pay heed to the object in such a representation, this is *cognition.*[h] Cognition is of two kinds, *intuition,*[i] *concept.*[j] *Intuitus* is a *singular representation.*[k]

In perception we do not relate our cognitions to the object. Through sensation, good feeling, pain – one does not cognize an object. This is only a mode of representation. But the representation is not distinguished by a particular object. In general, the relation of representation to the subject is called *sensation*, to the object, *cognition.* Logic occupies itself merely with cognition, but not with sensation.

A *conceptus* is a *repraesentatio communis*, which is common to many things. He who wished to have a representation of the color red first had to see the color red. When he compared the color red in the red of cinnabar, *carmoisin*$_F$,[l] and *ponceau*$_F$, however, he became aware that there is something general in the color red, that is contained along with other things in other representations of the color red, and he thought by red that

905

[c] "Gleichgültigkeit."

[d] "indifferent."

[e] "Anfänge."

[f] How many operations of the mind are there? Response. Three. Simple apprehension, judgment, and inference.

[g] "eine Vorstellung ist, repraesentatio."

[h] "*cognitio, Erkenntniß.*"

[i] "*intuitus, Anschauung.*"

[j] "*conceptus, Begriff.*"

[k] "eine einzelne Vorstellung, *repraesentatio singularis.*"

[l] carmine.

which was common to many objects, and this was a concept. A concept, then, is a representation that is common to many things. In the case of *intuitus*, I consider individual things. E.g., the sun, the earth. If I think of a certain genus of planets, however, then this is a *repraesentatio communis*, i.e., a *conceptus*. – Concept differs from intuition by virtue of the fact that all intuition is singular. He who sees his first tree does not know what it is that he sees. If he becomes aware that these objects have something common, then he omits everything they have that is different, and takes together what they have in common, and thus he has a *repraesentatio communis*, i.e., a *conceptus*. From this it becomes clear that one must not say *conceptus communis*, because this would be a tautology, because every *conceptus* is also *communis*. – Every *conceptus* is *empiricus* or *purus*. A *conceptus empiricus* is one that is produced through the comparison of objects of experience. A *repraesentatio empirica* is one that arises from the senses. This can become a *conceptus*, if I take that which is common to various empirical representations. It is easy to see that in the distinction between *empiricus* and *purus* what matters is the origin of the concept, and this is already a metaphysical investigation, then. For logic does not ask where concepts come from, but how they can be formed and ordered in accordance with the laws of the understanding. It pertains to logic, then, that a concept exists. It does not pertain to logic whether it is independent of experience or comes from experience. – There are many *conceptus empirici*, i.e., we often compare experiences and form from this a *repraesentatio communis*, and this is then called an *empiricus conceptus*. – For what is contradistinguished from a *conceptus empiricus* is a *conceptus purus*. A concept that has its origin independent of experience in the mere understanding is *purus*. E.g., the concept of cause, quantity, quality, etc. Whether there are such concepts is an investigation that belongs to metaphysics, because this is *cognitio pura*. – Our morals has many [*conceptus*] *puri*. The concept of *virtue* is not met with in experience, and if the world showed nothing but vice, we would nonetheless have a concept of virtue. – This [*conceptus*] *purus* can either arise from the understanding, and in fact if its ground is merely in the understanding, its object can still be represented *in concreto*. E.g., cause and effect [are concepts] of the understanding. One can distinguish the things in sense,[m] [can] sense what the talk is about in the case of effect, cause, etc., but the concept of causality lies merely in the understanding. Now the question arises, Can one encounter in experience the objects of this, his concept of the understanding? *Resp*$_{L}$. Yes. This happens through examples. An example of causality is: fire destroys wood. –

906

Or this *conceptus purus* is such that its object cannot be given in any experience. Then it is a concept not of the understanding but of mere

[m] Reading "im Sinne" for "im Verstande."

reason, i.e., one is not to understand the concept from experience; instead, I go beyond that to which experience leads me. – A *conceptus purus* is called *generaliter* a *notio*. A *notio* is more than a concept, then, for the concept of possibility, e.g., cannot be exhibited in experience. A *notio* whose object can be given in experience is called a *notio intellectualis*. If its object cannot be given in any experience, it is called a *notio rationis*, or an *idea*$_L$. Thus a *notio*, insofar as it cannot be given in any experience and also does not correspond to any experience, is actually an *idea*$_L$. The concept of the whole can be given in experience, *est notio intellectualis*[;] but if I make another new concept, e.g., the concept of a world that is the uncreated whole that contains all things, and in which all the parts stand in combination, one cannot give this in experience. If the world is eternal, what can comprehend all its eternity? The concept of the world is a mere idea, then. – The concept of the part is a *conceptus purus intellectualis, seu notio*.[n] But the concept of a part that is not composite is a *notio rationis, idea*$_L$. As long as my reason represents something divisible, that can always be divided further. But my reason finally demands the ultimate part, which cannot be further divided into parts, i.e., is simple. This concept cannot be shown in experience, and thus is a concept *a priori*, an idea. The concept of God is an idea. For experience cannot teach us whether all possible perfections may be united somewhere. – The whole of morals rests on ideas. We cannot encounter virtue among men. But my reason must nonetheless have a concept of virtue, as it must be in its complete perfection. We can perceive virtue in experience. But much must still be added[;] thus it is an idea. – The 907 doctrine of ideas is very important but actually belongs in metaphysics. Until now, it has been expounded wrongly. But if one does not distinguish it properly, then we cannot properly determine the use of our cognitions. Ordinary authors use the word *idea* completely wrongly. E.g., people speak of the idea of the color red, although this is not at all a *notio*. People speak of the idea of a triangle, although it is only a *notio*. In metaphysics it is shown that *notiones*[o] are either intellectual or sensitive. *Notiones*[p] *intellectuales* are necessity, cause, etc., which are labeled with the name categories. *Notiones*[q] *sensitives* are where an object of the senses is given, which I can cognize not in empirical intuition but in *pure intuition*. The concept of a triangle is a *notio sensitiva*, then. Ideas exclude all our cognitions.[r] They are drawn merely from reason, but they influence experience as rules in accordance with which one can obtain the most experiences.

How do *concepts arise*? I.e., how do representations become concepts?

[n] a pure intellectual concept, or a notion.
[o] Reading "notiones" for "rationes."
[p] Reading "Notiones" for "Rationes."
[q] Reading "Notiones" for "Rationes."
[r] "Kenntniße."

Logic does not concern itself with how *data*$_L$ for a cognition must be constituted, but rather merely with what the understanding does in connection with them[; it] pays heed to form, then, and not to the object. How does it happen, then, that a *repraesentatio singularis* becomes *communis? Resp. per comparationem, separationem, seu abstractionem.*[s] I compare things and attend to that which they have in common, and I abstract from all other things; thus this is a concept, through which all these things can be thought.

In logic it is a misuse for one to retain the expression *to abstract* so that one says *aliquidre abstrahe.*[t] E.g., as if, in order to have the concept of a tree, I took the concept of the leaves and of the trunk in particular, and abstracted from all differences among trees, and said that what has a trunk and leaves is a tree. No, I do not abstract the leaves and the trunk; rather, I retain them, and I separate them from everything else. I have to pay heed to that which a cognition has that is common, and *abstract from that* which it has that is different[,] e.g., from the magnitude or smallness of the tree. Accordingly, the word must not be so used that we say *aliquid abstrahere.* I abstract[u] from the remaining things. Abstraction does not add anything, then, but rather cuts off everything that does not belong to the concept, and notes merely what it has in common with other representations. The differentiation of a concept involves *comparatio*, then. I must pay attention to the agreement and identity of things, which is called wit, and secondly, *abstractio*. – It is wrongly expressed, then, when one speaks of *conceptus abstracti*, since *abstracti* means as much as *qui abstractus est a re.*[v] This is wrong, *nam non abstrahimus a re, sed separamus conceptum ab aliis rebus, conceptum abstrahimus a ceteris.*[w] We must abstract from many things[;] when in the case of scarlet cloth I think the color red, I already abstract from many colors[;] when in the case of scarlet cloth I think only an extended being, I abstract from many more things[;] if in this case I think merely that it is a thing, then I abstract from still more things. We should actually say, though, that the *use* of a concept is abstract. For every use of a concept is either *in abstracto* or *concreto*. I cognize a concept *in concreto* when I apply it to that which is contained under it. I think a concept *in abstracto* when I think it in general. From this we see that a cognition is abstract only[x] because the concept is thought *in abstracto*, without being applied to objects. E.g. People talk of education[y] and deal

908

[s] through comparison, separation, or abstraction.

[t] to abstract *something*.

[u] Reading "abstrahire" for "ignorire."

[v] which is abstracted from the thing.

[w] *for we do not abstract from the thing, but we separate the concept from other things[;] we abstract the concept from other things.*

[x] Reading "nur" for "nicht."

[y] "Erziehung."

merely with the early cultivation of man's faculties[z] without speaking of the application to child-rearing.[a] Here the concept is expounded not *in concreto*, but rather merely *in abstracto*.

BRIEF REPETITION OF THE FOREGOING

The form of a concept consists in common validity. *Repraesentatio, quae pluribus est communis.*[b] This constitutes a concept, then. – I cannot say *conceptus communis*, because this would be a tautology. A tautology is an enunciation where I make a concept distinct by means of it itself. For if a representation is not a *repraesentatio communis*, then it is not a concept at all. Since it already lies hidden in the concept, I must not add it. – But the use of a *conceptus* can be *singularis*. For what holds of many things can also be applied to an individual case. I think of a man *in individuo*, i.e., I use the concept of man in order to have an *ens singulare*. I can make use of a concept insofar as it is applied to many objects[;] then the concept is used as a *repraesentatio communis*, i.e., is used *in abstracto*, e.g., house. If I say of 909 all houses, now, that they must have a roof, then this is the *usus universalis*. It is always the same concept, however, and is here used wholly universally. For having a roof holds for all houses. This use of the concept is concerned universally with all, then. But a particular use is concerned only with many. E.g., some houses must have a gate. Or I use the concept only for an individual thing. E.g., this house is plastered in this way or that. We do not divide concepts into *universales*, *particulares*, *singulares*, then, but instead judgments, as we shall soon hear. In my judgment I can compare the thing with all, some, or an individual thing. This serves to determine our expressions exactly, and not to speak of everything in universal concepts. In kind, all concepts are universal and can always hold of others things in a certain way. E.g., plant holds for all grasses, but also for some bodies. The understanding has the faculty of concepts, and one can also define it thus. We said above that the understanding is the faculty of rules. But this is the same thing, for when I give a concept, I always give a foundation for rules.

Concepts arise *per comparationem, reflexionem, et abstractionem.*[c] In one consciousness I grasp many representations, in which I compare what is only a repetition of the other. From reflection, then, one cognizes that which many things have in common[;] afterward one takes away through abstraction that[d] in which they they do not agree, and then a *repraesentatio*

[z] "von der frühen Bildung des Menschen."

[a] "Kinderzucht."

[b] A representation that is common to many.

[c] through comparison, reflection, and abstraction.

[d] Reading "nimmt man durch die abstraction das weg" for "nimmt man die abstraction weg."

communis remains. No concept comes to be, then, without comparison, without perception of an agreement, or without abstraction. If I could not abstract I would not have any concepts, because something other than what is common to the individual representations[e] would always be occurring to me. E.g. If someone were such that in the case of the expression *house* what occurred to him was always just the *tavern* that he had seen, he would always preserve an *intuitus*. We see that no concept comes to be through omitting and abstracting; instead, this perfects a concept and makes it so that it does not remain a [*conceptus*] *singularis*. When a concept arises, the *positive* thing is comparing and reflecting, the *negative* thing is abstracting. For many a man it is hard to abstract, even if he can readily compare and reflect. When one has to do with such men one has a lot of trouble, therefore. Custom has led them to a point where it costs them great effort to omit that which does not belong to the concept. Most men have such bad principles because they think so vulgarly and cannot abstract the respectable, the proper, etc., from a concept of virtue. 910

An abstract concept is abstract only in use. It is less abstract when I say *in concreto* what I have said *in abstracto*. E.g., a body is an extension that has a figure. Now I give an example, i.e., I take all the things that I have omitted in the concept. The concept is used *in abstracto* when I omit all the differences that are common to the thing. A concept always arises through abstraction, consequently, but the concept itself is not abstract; rather, its use is. The use of a concept *in concreto* has its degrees, until finally the concept becomes *maxime in concreto* and belongs only to an *individuum*. In just the same way, I can always go further in abstraction, too. E.g., man, animals, living being, etc.

Every concept contains more possible concepts under itself and contains that which is common to various representations of several things. Thus if a concept contains something that is common to several things, it is itself contained in other possible concepts[;] it is a part of them, but contains only that which they have in common and omits what is different in them. Every universal concept is contained in the concepts from which it is abstracted, then. E.g., the concept *metal* belongs to gold, copper, etc.

Conversely, these things are contained *under* it, and this is just what constitutes the usefulness of a concept. In the case of intuition, I have no usefulness other than an individual object. Now the ground always contains the consequences under itself. Accordingly, every universal concept is a ground of cognition for many things, and furnished with a concept, I have a ground of cognition of many things. The concept itself is also contained in the things, however. For it constitutes a part of their representation.[f]

A concept is called a *higher* concept insofar as it contains others under

[e] Reading "den einzelnen Vorstellungen" for "der einzelnen Vorstellung."

[f] Reading "Vorstellung" for "Vernunft."

itself, and every concept is consequently a higher representation of others, because it always contains many under itself. A *lower* concept is a concept that is contained under others. E.g., man is an animal. The concept of animal belongs to all men and to still more things, too[;] consequently man is a *lower* concept than animal. – All *conceptus* stand in relation to each other in such a way that a *conceptus* is always *superior*$_{\text{L}}$ and *inferior*$_{\text{L}}$ relative 911 to the others, insofar as one is contained under another[;] and from this, finally, there comes a series of subordinate concepts. The *conceptus infimus* cannot be determined. For as soon as I have a concept that I apply to *individua*, it would still be possible for there to be still smaller differences among the *individua*, although I make no further distinction. Now in this gradation, one concept is always higher than another, until I come to the highest. The lowest cognition is intuition, because it is always concerned with something unique. I can set forth the *conceptus summus*, because there must be a concept in which I can omit everything. For if I wish to make a higher concept, I always have to abstract. If I cannot abstract, however, then no higher concept can be made[;] e.g., [the concept of] something. – The *conceptus superior*, in regard to the *inferior*$_{\text{L}}$, we call a *genus*$_{\text{L}}$. When we compare many things with one another, then, we can call every concept the *genus*$_{\text{L}}$ in regard to its *inferior*$_{\text{L}}$, *species*$_{\text{L}}$ in regard to its *superior*$_{\text{L}}$. *Genus*$_{\text{L}}$ and *species*$_{\text{L}}$ do not in themselves make any distinction among concepts, then, but only in the relation of concepts. Learned man is a *genus*$_{\text{L}}$ in regard to the philosopher, but learned man is a *species* in regard to man. Now we can think of a series of *genera*$_{\text{L}}$ and *species*$_{\text{L}}$, among which some will have to be *genera superiora*, until we finally come to a *genus summus*, namely, *something*.

Every *species* is at the same time a *genus*$_{\text{L}}$ in regard to the *species*$_{\text{L}}$ contained under it. A *species infima* is only comparatively *infima*, and is the last in use. It must always be possible to find another *species*$_{\text{L}}$, whereby this latter would in turn become a *genus*$_{\text{L}}$. But applied immediately to *individua*, a species can be called a *species infima*. – Here we can consider the *extension* and the *content* of a concept. The extension of a concept is a *sphaera*, and it is concerned with the multitude of things that are contained under the concept. We consider the concept as to content when we look to the multitude of the representations that are contained in the concept itself. The greater the extension of a concept, the smaller is its content, i.e., the less it contains in itself. E.g., the concept *man* has a large extension, but the concept *Negro* contains still more, namely, the concept of the color black, too, [and it] consequently has more content. Now the higher a concept is, the more one must abstract from the manifold, and the more 912 the content dwindles. It is a higher concept to the extent that it is contained in more things, and the more it contains that which belongs to more things. Now since in the case of the highest concept I have to omit so much that what remains to me is only what is common to *all* things, this concept therefore contains the least of all. From the highest concept, consequently, the lowest ones are determined, and this at the same time comprehends the correct determination of all things. A thoroughly determined concept is the lowest *under* all concepts. For it is not common to several things. A higher concept [is one] that is indeterminate *multimode*,[g] and the highest concept is that which is indeterminate in all things. The logical *sphaera* always grows, as a leaf of gold stretches when it loses in thickness, and just on this account is it so hard for man to go to the heights and to think things without content. The closer that concepts come to experience, on the other hand, the fuller or more concrete the representation is. The question arises, Which is better, a very concrete or a very abstract representation, so that one approaches the *individua* or the *genera*$_L$? *Resp*$_L$.: the one is as good as the other. It is lovely[h] if our representations have a large sphere. For a concept is always valid for what is contained under it[;] consequently the universality of cognition always rests on the sphere. But irrespective of this, the concept does lose in content, and this lack is unavoidable, and in regard to the human understanding is regrettable. Every lower concept is also called *angustior*,[i] every one that has a higher *sphaera* is called *latior*.[j] The *genus*$_L$ is always a *conceptus latior*, then, the *species*$_L$ a *conceptus angustior*. When two concepts stand next to one another and have the same *sphaera*, they are called *conceptus reciproci*. The chapter about *definitions* is the most important one in logic. For the greatest demand that one can put on a philosopher is always that he should define his concept. All logical perfection of our cognition consisted in the fact that our concept was distinct. The second perfection was that it also be complete, namely, that distinctness not rest on a few clear marks, but that it rest on as many marks as, taken together, constitute the concept. If, now, the concept is exhaustive, then no mark is lacking, of course. But although no mark is lacking, a mark could perhaps be superfluous, in that one mark could already be contained in another. This is an imperfection in the concept, if we multiply marks unnecessarily, and through tautologies make one mark into many marks. It also belongs to the logical perfection of a concept, accordingly, that the concept be precise, i.e., that the concept not contain more marks than are necessary to constitute the concept. Precise, *praecisus*, is not a good Latin expression. *Determinatus*, however, which is what the author calls precise, means nothing at all. For a concept that contains too little is *indeterminatus*[;] a concept would be *determinatus*, consequently, where more and more is added, and the concept is consequently exhaustive.[k] But in connection with plants, *prae-*

913

[g] in many ways.

[h] "schön."

[i] narrower.

[j] broader.

[k] Reading "ausführlich" for "nicht ausführlich."

cidere is used for cutting back, and thus it is with our concepts, too, which we cut back in regard to superfluous marks. If we take *completudo* and precision together, we can call a concept adequate. It is adequate to the object when the marks contain neither more nor less than directly constitutes the concept. The concept must be complete in order not to be too small, precise in order not to be too large. A definition is a *conceptus distinctus adaequatus*, then. But Wolff takes the word completely differently and calls a concept adequate where I do not merely have clear marks, but I cognize the marks themselves distinctly. These are intensive degrees of distinctness, however, of which we are not speaking here. Now if the marks are clear, then a definition is already present.[l] If I can also define the marks, then this is a definition of the parts of the definition. If a concept whose marks are merely distinct is called adequate by him, then he is already at the end. But one can still make the marks of marks distinct. For us, however, the expression adequate, or *conceptus adaequatus*, completes the definition and fits the object. Our definition, then, says as much as *definitio est conceptus distinctus completus praecisus.*[m]

DIVISION OF ALL DEFINITIONS

Definition has a certain perfection, which nothing can surpass. One could object, Won't you give marks of marks in the definition? *Resp*$_L$. One can also define marks of marks, and make a new definition from this. Since [definitions] constitute the greatest perfection of a concept, then, we have 914 to be acquainted with all the *requisita* of them, and we have to see to what extent it is possible to make them, how far we will get with this. All our concepts are either *given* concepts or ones that are *made*. A concept is given insofar as it does not arise from my faculty of choice. It can be given, however, either *a priori* merely in the understanding, or *a posteriori* though experience. I have many concepts that are given to me through the nature of my understanding, and which I have not fabricated. E.g., the concept of cause, time, etc. In just the same way, many concepts are given to us through experience. E.g., that water is a fluid body.

Conceptus dati[n] are contradistinguished from *conceptus factitii*, concepts that are made, which likewise are made either *a priori* or *a posteriori*. A concept is made *a priori* when it is made through pure reflection, without the objects being given through experience. E.g., I represent a 1000-sided figure, without ever having seen it. Such a concept is also called a *conceptus fictitius*, a fabricated concept. A concept that is thought up[o] seems [a] better [name] to me. I can also make a concept *a posteriori*, so that the

[l] "so ist es schon eine definition hinten her."
[m] A definition is a concept that is complete, distinct, and precise.
[n] Concepts that are given.
[o] "ein ausgedachter Begriff."

object is given to me in experience. E.g., I have a piece of metal[;] that is always given *a posteriori*, not made. If I want to have a distinct concept of it, however, then I have to test the metal for all its properties, and in this way I find them through various experiences, which do not lie in the concept[;] the nature of metal is thus a concept made *a posteriori*.

To make a concept *a posteriori*, then, is to trace given experiences further, and thus to draw out an adequate concept. – This would be nothing more, then, than to extend the concept. –

All our concepts, insofar as they are given to us, be it *a priori* or *a posteriori*, can be defined only through analysis.[p] For because it is given, I cannot make it distinct except by making clear the marks that lie in it, and that is just analysis. If this analysis is complete, then there comes from this a complete distinctness. If subsequently the marks are not too many, then it is precise, and thus arises a definition.

If concepts are not given but made, however, so that we are not merely to produce the distinctness of the concept but to make the concept itself, then we will be able to bring about a definition of the concept only *per synthesin*. E.g., if I want to represent a spirit, then I must make the concept for myself. I say I *want* to represent a thinking being that is not combined with any body. Here I have made the concept for the first time through the definition. Concepts that are made cannot possibly be defined, then, except *per synthesin*. All of mathematics defines *per synthesin*[;] it does not define given concepts, but concepts that are made. I want to think a figure, says the mathematician, that looks so and so, and is to be called such and such. We can also have a concept *a priori factitius*, the materials for which experience has given, while the concept itself has been made. E.g. Let one think an unconquerable fortification, the like of which does not exist at all. The materials, such as moats, stone – lie in experience. The concept itself is *factitius*. This is how it happens with someone who invents a new instrument.

915

A posteriori, however, there are also *factitii conceptus*. If I want to define a concept through experience[q] by clarifying, through experience, what is not contained in my concept, then this must also occur *per synthesin*. I want to produce a concept more extensive than I had[;] by this means I finally get a concept that consists of marks that I collected *per synthesin* from experience. – It is a universal rule, then, that all given concepts can only be defined analytically, all concepts that are made, be they made through the understanding or through experience, can only be defined synthetically. When can I say that a concept is defined in the *analysis*$_{L}$. When all its marks are complete and precise. When can we be certainly convinced that our analysis is complete? *Resp*$_{L}$. We never can be, because it can happen

[p] "per analysin . . . durch die Zergliederung."

[q] Reading "einen Begriff durch die Erfahrung" for "eine Erfahrung."

only through experiments, in which we can always overlook much[;] consequently all analytic definitions are combined with uncertainty. If a concept is a concept of experience, then it is harder to know[r] that I have analyzed correctly. Through analysis one never has apodeictic certainty. We cognize analytic definitions in such a way that one cannot set forth any sure *criterium*$_{\text{L}}$ for them.

Synthetic definitions, insofar as they have a fabricated object, can never err, because I say, in accordance with my faculty of choice, that I want to think this. – Synthetic definitions of concepts drawn from experience are completely impossible. We cannot make an object complete in experience

916 and set forth all the marks that constitute the concept. For experimental physics from time to time discovers still further properties of bodies.

Analytically, I make a given concept distinct by merely expounding the concept[;] *per synthesin*, however, I make a distinct concept. If we are to define a concept analytically, then it is just given us to, and we are just to make it complete and precise. – If this analysis is just incomplete, this is not a definition, but it is at least a degree of distinctness, which can be carried further and can approximate more and more to *completudo*. Before a concept becomes complete it must necessarily be incomplete beforehand, and secondly, it is also not always possible to attain complete concepts. Could there occur a distinct concept that is not yet complete? I can of course use an incomplete[s] analysis, too, because I do at least have some clear marks already. Hence it is not always possible, with every concept, for me to have defined it, and it is not necessary, in order to speak of an object, that one have defined it *per analysin*. For where I cannot say everything, I must at least say as much as I can say with truth. Definitions are not as necessary as people believe, consequently, and this is to be noted, because in most cases definition is extremely hard, and analytic completeness cannot always be expected. Because the incomplete analysis is nonetheless still a part of the definition, however, and consequently is at least true and correct, it becomes clear that we are certain that we cognize enough in the incomplete[t] analysis. E.g., when I say that virtue is a readiness in morally good actions, and in doing so I omit that it is also a mastery over our inclinations, I ask, Can nothing at all be inferred from the first, incomplete concept? [*Au*] *contraire*. Most philosophers have deduced all their morals from the first concept. I can draw consequences from every mark of a thing[;] if I cognize only a few marks in the thing, then a few consequences can be drawn[;] if I cognize everything, however, then all the consequences can be drawn. To begin initially with the definition, then, as happens in most philosophies, and not to commit oneself to

[r] "weniger merkclich zu wissen."
[s] Reading "incomplete" for "complete."
[t] Reading "incompleten" for "completen."

anything until one first has the definition, is actually to make all investigation impossible. For I must begin first from the imperfect. The endeavor of philosophers is of course to attain the greatest perfection through definitions. We must not say, however, that that of which no definition has been given does not deserve any treatment. For there are many things of which we cannot give a complete concept. E.g., jurists have never yet been able to give a definition of fairness. 917

Concepts that are given *a priori* independently of experience can be defined analytically. For here the concept concerns an object that I am to cognize through the understanding alone[;] consequently, whatever I am to say of it must be in my understanding, because we cannot go out of our understanding and seek elsewhere. Thus the whole of metaphysics and morals has to do with analytic definition. But although these two sciences are the true objects of analytic definitions, it is obvious nonetheless that definitions are not always unavoidably necessary[;] in the case of analytic definitions, rather, one must never begin by saying that this or that is a definition. For that all analysis is complete requires a proof[;] I must first show that the marks lie in the concept, and then show that taken together they constitute the concept.

It would be excellent and would give great worth to our cognitions if, in philosophy, we had concepts that are adequate to the object, and which also did not exceed precision, for this is the aim of our sciences. But since we are not in a position to accomplish such a thing, we must make do with as many clear marks as we can discover in our reason. Such incomplete concepts, which also occur in physics, we call descriptions.

To want to say straight away that this alone constitutes the concept is too dictatorial. For we first have to say how we have come to the *analysis*$_L$. What Wolff attempts in his philosophy is wholly false, then, and on this account each of his definitions is also false in philosophy. Concepts are commonly analyzed incompletely, although one cannot deny that he sets forth rather clear marks, and that he often comes quite close to the whole concept, and that regardless of [the incompleteness] his definitions in philosophy and in natural law can well be used, since they show much acuity. He learned to put definitions at the beginning in mathematics, where this is admittedly very good, because mathematics has synthetic definitions. One finds this even in society.[u] One speaks, e.g., of justice, and someone says, Define *justice* for me. He wants me to have probed all the depths of the concept, instead of engaging in reasoning[v] about what we know, and what lies in the concept, too. 918

Thus it happens that such definitions are always 99/100 false, and that

[u] "in Gesellschaften."
[v] "raisonniren."

Baumeister's defined philosophy[w] teems with errors.[32] – Of mathematical definitions not a single one is false, because the concepts are made arbitrarily[;] but all analytic [definitions] are given concepts. Can concepts of experience be defined analytically? When the inquirer into nature defines water, e.g., as a fluid body without taste or color, one readily sees how precarious the definition is. He who is not already acquainted with water will not thereby become acquainted with it. It is simply not necessary to define concepts of experience *per analysin*, however. For why do I need such a definition? For when I say the word *water*, others understand me. The definition, however, is completely unsuitable for acquainting others with water. For in the concept *water* there lies so little that I immediately go outside the concept and have to collect new marks through experience, i.e., I have to define the concept through exposition synthetically, and not analytically. An empirical concept can well be defined in accordance with that which lies in it. But one never seeks this, because so very little lies in it. It cannot be defined synthetically either, however, because we cannot be acquainted with all the possible marks that experience can teach concerning an object[;] consequently concepts of experience can never be defined.

The result of all that has been said, then, is that our concepts are either given or made. The given ones are either empirical concepts or concepts of the understanding. A given concept of experience cannot properly be defined[x] either *per synthesin* or *per analysin*, because in the first case I can only define[y] it through new marks, [while] in the latter case too little lies in the concept to be able to distinguish it from others. With concepts of the understanding, and in particular with ones that are given, a proper analytic definition is likewise impossible, which is due not to the thing, however, but to us, since it is hard to set forth the marks of a concept precisely. Arbitrary concepts can be made both *a priori* and *a posteriori*, but only synthetically. Only *conceptus arbitrarii* (*factitii*),[z] which are made *per synthesin arbitrariam*,[a] can be defined synthetically[;] these include all mathematical concepts. Indeed, what is still more, with a *conceptus arbitrarius* one always has to begin with the defini-

919

tion, because the very concept is produced through this, and because through this very thing I declare what I want to say through such a concept, which I have made arbitrarily[;] without definition, consequently, such a concept would be nothing.

A *nominal definition* is that distinct concept which suffices for differentiation of a thing from others. A *real definition* is that distinct concept which

[w] "definirte philosophie."

[x] "erklärt."

[y] "erklären."

[z] concepts that are arbitrary (made).

[a] through an arbitrary synthesis.

suffices for cognizing and deriving[b] everything that belongs to the thing[;] it suffices for explaining the thing internally, consequently, and for understanding what belongs to the thing.

It is essential and contains the concept of the essence of the thing. Nominal definition, on the other hand, is sufficient only externally, in comparison with others, in order to have insight into its identity or difference with others. It means almost nothing more than what the expression *nominal definition* says, a certain attestation to the name of the thing, in order to make the name of the thing distinct, but not to have better insight into the thing itself. It does not comprehend the essence of the thing, but only a comparison of a few marks of differentiation with others. Hence it can also have only comparative validity. E.g., when I say that man is an animal that has the faculty of speech. Here I can differentiate him from all animals (but not from the starling). Nonetheless, the concept is sufficient in comparison with other animals. –

How can I know that my concept is sufficient to distinguish the thing from all possible [other things]? *Resp*$_{L}$. Only those marks which, taken together, constitute the whole essence of the thing can suffice absolutely, for the whole essence of the thing cannot be – common to two things. And this is a real definition, then. Nominal definitions are valid only insofar as I make use of them. Real definitions are the actual definitions, then. When Wolff says that the genesis of the concept can also be comprehended from the real definition, this is false. For the genesis must be inferred subsequently from the real definition. For it makes possible the judgment as to how it could have arisen. His examples bring to light what we have said – as, e.g., he sets forth as a real definition that a circle is a curved line which moves around a fixed point, and whose parts are equally distant from the mid-point[;] the first is superfluous, because it can be inferred from the last. The genesis is only a deduction from the real definition. That is all Wolff says, too. Otherwise, real definition has nothing to do with the genesis, but only with the internal possibility of the thing. – If I cognize a thing in accordance with an *attributum proprium*, then I can also define it by means of such an *attributum proprium*. E.g., man is an animal that judges. Because the judgment is an *attributum proprium* of a man, it must necessarily flow from the whole essence of man. If it flowed only from a part, then many things, which are different in essence, could agree with the essence [of man] as to *this* part. The definition holds for the whole essence, then. For it cannot be understood except as of the whole essence. – Through the real definition the thing can always be distinguished, and from all other things. It is hard to distinguish the two, and often one regards as a real definition what was only a nominal definition. In the case of synthetic objects, definitions are always real. For the object is given *a priori* only

920

[b] Reading "abzuleiten" for "abzusondern."

through this one definition, and [only] through this definition is it possible to think it[;] but to make real definitions of given, analytic objects is very hard. I cannot even know whether my nominal definition is sufficient, because I can never find the marks to distinguish the thing from all possible other things, because I cannot compare it with all possible things[;] but only when I know that my marks exhaust the whole concept, i.e., when I can give a real definition, is a nominal definition also certainly sufficient. Such is the case with all definitions in natural science. – In morals, metaphysics, etc., on the other hand, there must be nothing but real definitions, because this is the aim toward which we must direct all our analysis, to bring about a complete concept. *Definition* is actually a complex of marks, a review or exposition of them, insofar as they contain the materials for a possible concept. Describing is not a determinate rule. One can be as long-winded as one wants, or one can be brief. We can accomplish much by thereby characterizing things beforehand. Nevertheless, descriptions always precede definitions for those concepts that are empirical[;] indeed, since we cannot define empirical concepts, they are only capable of description. Concepts *a priori*, on the other hand, if they are made *per synthesin*, e.g., in 921 mathematics, must always be defined. A given concept of reason need not always be defined, however; instead, we often put up with an incomplete concept. In concepts of reason, however, descriptions are not at all suitable. Thus, e.g., Lavater, who through the liveliness of his imagination more often gives excursions than he does exhaust things, sets forth very many of love's effects when he describes love.[33] But from all this one cannot get precisely the concept of what love is. Descriptions are not at all suited for speculative sciences, but only in *praxis*$_{L}$, where I can combine a lively image with my concept.

Distinctness is the all-important thing in definition. Then follows *completudo*. Precision, however, is not as important as *completudo*. This precision is in many cases hard, because without noticing we take one mark twice, because we hold things that have different names to be different. E.g., a body is an extended, divisible being. Here extension already lies in divisibility. In descriptions one does not take the whole at all exactly, because here one seeks only the proposition for a possible definition, which one perhaps does not want to make at all. Thus in the catechism I can give many descriptions of God as to his properties, although I see in the end that the precise concept of God is a being of all beings. Even in definition it does not matter at all if something is lacking in precision, and there is too much in the definition. That cannot do any harm, unless one violates the canon, *Quod fieri potest per pauca*,[c] etc. Precision is only a law of economy, and it makes the consciousness of

[c] What can be done by means of few things . . .

completudo easier. How do we pass judgment on a proffered definition? *Resp*$_{L}$. We ask:

1. Is the definition, as *a proposition*, *true*? Does that which is said of the thing in the definition actually belong to it? E.g., it is a true proposition that a ground is that on the basis of which I cognize why something is.
2. The concept must be distinct. If something is true as a proposition, it is not yet on that account distinct as a concept. Thus the example above does not become at all distinct through the definition. For *why* means as much as *through which ground*. Consequently, I would have said that a ground is that on the basis of which I cognize through which ground something is true. This is *idem per idem*,[d] then. This is a principal mistake, which is very common, and most definitions[e] in discourses are of this kind.
3. Once the concept is true as a proposition and is also distinct, then I can ask whether the distinct concept is also complete. Do the marks, taken together, constitute the complete concept? This is very hard. For how can we know that our concept lacks nothing more, and that we have left nothing out? To be sure, we do not notice that something is still lacking. But that is not a sufficient ground for calling the concept complete. For how often do we fail to notice something that we subsequently find? 922
4. The exhaustive concept must also be determined. This can still be done, and if it is not there, then this is not a great mistake. Precision is the reduction of definition *ad minimos terminos*[;] just as $^{12}/_{24}$ can be reduced to $^{1}/_{2}$, so too must I be able to cut back[f] the concept. It is lovely when we can do this, and when we know how to express all our definitions in sententious propositions. This is the elegance of a cognition.

A false definition can contain true propositions, accordingly, and be possible in spite of this, although it canot be held to be a concept adequate to the thing. Only I must convert it. Otherwise a mistake arises, since the one mark does not exhaust the whole thing.

Through what is a concept made distinct? Through clear marks. If these marks are tautological, however, i.e., if one is contained in another, then the concept does not in the least become distinct, although it sometimes seems to, because the tautology is hidden therein[;] something one must look carefully for in investigating the definition.

How are definitions found, then? It is obvious that this only applies to analytic definitions. For in the synthesis of an arbitrary concept, where I make a concept, the definition need not be found, because I say distinctly what I have invented in the understanding. Such definitions of the mathematician are actually only declarations of his willed opinion,[g] and mathematical definitions need no rule at all, consequently. For he need only say

[d] the same through the same.

[e] "Erklärungen."

[f] "praecidiren."

[g] "declarationen seiner Willensmeinung."

to anyone what sort of concept he wants to establish.[h] Nonetheless, *mathematici* sometimes go wrong concerning their concept, and in ancient times more seldom than in modern times. Euclid never did it. But Wolff brings all of philosophy into mathematics. When he gives the concept of similarity, he analyzes the concept. But here there can be a great risk that he has not made his analysis complete. Everything the *mathematicus* says, however, must be undoubtedly certain. Hence [Wolff] should have said that a similar figure, which I want to think, is, etc. Here, consequently, things must always be defined synthetically.

923

In the case of analytic definition the rules are the following: Seek true marks. You want to analyze, so attend to the marks and seek true ones, which actually belong to the thing. Those propositions which are found through the analysis of a concept, through which I become conscious of the marks of the concept, could be called elementary propositions, because they present the elements for definition. For although a definition does not yet come from these, they are nonetheless the representations for a definition, etc. E.g., if I say, Virtue is a readiness, a freedom in action, etc., here I seek through analysis one mark after another, in order thereby to attain the definition.

Now let us analyze the concept and seek as many elementary propositions as we can. Then we have to see whether this or that mark does not contain yet another, however[;] and here one must then guard oneself against ever placing a mark in the definition twice. – Now if I have sought true propositions, and in doing so have seen that these marks are different marks, then I collect them all again and compare them with the whole concept, and thus place them together again. But here we find the whole difficulty, namely, that the analysis can still be accomplished, but it is extremely hard to know whether the marks are present completely[;] and we have cause to be very distrustful about this. Since we cannot always maintain that our analysis is complete, then, we must attend to our definition with fear and trembling. And since the thing is so hard, I would say that I will define *as an attempt*, that I will establish a definition as an attempt, as it were, that I will not rely on it as on something free of mistakes, and that I intend to regard it as if it were not a definition. Here I can maintain, then, that even if it is not a definition it must nonetheless be (1.) a true proposition, (2.) a distinct concept, even if it is not a completely distinct concept.

I will be able to make good use of this presumptive definition. For I will always be able to say, *Cui competit definitum, ei competit definitio.*[i] E.g., he who is virtuous has a firm resolve to act. This *definitio* always belongs to the *definitum* of the virtuous. But I will not be able to say, conversely, *Cui*

[h] "etabliren und festsetzen."

[i] The definition agrees with that with which the defined agrees.

competit definitio, illi competit definitum.[j] I cannot say, conversely, that he who has a firm resolve to act is virtuous, and in fact I do not call him virtuous. I see quite well, then, that from a presumptive definition I can make any direct concept[k], but I will not be able to convert it, because I have not named everything, and have not cognized all the marks completely. I can say, e.g., that man is a rational animal, but not that every rational animal is a man. For in the definition something is lacking. – Now if I believe, finally, that I have all the marks completely together, and if I place them together, then I do not have to look to anything further, except that my definition be precise. This last is good and nice, but it does not constitute an essential *requisitum* of definition, so that even without precision such concepts have their sufficient usefulness. – If in the definition I have sought the first thing, namely, merely true propositions, then I define *obscurum per aeque obscurum*,[l] and one could call these tautological propositions. – With definitions, if they are otherwise simply true propositions, one can accomplish much, even if there is not an exhaustive concept. But he who wants to reciprocate, must have a complete concept. 924

Universal rules of definition.

1. One should not define *by means of a circle*. To define[m] by means of a circle is to define by means of a mark that presupposes the concept as *definitum*. E.g., if I define a ground as a cause of why something is, then my mark, *why*, i.e., *based on which ground*, is such a mark, which already means the concept of a ground. This *circulus vitiosus* occurs quite frequently. One takes a mark, and without examining further whether the concept by itself, independently of the concept, is clear *definitive*$_L$, one defines[n] *idem per idem*.[o]

2. *Definitio nec sit latior, nec angustior suo definito.*[p] I demand a complex of marks, which, taken together, exhibit the whole concept.[q] Hence one seeks not more marks, and not fewer, than are necessary, so that the *definitio* and the *definitum* are reciprocal, i.e., so that one can be put in place of the other. E.g., if I say that a body is an impenetrable being that is heavy, then the *definitio* is *angustior definito*.[r] For through the mark of heaviness, the concept of body is too restricted and narrow. For it is concerned only with bodies with which we are acquainted[;] consequently, if the definition has too much determination, it becomes *angustior definito*.[s] 925

[j] The defined agrees with that with which the definition agrees.
[k] "daß ich von einer praesumtiven definition mir jeden directen Begriff machen kann."
[l] the obscure through the equally obscure.
[m] "erklären."
[n] "erklärt."
[o] the same through the same.
[p] A definition should not be either broader or narrower than the defined.
[q] Reading "den ganzen Begriff" for "den ganzen Inbegriff."
[r] narrower than the defined.
[s] narrower than the defined.

The more indeterminate a concept is, however, the greater is its *sphaera*, *et latior est definitio definito*.[t] E.g., if I say figure, that applies to many things. If I say a *three-sided figure*, then it is already more restricted, etc. A *latior definitio*[u] is a concept which is determined enough by the definition[;] an *angustior* [*definitio*],[v] on the other hand, [is] when it is too hemmed in by too much determination.

OF LOGICAL DIVISION

On this we can be quite brief. A universal concept has a *sphaera*, and has lower concepts under itself. We investigate these lower ones insofar as the lower concepts are distinguished from one another. Division is thus the complete representation [of these lower concepts] insofar as they are considered according to their difference[s], in which, taken together, they are equal to the *sphaera* of the whole concepts. E.g., all beings on earth are organized or not organized. The organized ones are plants or animals. Logical division is nothing other than the taking apart of the *sphaera* of a concept. This dividing is something other than taking apart. In the case of division, I distinguish the manifold under the concept, i.e., the *sphaera*. In the case of taking apart, I analyze the concept. I do not analyze the concept itself [in division], but rather I only divide the *sphaera*, the lower concepts, insofar as they are contained under the universal.

The larger a concept's *sphaera* is, the less it contains in itself.[w] It contains all the more in itself, however, the less it contains under itself. In every division of a concept, then, we divide this concept into its parts without taking the concept apart, i.e., one divides the multitude of things that are contained under the universal concept. And this will be capable of being continued[;] the greater the *sphaera* that the concept has, the more members of the division there will be, and the smaller its *sphaera* is, the fewer members of the division there will be. Since every concept has a greater *sphaera*, the fewer parts it has, it follows that a concept can be divided all the more, the fewer parts it has. E.g. We represent many things under the concept of animals. There are animals that move on land, in the air, and in water, the mark of all of which is movement. We have not taken 926 the concept of animal apart here, i.e., analyzed it. For then we would have to have said that an animal is a material, which lives, etc. No, we divide the concept. We only see how many kinds are contained under the concept. In every division we represent, first of all, that a multitude of various things completely fills up the *sphaera* of a concept, i.e., [that they] are equal to the *sphaera* of the concept, consequently that no concept, as a part, is lacking.

[t] and the definition is broader than the defined.

[u] broader definition.

[v] narrower [definition].

[w] Reading "in sich" for "unter sich," in accordance with Lehmann's correction (24:1102).

Secondly, [we represent] that these various concepts, all of which are supposed to be contained in the *sphaera* of the concept, are different from one another, hence that one part of the *sphaera* is not contained in another. We say, then, in accordance with the example we used, that all animals, divided according to movement, are such as can move *either* on the earth, or in the air, or in water. This *either, or* expresses the fact that they are different, and that one kind is opposed to the other. Through the word *all*, however, one expresses the fact that together the marks constitute the concept. –

In every division, then, we have a *sphaera* and *membra dividentia*.[x] These latter must be opposed to one another and, taken together, must fill up the whole *sphaera* of the *conceptus*. E.g., if I say that all men are either virtuous or vicious, this does not hold. For there are men who have no character at all, as, e.g., a savage. Many rules appear in logic, and it is good that we indicate them, so that one may prove that one understands all the actions of the understanding that appear in connection with its operations. But these rules are of such a kind that one can easily dispense with these rules as precepts, because everyone observes them by himself, and later can also expound them *in abstracto*. Such is, e.g., this rule for division: the divided concept must not be wider or narrower than all the members of the division, when they can be taken together by means of an opposition[;] that is, the division must not lack a member. For if a member is lacking, then the concept would have a greater *sphaera*, because I would not have enumerated all the members, i.e., [the concept] would be broader. If I say more members than there actually are, then the divided concept has a smaller *sphaera*. Here one sees how hard it is to be able to give a rule of the understanding *in abstracto*. Everyone thinks it *in concreto*, however, without being conscious of this. In such cases, therefore, one must not think of the rules *in abstracto*, but rather of the examples *in concreto*, which one has before oneself. – The members of a division must also be opposed to one another. For otherwise I would not be able to say either, or. 927
From this we see everything that is already mentioned in the prolegomena, p. 14.[34] The common and healthy understanding is quite familiar with the rules. It cognizes only *in concreto*, however. The speculative understanding, on the other hand, can also prove them *in abstracto*. – In mathematics such rules are quite good. It is also a science, however, that cannot be thought at all without abstraction. A divided concept must not contradict any member of the division. E.g., if I say that all triangles are round or four-sided. In a division, the members ought to be contained under the concept, i.e., the concept of the division must be contained in them, which is not the case here, because neither round nor four-sided triangles are contained under the concept of a triangle.

[x] members of the division.

We have to distinguish *division*, *subdivision*, and *codivision*. Division in general is the representation of the manifold concepts that are opposed to one another and that fill up the whole *sphaera* of the concept. Now this can be continued. I can divide a concept in one *respectus* and then again in another *respectus*. All [humans] are virtuous or vicious as to character, men or women as to sex, young or old as to age, learned or unlearned as to cognition,[y] etc. This is *codivison*, where each time I only divide a given *conceptus*. I can also subdivide the concept, however. Then I divide the members of the division. Every subdivision is thus a division of a *membrum dividentium*. E.g., men are learned or unlearned. Learned men are learned in matters of reason [or] learned in matters of experience.[z] Those learned in matters of reason are philosophers or mathematicians, etc. For someone who accepts *species infima*, these *subdivisiones* will finally have an end. Since we have just shown, however, p. 373,[35] that in the nature of the thing every *species* can always contain further *species inferiores*, we will never come upon such concepts, whose sub-contained concepts cannot be divided again. Subdivision must proceed to infinity, then, although many a subdivision has an end, of course, *comparative*$_{\text{L}}$, for us.

Codivision also goes to infinity. E.g., I can divide the triangle, in regard to its *latera*, into equilateral and non-equilateral, in regard to its angles, into right-angled and oblique-angled. More cannot be set forth here. But 928 in regard to the things of nature, uncountably many codivisions can be given.

Quaeritur.[a] How does all division proceed, actually? Is division by means of our pure understanding always a pure division[b] only into two parts, and then into subdivisions, i.e., is it always a dichotomy, so that all other divisions are only subdivisions? Or can I divide a concept into more than two parts right at the beginning? *Resp*$_{\text{L}}$. It is obvious that every immediate division is a dichotomy. When we divide into several parts, this is polytomy, which is in every case a subdivision. E.g. If I want to take apart an apple into many pieces, I must nonetheless divide it first into two pieces. These may be different as to size or not. Afterward I can divide it into several parts. But these are subdivisions, then. Every immediate division is consequently a dichotomy. Dichotomy is brought about immediately by the pure word, not. E.g., triangles are either equilateral or not equilateral. Non-equilateral[c] triangles are either *aequicrura*[d] or *scalena*. When they divide triangles into *aequilatera*, *aequicrura*, and *scalena*, then, mathematicians have consequently brought the subdivision under the im-

[y] "Kenntniß."
[z] "Vernunft-Gelehrte, Erfahrungs-Gelehrte."
[a] It is asked.
[b] Reading "Eintheilung" for "Theilung."
[c] Reading "nichtgleichseitigen" for "gleichseitige."
[d] equal-legged (i.e., isosceles).

mediate division, and divided falsely. Since this is so extensive, however, it is not always observed, because with many subdivisions one loses sight of the *conceptus divisus*.

OF JUDGMENTS

A *judgment* is *generaliter* the representation of the unity in a relation of many cognitions. A judgment is the representation of the way that concepts belong to one consciousness universally[,] objectively. If one thinks two representations as they are combined together and together constitute one cognition, this is a judgment. In every judgment, then, there is a certain relation of different representations insofar as they belong to *one* cognition. E.g., I say that man is not immortal. In this cognition I think the concept of being mortal through the concept of man, and it thereby happens that this cognition, which constitutes the unity of two different representations, becomes a judgment.

Every judgment involves matter and form. The matter is the cognitions *generaliter* and the concepts, the form must constitute the combination and unity of the representation. If I say, e.g., that God is just, evil is punished, and if another man asked, Are these rhapsodies that you are bringing forth? then I would say, No! Because God is just, he therefore punishes evil, which then constitutes the form through which the cognition is brought to unity. All actions of the understanding that appear in a judgment reduce to 4, and all judgments are considered according to these.

929

Namely, first of all, as to their *quality*, they are divided into affirmative, negative, and infinite judgments. Even if the *logici* say that infinite judgments can be used as affirmative ones, that is a proposition which can be expounded in a special note. Basically, however, it is something different as to form, and in the beginning one must divide just as the distinction of the action[s] of our understanding is. How much is thought under this is something that belongs in a note.

2. As to *quantity*, our judgments are divided into universal, particular, and singular judgments, and even if the *logici* show that as far as the matter is concerned, singular judgments amount to universal judgments, a singular judgment is nonetheless distinct from universal ones, and this must be distinguished at the beginning, although one can say afterward that singular judgments belong to the universal ones. The *actus* of the understanding are obviously different, although one sees that the one use of the understanding holds as much as the other.
3. As to *relation*, judgments are divided[e] into categorical, hypothetical, and disjunctive judgments.
4. As to *modality*, into problematic, assertoric, and apodeictic judgments. Each of these 4 functions gives a particular kind of judgment, then.

[e] Reading "eingetheilet" for "getheilet."

Quality is the relation of concepts insofar as they stand in the relation of unity with one another[;] in accordance with this they are divided into affirmative judgments, if I combine one concept with the other positively, into negative judgments, if I separate one concept from the other, into infinite judgments, if I restrict one concept by the other. E.g., men are mortal[;] here I affirm mortality of men, or I think men as they stand under the concept of mortality. No man is mortal[;] here I deny mortality
930 of man. If I think man, I think him as he is distinct from all that which is mortal. *Anima non est mortalis,*[f] is a negative proposition. On the other hand, *Anima est non mortalis*[g] is an infinite proposition. – All affirmative propositions show their affirmation through the *copula*$_L$ *est*, which *copula*$_L$ indicates the relation of two concepts. When the *copula*$_L$ *est* occurs *simpliciter*, it means the connection of two concepts – when the *copula*$_L$ *est* is affected with the *non*, it means the opposition of the two concepts and indicates that the one concept does not belong to the other, or is not contained in the *sphaera* of the other. E.g., *anima non est mortalis*[;] here I represent that mortality does not include the soul. If I say, however, *anima est non mortalis*, then I say not merely that the soul contains nothing mortal, but also that it is contained in the *sphaera* of everything that is not mortal. In this case something special is said, then, namely, that I do not merely exclude one concept from the *sphaera* of another concept, but also think the concept under the whole remaining *sphaera*, which does not belong under the concept that is excluded. I do not actually say, *est immortalis*, but instead I say that the soul can be counted among all the concepts in general that may be thought outside the concept of mortality. And this actually constitutes infinite judgments. –

Affirmation and negation are qualities in judgment, accordingly. A negative judgment is not just any judgment that is negative, but a negative judgment where the negation affects the *copula*$_L$. A judgment is an affirmative judgment, accordingly, where it does not affect the *copula*$_L$ but rather the predicate, as occurs in an infinite judgment, and where the *copula*$_L$ is without any negation[;] consequently, all infinite judgments are affirmative, because the negation affects only the predicate. But although every infinite judgment has the nature of the affirmative, nonetheless, there is always a negation there, not of the judgment, i.e., of the relation of the concepts, but of the predicate.

The relation is the same, to be sure, as in an affirmative judgment, but the negation is still always there, and consequently infinite judgments are distinct from the affirmative judgment. In logic, this matter seems to be a subtlety. But in metaphysics it will be a matter of importance not to have passed over it here. For there the disinction between reality, negation, and

[f] The soul is not mortal.

[g] The soul is non-mortal.

limitation is greater. In the case of limitations I think something positive, but not merely positive, but rather negative, too, and it is something positive that is restricted. – They are called *judicia infinita* because they are unlimited. They only say what is not, and I can make uncountably many such predicates, for the *sphaera* of the predicates which, affected by *non*, can be said of the subject, is infinite. 931

The principle of all possible *praedicata contrarie opposita*[h] must come from the thing. This is the principle of thoroughgoing determination. This thoroughgoing determination of a thing is impossible, however, because it involves an infinite cognition to seek out all the predicates that belong to a thing[;] and hence I can proceed to infinity and still not determine the thing in a thoroughgoing way. E.g., the soul is corporeal, not corporeal. The soul is mortal, not mortal. In logical use they can count here as affirmative.

For every thing is distinct from others through determination. All other things that are affected with *non* can be said of this. E.g., the mark of stone is hardness. Now I can proceed to infinity and say that a stone is not metal, not wood, etc. Do I thereby say anything new? For what help is it that I know that everything else outside the concept is not stone? The *sphaera* of this everything else is infinite, and therefore these are called *judicia infinita*. The quantity of judgments is distinguished in such a way that there are *universal*, *particular*, and *singular* judgments. E.g., All men are mortal, Some men are mortal[,] Caesar is mortal. Here I have a *judicium universale, particulare,* and *singulare*. In every *judicium singulare* the predicate holds of the subject without exception[;] if I say, Caesar is mortal, no exception can occur here, because the concept Caesar is a singular concept, which does not comprehend a multitude under itself, but is only an individual thing[;] consequently it holds without exception in just the way that the *judicium universale* does, namely, because it has no *sphaera* from which something could be excepted. The [*judicium*] *universale* holds without exception because the *sphaera* comprehends everything, and consequently the *singulare judicium* is equal to the *universale* in use. There is a distinction here nonetheless, to which one must look, although in the formal use both can go together.

The *logici* have a custom of making the matter distinct by means of certain *vocales*[i] in the following verses:

Asserit A Negat E sed universaliter ambo.
Asserit I Negat O sed particulariter ambo.[j]

[h] predicates opposed as contraries.
[i] vowels.
[j] *A* affirms, *E* negates, but in both cases universally. *I* affirms, *O* negates, but in both cases particularly.

I.e., the *vocalis A* is *universaliter affirmans*. E.g., All men are mortal. *E* is
932 to mean a *judicium universaliter negans*. E.g., No man is mortal. *Particulariter affirmans* is *I*. E.g., Some men are learned[;] *particulariter negans* is *O*. E.g., Some men are not learned. This is used later on in syllogistic, where unintelligible words, e.g., *celarent*, *barocco*, which mean nothing, are used in order to show the quality of the proposition through the three *vocales*. – Thus we also have some school proverbs that must be noted. One asks: *Quae, qualis, quanta est propositio?*[k] *Quae propositio* relates to the relation, are they categorical, hypothetical, or disjunctive propositions? *Qualis propositio*, are they affirmative or negative? *Quanta propositio*, are they universal or particular propositions? From this the quality and quantity of judgments arise.

The author deals here with the condition of judgments. This is the determination of the subject in a categorical judgment, which [determination] contains the ground of truth. E.g., if I say that a man is deserving of punishment, then I see that this does not apply to the concept of man without condition. If I say, however, that a man who is vicious is deserving of punishment, then the viciousness is the determination of the subject. Actually this does not belong in logic, because logic does not occupy itself at all with content. – Analysis of the judgment consists in passing judgment on the judgment in accordance with the 3 *modi judicandi*. In earlier times one demanded these in the schools when one asked: *quae, qualis, quanta*?

According to the *relation* of judgments, all judgments are *categorical* or *hypothetical* or *disjunctive*. The matter of all categorical propositions consists of a concept, in which the concept of the subject belongs to the concept of the predicate. E.g., Man is mortal[;] the subject, man, belongs to the concept of the predicate, to be mortal. – In the case of hypothetical judgments the matter for the concept consists of two judgments. E.g., If God is just, evil is punished. Through a *propositio hypothetica* I want to say just that if the one is accepted, the other must also be accepted. One judgment holds under the condition of the other. – *Propositiones disjunctivae*, as to their matter, are two or more judgments which are always considered in opposition, and concerning which I represent that when they are taken together, these judgments constitute everything that can be said of the judgment. If one of them is true, then all the others[l] are false. If
933 all but one are false, then the one must be true. For because everything that can be thought is thought, and all the remaining ones are false, this one must be true. The matter of disjunctive judgments is various judgments, then, which are considered in opposition, however, so that all the judgments taken together constitute the whole judgment. We see that they

[k] What, of what quality, and of what quantity, is the proposition?
[l] Reading "alle anderen" for "alle."

constitute merely a logical division. For if I say, e.g., that all triangles are either isosceles or equilateral or scalene,[m] then the triangle is divided into as many members as it actually can be.

In the case of judgments, the form of the relation is that either the relation of a subject with the predicate is considered, or that of a ground with the consequence, or the relation of two or more judgments insofar as they fill up the *sphaera* of a concept *disjunctive*$_L$. – Categorical judgments constitute the *basis*$_L$ of all the remaining ones. Here the relation of subject with predicate is indicated. The hypothetical judgment is composed of two problematic ones; the disjunctive judgment, however, is composed of two or more judgments. In the hypothetical judgment I consider the combination of two judgments as ground and consequence. In the disjunctive judgment all the categorical judgments are members of the division[;] it is to be noted, however, that in the case of hypothetical and disjunctive judgments, the judgments cannot be transformed into categorical judgments again. – The matter of a categorical judgment consists of two concepts, the form in the relation in which the one concerns the subject, the other the predicate. E.g., All men are mortal. – In the hypothetical judgment the matter consists of two judgments. E.g., If the soul is corporeal, then there is no hope of the necessity of another life. The *if* expresses the relation. If a judgment is thought without saying what is true and not true, then this is a problematic judgment, which is accepted in order to see whether the other judgment follows if I accept this one. It is thought merely as to its possibility. I see only whether the judgment is possible, even if the thing itself is not possible, since on all sides men have hit upon strange propositions and have maintained them.

This is a judgment, then, that I do not regard as true as to modality, and it is called problematic. I say that there is no other life[;] I will merely think this in order to see how the proposition that I think would stand in connection with another one. The matter of hypothetical judgments consists of two propositions, then. Now I say that with these propositions things may be as they will, nonetheless, this much is certain, that if I accept that the soul is corporeal, then I cannot possibly say that it is immortal. In all hypothetical judgments there are two judgments which are thought problematically not assertorically, and which constitute the relation of a concept as ground to consequence. – Otherwise, the author says, things are said in the schools *per thesin*, i.e., assertorically, or *per hypothesin*, i.e. problematically. *Per thesin* means to say something categorically, *per hypothesin* to say something problematically, where the propositions are categorical, however, to the extent that the relation and the *nexus*$_L$ of the ground with the consequence is indicated. In all hypothetical judgments there are two problematic judgments. The form of these judgments

934

[m] Reading "ungleichseitig" for "gleichwinklich."

consists in the *consequentia*, according to which the one judgment is the consequence of the other. The ground in the hypothetical judgment is called the *antecedens*, the consequence is called the *consequens*[;] consequently the matter of hypothetical judgments consists of the *antecedens* and the *consequens*[;] the form, on the other hand, is the *consequentia*, i.e., what we deduce from the other.

It is good if we always have quite unique words for our concepts and do not need to make do with paraphrases. Thus *judgment* and *proposition* are actually distinct as to usage. When the *logici* say, however, that a proposition is a judgment clothed in words,[n] that means nothing, and this definition is worth nothing at all. For how will they be able to think judgments without words? Thus we prefer to say that a judgment considers the relation of two concepts insofar as it is problematic, while by propositions we understand an assertoric judgment. In judgment I test my proposition; I judge before I maintain. In the case of a proposition, however, I posit and I assert something, and the proposition consists in just this assertion[.] Hence we maintain that the *consequentia* of hypothetical propositions is called a proposition, because this deduction is certain and consequently is a positing.[o]

Some are of the opinion that we can transform hypothetical propositions into categorical propositions. One can do it. But what is maintained is no longer the same, then. This is to remove the hypothetical proposition and to put another in its place. It does seem to be the same if I say, All men are mortal, or, If something is a man, then it is mortal. But they are different. For in the second judgment it is problematic whether something is mortal. Being mortal is not maintained categorically but holds only when being man holds. Consequently it is completely different with categorical propositions than with hypothetical ones. In a hypothetical proposition it is not maintained at all that something is, but that it is if something, namely, the ground, is accepted.

935

In the case of categorical propositions, however, there is no settled condition. They are judgments essentially distinct from one another, then. With all hypothetical judgments I have two *modi*, a *modus ponens et tollens*. The *modus ponens is that if* the *antecedens* is true, the *consequens* is also true. The *modus tollens* is that if the *consequens* is false, the *antecedens* is also false. This will come up later in syllogistic.

The disjunctive judgment contains the relation of different judgments insofar as they are equal, as *membra dividentia*, to the *sphaera* of a *cognitio divisa*. E.g., All triangles, as to their angles, are either right-angled or acute or obtuse. – I represent the different members as they are opposed to one another and as, taken together, they constitute the whole *sphaera* of

[n] Reading "ein Satz ist ein Urtheil" for "ein Urtheil ist ein Satz."

[o] "eine position."

the *cognitio divisa*. This is in fact nothing other than a logical division, only in the division there does not need to be a *conceptus divisus*;[p] instead, it can be a *cognitio divisa*.[q] E.g., If this is not the best world, then God was not able or did not want to create a better one. This is the division of the *sphaera* of the cognition that is given to me. These are problematic judgments, of which it is said assertorically, however, that taken together they constitute the *sphaera* of the concept.

As for what concerns the modality of judgments, the ancients did not take the division as exactly as we do; instead they called every combination word *modality*. E.g., the world exists in a necessary way.[r] For them, the word *in a necessary way* was the modality. But can logic really judge whether a thing is necessary or not? No, for it has nothing to do with things and their necessity. Hence it can only ask whether a judgment is expressed with necessity or not. I ask only about the necessity that is to be met with in judgment. If the possibility is determined on the basis of the form, then it is a problematic judgment. If the possibility is actually there, then it is an assertoric judgment. And if it is combined with necessity, then it is an apodeictic judgment. An assertoric judgment can be merely contingently true or apodeictically true. The contingently true are empirical propositions. For experience only shows me how it is, but not that it must 936 be so. Apodeictic propositions, however, are propositions *a priori*, where at the same time I cognize the necessity of the propositions. *Judicia exponibilia*. E.g., if I say, A few[s] men are learned, then I can derive from this (1.) Some men are learned. For a few are some, of course. (2.) Many men are not learned, for a few is the opposite of many. These two propositions are included in the one proposition, which contains an affirmation and a negation, but expressed in the form of affirmation. These are exponible judgments.

Judgment can involve something that is not logical, but rather something that is aesthetical. A judgment is (1.) something logical that concerns the understanding. (2.) something sensible that concerns the senses. E.g., if I say that virtue's worth is greatest, that is logical[;] but [if I say that] virtue's worth exceeds everything to the point of *astonishment*, or if I add an Oh! or an Ah! then these additions are something aesthetic in the judgment. It would look quite ridiculous if someone wanted to bring in aesthetics in mathematics. In just the same way, someone who wanted to bring sarcasm into philosophy would not be writing *purely* logically, but aesthetically, too. One must distinguish these well and not confuse them. For the impression of the aesthetic often makes someone blind in regard to the logical. When the talk is about the truth of the matter, then every-

[p] divided concept.

[q] divided cognition.

[r] "die Welt ist nothwendiger Weise da."

[s] Reading "wenige Menschen" for "*wenn* wenige Menschen."

thing that excites the affects must be left out. One leaves this to those who want to win approval surreptitiously by means of beautifully turned expressions, and not through grounds.

Practical judgments contain an ought, the necessity of why something happens for some purpose or other. *Theoretical judgments* contain an is or an is not[;] I say whether they are or are not in a certain respect. A judgment that is capable of a proof is *provable*, demonstrable. One that is not capable of any proof is an *unprovable* judgment. Among all judgments there must be some that are not capable of any proof and are immediately certain, i.e., are unprovable propositions. Those that still need a proof, however, are provable. – However many propositions there may be that are mediately certain, there must in the end be some that are immediately certain. E.g., between two points I can draw only one straight line. –

Empty judgments. Among those that are immediately certain, some rest on identity, e.g., every body is extended. If I develop the concept of a body, 937 I find that I think the concept of extension in it. Here there is an identity of body and extension, then. For impenetrable extension is a part of the concept of body and lies in it. –

If the identity is *explicita*,[t] then such an analytic proposition, which rests on identity, is a tautological proposition. E.g., man is man. If I say, however, that man is a rational being, then the concept is the same *implicite*. Every proposition that is identical *implicite* is provable. For it can be developed in accordance with its parts. If a proposition is identical *explicite*, however, then it is wholly indemonstrable. Such a proposition can be called an empty proposition, e.g., Every body is corporeal. Propositions, on the other hand, that are identical *implicite*, are not empty propositions. For through them a mark that lay hidden is made clear. E.g., All bodies are extended. Here I need only make the identity distinct *per analysin*, and I see that it lies therein not tautologically but mediately. – It is false, however, and unworthy of so great a man, when the author says that all our cognitions of reason rest in the end on empty propositions. For then they would rest on nothing. No, they rest on propositions that are true but are identical *implicite*, and a large part rests on analysis, in accordance with which I have insight into the relation between subject and predicate. Propositions that are empty of sense are called empty, but so are those that are *fruitless* and without use. Identically tautological propositions are not *empty of sense*, but fruitless. All judgments serve only to give distinct concepts of things. E.g., Every man is a rational being. This is a distinct concept of man. Here I have made clear a mark of the concept, i.e., I have made it clear through its predicate[;] I have judged. Consequently we cannot have any clear marks except through a categorical judgment, and consequently judgments serve for attaining distinct con-

[t] Reading "explicita" for "explicata."

cepts. A judgment that does not produce a distinct concept is *empty*, however. It is not empty of meaning, but logically empty. Through them nothing useful is attained, because they do not yield a distinct concept, and do not fulfill the understanding's ends. Battology is similar to tautology[; it] is the vain[u] use of many words, where the concept . . . with many words . . .

[*Translator's Note*: The MS of the *Vienna Logic* breaks off at this point. It resumes in a different hand and in a very abbreviated style, continuing thus for another three pages (24:937–940). Because these last three pages are so difficult to interpret, they are not translated here. Instead, the corresponding section of the *Hechsel Logic*, which presumably contains what is missing from the *Vienna Logic*, appears next.]

[u] "unnütze."

The Hechsel logic

[*Translator's Note:* As noted in the Translator's Introduction, the latter half of the *Hechsel Logic* appears to have been identical with the latter half of the *Vienna Logic*. I translate a portion of the *Hechsel Logic* here to replace what is missing from the *Vienna Logic*. The translation begins on p. 86 of the Hechsel manuscript, three sentences before the point at which the translation of the *Vienna Logic* ends.]

. . . A judgment that does not produce a distinct concept is empty, however. It is not empty of sense, but logically empty. Through them nothing useful is attained because they do not yield a distinct concept, and do not fulfill the understanding's ends. Battology[v] (which has similarity with tautology) is the vain[w] use of many words, where the concept is said with many words, without these many words making the concept distinct. It gets its name from a certain Batto,[1] who observed[x] the opposite of laconism, and who exerted himself to combine many words with few thoughts. Tautology consists in *identitas explicita*.

87

We are speaking of mediately and immediately[y] certain judgments. An unprovable judgment that is not capable of further proof is immediately certain. One that it is still possible to prove in speculation is mediate. Proof is mediate certainty of cognition by means of another cognition. That every body is extended[z] no man can prove. This is an elementary proposition of a cognition, from which all other proofs are derived. These are either analytically unprovable or they are immediately certain propositions that are synthetic[.] E.g.: between 2 points only one straight line can be drawn. Synthetic propositions, then, are ones where I add one concept to another immediately. All immediately certain propositions *a priori* can be called principles. We can also have immediately certain propositions *a posteriori*. E.g.: This tree is made of wood[;][a] propositions that are immediately certain *a posteriori* are called propositions of experience. Principles need no proof because they are cognized[b] *a priori* and do not rest on

[v] Reading "Battologie" for "Bathologie," with Pinder.
[w] Reading "unnütze" for "nützliche," with Pinder.
[x] Reading "beobachtete" for "beobachtet."
[y] Reading "unmittelbar" for "untelbar," with Pinder.
[z] Reading "ausgedehnt" for "ausgelehrt," with Pinder.
[a] Reading "Dieser Baum ist aus Holtz" for "Dieser Baum, dieses Holtz," with Pinder.
[b] Reading "erkannt" for "erlernt," with Pinder.

experience. They are called principles because[c] they are not grounded in turn on others but instead provide the ground for others. They are also called *prima principia* because one cannot subordinate them to any other, and are cognitions such that all others are subordinated to them.[d] Principles are of 2 kinds, intuitive and discursive principles. An intuitive principle is called an *axioma*. There is no word in philosophy for discursive principles, because no one has ever made the distinction between intuitive and discursive principles. One could call it an *acroama*, however, a proposition[e] that can be expressed only through words and through *pure* universal concepts. An *axioma*, however, can only be exhibited in intuition. There are theoretical and practical principles. A postulate is a proposition in which is said what must happen when I act with respect to a given cognition. It is a representation of the nature[f] of an action in such a way that it is thereby presupposed that it is immediately certain, that it can be shown.[g] E.g.: [T]o draw a straight line. When one does not know immediately how the action is to be completed then this is a problem. E.g.: To have a perpendicular line fall on a point.

Judgments of experience are such insofar as they are given only *a posteriori* and we judge without proof. E.g. To judge that a body is heavy. An immediate *judgment of perception* is when . . . [2]

One must note how cognitions are combined in a system and how they fit together as members in accordance with the idea of a whole. In the case of an aggregate the concept of the parts is prior to the whole and hence one can say that every system has an arrangement of members where one part is always there for the sake of the other, and they are all related to the idea of the whole, as, e.g., the parts of an animal are[;] and [the parts] cannot be be increased at all, as happens in the case of a tree with its 88 branches, which on that account are not members of the tree, either, but rather parts. We will not call them merely parts then, either, but rather members. In a system the members have various names, in accordance with what their use is, and, indeed, in respect of their principal and secondary purposes in the system. What concerns the principal purposes are the definitions, the *axiomata*$_{L}$, which all relate to the principal purpose. *Membra principalia*[h] also include *theoremata*, i.e., theoretical judgments insofar as they are capable of a proof, and *problemata*[,] practical propositions which require a solution. When I have to show how it is possible to

[c] Reading "Grundsäzze, weil sie" for "Grundsäzze, nicht, weil sie," with Pinder.

[d] Reading "denen alle andern subordinirt werden" for "die allen andern subordirt werden," with Pinder.

[e] Reading "Mann könte ihn aber acroama nenen, ein Satz . . ." for "Mann könte ihn aber nennen. acroama ein Satz . . ."

[f] "Art."

[g] "praestiret werden."

[h] Reading "principalia" for "principiorum," with Pinder.

accomplish something, and have to prove that it has been accomplished in this way.

A *problema* needs first of all a proposition that represents the action that is to occur. E.g., when I ask to have a perpendicular line fall on a point. 2ndly there is the question of how it is to be proved[;] and then it must be proved that if I represent it as I have represented it, then I would[i] determine what the *questio problematis* says.

Included among the *principiae minores siue deriuatiuae*,[j] which concern the secondary purpose of the system, are[k] the *corollaria*. They are consequences of an *axioma* [or] *theorema* which are regarded not as principles but rather as *principia pertinentes res*.[l] They are not the basic parts themselves, but they still belong along with these. *Corollaria* are immediate deductions from the preceding propositions, and they are distinct from theorems in that they are inferred immediately from the preceding propositions. *Theoremata*, on the other hand, are drawn from a given judgment through a series of deductions. *Corollaria*, however, are immediate inferences from preceding propositions.

Scholia$_{L}$ are really not *principia* of a system but parts that are added to it, not in order to settle something, but rather to make the thing interesting and to embellish it. They tell the history of the proposition, mention examples, resolve scruples, and are concerned solely with secondary things, which do not extend the system, but rather its usefulness.

Now our author makes use of various expressions and says a lot that sounds great as it is proclaimed, but that does not develop the concept further. Thus he speaks, e.g., of how a problem is to be resolved and says: When the problem is given to you, seek all the possible actions through which it can be resolved, and then give a proof that the *quaesitum* has come about. One will become aware[m] of many delusions of this kind which prevail in many sciences, but which do not have the success that they promise. If culture did not refine man then we would see that most moralists and preachers have produced nothing better. Not because morals is not in a position to do this, but because they present nothing but tautologies and produce a lot of hot air, concerning what man already knows better by himself.

Of Inferences of the Understanding. If I am to deduce[n] one judgment from another, this is an inference. There are *mediate* and *immediate* inferences. A mediate inference is when, besides the concepts that are contained in 89

[i] Reading "würde" for "wurde."

[j] principles that are minor or derivative (reading "principalibus minoribus siue deriuatiuis" for "principiis minus deriuatuis").

[k] Reading "des systems gehen, gehören" for "des systems gehören," with Pinder.

[l] things pertaining to the principles.

[m] Reading "gewahr werden" for "gewant werden," with Pinder.

[n] Reading "folgern" for "folgen."

the judgment, I need still other concepts[o] that are not contained in the judgment in order to[p] derive a cognition. E.g., All bodies are divisible because they are composite. Here the inference will run thus: everything composite is divisible, consequently all bodies are divisible.[q] Here we need a third concept, namely, being composite,[r] in order to deduce from this that bodies are divisible. This is consequently a mediate[s] inference, then, when a third concept is sought out in order to draw a consequence from the judgment. If I say, however, All bodies are divisible, consequently some bodies are divisible, then these judgments are the same as to matter and they do not contain more than 2 concepts[;] such a deduction is called a *consequentia immediata*, an immediate inference. An immediate inference follows from the other [judgment] in such a way that it is distinct from the other only as to form[.] E.g., All men are mortal. Here I can infer immediately[,] merely as to form[,] Some mortal things are men, or consequently, No man is immortal. Such a deduction[,] where the *conclusio* differs from the *iudicium concludens* only as to form, is a *consequentia immediata*. One could also call it an inference of the understanding, in order to distinguish it from a *ratiocinium*, or an inference of reason. Where I need a *iudicum intermedium*,[t] because the one judgment is distinct from the other[u] *materialiter*[.] E.g., All men are mortal, consequently Cajus is mortal. Men[,] mortal constitute the matter of the first judgment. The judgment inferred from this is distinct from it as to matter, for Cajus does not occur in the concept of all men. Where 2 judgments are distinct as to matter, then, one cannot infer immediately;[v] rather, this is a mediate inference[w] or an inference of reason. Consequently immediate inferences[x] are essentially distinct from inferences of reason as *consequentia mediata*.[y] I can infer one judgment from the other immediately when it is not distinct[z] as to matter but rather as to form. They must be distinct as to sense, however, not merely as to expression, for I cannot derive *idem ex eodem*.[a]

Consequentiae immediatae[b] are divided into those where[c] the *consequentia*

[o] Reading "Begriffe" for "Urtheile."

[p] Reading "um" for "und," with Pinder.

[q] Reading "teilbar, folglich sind alle Körper teilbar" for "theilbar," with Pinder.

[r] Reading "das zusammengesetzt seyn" for "das zusammengesetzt sey," with Pinder.

[s] Reading "mittelbarer" for "unmittelbarer," with Pinder.

[t] Reading "iudicium intermedium" for "iudicium," with Pinder.

[u] Reading "vom anderen" for "von anderen," with Pinder.

[v] Reading "da nicht schließen" for "dar nicht schließen," with Pinder.

[w] Reading "mittelbarer" for "mittelbar," with Pinder.

[x] Reading "sind die unmittelbaren Schüße" for "sind da die unmittelbaren Schüße," with Pinder.

[y] Reading "consequentiis mediatis" for "iudiciis mediis," with Pinder.

[z] Reading "nicht unterschieden" for "noch nicht unterschieden," with Pinder.

[a] the same from the same (reading "ex" for "per," with Pinder).

[b] Reading "consequentiae immediatae" for "judicia immediata," with Pinder.

[c] Reading "solche, da die" for "solche die, die," with Pinder.

is derived *per iudicia aequipollentia*, or *per iudicia subalternata*,[d] or *iudicia opposita*, or *per conversionem iudiciorum*, or *per contrapositionem*.[e]

1. [An inference] *per iudicia aequipollentia*, as has already been mentioned, is really not an inference, for *per aequipollentia* I infer one judgment from another that is identical with it. They are distinct merely as to expression, but not as to sense. In logic, however, one holds to sense, not to words[.] E.g., if I say[,] Some men are not virtuous, consequently not all men are virtuous,[f] then this is not distinct as to sense. Rather, [it is] only expressed differently, and as to sense the very same thing [is] said. Nothing is without a ground, consequently everything has a ground. These are not really immediate[g] deductions, but mere substitutions. I can substitute one of these *iudicia* in place of the other. The first division drops out, then, but one must still be able to name it.

2. *Per judicia subalternata.*[h] Here, too, the matters are not distinct. In the case of [*iudicia*] *subalternata*,[i] however, the form concerns the quantity[.] E.g., All men are mortal, consequently some are mortal. The matter is the same but the quantity is distinct, for from the universal judgment a particular judgment is made. From the universal flows the particular, for if all men are mortal, then some men are so too. 90

3. A *consequentia immediata*[j] is *per iudicia opposita* when, from a judgment with the same matter, difference of form as to quality is expressed. E.g., All men are mortal, some men are not mortal.[k] The 2nd judgment is distinct from the 1st as to quantity, 1stly (for it is particular), as to quality, 2ndly (for it is negative). Or, e.g., some men are learned, some not. These 2 are distinct merely as to quality,[l] for the one is affirmative, the other is negative[;] hence they are called *iudicia opposita*, too, because affirmation and denial are opposed to one another. *Iudicia opposita* are *opposita* in 3 ways, namely, *contradictorie opposita*, *subcontrarie opposita*, and *contrarie opposita*.

2 judgments are opposed (1.) *contradictorie*, then, when one affirms universally and the other denies[m] particularly.[3] Wherever one of them is universal, the other particular, and wherever one is always affirmative, the other is always negative. E.g., All men are mortal, some [are] not. The *oppositio contradictoria*[n] is the kind that can be called genuine opposition.[o]

[d] Reading "subalternata" for "subaltera," with Pinder.
[e] Reading "contrapositionem" for "contraoppositionem," with Pinder.
[f] Reading "Menschen sind tugendhaft, so" for "Menschen, so," with Pinder.
[g] Reading "unmittelbare" for "untelbare," with Pinder.
[h] Reading "subalternata" for "subalterna," with Pinder.
[i] Reading "subalternatis" for "subalternis," with Pinder.
[j] Reading "immediata" for "inediate," with Pinder.
[k] Reading "sterblich, einige Menschen sind nicht sterblich." for "sterblich.," with Pinder.
[l] Reading "Qualitaet" for "Quantitaet," with Pinder.
[m] Reading "verneinet" for "verneinend."
[n] Reading "oppositio contradictoria" for "compositio contradicitoria," with Pinder.
[o] Reading "Opposition" for "contradiction," with Pinder.

For every opposition actually requires that when the one is posited, the other is removed, that both cannot at the same time be denied,[p] nor both at the same time affirmed. The positing of the one always excludes the other. *Affirmando unum, negat alterum, et negando unum, affirmat alterum.*[q] One must attend to this: What do I say when I affirm universally? That the thing holds of all. If someone wants to dispute this, then he has to say that this does not belong to all but rather to some[;] consequently he contradicts the universal negation by means of the particular affirmation, and he contradicts the universal affirmation by means of the particular negation, which constitutes true opposition. Thus if the one is true, the other is false[;] both cannot be true at the same time. If the one is false, then the other is true[;] both cannot be false at the same time. Apagogical proofs are ones where I infer from the falsehood of the opposite[r] to the truth of my proposition. Because in 2 *contradictorie opposita*, when the one is false, the other is true, they have the advantage[s] of proving the truth *indirecte*. In this connection, however, one must see that the propositions are actually[t] *opposita*, for in metaphysics one can prove very many propositions if it is a matter of showing that the opposite is false, because one can always draw a lot of absurdity from the opposite of a proposition. One thereby makes use of the absurdity of the opposite in order to put forward[u] the other 91 proposition, although one really cannot prove it[v] *directe*. Everyone triumphs, in that he has proved his proposition by having refuted the other one. This comes from the fact that propositions are held to be contradictory whose contradiction[w] is only illusory, and concerning which one is not certain. Nonetheless, one can use this means of inferring that contradictory propositions provide.

2. *Subcontrarie opposita* are found between 2 particular propositions that are the same as to matter. E.g., some men are learned, some not. They are not opposed to one another in the strict sense, however, and this does not occur in the case of true[x] oppositions. They are said to be opposed to one another, however, because they are opposed as to quality, although they agree as to quantity. Why can I not infer here that if the one is true,[y] the other is false?[z] Because they are not opposed to one another

[p] Reading "verneint" for "verneinend," with Pinder.

[q] Affirming the one negates the other, negating the one affirms the other (reading "negat" for "nega" and "affirmat" for "affirma," with Pinder).

[r] "des entgegen gesezten oppositi."

[s] Reading "den Vortheil" for "die Vortheile," with Pinder.

[t] Reading "wirklich" for "wilkürlich," with Pinder.

[u] "stoßen."

[v] Reading "ihn" for "sie."

[w] Reading "Contradiction" for "contradictionen," with Pinder.

[x] Reading "wahren" for "stricten," with Pinder.

[y] Reading "wahr" for "falsch," with Pinder.

[z] Reading "falsch" for "wahr," with Pinder.

stricte, in such a way that the one denies exactly what the other affirms. For if I say of a few that they are learned, then I have not said this same thing of the few of whom I say that they are unlearned, [not] of all, but rather only of the few, of whom I say that they are learned[a][,] only of a few. Accordingly, I simply cannot infer from the truth[b] of the one to the falsehood[c] of the other *per subcontrarie opposita*. Both cannot at the same time[d] be false, however; for if the one is false, that some men are learned, then the other must be true, that some are not learned. Both cannot be false, but both can well be true. Because both can be true, then, nothing can be inferred therefrom. I can of course infer that if the one is false, the other is true, but not that if the one is true, the other is false.

3. In the case of a *iudicium contrarie oppositum*, the opposition is universal, and the one *judicium* affirmative, the 2nd negative. The matter remains the same, however, as usual. E.g., All men are learned, no man is learned. These two judgments can both be false, because each judgment says more than is required for opposition. Of the proposition, All men are learned, the opposition is, Some men are not learned. He who says, then, No man is learned, says more than he should oppose, this is the source of the imperfection. Thus I can infer that both cannot possibly be true, but both can be false. The propositions are thus the opposite of the *subcontrarie opposita*[.]

4. *Per conversionem iudiciorum.* This *consequentia immediata* concerns the relation of judgments. I infer from a *iudicium conversum*[e] its *iudicium convertens*[f] if, while preserving the concepts, I infer from a judgment in such a way that what was the subject in the *judicium conversum*[g] becomes the predicate here.4 E.g., All men are mortal, consequently some mortals are men. All *conversio* is either *conversio simpliciter talis* or *per accidens*.[h] In the case of conversion, the *iudicium* is not altered[i] as to quality, and as the *conversum*[j] is, so must the *convertens*[k] be, too. It can be altered merely as to quantity and relation, then. In conversions, then, the differences are that the *convertens*[l] is the same as or different from the *conversum*[m] 92

[a] Reading "gelehrt" for "ungelehrt."
[b] Reading "Wahrheit" for "Falschheit," with Pinder.
[c] Reading "Falschheit" for "Wahrheit," with Pinder.
[d] Reading "nicht zugleich" for "nicht aber zugleich," with Pinder.
[e] Reading "converso" for "convertente," with Pinder.
[f] Reading "convertens" for "conversum," with Pinder.
[g] Reading "converso" for "convertente," with Pinder.
[h] conversion such that it is simple [or] by accident.
[i] Reading "nicht verändert" for "verändert," with Pinder.
[j] Reading "conversum" for "convertens," with Pinder.
[k] Reading "convertens" for "conversum," with Pinder.
[l] Reading "convertens" for "conversum," with Pinder.
[m] Reading "converso" for "converte," with Pinder.

as to quantity.[n] E.g., if it is different, then it is a *conversio per accidens*[;] but if the quantity[o] remains, so that, e.g., from one universal judgment another universal is converted, then it is *conversio simpliciter talis*[;] e.g., All men are mortal, consequently some mortals are men. Here the quantity[p] is different, hence it is a *conversio per accidens*. But this: No man is without enemies, consequently nothing without enemies is a man, is then *simpliciter talis*. Universal affirmative[q] propositions may never be converted[r] except *per accidens*. A universal negative judgment may always be converted *simpliciter*, however[;] e.g., All men are mortal[;] here I do not infer, consequently all mortals are men, but rather some mortals are men, and this because the subject is always contained under the sphere[s] of the predicate. In universal affirmative judgments, accordingly, the subject is a part of the sphere of the predicate[;] consequently I will say: the concept of men belongs only to some mortals, because only a part of the sphere of the predicate lies in the subject[;] consequently I can only convert *per accidens* here. Universal negative[t] judgments are converted *simpliciter*[;] because 2 concepts contradict one another in the whole extension, *b* contradicts *a*, as well as[u] *a* contradicts *b*. All particular judgments may be converted *simpliciter*, be they affirmative or negative[.] E.g., Some men are learned, consequently some learned beings are men, in which case they remain the same in sense.

5. *In the case of the consequentia immediata per contra positionem*, as in that of[v] conversion, a *metathesis terminorum*[w] is performed, but in such a way[x] that the quality is also altered at the same time.[y] All universal affirmative judgments may be contraposed. All men are mortal, nothing that is not mortal is a man.

We find, then, that in the case of the *consequentia immediata*, the alteration concerns only the form, and that *quoad qualitatem*[z] there are the *iudicia opposita*, *quoad relationem*[a] there is *conversio*. Contraposition concerns merely the modality of judgments, for it indicates nothing but the necessity of an affirmative judgment. If I have maintained a proposition as

[n] Reading "Quantitaet" for "Qualitaet," with Pinder.
[o] Reading "quantitaet" for "qualitaet," with Pinder.
[p] Reading "Quantitaet" for "Qualitaet," with Pinder.
[q] Reading "bejahende" for "besondre," with Pinder.
[r] Reading "umkehren" for "umdrehen."
[s] Reading "der Sphäre" for "den Spaehren," with Pinder.
[t] Reading "Allgemein verneinende" for "Verneinde."
[u] Reading "sowohl" for "wohl," with Pinder.
[v] Reading "wie bei" for "außer," with Pinder.
[w] transposition of terms.
[x] Reading "vorgenommen, aber so" for "vorgenommen, so," with Pinder.
[y] Omitting "ZE: Alle Menschen sind sterblich, also einiges nicht sterbliches ist kein Mensch.," with Pinder.
[z] as to quality.
[a] as to relation.

true, then through contraposition I make it undeniable,[b] in that I say, because it is true, it is thus undeniable.[c] E.g., if the proposition, All men are mortal, is to express necessity, then one would have to say, What is not mortal is not a man. Here one sees how nicely it is confirmed that these 4 functions of the understanding manifest themselves in the 4 kinds of alterations[d] of judgment, and one sees at the same time how nicely the ancients, in this division, have exhausted[e] all the *actus* of the understanding that occur in the possible alterations of judgments.

All *consequentiae immediatae* have the peculiarity that in them no subsumption under universal rules can occur except what would be[f] tautological. Because, however,[g] every tautological proposition would be empty, one simply omits it. E.g., All men are mortal, some men are men, hence some men are mortal.[h] On account of this, many logicians also say that immediate inferences are all short inferences of reason[;] they really are not, however, because a tautological subsumption is not a true subsumption.

93

Of Inferences of Reason[.] An inference of the understanding was[i] not inferred *per notam intermediam*, because the alteration lay only in form, the matter remained[j] the same. If I say, however, All men are mortal, consequently Cajus is mortal, then here a wholly new concept appears, which is not contained in the first judgment at all. Here I see, then, that I must have an intermediate judgment in order to be able to say that Cajus is mortal. I must presuppose, namely, that Cajus is a man. Cajus must lie under the principal concept of men, then, for otherwise I could not infer: hence Cajus is mortal[;] Cajus is a man[k] is the intermediate judgment and contains what must be cognized *per consequentiam mediatem*.[l] An inference of reason, or[m] a mediate inference, is where one judgment is combined with the other by means of an intermediate judgment; or an inference of reason is the truth of a judgment through the subsumption of its condition under universal rules[.][n] The concept of man must lie at the basis in the

[b] Reading "unleugbar" for "umlechtbar," with Pinder.
[c] Reading "unleugbar" for "umlechtbar," with Pinder.
[d] Reading "4 Arten von Veränderungen" for "4 Arten, und bey den Veränderungen," with Pinder.
[e] Reading "erschöpft" for "geschöpft," with Pinder.
[f] Reading "würde" for "würden," with Pinder.
[g] Reading "Weil aber" for "Weil also," with Pinder.
[h] Reading "Alle Menschen sind sterblich, einige Menschen sind Menschen," for "Alle Menschen sind sterblich," in accordance with Pinder's suggestion.
[i] Reading "wurde" for "würde," with Pinder.
[j] Reading "blieb" for "bleibe," with Pinder.
[k] Reading "Cajus is sterblich, Cajus ist ein Mensh" for "Cajus ist ein Mensch," with Pinder.
[l] Reading "mediatem" for "immediatem," with Pinder.
[m] Reading "oder" for "denn," with Pinder.
[n] Reading "allgemeinen Regel" for "andern Urteil," with Pinder.

case of Cajus, for if this does not lie at the basis, then I cannot say of Cajus that the truth holds of him as of other men.

In the case of inferences of reason, then, there occurs (1.) A rule, or the $major_{\mathrm{L}}$; sometimes, when it is the highest rule, it is called a *maxima*, or the rule of action[;] hence we can call every little rule a $major_{\mathrm{L}}$, and consequently this name from the ancient logicians is quite suitable. We can infer another judgment from the rule even without subsumption, and this occurs in the *consequentia immediata*. (2.) The *minor propositio* is the subsumption of the cognition under the condition of the rule. Every rule has its condition, under which it can be affirmed or denied. Here the condition of man is affirmed through[o] Cajus. If something is subsumed under a condition, then this is as much as to say that the predicate of the subsumption applies[;][p] to subsume means to cognize that something is contained under the condition of the rule. (3.) The proposition where the predicate of the rule is either affirmed or denied of the subsumption is the conclusion, the inference. Every inference of reason has two premises and a conclusion, then. The conclusion[q] is the proposition that is to be inferred from the first ones.[r] An inference of reason also has 2 premises, however, because 1stly there is a rule ($major_{\mathrm{L}}$)[;] then I must[s] also subsume under the condition of the rule, however, in that I say of what I have subsumed thereunder the very same thing that the rule says universally of its condition.[t]

The conclusion actually does not constitute a part of the inference, for if something follows from two given things, that which follows may not be taken as a part along with them; thus, e.g., if marks already suffice for a definition, then we may not cite the deduction from the marks. In an 94 inference of reason the conclusion is given just as soon as the *consequentia* from the premises is given. Thus we have only to weigh the truth of the two premises and the correctness of the *consequentia*. The truth of the two premises does not constitute the truth of the conclusion;[u] only the correctness of the *consequentia* from the premises does. All men are animals, All oxen are animals, are true premises, only the conclusion, All men are oxen, is nonetheless false. When, however, I have nothing to object to in either, then there is nothing more to object.[v] In an inference of reason one must not deny the conclusion, then, but one must reject either one of the premises or the *consequentia* from the concepts, i.e., he must say that what

[o] Reading "durch" for "wer," with Pinder.
[p] Reading "komt dazu" for "komt der Regel zu."
[q] Reading "Conclusion. Die Conclusion ist" for "Conclusion ist," with Pinder.
[r] Reading "den ersten" for "der ersten," with Pinder.
[s] Reading "ist (maior), dann muß" for "ist, den Major muß," with Pinder.
[t] Reading "ihrer Bedingung" for "ihren Bedingungen," with Pinder.
[u] Reading "Conclusion" for "Consequentz," with Pinder.
[v] Reading "einzuwenden" for "zu erinnern."

is derived from the premises[w] does not follow. The matter of inferences of reason is the premises, the form is the *consequentia.*[x]

Here we must recall that the matter of a categorical proposition consists of two concepts,[y] the matter of a hypothetical judgment of 2 or more propositions. The matter of an inference of reason consists of 2 judgments, however. Now if we want to divide inferences of reason, we cannot divide them as to quantity[z] into universal and particular inferences, for the major is only universal, in accordance with a special rule. The conclusion may be a universal[a] or a particular proposition, for nothing depends on the conclusion; rather, it depends on the way in which the *consequentia* of one judgment is drawn from another. There is no difference among inferences, furthermore, as to whether they are distinct as to quality, are affirmative or negative. They are not divided as to modality, either, into problematic, assertoric, and apodeictic propositions, because all inferences of reason have an apodeictic proposition as conclusion. For if I bring something forth through an inference of reason, then it is on that account necessary. Propositions can be true but contingently[b] true. E.g., that men in Africa are black is a true, contingent proposition, and it cannot be an inference, and is therefore not necessary.[c] Since they contain necessity, they are always apodeictic. Consequently inferences of reason cannot be divided at all, or they must be divided according to the differing relation of cognition, and they really are divided in accordance with this. All inferences of reason are either categorical or hypothetical or disjunctive inferences of reason. A categorical inference of reason is one whose[d] *major propositio* is a categorical proposition, i.e., where the relation of subject to predicate is indicated. A hypothetical inference of reason is one where the *major*$_{L}$ is a hypothetical proposition, and which expresses the relation of a ground to the consequence. A disjunctive inference of reason is one where the *major propositio* is a disjunctive proposition, and expresses the members of the division, which taken together constitute[e] the cognition. The division rests on the relation that is found in the *major*$_{L}$, then. Our author and all logicians talk as if all inferences of reason were categorical, or as if the *major*$_{L}$ contained nothing more than the relation of subject to predicate. This he calls an ordinary inference,[f] but the hypothetical and disjunctive inferences he calls extraordinary. But there is no

95

[w] Reading “Praemissen” for “praecisen,” with Pinder.
[x] Reading “Consequentz” for “Conclusion,” with Pinder.
[y] Reading “Begriffen” for “Urtheilen,” with Pinder.
[z] Reading “Quantitaet” for “Qualitaet,” with Pinder.
[a] Reading “ein allgemeiner” for “einer allgemeinen,” with Pinder.
[b] Reading “aber zufälliger Weise” for “oder gefälliger Weise,” with Pinder.
[c] Reading “deshalb nicht nothwendig” for “deshalb nothwendig,” with Pinder.
[d] Reading “dessen” for “der,” with Pinder.
[e] Reading “ausmachen” for “ausmacht.”
[f] Reading “Schluß” for “Schlüße,” with Pinder.

ground for this, for the last are just as ordinary as the categorical, since they are a wholly different way of inferring.

Since our author regards categorical inferences of reason as the essential ones, then, he proceeds, and all other logicians with him,[g] in the following way. In every categorical inference the *major*$_{\text{L}}$ is a categorical proposition. The *minor propositio* contains the subsumption of a concept under the condition of the *major propositio*, and the conclusion says of what I have subsumed in the minor what the rule says of the condition. In[h] every inference of reason what matters is the truth of the conclusion. This is a judgment that consists of two concepts. Now because the predicate cannot be immediately cognized of the subject, a middle concept must be involved. For if I say, Cajus is mortal, then I do not cognize immediately that he is mortal; rather, a middle concept[i] is involved, to which mortality belongs immediately,[j] so that I regard mortality as a mark of Cajus. I infer, then, Mortality belongs to man in general,[k] is a predicate of all men. To be a man is a concept of Cajus[;] consequently Cajus is mortal. There arises an inference of reason, then, since two *notae remotae* are combined through a *nota intermedia*, or a *medius terminus*. Every inference of reason involves 3 *termini*, then: subject, predicate, and *nota intermedia* or *medius terminus*. The logicians have named these 3 *termini* differently[;] the predicate of the conclusion is called the *terminus major*, because every predicate has a larger sphere than its subject. The subject of the conclusion is called the *terminus minor*, on the ground that it is contained under the sphere of the predicate[;] and the *nota intermedia* is called the *terminus medius*.

Furthermore, the logicians say that in every inference of reason the first proposition is called the *major*$_{\text{L}}$ because the predicate of the conclusion is contained in the first proposition. All men are mortal, and since the subject of the conclusion is the *terminus minor*, one calls the 2nd premise the *propositio minor*, because the *terminus minor* is contained therein. These names[l] do not apply to all syllogisms, however, but only to categorical ones[;] they do not suit hypothetical ones, because there the *propositio major* does not have 2 *termini*, but rather 2 *iudicia*[;] and in this way, then, the hypothetical inference would not have a *major*$_{\text{L}}$. The *major*$_{\text{L}}$ of a hypothetical inference runs thus. E.g., If God is just, the persistently evil will be punished. Here there are not 2 *termini*, but rather 2 propositions. From this it follows that the logicians' definition of *propositio major* and

96

[g] Reading "ihm" for "ihne."

[h] Reading "habe, was die Regel von der Bedingung sagt. In" for "habe, die Bedingung In," with Pinder.

[i] Reading "Mittelbegrif" for "unmittelbarer Begrif."

[j] Reading "unmittelbar" for "auch," with Pinder.

[k] Reading "komt dem Menschen überhaupt zu" for "komt dem Menschen Überhaupt zu seyn," with Pinder.

[l] Reading "Diese Benennungen gehen" for "Diese Benennung geht," with Pinder.

minor$_L$ simply cannot be admitted, and that[m] what we have said is more correct. The *propositio major* expresses a universal rule, the *minor*$_L$ subsumes under the condition of the rule,[n] and the conclusion affirms or denies the predicate of the rule. One can say, then, that even in[o] the *ratiocinium categoricum* the judgment that is[p] compared with the *medius terminus* is called the *major propositio*, because it happens that it[q] is always the rule. *Generaliter*, then, the *major propositio* is the rule. The matter of all inferences of reason is judgments, whose matter is concepts. In the categorical inference the matter consists of 3 concepts. In the hypothetical inference even more concepts occur. E.g., If God is just, then the persistently Godless will be punished. Here there are 4 *termini*, and here there is no division into *major*$_L$ and *minor terminus*.

Does the conclusion also occur in the *census*$_L$ of the matter? No, for if the premises are correct, and the *consequentia* from them is inferred correctly, then *eo ipso* it is true too. The truth is inferred from the premises, consequently it is not the material of the inference but only the deduction from the material. The matter consists of the two premises, then. The conclusion is not a part but only a deduction therefrom. For if we want to have constituent parts, then we do not want to have the consequences therefrom. Besides the matter, the *consequentia* is to be taken into consideration. The correct *consequentia* from the premises constitutes the form of the inference[;] on this account, one will never make an objection against the conclusion in a disputation;[r] rather, when the opponent has expounded an inference, then the respondent must say, *Syllogismus errat in materia* or *in forma*,[s] because unless something is mistaken either in the premises, i.e., in the matter, or in the *consequentia*, then the conclusion is correct.

In regard to truth, the *syllogismus* is divided into *verus et erroneus sive falsus*.[t] A *ratiocinium* can be false, in such a way that the error lies either *in materia* or *in forma*. *Ratiocinium laborat vitio in materia*[u] if one of the premises is false, or it is false *in forma* if the *consequentia* is drawn falsely from true premises.

Every *ratiocinium* is *vel purum, vel hybridum*, a pure inference, or a mixed or bastard one. A *ratiocinium hybridum* is when, besides the 3 propositions that constitute the inference, a further *consequentia immediata* is mixed in.

[m] Reading "und daß" for "undaß," with Pinder.
[n] Reading "under der Bedingung der Regel" for "unter der Regel der Bedingung," with Pinder.
[o] Reading "daß selbst in" for "daß die Ursach, weshalb selbst in," with Pinder.
[p] Reading "das Urtheil, das" for "das Urtheil, das Urtheil, das," with Pinder.
[q] Reading "es" for "er," with Pinder.
[r] Reading "Disputation" for "Disposition," with Pinder.
[s] The syllogism is wrong in matter [or] in form (reading "errat" for "erat," with Pinder).
[t] true, and erroneous or false.
[u] The inference suffers from an error in its matter.

E.g., Every substance has[v] a power to act. Every spirit is a substance, 97 consequently every spirit has a power to act, hence something that has a power to act is a spirit. Here the last proposition is converted *per accidens* and does not belong to the inference. Or one mixes something in in the middle. E.g., No thinking being is composite, consequently (*consequentia immediata*) nothing composite is a thinking being, *atqui*[w] all bodies are composite, consequently no bodies are thinking beings. Here we have 4 propositions. The 2nd proposition, which is the *propositio convertens*,[x] is actually the *major*$_L$ here, because according to a special rule, the *medius terminus in majori* is not the predicate, as in the 1st proposition. I have taken a proposition, then, and made of its *convertens*[y] the *major*$_L$, and from this composed the rest of the inference. These would be 4 propositions, then, of which, however, no *ratiocinium* can consist, and although the *syllogismus* is correct as to content and as to the *consequentia*, it is nonetheless not a *purus*, but rather a *hybridus*. For inferences of the understanding or *consequentiae immediatae* are in fact distinct from inferences of reason and are of a wholly different kind. This division is especially needed, then, just because we will show subsequently that all the artifice of the ancients with the 4 figures (excluding the first) consists merely in making *ratiocinia hybrida*, in that they falsely present as an inference of reason what is produced through one or more *consequentiae immediatae*, which are thought, however, only *tacite*.

The author speaks now of the principle of the principles of inferences of reason, of the formal principles, of course, for the material *principium* is always the *propositio major*. He mentions in this connection the principle of contradiction[;] this is to be regarded, of course, as the formal *principium* of all cognition, but it comes under consideration in connection with judgments and not with inferences, for it indicates that a predicate that contradicts a thing cannot be attributed to it[;] it holds[z] for propositions, then, and not for inferences of reason. There are as many formal *principia* of inferences of reason, then, as there are inferences of reason themselves. There are principles, accordingly, for categorical, hypothetical, and disjunctive inferences.

The *principium* of all categorical inferences (or as the author says, of ordinary inferences) is the *dictum de omni et nullo*, since I infer from the universal to the particular. Basically, however, this is not the principle of categorical, but also of all inferences of reason. For one can never infer otherwise than from the universal to the particular. For an inference of reason is the cognition of the truth of a cognition that stands under the 98 condition of a universal rule. If the condition of the rule occurs, then that

v Reading "hat" for "ist."

w but.

x Reading "propositio convertens" for "propositio conversa"; see MS pg. 91, above.

y Reading "convertens" for "conversum."

z Reading "gilt" for "gehört."

which stands under the condition of the rule must be just as true as what the rule says of the condition. E.g., If God is just, then the persistently godless will be punished. The condition of justice occurs, consequently the punishment occurs too. Thus it is also in the case of the disjunctive inference, and the inference from the universal to the particular is a *generales principium* of inferences of reason, and not of categorical inferences alone. However, if one explains the *dictum de omni et nullo* as the scholastics usually do, *Quidquid valet de genere vel specie valet quoque de omnibus sub isto genere vel specie contentis*,[5] then it can be regarded only as a *principium* of categorical inferences of reason, because here only the relation between a subject and predicate[a] is indicated. For this is as much as to say that what is affirmed or denied of the whole of the subject is affirmed or denied of all the other things that stand under the subject. The *minor*$_L$:[b] This or that also stands under the subject, *ergo*$_L$ it is affirmed or denied. Here there is merely a relation of concepts, namely, of subject to predicate, consequently it can be regarded in this relation[c] as a *principium* of categorical inferences. The *principium* of categorical inferences we now want to explain[d] in such a way that we will also, at the same time, provide a proof of it. A proposition that is to become the *principium* of the possibility of inferences of reason[e] cannot in turn be proved, for since it[f] lies at the ground of the possibility of all inferences of reason, one would have to presuppose it in order to prove it, in order to prove its possibility[g] based on it,[h] which would be an obvious circle. This highest *principium* of all categorical inferences, through which the *dictum de omni et nullo* can also be proved, is this: *nota notae est nota rei ipsius et repugnans notae, repugnans rei ipsi.*[i] What belongs to the mark of a thing belongs to all the things[j] that are contained under it.[6] E.g., nothing composite is a thinking thing, *atqui* all bodies are composite, consequently no body is a thinking thing, i.e., to be composite contradicts all thinking things. To be composite is a mark of bodies, *repugnans notae*, which is contradicted by the thinking being,[k]

[a] Reading "zwischen einem subiect und praedicat" for "einem subiect und praedicat," with Pinder.

[b] Reading "stehen. Minor:" for "stehen minor.," with Pinder.

[c] Reading "Beziehung" for "Bejahung," with Pinder.

[d] Reading "erklären" for "erlauben," with Pinder.

[e] Reading "Vernunftschlüße" for "Vernunft," with Pinder.

[f] Reading "er" for "es," with Pinder.

[g] Reading "seine Möglichkeit" for "eine Möglichkeit," with Pinder.

[h] Reading "aus ihm" for "aus ihn," with Pinder.

[i] The mark of a mark is a mark of the thing itself, and what conflicts with the mark conflicts with the thing itself.

[j] Reading "komt allen Dingen zu" for "komt allen Merkmaalen eines Dinges zu," with Pinder.

[k] Reading "welchem das denkende Wesen wiederstreitet" for "welches dem denkenden Wesen wiederstreitet," with Pinder.

consequently *repugnans rei ipsi*, consequently to be a thinking being contradicts all bodies. E.g., an affirmative inference. If one takes the proposition, All bodies are divisible, and it does not seem to be enough to show that 99 divisibility is a mark of body, then one seeks a *nota intermedia*, a *nota notae*. This immediate mark is being composite, and by means of this being composite I know that because it holds of all bodies,[l] divisibility must also hold of all bodies. Divisibility[,] a *nota notae*, is a *nota rei ipsius*, a mark of bodies[.] E.g., a negative[m] inference. No body is indivisible. To be indivisible contradicts all that is composite, and composite contradicts all that is divisible, consequently it also contradicts all bodies themselves,[7] *repugnans notae repugnat rei ipsi*. From this highest principle the *dictum de omni et nullo* is derived. The *genus*$_L$ and the *species*$_L$ are always the *nota* of the thing, the universal mark of things that are contained under them. Now *quidquid competit generi*,[n] i.e.,[o] every *nota* of the *genus*$_L$, or in other words the *nota notae*, is a *nota rei ipsius*[;] i.e., what belongs to the *genus*$_L$ belongs to the things contained under it, or to the *species*$_L$ of things that stand under it. These two propositions are the principles of all categorical inferences of reason, accordingly, and in fact are the highest principles, so that they in turn may not be proved, and cannot be.

In every conditioned judgment[p] there is an *antecedens* and a *consequens*[;] the *principium* of all affirmative hypothetical inferences, accordingly, is *a positione antecedentis, ad positionem consequentis valet consequentia*.[q] The *antecedens* remains that, *quo posito*[r] *ponitur conseqens*,[s] and the *principium* of negative hypothetical inferences is[:] *remoto consequente*,[t] *tollitur antecedens*,[u] if I remove the *consequens*[v] then the *antecedens*[w] cannot remain either.

The *principium* of all disjunctive inferences is, in every disjunctive proposition one can infer[x] from the truth of a member[y] to the falsehood of all other members, and from the falsehood of all other members to the truth of the one true one. This is the definition of all disjunctive inferences,[z] which consequently may not be proved in turn.

[l] Reading "Körpern" for "theilbaren," with Pinder.
[m] Reading "verneinender" for "verneinder," with Pinder.
[n] whatever agrees with the genus.
[o] Reading "d.i." for "die," with Pinder.
[p] Reading "Urtheil" for "Begrif," with Pinder.
[q] From the positing of the antecedent to the positing of the consequence the *consequentia* is valid.
[r] Reading "posito" for "positio," with Pinder.
[s] [that] by positing which the consequence is posited.
[t] Reading "consequente" for "antecedente," with Pinder.
[u] Reading "antecedens" for "consequens," with Pinder.
[v] Reading "consequens" for "antecedens," with Pinder.
[w] Reading "antecedens" for "consequens," with Pinder.
[x] Reading "geschloßen werden kann" for "geschloßen worden."
[y] Reading "eines Gliedes" for "des Grundes," with Pinder.
[z] Reading "Schlüße" for "Sätze," with Pinder.

Of the figures of inferences[;] the position of the *termini* in the premises of a categorical inference of reason constitutes the 4 figures. These 3 *termini* are the *terminus major*, *minor*, and *medius*. The premises are the two propositions, of which the one contains the *major terminus*, the other the *minor*$_L$[;] but because two *termini* are contained in every judgment, in the major there must also be a *terminus medius*[;] and since the *minor propositio*[a] must also have 2 *termini*, the *medius* must also be contained in it. The *medius terminus* appears in both premises, then, and in the four figures what matters is the position of the *medius terminus*. 100

It can stand 1. in the *locus subiecti* in the first premise and in the *locus praedicati* in the second, and that is the 1st figure[.]

2. it can stand in the *locus praedicati* in both premises, the second figure[.]

3. it can stand in the *locus subiecti* in both premises, the 3rd figure, and

4. it can stand in the *locus praedicati* in the first proposition and in the *locus subiecti* in the second, and this is the 4th figure.

The 4 positions[b] of the *medius terminus* can be cognized according to the following table.[8]

Fig. I.	Fig. II	Fig. III.
Med. term. Praed.	*Praed. med. term.*	*Med. term. Praed.*
Subiect med. term.	*Subiect med. term.*	*Med. term. Subiect*

Fig. IV.
Praed. med. term.
Med. term. Subiect

One sees quite well that the fourth is the first wholly converted, and the 3rd is the 2nd converted. Example *of the 1st figure*: The conclusion is to be, No body is a thinking substance. The *medius terminus* is because a body is composite[;] body is the *terminus minor*, thinking substance the *terminus major*. The inference, then, will run thus: Nothing composite is a thinking substance[;] here the *terminus medius* stands in the *locus subjecti*[;] *atqui*, all bodies are composite[;] here the *medius terminus* stands in the *locus praedicati*. *Ergo*$_L$, No body is a thinking substance. The predicate of the conclusion is the *major terminus*, the subject the *terminus minor*.

Example *in the 2nd figure*: The proposition is again to be, No body is a thinking being[;] *medius terminus*, because it is composite. Here the *terminus medius* must stand in the *locus praedicati* in both premises[;] hence the *major terminus*, thinking being, will be the subject in the *major*$_L$, and the 101

[a] Reading "propositio" for "Terminus," with Pinder.

[b] Reading "positionen" for "propositiones," with Pinder.

minor terminus[,] body, will be the subject in the *minor*$_{\mathrm{L}}$. Hence, no thinking being is composite, *atqui* all bodies are composite, *ergo*$_{\mathrm{L}}$ no body is a thinking being. Example *in the 3rd figure*. The proposition is: Some who are virtuous are imperfect[;] the *medius terminus*, because they are men. The *medius terminus*[,] man[,] will stand in the *locus subiecti* in both premises. The *major terminus* will be the predicate in the *major propositio*, and the *minor terminus* will be the predicate in the *minor*$_{\mathrm{L}}$. Thus: All men are imperfect, some men are virtuous, consequently some who are virtuous are imperfect. *Example in the 4th figure*[:] The conclusion is to be: Something that has a power to act is a spirit[;] the *medius terminus*, because it is a substance. The *medius terminus*[,] substance, will be the predicate in the *major*$_{\mathrm{L}}$, the subject in the *minor*$_{\mathrm{L}}$. Spirit will be the subject in the *major*$_{\mathrm{L}}$ and having a power to act[c] will be the predicate in the *minor*$_{\mathrm{L}}$. Thus: Every spirit is a substance, every substance has a power to act, hence something that has a power to act is a spirit.

All inferences of reason must have as their basis the correct rule: that I can proceed from a *nota remota per notam intermediam*[d] to the thing, according to the rule above:[e] *nota notae est nota rei ipsius*, in the case of affirmative inferences. The *major*$_{\mathrm{L}}$ says this is a *nota*, the *minor*$_{\mathrm{L}}$ says this *nota* belongs to a thing, *ergo*$_{\mathrm{L}}$ what is attributed in the *major*$_{\mathrm{L}}$ to the mark of the thing must be attributed to the thing itself in the conclusion. And in negative inferences of reason the rule holds: *repugnans notae, repugnat rei ipsi.*[f] E.g., No body is a thinking substance, because it is composite. 102 The *major*$_{\mathrm{L}}$ says that a thinking substance[g] contradicts all being composite. The *minor*$_{\mathrm{L}}$ says that being composite is a mark of bodies, the *conclusio* that what contradicts the mark of the thing contradicts the thing itself. Being composite contradicts thinking, [but] being composite is a mark of body, consequently thinking being contradicts body. Or an affirmative example: All who are learned are mortal[;] to be mortal is a mark of all men, and to be a man is a mark of all who are learned. Conclusion: hence to be mortal is also a mark of all who are learned, *nam nota notae est nota rei ipsius*.

The *terminus medius* has the position of a *nota intermedia* only when it stands in the *locus subjecti* in the *major*$_{\mathrm{L}}$ and in the *locus praedicati* in the *minor*, otherwise it never does. We saw this in our example in the 1st figure. Thinking contradicts body[;] thinking is the *nota remota*, this contradicts the *nota intermedia*, being composite, consequently it must also contradict body.[h] In the *major*$_{\mathrm{L}}$ it has to be the subject because I want to say of

[c] Reading "eine Kraft zu handeln haben" for "Kraft zu handeln, seyn,."

[d] from a remote mark through an intermediate mark.

[e] Reading "obigen Regel" for "Übrigen Regel," with Pinder.

[f] What conflicts with a mark conflicts with the thing itself.

[g] Reading "substantz" for "substantz,".

[h] Reading "Körper" for "denkenden Wesen," with Pinder.

the predicate that it belongs to or contradicts the subject. In the *minor*$_{\text{L}}$ it has to be the predicate, because it is a *nota* of the *terminus minor*, and a *nota* is always just exactly a predicate[;] consequently[i] if the *medius terminus* is to represent a[j] *nota intermedia*, it must be placed as it stands in the 1st figure. In the 2nd figure it simply does not stand in the position of a[k] *nota intermedia* in the *major*$_{\text{L}}$, for there the *nota remota* is supposed to be compared with the *intermedia*; hence it has to stand in the *locus praedicati*, because a *nota* is exactly a predicate. If we recall our example above, then we see that it does not follow as in the first figure, and we make leaps. In both cases we compare thinking and being a body with being composite,[l] and hence we do not infer from the *nota remota* through the *intermedia* to the thing. If being composite is to be a *nota intermedia*, then it has to stand 103 in the *locus subiecti* in the *major*$_{\text{L}}$[;] for if everything stands in proper order, then I say that what contradicts the mark contradicts the thing itself. All bodies are composite, consequently thinking contradicts body. *Repugnans notae, repugnat rei ipsi.* So too in the 3rd figure[;] I infer in our example above from man to the imperfection of those who are virtuous. Through leaps, and not at all through a *nota intermedia*. The *minor propositio* would really have to be converted *simpliciter*, so that the *intermedia* would obtain the *locus praedicati*. Thus all men are imperfect, some who are virtuous are men,[m] consequently some[n] who are virtuous are imperfect. The difference in the 4th figure comes because I slip a *consequentia immediata* into a *ratiocinium*, and thereby make a *ratiocinium hybridum*[;] and from this it follows that we always infer in the 1st figure, that we only need a *metathesis terminorum*[o] in thought, whereby reason is brought again to the first figure. E.g., the inference in the 2nd figure: No thinking being is composite, conversely, nothing composite is a thinking being, *consequentia immediata*[;] *atqui* all bodies are composite, consequently no body is a thinking being. Here I have converted *simpliciter* and have thereby reduced the inference to the 1st figure. E.g., our inference in the 3rd figure[;] the *major*$_{\text{L}}$, All men are imperfect, stands as in the first and remains[;] the *minor*$_{\text{L}}$, Some men are virtuous, is converted *simpliciter*. Some who are virtuous are men[;] consequently some who are virtuous are imperfect. The *minor terminus*[p] is transported[;] thus it[q] comes to stand in the position

[i] Reading “als praedicat folglich” for “als praedicat folglich, folglich,” with Pinder.
[j] Reading “eine” for “ein,” with Pinder.
[k] Reading “einer” for “eines,” with Pinder.
[l] Reading “mit dem zusammengesezt seyn” for “mit dem zusammengesezt seyn des einen praedicat.”
[m] Reading “einige Tugendhafte sind Menschen” for “einige Menschen sind Tugendhafte,” with Pinder.
[n] Reading “einige” for “alle,” with Pinder.
[o] transposition of terms (reading “Metathesis” for “Mathesis,” with Pinder).
[p] Reading “Minor terminus” for “Minor: terminus,” with Pinder.
[q] Reading “er” for “minor,” with Pinder.

of[r] the *nota intermedia*. In the 4th figure several alterations occur: firstly, the *minor*$_L$ is made the *major*$_L$. Thus I infer: Every substance has a power to act, every spirit is a substance, consequently every spirit has a power to act. 2ndly the conclusion is converted *per accidens*. Thus I say: Something that has a power to act is a spirit. I see from obscure perceptions that I have to infer in this way, because otherwise there would be no sense[s] in the inference, and I would not know how I came to it.

Inferences in the last 3[t] figures are all correct inferences, but they are not logically perfect, insofar as the *ratiocinium* is not *purum* but rather *hybridum*, since a *consequentia immediata* has slipped in[;] and although I can include such a *consequentia immediata*, it is nonetheless not a real *ratiocinium*. We see, then, that the first figure prevails through all the other figures, that the *medius terminus* must always be the *nota intermedia*, that one can bring it into this position[u] in the 3 remaining figures through conversion, *simpliciter* or *per accidens*, or *per metathesin* in the 4th figure.

Of the modi of inferences of reason[.] The *modus* in an inference of reason consists of the qualities and quantities[v] of the 3 propositions of an inference. Because the quality and quantity are indicated by the 4 letters

104 A:E:I:O, we will present[w] them in every inference by 3 of these letters, because there are only three propositions. E.g., A:A:A, i.e., the *maior* is *universaliter affirmans*, the *minor*$_L$ *universaliter affirmans*, the *conclusio universaliter affirmans*[;] one expresses this *bArbArA*, and adds the consonants only for the sake of making it sound good, although they mean nothing. Or E.A.E., i.e., the *maior* is *universaliter*[x] *negans*, the *minor*$_L$ *universaliter affirmans*, the *conclusio universaliter*[y] *negans*; or A.I.I.[,] *universaliter*[z] *affirmans, particulariter affirmans, particulariter affirmans.*[a] E.I.O.[,] and so forth[;] one can begin with A[:] A.E.A.[,] A.E.I.[,], A.E.O.[,], *pp*;[9] because there are 4 letters, each can be altered 16 times, and there arise 64 *modi* of inferences of reason, which, however, except for a few, have no further names. According to the adjoining table.

[r] Reading "an die Stelle" for "an statt der Stelle," with Pinder.
[s] "kein Verstand."
[t] Reading "in den 3 letzten" for "in den 4," with Pinder.
[u] Reading "in diese Stellung" for "in dieser Stellung," with Pinder.
[v] Reading "Qualitäten und Quantitäten" for "Qualiteten," with Pinder.
[w] Reading "angeben" for "angegeben," with Pinder.
[x] Reading "universaliter" for "universalis," with Pinder.
[y] Reading "universaliter" for "universalis," with Pinder.
[z] Reading "universaliter" for "universalis," with Pinder.
[a] Reading "particulariter affirmans, particulariter affirmans" for "particulariter affirmans," with Pinder.

A.A.A.	I I I.	E.E E	O O O
A.E.A	I E.I.	E A E	O E O
A E.I	I E A.	E A.I.	O E I.
A.E.O	I E.O	E A O	O E A
A I E	I A.E.	E I A	O A E
A.I O.	I a O	E I O.	O A I
A A E.	I I.E.	E E A	O O E.
A O A	I O.I.	E O E	O I O
A O E	I O E.	E O A	O I E
A O I	I O.A	E O I	O I a
A O O	I O O.	E O O	O I I.
A I I.	I a a.	E I I	O A A
A.E E	I E E.	E a a.	O E E.
A I A	I I A	E I E	O A O.
A A O.	I O O.	E E O	O O I.
			O O A.

Among these many are excluded because they contradict the universal rules of inferences of reason; but in the end, then, 19 of 64 must still[b] remain, which are composed in accordance with the universal rules of inferences of reason.

The universal rules of inferences of reason are.

1. There must not be more than 3 *termini* in the inference[.]

2. The *medius terminus* must be only in the premises.

3. *Ex puris negatiuis nihil sequitur*[;][c] the ground of which is that in every inference of reason there is a rule and a subsumption under the rule;[d] now it may be affirmative or negative, but I have to subsume *affirmatiue*, for I can always say *affirmatiue* that this concept stands under the condition of the rule[.] Every proposition that says whether something stands under the rule is affirmative; accordingly, every subsumption in accordance with the nature of the inference of reason must always be affirmative. If it were negative there would be no subsumption under the condition of the rule.[e]

4. *Ex puris particularibus nihil sequitur.*[f] If there were only particular propositions, there would be no rule, since every rule must of course be universal.

5. *Conclusio sequitur partem debiliorem.*[g] The conclusion follows the part of the premises that is negative or particular and arranges itself according

[b] Reading "müssen doch am Ende noch" for "muß doch am Ende doch," with Pinder.

[c] From negatives alone nothing follows.

[d] Reading "der Regel" for "den Regeln," with Pinder.

[e] Reading "subsumzion unter der Bedingung" for "subsumzion nach der Natur der Vernunftschlüße immer bejahend seyn. Wäre sie verneinend so wäre sie gar keine subsumzion under der Bedingung," with Pinder.

[f] From particulars alone nothing follows.

[g] The conclusion follows the weaker part.

to it. The *pars debilior*[h] means a negative or a particular proposition. That the rule is certain becomes clear from the fact that if one of the premises is particular, the subsumption is certainly particular. But if I have subsumed particularly, then I can only say of some that the predicate belongs to them. The conclusion always follows the subsumption *quoad quantitatem*,[i] then. *Si praemissorum una est negatiua, conclusio etiam est negativa*[;][j] for if I say, No man is without errors, all who are virtuous are men, then the conclusion must be negative too, because the rule says that everything that is under the condition is to be denied. Hence the conclusion must contain the negation too.

Given these rules, only 19 of the remaining 64 *modi* are left, and of these 9 are also excluded, so that we have 10 *modi utili*, because among the 19 inferences of reason that it is possible to conceive, 9 are useless

105 *translationes* of the truth.

Logicians present rules in the case of every figure.[k] The rule for the first is[l] *maior sit universalis, minor affirmans.*[m] One can see, however, that the former has to be a rule for all inferences of reason, for[n] every rule must be universal. The $minor_{L}$ is the subsumption under the rule[;] every subsumption is affirmative, however, consequently the $minor_{L}$ must be *affirmans*[;] this also holds for all inferences of reason.

In the first figure we can have conclusions of any quality and quantity[;] we can have universal affirmative, universal negative, and particular affirmative and negative propositions[;] but in all the other figures only conclusions of a certain kind can be inferred, and not in every quality and quantity. In the 2nd figure the conclusion is always negative, in the 3rd it is always particular, and in the 4th figure it is always particular or negative. A universal affirmative simply may not be thought in the 4th figure. The restriction already indicates that in the inferences in other figures there are certain conditions, under which they can be brought into the first figure, and these conditions make the conclusion be restricted to certain conditions. E.g., in the 2nd figure. No thinking being is composite, all bodies are composite, consequently no body is a thinking being. In the $maior_{L}$ the *medius terminus* stands converted, and not as it is in the 1st figure[;] in the *minor* it stands correctly. If this[o] inference is to be brought into the 1st figure, then, it must be preceded by a *metathesis terminorum* in the *maior*, and the *medius terminus* must stand in the *locus subjecti*. We say,

[h] weaker part.

[i] as to quantity.

[j] If one of the premises is negative, the conclusion is negative too.

[k] Reading "bey jeder Figur" for "bey jeder Vernunft and Figur," with Pinder.

[l] Reading "Die Regel für die erste ist" for "Die Regel ist die erste," with Pinder.

[m] The major should be universal, the minor affirmative.

[n] Reading "denn" for "und," with Pinder.

[o] Reading "dieser" for "diesen," with Pinder.

then, that nothing composite is a thinking being, *atqui* all bodies are composite, consequently no body is a thinking being. Now the inference is correct. The rule of the 1st figure is, the *major*$_L$ is to be universal, hence if a *metathesis* is to occur, the transposition of the *termini* must be such that the universality is not lost. No *conversio per accidens* can take place, then, because through this the *major*$_L$ would become particular[;] consequently the *major propositio* in the 2nd figure simply cannot be affirmative, because an affirmative proposition can only be converted *per accidens*, and then the *major*$_L$ in the first figure would not come out universal. Hence in the *secunda figura* the *major*$_L$ must always be a negative proposition. One can also convert the *major*$_L$ through *contrapositiones*, for from this there always emerges[p] a negative proposition. Now it is said that *conclusio sequitur partem debiliorem*[;] where the *major*$_L$ is negative the conclusion will be negative too. The *consequentia immediata* that I draw in the 2nd figure is to contain a universal proposition. Now since an affirmative proposition can never be converted *simpliciter*, the *major*$_L$ in the 2nd figure cannot be affirmative. No affirmative proposition can arise through *metathesis*$_L$, for if an affirmative proposition is to be converted, it would have to be converted *per accidens*[;] consequently it must either be a negative proposition or, if it is affirmative, it has to[q] be contraposed[;] i.e., if the proposition will also be negative, then the conclusion will consequently always be negative. The 2nd figure does not infer purely, then, because the *major*$_L$ must always be converted, and the cause of the fact that the conclusion must always be negative lies in this, that the 2nd figure does not infer immediately 106 through its *major*$_L$, but rather by a universal negative proposition being inserted. Example in the 3rd figure. All men are imperfect, some men are virtuous, consequently some who are virtuous are imperfect. The *major*$_L$ stands correct. In the *minor*$_L$ the *medius terminus* stands incorrectly[;] here a *metathesis terminorum* must occur, then. In the first figure[r] the *minor*$_L$ is *affirmans*, consequently the transposition must occur in such a way that the proposition that comes from it is always affirmative and never negative. Hence it will not be possible to convert it *per contrapositionem*, because from this a negative proposition arises, but rather *per conversionem*. Hence the proposition that comes from this must be affirmative. Now if the *minor*$_L$[s] in the III *figura* is universal, only a particular proposition can emerge from this, because affirmative propositions may only be converted *per accidens*. If the *minor*$_L$ is particular, then it is converted *simpliciter* and remains particular. *Conclusio sequitur partem debiliorem*[;] the conclusion must always be particular, then. We see, then, that

[p] Reading "wird immer" for "wird immer wieder," with Pinder.

[q] Reading "muß . . . contraponirt werden" for "muß . . . contraponirt werden müßen," with Pinder.

[r] Reading "In der ersten Figur" for "In der Figur," with Pinder.

[s] Reading "minor" for "major," with Pinder.

the 1st figure infers in the 3rd, since[t] the *termini*[u] are transposed through a *consequentia immediata* that is inserted in thought. In the 4th figure there are no universal affirmative conclusions. Here one has to convert 2 times; one converts either both the premises or the conclusion and one premise. All logicians admit that the inference in the 4th figure is unnatural, because 2 *consequentiae immediatae* that occur in thought have to be inserted. To insert one, as occurs in the 2nd and 3rd figure, is still natural, but when one is to do it 2 times, then one finds difficulty. This is mentioned in order to show that this game of the 4 figures is nothing but an artifice for confusing, in that one hides the simple under the complicated.

To make possible the reduction[v] of inferences to the 1st figure, logicians have sought out some barbaric words[,] in order to determine, in accordance with the 4 vowels A.E.I.O.[,] the qualities and quantities that occur[;][w] the *consonantes*, however, are not merely for the sake of euphony, but in order to indicate, in the case of figures other than the 1st, through what kind of *metathesis*$_L$ the reduction to the 1st figure is possible. Toward this end, the following verse is to be noted. *S. vult simpliciter verti, P. vero per accidens, M. vult transponi, C. per impossibile duci*[;] i.e., a proposition in which an *S* stands is to be converted *simpliciter*, where a *P* stands *per accidens*, where an *M* stands it is to be converted, and where a *C* stands contraposed. These words are in the 1st figure: *bArbArA*, *cElArEnt*,[x] *dArII*, *FErIO*. Here the consonants mean nothing, because they are already in the first figure. In the 2nd figure: *cEsArE*, *cAmEstrES*, *fEstInO*, *bArOccO*. In the 3rd figure *dArAptI*, *fElAptOn*,[y] *dIsAmIs*,[z] *dAtIsI*,[a] *bOcArdO*, *fErIsOn*. In the 4th figure *cAlEmEs*,[b] *bAmAlIp*,[c] *dImAtIs*,[d] *fEsApO*,[e] *frEsIsOm*.[f] These are together the 19 possible inferences in all figures, for although one has calculated 64 *modi*, there remain after the usual rules only 19, and of these[g] only 10 are useful, as the logicians admit, because the remaining 9 only infer quite *indirecte*. It is to be noted that in the words the consonants are always connected with the preceding vowels[;] I must not say *ce-sa-re*

[t] Reading "indem" for "indem ein Gedannke," with Pinder.
[u] Reading "Termini" for "Säzze," with Pinder.
[v] Reading "Reduktion" for "Relazion," with Pinder.
[w] Reading "die vorkommenden Qualitaeten und Quantitaeten" for "die vollkommen die Qualitaeten und Quantitaeten," with Pinder.
[x] Reading "cElArEnt" for "cESArEnt," with Pinder.
[y] Reading "fElAptOn" for "fEcAptOn," with Pinder.
[z] Reading "dIsAmIs" for "dIFAnIs," with Pinder.
[a] Reading "dAtIsI" for "dAtIFI," with Pinder.
[b] Reading "cAlEmEs" for "cAEemEs," with Pinder.
[c] Reading "bAmAlIp" for "bOmAlIp," with Pinder.
[d] Reading "dImAtIs" for "dImAeIS," with Pinder.
[e] Reading "fEsApO" for "sEsApO," with Pinder.
[f] Reading "frEsIsOm" for "frEsIsO," with Pinder.
[g] Reading "von diesen" for "von diesem," with Pinder.

but rather *ces-ar-e*, not *ca-me-stres* but *cam-estr-es*, and so forth. This indicates that in *camestres*, in the *major*$_{\text{L}}$, because *M* stands there, the proposition must be transposed, then *S: vult simpliciter verti*[;] the *conclusio* (*es*) *S: vult simpliciter verti*[.] E.g., *fest-in-o*. In the *major*$_{\text{L}}$ there is to be a conversion *S: simpliciter*.[h] 107

Besides categorical inferences, about which the logicians make such a fuss, there are[i] hypothetical and disjunctive ones. A hypothetical inference is one whose *major*$_{\text{L}}$ is a hypothetical proposition, in[j] which [there is] an *antecedens* and a[k] *consequens*, a proposition that contains a ground and another that contains a consequence. E.g., If God is just, then the persistently godless will be punished. The *minor*$_{\text{L}}$ can subsume in 2 ways, *ponendo antecedens*[l] and *negando consequens*.[m] In the case of hypothetical syllogisms, then, there are 2 *modi*, a *modus ponens* and *tollens*. The *modus ponens* infers *a positione antecedentis ad positionem consequentis*.[n] The *modus tollens* infers *a remotione*[o] *consequentis ad remotionem antecedentis*.[p] *Per modum ponentem* I infer: *atqui verum est prius, ergo et posterius*.[q] God is just, conclusion, hence he punishes the wicked. *Per modum tollentem* I infer: *atqui falsum est posterius, ergo et prius*[.][r] He who is beheaded is dead, It is false that he is dead, consequently it is also false that he is beheaded. In the case of *modus tollens* I cannot infer from the falsehood of the *antecedens* to the falsehood of the *consequens*, but rather conversely[;] for the ground can be false, and the thing itself nonetheless true, and this based on a different ground[;] for even if someone is not beheaded, he can have died from disease.

In the disjunctive inference there is always a disjunctive proposition, in which the *membra disjunctionis*[s] are contained. Here we infer either *per modum ponentem*, *atqui*, one of the *membra* is true, consequently all the others must be false, or *per modum tollentem*. All the *membra* are false except one, consequently that one must be true. E.g., The soul is simple or composite, but it is not composite, consequently it is simple.

A *dilemma*$_{\text{L}}$ is an inference of reason that is composed of a hypothetical and a disjunctive inference, where the major is a hypothetical proposi-

[h] Reading "simpliciter" for "simplex," with Pinder.
[i] Reading "giebt es" for "giebt," with Pinder.
[j] Reading "der, dessen major ein hypothetischer Satz ist, in" for "der, in," with Pinder.
[k] Reading "und ein" for "zu einer," with Pinder.
[l] by affirming the antecedent.
[m] by negating the consequent.
[n] from the positing of the antecedent to the positing of the consequent.
[o] Reading "a remotione" for "ad remotionem," with Pinder.
[p] from the removal of the consequent to the removal of the antecedent.
[q] but the first is true, therefore the second is too.
[r] but the second is false, therefore the first is too.
[s] members of the disjunction.

tion, whose *consequens*,[t] however, is a disjunctive[u] judgment[.] E.g., If this world is not the best, then God was not able to create a better one or he did not want to. Now I infer *a remotione consequentis ad remotionem antecedentis*. I reflect on[v] the *consequens per omnia membra*. I say: He *could* have created a better world, for God is omnipotent[;] he wanted to create a better world, for he is good[;] consequently it is false that this world is not the best. A *dilemma*$_{\text{L}}$ is thus a hypothetical inference, for the *major propositio* contains a hypothesis, but the *consequens*[w] of this proposition is disjunctive and has to be negated *per omnia membra*. The ancients made much of this *dilemma*$_{\text{L}}$ and called it[x] a horned[y] inference, *syllogismus cornutus*. They commonly said, then, if you maintain this, then you must also maintain this and that. But these propositions are false, consequently what you maintain is also false[;] all the ways you can go are false,[z] consequently you have no way to go. In metaphysics, especially, one can show difficulties[a] with a multitude of claims,[b] turn where one will. Since certain cognitions are such that they produce difficulties in application *in concreto*. E.g., If the human will is free, then it must be bound neither by nature nor by moral laws. If it is an exception to the law of nature, then

108

this is combined with great difficulty, because then[c] one would not be able to see how free actions are possible. If free actions are not bound by the moral law, then every free action will be contingent, and all morality will disappear. Here difficulties appear on all sides, and it is a sophistical trick not to maintain the opposite but always just to point out individual difficulties. By this means one can make even experience doubtful, which, however, is the ground of all our certainty. The skeptics were sophists who denied the certainty of all claims. They said: If you maintain that, then you end up in all these difficulties, and they made the other quite confused. One can maintain his principal propositions by proving them *apagogice* from the opposite[;] but because the incomprehensibility[d] of the opposite only indicates a difficulty with the opposite, and because incomprehensibility and impossibility are hard to distinguish, there is always something misleading in this, and it leans toward sophistry when[e] one proves merely from the opposite. E.g., If someone has bought stolen goods, then he must

[t] Reading "Consequens" for "Consequenz," with Pinder.

[u] Reading "disjunctives" for "hypothetisches," with Pinder.

[v] "Ich reflectire."

[w] Reading "Consequens" for "Consequenz," with Pinder.

[x] Reading "es" for "ihm," with Pinder.

[y] Reading "gehörnten" for "gehörten," with Pinder.

[z] Reading "sind falsch, folglich" for "folglich."

[a] Reading "Schwierigkeiten" for "Schwierigkeit," with Pinder.

[b] Reading "Behauptungen" for "Behauptung," with Pinder.

[c] Reading "denn" for "den," with Pinder.

[d] Reading "Unbegreiflichkeit" for "Unmöglichkeit."

[e] Reading "Sophysterey, wenn" for "Sophysterey. wenn."

either surrender them to the owner, or he must keep them for himself. If I assume the first, then I can say, how can I know whether or not I am buying stolen things[;] I am never certain whether the salesman hasn't stolen the wares from someone else. Hence it is an absurdity if I am to surrender them. If I say I am keeping them, then an absurdity also emerges, and through such proofs the thing would cease to belong to the owner; but the way of arguing is so deceitful that through the indicated difficulties one can attack even true propositions. Hence all sophists have used *dilemmata* extensively, and even the most honest men may argue for good things through crookedness[;] of this sort are the holy *piae fraudes*,[f] where one presents legends as true, because pious decisions are thereby achieved[.] But one must look not only to the intention but also to the means, whether they are rightful. Thus they have[,] e.g., an *argumentum a tuto*,[g] that one achieves the most security[h] if one chooses one party. But here the question is not what produces the greatest advantage, but what is true. They say it cannot harm a man at all if he believes something that he cannot get to the bottom of; rather, it helps him. But basically these are intrigues, and one ought to say to what extent one has insight into the thing. The honest man must not disguise anything, must not affect speculations where there are none, and he must call all things by their names[;] good intention does not come into consideration here. Quintilian gives orators a rule that does not give one an all-too-favorable idea of *oratores*: that they are to present many *argumenta*, even if weak ones, so that the people will finally be persuaded by such a mass of grounds.[10] It is not the advice of an honest man to state many *argumenta* that prove nothing – *tamen valent.*[i] *Alteri* – [11] This art of making deceptions can be lucrative, but it cannot be united with honesty, and arts of this kind must be banished from philosophy[;] and the simpler an object is, the more directly one must speak. The multitude of the arguments counts for nothing. 109

There are formal and covert inferences. An inference that contains all the propositions from which an inference of reason can come about, but in which the form is not expressed but rather thought, is covert. E.g., All bodies are divisible because they are composite. This is a *syllogismus crypticus*. The formal inference is called [*syllogismus*] *formalis*. One leaves out a proposition because it would be too extensive always to infer formally. But no man infers anything without thinking formally, and in our reason itself every inference is formal[;] when we communicate, however, and make ourselves understandable *explicite*, then we can leave out some

[f] pious deceptions.
[g] argument based on security.
[h] Reading "das sicherste Teil" for "das schwerste Teil," with Pinder.
[i] but are valid all the same.

expressions[j] that must be met with in our thought, because if we were not to think thus, then there might be no connection among our thoughts. Reason always infers formally, however, as soon as the inference indicates anything to a man[;] thus it can occur through a cryptic inference, which is also called an *enthymema*, since the premise or the conclusion is left out, which one can complete in thought.

There are 2 kinds of inferences that actually do not belong to logic but really have no other place, namely, *per inductionem* and *per analogiam*. We infer *per inductionem* when we take it as a basis that what belongs to many things of the genus[k] belongs to the remaining things of that genus. This is not really a pure inference, of course, for I cannot infer from the particular to the universal. However, there is no other way that we can determine our universal judgments through experience. Who can be acquainted with[l] all things that belong under a certain genus? However, I must know the properties of the genus[m] through which it is a genus, because only then can I represent it to myself. E.g., All bodies are heavy is a true, but nonetheless not a certain proposition. For although Euler[12] admits that all bodies are heavy, he nonetheless suspects that the upper ether is not heavy,[n] and this proves that one may not maintain heaviness of all matter with certainty, and then the proposition is not universal. The *medicus* and the *anatomicus* call that a *casus praeternaturalis*. Induction is a crutch, however. We infer that we have cognized the thing in so many *species*$_{L}$ of the genus, so it will belong to the remaining *species*$_{L}$ too. Given the many things in which we have been able to consider the matter, we say that it will belong to the remaining ones too. According to induction, from a great multitude of things that belong to a genus we can well presume that this mark will belong to all the remaining things that belong to the genus[;] but this is always only an empirical universality. Rational universality is strict[;] here what I attribute to the concept universally actually does belong to all the things without exception. Empirical universality, on the other hand, is a broad universality[;] I say that I may maintain something universally because I act correctly in doing so. However, this is quite uncertain. I infer according to analogy thus: when two or more things from a genus agree with one another in as many marks as we have been able to discover, I infer that they will also agree with one another in the remaining marks that I have not been able to discover. When things agree on many points, then I say that they will also agree in the remaining marks[o]

110

[j] Reading "so könen wir einige Ausdrükke weglaßen" for "so könen wir einige Ausdrükke verständlich machen; so könen wir einige Ausdrükke weglaßen," with Pinder.

[k] Reading "Gattung" for "Gattungen," with Pinder.

[l] Reading "kennen" for "könen," with Pinder.

[m] Reading "Gattung" for "Gattungen," with Pinder.

[n] Reading "schwer" for "schwerer," with Pinder.

[o] Reading "Merkmalen" for "Vernunft theilen," with Pinder.

with which I am not yet acquainted[;] I infer, then, from some marks to all the other ones, that they will also agree in these. E.g., The moon has mountains and valleys, day and night, our earth has day and night,[p] and so forth; since the moon has much similarity with our earth, I will attribute to it many of the properties of the earth. We must proceed empirically in accordance with analogy or we will not acquire extended cognition, and without universal rules we cannot draw a universal inference. One cannot possibly examine an object regarding all its properties. Thus if 2 things agree in as many things as one is acquainted with,[q] one infers that they will also agree in the remaining points. That really does not hold,[r] but what else are we to do? Induction and analogy are inseparable from our cognitions, and yet errors for the most part arise from them. We are always acquainted only with something in things, and we infer that here it will be as nice as it is in other things. Since we cannot do without a crutch for the human understanding, we must pay heed to whether a mistaken inference is made here.

The propositions in an inference can be true, but the inference can nonetheless be false as to form, i.e., a fallacy. Here one can either be deceived oneself, so that one misleads oneself and does not observe the logical form, and then it is[s] a *paralogismus*; or insofar as one seeks intentionally to mislead others, and then it is a *sophisma*[;] for when I do not have the intention of misleading others, then it is a *paralogismus*. Those in the Megaric school, and subsequently also the stoics, exerted much effort and occupied themselves much with these conjurer's tricks,[t] with making sophisms, through which they embarassed the *logici*.

The logician is required not only to cognize that an inference is false; rather, he must also state the rule that is contrary to the inference. Hence they sought names where this violation of the rule was hidden and could not easily be discovered. Thus they had *sophisma*[u] *sensus compositi et diuisi*,[v] *a dicto secundum quid*[w] *ad dictum simpliciter*,[x] *pp*[.] E.g. A farmer's son came home to his father in the evening[;] since the father could not prepare anything else for him quickly, he cooked 3 eggs. The young man wanted to show his learnedness and began to philosophize: Where there are 3 there are also two, two and 3 make 5, consequently there are 5 eggs lying there[;] the father was startled by his son's learned mind, ate up the 3

[p] Reading "unsre Erde hat Tag und Nacht, und sofort" for "unsre Erde hat des Nachts einen Mond und sofort."
[q] Reading "als man kennt" for "als man könt," with Pinder.
[r] Reading "nicht an" for "nicht anders an," with Pinder.
[s] Reading "und dann ists" for "und ists," with Pinder.
[t] Reading "Taschenspielkünsten" for "Taschenspielkünstlern," with Pinder.
[u] Reading "Sophism" for "Sophisma," with Pinder.
[v] Sophisms of composition and division.
[w] Reading "secundum quid" for "secundum, und," with Pinder.
[x] from what is said with qualification to what is said simply.

eggs, and told the son to eat the remaining 2, which was quite the best way to refute this *sophisma*. As soon as one tried to clothe this in the form of a syllogism, the *vitium* would at once strike the eye.

The *sophisma figurae dictionis*[y] is where the *medius terminus* is taken in different meanings. E.g., A philosopher is a kind of learned man. Leibniz was a philosopher, consequently Leibniz was a genus of learned man. *Vox medii termini*,[z] *philosopher*, is taken in different meanings[;] one time it is taken as a predicate, and the other time as a multitude of things to which the predicate belongs. When the *medius terminus* in the two premises is taken in different meanings, then this always yields a *fallacium*. E.g., no[a] artist is born; some men are artists[;] hence some men are not born. In the *major*$_{\mathrm{L}}$ the *medius terminus* means the art, and in the *minor*$_{\mathrm{L}}$ the man.

111

Sophisma a dicto, secundum quid, ad dictum simpliciter[;] one could almost allow this, but with some restriction. E.g., He who says you are an ass says you are an animal, consequently he who says you are an ass speaks the truth. He says the truth in part, for in saying that I am an ass he also says that I am an animal[.] Or, e.g., He who says that the respondent is a man speaks the truth[;] he who says that a Moor is a man speaks the truth[;] consequently he who says that the respondent is a Moor speaks the truth. But even this can be granted in part; he says more than that the respondent is a man, of course, but in saying that he is a Moor he also says that he is a man. What he ought to accept *secundum quid*[b] he understands *simpliciter*.

An example of a *sophisma figurae dictionis* can also be this. A lady was traveling with some learned men, and since they lost their way they asked a farmer which way to go. The farmer asked them if they understood Latin, and since they said they did, the farmer answered that they should just go straight ahead; but soon they came to a morass, where they quickly got stuck. Hence they turned around and asked the farmer about his advice. What? replied the farmer. One can go through the whole world with Latin, and you cannot even go through this swamp? The farmer took the word *world* on one occasion for the society of men, and on the other in its geographical meaning.

A *sophisma heterozeteseos*[c] is when someone who[d] wants to prove a proposition proves something else[;] e.g., he is supposed to prove that the soul is immortal, and he only proves that it is simple. The persistence of a simple being after death still does not prove immortality, which indicates the

[y] sophism of the figure of speech.

[z] The expression for the middle term.

[a] Reading "kein" for "ein," with Pinder.

[b] with qualification.

[c] sophism of misdirection (reading "sophisma heterozeteseos" for "sophima a heterozeteseos," with Pinder).

[d] Reading "jemand, der einen" for "jemand einen," with Pinder.

continuation of its life. In just the same way one commits a *sophisma* in the concept of the existence of God when one pretends to give a proof of it. They do prove that a being of many perfections[e] must be the cause of the world, but it must also be proved that the cause of the world is not just any being of great perfection but that it is a single being. It must be proved not merely that it is inexpressibly great, but that it has all power, not merely that it has a great understanding but that all cognitions belong to it. The whole of nature cannot prove this much to us, however, hence there is a *sophisma heterozeteseos* here, in that I answer something other than what I was asked. I prove the existence of some sublime cause,[f] which must be very great, but the question here is not about this but about the primal being.[g]

The *sophisma ignorationis elenchi* is when someone means to dispute something but does not refute the other; rather, he refutes what he imagines to be the other's opinion. He refutes his own fancy, then, which he imagined based on the other's propositions[;] e.g., when I say that the apodeictic proof of the immortality of the soul is not given in philosophy, then someone else would commit a *sophisma ignorationis elenchi* if he were to come and say that we have no grounds at all for accepting the immortality of the soul, but only probable supposition. There is no talk here of its not being possible to prove the proposition speculatively, however, but only of its mode of proof. An *elenchus*$_{\mathrm{L}}$ is the distinct representation of the purpose of a claim[;] I must know exactly[h] what our dispute is about, otherwise I commit a *sophisma ignorationis elenchi*.

Most of the business of the Megaric[i] school was with sophistries, and most of the tricks were applied by them for miserable purposes, for the tying of knots,[j] in order to give others the trouble of resolving them. Euclides was the founder of this school, not the mathematician, however, but Euclides of Megara.[k] They had, for example, the following sophistries. The Liar[,] *mendax*[,] got its name from its *medius terminus*. It runs thus: If you say you lie, and in saying this you speak the truth,[l] then you speak the truth in lying. This is incorrect, however[;] it really should run thus[:] If you say you lie, and in saying this you speak the truth,[m] then you speak the truth in saying that you lie[;] and this is then correct. 112

[e] Reading "viel Vollkommenheiten" for "Unvollkommenheiten," with Pinder.

[f] Reading "irgend einer erhabenen Ursach" for "irgend 1 erhabene Ursach," with Pinder.

[g] "Uhrwesen."

[h] Reading "genau" for "genant," with Pinder.

[i] Reading "megarische" for "maligarische," with Pinder.

[j] Reading "Knoten" for "Karten," with Pinder.

[k] Reading "Megara" for "Magorra," with Pinder.

[l] Reading "und indem du das sagst, die Wahrheit sagst" for "und jedem du das sagst, und zwar die Wahrheit sagst," with Pinder.

[m] Reading "und indem du das sagst die Wahrheit sagst" for "und jedem du die Warheit sagst," with Pinder.

Epimenides says, All Cretans are liars[;] he himself is a Cretan[;] hence he himself lies in saying that Cretans are liars, and so it goes round and round. Philetas,[n] trying to resolve this liar, racked his brains so much that he had to wear lead soles so that the wind would not blow him off the bridge. This is the *obvelatus*:[o] Do you know your father? Yes[;] but I present him to you *obvelatus*. Now do you know him? No[;] consequently you know your father and you do not know him. This is the *acervus*:[p] I put a pile of grain before you[;] is it still a pile if I take away one grain? Yes[;] if I take away 2? Yes[;] and so forth[;] consequently it does not cease to be a pile until I take away the last grain. One commonly commits such [fallacies] in the case of indeterminate defininitions.[q] E.g., he who is much too thrifty is miserly. Here I cannot really know where thriftiness ends, and this is an actual *acervus*, then. This is the *caluus*:[r] When someone has lost his hair he is called bald. With which hair does he begin to be called bald? With the first? No[;] with the second? No[;] *pp*[;] consequently one will not be bald as long as one still has one hair. The *cornutus*[s] runs thus: What you have not lost you still have. You have not lost any horns,[t] consequently you still have horns.

One can scarcely think of a more pitiful[u] game, yet at that time someone who knew how to invent such things was[v] held to be a fine guest. Peter Abelard, who was always first among the scholastic philosophers, was once traveling with a clergyman[;] the clergyman said, Look! there is an ox flying. Abelard asked, Where? The cleric started laughing and asked, How could such a great philosopher believe that? *Abelard* answered, I believed it more possible for an ox to fly than for a clergyman to lie. We have quite different inferences which are mentioned in metaphysics, which belong[w] under the nature of metaphysical reason, and which no man can avoid, and which he can cognize only by seeing that he ends up in conflict with his arguments. We badly need to discover this source, because of which men have always followed this inference. Discovery of it enlightens the understanding and gives us a sure foundation. Such a natural sophistication is a real accomplishment, then, and it enlightens the understanding.

A *sorites*$_{\mathrm{L}}$ or *acervus* is a chain of inferences that are subordinated to one another. It is a chain of inferences of reason, where the conclusion of

[n] Reading "Philetas" for "Phylotas," with Pinder.
[o] the veiled one.
[p] the heap.
[q] "bey dem unbestimten definiren."
[r] [the] bald one.
[s] [The] horned one.
[t] Reading "keine Hörner verloren" for "keine Hörner," with Pinder.
[u] Reading "erbärmlicheres" for "erbärmleriches," with Pinder.
[v] Reading "indessen wurde" for "indessen würde," with Pinder.
[w] Reading "gehören" for "gehört," with Pinder.

one inference becomes the premise of the one following, and it is also called an *enarratio syllogistica.*[x] E.g., Everything that thinks is simple, the soul thinks, hence it is simple. Everything that is simple is indivisible. The soul is simple, hence it is indivisible. What is indivisible is imperishable. The soul is indivisible, hence it is imperishable. What is imperishable persists, the soul is imperishable, hence the soul persists. In this way I can make a whole chain of inferences, where I always make the conclusion into the premise of the following inference. This *sorites*$_L$ is of two kinds, either downward toward the following premises, or upward toward grounds. The first occurs when the conclusion of the one becomes the premise of the other, and is called an *episyllogismus*. But when the premise of the one becomes the conclusion of the other, then it is called a *prosyllogismus*[.] E.g., Everything imperishable is indivisible, the soul is imperishable, hence it is indivisible. Everything that persists is imperishable, the soul persists, hence the soul is imperishable. In all disputations[y] the *prosyllogismos*[z] is disputed.

The opponent must have an argument that is directly opposed to the disputation. Now the respondent allows him to prove one of the premises through a new inference, and this is then a *prosyllogismus*. It does not work *per episyllogismum*. If, e.g., we had proved the proposition,[a] All laws follow from the law of nature, and the opponent were to begin[:] What follows from nature is in accord with wisdom's purpose, consequently the laws of nature are in accord with wisdom[;] then the respondent would say that the inference is not contrary to my disputation. Here one does not allow inference *per episyllogismum*, then, for the respondent would simply not know where the chain of inferences was to run, and would allow things that he would later want to take back. When the *propositio major* of a chain of inferences is left out,[b] then this is called a *sorites*$_L$[.] E.g., Everything that thinks is simple, what is simple is indivisible, what is indivisible is imperishable, what is imperishable persists, consequently since the soul thinks it persists. This *sorites*$_L$ is *categoricus* if it consists of nothing but categorical propositions[;] the two are essentially different, then. A *sorites categoricus*[c] is a chain inference through which the chain of subject and predicate is given. 113

A *saltus in probando*[d] is the connection of a premise with the conclusion, where the other premise can be left out. It is called a *saltus legitimus* if each of them can be inserted into the thing, since it accords with the

[x] syllogistic explanation.
[y] Reading "disputationen" for "disputation," with Pinder.
[z] Reading "prosyllogismus" for "per syllogismos," with Pinder.
[a] Reading "den Satz" for "denn Satz," with Pinder.
[b] Reading "propositio major ausgelassen wird" for "propositio, major wird," with Pinder.
[c] Reading "Sorites cathegorikus" for "Sorites oder cathegorikus," with Pinder.
[d] A leap in proof (reading "saltus" for "faltus," with Pinder).

natural understanding to add the the *minor propositio* in thought. A *saltus illegitimus* is one where this is not so clear, and where I make a leap in that I pass to a thing from a distant cognition without traversing the *nota intermedia*.

In all kinds of proof and in all arguments the ground of proof can be taken *gratis*$_L$, without proving it[.] E.g., it need not be proved that everything contingent has a beginning when one uses the proposition in philosophy; but one seeks the proof, and this is called *petere principium.*[e] *Petitio principii*, then, is the acceptance of an immediate proposition that still needs a proof. A *circulus in probando*[f] is when I put at the basis of the proof of a proposition that which is supposed to be proved[.][g] E.g., if we proved, based on the holy scripture, that this is the word of God. From revelation alone I cannot prove this. Sometimes the proposition is put at the basis but remotely, and frequently it is hard to discover. Some people in their writings save a proof for another place, but when they come to that place they say that we have just proved it.[h]

It happens that one proves too much or that one proves too little. He who is supposed to prove, e.g., that the soul is immortal, and who only proves its persistence, proves too little. He proves too much if he also proves something that is false. If a proof contains too little, that little can be true, but if it proves too much, then it proves more than is true, and this is false, then, and then it proves nothing at all[;] and one must guard against this carefully. E.g., If we have not given life, then we may not take it, either. We have not given it ourselves, hence we cannot take it, either. We have not given it to a chicken, hence we cannot take it from a chicken, either.

A *locus*$_L$[i] is nothing other than a universal kind of cognition under which a given cognition can be brought. I am acquainted with movement, as something belonging to natural science, also insofar as it belongs to metaphysics in its effects, and this is then the metaphysical place[j] of motion. A *locus*$_L$ in the metaphysical sense is thus a title of a genus of cognitions under which a given cognition can be brought, and *topica* is the science of the places that one cognition has under others, *est positus cognitionis in quadam cognitioni generali.*[k] Every universal cognition has places, for a particular cognition and every system has determinate places for the parts of the system. It is shown, however, how common and learned cognition differ, in that common cognition contains an aggre-

[e] to beg the question (literally, to beg the principle).

[f] A circle in proving.

[g] Reading "lege, was bewiesen werden soll, ZE" for "lege, ZE," with Pinder.

[h] Reading "haben." for "haben," with Pinder.

[i] place, or topic (reading "Ein locus" for "Eine Wißenschaft," with Pinder).

[j] Reading "der metaphysische Ort" for "die metaphysische Art," with Pinder.

[k] it is the position of a cognition in a certain general cognition.

gate of cognitions, learned cognition a system; or in that a science is brought into a system.

A system presupposes[l] the form of the whole before the parts, where the parts have to be determined in accordance with the idea of the whole.[m] Hence topic would be the determination of an individual cognition's *locus scientificus* in its system, and the art of indicating for various cognitions[n] their place in the system. This art would not be bad; Aristotle started it, but thanks to the scholastic stuff it was again forgotten. E.g., one gives virtue a place in politics as a doctrine of prudence, in morals as a doctrine of morality[;] hence what matters is the place to which each member of the system belongs, because otherwise this would at once become an aggregate.[o] The *locus grammaticus* would be if, e.g., I taught about philosophy grammatically, that according to its etymology the word means love of wisdom. In the case of the *locus logicus* I consider the scientific connection, and I thereby[p] define philosophy. The *locus logicus* involves definitions, *axiomata*$_L$, the power of cognition, whether a cognition belongs to concept or to judgment, whether something is cognized *ab oppositis*[;][q] these are nothing but *loci logici*. A *locus metaphysicus* is, e.g., the matter of the *nexus effectiuus*,[r] of the whole and the parts[,] of effects and causes. The *locus moralis* is when I describe something in accordance with morality. The *locus iuridicus* is when I consider whether something is really right.[s] *Locus topicus*[t] is a tautology, but it is common[.] A topic is not bad if, after one has gone through a science, one can add a topic and see what belongs to it, and can thereby distinguish[u] all cognitions[;] for in morals, e.g., much depends on the place in which a cognition comes to stand.

114

The 2nd part of logic, Of the Method of Cognitions. Logic has to do neither with the observation of things and objects, from which no rules[v] for method can be gained, nor with the observation of the end of cognition, nor[w] with the cognition of the subject. Logic ignores all[x] of this and deals merely with the form of the understanding and of reason[;] it ignores the

[l] Reading "setzt . . . voraus" for "sagt . . . voraus," with Pinder.
[m] Reading "nach der Idee des gantzen" for "nach dem Idee den gantzen," with Pinder.
[n] Reading "den mancherley Erkentnissen" for "in mancherley Erkenntnissen," with Pinder.
[o] Reading "ein Agregat" for "eine Kette und ein Agregat."
[p] Reading "dadurch" for "durch," with Pinder.
[q] from its opposite (reading "ab oppositis" for "oppositio," with Pinder).
[r] Reading "nexu effictiuo" for "nexu affectiuo," with Pinder.
[s] Reading "etwas danach betrachte, was eigentlich recht ist" for "etwas betrachte, was eigentlich recht ist," with Pinder.
[t] Topical topic, or topical place.
[u] Reading "unterscheiden" for "unterscheide."
[v] Reading "keine Regeln" for "allein Regeln," with Pinder.
[w] Reading "noch" for "auch," with Pinder.
[x] Reading "von dem allen ignorirt" for "von dem allein ignorirt," with Pinder.

subject, for it speaks of reason in general. It ignores the final end, for it asks only[y] if cognition is in conformity with the condition of the understanding, and what are the rules in conformity with which one can determine the conformity[;] hence the doctrine of method[z] is what belongs in logic. This should be the last thing in any science, for much is required to show the way on which one is to proceed in a science, and many sciences are so tangled together that one simply does not know how to distinguish them. Basically, however, method will here mean nothing but the title and the *termini technici* in the case of method[;] logic cannot do more, for it is a propaedeutic to all sciences and consequently cannot know what belongs to each in particular.

Method is the unity of a whole of cognition according to principles. A unity of cognition can be empirical, which experience teaches, insofar as it is in accordance with purpose, i.e., is a unity[a] in accord with rules that can[b] be drawn from experience. But there is also a unity in accordance with universal principles of experience, where we can produce a thoroughgoing connection, and can produce a system, in that we discover the nature of the whole[c] through the connection of the manifold. Insofar as the unity of cognition rests on empirical rules, it is called manner[,] in Latin *modus*. But the unity of the manifold insofar as it rests on principles of reason is called method.[d] There must be a certain connection of cognitions in that they constitute a whole[;] there must be a rule of unity. If mere modernity is the rule of unity, then it is called *fashion*, where the rule is accepted by the multitude. Horace says, You should be *suaviter in modo*, i.e., pleasant in manner, *sed fortiter in re*, i.e., thorough in method.[13] The first is aesthetic perfection, the second logical. Both perfections concern manner, basically. One can have a thoroughness insofar as experience has instructed us thereof, or one can have a thoroughness according to principles, and we wish now to treat of this latter,[e] namely, of method. *Methodically* observed is something different from methodically expounded. One can distinguish method or the mode of cognition from exposition or style. The mode of cognition is that mode of connection of cognition[f] whose unity constitutes the cognition itself. How is the nature of the manifold in a cognition to be made more comprehensible and broken into sections[;] these two expressions are often confused. One needs method for thought, style for exposition. It is not a matter of indifference how one expounds, but the most

[y] Reading "nur" for "mich," with Pinder.
[z] Reading "Methodenlehre" for "Methode Lehre," with Pinder.
[a] Reading "d.i. eine Einheit" for "die eine Erkenntnis," with Pinder.
[b] Reading "können" for "köne," with Pinder.
[c] "die Art des Gantzen."
[d] "methodus, Lehrart."
[e] Reading "von dieser letzten" for "von diesen letzten," with Pinder.
[f] Reading "Erkenntnis" for "Einheit," with Pinder.

important thing is how one is to think[.] The method of thought has to be grounded on certain cognitions that are suited to the cognition of unity.

Some have thought well as to method but did not have the talent of exposition, which belongs more to aesthetic perfection[,] really not to . . . ,[14] but belongs instead to exposition, the way I make a cognition simple, that is, make[g] clear and lively what I have thought through the understanding and reason, and excite an interest in it. Eloquence concerns exposition only in regard to language and in regard to grammatical laws. Oratory is the art of speaking and making an illusion[h] in order[i] to persuade someone else. Exposition[,] *ratio dicendi,*[j] is the art of expressing something, of thinking in a way that is adequate to method. Style is frequently nothing but a trick that amounts to nothing but pleasing the ears[;] exposition, however, is a wonderful thing[;] here there can also be aesthetic perfection, which agrees, however, with logical perfection. A preacher must observe method, in that he[k] makes a selection from the connection of his dogmatic propositions and makes these comprehensible. When he has sought out such propositions and seen to it that they are comprehensible propositions and not abstract ones, then he looks to see that his exposition is uniform, for if artificial it would not be in accord with the dignity of a holy discourse. But the exposition must nonetheless exhibit the matter in a brighter light, so that the healthy eyes of the common understanding also comprehend it, otherwise such an exposition would not be worthy of religion. Toward this end read Demosthenes. Cicero shows an affected taste and art of speaking. One forgets this if the exposition has energy[;] then we are charmed and transported by the exposition. Where man is merely entertained, it is not an exposition[;] that is a game[;] but where man is also instructed, that is an exposition.

115

Method can be critical, scholastic, also popular. In scholastic[l] method the exposition is composed methodically[,] i.e., where the parts of the method, and meticulousness of observation, shine forth. This method reigns in all the sciences. Popular method does not have the purpose of furthering science but instead of furthering interest, without aiming at knowledge. It is distinct from[m] scholastic method, then. As far as the popular is concerned, one has to attend to the fact that popular exposition and popular method are not the same. The exposition can be popular, but not the method. E.g., Gottsched's compendium[15] is popular[,] but its

[g] Reading "mache" for "machen," with Pinder.

[h] Reading "einen Schein" for "ein Schein," with Pinder.

[i] Reading "um . . . zu Überreden" for "ohne . . . zu Überreden," with Pinder.

[j] manner of speaking.

[k] Reading "indem er aus dem Zusammenhang" for "indem er aus dem er aus dem Zusammenhang," with Pinder.

[l] Reading "scholastischen" for "Socratischen," with Pinder.

[m] Reading "von" for "vor," with Pinder.

method is scholastic. The French all have popular exposition. Accordingly, popular method needs to regard[n] not merely exposition but also order, so that one knows where one is to stop and where to start. Not everyone can combine such lucid exposition with simplicity, as, e.g., Voltaire and Fontenelle do. In a philosophical encyclopedia there should not be merely a rhapsody of philosophical propositions, but rather a popular[o] exposition of philosophy. There has never been a lack of those who have thought about making method popular, and yet preachers need nothing in the world more than popularity, namely, the way of ordering thought so that it becomes popular. A treatise on method would put the crowning touch on the world. Cartesius sketched a treatise, which is affected,[p] however. To discover this will be most difficult, but then it will order all our cognitions and lead us to discoveries.

In the case of the method of cognitions of reason, concepts are taken as the basis, with cognitions of experience *facta* are[;] if historical cognition is to constitute a science it has to be a system, and as a system it needs a method, although[q] the things themselves are not grounded on reason. The order in the exposition must be related to grounds,[r] however. The method of cognition of reason is scientific,[s] however, if it is scholastic, if the form of this science shines forth distinctly, so that the science has a principal purpose, to which one attends. This is distinct from popular method. Where I expound cognition in such a way that it is to be of universal use, then I do not make use of scientific method, but rather of a different one, in which things scholastic[t] are not so evident. For then scientific form is surrounded by a wall, so that it accommodates universal taste and becomes popular. Scientific form in metaphysics does not really accord with present taste, but if it deals with nature or reason it is much needed. In short, there is no science that does not need to be expounded scientifically, although subsequently I can hide the scientific form somewhat if I wish to accommodate others.

Scientific method is divided into synthetic[u] and analytic method. With synthetic method one begins with principles of reason and proceeds toward things that rest on principles[;][v] with analytic method one proceeds toward principles from things that rest on principles.[w] Synthetically, I

[n] Reading "anzusehen" for "angesehen werden."
[o] Reading "ein populärer Vortrag" for "ein pulaerer Vortrag," with Pinder.
[p] Reading "gesucht" for "versucht," in accordance with Pinder's suggestion; but the reading is uncertain.
[q] Reading "oblgleich" for "daß obgleich," with Pinder.
[r] Reading "Gründe" for "Grund," with Pinder.
[s] Reading "scientifisch" for "synthetisch," with Pinder.
[t] "die Schule."
[u] Reading "synthetische" for "scientifische," with Pinder.
[v] "zu den Principiaten."
[w] "von den Principiaten."

begin with definitions and proceed to axioms, corollaries, with all their consequences[;] thus this method, when I proceed from the simple to the composite, is synthetic. Analytic method is always combined with popularity,[x] for one gets used to abstract cognitions[y] when one ascends to principles rather than having to begin with them. Synthetic method is the most perfect of all[;] but when I accommodate myself to the capacity of other men, then I begin with their common concepts, seek a rule based on these, then seek to draw a common *principium,* and thus I climb from lower cognitions to high ones. When one has climbed by analysis to abstract cognitions[z] then one can cognize them much more easily *in concreto.* For one need only attend to the cognition that one had previously taken as ground. Analytic method is also a means of discovery and of exposition,[a] in that I speak popularly. The true method of exposition is synthetic, however, for even if I have thought the thing analytically, the synthetic method is what first makes it a system. All cognitions must be systematic, however, because I cannot myself know whether I have a complete whole, for one member in the system serves to justify the correctness of the other and to rectify it.

116

The author distinguishes art and science from one another. Art means an ability to do,[b] science means knowledge.[c] Many a man knows something but cannot bring into being what he knows. Many a man can do something but does not have the relevant *knowledge*[;] he cannot make distinct and comprehensible the way that he brings it into being. The common man says: This is not art but science, i.e., if one knows, then one has the ability. But art requires that one actually be able to do what one knows, then one has the ability. But art requires that one actually be able to do what one knows, too. There are many arts that are far removed from sciences, and which men cannot make into science. E.g., people always try to make the art of painting, music, into a science. Art is concerned with completion, science with the content of cognition. People divide the arts into bread-winning arts and liberal arts.[d] [They are called] bread-winning arts insofar as their worth does not lie in the arts themselves, but instead they are regarded as a means of commerce[;] certain arts can be encouraged[e] in such a way, and thus some arts are treasured because they nourish us, and just for this reason other arts enjoy no great esteem. The liberal arts have an inner worth, without serving for gain[.] E.g., the art of

[x] Reading "Mit der Popularitaet" for "Bey der Popularitaet," with Pinder.
[y] "Kentnißen."
[z] "Kentnissen."
[a] Reading "des Vortrags" for "Vortrags des Vortrags," with Pinder.
[b] "ein könen."
[c] "ein wißen."
[d] "in Brodt und freye Künste."
[e] Reading "encouragiert" for "ancuragirt," with Pinder.

the carpenter, of the builder, are arts for earning one's bread[;] other arts have a worth in themselves. E.g., poetry, oratory. These have an immediate pleasantness in themselves and need no *auctoramentum*[;][f] these are liberal arts, because they have an inner worth by themselves. If liberal arts are used as arts for earning one's bread, then their inner worth, i.e., their dignity, is[g] degraded. One gives them the worth of a means, although they have an unconditioned worth. In this way poetry often loses its prestige. Nonetheless, the art of poetry can well be used for gain.

The author distinguishes natural from artificial method. But every[h] method is artificial, namely, an artificial way of combining cognitions. This is a tautology. But we can distinguish natural from affected[i] method, *methodus affectata,* in which one merely wishes to show his art, but which is not suited[j] to the character of the cognitions. Man is affected when he shows an art that is not suited to the end. A method is natural, however, that is in conformity with ends. Many ponder over things with so much labor, not in order to reach the end, but rather in order to show their art. This includes, for example,[k] verses that can be read backwards and forwards, also affected sermons[;] nothing should be affected, however, consequently no method, either.

Syllogistic exposition is where one expounds a cognition through a whole chain of episyllogisms[;] this is, as it were, a way of spelling out our reason, and it can only be used in the beginning, in order to make it attentive to all of reason's steps. By tabular method one can show a system in all its connection, as the *anatomicus* shows the skeleton of the body in accordance with all its articulation.

Method is divided into acroamatic and erotematic method. It is acroamatic if I merely imagine a listener[;][l] it is erotematic if at the same time I ask questions, since from the asking a conversation finally comes about; thus the erotematic method can also be called dialogic. Dialogues are either Socratic or catechistic. The method in an *examinatorio* would be wholly erotematic, but in the case of the dialogic, questions alternate. In Socratic method the one who asks questions is the teacher, but one must presuppose of him who asks that he does not know what he asks, for otherwise he would not be permitted to ask questions[;] or, one can also ask others, in that someone must render an account of what he has learned. In genuine dialogue, however, the one who asks questions is always the one who learns. But in the case of our catechism, the child is

117

[f] wages.
[g] Reading "wird" for "würd," with Pinder.
[h] Reading "eine jede" for "eine."
[i] "gekünstelten."
[j] "angemessen."
[k] Reading "zum Beispiel" for "zum Beweise," with Pinder.
[l] "wenn ich nur einen bloßen Zuhörer vorstelle."

the one who learns, which is backwards; if it is a matter of a historical cognition, then it is all right, of course, for there there are concepts of memory, which I examine. In the case of cognitions of reason, however, where one does not proceed historically, that catechistic method is completely contrary to the end. Hence it is used completely wrongly in religion, since one transforms a cognition of reason in a historical cognition. In himself, man does not become smarter in religion, because here everything is cognitions of reason and nothing[m] depends on *facta.* Thus the catechistic method is natural insofar as the pupil is supposed to acquire actual concepts. One can catechize the historical[;] this belongs to revealed religion[;] but in religion one must[n] also have reason, consequently the erotematic method that is catechistic is wholly inappropriate in the case of cognitions of reason. The teacher asks questions of the one who is learning things that he did not think out, and yet he has to say to him in a determinate *terminus* what he has committed to memory[;] consequently it is mere memory work. What belongs in place of catechistic[o] method is the Socratic method[;] on this, read Gedike's translation of 4 Platonic conversations.[16] Socrates speaks of matter of reason. Now he asks questions of his followers as one who really does not know the thing, and as if he were learning from the other[;] but what matters in this connection is that he knows[p] how to ask so cleverly[;] he thereby developed the cognition that lay in him. In the end the listener figured out everything by himself, so that the teacher could even be completely ignorant and could learn with the other, if only he knew how to ask questions well. One ought to treat religion in this way with the pupil and draw out of him everything that lies in him with regard to God and morality. For this is truly the erotematic method[;] here the pupil commits nothing to memory, but instead learns the order of his own reason, while the catechistic method, on the other hand, is a mechanical thing, in which he has thought out nothing.

The distinction between geographical and historical method rests on the fact that the one determines differences of space, the other differences of time. -"- - - -[17]

To *meditate* means not merely to think something out,[q] but also a reflection. All thought occurs *tumultuously*[;] afterward, however, I have to meditate with reflection. In thought[r] one first proceeds tumultuously[;] afterward, when one has considered something, one then brings in an order and connection, and thus there arises a universal and complete whole.

Among the *termini technici* are included the *termini familiares*[;]

[m] Reading "nichts" for "nicht."

[n] Reading "aber man muß" for "aber muß," with Pinder.

[o] Reading "der catechistischen" for "der kategorischen," with Pinder.

[p] Reading "weißt" for "wißen."

[q] Reading "etwas ausdenken" for "etwas ausdeuten," with Pinder.

[r] Reading "Beim Denken" for "Beim meditiren," with Pinder.

these are expressions that cannot be understood, which one believes one understands because one has used them so often.

Merchandising of words[s] among the learned is where they sell merely words instead of things[;] they are called on this account *logodaedali*, because they only fabricate words.

A *terminus inanis* is one that has no meaning at all. A *terminus vagus*[t] is one whose meaning is not determined exactly. *Synonyma* are words that mean the same.

A *homonym* is a word that has various meanings. Experience[u] teaches that there are not 2 *synonyma* in a language. One uses different words, of course, but if one investigates them exactly, every word has a different determination. It is pleasant thus to distinguish words in a language.

Reason has nothing at all to do with *style*, except with the purity of it. For in the case of cognitions of reason, everything aims at attending to precision and to the appropriateness[v] of things to one another.

Speech means the aesthetic art, which is added to expression; the art of giving the expression perfection. This requires[:]

118

1. Being well spoken,[w] that one has a manifold of words in one's head.
2. Eloquence, i.e., style.
3. Oratory is an art of persuasion and of bringing someone else to possess a cognition by speaking, without convincing him through reason. Men must not be persuaded,[x] however, but convinced[.]

Didactic method[y] involves the ability to descend and to ascend[.][z] One places oneself[a] in the middle[;] hence one must know how to raise oneself to those who have more capacity, and how to descend[b] to those who have lower capacities. To write thus is a great art[;] but the higher must have more ability to ascend than to descend, without which it does not amount to much[;] without this one does not lose much, either.[18] . . .

Disputations, whether they be carried out orally or in writing, always have a *status controversiae*, where the *sophisma ignorationis elenchi* must be avoided.[c]

One can refute the opponent by an argument κατ' ἄνθρωπον,[d] in that

[s] "*Wortkrämerey.*"
[t] Reading "vagus" for "vastus," with Pinder.
[u] Reading "Erfahrung" for "Erfindung."
[v] "Angemessenheit."
[w] "Die Beredheit."
[x] "beredt."
[y] Reading "In der didaktischen Methode" for "in der dialectischen," with Pinder.
[z] Reading "condescendenz und coascendenz" for "condescendenz."
[a] Reading "stelt sich" for "stelt sich seinen Leser," with Pinder.
[b] Reading "herabzulassen wissen" for "herablassen zu wissen," with Pinder.
[c] Reading "vermieden" for "verneind," with Pinder.
[d] based on the man.

I accept my opponent's opinion and from it infer something contrary to him, or by an argument κατ' ἀλήθειαν,[e] when I take as a basis something that is true. Locke mentions in addition the following. E.g., the *argumentum ad crumenam,*[f] when I say that I bet[g] that it is true. The *argumentum ad verecundiam,*[h] when one says: You can hardly know better than Wolff and Leibniz, i.e., than the learned.

One can also defend oneself by *retorsiones*[.] E.g., by the *argumentum ab adio* or *ab inuidia,*[i] where one says what would arise from the thing if one draws such consequences. Theologians make much use of these, and from this the *odium theologicum*[j] has arisen, when[k] one has a personal hatred toward something and seeks to rally all men against him. Hence[l] one must avoid this *argumentum ab odio.*

One defends oneself against this argument by apologies, which are a defense against an insult.

Hechsel – Pomeranus

Finis
1782.

[e] based on truth.
[f] argument based on wealth.
[g] Reading "wette" for "wollte," with Pinder.
[h] argument based on modesty (i.e., an appeal to authority).
[i] argument from hatred [or] from envy.
[j] theological hatred.
[k] Reading "enstanden, wenn" for "entstanden. Wenn," with Pinder.
[l] Reading "sucht. Deshalb" for "sucht, deshalb," with Pinder.

PART III

The Dohna-Wundlacken logic

Logic

according to
the lectures of Professor Kant
in the summer semester, 1792

The 23rd of April, 1792

EXPLANATION OF SYMBOLS

Unreadable passages have been restored by conjecture and have been signified regularly by "†", those passages for which no acceptable conjecture occurred to me, by ". . . †". All additions between the lines and in the margin, as well as the appended notes, I have incorporated in the main text, although the various types of additions are indicated by special signs: those written above the lines by "< >", the marginal notes by "{ }",[1] the appended notes by "| { } |". Where I had to make my own interpolations, in order to close small gaps in the manuscript, I have used "| |". By this means I hope to a wide extent to be able to make the structure of the original notebook obvious to readers.

A. Kowalewski, *Immanuel Kant's Principal Lectures on Philosophy*, 1924, p. 52

{FIRST HOUR, THE 23RD OF APRIL, FROM 7–8} 693

Prolegomena

{All things between heaven and earth occur and act according to rules, e.g., bodies according to the laws of gravity.}

One must reflect on his thought, i.e., do it according to rules. Every language is bound to certain particular rules. This is so above all in the case of dead languages, where one can actually designate the rules. One can also use the rules without actually giving them names. One learns[a] these rules gradually through attempts. The first ones fail[;] finally one attains skill. Among the rules of thought there are universal ones, which apply to particular objects without distinction. Thus there are universal rules of language, too. Such a grammar does not contain words, not a *copia vocabularum*,[b] but rather only the form of language. We will be able to represent to ourselves a universal doctrine <of thought>. This universal doctrine of thought is called *logic*, doctrine of the understanding. It is a preparation for thinking about objects.

The *understanding* is the faculty of thinking <of understanding something>, of rules, the *power of judgment* the faculty of subsuming, *reason* of inferring what pertains to something <of having insight into it>. A *rule* is a concept under which much, a manifold of representations, is contained.

We can distinguish:

1. the *necessary*[c] universal rules of thought, without distinction as to what it deals with. If they were not universal they would not be necessary.

{2. the contingent ones.}

These rules concern only the form of all rules of thought.

{E.g. If men are mortal, then they must † have existed <once>, too. If the one proposition is true, so too is the other. Such a judgment [is] a hypothetical, conditioned judgment.}

The content of a cognition is the object or the matter and is distinguished from the form. A universal logic must abstract from all objects of thought.

The necessary, universal rules of thought must be *a priori*, moreover, not derived from experience. Everything that comes from experience <*ex*

[a] "lernt {exercitat}."

[b] a supply of words.

[c] "*notwendigen* {necess.}."

cognitione oriuntur> is called empirical and is opposed to <transcendental> cognition *a priori*. We use empirical cognition[d] to aid the latter, to be sure. But that is never good[;] it is always better if one cognizes everything from reason.

694

Logical rules are not ones according to which we think, but according to which we ought to think. {Logic contains no matter at all, only form of thought.} Logic must contain principles *a priori*. {Therefore logic is a science and grammar is *not*, because its rules are contingent.} Hence every logic in which rules from experience occur is no longer pure. {Rules concerning the sensibly perfect are contained in aesthetics.}

That is universal[e] which is universal[f] according to reason[;] empirically universal, only insofar as it is always so in experience. *Paedeutica* (child-rearing) {παιδευτική}. A doctrine concerning practice[g] is no longer pure logic, but only its more refined employment, application. {A distinct concept is one, of whose marks I am conscious. Without these universal rules (even if one is not conscious of them) thought in general is not possible – therefore logic is a propaedeutic to all the sciences, the highest touchstone that something conforms to the laws of the understanding.} All psychological observations must be excluded from <pure> logic. All rules that are logically provable in general are in need of a ground from which they are derived. Many propositions (e.g., that of contradiction) cannot be proved at all, neither *a priori* nor empirically.

{Is there a natural logic? *Logica est scientia. Omnis scientia est artificialis. Ergo –* [h]}

A proof that is made fully *a priori* {at the same time intuitively[,] with insight into necessity} is called a demonstration. Now what is not capable[i] of any demonstration is empirical.

We can consider this science, whether it is doctrine or critique { – depends on use – } or both together.

{Logic as doctrine can be called a canon of the understanding and of reason. A canon is a demonstrated critique (in Greek [the word] indicates a *rule*).}

Logic is a doctrine, it provides rules,[j] it is a demonstrated theory.

A doctrine {is a complex of rules, where the rules must precede the product[.] (Critique is the use of the power of judgment, where the product precedes the rule)[.]} [It] contains the ground for passing judgment as to whether something is true or false. It can have two uses, one

[d] "Kenntnis."
[e] "Universell."
[f] "allgemein."
[g] "Uebungslehre."
[h] Logic is a science. Every true science is artificial. Therefore . . .
[i] "fähig <dignum>."
[j] "sie gibt <praebet> Regeln an die hand."

only as critique, the other as organon. The first case[,] e.g., the doctrine of taste, only critique {serves for passing judgment on something, e.g., a poem}, does not teach us to make something tasteful ourselves. {Critique requires that the product already be there, whereas technical rules can be given in advance.} 695

Mathematics is a doctrine but at the same time an organon {through which a cognition becomes possible as to content} of wide extent, namely, e.g., arithmetic. Is logic also an organon? No, it serves only for critique, as grammar does (which has much similarity with logic), from which one really cannot learn the language[;] this also requires a wealth of words.

A doctrine is a demonstrated discipline {a system,[k] a principle of production}. Logic does not suffice for an organon, it does not have objects. When, notwithstanding, a logic is misused as an organon, it is called dialectic. {The art of speaking about any object *pro et contra*. Reason can deceive itself unintentionally when it oversteps the laws of logic.} If it is to serve merely for passing judgment, however, then it is called analytic or a logic of truth. Dialectic, on the other hand, [is] only a logic of illusion.

{The use of logic is analytical when it is used only as canon, dialectical when it is also used as organon[;] then it is a logic of illusion and deceives us. Logic as canon is called *analytic* (logic of truth). Zeno of Elea, a great dialectician.}

{2ND HOUR}

To think is to represent something to oneself in a concept. Logic can be called a doctrine of reason,[l] not just a rational doctrine[m] {a science of reason[n] as to matter,[o] because its object is only human reason. Mathematics, physics, morals are also sciences of reason, to be sure, but only as to form, not as to matter.} Logic is occupied only with the formal rules of thought. {The object is the matter, the subject the form.}

Can instruction in the fine arts be doctrine? The rules of these arts can serve only for passing judgment. Aesthetics allows no doctrine, only a critique. Sciences, however, allow doctrine. Fine art has no rules as the touchstone of correctness of the judgment of taste, but doctrine has rules.

By barbarism is understood not only the spread of total ignorance but above all the corruption of taste, too. We would have to fear this if we did not still have such excellent models from antiquity. {Namely, poets, beaux-esprits,[p] e.g. Horace, etc. Taste can be cultivated and maintained 696

[k] "Institution."
[l] "Vernunftlehre."
[m] "vernünftige Lehre."
[n] "Vernunftwissenschaft."
[o] Reading "der Materie nach" for "nicht der Materie nach."
[p] "schöne Geister."

only through examples, not through rules. Note: Polyclitus, a famous sculptor of antiquity, made a statue which was subsequently always used as a model. Archetype,[q] lies in everyone's mind, which must approximate to it.}

Fine art needs a model (*exemplar*), then, but not so science[;] it needs rules. A doctrine, insofar as it can be demonstrated, is called a canon. Logic is a canon, not only a critique[;] it is also only a means for passing judgment. {A canon is an inviolable law. Thus it could not be brought about in the case of taste, where everything depends on custom and the satisfaction of others.}

Is logic as a canon also a means for acquiring science? No. Logic abstracts from all content, hence also from all cognition, {it only makes our thought be correct} and it is not an organon. But mathematics is not only a canon but also an excellent organon. {Indeed, certainly the greatest one, for it occupies itself with matter, with the measurement of time and of space.} Natural science also involves mathematics.

Logic is divided, now,

1. into *logica naturalis* (natural) and (only a complement)
2. into *logica artificialis* (artificial). This is the logic that is the use of our understanding actually *explicite* not *implicite*. {Basically there is only an artificial logic, for basically there is no natural logic – natural grammar.}

It is expounded (1.) scientifically, as a science is always expounded, (2.) scholastically-popularly, with scholastic correctness, congruent with the subjective ground of the faculty of cognition of everyone. {Popularity begins with perfection.}[r] Every science must be expounded scholastically correctly. This is a *consequens*[s] of perfection.

Now we can divide logic into

1. the logic of the healthy understanding, *sensus communis*,
2. the logic of the speculative understanding[; this] gives rules *in abstracto*.

The common understanding is the faculty of being able to judge according to rules *in concreto*. {Not the plain[t] [understanding]. This word 697 is absurd.}[2] The common understanding is called healthy when it is correct. Morals must be cognized wholly *in concreto*, but physics also has *abstracta*.

A logic ought to be expounded *in abstracto*. It is a propaedeutic {a preparatory exercise for the sciences} to all the sciences, something that concerns their content, e.g., in regard to physics and morals.

[q] "Archetypon, Urbild."

[r] Reading "geht von der Vollkommenheit aus" for "geht von der Vollkommenheit ab."

[s] Reading "consequens" for "Konsequenz."

[t] "der schlichte."

{3RD HOUR, THE 26TH OF APRIL, 1792}

Can it also be <regarded> as a propaedeutic to philosophy? No. For it is itself a part of philosophy, {and in fact the part with which we are supposed to begin}, as we will soon hear.

All our cognition is either (as to its mode of acquisition)

1. rational, insofar as it is derived *a priori* from reason (e.g., pure mathematics, metaphysics),
2. historical[;] as such it is:

a) subjectively historical, when the cognition in the subject rests on empirical grounds;

b) objectively historical, when the ground of cognition can never be other than historical. Cognitions that are <objectively> rational can nonetheless be subjectively historical. {Logic itself is a system. Cognitions that conform to it are partly systematic, partly fragmentary. – Opposed to methodical cognition is tumultuous cognition.} In mathematics there can be a subjectively historical cognition, even if it is certainly objectively rational, which occurs above all in the case of surveying. Also, unfortunately, in the case of natural religion {which many believe merely out of lazy trust in the reason of others, in order not to rack their brains. If they forget the words, then the thing is forgotten too.}

{What is philosophy?} All cognition of reason is either (1.) a cognition through concepts, (2.) one through construction of concepts. The latter is called exhibiting[u] a concept. This is a cognition of reason only insofar as the concepts correspond with one another *a priori* <in intuition>. A cognition of reason through concepts is called philosophical. Thus a system through concepts is philosophy.

{To construct a concept is to give it a corresponding intuition *a priori*.} A cognition of reason through construction of concepts is called mathematical. Thus a system – – mathematics.

A system must always be thought through, a manifoldness in connection, a combination of cognitions based on a common[v] principle. Hence we can learn much geography, but not in a system, only as an aggregate. The philosopher can be considered as {an} artist of reason[w] and teacher of wisdom. Philosophy <in the practical sense> is the science of the final ends of human reason. Philosophy as art of reason[x] is called speculative, as doctrine of wisdom[y] practical. The ancients always called philosophy the doctrine of wisdom.

698

[u] "darstellen, exhibere."

[v] "gemeinschaftlichen."

[w] "Vernunftkünstler."

[x] "Vernunftkunst."

[y] "Weisheitslehre."

{4TH HOUR, THE 27TH}

One can make a distinction between the two expressions, to learn *philosophy* and to learn *to philosophize.* To learn is to imitate the judgments of others, hence is quite distinct from one's own reflection. {Not to learn philosophy – but rather to learn to philosophize, otherwise it remains only imitation – but to attain it oneself through exercise of the understanding, that is what matters. Only he who is capable of the self-use of his reason is called a philosopher. Philosophy is scientific cognition *in abstracto* – it is itself science.} To learn to philosophize means one must learn to use his reason himself, and here of course there is a use of healthy and of speculative reason. We must exercise it in concepts. Practical cognition, insofar as our understanding aims at cultivation and an end; and practical reason is the final end of human |wisdom|. Philosophy as doctrine of wisdom presupposes a teacher of wisdom. The ancients demanded of a teacher of wisdom that he also be a wise man in practice. {Wisdom is agreement with the final ends of all things. All other cognitions have their value only as means – only philosophy leads to the ultimate final end – wisdom. (The doctrine of the highest good.) Philosophy – love for wisdom.} The cynics {the name derives from *kynosarges*,[z] a building where they customarily met} took the short way, as they called it, to happiness, by practicing being able to do without everything.

Now we wish to speak somewhat of philosophy as a complex of cognitions, and of its history.

The first philosophers were poets. It took time, namely, to discover words for abstract concepts[;] hence in the beginning supersensible thoughts were represented in sensible images. Pherecydes first wrote 699 philosophy in prose. {The founder of the Ionian school is Thales. The Eleatic school included Parmenides, Xenophanes. On account of the poverty of language, one could only philosophize in poetry at that time.}

The most famous sect is the Platonic one, then the Aristotelian. The latter were called *peripatetici*[a] {they spent their time in the Lyceum[;] this was a colonnade where things were taught *ambulando*[b]}[;] the former [were called] Academics. The Stoics <under Zeno of Citium> got their name from στοά, *porticus.*[c] The Epicureans – (h*orti*[d]) {Epicurus taught there}.

The so-called Academy (i.e., Plato's school) was in the beginning wholly dogmatic, but it degenerated later into addiction to doubt,[e] skepti-

[z] From κῦνόσαργης, a gymnasium for those who were not pure Athenians.

[a] From περιπᾰτετικοί, ones who walk around.

[b] while walking.

[c] Both words mean "porch."

[d] gardens.

[e] "Zweifelsucht."

cism. Carneades cannot be regarded as the founder of a new school but only as an extraordinary orator. Arcesilaus founded a new one, however.

{Anaxagoras was the first philosopher who also taught theology.} The ancients divided the whole of philosophy into three parts, namely, logic, physics, and ethics. But one must still consider whether a dichotomy would not be better here than a trichotomy. {Practical |philosophy|: (1.) Ethical[;] Socrates never purported to be a philosopher. His fragmentary doctrines were brought into a system by Plato. (2.) Political, rules of prudence, Pythagoras. With respect to him everything still lies in obscurity. A term of the subdivision enters into the superdivision.}

We have now actually divided philosophy into:

1. formal philosophy[;] this is logic.
2. material philosophy. This can be divided into theoretical and practical.

Ethics in modern times has been called the doctrine of virtue. Physics can also be considered in two ways.

1. As *physica rationalis*, pure doctrine of nature {pure is the opposite of empirical} [;] since Aristotle this is called metaphysics.
2. As *physica materialis*[,] or as metaphysics and empirical physics. Any cognition is *pure* when there is no influence of empirical cognitions[f] in it.

Physica empirica can be divided again

1. into the doctrine of bodies, *physica specialis* † and
2. into the doctrine of soul, *psychologia specialis* †.

If we regard philosophy as the complex of several sciences, then first we want to look at the 7 so-called liberal arts:[g] (1.) grammar, (2.) rhetoric, (3.) dialectic, (4.) arithmetic, (5.) music, (6.) geometry, (7.) astronomy. {This division was made by Rabanus Maurus (at the time of Charlemagne) on behalf of theology. – At that time all the sciences were divided into A) a higher faculty: (1.) preservation of blessedness,[h] (2.) of freedom and of property, (3.) of life and health, of *esse* in general; B) *melius esse*, the lower faculty}.[3]

700

[f] "Kenntnisse."

[g] "freien Künste."

[h] "Seligkeit."

{5TH HOUR, THE 30TH OF APRIL}

Tractatio ipsa

Logic is the science that contains the formal rules and principles of thought. It is customarily divided into:

1. theoretical logic,
2. practical logic[;] but there is no such division, for in that case it would have to be applied to objects, which is not the case at all, however, for it contains only the formal rules of thought.

One can | divide | it rather into:

1. the doctrine of elements[; this] contains rules in general,
2. the doctrine of method[; this] contains the principles of science.

The doctrine of method is the complex of cognitions,[i] insofar as they are made into a system { – It contains directions for the way in which a system of cognition is to be attained}. It constitutes the so-called practical part.

In the history of logic the most outstanding phenomenon is where it battled with itself as to whether any cognition is certain. He who believed that it could be completely proved was called a dogmatist, but the doubters were called skeptics. {Skeptics wanted to *prove* that one cannot attain certainty about anything at all, and thus they fell into contradiction with themselves – a cathartic, which annuls itself. – Their acuity, with which they attacked the scholastics, is admirable.} They were in the end a valuable sect. {Pyrrho was the earliest of all the skeptics – later Arcesilaus, Carneades.}

We have no one who has exceeded Aristotle or enlarged his <pure> logic (which is in itself fundamentally impossible) just as no mathematician has exceeded Euclid.

| {*Something about the history of logic.* The Greeks, among all oriental peoples, have the greatest merit for developing philosophy. Subsequently its study declined almost wholly in the time of the middle ages, until in the 701 12th century the scholastics arose in Paris. Actually all their distinctions concerned only theology, hence also the many useless rules and barbaric expressions here.[j] In the end people made do with digging the ancient

[i] "Kenntnissen."

[j] Ak, "daher auch"; MS and Ko, "daher auch hier."

authors out of the scholastic chaos and the ruination of language that <resulted> from it. – Locke became famous through his *Essay Concerning Human Understanding* – he speaks there of the origin of concepts, <but> this really does not belong to logic, but rather to metaphysics. The result of his investigations: Everything derives from experience. But it does not follow at all from this that concepts can be *displayed* only in experience. – Then Leibniz entered the picture. Although actually having written no logic, he nonetheless did much to illuminate concepts (he wrote in defense of his countrymen against the Englishman Locke). In his works he expressed ideas which subsequently moved Wolff to his system. Thorough description of this is to be found in Reusch, *Systema logicae*,[4] and in Corvinus.[5] Crusius[6] provides much nourishment for the understanding.} |

A principal point in logic will rest on the criterion of truth. Now we begin.

I. The doctrine of elements

{It treats the concepts of the understanding in general. The division of all thought – which has various forms that may be exhausted and brought into a system. The general thing that lies at the basis of all cognition is *representation* – a fundamental concept that cannot be explained. *Cognition* is relation of representation to an object – combined with an *actio* in the mind – consciousness (representation of our representation), which is lacking in obscure representations.}

The ancients divided it into (1.) *apprehensio simplex*, (2.) *judicium*, and (3.) *ratiocinium.*[k] Our cognition involves two things, *intuition* and *concept*. Representations can also be related to something other than cognition, namely, to the feeling of pleasure and displeasure (the way in which we are affected by things). All our intuition belongs to sensibility, every concept to the understanding. Sensibility contains two faculties, sense and imagination {this is the magical power of the human spirit}, or the faculty for intuition of an object insofar as it is not present[;] but sense is that faculty insofar as the object is present.

702

{All our representation is (1.) sensation – its relation to the subject, (2.) cognition – relation to the object. (1.) e.g., pleasure – lies merely in me – not in the object.}

Of the consciousness of representation, or apperception

This is the faculty of representation in relation to an object {that belongs to our condition}, which in the case of apprehension is still not present at all, but instead is, as it were, produced <grasped[l]>. In the thought that man can say, I think – there lies exceptionally much. *Consciousness* of our concepts is always hard. {It is required above all for concepts. Due to the lack of consciousness, even animals are not capable of any concept – intuition they do have. – Consciousness is a wholly separate dimension of the faculty of cognition (therefore gradation from animals to man does not occur).} A concept contains what is universal for many <(various)> representations. A concept is called

[k] (1.) simple apprehension, (2.) judgment, and (3.) inference.

[l] "gegriffen."

clear, of which one is conscious. (The savage would ask, What is a house?)

distinct, when one is conscious not only of the total concepts but also of the partial concepts.[m] We need distinctness in all concepts that we wish to communicate to others. One cannot demand <distinctness> of any concept that contains no manifoldness (partial representations). E.g., time. {With this concept one can only demand clarity – it is only a simple representation.}

When a representation that is clear as a whole is obscure *particulariter*, then it is indistinct. {Indistinct representations are called confused.[n] But actually they come from the weakness of the representation. If there is order in |representations|, however, then it arises out of confusion. Only when the representation is composite can it be confused.} Concepts of which one is not conscious are obscure. It holds, however, only for obscure representations. These are either

1. merely clear, and then either
   a) simple or
   b) composite, or
2. merely distinct. This distinctness is 703
   a) distinctness of intuition,
   b) distinctness of concepts. (In the author, only this latter appears, but the corresponding intuition, exhibition,[o] is just as necessary.)

{Order in representations and concepts is of the greatest importance. There are three relations:

1. subject to predicate,
2. dividing members to the divided concept,
3. the relation of ground to consequence.}

Not even philosophers have succeeded in wholly explicating the concept of virtue. One has it in oneself but cannot express it. –

{6TH HOUR, THE 1ST OF MAY}

§ 15 and § 16 in our author do not really belong to logic at all. {P. 11. 12}[7]

§ 17. Rational cognition, a distinct way of cognizing something from grounds. A cognition from concepts is really cognition of the understanding. To think means to represent something to oneself *discursive*$_L$[; it is] distinguished from intuition, to represent something to oneself *intuitive*$_L$. Reason, the faculty of inferring[;] this involves judgments, and these cannot occur † without concepts. Receptivity[p] is distinct from spontaneity {self-activity}. Understanding is the higher faculty of cognition. {It is,

[m] Reading "Totalbegriffe . . . Teilbegriffe" for "Teilbegriffe . . . Totalbegriffe."
[n] "verworrene <konfuse>."
[o] "Darstellung, exhibitio."
[p] "Die Empfänglichkeit, Receptivität."

namely, the faculty of rules[,] and these are already concepts.} Then one comes from representations to concepts <*facultas concept . . .* >, then to judgments, then to inferences.

{The higher faculty of cognition contains:

1. understanding,
2. power of judgment,
3. reason.}

The *understanding* is the faculty of representation of the universal as such. {E.g., definition of man in general.}

The *power of judgment* is the faculty of representing the particular as contained under the universal {Caius is a man}[,] or the faculty of subsumption.

Reason is the faculty of the *derivation of the particular from the universal* or cognition *a priori*. {All men are mortal. Sempronius is a man, too. Sempronius is mortal.

704

In the *first two*, understanding and power of judgment, one can teach, in the *latter* only practice.}

The definition of logic, *cognitio rationalis*,[q] is not the best[; it] could only hold if it has for its object the use of the rules of the understanding and of reason.

All cognition must be rational.[r] The author should say, then, cognition of reason.[s] Now what is not *cognition of reason* is *historical* cognition, rests on empirical grounds. {Scientific cognition is that of which rules *in abstracto* are possible. Cognition is common insofar as it is not scientific.}

One must exert oneself to learn *to philosophize*, not merely to learn *philosophy*. For if we did the latter our cognition would be merely historical and not drawn from ourselves. A complex of cognitions as a system is a science, and here a main principle, from which everything else is derived, also lies at the basis. A cognition is called common insofar as it is not science. It can sometimes be very vast, but has no system, no unity of the whole. He who possesses such a cognition is opposed to him who has science not as to matter but as to form. Indeed, as to matter he can even be richer, but everything is thrown together randomly. We may count philosophical cognition a part of learnedness, insofar as we provide a philosophical history of what all philosophers ever have said. But he who can do this is not on that account a philosopher. One is this only when one can philosophize. Historical cognition as science is learnedness. A teacher of reason[t] can be a philosopher or a mathematician. He who possesses all historical cognition as a science is called a polyhistor.

[q] rational cognition.

[r] "Vernünftig."

[s] "Vernunfterkenntnis."

[t] "Vernunftlehrer."

In the concept of the philosopher one can think a twofold distinction: (1.) as artist of reason, (2.) as wise man or legislator.

Philosophy proper (which should not be merely an art of reason) includes nothing but metaphysics and morals. These serve as means for cognizing our existence as rational beings and for cognizing the ultimate end, our aim {– the highest good –}, the most sublime that we have. From this it becomes clear that the *physicist* does not have a *science* at all, although one always counts physics among the sciences. 705

Our author treats now

Of beautiful cognition

{There really is no beautiful cognition.[u] In cognition it is only a matter of the relation to the object – if it is met with, then it is *true*, but only the *exhibition* can be *beautiful.*

Sensibility is the faculty of intuition:

A. sense, faculty of intuition in the present,
B. imagination, faculty of intuition in the absence of the object.}

If I call something beautiful, then I thereby express my satisfaction, my pleasure (the relation of the object to the subject, which produces a pleasant representation, which determines the mind itself to the preservation of that representation) in the object. The basis of the definition. In everything beautiful we understand only relation of cognition to the subject, not to the object itself. E.g., in the description of beautiful objects one describes only how one is affected by them. One cannot possibly depict the object itself. There simply is no beautiful cognition, then.

{7TH HOUR, THE 3RD OF MAY}

Perfection is divided into

1. logical perfection in the agreement of the faculty of cognition with the object,
2. aesthetic perfection[;] | it | consists in the agreement of the object with the subject's faculty of cognition.

{Aesthetic perfection is the subjective agreement of the understanding with sensibility – which enlivens the representation of an object. Because the agreement is only subjective, it will also be possible only through sensation. A feeling of pleasure arises with this[,] just as a feeling of displeasure does in the sensation of opposition.}

Imagination and understanding are the only two active faculties of cognition of the human mind. But the senses are wholly passive, they necessarily require an object[;] imagination provides objects for itself. 706

[u] "Schönes Erkenntnis."

All our cognitions involve the following two things {two elements, one of which without the other yields no cognition}:

1. intuition (the interpretation[v] of the concept, of thought);

2. concept. A pure concept like a pure rule does not yet yield any distinctness of cognition[;] this requires intuition, too. Conversely, intuition without concept is likewise nothing. For without [a concept] it would be as if it had seen nothing. E.g., tasteful poetic descriptions of regions, which produce only intuition, do not serve at all for cognition, are only cosmetic.

If I look only to beauty, however, then I do not demand instruction but only pleasing entertainment. This satisfaction can excite the mind itself[;] in that case it remains in spontaneity. Taste is supposed to be the faculty of taking satisfaction in the object on the basis of the subjective agreement of the powers of cognition.

{Since beauty can never be cognized through concepts, only through feeling, but this is not as communicable as concepts, which, since they deal with the object, [and are] the same in all subjects – no objective rules concerning it may be given, then. Nonetheless the beautiful is distinct from the pleasant through the fact that the former holds for all with subjective universality, while the latter reaches only to individual subjects. With matters of the *pleasant* one will not demand that anyone make the same judgment – as in the case of objects of the *beautiful*, where the judgment of *taste* is universally valid. – The aesthetically beautiful is not to be elucidated through rules but merely through examples – hence the worth of the classical authors.}

In regard to satisfaction in objects, cognition is of two kinds.

1. The beautiful[;] the faculty of distinguishing the beautiful is called taste.
2. The sublime[;] the faculty of distinguishing |the sublime| is called feeling.

Taste belongs to the power of judgment. For it is not |a| means for producing objects but only for passing judgment on them.

Now the power of judgment is also of two kinds:

1. logical,

707 2. aesthetic. The latter is taste {understanding in union with imagination}. An empirical judgment is produced through the immediate impression that the <representation of the> object makes on our mind, produces {in regard to the feeling of pleasure and displeasure}. The logical power of judgment always has established rules. But those of the aesthetic power of judgment rest only on empirical grounds. To quarrel about the pleasure that arises from the senses (e.g., to be astonished that sauerkraut does not taste good to someone else) would be quite foolish. Hence in *this* case the proverb, *Chacun à son goût*,[w] would be correct if it

[v] "die Interpretation."
[w] French: Each to his own taste.

had this meaning. But since this is not so {for here we do not understand by taste the stimulation of the palate but rather the aesthetic power of judgment}, then it is false in every other respect. For taste is the aesthetic power of judgment and is *universally valid.* This can put us on the trail of where taste is really to be posited. {Everything that belongs to sensation is subjective, everything that belongs to intuition objective.} Everything that does not rest on the relation of our faculty of representations to the object, but rather to the subject, to the representing faculty, is *aesthetic.* Insofar as we find imagination and understanding enlivened harmoniously through a certain feeling, we have taste. {The freedom of imagination agreeing with the concept of the understanding. Without the former, which gives it intuition, the latter would accomplish nothing – the object would disappear for it. The understanding comes to the aid of imagination and brings uunity into its products.}

|{*Taste* is art. The understanding and imagination, which have to unite in this, are like two friends, who cannot stand each other and yet cannot part from each other – for they live in perpetual strife and yet are mutually indispensable. As follows from the above, there are no beautiful sciences,[x] but only an *art of the beautiful.* In order to produce it, *genius* is required – e.g., a good poem cannot be ordered, it comes about only when the poet has the mood – the fortunate disposition of the mind – for it[;] rules are not enough for this. There are poets rather than rules for poetry.}|

{8TH HOUR}

The logical perfection of representations consists in the fact that they represent particular representations as in the universal { – or formal completeness is the requisite for logical perfection (as material is for aesthetic) – it seeks out the particular under the universal.} But in the case of the aesthetic it is just the converse. There, that is, universal representations are represented in the particular. In a logical judgment, then, I look then only to the fact that particular representations are represented in the universal. {With aesthetic judgment, again, it is just the converse.} Logical perfection requires bringing intuition to concepts, aesthetic perfection bringing concepts to intuition. Logical perfection consists in the agreement of cognition with the object, aesthetic perfection in that with the subject and its faculty of cognition. 708

Our author opposes ugliness <*deformitas*> to beauty {ugliness is just as positive as beauty – an object that I hate, the maximum disgust}[;] but there is a middle term, dryness <*jejunum*> {it is a grade of perfection that mathematics possesses, because it has dryness}, and in fact dryness and

[x] "schönen Wissenschaften."

beauty can exist together {e.g., in a sermon which begins dryly but contains many beauties in what follows.}

Beauty can only concern exhibition, intuition, not really the concept. The great business of propagation extends throughout the whole of nature. – The expression[,] beautiful cognition[,][y] is not fitting at all.

The faculties of our mind may be brought into the following three classes:

1. faculty of cognition,
2. feeling of pleasure and displeasure,
3. faculty of desire.

Our cognition is a representation, and

1. In relation to the faculty of cognition it is called *logical* perfection {in relation to the *understanding* – truth is a judgment, not a feeling}.
2. In relation to the feeling of pleasure and displeasure it is called *aesthetic* perfection {in relation to the *power of judgment*}.
3. That it agrees with our faculty of desire – *practical* perfection {in relation to *reason*}.

709

Of the perfections of cognition

We can have perfection in cognition:

1. in quantity – universality –
2. in regard to quality – *distinctness* through concepts {i.e., through consciousness of marks},
3. in regard to relation – relation <of representation> to an object. Truth[,] agreement of the judgment with the mode of thought. {Truth is here the logical perfection.}
4. in regard to modality (rests on whether it is contingent or necessary). {Here it is the necessity that is cognized *a priori*.}

Logical perfection <as to quantity> consists in the *universality* of representations, that concepts become distinct. This universality was objective {and aimed at representing the particular in the universal *in abstracto* – }. But aesthetically it is subjective and this subjective universality is called popularity. {Thus aesthetic perfection aims, on the contrary, at representing the universal *in concreto* – this [is] popularity – to make concepts of the understanding congruent[z] with the *sensus communis* (i.e., with the healthy common understanding. – }

The 2nd logical perfection is *distinctness* through concepts. This is effected through few marks {in which I am conscious of the partial representations, too, however}; aesthetic distinctness [is effected] through

[y] "schöne Erkenntnis."

[z] "angemessen."

many marks. Logical distinctness arises from the fact that I represent little in many things, aesthetic distinctness from the fact that I represent much in <few>. Aesthetic distinctness is called liveliness in the combination of many representations. For logical distinctness abstraction is required. Aesthetic [distinctness] involves a swarm of coordinate representations.

The 3rd perfection is relation to the object – *truth* {agreement with the object}. That which holds according to appearance is aesthetically true – the agreement of a judgment with the subject's mode of thought. Thus the poet is concerned with universal illusion, with subjective truth. The poetic is always true aesthetically, seldom logically. E.g., thunder rumbles. {Truth is agreement of the judgment with the mode of thought.}

Now the 4th <perfection>. Modality rests on whether it is a necessary or merely a contingent judgment. An aesthetic necessity, namely, [is] when it is necessary to represent the thing in accordance with laws of imagination, not according to laws of reason. Aesthetic necessity is only subjective necessity. Aesthetic perfection is the understanding's condescension to sensibility. 710

{9TH HOUR}

An object is given through intuition, thought through concepts. When intuition and concept agree, tending to enliven the cognition itself, then they produce a satisfaction in us, and this is then called beautiful cognition.[a] One must exert oneself to get understanding and imagination to agree in reference to a common enterprise. This is no longer play, however. With a beautiful product a new cognition is not required, but only the enlivening of the powers of cognition. Production of the beautiful is in general not science, but rather free play of imagination. Imagination and understanding are two friends who cannot do without one another but cannot stand one another either, for one always harms the other. The more universal the understanding is in its rules, the more perfect it is, but if it wants to consider things *in concreto* then | it | absolutely cannot do without the imagination.

The imperfections of cognition are (1.) either imperfections of lack (*defectus*) or (2.) imperfections of deprivation (*vitium*), better, of transgression (*reatus, transgressio legis*, it is *reus*[b]).[8]

{Ignorance resembles a *tabula rasa* – error a scribbled tablet. Here one has in addition the labor of wiping away the false in order to come once again to ignorance.

Truth	Ignorance	Error
+a	o[c]	−a }

[a] "schönes Erkenntnis."
[b] accusation, transgression of the law, [it is] the accused.
[c] Reading "o" for "a."

For even if one does not say everything that is true, everything that one says must still be true. Opposition is not only something negative, but actually something positive, which in mathematics would have the minus sign. E.g., if a doctor does not merely |not| replenish a sick man's lack of health but wholly destroys it for him. From this we even see that among all the imperfections of human existence one must protect oneself most of all against that of opposition, because it has the horrible property not only of not being valuable but even of damaging. For if one has learned something false, it costs unspeakable effort to transpose oneself once again into the condition one was in, as if one knew nothing of it, so as to become acquainted with the truth.

711

{10TH HOUR}

Of the extensiveness of learned cognition

{The horizon is the complex of those cognitions that belong to a man's end.}

Extensive cognition rests on manyness,[d] but intensive cognition on degree. The last is a quantity of unity. The first is called by the author extensiveness of learned cognition.

Of the horizon of human cognition. – The horizon {horizon, the circle that limits all objects} is the congruence <agreement> of the limits of any cognition whatever with the limits of human perfection. This latter is limited, would fall prey to chimeras if it were extended beyond the limits. Nothing can be invisible to us beyond the horizon. Hence this way of speaking is wrong. It is only what lies beneath our horizon that we cannot know. We can divide our horizon:

{Only this belongs in our field. We divide: things that are beyond, outside, and beneath our horizon – outside it, what we do not need to know; beneath it, what we ought not to know. This is concerned with the end, with the practical.}

1. logically, the determination of our logical horizon { – relation to the faculty of cognition requires distinctness of abstraction. This would harm the imagination. Aesthetics needs only clarity, therefore}.
2. aesthetically, as to agreement with our taste.
3. practically, as to the congruence[e] of our cognition with our ends.

We can divide the logical horizon into:

1. the historical horizon, and it can be a) objective {e.g., natural history, history}, b) subjective.

[d] "Vielheit."

[e] "Angemessenheit."

2. the rational horizon {objectively rational, insofar as one can have insight into it *a priori*}.

The historical horizon is incomparably more extensive than the rational {either that of pure reason or metaphysics or (2.) that grounded on experience[,] or physiology}. In mathematics the latter is the most extensive, in philosophy the former. The field of mathematics is unsurveyable. Critique is the determination of the <rational> horizon of human cognition. {There is a universal horizon of the cognitions of the human race. The horizon of human cognition that concerns experience is called physics. Physics also has its limits, insofar as we do not have insight with reason as to whence this or that object comes.} 712

To determine the rational horizon of human cognition is one of the noblest and hardest occupations of the human spirit. Here metaphysicians usually go astray. – Only metaphysics or its <foundation, the> critique of pure reason[,] can show where the limits of reason begin and where all its faculty ceases. One can occupy oneself |with| the universal horizon of humanity and [also] treat the individual man. It is maintained by some, quite without right, that there are certain cognitions we can know, but |they| would not be of value to us. {Many cognitions and sciences would not have reached the [current] level if one had asked right at the beginning about their use. This often shows itself only when they have attained perfection.} *Quaerit delirus et non respondet Homerus.*[f] The human race must learn all cognitions useful to us {in order thereby to cultivate its understanding. – No knowledge of any kind whatsoever can be wholly contrary to ends (universally)}. Admittedly, something can perhaps be dispensable for individual men. Men divide cognitions[g] into various fields. For each there are lovers, accordingly as they have inclinations toward this thing or that.

{11TH HOUR, THE 10TH OF MAY}

{Further, one can divide the horizon of human cognition into:

1. the horizon of healthy reason,
2. of the sciences.}

In a certain way we can say that the beginning of the world is when the art of writing arose. There are no cognitions[h] at all that we ought not to know, for it is our duty, universally, to know everything if only we can know it. But there are of course cognitions[i] that we can do without and

[f] A madman asks and Homer does not reply.
[g] "Kenntnisse."
[h] "Kenntnisse."
[i] "Kenntnisse."

therefore need not know {which are outside our horizon, according to the explanation above} (as, e.g., the doctor can do without Hebrew. Hence need not know it).

713 The manner in which cognitions[j] are taught in universities is called factory-like,[k] because there are many who work here communally on one end.

Quantity of Cognition. Here it is not a matter of multitude but of degree. {*Non multa, sed multum.*[l] The external extensive quantity of cognition indicates the universal extension of it among many men. – This is the situation today – – *Enlightenment* – the degree of culture – which, according to the talents of the subject, makes man capable of his ends as man and as citizen.}

Practical rules in regard to the horizon of human cognition. One must not determine the horizon of one's cognition too early, for one does not know for what one will have a particular talent in the future. Inclination can alter even more. {First learn a great deal, in order then to see in what one takes the most pleasure – but not in a desultory fashion – from one to the other. – All study in accordance with rules cultivates the understanding – hence grammar [is] valuable even to the future artist. Usually one learns to act in conformity with, one even becomes acquainted with, his talents, inclinations, and situation † only when it is too late.} But once one has accepted the horizon of his cognition determinately, one must not alter it easily. One must not measure the horizon of others by his own. Above all, one must not call valueless what seems to us in a particular respect to be dispensable. If people had always wanted to grasp value with their hands, they would never have advanced in any science. Can there be things of which one can say that we ought not[m] to know them? – Praiseworthy ignorance? Ignorance is never praiseworthy. {Thus there is an *ignoratio inculpabilis* (inculpable), but never an *ignorantia laudabilis*.} Not that, but rather acquaintance with one's ignorance is praiseworthy {and it requires much cognition[n]}. He who comes this far makes the step from the field of science to the field of wisdom. Those who are inflated by conceit are usually called idiots by others. Thus are men called who, even if they have many cognitions[o] – still do not have science[;] he who does not have the former either is called ignorant. In general, he who lacks knowledge[p] in regard to the science from which he profits, is called ignorant.[q] – An idiot is to one

[j] "Kenntnisse."
[k] "fabrikenmäßig."
[l] Not many, but much.
[m] Ak, "wollen"; MS and Ko, "sollen."
[n] "Kenntnis."
[o] "viel Kenntnisse."
[p] "unwissend ist."
[q] "Ignorant."

who knows much what the *laicus* is to the *clericus* or what the *literatus*, one who can read and write, . . . – at that time, much!}[9] Polyhistory is knowing 714 a lot historically[;][r] knowing a lot rationally would be called polymathy {this includes philosophy and mathematics}[;] and <both taken together>[,] knowing a lot about everything (if that can be thought)[,] would be called pansophy.

The polyhistor must be (1.) a *humanist*, i.e., he must be well-acquainted with the ancients and the fine arts (poetic and rhetorical art).

{The *humaniora* are advantageous for cognition[s] of taste and for participation in the sensations of others. This latter, namely, the faculty to communicate one's sensations <cognitions[t] † and feelings> to others, constitutes exactly what is characteristic of the humanist. – The humanist is such through the fact that his cognition is science, learnedness. – }

What corresponds to the humanist is the belletrist. He is not concerned, like the former, with the independently beautiful, but only with what is alterable in accordance with the variety of taste that follows fashion.

{The belletrist is only one who apes the humanist – a mere dilettante. We have to decide for one or the other. In order not to become a pedant, the belletrist pursues merely gallantry.[u] The gallant manner is nothing other than tasteful popularity. Scholastic perfection (congruence[v] with rules <with the object>[)] always remains the first requisite for cognition, just as in the case of language grammatical correctness is required first –
then elegance. Popularity <congruence[w] with the subject> must be the descent[x] of a cognition, insofar as it already has scholastic perfection. He who holds |scholastic perfection| <in social intercourse> to be the only perfection is called a *pedant*; he can never communicate except with someone who has also been schooled in the same way.[y] Gallantry is just as much a mistake.}

The polyhistor must be

2. a *linguist*, one well-acquainted with ancient languages, because here it is a matter of independent, lasting models.

3. The *literator* is someone well-acquainted with books (Magliabecchi,[10] a famous book-collector[z] in Florence, had a terrific memory). Philology is the complex of all instruments of learnedness. The philologist is the

[r] "historische Vielwisserei."
[s] "Kenntnis."
[t] "Kenntnisse."
[u] "galante Studia."
[v] "Angemessenheit."
[w] "Angemessenheit."
[x] "Herablassung."
[y] "der die Schule mitgemacht."
[z] "Buchführer."

connoisseur of the tools of learnedness,[a] the humanist is the connoisseur of the cultivation of taste. Humanity is always at the same time popular. Only dead languages can become models of taste, not living ones, for the latter simply change too often, and words whose meaning was noble have 715 a lower meaning. To have lasting taste, one must study the ancients. If the ancients were to be lost, one has to fear the spread of barbarism. In Hindustan there is a language that was once in use there but is now dead {its origin unknown} (Sanskrit), which is quite perfect, but is only spoken by a few Brahmins. The belletrist is called a dilettante[;] he finds pleasure and taste in the fine arts.

We can divide the talent of man inasmuch as it is inclined:

1. toward science or
2. toward art {all culture rests on these two things}.

The latter | art | can now be divided into:

a) liberal arts, *artes liberales* or *ingenuae*[b] {a liberal art is skill that pleases immediately},
b) into wage-earning arts,[c] *artes mercenales*[,] serviles,[d] which can please only as a means to some self-serving end {wage-earning arts always please only mediately, for other purposes, and just so all the sciences, too. They almost always please only on account of their usefulness[,] etc. Mathematics pleases immediately, to be sure, but to this extent one could also reckon it among the free arts. Wage-earning art can be made to order – not liberal art – | we | cannot make its products according to rules like the former.}

This division of talent must be handled carefully. The beautiful is that which pleases through itself. With this one simply does not ask about use. If, with an art, one asks about the use, then it is an art for earning one's bread.[e]

As for what concerns the sciences, these may be divided into

1. historical sciences and
2. sciences of reason.

The complex of historical sciences is learnedness. The complex of sciences of reason has no particular name, for its parts[,] philosophy and mathematics[,] are simply too very different. The complex of all sciences is called polyhistory, of which we spoke above.

The author speaks now of the pedant. He is (1.) scholastic pedant, (2.)

[a] Ak, "Gelehrsamkeit, der Humanist"; Ko and MS, "Gelehrsamkeit. Der Philolog ist der Kenner der Werkzeuge der Gelehrsamkeit, der Humanist."

[b] liberal arts [or] ones worthy of a free man.

[c] "Lohnkünste."

[d] arts that are hired, servile.

[e] "Brotkunst."

pedant in matters of politeness.[f] E.g., someone speaks like a book, always under the compulsion of rules. {One finds such people at courts, e.g., chamberlains.}

Of pedantry

716

{p. 24, § 65.}[11]

By a pedant we do not understand one who is ignorant (thus the author's explanation is incorrect). But he is laughed at. How does that happen? The word *pedant* comes from Italian and means actually *magister pedarius*.[g] Now this latter was merely a schoolman, not for the world at all, because he did not come to the master's table but was for the most part with the servants.

{Pedantry is fussiness in form. No nation is so inclined to this as the German nation is. Pedantry exists in all fields, above all in the military and among jurists. – A charlatan [is] one who ostentatiously displays a meager cognition.}

Pedantry is useless exactitude <fussiness> in formalities. Purposive exactitude <meticulousness> in formalities is thoroughness. The two have a certain similarity, then. In many cases there is much that is arbitrary in formalities. For scholastic purposes they are useful, but not for popular ones, i.e., in social intercourse. Fussiness and meticulousness are thus to be distinguished.

It is very true that the transition from meticulousness to fussiness is quite easy. One cannot possibly learn everything according to formalities, e.g., to write a letter. Thus one sees the great difference between the pupil's wooden letter and his sister's flowing one {although the latter one may not be at all orthographic}. The Muses do need the society of the Graces, then, and these latter consist in the fact that the dust of the school, the scholastic, is wiped away from the cognition and it becomes popular, universally comprehensible. {Therefore the ground of the cognition must be scholastically correct, however.}

Pedantry is not unique to the scholarly estate but peculiar to all classes. A *dummy*[h] is one who cannot create anything from himself but can merely imitate, and when he wants to produce something from his cognitions cannot depart at all from the scholastic formulas. {*D.; umbraticus*[12] – the sign of a pedant. – Gallantry means a beautifying of that which is not in itself a beautiful object.} Charlatanism is boasting and ostentation. Belletrism belongs to the fashionable *studium*, which alters

[f] "Höflichkeitspedant."

[g] a teacher of inferior rank, who must travel on foot (reading "pedarius" for "pedanius").

[h] "Pinsel."

so often. The more a science is extended <not> as to content but rather as to space the shallower it becomes.

717

Of the quantity of learned cognition

Extensiveness consists in extensive quantity in the manifold {to know about *many* things}. Intensive quantity is concerned with degree {to know *much* about *one* thing. *Non multa, sed multum.* The quantity of the extension weakens the degree – produces shallowness. There is more value on the whole when some few have deep cognition in the science – which they treat with thoroughness – than when it is[i] distributed universally.}

Mathematics, e.g., is extensive quantity. One must restrict[j] the manyness of cognitions in order to produce a unity.

The author always speaks of learned cognition. But this expression is improper. Cognition can be called scientific[k] if it is scientific[l] and systematic. Now this involves a main principle, just as in history one accepts the civil constitution[m] as a main principle. History can also be regarded as a science, then, if it is brought into a system, which one derives from a main principle.

The whole doctrine of elements is nothing more than common cognition, and the whole of logic should be treated thus, so that the common man can understand it without other cognitions. In regard to objects, a cognition can be extensively great, in regard to objects – their manyness and manifold application, as in mathematics. Even popularity deals not with how much[n] <*quantum*> but rather with how many things[o] <*quot*> we know. This contributes to using it in society. In one age enlightenment can be extensively great, namely, when it reaches all, but intensively small, namely, because no one has very much of it, but all simply know some little[;] they are so-called *bureaux d'esprit*,[p] e.g., like Madame Geoffrin,[13] who was famous on this account. Just as when one beats gold[q] very flat it then takes up a great space, but on the other hand it is thin and can easily be damaged. The extensive quantity of enlightenment can also be called subjective, since it stretches to all subjects, but the intensive can be called objective, which deals with degree.

[i] Reading "ist" for "sind."
[j] "restringiren."
[k] "scientifisch."
[l] "wissenschaftlich."
[m] "bürgerliche Verfassung."
[n] "wieviel."
[o] "wie vielerlei."
[p] French: obsolete expression for societies, or clubs, of intellectuals.
[q] Reading "Gold" for "Geld."

The author speaks further now:

Of the fruitfulness and importance of a cognition

Fecunditas et dignitas.[r] Both have to do with the intensively great. Former rests on the multitude <of the consequences>, latter on the {importance of the consequences}. But we also have[s] cognitions that are at the same time fruitful and important. {Everything that cultivates the understanding is logically important. Hence mathematics is so to an exceptional degree, on account of its clarity, distinctness, certainty. – Distinctness: where the concept's marks are clear. When the marks of the marks are so, Wolff called this completeness – however, the partial concepts can always have still others in[t] themselves, and here there is | no | limit, then, until the simple representations.} 718

Now we come to a material that does belong to logic proper, namely,

Of the truth of learned cognition

Logic begins with clear concepts but gives no rules for how they are made clear. For logic presupposes consciousness of representations. Thus logic properly teaches only of the *distinctness of concepts.*

Now we have spoken of the quantity and quality of cognition and we come now to

III. *the relation of representations* in our cognition. The agreement of representations with their object is called truth. – Now in this chapter we wish to have a criterion of truth that holds without distinction in all cognitions. {The skeptics said all judgments were made haphazardly – διαλλήλη,[u] always the grounded on the ground and this again on the grounded, hence in a circle.}

{There is a universal formal criterion of truth, however, agreement of [cognition] with itself – a material criterion, agreement with the object[,] cannot be possible universally – for (if it were universal) it would also have to occur when I abstract from all matter, – and the agreement of my cognition of the object with my cognition of the object would be <a> tautological criterion. Hence the skeptics overturned the latter[;] the former they were not able to attack.}

The universal criterion of truth will really always be only formal, will abstract from all content and difference of cognition. It will never say to me, then, whether my cognition agrees with the object, but whether my

[r] Fruitfulness and worth.

[s] Ak, "Wir haben auch"; MS and Ko, "Wir haben aber auch."

[t] Reading "in" for "unter."

[u] diallelon.

cognition agrees with me myself. The universal criterion of truth will not
719 be an organon but only the *conditio sine qua non*, the unavoidable condition of truth. This is that we are in agreement with ourselves in thought. How could a cognition that <is not at one with itself agree with the object>? The criterion must consist in the rule with which alone the understanding agrees with itself in thought. It is not sufficient materially, but it is still unavoidably necessary. A material criterion of truth cannot possibly be universal and hold for all objects. One can of course have material criteria of truth, but they cannot be universal †. They would be those that we have from the character of the object in respect of the senses.

{HOUR}

Through intuition the object is given and through concepts it is thought. The universal criterion of truth is merely negative. The skeptics can be divided into Pyrrhonists and Academics, the latter of whom pursued it furthest. The principle of contradiction is the first formal criterion of truth. For truth it is not enough that a judgment be possible – truth could be called *logical actuality*. If one says *posito*[v] a triangle has 6 sides, then this is a problematic judgment[;] if one says a hexagon has 6 sides, then it's a proposition.

The *first* criterion of truth (after the principle of contradiction) is the principle of the problematic judgment – possibility. The 2nd is the principle of assertoric judgments, in which logical actuality { – truth}. The 2nd principle is the principle of sufficient reason. {Cause is that which lies at the ground of all appearances.}

3. Every cognition has some consequence or other, and if only one consequence is false, then the cognition is false too. If all the consequences are true, then the cognition is true – but who can know all the consequences? That involves omniscience. One can infer from the consequences to the grounds, then. From the falsehood of the consequences one can infer only to the falsehood of the ground, but from this to the truth of the opposite. { – 106}

{*ad* § 109.} A false judgment is always an error. In this case one must
720 prove, however, that it conflicts with the criterion of truth. Error requires that we hold a false judgment to be true. Unfortunately we are filled with errors, but to take precautions against them we must first know whence they have sprung.

[v] I posit [that].

{Truth and error cannot possibly be contained in intuitions – but rather in judgments. Hence [there are] more errors in an academy of sciences than in a village full of farmers, because more judging occurs there – he who never judges will never err either.}

Neither truth nor error rests on the concepts of our understanding, but rather only on its <judgments>. Judgment is an action of the understanding. Truth, however, according to its formal criterion, is the agreement of a judgment with the laws of the understanding. But error is a deviation of judgment from the laws of the understanding. – {If I isolate the understanding, then, so that I take away sensibility, then it could not err (for no power can produce an effect except according to certain laws) – only when I hold an influence of sensibility to be an *actus* of the understanding is it error. All our errors are turnings of judgments to the diagonal – crosswise[w] (the [German] word [for this] comes perhaps from the English [word] square[x]) – }.

How is it possible for a power to depart from its own laws? – The restrictions on the human understanding are not the ground of errors. They are grounds of a great lack in our cognition < – of ignorance (which we cognize only after [acquiring] much science of reason)>, but not of contradiction. Now since it is nothing negative, and the understanding alone by itself cannot err, it must be something positive – sensibility. The *oppositum* of the understanding does not judge at all, however. Now we have no other source. We see, then, that it occurs through the combination of the understanding and sensibility {thus we call the subjective in our representations}. Insofar as this ground lies in sensibility, we call it illusion. This is usually explained as the subjective that is falsely held to be something objective. {The ground of all error [is] a subjective ground of our judgment that we regard as an objective one. A man readily believes what he wishes. Wish is a subjective | ground, | but for belief one must have an objective one.}

Sensibility also has its own laws. Combined in a judgment, they can of course agree with one another. Solely in the combination of two heterogeneous grounds of determination. The matter of errors is thus neither true nor false. 721

{*Porismata:*[y] We are responsible for all errors – for all judgments are arbitrary and only through judgments are errors possible.

No error is a wholly false judgment. The judgment can be correct in form.}

[w] "in die Quere."

[x] "aus dem englischen square – Quadrat."

[y] Corollaries.

{HOUR, FRI., THE 18TH OF MAY}

Every error must be explained. We have *internal marks* of truth, which are grounded in our understanding, and 2ndly *external marks*. The former include *the principle of contradiction* <the logical criterion of possibility (problemat.)> and the 2nd principle, that the judgment as proposition must always be grounded <the logical criterion of actuality (of assertoric judgments), the principle of sufficient reason>. The 3rd <the logical criterion of truth <necessity>>, that if one cannot cognize the truth of a proposition from its grounds, then one can from its consequences. {One cannot judge here through a sense of truth[z] – as little as one can judge duty through moral feeling. One can never judge through the senses but only through the understanding. – }

The external criteria (marks) of truth consist in the agreement of the judgments of others with our own. This is actually not a logical, but rather a psychological criterion. Merely by comparing one's judgment with that of another, one cognizes whether the ground of determination of our judgment is subjective or objective[;] the latter is universally valid, | the | former not. {(Many exceptions to a rule indicate its defectiveness.)}

In logic sensibility is called the subjective in our † cognition.

{*Principium rationati: nihil sine ratione*,[a] everything must have its ground. This is the criterion from consequences. It is negative and sure. If the consequences are false, then certainly the ground is so too. One cannot infer conversely. If the consequences are true, etc. For there can be several grounds. *Principium rationis*:[b] every proposition is itself a ground, has its consequences.}

{There is a natural drive, a vocation, to communicate one's cognitions to others – hence freedom of communication is a human right (only if it could be wholly contrary to the interest of the state might there be a prohibition by the authorities.)

722 Possession of the power of judgment is the greatest gift of nature. There can be a lack of it even in an understanding that is otherwise good.}

In a certain way one can say of all cognitions that one only understands them rightly when one can make them himself, i.e., not merely copy them but derive them from himself.[c]

No judgment could be found that would be *wholly* false. This cannot occur as long as our judgments are derived from the understanding.

One cannot really convince anyone of the opposite of his opinion unless one says to him *how* he came to it from his own particular viewpoint, that

[z] "durch Wahrheitssinn."

[a] Principle of the grounded: nothing without a ground.

[b] Principle of the ground.

[c] "aus sich ableiten."

his judgment is not objective, then, but merely subjective. According to our subjective judgment, then, our final end would be happiness[;] that suits us, we *want* that. But if we concern ourselves with what we *ought* [to do], with the objective, then morality, duty, must occupy this place. Through the method just set forth one gains in critical faculty of understanding. Thus it is said that in a great book there are great errors, and this is quite natural.

Now there follows a distinction between

1. *partial* truth (true *tolerabiliter*, e.g., in measurements) {since the acceptance of the partially true as totally true does not contradict the end – although this involves a certain incorrectness. – } and
2. *total* truth.

Someone can speak the truth but not the whole truth. But one must see that it does not run counter to the ends of cognition.

Now the author speaks of

exact and *crude* cognition. The latter does not indicate that it contains something false, but only that it is not wholly true. Every cognition is either *cognitio vaga* or *cognitio determinata*. Thus, e.g., *medium tenuere beati*,[d] what is good and what is too much or too little, such men do not know this. This is a *regula vaga*,[e] which is not at all determinate, merely tautological wisdom. Be wise, make yourself perfect. Now in what does this consist? One takes it in one way, another in another. Even determinate rules can be *regulae late* or *stricte determinatae*.[f] Many definitions are of the first kind. A cognition is called exact when no free play for error is contained in it. A cognition that requires much attention is called exact in regard to the object, is called subtle in regard to the subject. He who inappropriately employs his cognition on the small is called a micrologist. If something is practical, one cannot find fault with subtlety. 723

{HOUR, THE 21ST OF MAY}

Casuistry consists in a multitude of useless subtleties, where one has thought out cases that simply do not occur in common life. There have been ages in which subtleties and micrology held sway to an astonishing extent.

There is a certain smallness of mind[g] that is not always noticed. The people who possess it can never apply a part of cognition to the whole system of it. This is a great touchstone, from which one can infer immedi-

[d] to hold to the golden mean.
[e] vague rule.
[f] rules that are determined broadly [or] strictly.
[g] "Kleingeisterei."

ately to a man's mind. There are differences between mind[h] and spirit.[i] Mind, the faculty of the understanding, but spirit, the faculty of principles.

{That which agrees with universal illusion is aesthetically true, e.g., the rising and setting of the sun – thus it is quite distinct from logical truth. One does not go directly from error to truth, but rather only by way of the consciousness of ignorance.}

A cognition that is exact (*exacta*) in regard to the object is opposed to a rough one (*rudi*). *Cognitio vaga*[:] do not add[j] too much to anything, nor too little[;] here almost nothing at all is said. Those who believe that the legislator commands too strictly, that there is still free play between his laws and their transgression, are called latitudinarians. Here of course there is nothing fixed, and we must always make an effort to have our cognition be strictly, exactly determined. This is geometry's merit.

Then there is also a *cognitio crassa*[k] – rough and ready,[l] an estimate of the whole, without passing particular judgment on the individual. {Coarse-grained cognition not only has no *exactitudo*, it also spoils men by giving occasion for errors.}

Truth can be used *substantive*$_{L}$ and *adjektive*$_{L}$, e.g., when we think of truth in general or the truth of a proposition. A cognition that is determinate in regard to the object is called truth. This rational cognition is 724 always *apodeictic*, because we are conscious not only of its truth but also of its necessity. An apodeictic cognition is either through concepts or through construction of concepts. In the former case it is dogmatic, in the latter mathematical. A cognition that is apodeictically certain from concepts is called a *dogma*$_{L}$, a cognition that is apodeictically certain from the construction of concepts is called a *mathema*. –

{An apodeictic proposition: Everything is contingent – (has a cause) – $2 \cdot 2 = 4$.[m] The latter is intuition, in the other case only a concept. Both are equally certain objectively, but subjectively there is a great difference. The mathematician can rest in his work, he still has intuition – this is not the case for the philosopher, hence his work is far more tiring.}

The propositions of morals and metaphysics are all *dogmata*$_{L}$.

Because physics is only an application of the latter cognitions, it has an apodeictic certainty. A system is a whole <of dogmatic truths> from principles. {A system is distinct from an aggregate, in that the latter is the whole which is preceded by the parts.}

The principle of history is time – chronology.

[h] "Kopf."

[i] "Geist."

[j] Ak, "tun zu"; MS and Ko, "zu tun."

[k] coarse-grained cognition.

[l] "über Pausch und Bogen."

[m] Ak, "$2 \cdot 4 = 4$"; MS and Ko, "$2 \cdot 2 = 4$."

{HOUR, THE 22ND OF MAY}

One cannot say of any error that it is unavoidable in itself, but this may well be said of ignorance. For we have no need to judge about everything, and if we do so, it still need be only problematically. {There is no *error invincibilis* – but [there are] errors that are hard to avoid practically – Mark: incompatibility with the judgment of others.} An unavoidable error always presupposes the necessity of judgment. {If the judgment were not necessary, that is, then one could easily avoid the error by not judging at all. – }

He who accepts an obviously absurd judgment acts stupidly. {What the *sensus communis* recognizes as such – what does not even have illusion on its behalf. – (Considered logically, no error is dangerous – here we do not look to the matter) – if one ever declares someone's judgment | to be | stupid, thus denying he has understanding, then no *discours* will help to bring him away from it. He who engages in this, then, acts stupidly himself.}

Error is not possible in regard to the obviously false, only in judgments where falsehood lies hidden. Mathematics has the *peculiarity* that one instantly perceives the falsehood of a proposition there. To remove the hidden ground of an error is called clearing up the illusion.[n] If someone maintains something, the falsehood of which he well sees yet without abandoning it, then the fault lies more with his will than with his understanding. A crude error is one, avoidance of which is easy – it is not the same thing as a stupid one. A dangerous error, when we are not merely concerned to extend our cognition but rather, e.g., we always ask first about the use {into which we perhaps cannot have insight then. The shallowest minds usually do this.} He who shows the disadvantage of a cognition when he is supposed to point out its falsehood is called a *consequentarius*, because he always infers from the consequences to the ground { – he starts with the practical}. –

725

The author now speaks in the *5th section*

Of the clarity of cognition

Clarity is consciousness <not> only of representations in the whole but also of their partial representations. A mark is a partial representation insofar as it is a ground of cognition of the whole representation. A ground of cognition is of two sorts:

1. a ground for cognizing a thing in itself[,] or the *internal* ground of cognition;
2. a ground for cognizing a thing based on other coordinate things[,] or the *external* [ground of cognition]. –

[n] "den Schein entwickeln."

In the comparison with others we cognize either

1. through the *nota* {*nota*, a partial representation which lies at the basis of the concept as mark} *identitatis* {mark, characteristic} and
2. through the *nota diversitatis* {sign of differentiation, e.g., between man and animal}.

Partial representations as grounds of cognition can be partial concepts and partial intuitions. The latter do not occur in logic.

A concept is the representation of that which comprises *many representations*. The author makes a distinction between mediate and immediate representations. All combinations are either combinations of coordination or of 726 subordination. The former produce a whole that is called an *aggregate*. They arise through connection of the manifold. Insofar as it involves subordination of one thing to another,[o] it is called a *series*. Now there is a *terminus a priori* and one *a posteriori*[;][p] in logic, [there is] only the one *a parte ante*[q] not the latter *a parte post*.[r] {A mediate mark is a *nota notae*, a mark of a mark. When in the series of representations subordinated to one another one finally comes to an *indivisible* one, this is called the *terminus a parte ante*. This latter can be divided[;] e.g., *quidquam*.[14] One cannot prove *a parte post*, only illustrate.}

Marks can here be divided into

1. affirmative and

2. negative. But this pertains really more to judgment than to marks. {Negative marks, whereby I signify something as an error into which no one would fall anyway, are superfluous – just as affirmative ones that say nothing new or unfamiliar – tautologous.} The expression negative marks implies the matter, and this does not pertain to logic. All negations presuppose affirmations. Thus among savages there isn't any poverty, since this would occur only in comparison with the wealthy. Since they are not acquainted with the positive, they do not form any representation of the negative. Thus, too, no person <born> blind can form a representation of darkness, because he is not acquainted with light.

A mark is *important* when it is a ground of cognition of great consequences. {Marks in comparison with others (as to diversity or identity) are not as important as those through *derivation*, *internal* marks. Importance is: (1.) logical, e.g., 3 *termini* in a syllogism; (2.) practical. – Thus logical, grammatical incorrectness can be practically unimportant (in a certain respect).}

If it serves for differentiation of a ground of cognition that itself is great as to degree, then (where the mark is determined as to degree) this is

[o] "Sofern es einander subordiniert ist."

[p] a terminus on the preceding side [and one] on the posterior side.

[q] on the prior side.

[r] on the posterior side.

called *intensive*, [but] when a mark has reference to multitude, manifoldness {in general, to extension} – *extensive*. A mark is *sufficient* when it contains {suffices for derivation [of]} the ground of all differentiating marks, *insufficient* when it only contains the ground of a few signs of differentiation. But an insufficient ground is not to be rejected. For it 727 always contains a part of the ground – as guesses {without these latter we never arrive at certainty}.

Marks are divided further into:

1. absolutely necessary, unchangeable ones and
2. contingent ones.

Those without which the thing absolutely cannot be thought are necessary. One attains them through the mere analysis of the concept. {Essence [is] the complex of the highest marks of a thing, *complexus notarum conceptum aliquem primitive constituentium.*[s] First, *completudo* is required; (2.) that the marks are not derived from others but rather are primitive – and inseparable – the logical essence the inner possibility.}

In logic the talk is never of the marks of things. In that case logic would occupy itself with matter. But it deals only with the marks of the concept. What is physically necessary can be logically only contingent. E.g., it is physically necessary that all bodies fall, but this lies only in the thing and logically is only contingent. The *notae logicae necessariae*[t] belong to the *esse* of the concept. These are *ad esse conceptus necessariae, pertinent ad essentiam.*[u] {Man is mortal, can err – *extraessentiale* – what does not belong essentially to it.} *One cannot remove these marks without removing the thing itself. – Melius esse logicum* (like *beatitudo juridica*, when it is a matter of *beati possidentes*).[15]

The necessary marks of things belong to the thing itself {or *ad* † *esse*}:

1. either *as constitutiva*, as *constituents* <*essentialia*> {essential parts} – *originarie*[v] | belonging to the concept | {*originarie*: extension}[16]

2. or as *rationata*, as *consequences* <*attributa*> which belong to the concept *derivative*$_{\text{L}}$, e.g., the concept triangle – the consequences are whether the angles [are] right † or etc.

With corporeal things, divisibility is a mark, *quod pertinet ad essentiam*,[w] not as *constitutivum*,[x] however, but rather as *rationatum*.[y] {From the mark that the creature is corporeal, divisibility can be derived.}

[s] the complex of marks that constitute a concept primitively.
[t] logically necessary marks.
[u] necessary to the being of the concept, they pertain to the essence.
[v] original [marks].
[w] which pertains to the essence.
[x] something constitutive.
[y] something grounded.

The former are also called *essentialia*, essential parts[z] {the complex of all essentials is called the essence}, the latter *attributiva* (properties) {these are (1.) *communia*;[a] (2.) *propria*}.[b]

728 Contingent marks are either:

1. *notae internae contingentes*[c] – *modi*, e.g., learnedness | or |
2. *notae externae contingentes – sive relationes*.[d]

The tabular division of marks <predicates> would thus be

1. *ad essentiam pertinentia*,[e] without which the thing cannot be thought.
   a) *ut rationata sive attributa*;[f]
   b) *ut constitutiva sive essentialia*.[g]

{One can often derive one concept from another, they reciprocate.[h] That gives the most certain mark.}

2. *extraessentialia* {without which the concept | can be thought |}, e.g., a triangle – there the angles are undetermined.
   a) *externa* – relation, the *external* determination, whether he [is] father or son {the external determinations of marks are always contingent};
   b) *interna*, the *internal* determinations of a thing, insofar as they are not necessary, are called *modi*, e.g., learned or not learned.

When we speak of the essence of things, then we do so of the logical essence (that consists in the concept), not of the real essence (nature), which is treated in metaphysics. {[The] complex of all those internal determinations that contain the first ground of the existence of a thing is called the natural essence. – Into this it is very hard to have insight, [but] into the logical essence it is easy, it lies merely in the concept. – }

Essentia est complexus notarum conceptum aliquem primitive[i] *constituentium*.[j] The logical essence is the complex of those marks that are sufficient to derive what belongs to the essence. The logical essence is easy to cognize. For with this one has nothing to do but analyze concepts. We can never have complete insight into the real essence, e.g., we can never experience *all* the marks of water no matter how far physics advances. All the same, some logical concepts are hard to define, e.g., the concept of virtue. There we are far short of having found all the marks. We name the following: a

[z] "wesentliche Stücke."
[a] common.
[b] proper, peculiar.
[c] contingent internal marks.
[d] contingent external marks – or relations.
[e] things pertaining to the essence.
[f] as things grounded, or attributes.
[g] as things constitutive, or essential things.
[h] "reciprocieren."
[i] Ak, "primitive"; MS and Ko, "primitivum."
[j] The essence is the complex of marks that constitute a certain concept primitively.

readiness[k] in lawful actions that are done freely[;] but this is still not enough {it is moral strength in pursuit of these, with struggle against obstacles}. Body can be defined perfectly – a filling of space indicates only matter, but the description of its figure in accordance with the three dimensions indicates bodies.

Now the author speaks

Of obscure representations 729

Let us suppose the representation is distinct, i.e., its partial representations are clear[;] e.g., justice[;] there is compulsion here[;] fairness is distinct from this[;] it is very hard to have insight into this. We can make obscure representations clear through examples, but this clarification is not logical, only aesthetic.

{Obscurity is subjective if the ground lies in the subject – objective if in the object. – An obscure representation – that of which one is not conscious[;] this seems to be a contradiction – one cannot | comprehend | it immediately, but one can do so mediately through inference.}

We often call an exposition obscure because it is logically distinct but does not have enough clarity aesthetically – no suitable examples can be given {e.g., body, extended impenetrable figure}. Virtue can be distinguished from holiness; for with the latter no temptations toward evil occur {e.g., the angels}. This has generally been forgotten. In our distinct cognition we can think another perfection, *completudo* <exhaustiveness – exhaustive distinctness> {in a concept, where there are *coordinate* marks, as well as *depth* through subordinate marks – if here I have even just a single [mark], it can still be a *nota superior* – [they] may be traced back to simple concepts.} The greatest distinctness through subordinate marks is called *depth* of cognition. Both together constitute *thoroughness.*

{NTH HOUR}

Deep distinctness is always harder to understand, because it is more abstract. To attain full distinctness one must seek out marks of marks, until at last one attains the highest marks, the simple concepts. We can compare this with lively cognition or rather with the lively mode of representation <consciousness is in this case lively>. {The more this representation produces alterations in the subject, the livelier is this science † through examples.} We can call this aesthetically greater clarity liveliness. Logically greater clarity is distinctness.

{Comprehensibility and clarity are to be distinguished. Through the resolution of marks a concept becomes harder to comprehend – on ac-

[k] "Fertigkeit."

730 count of subtlety. All making distinct[l] rests on the development of partial representations (insofar as these are not of themselves clear).}

All our representations can have two relations, first to the subject, then they are called sensations, second to the object, – – – cognition.

Cognitions can become lively:

1. if they are related to the material, sensibility <sensation> (subj.);
2. if they are related to the formal, intuition (objective).

{A representation that enlivens must exhibit the object as present.

It is different 1. *to make* a cognition *distinct* (here nothing is added, only raised to distinctness, this [is] | analytic |,

2. to make a *distinct cognition* – where previously there was none, this [is] | synthetic |.}

With logical distinctness it is not at all a matter of the multitude of the marks <See p. 42 . . . †>,[17] but with aesthetic distinctness it is precisely a matter of their manifoldness[m] (e.g., description of spring). The origin of distinctness is of two kinds, analytic and synthetic. The mathematician has this last manner.

Now the author speaks

Of the comprehensible and the incomprehensible

Feelings can never produce a cognition. {The word representation may not be explained at all. For one would thereby have to presuppose the concept of it.}

We begin (1.) with *representing*. The 2nd is then *to perceive* something – *percipere* – to represent something with consciousness[;] the third – *to be acquainted with* something <*noscere*>, i.e., so to cognize that one is acquainted with it in comparison with others as to their identity and diversity. *To understand* something <*intelligere*>: to represent something *through the understanding*, through concepts {so that one can explain oneself concerning it, state its marks}. To cognize the thing *from reason* {i.e., *a priori* through the understanding, even if it were not given}, from universal principles according to its grounds, is called *having insight* {*perspicere*}.[n] Hence . . . to have insight *a priori* is to cognize not only that it is so <as, e.g., dissolution of

731 salt by water> but that it must be so <e.g., a solar eclipse (mathematically) {even if we had not seen it}>. The last step is to *comprehend*, to have insight into something sufficiently <for a certain purpose>. To comprehend *absolutely* <in every respect>, *comprehendere*, <is for us impossible> {*not* moral rules}. One can comprehend perfectly various hydraulic phenomena of water, e.g., and have insight into this *a priori* {as soon as we accept fluidity as

[l] "Alle Deutlichmachung."

[m] "Vielfältigkeit."

[n] "*einsehen* {einsehen perspicere}."

a hypothesis – to have insight requires consciousness of truth throughout}. But one can <not> have insight *a priori* into that which is fluid.

Examples contribute to understanding only aesthetically.[18] Often we believe that we have insight into something that fundamentally we can only explain – understand according to its possibility.

We always understand best that which we can make ourselves.

A distinct concept becomes complete when all marks are contained therein {exhaustively distinct, insofar as it contains all coordinate marks.} {Totality in regard to subordinate marks is called by the author completeness.} One must not make his concept excessively full,[o] for one makes it hard for oneself if one takes up superfluous | marks |. A concept where all dispensable marks are left out is called precise.[p] A concept that contains not too much, not too little, is called adequate {since we cognize not only the marks themselves but also the marks of the marks, but the concept adequate does not fit until the series is wholly brought to an end.}

The first grade of subordination is a mark of a mark. An adequate concept rests on coordination.

{When the sum of the marks does not contain too much – precise – when it does not contain too little – adequate. Distinctness of the understanding is that through concepts. Distinctness of the power of judgment [is] that with examples through intuition. Distinctness of reason [is] that through mediate marks (as distinctness of understanding [is that] through immediate ones). All concepts that are not precise [are] indeterminate, vague.[q]}

A lucid mind [is one] that always knows what it wants.

SIXTH DIVISION

Of the certainty of cognition

Here the talk is not of truth but of holding-to-be-true. {Objectively, all propositions are certainly true or certainly false.} This is judgment in relation[r] to the *subject*. We want in this case to know not the grounds of the truth but those of the holding-to-be-true. The degrees are: (1.) opining, (2.) believing, (3.) knowing. We can call these three concepts the modalities of the *sensus veri et falsi*.[s]

732

Opining is a holding-to-be-true that is, with consciousness, both subjectively and objectively insufficient. An insufficient holding-to-be-true is

[o] "Superabundant."
[p] "präzis."
[q] "vag."
[r] "im Verhältnis und der Beziehung auf."
[s] sense of the true and the false.

what does not suffice to exclude the opposite. He who only opines is still open to opposing grounds.

If <one> believes, however, then this is no longer so. {It is an assertoric holding-to-be-true, which we nevertheless still do not cognize with the consciousness of necessity (hence we have to admit that modifications are possible).} Belief is a holding-to-be-true that is subjectively <sufficient> but objectively insufficient, with consciousness. Believing is distinct from knowing, then, in that it is incapable of proof. Believing is a private holding-to-be-true, sufficiently certain only for me. Hence I cannot yet say that I know it.

Knowing is a holding-to-be-true that is sufficient both subjectively and objectively. {I hold the opposite to be impossible. Opining is a holding-to-be-true that is both objectively and subjectively insufficient, with consciousness. The concept of belief is best grasped in a practical respect (although this influence on the will does not pertain to logic).} It can be empirical through experience or apodeictic *a priori*. The holding-to-be-true of an apodeictic proposition can be apodeictically certain.

What I *opine*, this judgment I pronounce only problematically[;] hence the holding-to-be-true is (1.) *problematic*, namely, when it is accepted in such a way that it is still to be proved †. It is called problematic because it only serves for finding, among various grounds, the sufficient one.

Now in belief the holding-to-be-true is (2.) *assertoric*. For I say that it is sufficient for me <subjectively>, but I do not settle whether it is objectively sufficient. Many representations of a future state are mere products of imagination[;] some ideas that please us greatly (e.g., of male and female light[19]) [are] only ideas in the subject.

In knowledge the holding-to-be-true is (3.) *apodeictic*. {*Intuitio* in mathematics. Conviction. Persuasion is the illusion of conviction, uncertain whether subjective or objective.}

733 The propositions held to be true[l] can be empirical and the holding-to-be-true be apodeictic. The holding-to-be-true is combined either with the consciousness of subjective necessity or with that of the contingent. In the latter case, when it is subjectively and objectively insufficient, [it is] opining, but when it is subjectively sufficient and objectively insufficient – believing. Hypotheses are opinions. In mathematics there is neither opining nor believing but only knowing – or nothing – and in merely speculative metaphysics it is the same.

{Something is a matter of opinion if it simply cannot become an object of knowledge, neither objectively nor subjectively (e.g., whether there are inhabitants of the moon). – Concerning the possibility of animals' reproduction of their own kind we will never have more than opinions. – Matters of belief, where there is for us † only a subjectively sufficient ground for

[l] "Die Sätze des Fürwahrhaltens."

holding-to-be-true. – Everything that we accept based on ends is for us only subjectively sufficient – (i.e., I must accept that this is so, or else I make no progress with my reason here – this I cannot accept as holding objectively, of course, but it is sufficient for me.)

Where † knowledge is *possible*, this is already a matter of knowledge, e.g., geography. – Only objects of rational belief[u] can be called matters of belief.}

What are objects of opinion, belief, and knowledge? Are objectively historical propositions objects of opinion, of belief, or even of knowledge? They are objects of knowledge. For there are cases where we can use the experience of others as our own. Are mathematical propositions objects of opinion, etc.[?] Because they are *a priori*, they are all objects of knowledge. (Concepts are called transcendental when we have them *a priori*.) Can't one also accept propositions *a priori* on belief? Yes. Mathematics is also of this kind. {One believes mathematicians because it is not possible that they can err, since they would hit upon false consequences at once. In philosophy, however, there is no belief.

He who is capable of rational belief [is] a believer.[v] The morally practical rests merely on reason. What is either itself a duty, then, or stands in close connection[w] with it – this [is] the object of belief (of practical holding-to-be-true) – he who does not, etc., [is] an unbeliever[;][x] he who believes everything else [is] credulous.[y]}

That for whose opposite one has no grounds is a matter of opinion. There are objects of opinion that can become objects of belief and of knowledge, e.g., in physics, what Newton opines about the origin of the planets, etc. There is a belief that is valued the same as knowledge in a practical (not in a speculative) regard, e.g., some of the propositions of the ancient philosophers – probabilism. The certainty that <pertains> to cognition[z] of the commandment to perform or not to perform[a] an action is moral. That which is certain according to rules of prudence can be <called> not morally, but rather pragmatically certain. The concept of moral certainty is misused when one often has nothing more than a practically sufficient ground of truth {e.g., in the case of bets}[;] it need not be theoretically certain. {Logical certainty (apodeictic) is (1.) philosophical, (2.) mathematical.} Moral certainty relates to conscience. E.g., in the case of dogmas of Catholicism, which some accept without consulting conscience. When one does something at the risk of erring, then one is

734

[u] "Gegenstände des Vernunftglaubens."
[v] "Gläubig."
[w] "in connater Verbindung."
[x] "ungläubig."
[y] "leichtgläubig."
[z] "Kenntnis."
[a] "des Gebots oder Verbots."

never morally certain. In the word *belief* one always thinks of voluntary[b] approval, in the word *opinion* of approval that is decided.[c] A matter of belief is that which ought to be held true, and of which there is no knowledge. It is regarded as a holding-to-be-true that depends on my wish.[d] Rational belief is called simply *fides*. It is a complicated concept. {For a believer[e] we actually have no Latin word – *fidelis* – faithful – .} There are certain transcendent judgments,[f] which lie outside the boundaries of our cognition, which one can only believe. He who is not convinced even by moral grounds is an unbeliever. In the theological sense, an unbeliever is one who does not have insight into the supersensible and will not accept it, even if morally it is actually necessary, because it cannot be proved theoretically with reason <it is uncertain>. He who does not accept even what is historically certain, just because the certainty is not apodeictic, is called disbelieving.[g] Certainty is the objective sufficiency of holding-to-be-true. In the case of belief it is subjective. There I can only say: *I am* certain. But in the case of certainty: *It is* certain, this is universally valid.

A rational cognition[h] is different from a cognition of reason[i][;] the former must be the property of all cognitions. As for the distinction of mathematical certainty, it is a matter not of degree but of quantity.

All certainty is either

735

1. empirical, is that which derives from experience, | or |
2. rational, is that whose origin is *a priori*. It is considered, again, in two respects: objectively a) logical, in respect of the theoretical faculty of cognition; subjectively b) practical, in respect of moral use.

Rational logical certainty is called *generaliter* an apodeictic certainty, for it is cognized from grounds *a priori*. {We have conviction about a thing when we cognize it as true with the consciousness that our judgment is objective.} One cannot say that mathematical certainty is greater than philosophical certainty. The difference lies only in the fact that it is intuitive, while the philosophical is only discursive. Philosophical certainty can still attain the same degree, but <never> the property of being intuitive. In the case of philosophical propositions it is customarily said that they are as certain as 2 times 2 [=] 4[;] but this is not determinate, for the latter is mathematical, not philosophical certainty. {The degree of both certainties is the same, but they are of different kinds.}

[b] "freiwilligen."
[c] "einen entschiedenen Beifall."
[d] "Belieben."
[e] "Für Gläubig."
[f] "überschwengliche Urtheile (transcendent)"
[g] "ungläubisch."
[h] "Ein vernünftiges Erkenntnis."
[i] "Vernunfterkenntnis."

{HOUR, MONDAY}

Acceptance is a contingent approval that has sufficient ground in regard to a certain purpose. *Settled*[:] this presupposes a dispute, since the matter was uncertain. One cannot say of mathematical propositions that they are settled; for who can dispute about them?

{Sometimes it is said that something is *indisputable*. But this means no more than undisputed – no one has ever been found who has rejected it.}

No cognition but the mathematical can be presented *evidently*.[j] Nothing else, namely, can bring about an *intuitus a priori*.

{A cognition is called *thorough* insofar as it is secured against doubt by logically sufficient grounds.} A *thorough* cognition must be derived from sure principles. Thorough history can only be attained through chronology.

Coherent means the same as *consequent*, that everything stands in connection.[k] The coherent is the highest thing in the use of our cognition – to be consequent. {*Consequent* means *correct in consequences*[l] when the connection of the consequences with the ground is in accordance with logical laws. *Coherent*, this proposition fits together with the previous ones in the series of a system. – The more consequent a man is with respect to dangerous maxims, the more harmful he is. – }

736

When the mathematician demonstrates, he compels everyone who understands him to approve. We really cannot say here, then, that we *give* him *approval*. {The expression, *to give approval*,[m] seems not to lie in our will. Can we withhold our approval of a mathematical proof? Holding-to-be-true pertains to the understanding, but investigation to the faculty of choice.}

In *suspensio judicii* there lies some freedom. One can also give his approval and yet, in judging, not make a decision – which still awaits further grounds – where one accepts the opposite as still possible. I am free when I accept a proposition in a practical respect for the good that can follow from it. One can say, then, that there are things in matters of religion, e.g., our eternal continued existence, which we accept just for this good, for this life is not at all adequate to the idea of the highest good.

Suspensio judicii consists in this, that when all the grounds on both sides are equally insufficient, none is predominant. It can be (1.) *ob indifferentiam*[n] – (2.) *ob aequilibrium*.[o] To hold oneself in *suspensio judicii* by choice {this is the mean between holding-to-be-true and rejecting – it remains

[j] "*Augenscheinlich*."

[k] "im nexu, im Zusammenhang."

[l] "*folgerecht*."

[m] Reading "zugeben" for "zu geben."

[n] on account of indifference.

[o] on account of equilibrium.

only a problematic judgment} shows a very great mind and is extremely hard on account of the fact that the inclination toward immediate judgment of the understanding interferes. *Ob aequilibrium*[,] to be and to remain inconclusive[,] gives evidence of weak minds.

Argumentum ad crumenam,[p] because he who does not have a full purse cannot take part in the wager. {Of him who will not take part in a wager it is assumed that he is uncertain of his matter.}

Argumentum ad verecundiam.[q] Because a great man has maintained it, and one can hardly wish to know it better. {A bad argument.}

The best argument is always the *ad tutum*,[r] namely, in case one accepts the most certain. It is cunning, but it does not always lead to the true.

As for what concerns *suspensio judicii*, it is:

1. *critica* or *indagatoria*,[s] a postponement of judgment for closer investigation {until a ground for holding-to-be-true presents itself};
2. *sceptica*, [which] is the renunciation of an assertoric judgment. {A total renunciation of all certainty. The principle, always to postpone one's judgment, is called ἐποχή[t] – *status indifferentiae*.}[u]

737

We come now to the doctrine

Of prejudices

A provisional judgment {*judicium praevium*} has in common with prejudice only the fact that it is likewise made before the investigation of the matter. {*Praejudicium* is not distinct from . . . . † the two are the same. The latter is actually appeal to a judgment, hence <through> experience[;] this contributes, meanwhile, to culture. A *judicium praevium* is a judgment that precedes investigation[v] – there can be no judgment without reflection, but there can without investigation[;] what is immediately certain permits none. – } A *judicium reflectens*[w] is where one sets a judgment as a problem, in order to investigate its truth. Even for seeking, one must have a particular principle. To seek this out pertains to the faculty of judgment. One cannot teach this. For if one wanted to give it rules, he would already use the faculty of judgment in order to subsume under these. A *judicium praevium* precedes investigation, then; but it must always occur simultaneously with reflection.

{Provisional judgments arise from grounds that are insufficient, with

[p] An argument directed to the purse.
[q] An argument directed to modesty or awe (i.e., an argument from authority).
[r] [An argument] directed to security.
[s] critical [or] investigative.
[t] suspension of judgment.
[u] the condition of indifference.
[v] Reading "Untersuchung" for "Ueberlegung."
[w] a judgment to be reflected upon.

consciousness. – *Skill in provisional judgments is a kind of prudence.* This chapter has until now been neglected in logic. Every inventor must judge provisionally.}

I reflect on something when I compare it with the laws of the understanding. There are propositions, which are *judicia determinantia* (determining judgments) even before any investigation, e.g., between two points only one straight line is possible. They are also called *judicia indemonstrabilia* – without proof, immediately certain, unprovable[x] – we will speak of this more in what follows.

{The inclination to judge, to make objectively universal principles, from subjectively universal causes, is prejudice. – }

Judicia reflectentia[y] are those which introduce investigation, which show (1.) whether a matter needs investigation, (2.) how I ought to investigate a matter. Prejudice is a maxim of judging objectively from subjective grounds. A prejudice is never an individual proposition, e.g., the apple doesn't fall far from the tree. This is not yet a prejudice, but only a consequence from another one. For a prejudice is not a proposition *but only a maxim for drawing propositions from one.* A maxim means a subjective principle.[z] An objective one is called a principle.[a] A rule that the subject makes his principle[b] is called a maxim. Thus many men make a rule subjectively their maxim which is objectively false. The maxim is grounded here on an illusion, which we defined above in such a way. Prejudice is thus a maxim of holding to be true rules that are grounded on illusion. The formulas are either (1.) *mottoes* | or | (2.) aphorisms – sentences | or | (3.) rules[c] or | (4.) | proverbs.[d] {A saying is a proposition that is tied to a customary expression, so that this makes remembering easier. Rules or *canones*. Sentences are aesthetic formulas. – *Canones* are classical ones. – *Dicta*$_L$ are holy formulas.} One will best cognize the national spirit of a people on the basis of its proverbs. –

738

The prejudice that we mentioned first, Like father, like son, or something similar, is actually grounded on the fact that one has accepted as universally valid the maxim that there is much similarity between men and animals. And this prejudice is based on the subjective ground that what the whole world says is true.

Sentences could be called aesthetic formulas, just as proverbs could be called *formulae vulgares*. *Sentences* are customarily formulas for wisdom. *Canones* are formulas for science. Classical formulas are called, in the

[x] Reading "unbeweisbare" for "nicht unbeweisbare."
[y] Judgments to be reflected upon.
[z] "Grundsatz."
[a] "Prinzip."
[b] "Prinzip."
[c] "Lehrsprüche."
[d] "Sprichwörter, proverbia."

juristic sense, *brocardica*.[e] {They have authority and declare all investigation to be superfluous. Proverbs are called *loci communes*[;][f] because everyone speaks thus, it ought to be true – proverbs are the concentrated (common) folk wisdom. Hence those [who] always want to utter proverbs [are] vulgar.} *Dicta*$_{\text{L}}$ are sayings κατ᾽ ἐξοχήν.[g]

In the case of all merely subjective grounds we are always passive, e.g., with inclination, with custom – the tendency toward imitation. The tendency toward prejudice is a tendency toward mechanism in the use of reason. There are sentences that announce themselves as prejudices.

Prejudices can be divided in general into

1. the *praejudicium*[h] *hominis*;[i]
2. that of the occasion of our <judgments> a) *loci vel* b) *temporis*.[j]

The *praejudicium hominis* is again of two kinds:

1. *praejudicium vel personae* (for a person)

739 2. *praejudicium – multitudinis* (for the multitude) – this is peculiar to women and is also quite well suited to them. {What all the world says is true.} One who has the *praejudicium multitudinis* distrusts his own reason. {The prejudice of prestige, e.g. of antiquity, which has its ground, e.g., in thankfulness.} | {Prejudices of prestige[,] e.g. for great men[,] are often harmful to the sciences, since by their greatness they frighten others from competition – everyone who would like to choose this field to work in despairs of reaching this ideal, much less of going beyond it. – Sometimes we admire out of contempt, since what someone did was really a lot, for the scanty representation that we had of him. Thus Mercier[20] admires the Germans, thus one admires women who accomplish something scientific.

A distinction between admiration[k] and wonder.[l] We admire the ancients not on account of the degree of their cognition, but rather for how they advanced it so far, relative to the few aids they had. – Learnedness. Acquaintance with the ancients. Of the respect that it deserves, we always let much fall on the ancients themselves. – Prejudice in favor of the ancients has some causes. One is not acquainted with the new, does not want to be acquainted with it, due to laziness. In matters of fine art the ancients are actually still models – in the case of other objects we have made many advances since then. In the aesthetic, in matters of sensation[,] the ancients were able to advance things further than we can

[e] From Italian: *broccardo*, a legal rule or axiom.

[f] commonplaces.

[g] par excellence.

[h] "Vorurteil, praejudicium." (Ak, "praejudicium,'; MS, "praejudicium.")

[i] prejudice *concerning the man*.

[j] a) of place or b) of time.

[k] "Bewundern."

[l] "Verwundern."

on account of their civic condition."[m] Speeches to a cultivated, <re-fined> people in regard to the constitution of the state had to attain a high degree of perfection < – energy – >. – Here is one basis. Thus the opinion does not rest on mere prejudice. If these works were to be lost we would not get them back, because we cannot reach this condition. Only a dead language can become a model of representation[;] living ones suffer alterations too often.} |

The *praejudicium multitudinis* is also of two sorts[:]

1. *praejudicium eruditorum* {the prejudice in favor of the learned}[;] thus the common man trusts the learned.

2. *praejudicium sensus communis*. The common understanding is a kind of sense <(*praejudicium empirismi*[n])> [,] which, as it were, has an intuition. {Often even learned men have a particular regard for it.} In medicine it is the opposite, however, because they believe that it is dangerous to make use † of learnedness haphazardly. {They believe, namely, that those learned in medicine never come up with † anything based on experience †.} 740

The author treats now

Of logical egoism

{Logical egoism is a *selfish prejudice*.} This is not merely conceit but rather a kind of logical principle, which takes as *dispensable* the criterion of truth, *to compare one's opinions with those of other men*. {The mathematician can never risk this – *vitium subreptionis*,[o] based on subjective grounds. – } The principle of the indifference, etc., of the judgments of others in comparison with my own is the principle of logical egoism. It is unfair to condemn[p] people to keep all their judgments to themselves. For they have to communicate if they are not to lose the strong criterion of truth, to compare their judgments with the judgments of others.

The author speaks further of the *prejudice in favor of someone else* – this is exactly the opposite of the one mentioned previously. Sometimes, namely, one elevates a great man in order to hide one's weaknesses from [one's] contemporaries – it is a means of comparing and removing the difference. Such an idol, whom one has raised for admiration, e.g., Aristotle, has harmed mankind extraordinarily and always held it bound. For no one believed that one could ever surpass this great man, hence people only imitated. Thus the greatness of a man harmed posterity {*vid.* also p. 57[21]}, which did not have the courage to surpass him.

[m] "bürgerlichen Zustandes."

[n] prejudice in favor of empiricism.

[o] error of subreption.

[p] Reading "dazu zu kondemnieren" for "dafür zu kondemnieren," in accordance with a suggestion by Hinske.

We come now specially to the prejudice of antiquity, the *praejudicium antiquitatis*. We have the prejudice that at the time the ancients lived nature had not yet deteriorated so much. There are also other causes. The high estimation of antiquity is found above all among those who have studied the ancients, <without> which study one simply cannot lay claim to the title of learned man – among others, [it is] merely based on imitation. {To have accepted a provisional judgment as decisive is prejudice.} We also admire the ancients because even in the childhood of the human race they had already come a long way. Further, it is in accordance with thankfulness that we praise them on account of their great merits and 741 forget and overlook their weaknesses. – We ourselves, so to speak, can someday become ancients ourselves †, if we leave behind such products as they did, etc.

The prejudice of modernity arises from inclination. For the first man to communicate some such thing finds merit therein. The true provisional judgment would be that writings that have been preserved through so long a time merely on account of their inner worth and excellence must of course have something persisting and lasting.

{When we have attained certain cognitions with effort, and these, in connection with others, constitute in a certain combination as a whole a system, then we have a certain predilection for them. – This flows from the nature of man[;] we † infer their truth from the connection. An accepted ground can well serve for the explanation of many consequences without being the correct ground.}

The prejudice of accepted dogma, *praejudicium systematis*. People frequently write against this. A system allows a provisional favorable judgment to its advantage. The conformity of a proposition to the whole system proves <its> truth.

There are many *volontaires* in the sciences, who do not wish to stand under any command of the school (so to speak). We must not declaim too much against systems. Some French writers have done this. Subsequently there is a prejudice of <lazy> trust, of easiness.

One can pass judgment on the universal validity of a rule only from rules *in abstracto*. E.g., One wishes to have a principle for the concept of a lie. One must judge about this *in abstracto*. For if one were to look to individual cases, many lies could be useful, e.g., Themistocles' suggestion – Aristides.[22] But all infidelity is harmful.

The prejudice of shallowness. It consists in one's not going into the depth of the cognition – namely, to subordinate marks. {Genius is completely required for a good provisional judgment.}

After this the author speaks of *opposed prejudices*, namely, when one has distrust toward certain things. {Thus we can think of a prejudice against the ancient, as well as one against the modern – Distrust toward the whole of human cognition is called misology.} This can also apply to oneself.[q] It is destructive for man if it frightens off his courage for every task whatsoever; but when it is only such † that we distrust our own powers in every occupation, then that is the most excellent situation of the human mind. 742

Now we come to the doctrine

Of the probable

{A chapter in which logic can never advance much.} If I say that something is probable (even if it should be only subjective), then this concerns quality. But if I ask how great the probability is, then I consider it *as to degree*. The relation of the grounds for the truth to grounds of the opposite is plausibility[r] (*verisimilitudo*). But the relation of the grounds for the truth to the sufficient grounds[s] is probability. If I only have a ground of holding-to-be-true and no ground for proof of the opposite, then this is *verisimilitudo*. {The *verisimile* is the plausible – [the] *probabile* [is the] acceptable.[t] Judgment concerning *verisimilitudo* rests on comparison of the judgments for the truth to the grounds of the opposite. With probability, the grounds of holding-to-be-true constitute more than half – they outweigh.} The sufficient ground is the sum of all cases that could happen at all. Only in mathematics can one indicate determinately the grounds of holding-to-be-true.

{HOUR, MONDAY <. . . . .†>}

{All probability is found *numerando*[,] by counting up[,] or *ponderando*.[u] The first way requires homogeneity, e.g., throw of the dice, just as easily 3 sixes as 3 eights. I am to throw 8 with 2 dice. Here 5 cases are possible. The probability can be counted up, is = 5/36. But when something [is] to be figured out by guesswork,[v] e.g., testimony, then the grounds have to be pondered, e.g., a man of good upbringing, etc. Where the grounds are enumerated, I can say that it is probable, but where they are pondered, only that it is probable *to me*. Likewise, one can never say this is morally certain, but rather <I am> morally certain, i.e., it rests with me on practical grounds[;] otherwise one may not use the word *moral* at all – otherwise it is better to say certainty based on physical grounds – theoretical.}

[q] "auf sich selbst Bezug haben."

[r] Reading "ist die Scheinbarkeit (verisimilitudo)" for "(verisimilitudo)."

[s] Reading "der Gründe für die Wahrheit zu den zureichenden Gründen" for "der Gründe für die zureichende Wahrheit."

[t] "annehmbar."

[u] by weighing, estimating.

[v] "Wenn aber etwas zu erraten."

A proposition can be called *probable* only insofar as it lies on the way 743 toward certainty and produces certainty increasingly through homogeneous grounds. Judgments that are concerned with the supersensible (or with the transcendent[w] in contrast to the immanent, which is grasped with the senses, remains in representation). Hence in metaphysical things, in all things *a priori* in general, there is no probability in the theoretical. Here we must know or there is nothing. For our suppositions cannot be brought to certainty in this way. Not even if several different grounds are available. This indicates nothing further, namely, than the fact that there are many insufficient grounds, which can never yield a universally valid proof, and it is always a proof of uncertainty when, instead of naming a sufficient ground, one gives several that are not sufficient. *Probability* is approximation to certainty, and several grounds, when they hold, are supposed to be combined in a proof. What is lacking in such cases, where we are on the way toward certainty, is only a *complementum*.

{*ad* § 176 p. 55}[23] The author speaks further of *doubt*. We acquire a doubt – *dubitatio* – subjectively when our holding-to-be-true is not determined (stands *in aequilibrio*). In the case of *suspensio judicii* the grounds must still allow a doubt. Doubt (*dubium*) as an objective ground of holding-to-be-true is the judgment that I make concerning truth, or a relation of the judgment to the subject, insofar as the subject holds something to be true. – Doubt is an objective ground, however small it may be, for holding the opposite to be true. {The condition of holding-to-be-true with consciousness of insufficiency is called the condition of doubt.} An objection is a *dubium* of which I am conscious, i.e., insofar as it is put forth in concepts of the understanding – insofar as it is *represented obscurely*, [it is] a *scruple*. {This scruple can become a determinate doubt.} This can in some cases be raised to the clarity of an objection. There are frequent objections against judgments of the understanding that lack distinctness {they have been answered, but they have not yet been given an answer},[x] hence the handling of a scruple requires development. One has to present what it is that the other is running up against. {When this becomes clear, it contributes very much to the perfecting of the holding-to-be-true.} Often one cuts a knot without untying it[;] e.g., in the quarrel about the assertion that this world is the best one, the opponents point out that there is so much trouble in it, particularly for man, that the world could not possibly 744 be called good[;] and without uncovering the falsehood of this, people customarily show that the world, <the work> of an all-wise being, cannot be bad. {Leibniz answers the objection thus: there is a creator, whom I cannot think otherwise than as the best, wisest being.} *Difficultatem dif-*

[w] "aufs Ueberschwengliche, Transcendente."

[x] "man hat ihnen geantwortet, sie sind aber noch nicht beantwortet."

ferre, non auferre,[y] when difficulties, even ones removed by grounds of cognition, yield to similar difficulties. {E.g., the Fall [explained] by the devil. (Dice – 36 [cases])} Another expression: *obnubilare, non diluere*[z] – to obscure the truth still more.

{HOUR, TUESDAY}

We come now to the condition of doubt – condition of the mind insofar as it is conscious that it is undetermined in regard to holding-to-be-true. Dogmatism and skepticism are opposed to one another. {The skeptical method is that of postponing one's approval, where one is equally open to opposing grounds.} Universal skepticism is the prejudice of accepting all cognition in general as uncertain. Dogmatism is the prejudice of accepting the <full> certainty of cognition without holding the critique of our faculty of reason to be necessary { – detrimental to reason}. {Dogmatic skepticism, which declares all certainty to be impossible.}

{There are no *logice dijudicata*[a] – here there are not truths fully settled. We must at least always answer the possible doubts against them.

Criticism is the principle of not holding judgments *a priori* to be true until we have compared them with the laws of our faculty of reason. This method is applicable and necessary only in cognitions *a priori* through concepts.}

Mathematics and natural science do not need the critique of our reason. Here we do not need to investigate where the limits of these cognitions are, because everything can be set forth through intuition. – The prejudice of dogmatism is grounded on the accomplishment of many cognitions *a priori* without critique through reason. Here reason succeeds magnificently, and hence people believe that it will also succeed in other cases. One cannot blame Plato for coming to fantastic ideas[b] through reflection on mathematics – if only the Platonists had not subsequently carried things too far. Our concepts, as mentioned above, are mathematical and philosophical – the former are confirmed by themselves through intuition, but this simply cannot occur with the latter. *To elucidate* is merely to analyze one's concepts, but *to extend* [is] when one goes out beyond[c] the usual concepts. If one wishes to extend his cognition of reason through mere concepts, then if no further critique occurs, one is a dogmatist. {Hypothesis: inference that a ground is the correct one, from the sufficiency of that ground for given consequences – this supposition, in order to be able to explain those consequences from it. *ad* p. 68.}[24]

745

[y] to postpone the difficulty, not to remove it.

[z] to obscure, not to resolve.

[a] things adjudicated logically.

[b] "schwärmerische Ideen."

[c] Ak and MS, "hinausgeht'; Ko, "inansgeht."

Quite often the opposite has just as many grounds as the proposition itself. An example – Proposition: the world has a beginning[;] opposite: the world has no beginning. Then what would the being that made it have done through all eternity? Metaphysics is the extension of our cognition through concepts *a priori* – through construction of these – mathematics. Our reason in its pure use is dialectical. –

The strictest skeptic, who simply is not critical any longer, can rightly be called a dogmatic skeptic, although this appears to be contradictory. One can catch them easily. They wish to demonstrate that no truth can be demonstrated. They reject the arguments of the dogmatists and yet accept certainty – in the end they say that everything in the world is uncertain, even that everything in the world is uncertain[;] they call this cathartic or purgative, which does away with itself as well. The skeptics usually had much dialectical acuity, as one can see from their writings. {Persiflage – Plato's disciple Speusippus, Arcesilaus, Carneades [are] skeptics – partial <Pyrrho> – nothing <academic doubt>.}

The mathematician need never investigate why his propositions are *a priori*. Criticism is the middle way between dogmatism and skepticism, the principle of a rightful trust in one's use of reason. That which cannot be put forth through any experience or sensible evidence is transcendent. Just on account of this ground one can never hit upon an error, except in the case where one can oneself prove the opposite. In these cases critique is thus thoroughly necessary, not in mathematics, because there there are actual *facta*. – Skepticism is then plainly objectionable – but the skeptical method of testing and investigating a thing more and more has very many advantages – the doubt of postponement – *indagare*.[d] – {This is the doubt

746 that has the most useful consequences for the investigation of truth.} *Academic* doubt was dogmatic. They held, namely, that nothing is certain. *Pyrrhonic* doubt appears <to> have been more a doubt of postponement. At least it was certainly not as universal as academic doubt.

{| ad | § 181 p. 57}[25] *Hypothesis* – Presupposition. It is a judgment which infers from the sufficiency of a judgment for given consequences to the actuality of the ground. Every hypothesis is in the end mere opinion – from the sufficiency of a ground for a given consequence one cannot infer the truth of the proposition. For other grounds could also be sufficient for the <consequences>. {The sufficiency of the ground based on certain given consequences still does not give a perfect inference to its truth.}

We need hypotheses and in natural science simply cannot do without them. {Hypothesis is more than opinion[; it is] actual presupposition.} But, what is peculiar, metaphysics also has hypotheses – not in a theoretical respect, but in a practical one.

[d] to investigate.

| 1. | The ground that I accept *per hypothesin*, of this the possibility must be certain {otherwise one proceeds with just empty fictions}, e.g., a central fire.[26] {Pickles in the honey pot.[27] Conring thinks he has found Isis.}[28]
2. The consequence from the assumed ground must be given, hence it must be actual – the cause need only be possible.
3. The *consequentia* <of the consequences> from their cause must be wholly certain as well. Otherwise, how can one infer from it?

The 4th *requisitum* [is] the unity of the assumed ground in its sufficiency in regard to the consequences. { – All the consequences must flow from this one assumed ground. If it is not so, then one takes aid from another new | hypothesis |. *Hypothesis*$_L$ *subsidiaria* – {thus one † seeks . . . †) e.g., certain medicinals cure certain diseases. The sufficiency of a ground for all the consequences remains uncertain, however, hence every hypothesis [remains uncertain].}

A hypothesis, as long as it remains a hypothesis, never acquires full certainty, i.e., no apodeictic certainty (where the opposite would be impossible)[;] it can acquire empirical certainty. We speak here only of hypotheses of theoretical cognition. But there are also morally practical hypotheses, which are necessary in that they occur constantly according to certain laws. But a hypothesis in a theoretical respect is never necessary. In a moral respect [it is], however[;] e.g., duty is objectively necessary and happiness subjectively necessary, certain, etc. 747

{ad § 184 p.58}[29] *Of Persuasion and Conviction*. {*Persuasio male significat*[e] . . . .†}

The distinction between persuasion and conviction is precarious. Persuasion is actually holding-to-be-true based on grounds, without investigating whether they are objective or subjective. Holding a proposition to be true, without being able to distinguish whether it occurs from subjective or objective grounds. Even an honest man is incapable, as judge, of distinguishing the subjective grounds of his judgment from the objective ones when he is inclined favorably toward his friend's case.

We have already spoken above of science. {A cognition is systematic when the combination it has in a whole is necessary. A system is a whole insofar as the consciousness of its totality is possible only according to principles. – } It | *sc.* science | is actually the complex of cognitions, insofar as they are combined in a system. This does not require that they be rational. One must carefully distinguish *art* from *science*, however. *In sensu stricto*, it is that skill of producing something such that, even if one knows it, one still cannot make anything. It would be called *mechanical* art, or manual art, if one can [produce things] just by knowing it. Art, however, in distinction from common skill, [is] that skill defined above *in sensu stricto*.

[e] [The word] persuasion signifies something bad.

{HOUR, MONDAY}

Art is the system of nonhomogeneous skills. Outside the mathematical or intuitive and the philosophical or discursive there is another certainty that is not objective. The ground is really subjective – it is a practically valid certainty, namely, which must be called not moral but rather *pragmatic*[;] when one accepts something, that is, not so much according to rules of morality, but rather according to rules of prudence. A technical rule is a rule of art, a pragmatic rule one of prudence, a moral rule one of morality, of virtue – duty. Practical certainty also includes moral certainty. –

748 The author speaks here of a mathematical certainty of the first and the second degree. But there is no distinction here except that between mathematical and discursive certainty. {Merely absolute necessity is not by any means mathematical certainty – 2 · 2 = 4. For although what is true cannot be more true, there still remains always variety in the degree of certainty, because there there is proof through concepts alone, but here through intuition.}

A hypothesis means in most cases a merely arbitrary positing. Thesis, a firm proposition.

Now the author comes to the section

Of proofs

The *constitutiva* of every proof are:

1. The proof,[f] *probatio*,
2. That which is supposed to be proved, *probandum*. This is the material of the proof.
3. The relation between the two, that a correct *consequentia* follows therefrom; e.g., everything extended is divisible, all bodies are extended, hence all bodies are divisible, and after this the further inferences, etc.

We can call unprovable, first, that which is wholly false, and that which is immediately certain. The latter propositions are indemonstrable, the mediate ones demonstrable.

{HOUR}

To prove is to hold something to be true on account of a ground. We can divide all proofs into *direct* {or ostensive} ones and *indirect* or apagogical ones. The latter are those that one <derives> from the falsehood of the opposite. Apagogical proofs have almost more *intuitus* in them than the direct ones, because contradiction is always striking. {Apodeictic proofs –

[f] "Die Beweisführung."

with consciousness of necessity – *demonstratio*, a proof combined with intuition.

One can prove much apagogically *ex concessis*,[g] namely, when the other has already conceded something. These are *argumenta ad hominem*. In mathematics there are many such proofs. They are always excellent.

Now we want to see how they are suited for philosophy. When an accepted concept itself contains a contradiction, then the predicate can conflict with the concept and the opposite of the predicate can too. {Apagogical proofs are very unreliable[h] in philosophy.} One can prove quite different propositions simultaneously. This often happens in philosophy. Someone can refute his opponent apagogically and be refuted by him just as forcefully by being also reduced *ad absurdum*. The human will is free. This proposition is indispensable in morals. For if men could not act otherwise than they do act, then all laws would be in vain. The opinion of the opposite of this proposition is called fatalism, that all men act only according to certain laws determined by nature. Priestley and Price[30] had a long dispute over this. Each brought the other *ad absurdum* and nonetheless nothing came to an end. {No one proves his proposition *directe*, but always only the falsehood of the opposite. In philosophy that can easily deceive, for one can just as well err oneself in the matter, even if one proves that the other errs – both can quite easily be wrong.} The given multitude of all parts is finite or infinite, i.e., all the parts of a body taken together, and we can never do this, for every body is infinitely divisible, one would never be finished. Hence taking all the parts together is a *contradictio in adjecto*. –

749

The result of all this is that one cannot make use of apagogic proofs in philosophy, because here one cannot present them in intuition.

An aesthetic demonstration would be one that occurs by means of a *bon mot* {but is not always true}.

Now we come to the section:

Of the sources of our cognition

{The author has 3, experience, reason, and belief.} They are not of 3 kinds but only of 2 kinds: (1.) rational, (2.) empirical. {There is a belief of reason, but merely in a practical respect – hence this is not a separate source but always only reason, which is either theoretical or practical. All experience is of 2 kinds, immediate or mediate. This latter kind is historical belief.} As for what concerns belief, historical belief can also be called empirical[;] it is always grounded on someone else's testimony and experience. But no theoretical cognition is grounded on belief of reason; this is sufficient only

750

[g] from things conceded.

[h] "mißlich."

for practical purposes. A comparison and combination of truth toward a cognition. Experience is an operation of the understanding, hence perception does not at all suffice. Historical belief is connection of the experiences of others with my own. {It is a matter of determining what justifies me in respecting mediate experience as immediate – on what authority rests.} The witness who is an eyewitness, *testis oculatus*, {who has immediate experience himself,} is authentic. He is irrefutable when he *can know* the truth and *wants to say* it. Thus *capacity* and *integrity* are both *requisita*.

Testis auritus.[i] In the series of such witnesses there is often nothing but rumor – *rumor* <*sine capite*>[j] – the more of these there are, the more uncertain is the rumor. It is like the copy of a copy. {The longer the chain, the more uncertain. Tradition [is] where the first witness is unknown. If you believed, you would not trace the rumor back to the first ground. The competence is simply not to be settled. – } But the greater the multitude of coordinate witnesses, the more believable the rumor is. – The best means for passing judgment on the integrity of a person with whose character one is otherwise unfamiliar is not by whether he had an interest in the matter or not. Many rules of prudence are involved here, which may not be introduced in logic, however.

Now we want to touch on the concept of belief insofar as it is not a source of cognition but rather a mere judgment of reason, insofar as it no longer has a theoretical but rather a merely practical purpose. {*Unbelieving*[k] with respect to the practical – to belief of reason[;] *disbelieving*[l] with respect to the theoretical, to historical belief. In Latin there is no word for unbelieving. Someone is unbelieving who does not want to accept something based on moral grounds (which are sufficient as springs of morality), e.g., the existence of a highest being. – }

A hypothesis, which one holds to be necessary in a practical respect, e.g., a businessman finds a ground that is sufficient for undertaking something. E.g. A general must necessarily judge and decide something when 751 he faces the enemy. Here hypothesis is not optional,[m] then, in order to explain something, but instead is necessary in a practical respect. In the first case the purpose would be theoretical, however. All practical purposes (– legislations of reason) are either (1.) pragmatic or (2.) moral, i.e., either rules of prudence or laws of morality. Thus that general's purpose is pragmatic. Belief, regarded as a hypothesis, becomes necessary for a moral purpose, [and] can be called pure belief of reason.[n] The concept of

[i] A hearsay witness.
[j] rumor <without a source>.
[k] "*Ungläubig*."
[l] "*ungläubisch*."
[m] "beliebig."
[n] "reiner Vernunftglaube."

duty is wholly distinct from that of advantage. The posited end of fulfillment of duties is furtherance of the highest good, insofar as one can attain it here, the happiness of man[;] the unification of morality, worthiness to be happy, with happiness itself, does not lie in any man's power. If we see that our sources of cognition do not suffice for cognizing God as moral being, then we can nonetheless have a moral belief thereby. {Practical belief does not extend cognition, it is only the transition from the theoretical to the practical.}

Our author speaks now of the perfection of practical cognition, a chapter that actually does not especially belong to logic.

Of practical cognition

One sees that what he says about it does not actually belong to logic. It would be good to leave merely speculative things to religion. A *speculative* cognition is that which has no application practically. Practical propositions are either imperatives – then they are opposed to theoretical ones – or they are grounds for possible imperatives, and then they are opposed to merely speculative ones. E.g. There is a God[;] this is no merely speculative proposition but rather a practical one. For it contains grounds for possible imperatives.

{Practical propositions <are ones that> contain grounds of cognition for possible imperatives. The proposition, There is another life, is practical, because it contains grounds for possible imperatives. – Theoretical propositions are also called practical when they contain such grounds. Those propositions that contain no such grounds at all are also speculative. Imperatives determine to action.}

Now we go to a new section:

Of concepts

752

All cognition is through intuition or concept – representation is an elementary expression which cannot be further analyzed. Representation may be combined also with apperception – the consciousness of the representation.

{ad p. 14}[31] A representation combined with consciousness is called perception, *perceptio*. This *perceptio* becomes *cognitio* insofar as the representation is related with consciousness to an object. Now this representation is again of two kinds:

1. *intuitus* – this is not yet a cognition,

2. *conceptus*, contains that which is common to several objects, *nota communis*. A concept, considered by itself, is:

a) *conceptus empiricus* – when there is sensation in its representation

{for whose existence it is required that experience precede. The material of all empirical representation is sensation.}

b) *conceptus purus*, this is called a *notio*. It can be called a pure concept of the understanding. The concept of a triangle is a *conceptus* | *a* | *priori*.

{A concept is a *repraesentatio discursiva*. – The action whereby we give to a concept the corresponding intuition is called exhibition.[o] Cognition is more than *conceptus*, more than *intuitus*, it is both together. We seek objective reality, which we attain through application to intuition.}

An *idea*$_{L}$ is a concept of reason for which no object can be given adequately in intuition.

Representation, if it arises from the understanding, is always a concept. But the intuition of *red* does not yet give any concept of the understanding. – The representation of something as cause can only occur through the understanding, hence is a *notio*. {One can never experience a cause – for causality is a *notio*.} All intuition is only a representation of that which is given to us through the senses. Where it occurs – e.g., with mathematical concepts – there are never any *notiones* – pure concepts of the understanding[;] but of course [there are] *conceptus a priori*. {*Conceptus purus*: (1.) *intellectualis*, (2.) *rationalis*. A *conceptus purus intellectualis* is called a *notio* – e.g., virtue. A *conceptus purus*, to which no corresponding intuition can be given, [is called an] *idea*$_{L}$, e.g., of God. – I can give examples of virtue. Nonetheless it is not a concept of experience. Ontology has to do with nothing but notions. – Concepts, as to their matter, are 753 *dati* or *factitii*.[p] The former are called *notiones*, the latter empirical concepts. (*Conceptus arbitrarii*, arbitrary ones). Every concept of experience is made. Perception is only subjective – not yet experience. This is cognition with consciousness of the relation to the object.}

Sensibility involves two things, *sense* and *imagination*. There are merely logical concepts – so-called aesthetic concepts are merely representations without a concept. There are *a priori* pure concepts of the understanding, but also sensibly determined concepts of the understanding. {ad § 255}.

Experience means empirical cognition. With an empirical representation something must be perceived (sensed with consciousness). Hence experience presupposes empirical intuition and a concept. Sensation is indispensable for this. Transcendental philosophy, which must precede metaphysics, deals with the origin of pure concepts of the understanding. Logic does not do this. It is occupied only with actual actions. For the *use* of a concept abstraction is required, but the concept is still not made thereby. The latter occurs (1.) through the fact that something is considered as a partial representation, which can be common to several, e.g., the red color. (2.) When I consider the partial representation as a *nota*, as

[o] "Darstellung, exhibitio."

[p] given [or] made.

ground of cognition of a thing, e.g., I cognize blood, a rose, etc., through *red*. The 3rd action is abstraction, to consider[q] this partial representation as ground of cognition, insofar as I ignore all other partial representations. A concept is thus a partial representation, insofar as I thereby abstract from all others.

{To abstract is in the philosophical sense a negative concept – not to attend. There are not *abstract concepts*. We can only abstract *from something*, from certain differences, marks of things. The distinction between *abstract* and *concrete* lies not in the concept but in the *usus conceptuum*.[r]

A concept can be contained in other concepts (a part of them), but the others can at the same time be under it, it can be their ground. These two are only the various relations of the same concept, which can quite well be at the same time part and ground of something. Man is the partial representation of Negro, of someone learned (for a part of the concept of this, etc., is of course always that he is a man), but at the same time this concept is also the ground of cognition, under which the white man, the Negro, the learned man belong.}

754

Through abstraction, however, nothing is produced, but rather left out. We must not say that I *abstract a representation*, but rather that I *abstract from a representation*. I can either abstract from the variety of the things to which this concept is common, or I can attend to this in comparison with others. This is actually the use of the concept, in the first[s] case *in abstracto*, in the second case *in concreto*.

The faculty for the use of concepts *in concreto* is called the common understanding, the faculty, etc., *in abstracto*, is called the speculative understanding. The abstract concept <is> contained <in the> concrete one and itself <contains> the concrete one under itself. A higher concept is one that comprehends several in itself. *Repraesentatio singularis* – has an *intuitum*, indicates it immediately, but is at bottom not a *conceptus*. E.g., Socrates is not a *conceptus*.

{HOUR, MONDAY}

As soon as I make use of words, the representation is an individual concept. If the concept is expressed with particularity,[t] however, one considers it[u] *in abstracto*. Then it is no longer called a *conceptus universalis* but rather *communis*. A *conceptus communis* can be called *superior*$_{\text{L}}$ in regard to other concepts that are contained under <it>[v] {a higher concept}, *infe-*

[q] Reading "als Erkenntnisgrund zu betrachten" for "als Erkenntnisgrund."
[r] use of concepts.
[s] Ak, "im erstern"; MS and Ko, "im ersten."
[t] "Wird aber der Begriff ganz besonders ausgedrückt."
[u] Reading "ihn" for "es."
[v] Reading "unter <ihn>" for "in <ihm>."

rior$_{\text{L}}$ in regard to those under which[w] it is contained. {The *inferior*$_{\text{L}}$ (lower) always contains more in itself, the former | i.e., the *superior*$_{\text{L}}$ | more under itself but less in itself. For the *conceptus superior* is wholly universal just by virtue of the fact that it contains little in itself, e.g., the concept [of] man under that of animal. Hence this latter [is] a *conceptus superior*, since it contains more under itself, although it contains less in itself. Here we ignore the property of the understanding (in man). The higher the concept – the simpler. Living corporeal being – still higher[,] corporeal being[;] simple. The highest: being, thing[;] the simplest. If we look to the *content* of a concept, then we consider it *in concreto*. If we look to the *sphaera*, then we consider it *in abstracto*. – Of the first kind is cognition of practical people[x] – (with mole's eyes – merely on the spot[y]).}

Every *conceptus communis*, in regard <relation> to the *conceptus* under <which it> is contained, is called *species*$_{\text{L}}$[;] in regard to those that are 755 contained under it, *genus*$_{\text{L}}$. {The concepts of *genus*$_{\text{L}}$ and *species*$_{\text{L}}$ are different merely in respect of relation.} Now what was called *genus*$_{\text{L}}$ in one *respectus* I can call *species*$_{\text{L}}$ in another, [;] e.g., man [is] in numerous respects a *genus*$_{\text{L}}$, but in relation to animal [is] nonetheless a *species*$_{\text{L}}$. Can we find a *genus summum*? The *genus summum* is that which is contained under no other, is not a partial concept, i.e., has no further part. Now if there is a *genus summum*, an object in general, can one also find a *species infima*? One must assume that there are *conceptus communes* under which one cannot subsume any others. But it remains merely arbitrary, and hence one cannot say that a *species infima* can be found.

In the subordination of human concepts we begin with the lowest step, with the *individuum* – this is reckoned as a *conceptus singularis*. From there we go to the *conceptus superior* – or *communis*. E.g., oak tree {*ilex* in Spain, the wonderful acorns that taste like chestnuts} – growing things – plants – bodies – substances. Finally we come *per analysin* to the concept of a *thing*. The *conceptus superior* is always only a part of the *inferior*$_{\text{L}}$, so that the *conceptus summus* [contains] the least of all in itself – object, where one has not determined at all what – but it contains everything else under itself.

Our cognition gains uncommonly [much] if we always go to the *conceptus superior*. The multitude of things that are contained under the concept is called the logical *sphaera* of the concept. The greater this is, the smaller is its content. {The *sphaera* is *latissime patens*,[z] the simpler and more abstract the concept is. We understand by this not the content but rather the circle of application, a line that has in itself no breadth but nonetheless comprehends a great space. A concept that has no *sphaera* at all, e.g., that of the individual Julius Caesar is = to a point.}

[w] Reading "unter die" for "in denen."

[x] "der Praktiker."

[y] "bloß auf dem Fleck."

[z] open to the broadest extent.

Some concepts have one and the same *sphaera*, like the concept of the necessary and the unalterable. Such concepts are called *conceptus reciproci*, convertible concepts. *Latior* | *conceptus* |,[a] when | one | understands still more thereunder. If one wished to undertake a consideration and a comparison between metal and wood, then these are *conceptus heterogenei*, have no *respectus* at all in regard to their quantity, e.g., 100 years – German miles, {because none of these concepts that are compared with one another stands under the other. – } *Conceptus reciproci* must be homogeneous. One really should not say *conceptus universalis*. Only the application can be used *in abstracto*, and then the concept is *quoad usum universalis* or *particularis*,[b] etc. A *conceptus* is always a *repraesentatio communis*[;] in logic there are no others. 756

There are various kinds of *differentia*$_{L}$. They are, namely:

1. *generica* – [this] is the variety of genera,[c] e.g., physicians name several diseases –
   materiae sui generis.[d]
2. *specifica* – [this] is the differentiation of things that belong to a common *genus*$_{L}$ – in the *species*$_{L}$ there must be something that was not contained in the *genus*$_{L}$.
3. *numerica* – i.e., the distinction of the *conceptus singulares*, insofar as they are not common to several. Among men we indicate them by *nomina propria.*[e]

Of definitions

The logical perfection of definition consists:

1. in distinctness[;] it is the highest requirement of definition.
2. in *completudo* or in distinctness through sufficient marks.
3. *praecisio* – precision, i.e., the separation of everything else that is not required for sufficient distinctness.

{Precision is a requirement of the 2nd degree for definition. No more marks than necessary. Definition is the highest logical perfection of a concept.}

Conceptus adaequatus in minimis terminis – *conceptus completus, praecise determinatus.*[f] If the concept has these requirements, then it is a *conceptus rei adaequatus.*[g]

Now we will show how definitions are made.

All concepts are of two kinds, namely:

[a] Broader | concept |.
[b] universal [or] particular as to its use.
[c] "der Gattungen, generum."
[d] [Their] matters [are] distinct, each of its own kind.
[e] proper names.
[f] A concept that is adequate, in minimal terms – a complete concept, determined precisely.
[g] concept adequate to the thing.

1. *conceptus dati*, and these are either
   a) *empirici* – given *a posteriori*,
   b) *rationati* – given *a priori*. – {E.g., concept of cause, quantity, substance, action, time, and space. We cannot observe space[.] – – It is not an empirical representation. For this latter always rests on perception.}

2. *conceptus factitii* < – made – fabricated – > – they can be made[h]
   a) *ex datis a posteriori*,[i]
   b) *ex datis a priori*.[j]

757 All *definitions of given concepts*, if they are given *a priori*, are always *analytic*, all *definitions of concepts that are made* are without distinction *synthetic*.

{A synthetic definition, one that arises from many concepts taken together. I make for myself the concept of a *quadratum* (*est rectangulum quadrilaterum aequilaterum*)[k] through the definition. This latter precedes the concept, then. It is always so in synthesis.

Analysis. I seek out marks in the concept that I already have. This requires: (1.) <Exposition of the concept> (e.g., body. Through the exposition we attain the elementary propositions for the definition. Here, too, the 3 *requisita*. Body. Extended, composite, divisible [– this] lies in it already.)

Mathematical definitions can never be false, because mathematics makes its concepts itself. – Definitions of concepts of experience are synthetic. They can actually never be defined, only described.}

An empirical concept can also be defined[l] analytically. In this case not merely is the concept given, but also the object. If, e.g., one wished to define *water*, then one would <only> define one's concept of it, not the object itself. It is the same with all other concepts of experience. One can of course define them themselves, but not the object, because we cannot find *all* the marks. With all concepts of experience, the definition of the concept is in and of itself wholly dispensable. – (It is in fact wholly subjective.) *Conceptus dati* can usefully be defined only insofar as they are given *a priori*. – My definition never becomes complete in regard to the object and *eo ipso* never becomes a definition.

Thus far we have treated of *given* concepts and we come now to those that are *made*. All definitions here are synthetic, for at the basis there always lie *data*$_{L}$ that are put together. All mathematical definitions are synthetic. All approximations to concepts of experience, observations, are synthetic. But the synthesis is not arbitrary, the concept is thus not *arbitrarie*

[h] Reading "gemacht" for "gegeben."
[i] from things given a posteriori.
[j] from things given a priori.
[k] square (it is a four-sided equilateral rectangle).
[l] Reading "definiert" for "gegeben."

factitius.[m] The mathematician can never err, only lack in precision. E.g., Wolff in the definition of the circle, which one can comprehend more concisely than he did. Hence he did not err but only failed in precision.

{HOUR} 758

Definition is the declaration of the representations that I make for myself of the object. Concepts that are made also include those that arise from perceptions. If a definition of these is possible, it cannot be other than synthetic. But we can define concepts of experience only nominally {describe [them]. Description differs from definition in not having the requirements of *completudo* and precision.}

Now we proceed to concepts given *a priori*. All definitions of concepts given *a priori* are defined *per analysin*. {The beginning here is always exposition – (not definition).} E.g., the concept of right. It is not innate in us, of course[;] <rather,> to produce it we had to reflect concerning it – in the concept of virtue is contained, first – lawfulness for actions, then lawfulness for right actions, then in addition freedom. {Which stands in conflict with the inclinations, – in this it is distinct from holiness.}

In the analysis of a concept the 1st thing – the exposition – is gradually to become conscious of the manifold that is contained in my consciousness[;] 2ndly – definition, when the exposition is complete. But now how can we ever become certain whether we have expounded a concept perfectly? In such cases one must be very cautious, e.g., in those of substance and cause – concepts that are pure *a priori*. {In philosophical definitions one can never be fully conscious of *completudo* – not to be conscious that something is lacking is quite different from being conscious that nothing is lacking.}

Note. In the case of given concepts, one must never begin with definition but always with exposition. But with concepts that are made – *conc. factitii,*[n] e.g., mathematical ones, definition must always precede. Exposition begins with elementary propositions. In regard to coordinate concepts, there can never be any definition or demonstration, if one takes the words strictly. These words pertain actually only to † mathematics. Nevertheless, insofar as we suspect *completudo*, we call it in philosophy – definition. It is not always necessary to define. –

Now we proceed further and will treat

Of the rules for definitions 759

Passing judgment on definitions involves the following rules:

[m] made arbitrarily (reading "factitius" for "facticius").
[n] concepts that are made (reading "factitii" for "facticii").

1. whether the proferred definition, as a proposition, is true,
2. whether the definition, as a concept, is distinct. –

Two things hamper the distinctness of a concept, namely,

a) when the marks are tautological [and] I explain *idem per idem.*[o]
b) when I explain *obscurum per aeque obscurum.*[p]

The 3rd criterion is whether the concept, as a distinct concept, is exhaustive {*completudo*},

the 4th, whether the concept that I regard as exhaustive is precise {precision}. How are definitions to be made?

1. Seek several elementary propositions (here the talk is of analytical [definitions]).
2. See to it that the predicate is not just as obscure as the concept that you want to explain. –
3. Collect several such predicates, until you are certain that together they exhaust the whole concept.
4. See to it that one mark does not already contain another and hence can be dispensed with. (Through this one still does not learn to make definitions.)

The most useful of all the rules is that one must begin with exposition, through which one attains elementary propositions of a definiton. In the case of an analytic definition we always reserve the right to extend our concept and perhaps even to opine the opposite in the future. If no concept lies at the basis, then I cannot speak of the thing at all. But this is always possible when we have made the concept clear. One must be especially cautious about making a definition that does not reciprocate, that does not convert. All definitions in philosophy must be regarded as *tentamina*[q] for philosophizing.

As for what concerns quantity, the perfection of a definition rests on the fact that the *definitio* is reciprocal with the *definitum*, that one can put one in place of the other. {When the *sphaera* of a definition is equal to the *sphaera* of the *definitum.*} *Definitio nec sit latior nec angustior definito.*[r] A *conceptus* is *latior* than another when it contains fewer, *angustior* when it has more determinations. This is the consequence, namely, of the narrowing of the concept.

Quality in logic – distinctness. The logical requisite:

760 *Ne definiatur obscurum per aeque obscurum.*[s]

2. Logical relation is the relation of the marks in the definition to the concept of a *definitum*. Every ground *generaliter* must be something

[o] the same by the same.
[p] the obscure by the equally obscure.
[q] attempts.
[r] The definition should be neither broader nor narrower than the thing defined.
[s] The obscure is not to be defined by the equally obscure.

other than the consequence[;] without this it is not a ground. The third rule is

3. *Non definiendum in circulo*, i.e., [do not] explain *circulo, idem per idem.*[t] When the identity is obvious, then this is called tautological. {As in: *Ratio est id, per quod cognoscimus, cur aliquid sit.*[u] *Cur*[v] means, however, *quam ob rationem.*[w] The explanation is thus wholly tautological, says nothing new.} But if it is hidden, then we call this method explaining in a circle. The fourth rule:

4. Modality – necessity is here the logical perfection. An empirical proposition does not contain it. Empirical concepts cannot be defined at all.

Definitions can be divided into

nominal and – for distinction from the other – real definitions,[x] which are sufficient for derivation of all predicates and concepts. Through real definitions[y] we have insight into the possibility of things. Nominal definitions[z] serve merely | to | distinguish a thing. A nominal definition that would be sufficient for distinguishing the thing from all others would be just as good as a real definition. Mathematical definitions are all real. Description is distinct from definition in that it contains only the historical.[a] The exposition of a concept in which it remains undetermined whether it is complete or precise is a description.

{HOUR, MONDAY}

Of the division of concepts

{It consists in the distinct representation of all lower concepts, insofar as they are contained under a higher one and are opposed to one another.} Logical division[b] is called division[c] and is distinct from the taking apart[d] or analysis of the concept. By *divisio logica* is understood not the taking apart of the concept itself (*divisio realis*) but rather – of its *sphaera*. E.g., the concept of man has a *sphaera* – not a manifoldness in itself, but rather it comprehends many others under itself. {A division of trees, e.g., into crown, trunk, root, would be *partitio*, not *divisio*.

[t] circularly, i.e., the same by the same.
[u] A ground is that through which we know why something is.
[v] Why.
[w] because of what ground.
[x] "Realerklärungen."
[y] "Sacherklärungen."
[z] "Nominalerklärungen."
[a] "nur Historisches."
[b] "Division."
[c] "Einteilung."
[d] "Teilung."

761 *Partitio* is different from *divisio* – the latter divides merely the concept. Logical division is always dichotomy, *a* or *non a*. All living beings are mortal or non-mortal. This is analytical division according to the principle of contradiction. The principle of all logical divisions is the *principium exclusi medii inter duo contradictoria.*[e] Synthetic division is into *a* and *b*. Polytomy presupposes real cognition, not merely cognition of form. – In this case one can never become certain of the completeness of his division. To be fair one would have to be able to survey how much [is] *possible*. But there are concrete concepts, objects of experience. Here only *partitio* is possible.}

All division can occur into *opposita* or into *disparata*. The first can also be made *a priori*, but empirical division (division of experience) is only into *disparata*, e.g., the various races of man, red-brown, yellow, etc.[;] | one | into *opposita* would be if I said, All men are either white or non-white.

Now we want to go through the points that pertain to the division of a concept.

1. The divided concept, *conceptus divisus*, whose sphere can be divided.

2. The *membra dividentia*, the lower ones, which are contained under the higher ones. They are members of the division, which, put together, form a complete whole. One cognizes this when they are adequate to the sphere. A division expresses, then, that lower concepts subordinated to higher ones are together equal to the whole sphere of the concept.

A given division can be considered in relation to its subdivisions[f] <division of a member of the division>, which go quite far, to the *individuum* and to its codivisions,[g] e.g., men, *respective*$_{\text{L}}$ to <1.> learnedness, <2.> sex, <3., 4.> etc. The members of the codivision are called *membra codividentia*.

We come now to the actual rules. The first is:

1. The *conceptus* must not be *latior*[h] than all the *membra dividentia*[i] taken together[;] the less in itself, the more under itself. {Then it contains too much.}
2. The *conceptus* must not be *angustior*[j] than the *membra dividentia* either.
3. Between the terms of the division there must be oppositions, and these are 762 taken together *disjunctive*$_{\text{L}}$, i.e., through either or. {The *membra dividentia* must be opposed to one another or else it is not logical division.}
4. The divided concept must not contradict the concept of the division.
5. The members of the subdivision must not come under the members of the superdivision, that would be contradictory. E.g., to the ignorant we must oppose, not the learned, but rather him who has science.

[e] principle of the excluded middle between two contradictories.

[f] "Untereinteilungen, Subdivisionen."

[g] "Nebeneinteilungen <Codivisionen>."

[h] broader.

[i] members of the division.

[j] narrower.

6. I must derive the number of the members of the division from the nature of the divided concept. Every empirical division can be called partition rather than *divisio logica*. {With the latter, one must know that there are neither more nor fewer terms of the division[;] with empirical division this need not be so. – }

Logical division <which abstracts from all content> cannot be other than dichotomy <2 terms> – *a* – *non a* – according to the principle of contradiction. {This is the principle of all analytic judgments.} Polytomy, trichotomy, etc. – divisions that are not made according to this principle – are always synthetic. {Synthetic divisions – trichotomy, polytomy in general. – It is striking that trichotomy appears so often, subst. . . . .† God: (holiness, goodness, justice). Here there is, as it were, a highest proposition or a condition <a conditioned> a consequence † [;] unity [is] the condition, manyness the conditioned, allness the consequence, combination {allness – manyness as unity) of both together.}

Of judgments

The representation that is universal through its consciousness as the representation of a mark is a clear concept. The consciousness of a universal representation (*repraesentatio communis*) is called not merely a concept, then, but a clear concept. A concept that becomes clear through a judgment is called a distinct concept, and a concept that becomes distinct through an inference of reason is called a concept of reason (according to Wolff, a complete concept).

{Judgment is the representation of the unity of given concepts, insofar as one is subordinated to the other or excluded from it. –

1. Clear concept, through consciousness of universality.
2. Distinct concept, not merely through *apprehensio*, but rather – *judicium*. 763
3. Concept of reason.

3 Judgments:

1. Where one [is] under the other as † subject under predicate: *categorical*.
2. The judgment where one concept [is] under the other as conditioned under the condition †, as consequence under the ground: hypothetical.
3. The judgment that contains a consequence which can † be divided disjunctive: QPJ.}[32]

To act means to separate the cause from the effect. If a concept is to become distinct, then one must always make a *judicium*. The mark becomes at once the predicate of the judgment, e.g., man is an animal. This distinct concept comes to be only through a judgment. From this we see that before one gets to distinct concepts, one must treat judgments.

A concept of reason arises out of an inference of reason. E.g. All men are living beings, all living beings are animals, *ergo*$_{L}$ † all men are animals. One can infer † a *nota remota*, then, only through a *nota media*, through an inference of reason. Hence one should rather treat inferences, should take up the three operations of thought right at first. This was Aristotle's manner – very stringent. – It was Wolff who broke it off.

A judgment is the representation of the relation of concepts among one another, through which a cognition becomes distinct. A great mistake in this logic, that the author speaks immediately of subject and predicate {before, that is, the more necessary † prior cognitions[k] are set forth[;] it is thus in every † logic}. Our author's definition of judgment fits only categorical ones. {We do not have just one kind of judgment – } But there are also hypothetical ones, problematic ones. {3 relations: (1.) of inherence, (2.) of dependence, (3.) of parts to each other, which together make a whole.}

All judgments may be reduced to 3 kinds: 1. categorical † ones, which contain the relation of predicate to subject.

2. hypothetical † ones[;] they contain the relation of ground to consequence. <If the soul is not composite, then etc.>

{What is not composite is not perishable. The soul is not composite, the soul is not perishable.}

764

3. disjunctive ones[;] they contain the relation of a divided concept to the whole sphere of the division <e.g., all men are learned or non-learned>. These judgments are of a completely different kind but have this in common, that <they> can always be expressed categorically, too (nonetheless, it might not always work).

{There are kinds of difference, numerical – specific – *toto genere* different. – We went thus upwards from below. Learned men are specifically the same and generically, too, and nonetheless numerically different[,] as C. and J.}[33]

We proceed now to

Categorical judgments

In logic, matter is the given. {Form, in logic, is the way of putting together and connecting given concepts.} In categorical judgments the subject and the predicate must be given. In all categorical judgments negation <the sign of negation> must affect the copula <not the predicate>, or else they are not negative judgments. {*Anima non est <copula> mortalis*,[l] would be a negative judgment. *A. est immortalis <non mortalis>*[m] would be affirmative.} Judgments whose predicates are merely negative {e.g., *non-*

[k] "Vorkenntnisse."

[l] The soul is not <copula> mortal.

[m] The soul is immortal <non-mortal>.

m. – that which | is outside | the sphere | *m.* |} are called infinite judgments <*judicia infinita*> {because there is no end of those things that are *non a*[;] but *a* can be determined}.

Of the condition of unconditioned judgments

{Every judgment has the condition of truth – the ground for one's attributing to it a predicate.} In every judgment there must be something in the subject that makes the predicate be attributed to it, and this is called the condition. E.g., every body, as an extended being, is divisible. Or another example: all men, as finite beings, are capable of mistakes (*faillible*). Now this, again, is not called a conditioned judgment, but a restricted one. If the latter is removed, then it becomes conditioned. The restriction is called the determination of the judgment.[n] – Sometimes these determinations lie in the concept, sometimes they are added.

We come now to the division of judgments[:]

765

1. as to *quality* they are either affirmative or negative <and infinite>, e.g., some men are not learned – a negative judgment
2. as to *quantity* all judgments are either
   a) *universalia*, are expressed by *all*,
   b) *particularia*[;] instead of this expression rather plural[o] judgments.

We can consider every predicate in itself as a *terminus major*. There are universal judgments that are expressed not universally, only plurally, e.g., All rational beings are thinking beings,[p] some men are rational beings, some men are thinking beings, etc. There are 3 sorts of judgments as to quantity, namely, universal, particular, and singular. A *judicium singulare* permits no exceptions because it has no *sphaera*.

| {The *judicium generale* is in general distinct from the universal judgment.[q] It occurs where there are only a few exceptions, where by this judgment one[r] runs the least risk of erring, hence one can say it *generaliter*. Such judgments can occur only in the empirical.} |

A categorical judgment has either 2 subjects and one predicate or 2 predicates and one subject or only one subject and only one predicate. We come

3. to *relation*[;] as to this, we divide[s] judgments into
   a) categorical ones. The relation of subject to predicate.
   b) hypothetical ones. The relation of ground to consequence. {– 2 judg-

[n] "die Bestimmung des Urteils (determinatio judicii)."

[o] "pluralistische."

[p] Reading "Wesen" for "Menschen," following a suggestion by Hinske.

[q] "vom allgemeinen <universellen> Urteil."

[r] Ak, "wo durch man diese Urtheil"; MS, "wo man durch dieses Urtheil."

[s] Reading "teilen wir die Urteile ein" for "teilen wir die Urteile."

ments are in the relation where one grounds the other. If the one is true, then so is the other. With the hypothetical judgment there can only be 2 propositions, – with the disjunctive there can be several.}

c) disjunctive ones. The relations of members of the divided concept, of parts of the sphere to the whole sphere.

The categorical † <absolute> judgment contains only the relation of 2 concepts, but the hypothetical and the disjunctive of two or more judgments †. {A proposition[t] is an assertoric judgment.}

That which is the ground in a *judicium hypotheticum* is called *antecedens*, the connection with the last is called the copula, the <inference[u]> following from the two judgments is called the *consequentia*. The matter of the 766 hypothetical judgment consists not of 2 concepts but of two judgments, whose relation is the *consequentia*. {A hypothetical judgment consists of two problematic ones – these are its matter. The inference[v] of the *consequens* from the *antecedens* is called the *consequentia*. The hypothetical judgment does nothing but draw the *consequentia* from the two problematic propositions.}

Now an example of the *judicium disjunctivum*: All bodies are either fluid or solid. <If this world is not the best, then | God | either was unfamiliar with a better or did | not | wish to create it or could | not create | [it], etc.> {Together these constitute the whole *sphaera*.}

4. *Modality* (determination of the connecting concept).[w] The 3 determinations of the copula {or of the connecting concept} (above all for categorical judgments) are:
   a) problematic judgments, contain logical possibility,
   b) assertoric judgments, contain logical actuality {truth},
   c) apodeictic judgments, contain logical necessity.

{HOUR, FRIDAY}

The author says that a *judicium* without modality is a *judicium purum*. A judgment is called *exponibile* because a thought or concept is expressed as simple, although in fact it is composite, and in fact is composed of an affirmative and a negative, e.g., few men are virtuous. {This means that some men are virtuous, many men are not virtuous, hence an affirmative and a negative judgment.} {A composite judgment, where 2 judgments have one predicate.} Those judgments which {are aesthetic}[,which] merely represent the subjective in relation to a faculty of cognition, are not <purely> logical. E.g., when one makes a description of mountains and

[t] "Propositio oder Satz."
[u] "Schlußfolge."
[v] Reading "Schlußfolge" for "Folge."
[w] "Verbindungsbegriff."

in doing so relates not universally valid concepts of their size and position, but rather merely the sensations produced by them in us.

{Theoretical judgments are those that determine an object as possible. Practical ones signify the actions for making it actual.}

Practical propositions relate to actions, through which the proposition becomes possible.

{An unprovable judgment can nonetheless be true. – All immediately certain propositions are unprovable.} To demonstrate can have 2 meanings. – 767

An empty judgment {what contains no ground of any cognition, thus tautological judgments} is a judgment which contains no concept, which is wholly indistinct, when I explain *obscurum per aeque obscurum*.[x] An empty judgment can be obviously or covertly [empty]. {Identical judgments are not on that account empty. – All definitions are identical with the defined concept. Identity can also be cognized through analysis.}

If the *identitas* [is] *explicita*, then the judgment is tautological – if one mark is named twice. Not everything unprovable is an identical proposition. Synthetic propositions are included too. When I have transformed *identitas implicita* into *explicita*, then I have accomplished the analysis.

The author speaks now of unprovable judgments. *Axioms* are unprovable <immediately certain> propositions. {They are possible only in mathematics.} Even if some things should be discoverable *per analysin*, the mathematician does not want this. For this is not his business, since he produces everything through construction of concepts in intuition. {Axioms are always synthetic propositions, namely, those that one can put forth in an intuition <through> *intuitus purus*. Analytical propositions are not identical | with these |.}

A postulate is a practical proposition concerning what is to be done, without showing the way, because it assumes that everyone can do what it recommends as imperatives. {For in logic it depends not on matter but always on form.}

Judgments are either intuitive (insofar as it is concerned with an object that may be exhibited in intuition) or discursive (whose object is exhibited through a concept).

A judgment of perception is intuitive (not discursive). An empirical judgment is intuitive, but experience is nonetheless discursive. Judgments of experience are always discursive, because we always connect perceptions with them. [It is] a *vitium subreptionis*[y] if one holds what is only a judgment of perception to be a judgment of experience.

A *theorema* is a theoretical proposition insofar as it is capable of a proof. {A deduction that one draws through an inference is a *corollarium*

[x] the obscure through the equally obscure.

[y] error of subreption.

consectarium.} A problem[z] is a practical proposition, since one must accept what one is ordered to do.

768 {HOUR, MONDAY}

An *axiom* [is] a proposition that comes immediately from the definition. It presupposes intuition, really, or at least immediate certainty *a priori*. A practical proposition that needs and is capable of a solution is called a *quaestio problematis* {a proposition that determines the action that is supposed to happen}. The representation of the way in which the object is brought to be is called a *resolutio*. The proof that – when one has proceeded thus – this follows: *demonstratio*. A *postulate* is capable neither of a resolution nor of a demonstration. The resolution of the problem is complete when everything is contained therein, [e.g.,] when the proportion has been completely resolved. This does not always apply in mathematics, but one can approximate it as much as one wishes, e.g., the measuring of the diameter of the earth. – Exactitude – precision presupposes that it [is] complete – that it does not contain too little, nor too much.

In the case of resolutions in things practical, one does not take things so exactly and is satisfied when one has the means, whose power one prefers to be too strong rather than too weak. {E.g., levers, pullies, preferably too much power rather than too little. – Test – to bring back to the given – what one has analyzed. – }

Qualitas occulta, a method common in scholastic philosophy, according to which they held the name of the effect of the cause to be insight into the cause itself. {Tautology in the determination of the cause – e.g., instinct, *horror vacui*,[a] idiosyncrasy, etc. – one is often deceived through this. – Nothing is cause of itself[b] – the cause must always be something else than the *causatum* – the effect.} ἐντελέχια[c] – the name of a cause unknown to us.

We are still naming certain propositions in a system {and, indeed, in a dogmatic system}. A *corollarium* is a proposition that can be deduced from another proposition through a single inference. *Corollaria* can be theoretical or practical. The author often presupposes cognitions[d] on the part of his readers and makes corollaries which would still be theorems for beginners. This is always relative to capacities. *Wolff* translated *corollarium* as *addition*[e] <better, deduction[f]>, *scholion* as *note*.[g] *Scholion* – a resting place[;] by this is

[z] "Eine Aufgabe."
[a] abhorrence of a vacuum.
[b] "von sich selbst Ursach."
[c] entelechy (i.e., that which gives form or actuality to a substance).
[d] "Kenntnisse."
[e] "Zusatz."
[f] "Folgerung."
[g] "Anmerkung."

understood that which is regarded not as a constituent part of a system but rather as explanation. *Scholia*$_{\mathrm{L}}$ can also contain the value, the reality, and the history of the proposition, who said it first. Finally comes the name *lemma*$_{\mathrm{L}}$[h] {where one takes something from another system}[; it] does not belong to the *territorio* of the discipline; *est peregrinum aliquid*[i] { – a digression[j] – }.

769

Immediate inferences (*consequentiae immediatae*) are deductions of one proposition from another, the two being distinct from one another not as to matter but <merely> *as to form*. These have no *medius terminus*. Immediate inferences are inferences that cannot be transformed into inferences of reason except through tautological subsumptions. {E.g. All men are mortal, some mortals are men[;] this is a *consequentia immediata*. An inference of reason: All men are mortal is the *major*$_{\mathrm{L}}$, *atqui*[k] some mortals are mortal, this is the *minor*$_{\mathrm{L}}$, a tautological subsumption. *Ergo*$_{\mathrm{L}}$ some mortals are men, the conclusion. Now since tautological propositions are empty, we leave out the *minor*$_{\mathrm{L}}$ and the conclusion follows immediately.} Tautological judgments can be regarded as empty because they contribute nothing at all to distinctness, e.g., all men are mortal, some men are men (tautological), some men are mortal.

According to our author the first *consequentia immediata* is to be called

1. *per judicia aequipollentia.*[l] I infer from one judgment to another that means just the same. The ground must always be distinct from the consequence.

Now we will go through 4 *consequentiae immediatae*. The first – *per judicia subalternata*, where I infer from the universal to the particular. {*quoad quantitate*[m]}

2. *Per judicia opposita,*[n] where I infer from | one of | 2 mutually opposed judgments to the other.
3. *Per conversionem judicii,*[o] where I convert the *termini* of the judgment, only the relation, not the quality.
4. *Per contrapositionem,*[p] where again the quantity is not altered, only the quality. What was predicate in the first proposition becomes now subject, but the quantity, the affirmative and the negative[,] remains. (*Metathesis*$_{\mathrm{L}}$.) {In every affirmative judgment I can contrapose – one need only convert.}

Now we will go through the individual *consequentiae*.

1. *Per judicia subalternata* – what belongs to all belongs to some, e.g., all men are mortal, consequently some men are mortal.

[h] "Lemma – Lehnurteil."
[i] it is something foreign.
[j] "Episode."
[k] but.
[l] through equivalent judgments.
[m] as to quantity.
[n] through opposed judgments.
[o] Through the conversion of judgments.
[p] Through contraposition.

770 2. All *oppositiones* in logic have 3 distinct kinds. They are:

1. *contradictorie opposita* to one another – {contain everything required for opposition – }[;] or they contain less than is required for opposition, the *judicia*
2. *subcontrarie opposita* {hence they can both be true} or
3. *contrarie opposita* {contain more than is required, hence can both be false.}

Now we proceed to their rules.

The rule of the first [kind]: No proposition is opposed to another *contradictorie* except the universal affirmative to the particular negative. –

People have accepted certain symbols. Universal affirmatives are signified[q] with *a*, universal negatives with *e*, *particulariter* affirmatives *i*, *o* particular negatives. This is expressed thus:

Asserit a, negat e, sed universaliter ambo –

Asserit i, negat o, sed particulariter ambo.[r] –

If one of 2 contradictory judgments is true, then the other is false, and conversely.

We come

2. to judgments *subcontrarie opposita.*[s] Particular judgments are opposed to one another *subcontrarie.*
3. Judgments *contrarie opposita* are those where two universal judgments are opposed to one another as *a* and *e*.

With universal judgments one says more than is needed for opposition. For opposition, however, nothing more is required than that *a* and *o*, *e* and *i*, are in opposition.

3. *Conversio judicii* consists in the inference of one judgment from another through *metathesis terminorum*[t] {since one makes what previously was subject the predicate}, but through preservation of the quality of the judgment. The *judicium conversum* is given, the *convertens* must be deduced from the *consequentia immediata. Conversio simplex* † is where the quantity remains the same. The concept of the subject is considered as if it stands under the predicate as *locus geometricus.*[u] {Hence one cannot convert these propositions, that would bring the *latior* under the *angustior.*} Universal 771 affirmative judgments can actually be converted only *per accidens*, but particular affirmatives <*simpliciter*>. All negative judgments may be converted *simpliciter* – the opposition is always reciprocal. All universal affirmatives, etc. Contraposition through *metathesis*$_{L}$.

{N.B. Tuesday the 17th. Kant took a vacation here of more than 4 weeks.}

[q] Reading "Allgemein bejahende werden . . . partikulär verneinende bezeichnet" for "Allgemein bejahende . . . partikulär verneinende."

[r] *A* asserts, *E* negates, but in both cases universally *I* asserts, *O* negates, but in both cases particularly.

[s] Reading "opposita" for "oppositae."

[t] transposition of terms.

[u] geometrical locus or place.

{MONDAY THE 20TH AUGUST}

An *inference of the understanding* is the *consequentia*[v] of one judgment from another, *absque judicio intermedio.*[w] An inference of reason is the cognition of the necessity of a proposition through the subsumption of its condition under a universal rule. This is called a *judicium intermedium.*

{An inference of reason is the consequence of one inference of the understanding from another through a *judicium intermedium*. Inferences of the understanding infer from the universal to the particular, inferences of the power of judgment from the particular to the universal. [The power of judgment] substitutes: *atqui*[x] this is a case of the universal rule. Its inferences are never strict – only an attempt *in subsidium*[y] – thus analogy and induction.}

Everything extended is divisible, consequently bodies are divisible, is not a *consequentia immediata*. In the case of a universal inference of reason it is necesary that it be brought under a universal rule, and secondly that one subsume the condition under the universal rule. E.g. Everything extended is divisible, *atqui* all bodies are <extended>, *ergo*$_L$ all bodies are divisible. Every inference of reason consists of 3 propositions:

1. the *universal rule*, i.e., the major proposition, *major propositio,*
2. the condition of the subsumption of a certain proposition under a universal proposition, the *minor*$_L$,
3. the proposition that is to be understood through the subsumption under a universal rule, the *conclusio*.

Analogy and *induction* are inferences of the power of judgment. In inferences one can never infer <surely> from the particular to the universal. An inference of <induction> is when I infer from some things that belong to a certain species to all the things of the species, that it belongs to all the others. {To know how one ought to seek variety, how one reflects, this one cannot teach. – } 772

According to the inference by analogy, if 2 things agree under as many | determinations | as I have become acquainted with, then I infer that they agree † also | in | the other | determinations |. I infer, then, from some determinations, which I cognize, that the others belong to the thing too. This is an inference of a provisional judgment. One reserves the right to change it. {An inference according to analogy, that animals have souls – But . . . † why? If wasps have drunk from the forbidden honey and now wish to sting, then they fall, but they have . . . † Faculty of desire. This holds for plants, too, the fly-trap. They seek air and sun and water.†}

[v] Reading "Konsequenz" for "Folge."
[w] without an intermediate judgment.
[x] but.
[y] in support.

No logician has yet developed analogy and induction properly. This field still lies open. A judgment which settles what is true or false is called determinative . . . †

There are three kinds of *inferences of reason*, categorical, hypothetical, and disjunctive. In the first there are only 3 *termini*. The ground of this lies in the fact that in all inferences of reason there must lie at the basis a rule, under which one subsumes. The 3rd is the application – *conclusio*. In every inference of reason we have matter and form. The first consists of the premises {the premises are called the matter of the inference of reason}, the latter of the *consequentia*. Logic does not have to concern itself at all with falsehood *quoad materiam*.[z] If one has concluded correctly, even from false premises, then the conclusion is nonetheless correct. No rational being is infallible. Man is a rational being, therefore no man is infallible. The conclusion is correct, the premises false. What pertains to logic is only the argumentation and the *error aut veritas ratiocinii quoad formam*.[a]

The *major propositio* is always an assertoric proposition. {The *major propositio* contains the rule, the *minor*$_{\mathrm{L}}$ the subsumption, the *conclusio* the consequence. An inference of reason [is] the consciousness of the necessity of a proposition through subsumption under a universal rule. – }

Each of these inferences of reason has its special principle. Categorical inferences of reason infer according to the *dictum de omni et nullo*. Hypothetical inferences of reason according to the rule *a ratione ad rationatum valet consequentia*[b] or *a negatione rationati ad negationem rationis valet consequentia*[c] <*posita ratione ponitur rationatum*[d]>.

773 The *dictum de omni et nullo* is a consequence of the *principium contradictionis* {the principle of contradiction is the principle of judgments, not of inferences of reason}. It says:

Quicquid valet de genere aut specie,[e] *valet etiam de omnibus sub genere aut specie – quicquid non valet de genere aut specie, non valet etiam de omnibus sub isto genere aut ista specie contentis.*[f]

I can infer thus, for the concept of the whole contains the marks of the individual. Kant expresses this:

Nota notae est nota rei ipsius[g] <the universal principle of all affirmative

[z] as to matter.

[a] error or truth of the inference as to form.

[b] from the ground to the grounded the *consequentia holds*.

[c] from the negation of the grounded to the negation of the ground, the *consequentia* holds (reading "a negatione rationati ad negationem rationis valet consequentia" for "a negatione rationati").

[d] in positing the ground one posits the grounded.

[e] Reading "de genere aut specie" for "de genere."

[f] Whatever holds of the genus or species holds also of all those things under the genus or species – whatever does not hold of the genus or species also does not hold of all the things contained under that genus or that species.

[g] A mark of a mark is a mark of the thing itself.

inferences> – *Repugnans notae repugnat rei ipsi*[h] <the principle of all negative inferences>.

{E.g., All bodies are alterable. I seek the *nota intermedia divisible*, a more proximate mark of all bodies. *Alterable* is a mark of divisible, divisible a mark of bodies, hence alterable is a mark of bodies.

divisible

bodies	–	alterable
divisible	–	alterable
bodies	–	divisible
–	–	alterable

according to the principle of all affirmative inferences.34

Inferences of reason consist, then, in the fact that we compare a *nota notae* with the *nota rei ipsius per notam intermediam.*[i]}

In the case of disjunctive propositions, the *membra disjunctionis*, no matter how many they are, must <be> considered as one term <according to the *principium exclusi medii inter duo contradictoria*[j]>, for with contradictory judgments there can only be 2 propositions, *a* and *non a*.

We come to the doctrine

Of categorical inferences of reason

They deal merely with categorical propositions. – The *major terminus* is the predicate, the *minor*$_{\text{L}}$ the subject, and | in addition | [there is] the *medius*. There can only be 4 conclusions. *Medius terminus est*[k] *in majori <propositione loco> subjecti* and *in minori <loco> praedicati.*[l] Every *conclusio* consists of a subject and a predicate. We will now exhibit the 4 different syllogistic figures.

774

I	II	III	IV
All M. err M.P.	Bodies[m] are divisible P.M.	M.P.	P.M.
Learned men are M. S.M.	The soul is not divisible S.M.	M.S.	M.S.
Learned men can err S.P.	The soul is not corporeal S.P.	S.P.	S.P.

[h] What conflicts with a mark conflicts with the thing itself.

[i] [we compare a] mark of a mark [with the] mark of the thing itself through an intermediate mark.

[j] principle of the excluded middle between two contradictories.

[k] Reading "est" for "ist."

[l] In the major <proposition> the middle term is <in the place> of the subject [and] in the minor it is <in the place> of the predicate.

[m] Reading "Körper" for "Korper."

{One has to represent this to oneself as a chain of three terms. –

– Bodies are divisible.

The soul is not divisible.

– – – – corporeal.

For the *major*$_L$ is the rule. The *minor*$_L$ is always affirmative. For I say: *atqui* this is contained under the rule.}

In the 2nd figure one always finds a negative conclusion. For here one never infers immediately, but rather one must put in a *conclusio immediata*.

The *major propositio* must always <in all categorical inferences of reason> be universal.

In the 3rd figure we can only have a particular conclusion.

The 4th figure never has a universal affirmative or universal negative conclusion. Inference in the 2nd, 3rd, or 4th figure must always be reduced in thought to the first.

{Only inferences according to the first figure are categorical. The others are all *ratiocinia impura*. – With the categorical inference of reason, namely, the predicate of the *conclusio* must be related to the *medius terminus*. *Ratiocinia hybrida*, where besides the premises and the *conclusio* [one needs] also a *consequentia immediata*. – }

Now we must go through the universal rules of inferences of reason.

775 In any inference of reason there can only be 3 *termini*. If a *terminus*$_L$ is taken in two meanings, then the inference in fact has 4 *termini*. Thus the expression in the schools: The inference goes on 4 feet. The *terminus medius* must lie in the premises.

Now come a few errors that are easily committed:

1. *Ex puris negatives <praemissis> nil sequitur*[n] {for the *minor propositio* must be affirmative,}
2. *Ex puris particularibus nil sequitur*[o] {[this] follows from the concept of an inference of reason. At least the *major*$_L$ must be *universalis*}.
3. *Conclusio sequitur partem debiliorem*,[p] which is as much as to say that one of the premises is called the *pars debilior* if it is negative or particular, then the *conclusio* is also either particular or negative. { – Only the *minor*$_L$ can be particular. – }

Negation is opposition, contradiction.

We come now to the special rules for inferences of reason of the first figure. They are called

Major sit universalis, *minor affirmans*[q] – this fits all categorical inferences. Now further *minor sit affirmans* holds for all as well. The *minor pro-*

[n] From purely negative <premises> nothing follows.

[o] From purely particular [premises] nothing follows.

[p] The conclusion follows the weaker part.

[q] The major should be universal, the minor affirmative.

positio ought, indeed, to express that the condition belongs to this or to that. All inferences in the remaining figures are not *ratiocinia pura*, but *hybrida* – i.e., ones that do not actually [consist] of 3 propositions, but where a 4th is mixed in *per consequentiam immediatam*. {Another term in the *ratiocinium* is called the 4th foot.} It is only an artificial trick to produce a correct inference through transposition of the *medius terminus*. {Transposition, *metathesis terminorum*, is of two sorts, *per contrapositionem*, *per conversionem*. The *conclusio* in the 3 remaining figures is never universal affirmative – in accordance with the first one has all 4 kinds (univ. <and> part.[,] affirmative and negative). This shows that the other ones walk on stilts.}

In the 2nd figure, *Major <sit> universalis, conclusio negativa.*[r]

In the third figure, *Minor*$_L$ <because it is the subsumption> *affirmans, conclusio particularis.*[s] {The alteration occurs in the *minor propositio*. If this is universal <or particular> *affirmative* before [the alteration], as always, then it can only <be> converted *per accidens* – if [the *minor*$_L$] had been particular affirmative, then: *conclusio sequitur partem debiliorem*,[t] hence it is particular too.}

In the 4th figure: *Conclusio vel negativa vel particularis.*[u]

776

Reusch's logic.[35] The conclusion of the 2nd figure is negative, because the syllogism cannot be made into the first figure. In the 3rd figure a *metathesis terminorum* must be performed on the *minor propositio*. A universal affirmative proposition can only be converted *per accidens*. The inference in the first figure is the only pure one. (*Ars non habet osorem nisi ignorantem.*[v])

The *modus* of a proposition is the quality and quantity. In the first figure one can infer in *Barbara* {ad p. 110}.[36] One writes thus: *Cel – ar –* ent. In the syllables where there is an *s* I must convert the proposition *simpliciter*, *p per accidens*, where there is an *m*, there must be conversion, where there is a *c*, there must be contraposition.

The *modi* come altogether to 64 various kinds from the 4 vowels *a – e – i – o*.

For each there are 16 different inferences. But 28 are left out according to the rule: *Ex puris negativis nihil sequitur.*[w] 18 are left out according to the rule: *Conclusio sequitur debiliorem.*[x] 8 are excluded according to the rule that a negative conclusion

a a e
a a i
a a o
a e a
a i a
a o a
e a o
e i o
e o o
etc.

r The major <should be> universal, the conclusion negative.

s The minor. . . . [should be] affirmative, the conclusion particular.

t The conclusion follows the weaker part.

u The conclusion is either negative or particular.

v Art has no enemy but ignorance.

w From purely negative [premises] nothing follows

x The conclusion follows the weaker part.

cannot follow from merely affirmative premises. There remain no more than 10 *modi*, of which only 8 *modi* are *utiles*. –

The *hypothetical inference of reason* is one where the *major propositio* is a conditioned proposition. *Modus ponens* infers from the ground to the consequence. *Modus tollens* from the consequence to the ground. It cannot happen that I infer *a consequente sublato ad antecedentem.*[y]

The dilemma is a hypothetical <judgment> whose consequence is a disjunctive judgment. {E.g., if this world is not the best, then either God was acquainted with none better, or he was unable or unwilling to create a better one.}

Now a formal inference of reason is an enunciation, where something is expressed *explicite*. Among the *ratiocinia cryptica* is included the enthymeme. {E.g., all animals are mortal, consequently all men are too. The *medius terminus* is lacking.}

An inference of reason is cryptic *per transmissionem praemissarum*[z] or *per omissionem praemissarum.*[a]

A *syllogismus contractus* is when I infer *per medium terminum.*[b]

All inferences of reason ought to give necessity in their conclusion. If 2 things that stand under the same genus agree in all respects with which I am acquainted, then this is so in the case of the others too. I infer from the identity of some properties to the identity of all. An inference can never produce a cognition from empirical propositions. {The inferences by induction and analogy are only crutches for human reason.} Only from universal premises can we infer. But no proposition of experience gives us *universitas*[c] *simpliciter*, but only *secundum quid*,[d] as far as we are acquainted. The inference, | when I | infer from some predicates of the things to all the remaining ones, that is an inference by analogy. E.g., Mercury, Venus, Earth, Mars, Jupiter, Saturn, Uranus are dark planets. Now I infer through induction that the remaining planets, which perhaps can still be discovered, might also be dark. The inference by induction is also called *ob paritatem rationis.*[e]

777

Exempla illustrant, non probant.[f] There is no inference by example,[g] then.

An inference of reason that is false in <matter> is called a fallacy, and if it is false *in <forma>* – a paralogism. A *sophisma* is an inference that is

[y] from the consequence to the antecedent by denial (Ak, “antecedentem schließe”; MS and Ko, “antecedentem schließe.”

[z] by passing over premises.

[a] by omission of premises.

[b] through the middle term.

[c] the whole.

[d] with qualification.

[e] because of the equality of the ground.

[f] Examples illustrate, they do not prove.

[g] “Exempelschluß.”

false in *forma*. {The word sophist did not always have the bad meaning, *specious reasoner.*[h]}

It is believed of many false inferences that they are so *in forma*, but quite often they are so *in materia*. The ancient Megaric school, founded by Euclides the Megaric (not the geometer), occupied itself with such inferences, turned many people around in this way.[i]

Achilles, Cretensis, Acervus. {Cf. Daries, Logic.37}

{If you say you lie, and in saying this you speak the truth, then you speak the truth by lying – [this] is false *in materia*, in that *you say* that you lie. –

Epimenides says: All Cretans are liars. *Ipse vero est cretensis – ergo ipse est mendax*,[j] hence his claim would be a lie.}

One adds more and more[;] how many grains make a heap? With gradual increase there is no transition to another genus. {For concepts of comparative quantity there is no specific difference at a determinate place. This serves principally in morals to warn against defects of the *medius*[k] <of mediocrity>. In the case of things that are specifically different, let us be careful to make a distinction according to degree.}

Cornutus.[l] *Quicquid non amisisti, habes. Cornua non amisisti. Ergo habes.*[m]

Calvus.[n] How many hairs [must be] removed before a head is bald? – I cannot define anything through *more* or *less*. –

The *sophisma heterozeteseos*,[o] when it concerns a disputed question, is called a *sophisma ignorationis elenchi*. – E.g., the proof of the immortality of the soul – one would prove a future life.38 778

Ratiocinia can also be *composita*, insofar as they are subordinate to one another.

Ratiocinatio episyllogistica[p] occurs when the conclusion of a syllogism is the premise of a given one. In all academic disputations one infers *per prosyllogismos*.

{*Sorites*, a series of inferences of reason according to episyllogistic order.} There are still some explanations to be added:

A *saltus in probando*,[q] when one connects a ground with a remote consequence without a mediating proposition. – {One can leap *legitime*, when the mediating proposition is understood of itself. – }

[h] "Vernünftler."
[i] "wendete viele artig."
[j] He himself is in fact a Cretan – therefore he himself is a liar.
[k] middle.
[l] The horned one.
[m] Whatever you have not lost, you have. You have not lost horns. Therefore you have them.
[n] The bald one.
[o] sophism of misdirection.
[p] Episyllogistic reasoning.
[q] leap in proof.

Circulus in probando,[r] when one introduces into the ground of proof that which is supposed to be proved.

Petitio principii – to assume *gratis*$_{L}$. –

One says of proofs that are erroneous that they say too much or too little, the former is a *vitium,*[s] the latter a *defectus.*[t] He who proves too much proves nothing at all. Just as he who says less than the truth does not lie, but he who says more than the truth certainly lies.

{*Topics*, the science that shows how one ought to determine logical places.} *Topic* is the art of bringing † one's concepts under certain principal concepts <fields>: *generalia capita argumentorum aut genera in quibus reperiuntur.*[u] A particular sentence is called a *locus topicus*[v] or, since that is tautological, *locus communis.*[w] Thus a canon is something like, You cannot teach an old dog new tricks.[x] *Locus grammaticus,*[y] e.g., etymology[;] *locus logicus*[,][z] like the *dictum de omni et nullo* – Inference *a toto ad partes*[a] etc. *Locus metaphysicus, ethicus*[,][b] whether I derive something from *utili* or *honesto. Argumentum ab utili,*[c] etc. *Locus physicus* – from the purposes of nature. The name may well have come from the *locus geometricus*, i.e., when a problem can be divided into infinitely many kinds. {Parallels, the *locus geometricus* of equal triangles on one base.}

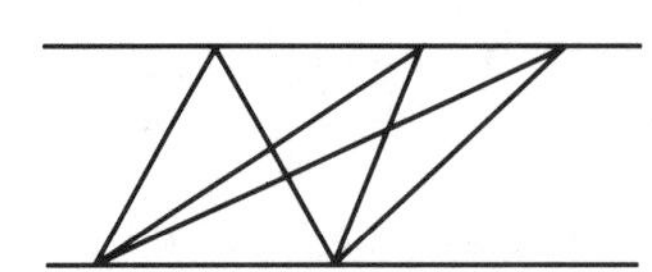

It is impossible, however, for philosophy to make itself equal to mathematics in this.

779 In accordance with our division, we proceed to the last part of logic, which can also be regarded as a brief appendix:

[r] A circle in proof.
[s] error.
[t] defect.
[u] general headings for arguments, or genera in which they are found.
[v] topical topic.
[w] common topic, or commonplace.
[x] "jung gewohnt, alt gethan."
[y] A grammatical topic.
[z] a logical topic.
[a] from the whole to the parts.
[b] A metaphysical topic, an ethical topic.
[c] Argument from usefulness.

II. The doctrine of method

This is also called the practical part. There really is no practical logic, however. For it is not an organon, only a canon. This appendix serves for the critique of cognition.

The doctrine of method contains the precepts for the possibility of a system of cognition of the understanding and of reason. It is, then, the doctrine of *methodus*. {*Methodus* – the way a cognition can attain scientific form.} Method is combination of thoughts. – We can think of it in two ways, as *methodus logica* {not merely the way of teaching but the way of thinking}[;] this could be called manner, it rests wholly on rules; *methodus aesthetica* rests merely on taste and may not be brought to any rules.

The word *methodus* is not translated sufficiently by [the German word for] *method*.[d] For there is a method as mode of *thinking* as well | as | of *teaching*.

{Exposition
1. systematic
2. fragmentary
   1. methodical
   2. tumultuous.}

Now come the various methods.

The first division is into synthetic and analytic. The latter is where I go from consequences to grounds, the former where I go from grounds to consequences. {A division is unsystematic if one cannot see from it why there could not be still more terms of the division.} In philosophizing one can proceed synthetically or analytically. The mathematical method is a synthetic method. It differs from all others in that it presents through intuition. A way of thinking[e] is always something moral. But one could say that a mode of thought[f] is the *methodus*. Method is

1. popular – this is for the common understanding – *in concreto*.
2. scholastic – belongs to the sciences – *in abstracto*.

To *orient oneself*, means to put oneself in a certain standpoint where one can easily consider the things *in concreto* †.

[d] "Lehrart" (literally, "mode of teaching").
[e] "Denkungsart."
[f] "Denkart."

780 *Methodus syllogistica.* Many have even made an effort to expound mathematics in this way. – {Basically, however, this is only a mere subtlety.}

The method of tables – a certain tree, which has many principal and secondary branches.

A science is a cognition that [is] derived from certain principles and fits together in a system.

The Socratic method – the Platonic. –

Methodus vel est acroamatica {where someone expounds alone, without asking or answering} *vel erotematica*[g] {in question and answer}. The latter is catechistic or dialogical. In the former the one who asks is always the teacher, in the second the one who is asked. The acroamatic method is also the Platonic.

Philosophical materials should never be expounded catechistically. Catechism can be mechanical or *judicieuse* {through association of representations – this cultivates the understanding}.

Can one expound religion catechistically? {It is thereby led astray into prejudices.} Actually this is not the best method, that would be the dialogical. The common man cannot very well grasp a coherent exposition. Historical cognitions can be expounded catechistically. –

Socrates said: I am the midwife of someone else's thoughts. He derived everything from their concepts, which they were simply not able to develop suitably. – {This kind of catechistic method is the only one that may be applied in philosophical objects. It is basically erotematic catechism, although it is called dialogical. – Catechisms ought to be arranged thus – first, derive everything from reason and on this build positive religion – for man as he now is.}

One can think tumultuously or methodically. The latter, when we wish to produce a cognition, is called meditation. But before one thinks methodically, one must always think tumultuously too, ramble around, seek out everything that occurs to one.

1. [W]hat do I want? – {Many who wrote books did not know this at all, or only obscurely. – }
2. [W]hat is important in this connection.

These 2 points indicate the man who is *judicieuse*. –

{*Homonyma*, expressions that mean many things, are proofs of the pov- 781 erty of a language.} Signification of cognition, speaking, writing[.] – But what the author says about this does not belong to logic. – One must not forge *termini technici* without need. Nonetheless, scholastic strictness does sometimes require them. One does not understand a thing until one can communicate it to others. Words with which one cannot combine any distinct concept (e.g., *entelechia*) are called *termini inanes*.[h] A *conceptus*

[g] Method is either acroamatic . . . or erotematic.

[h] empty terms.

deceptor, a deceptive concept, usually contains 2 concepts that in and of themselves are distinct – but together are not understandable. {| Concepts | which seem to mean something but in the end mean nothing, like apathy and idiosyncrasy.} Moreover, a *terminus familiaris* {a commonly used expression} – ones that occur in common life.

{Logomachy, conflict through misunderstanding of words, verbal conflict. Such a thing cannot last long. One would have discovered it long since, as, e.g., the dispute between | defenders of | freedom and defenders of natural necessity.}

Quite often people believe they understand one another just when they are furthest removed from each other.

Terminus ambiguus {ambiguous}, *vagus*, an expression about which one never rightly finds out what is to be thought thereby – fortune – such a thing can be determined. Proposition – *judicium verbis prolatum*[i] – no – only assertoric <judgments are> propositions. { – A *propositio* is a *judicium categoricum*, hence a kind of *judicium*, and *judicium* is not synonymous with *propositio*.}

A syllogism is a *ratiocinium formale*, not *verbis prolatum*.[j] One must of course always express it with words, loudly or softly. {It is only a matter of the expression of concepts <through> thought or words.}

{What logic is in regard to thought, style is in regard to the signification[k] of thought. Logical perfection of style is scholastic perfection – opposed to it is aesthetic perfection.}

Purity, elegance of style, is called purism when one exaggerates it. Elegance.[l] Glittering words:[m] . . . .†, longimetry, half Greek, half Latin. Not loquacity – ornatus[n] – (no sonority). A speech – *sermo* – *oratio*, if it is festive. Eloquence[o] is suitable for all writings. Oratory,[p] *ars persuadendi*,[q] to win approval for the present moment.

In the case of learned exposition – the ability to descend and the ability to ascend.[r] {Glibness, *copia*[s] of words, eloquence – art of applying this *copia*. Rhetoric, the skill of leading others with this art according to one's purposes, of making the false seem true.}

Sermons must be universally understandable. In them there must reign 782 a power to have an effect on every soul. They come together out of a

[i] a judgment set forth in words.
[j] a formal inference, [not] one merely expressed in words.
[k] "Bezeichnung."
[l] "Concinnität."
[m] "Zwitterwörter."
[n] ornate, embellished.
[o] "Wohlredenheit."
[p] "Beredsamkeit."
[q] the art of persuasion.
[r] "Descendenz und Coascendenz."
[s] abundance.

common end. *A. Hermann Francke*39 says that sermons should be such that if a man has heard only one of them, he finds perfect morals. The ability to descend[t] and the ability to ascend[u] are a great gift, to distinguish, to choose, what this and what every listener needs. It requires much genius, to teach a little to someone who can learn little. In an *auditorium*$_L$, as in the writing of a book, one must be able to ascend, concern oneself with the higher abilities, which will develop into something at some time in the future.

We have two kinds of exposition

(1.) didactical and (2.) polemical. The first is instructive (dogmatic), the second merely frees from errors.

We refute[v] someone when we *refute*[w] his claim. <to answer and to provide an answer – different.> It falls to him who says that the other is wrong to prove it.

In every dispute we have *thesis* and *antithesis* – *thesis <status> controversiae.*[x] The determination of the question {this often involves great difficulties} is called the *forma controversiae.*[y] Here one often discovers a logomachy – verbal dispute. But a logomachy does not usually ever last long. –

Argumentations are divided into

1. *argumentationes* κατ᾽ ἀλήθειαν,[z] based on objective grounds,
2. *argumentationes* κατ᾽ ἄνθρωπον,[a] based on subjective ones {i.e., based on assertions of the subject, as, e.g., in the gospel, that there are spirits, because they believe in ghosts. – }

A bet is an agreement on punishment for him who fails. The *argumentatio ad crumenam*[b] is wholly fair. The *argumentum a verecundia*[;][c] there the monk Abelard said: *Si omnes patres sic – ego non sic.*[d] – Instance, a particular proposition that contradicts a universal one. Retort, when one proves conversely, namely, makes a consequence from my proposition that affects the opponent. –

A *consequentarius*, one who, from the theoretical assertions of someone else, draws consequences that bring danger. {A *consequentarius* is one who draws from my propositions consequences that are disadvantageous to the person of someone. – }

[t] "Condescendenz."
[u] "Coadescendenz."
[v] "refutieren."
[w] "*widerlegen*."
[x] the thesis <answer to the question brought> of the controversy.
[y] form of the controversy.
[z] arguments based on truth.
[a] arguments based on the man.
[b] argument directed to the purse.
[c] argument from modesty (i.e., an appeal to authority).
[d] If all the fathers [say] so – I [say] not so.

783

An *apology* is a defense against a consequentarian.[e] A formal disputation – there the *acteurs* are the respondent and the opponent. To make things immediately comprehensible for the respondent, one speaks in inferences. The rule contains principally this, that the conclusion of one's argument will directly contradict the thesis of the respondent – *per prosyllogismos*. The *praeses*,[f] as assistant to the respondent, seeks to even out the dispute. –

That which makes one prudent is pragmatic. Passing judgment on the effects based on their causes.

A *compilator* is one who makes one book out of many. {It is much harder to express oneself briefly and coherently, e.g. in a letter – manual – than extensively.} An *epitomator*[g] is one who makes a small thing out of a large one. {He must be an expert, in order not to injure the spirit of the work in his selection.} A *plagiarius* is a learned thief, who steals his thoughts from another.

The author speaks lastly of the character of the learned man. A naturalist is one who acquires cognitions that do not constitute a system. Metaphysics and morals are the hobby horses of such people. {There can be naturalists in all fields. – }

An *autodidactos*, one who has science without teachers {like Lambert[40]}, who either has created everything by himself or at least has been his own commentator in reading scientific books.

Actually there are no synonyms in any language. For when words were invented one certainly wanted to signify with each of them a particular concept, which one will always find on more exact investigation of the word. E.g., steed <rider>, horse <genus>, nag, jade <work>, (hack,[h] [the German word for] which comes from[i] *caballus*)[;] each brings with it a particular concept.

While enumerating methods earlier we forgot the *mathematical*. This is none other than the synthetic method, which proceeds from the first grounds of a cognition and stops at the last consequences. The first thing with this method, now, is definition, then axiom, theorem, problem, etc.

{*Scholion*, *corollar*. Wolff expounded philosophy in accordance with this method, which cannot be done.}

Note. In conclusion, Kant added some more about meditation, methodical thinking. He said, namely, that it is principally a matter (as mentioned above) of two things:

1. to know exactly what one really wants, and then
2. what is important for that. Then he brought up how much effort it

[e] "Konsequenzmacher."

[f] guardian (a formally prescribed role in the defense of a thesis).

[g] one who makes an epitome or abridgement.

[h] "Kobbel."

[i] Reading "das von caballus kömmt" for "davon kömmt caballus."

was for him, e.g., when he was occupied with the thought of writing the
784 *Critique of Pure Reason*, to know what he really wanted. In the end he found that everything could be captured in the question, Are synthetic propositions *a priori* possible? – Yes. But it depends on the fact that we can give them corresponding intuitions. If this cannot occur, however, then they do not have this property. From this one sees how much easier meditation is made by this method.

{This occurred in the *repetitorium* Saturday[;] the *collegium* was closed on Friday. – }

End of Kant's Logic
Saturday, the . . . . st of September, 1792

PART IV

The Jäsche logic

Immanuel Kant's
Logic
A manual for lectures

edited by Gottlob Benjamin Jäsche

Preface

It is a year and a half now since *Kant* commissioned me to prepare his *Logic* for publication, as he expounded it to his listeners in public lectures, and to transmit it to the public in the form of a *compendious manual.* For this purpose I received from him his own manuscript, which he had used in his lectures, with the expression of special, honorable confidence in me, that, being acquainted with the principles of his system in general, I would easily enter into the course of his ideas, that I would not distort or falsify his thoughts, but rather would present them with the required clarity and distinctness and at the same time in the appropriate order. Now since, as I thus accepted the commission and have sought to carry it out as well as I was able, in conformity with the wish and the expectation of that *praiseworthy wise man*, my most honored teacher and friend, everything that concerns the *exposition*, the clothing and the execution, the presentation and the ordering of the thoughts, is in part to be reckoned to *my* account, I am naturally obliged to provide an account to the readers of this new Kantian work. On this matter, then, a few closer explanations here.

Since the year 1765, Professor *Kant* has based his lectures on logic, without interruption, on *Meier's* textbook as guiding thread (Georg Friedrich Meier's *Excerpts from the Doctrine of Reason*, Halle: Gebauer, 1752), for reasons he explained in the program he published by way of announcement of his lectures in the year 1765.[1] The copy of the mentioned compendium that he himself used in his lectures, like all the other textbooks he used for the same purpose, is interleaved with paper; his general remarks and elucidations, as well as the more special ones that relate in the first instance to the text of the compendium in its individual sections, are found partly on the interleaved paper, partly on the empty margin of the textbook itself. And what has been written by hand here and there in scattered remarks and elucidations, taken together, constitutes now the *storehouse of materials* which Kant built up in his lectures here, which in part he expanded from time to time through new ideas, and which in part he again and again revised anew and improved in regard to various individual materials. Hence it contains at least the essentials of what the famous commentator on Meier's textbook was accustomed to communicate to his listeners concerning logic in lectures that were given in a free manner, and that which he esteemed worthy of writing down.

4

Now as for what concerns the presentation and ordering of things in this work, I believed that I would put forth the great man's ideas and principles most fittingly if, with respect to the economy and the division of the whole as such, I held myself to his express explanation, according to which nothing more may be taken up in the proper treatment of logic, and in particular in its *Doctrine of Elements*, than the theory of the three essential principal functions of thought: *concepts*, *judgments*, and *inferences*. Hence everything that deals with cognition in general and with its logical perfections, and which in Meier's textbook precedes the doctrine of concepts and takes in almost half of the whole, must accordingly be reckoned to the introduction. "Previously," Kant says right at the outset of the eighth section,[2] in which his author expounds the doctrine of concepts – "Previously cognition in general was treated, as *propaedeutic* to logic, now *logic itself* follows."

In consequence of this explicit pointer, I have placed everything that occurs before the mentioned section in the Introduction, which for this reason contains a much greater extension than it customarily includes in other logic manuals. The consequence of this was then also that the *Doctrine of Method*, as the other principal part of the treatise, had to turn out that much shorter, the more the materials that had already been treated in the Introduction, as for example the doctrine of proofs, etc. – which, by the way, are now rightly included in the sphere of the doctrine of method by our modern logicians. It would have been a repetition as unnecessary as improper to give mention to this material yet again in its proper place, only in order to make the incomplete complete and to put everything in its proper place. I have done the latter with respect to the doctrine of *definitions*, however, and of the *logical division of concepts*, which in Meier's compendium belongs to the eighth section, namely, to the doctrine of elements of concepts, an order which even *Kant* left unaltered in his exposition.

It is surely obvious that the great reformer of philosophy and, as concerns the economy and external form of logic, of this part of theoretical philosophy in particular, would have worked on logic according to *his* architectonic plan, whose essential outlines are sketched in the *Critique of Pure Reason*, if it had pleased him to do so, and if his occupation with a scientific grounding of the whole system of philosophy proper – philosophy of the really true and certain, which is an occupation immeasurably more important and more difficult, and which in the first instance only he and he alone could carry out with his originality – had permitted him to think of preparing a logic himself. But this work he was quite able to leave to others, who, with insight and with unbiased judgment, could use his architectonic ideas for a truly purposeful and well-ordered arrangement and treatment of this science. This was to be expected from several thorough and unbiased thinkers among our German philosophers. And in this expectation *Kant* and the friends of his philosophy were not disappointed. Several recent textbooks on logic are to be regarded, in respect of the economy and the disposition of the whole, more or less as fruit of those *Kantian* ideas on logic. That this science has really gained through this; that it has become, though not richer or really more solid as to its content or in itself better grounded, yet *more purified*, partly from all its foreign components, partly from so many useless subtleties and merely dialectical tricks; that it has become *more systematic* and yet at the same time, with all scientific strictness of method, *simpler* – of this everyone must be convinced, even by the most fleeting comparison of older textbooks of logic with modern ones worked out in accordance with Kantian principles, if only he has correct and clear concepts of the proper character and the legitimate limits of logic. For however much many of the older manuals on this science may stand out for scientific strictness of method; for clarity, determinateness, and precision of explanations; and for conciseness and evidence in proofs; still there is scarcely a one of them in which the limits of the various spheres that belong to universal logic in its broader extension – the merely *propaedeutic*, the *dogmatic* and *technical*, the *pure* and the *empirical* – do not run into and through each other, so that the one cannot be determinately distinguished from the other. 6

Herr *Jakob*, in the Preface to the first edition of his logic,[3] does observe: "Wolff grasped the idea of a universal logic exceptionally well, and if this great man had thought of expounding pure logic in complete separation, he would certainly, by means of his systematic mind, have presented us with a masterpiece, which would have made all further work of this kind unnecessary." But he did not execute this idea, and none of his successors developed it either, however great and well-grounded in general the merit may be that the *Wolffian* school has attained concerning the properly *logical*, the *formal* perfection in our philosophical cognition.

But irrespective of what was able to happen and had to happen in regard to external form for the perfection of logic by the necessary separation of pure and merely formal propositions from empirical and real or metaphysical ones, when it comes to passing judgment on and determining the inner content of this science as science, there is no doubt about *Kant's* judgment on this point. He frequently explained, determinately and expressly, that logic is to be regarded as a separate science, existing for itself and grounded in itself, and hence that from its origin and first development with *Aristotle*, right down to our times, it could not really gain anything in scientific grounding. In conformity with this claim, *Kant* did not think either about grounding the logical principles of identity and contradiction on a higher principle, or about deducing the logical forms of judgment. He recognized and treated the principle of contradiction as a proposition that has its evidence in itself and requires no derivation from a higher principle. He only restricted the use, the validity, of this principle 7 by banishing it from the sphere of metaphysics, where dogmatism sought to make it valid, and restricting it to the merely logical use of reason, as valid only for this use alone.

But now whether the logical principle of identity and of contradiction is really incapable of or does not need any further deduction, in itself and without qualification, that is of course a different question, which leads to the highly significant question of whether there is in general an *absolutely first* principle of all cognition and science, whether such a thing is possible and can be found.

The *doctrine of science*[4] believes that it has discovered such a principle in the *pure, absolute I*, and hence that it has grounded all philosophical knowledge perfectly, not merely as to form but also as to content. And having presupposed the possibility and the apodeictic validity of this absolutely one and unconditioned principle, it then proceeds completely consistently when it does not allow the logical principles of identity and of contradiction, the propositions $A = A$ and $-A = -A$, to hold unconditionally, but instead declares them to be subaltern principles, which can and must be established and determined only through it and its highest proposition: *I am*. (See the *Foundation of the Doctrine of Science*, p. 13f.) In an equally consistent way *Schelling*,[5] in his system of transcendental idealism, declares himself against the presupposition of logical principles as *unconditioned*, i.e., as not derivable from any higher principle, since logic can arise in general only through abstraction from determinate propositions and, insofar as it arises in a scientific way, only through abstraction from the *highest* principles of knowledge, and since it consequently presupposes these highest principles of knowledge and with them the doctrine of science itself. Since, however, from the other side, these highest principles of knowledge, considered as *principles*, just as necessarily presuppose logical form, there arises here that circle which cannot be broken by science, but which can at least be explained, explained by recognition of a principle of philosophy that is first both as to form and as to content (formally and materially), in which these two, form and content, reciprocally condition and ground one another. In this principle is supposed to lie 8 the point in which the subjective and the objective, identical knowledge and synthetic knowledge, are one and the same.

Given the presupposition of such a dignity, which must undoubtedly belong to such a principle, logic would accordingly have to be subordinated, like every other science, to the doctrine of science and its principles.

But whatever the situation may be here, this much is settled: In the inner part of its sphere, as concerns the essential, logic remains in every case unaltered; and the transcendental question as to whether logical propositions are still capable of and require a derivation from a higher, absolute principle has as little influence on logic and on the validity and evidence of its laws as the transcendental problem, How are synthetic judgments *a priori* possible in mathematics? does on pure mathematics in regard to its scientific content. Like the mathematician as mathematician, the logician as logician, within the sphere of his science, can also continue confidently and certainly to explain and to prove, without permitting himself to worry about the transcendental question, which lies outside his sphere, as to *how pure mathematics or pure logic is possible as a science.*

Given this universal recognition of the correctness of universal logic, the battle between the skeptics and the dogmatists concerning the ultimate grounds of philosophical knowledge has never been conducted in the domain of logic, whose rules were recognized as valid by every rational skeptic as well as by the dogmatist, but rather has always been conducted in the sphere of metaphysics. And how could it be otherwise? The highest task of philosophy proper concerns not subjective but objective, not identical but synthetic, knowledge. In this, logic *as such* remains completely on the sidelines; it could not occur either to critique or to the doctrine of science – nor will it be able to occur at all to a philosophy that knows how to distinguish determinately the transcendental standpoint from the merely logical – to seek the ultimate grounds of real philosophical knowledge inside the sphere of mere logic, and to wish to cull a *real object* from a proposition of logic, considered merely as such.

He who has grasped the enormous difference between logic proper (universal logic), as a merely formal science, the science of mere thought as thought, and transcendental philosophy, this sole material or real pure science of reason, the science of knowledge proper, and who never again fails to heed this difference, will thus easily be able to pass judgment on the question of what is to be said concerning the recent attempt lately undertaken by Herr *Bardili* (in his *Outline of Primary Logic*[6]) to make out a *prius*[a] for logic itself, in the expectation of finding on the path of this investigation "a *real object*, either posited by *it* (mere logic) or nothing can be posited at all; the key to the essence of nature, either given by *it*, or no logic and no philosophy is possible." In truth, however, one cannot see in what way Herr *Bardili* could discover a real object based on the *prius* of logic that he advances, the principle of the absolute possibility of thought, according to which we can repeat *one* as *one and the same in the many* (not the manifold) infinitely many times. This *prius* of logic, supposedly newly discovered, is in fact obviously nothing more and nothing less than the old, long recognized principle of identity, established within the sphere of logic and placed at the head of this science: *What I think, I think*; and it is only this and nothing else that I can *think repeated to infinity*. – Who, after all, in the case of the well understood logical principle of identity,[b] will think of a manifold and not of a *mere many*, which of course arises and can

9

[a] prior (i.e., claim to priority).

[b] "Satze der Identität."

arise through nothing other than the mere repetition of one and the same thought, the mere repeated positing of an $A = A = A$, and so on to infinity. It would be difficult, then, on the path that Herr *Bardili* has taken, and by the heuristic method that he has used, to find what philosophical reason seeks: the *beginning and ending point*, from which it may set out in its investigations and to which it may again return. The principal and most significant objections that Herr Bardili has lodged against *Kant* and his method of philosophizing could not so much touch *Kant* the *logician*, then, but rather *Kant* the *transcendental philosopher* and *metaphysician*. Here, 10 then, we can let them be deferred entirely to their proper place.

Finally, I wish to mention here that as soon as leisure permits I will work up the Kantian *Metaphysics* in the same manner and publish it, for which I already have the manuscript in hand. Königsberg, the 20th of September, 1800.

Gottlob Benjamin Jäsche

Doctor and Private Docent at the University in Königsberg,
Member of the Learned Society of Frankfurt on the Oder.

Introduction

11

I.

Concept of logic

Everything in nature, both in the lifeless and in the living world, takes place *according to rules*, although we are not always acquainted with these rules. – Water falls according to laws of gravity, and with animals locomotion also takes place according to rules. The fish in water, the bird in the air, move according to rules. The whole of nature in general is really nothing but a connection of appearances according to rules; and there is *no absence of rules* anywhere. If we believe we have found such a thing, then in this case we can only say that we are not acquainted with the rules.

The exercise of our powers also takes place according to certain rules that we follow, *unconscious* of them at first, until we gradually arrive at cognition of them through experiments and lengthy use of our powers, indeed, until we finally become so familiar with them that it costs us much effort to think them *in abstracto*. Thus universal grammar is the form of a language in general, for example. One speaks even without being acquainted with grammar, however; and he who speaks without being acquainted with it does actually have a grammar and speaks according to rules, but ones of which he is not himself conscious.

Like all our powers, *the understanding* in particular is bound in its actions to rules, which we can investigate. Indeed, the understanding is to be regarded in general as the source and the faculty for thinking rules in general. For as sensibility is the faculty of intuitions, so the understanding is the faculty for thinking, i.e., for bringing the representations of the senses under rules. Hence it is desirous of seeking for rules and is satisfied when it has found them. Since the understanding is the source 12 of rules, the question is thus, according to what rules does it itself proceed?

For there can be no doubt at all: we cannot think, we cannot use our understanding, except according to certain rules. But now we can in turn think these rules for themselves, i.e., we can think them *apart from their application* or *in abstracto*. Now what are these rules?

All rules according to which the understanding operates are either *necessary* or *contingent*. The former are those without which no use of the understanding would be possible at all, the latter those without which a certain determinate use of the understanding would not occur. The contingent rules, which depend upon a determinate object of cognition, are as manifold[a] as these objects themselves. Thus there is, for example, a use of the understanding in mathematics, in metaphysics, morals, etc. The rules of this particular, determinate use of the understanding in the sciences mentioned are contingent, because it is contingent whether I think of this or that object, to which these particular rules relate.

If now we put aside all cognition that we have to borrow from *objects* and merely reflect on the use just of the understanding, we discover those of its rules which are necessary without qualification, for every purpose and without regard to any particular objects of thought, because without them we would not think at all. Thus we can have insight into these rules *a priori, i.e., independent of all experience*, because they contain merely the conditions for the use of the understanding in general, *without distinction among its objects*, be that use *pure* or *empirical*. And from this it follows at the same time that the universal and necessary rules of thought in general can concern merely its *form* and not in any way its *matter*. Accordingly, the science that contains these universal and necessary rules is merely a science of the form of our cognition through the understanding, or of thought. And thus we can form for ourselves an idea of the possibility of such a science, just as we can of a *universal grammar*, which contains 13 nothing more than the mere form of language in general, without words, which belong to the matter of language.

Now this science of the necessary laws of the understanding and of reason in general, or what is one and the same, of the mere form of thought as such, we call *logic*.

As a science that deals with all thought in general, without regard to objects as the matter of thought, logic

1. is to be regarded as *foundation* for all the other sciences and as the *propaedeutic* to all use of the understanding. Just because it does abstract wholly from all objects, however, it also

2. cannot be an *organon* of the sciences.

By an *organon* we understand, namely, a directive as to how a certain cognition is to be brought about. This requires, however, that I already be acquainted with the object of the cognition that is to be produced according to certain rules. An organon of the sciences is thus not mere logic,

[a] "vielfältig."

because an organon presupposes exact acquaintance with the sciences, their objects and sources. Thus mathematics, for example, as a science that contains the ground for the extension of our cognition in regard to a certain use of reason, is an excellent organon. Logic, on the other hand, as universal propaedeutic to all use of the understanding and of reason in general, may not go into the sciences and anticipate their matter. It is only a *universal art of reason* (*canonica Epicuri*) for making cognitions in general conform to the form of the understanding in general, and hence is only to this extent to be called an organon, which serves of course merely for *passing judgment* and for *correcting* our cognition, but not for *expanding* it.

3. As a science of the necessary laws of thought, without which no use of the understanding or of reason takes place at all, laws which consequently are conditions under which the understanding can and ought to agree with itself alone – the necessary laws and conditions of its correct use – logic is, however, a *canon*. And as a canon of the understanding and of reason it may not borrow any principles either from any science or from any experience; it must contain nothing but laws *a priori*, which are neces- 14 sary and have to do with the understanding in general.

Some logicians, to be sure, do presuppose *psychological* principles in logic. But to bring such principles into logic is just as absurd as to derive morals from life. If we were to take principles from psychology, i.e., from observations concerning our understanding, we would merely see *how* thinking does take place and *how* it *is* under various subjective obstacles and conditions; this would lead then to cognition of merely *contingent* laws. In logic, however, the question is not about *contingent* but about *necessary* rules; not how we do think, but how we ought to think. The rules of logic must thus be derived not from the *contingent* but from the *necessary* use of the understanding, which one finds in oneself apart from all psychology. In logic we do not want to know how the understanding is and does think and how it has previously proceeded in thought, but rather how it ought to proceed in thought. Logic is to teach us the correct use of the understanding, i.e., that in which it agrees with itself.

From the given explanation of logic, the remaining essential properties of this science may now also be derived, namely, that it

4. is a science of reason not only as to its mere form but *as to its matter*,[7] since its rules are not derived from experience, and since at the same time it has reason as its object. Logic is thus a self-cognition of the understanding and of reason, not as to their faculties in regard to objects, however, but merely as to form. In logic I will not ask what the understanding cognizes and *how much* it can cognize or *how far* its cognition goes. For that would be self-cognition in regard to its *material* use and thus belongs

to metaphysics. In logic the question is only, *How will the understanding cognize itself?*

Finally, as a science that is rational as to matter and to form, logic is also

5. a *doctrine* or a *demonstrated theory*. For since it is occupied, not with the common and as such merely empirical use of the understanding and
15 of reason, but rather merely with the universal and necessary laws of thought in general, it rests on principles *a priori*, from which all its rules can be derived and proved, as ones with which all cognition of reason has to be in conformity.

By virtue of the fact that logic is to be taken as a science *a priori*, or as a doctrine for a canon of the use of the understanding and of reason, it is essentially distinct from *aesthetics*, which as mere *critique of taste* has no canon (law) but only a *norm* (model or standard for passing judgment), which consists in universal agreement. Aesthetics, that is, contains the rules for the agreement of cognition with the laws of sensibility; logic, on the other hand, contains the rules for the agreement of cognition with the laws of the understanding and of reason. The former has only empirical principles and thus can never be science or doctrine, provided that one understands by doctrine a dogmatic instruction from principles *a priori*, in which one has insight into everything through the understanding without instruction from other quarters attained from experience, and which gives us rules, by following which we procure the required perfection.

Some, especially orators and poets, have tried to engage in reasoning[b] concerning taste, but they have never been able to hand down a decisive judgment concerning it. The philosopher *Baumgarten* in Frankfurt had a plan for an aesthetic as a science.[8] But *Home*,[9] more correctly, called aesthetics *critique*, since it yields no rules *a priori* that determine judgment sufficiently, as logic does, but instead derives its rules *a posteriori*, and since it only makes more universal, through comparison, the empirical laws according to which we cognize the more perfect (beautiful) and the more imperfect.

Logic is thus more than mere critique; it is a canon that subsequently serves for critique, i.e., as the principle for passing judgment on all use of the understanding in general, although only on its correctness in regard to mere form, since it is not an organon, any more than universal grammar is.

Now as propaedeutic to all use of the understanding in general, universal logic is distinct also on another side from *transcendental logic*, in which the object itself is represented as an object of the mere understanding; universal logic, on the contrary, deals with all objects in general.

16 If we now join together all the essential marks that belong to a complete

[b] "vernünfteln."

determination of the concept of logic, then we shall have to put forth the following concept of it:

Logic is a science of reason, not as to mere form but also as to matter; a science a priori of the necessary laws of thought, not in regard to particular objects, however, but to all objects in general; – hence a science of the correct use of the understanding and of reason in general, not subjectively, however, i.e., not according to empirical (psychological) principles for how the understanding does think, but objectively, i.e., according to principles a priori for how it ought to think.

II.

Principal divisions of logic – Exposition – Use of this science – Sketch of its history

Logic is divided

1. into *analytic* and *dialectic.*

Analytic discovers through analysis all the actions of reason that we perform in thinking. It is thus an analytic of the form of the understanding and of reason and is rightly called the logic of truth, because it contains the necessary rules of all (formal) truth, apart from which our cognition is untrue in itself, regardless of its objects. Thus it is also nothing more than a canon for adjudication (of the formal correctness of our cognition).

If one were to use this merely theoretical and universal doctrine as a practical art, i.e., as an organon, then it would become *dialectic.* A *logic of illusion* (*ars sophistica, disputatoria*[c]), which arises out of a mere misuse of analytic, insofar as the illusion of a true cognition, the marks of which have to be derived from agreement with objects and thus from *content*, is fabricated according to *mere logical form.*

In earlier times dialectic was studied with great industry. This art expounded false principles under the illusion of truth and then sought, in conformity with these, to maintain things in accordance with illusion. Among the Greeks the dialecticians were the lawyers[d] and orators, who were able to lead the people wherever they wanted, because the people allow themselves to be misled by illusion. At that time dialectic was thus the art of illusion. For a long time, too, it was expounded in logic under the name of the *art of disputation*, and as long as it was, all of logic and philosophy were the cultivation of certain garrulous souls for fabricating any illusion. Nothing can be less worthy of a philosopher, however, than the cultivation of such an art. In this sense it must be done away with,

17

[c] a sophistic art, an art of disputation.

[d] "Sachwalter."

then, and instead of this a critique of this illusion must be introduced into logic.

We would have two parts of logic, accordingly: *analytic*, which would expound the formal criteria of truth, and *dialectic*, which would contain the marks and rules in accordance with which we could recognize that something does not agree with the formal criteria of truth, although it seems to agree with them. Dialectic in this sense would thus have its good use as *cathartic* of the understanding.

It is customary to divide logic further into

2. *natural* or *popular* logic and *artificial* or *scientific* logic (*logica naturalis, log. scholastica s. artificialis*).

But this division is inadmissible. For natural logic, or logic of common reason (*sensus communis*), is not really logic but an anthropological science that has only empirical principles, in that it deals with the rules of the natural use of the understanding and of reason, which are cognized only *in concreto*, hence without consciousness of them *in abstracto*. – Only artificial or scientific logic deserves this name, then, as a science of the necessary and universal rules of thought, which can and must be cognized *a priori*, independently of the natural use of the understanding and of reason *in concreto*, although these rules can first be found only through observation of that natural use.

3. Another division of logic is that into *theoretical* and *practical* logic. But this division is also incorrect.

Universal logic, which as a mere canon abstracts from all objects, cannot have a practical part. This would be a *contradictio in adjecto*, because a practical logic presupposes acquaintance with a certain kind of object, to 18 which it is applied. Thus we can call every science a *practical logic*; for in each we must have a form of thought. Universal logic, considered as practical, can thus be nothing more than a *technique of learnedness in general*, an *organon of scholastic method*.

In consequence of this division logic would thus have a *dogmatic* and a *technical* part. The first would be called the *doctrine of elements*, the second the *doctrine of method*. The practical or technical part of logic would be a logical art in regard to order and to logical terms of art and logical distinctions, to make it easier for the understanding to act.

In both parts, both the technical and the dogmatic, it would be impermissible to give the least consideration either to the objects or to the subject of thought. In this latter relation logic could be divided

4. into *pure* and *applied* logic.

In pure logic we separate the understanding from the other powers of the mind and consider what it does by itself alone. Applied logic considers the understanding insofar as it is mixed with the other powers of the mind, which influence its actions and misdirect it, so that it does not proceed in accordance with the laws which it quite well sees to be correct. Applied logic really ought not to be called logic. It is a psychology in which we consider how things customarily go on in our thought, not how they ought to go on. In the end it admittedly says what one ought to do in order to make correct use of the understanding under various subjective obstacles and restrictions; and we can also learn from it what furthers the correct use of the understanding, the means of aiding it, or the cures for logical mistakes and errors. But propaedeutic it simply is not. For psychology, from which everything in applied logic must be taken, is a part of the philosophical sciences, to which logic ought to be the propaedeutic.

It is said, to be sure, that technique, or the way of building a science, ought to be expounded in applied logic. But that is futile, indeed, even harmful. One then begins to build before one has materials, and one gives form, but content is lacking. Technique must be expounded within each science.

Finally, as for what concerns

5. the division of logic into the logic of the *common* and that of the *speculative* understanding, we note that this science simply cannot be thus divided. 19

It cannot be a science of the speculative understanding. For as a logic of speculative cognition or of the speculative use of reason it would be an organon for other sciences and not a mere propaedeutic, which ought to deal with all possible use of the understanding and of reason.

Just as little can logic *be a product of the common understanding.* The common understanding is the faculty by which we have insight into the rules of cognition *in concreto*. Logic, however, ought to be a science of the rules of thought *in abstracto*.

Nonetheless we can accept the universal human understanding as object of logic, and to this extent it will abstract from the particular rules of speculative reason and thus be distinct from the logic of the *speculative understanding*.

As for what concerns the *exposition* of logic, it can be either *scholastic* or *popular*.

It is *scholastic* insofar as it is adequate to the curiosity, the capabilities, and the culture of those who want to treat the cognition of logical rules as a science. *Popular*, however, if it condescends to the capabilities and needs of those who do not study logic as science but only want to use it to enlighten their understanding. – In the scholastic exposition the rules must be presented *in their universality* or *in abstracto*; in the popular, on the other hand, *in the particular* or *in concreto*. The scholastic exposition is the foundation for the popular, for the only one who can expound something in a popular way is one who could also expound it more thoroughly.

Here we distinguish *exposition* from *method*, by the way. By *method* is to be understood, namely, the way to cognize completely a certain object, to whose cognition the method is to be applied. It has to be derived from the nature of the science itself and, as an order of thought that is determined thereby and is necessary, it cannot be altered. *Exposition* means only the
20 manner of communicating one's thoughts in order to make a doctrine understandable.

From what we have previously said concerning the nature[e] and the end of logic, the worth of this science and the use of its study can be evaluated in accordance with a correct and determinate standard.

Logic is thus not a universal art of discovery, to be sure, and not an organon of truth – not an algebra, with whose help hidden truths can be discovered.

It is useful and indispensable as a *critique of cognition*, however, or for passing judgment on common as well as on speculative reason, not in order to teach it, but only to make it *correct* and in agreement with itself. For the logical principle of truth is agreement of the understanding with its own universal laws.

As for what concerns the history of logic, finally, we want to cite only the following:

Contemporary logic derives from *Aristotle's Analytic*. This philosopher can be regarded as the father of logic. He expounded it as organon and divided it into *analytic* and *dialectic*. His manner of teaching is very scholastic and has to do with the development of the most universal concepts, which lie at the basis of logic, but one has no use for it because almost everything amounts to mere subtleties, except that one [has] drawn from this the names for various acts of the understanding.

From Aristotle's time on, logic has not gained much in *content*, by the way, nor can it by its nature do so. But it can surely gain in regard to *exactness*, *determinateness*, and *distinctness*. There are only a few sciences that can attain a permanent condition, where they are not altered any more. These include logic and also metaphysics. Aristotle had not omitted any moment of the understanding; we are only more exact, methodical, and orderly in this.

21 It was believed of *Lambert's Organon*[10] that it would augment logic

[e] "Wesen."

considerably. But it contains nothing more except for subtler divisions, which, like all correct subtleties, sharpen the understanding, of course, but are of no essential use.

Among modern philosophers there are two who have set universal logic in motion: *Leibniz* and *Wolff.*

Malebranche and *Locke* did not treat of real logic, since they also deal with the content of cognition and with the origin of concepts.

The universal logic of Wolff[11] is the best we have. Some have combined it with the Aristotelian logic, like *Reusch*,[12] for example.

Baumgarten, a man who has much merit here, concentrated the Wolffian logic,[13] and *Meier* then commented again on Baumgarten.

Crusius[14] also belongs to the modern logicians, but he did not consider how things stand with logic. For his logic contains metaphysical principles and so to this extent oversteps the limits of this science; besides, it puts forth a criterion of truth that cannot be a criterion, and hence to this extent gives free reign to all sorts of fantastic notions.

In present times there has not been any famous logician, and we do not need any new inventions for logic, either, because it contains merely the form of thought.

III.

Concept of philosophy in general – Philosophy considered according to the scholastic concept and according to the worldly concept – Essential requirements and ends of philosophizing – The most universal and highest tasks of this science

It is sometimes hard to explain what is understood by a science. But the science gains in precision through establishment of its determinate concept, and in this way many mistakes are avoided which otherwise creep in, for certain reasons, if one cannot yet distinguish the science from sciences related to it.

Before we try to give a definition of philosophy, however, we must first investigate the character of various cognitions themselves, and since philosophical cognitions belong to the cognitions of reason, we must explain in particular what is to be understood by the latter. 22

Cognitions of reason are opposed to *historical* cognitions. The former are cognitions *from principles* (*ex principiis*), the latter cognitions from *data* (*ex datis*). – A cognition can have arisen from reason and in spite of that be historical, however, as when a mere literator learns the products of someone else's reason his cognition of these products of reason is then merely historical, for example.

One can distinguish cognitions, then,

1. according to their *objective* origin, i.e., according to the sources from which alone a cognition is possible. In this respect all cognitions are either *rational* or *empirical*;
2. according to their *subjective* origin, i.e., according to the way in which a cognition can be acquired by men. Considered from this latter viewpoint, cognitions are either *rational* or *historical*, however they may have arisen in themselves. Hence something that is *subjectively* only historical can be *objectively* a cognition of reason.

With some rational cognitions it is harmful to know them merely historically, while with others it makes no difference. Thus the sailor knows the rules of navigation historically from his tables, for example, and that is enough for him. But if the jurist knows jurisprudence merely historically, then he is fully ruined as a genuine judge, and still more so as a legislator.

From the stated distinction between *objectively* and *subjectively* rational cognitions it is also clear now that one can in a certain respect learn philosophy without being able to philosophize. He who really wants to become a philosopher must practice making a free use of his reason, then, and not a merely imitative and, so to speak, mechanical use.

We have explained cognitions of reason as cognitions from principles, and 23 from this it follows that they must be *a priori*. But there are two kinds of cognitions, which are both *a priori*, but which nevertheless have many noteworthy differences, namely, *mathematics* and *philosophy*.

It is customary to maintain that mathematics and philosophy are distinct from one another *as to their object*, in that the former deals with *quantity*, the latter with *quality*. But[f] this is wrong. The distinction between these sciences cannot rest on the object, for philosophy deals with everything, hence also with *quanta*, and mathematics does so in part too, insofar as everything has a quantity. The specific difference between these two sciences is constituted only by the *different kind of cognition of reason, or of the use of reason*, in mathematics and philosophy. Philosophy is, namely, *cognition of reason from mere concepts*, while mathematics is *cognition of reason from the construction of concepts*.

We *construct* concepts when we exhibit them in intuition *a priori* without experience, or when we exhibit in intuition the object that corresponds to our concept of it. – The mathematician can never make use of his reason in accordance with mere concepts, the philosopher never through construction of concepts. In mathematics one uses reason *in concreto*, but the intuition is not empirical; rather, here one makes something the object of intuition for himself *a priori*.

[f] Reading "Allein" for "Alles," in accordance with the published list of printer's errors (KI, xli).

And as we see, mathematics has an advantage over philosophy here, in that the cognitions of the former are *intuitive* cognitions while those of the latter are only *discursive*. The cause of the fact that in mathematics we consider quantities more lies in this, that quantities can be constructed *a priori* in intuition, while qualities on the other hand cannot be exhibited in intuition.

Philosophy is thus the system of philosophical cognitions or of cognitions of reason from concepts. That is the *scholastic concept*[g] of this science. According to the *worldly concept*[h] it is the science of the final ends of human reason. This high concept gives philosophy *dignity*, i.e., an absolute worth. And actually it is philosophy, too, which alone has only *inner* worth, and which first gives a worth to all other cognitions. 24

Yet in the end people always ask what purpose is served by philosophizing and by its final end[,] philosophy itself considered as science in accordance with the *scholastic concept*.

In this scholastic sense of the word, philosophy has to do only with *skill*, but in relation to the worldly concept, on the other hand, with *usefulness*. In the former respect it is thus a *doctrine of skill*; in the latter, a doctrine *of wisdom*[,] the *legislator* of reason[,] and the philosopher to this extent not an *artist of reason*[i] but rather a *legislator*.

The artist of reason, or the *philodox*, as *Socrates* calls him, strives only for speculative knowledge, without looking to see how much the knowledge contributes to the final end of human reason; he gives rules for the use of reason for any sort of end one wishes. The practical philosopher, the teacher of wisdom through doctrine and example, is the real philosopher. For philosophy is the idea of a perfect wisdom, which shows us the final ends of human reason.

According to the scholastic concept, philosophy involves *two* things:

First, a sufficient supply of cognitions of reason, and *for the second thing*, a systematic connection of these cognitions, or a combination of them in the idea of a whole.

Not only does philosophy allow such strictly systematic connection, it is even the only science that has systematic connection in the most proper sense, and it gives systematic unity to all other sciences.

As for what concerns philosophy according to the worldly concept (*in sensu cosmico*), we can also call it *a science of the highest maxim for the use of our reason*, insofar as we understand by a maxim the inner principle of choice among various ends.

[g] "*Schulbegriff.*"

[h] "*Weltbegriffe.*"

[i] "*Vernunftkünstler.*"

For philosophy in the latter sense is in fact the science of the relation of all cognition and of all use of reason to the ultimate end of human reason, to which, as the highest, all other ends are subordinated, and in which they must all unite to form a unity.

25 The field of philosophy in this cosmopolitan sense can be brought down to the following questions:

1. *What can I know?*
2. *What ought I to do?*
3. *What may I hope?*
4. *What is man?*

Metaphysics answers the first question, *morals* the second, *religion* the third, and *anthropology* the fourth. Fundamentally, however, we could reckon all of this as anthropology, because the first three questions relate to the last one.

The philosopher must thus be able to determine

1. the sources of human knowledge,
2. the extent of the possible and profitable use of all knowledge, and finally
3. the limits of reason.

The last is the most necessary but also the hardest, yet the philodox does not bother himself about it.

To a philosopher two things chiefly pertain: 1) Cultivation of talent and of skill, in order to use them for all sorts of ends. 2) Accomplishment in the use of all means toward any end desired. The two must be united; for without cognitions[j] one will never become a philosopher, but cognitions[k] alone will never constitute the philosopher either, unless there is in addition a purposive combination of all cognitions and skills in a unity, and an insight into their agreement with the highest ends of human reason.

No one at all can call himself a philosopher who cannot philosophize. Philosophizing can be learned, however, only through practice and through one's own use of reason.

How should it be possible to learn philosophy anyway? Every philosophical thinker builds his own work, so to speak, on someone else's ruins, but no work has ever come to be that was to be lasting in all its parts. Hence one cannot learn philosophy, then, just because it *is not yet given*. But even granted that there were *a philosophy actually at hand*, no one who learned it would be able to say that he was a philosopher, for *subjectively* his cognition[l] of it would always be only *historical*.

26 In mathematics things are different. To a certain extent one can probably learn this science, for here the proofs are so evident that anyone can

[j] "Kenntnisse."
[k] "Kenntnisse."
[l] "Kenntniß."

become convinced of them; and on account of its evidence it can also, as it were, be preserved as a *certain* and *lasting doctrine*.

He who wants to learn to philosophize, on the other hand, may regard all systems of philosophy only as *history of the use of reason* and as objects for the exercise of his philosophical talent.

Thus the true philosopher, as one who thinks for himself, must therefore make a free use of his reason on his own, not a slavishly imitative use. But not a *dialectical* use, i.e., not one that aims only at giving cognitions the *illusion* of *truth* and *wisdom*. This is the business of the mere *sophist*, thoroughly incompatible with the dignity of the philosopher, as one who is acquainted with and is a teacher of wisdom.

For science has an inner, true worth only as *organ of wisdom*. As such, however, it is also indispensable for it, so that one may well maintain that wisdom without science is a silhouette of a perfection to which we shall never attain.

He who hates science but loves wisdom all the more is called a *misologist*. Misology arises commonly out of an emptiness of scientific cognitions[m] and a certain vanity bound up with that. Sometimes, however, people who had initially pursued sciences with great industry and fortune, but who found in the end no satisfaction in the whole of their knowledge, also fall into the mistake of misology.

Philosophy is the only science that knows how to provide for us this inner satisfaction, for it closes, as it were, the scientific circle, and only through it do the the sciences attain order and connection.

For the sake of practice in thinking for ourselves, or philosophizing, we will have to look more to the *method* for the use of our understanding than to the propositions themselves at which we have arrived through this method.

IV.

27

Short sketch of a history of philosophy

There is some difficulty in determining the limits where the *common* use of the understanding ends and the *speculative* begins, or where common cognition of reason becomes philosophy.

Nevertheless there is a rather certain distinguishing mark here, namely, the following:

Cognition of the universal *in abstracto* is *speculative* cognition, cognition of the universal *in concreto* is *common* cognition. Philosophical cognition is speculative cognition of reason, and thus it begins where the common use of reason starts to make attempts at cognition of the universal *in abstracto*.

[m] "Kenntnissen."

From this determination of the distinction between common and speculative use of reason we can now pass judgment on the question, with which people we must date the beginning of philosophizing. Among all peoples, then, the *Greeks* first began to philosophize. For they first attempted to cultivate cognitions of reason, not with images as the guiding thread, but *in abstracto*, while other peoples always sought to make concepts understandable only *through images in concreto*. Even today there are peoples, like the Chinese and some Indians, who admittedly deal with things that are derived merely from reason, like God, the immortality of the soul, etc., but who nonetheless do not seek to investigate the nature of these things in accordance with concepts and rules *in abstracto*. They make no separation here between the use of the understanding *in concreto* and that *in abstracto*. Among the *Persians* and the *Arabs* there is admittedly some speculative use of reason, but the rules for this they borrowed from *Aristotle*, hence from the Greeks. In *Zoroaster's Zend-Avesta* we find not the slightest trace of philosophy. The same holds also for the prized *Egyptian* wisdom, which in comparison with Greek philosophy was mere child's play.

As in philosophy, so too in regard to *mathematics*, the Greeks were the first to cultivate this part of the cognition of reason in accordance with a speculative, scientific method, by demonstrating every theorem from elements.

28 *When* and *where* the philosophical spirit first arose among the Greeks, however, one cannot really determine.

The first to introduce the speculative use of reason, and the one from whom we derived the first steps of the human understanding toward scientific culture, is *Thales*, the founder of the *Ionian* sect. He bore the surname *physicist*, although he was also a *mathematician*, just as in general mathematics has always preceded philosophy.

The first philosophers clothed everything in images, by the way. For poetry, which is nothing other than a clothing of thoughts in images, is older than *prose*. Thus in the beginning one had to make use of the language of images and of poetic style even with things that are merely objects of pure reason. *Pherecydes* is supposed to have been the first author of prose.

The *Ionians* were followed by the *Eleatics*. The principle of the Eleatic philosophy and of its founder, *Xenophanes*, was: *In the senses there is deception and illusion, the source of truth lies only in the understanding alone.*

Among the philosophers of this school, *Zeno* distinguished himself as a man of great understanding and acuity and as a subtle dialectician.

In the beginning *dialectic* meant the art of the pure use of the understanding in regard to abstract concepts separated from all sensibility. Thus the many encomia of this art among the ancients. Subsequently these philosophers, who completely rejected the testimony of the senses, necessarily fell, given their claim, into many subtleties, and thus dialectic degenerated into the art of maintaining and of disputing any proposition. And so it became a mere exercise for the *sophists*, who wanted to engage in reasoning[n] about everything, and who devoted themselves to giving illusion the veneer of truth and to making black white. On account of this the name *sophist*, by which one formerly meant a man who was able to speak about all things rationally and with insight, became so hated and contemptible, and the name *philosopher* was introduced instead.

Around the time of the Ionian school there appeared in *Magna Graecia* a man of strange genius, who not only founded a school but also outlined and brought into being a project, the like of which had never been before. This man was *Pythagoras*, born on[o] *Samos*. He founded, namely, a society of philosophers who were united with one another into a federation through the law of silence. His divided his hearers into two classes: the *acusmatics* (ἀκουσμαθικοί), who had simply to listen, and the *acroamatics* (ἀκροαμαθικοί), who were permitted to ask too.

29

Among his doctrines there were some *exoteric* ones, which he expounded to the whole of the people; the remaining ones were secret and *esoteric*, determined only for the members of his federation, some of whom he took into his trusted friendship, separating them wholly from the others. He made *physics* and *theology*, hence the doctrines of the visible and the invisible, the *vehicle* of his secret doctrines. He also had various *symbols*, which presumably were nothing other than certain signs that allowed the Pythagoreans to communicate with one another.

The end of his federation seems to have been none other than *to purify religion of the delusions of the people, to moderate tyranny, and to introduce more lawfulness into states*. This federation, which the tyrants began to fear, was destroyed shortly before Pythagoras's death, however, and this philosophical society was broken up, partly by execution, partly by the flight and the banning of the greatest part of its members. The few who remained were *novices*. And since these knew little of the doctrines peculiar to Pythagoras, we can say nothing certain and determinate about them. Subsequently many doctrines that were certainly only invented were attributed to Pythagoras, who by the way was also a very mathematical mind.

The most important epoch of Greek philosophy starts finally with *Socrates*. For it was he who gave to the philosophical spirit and to all speculative

[n] "raissoniren."

[o] Reading "auf" for "zu," with the published list of printer's errors (KI, xli).

minds a wholly new *practical* direction. Among all men, too, he was almost the only one whose behavior comes closest to the *idea of a wise man.*

Among his disciples the most famous is *Plato*, who occupied himself
30 more with Socrates' practical doctrines, and among Plato's disciples *Aristotle*, who in turn raised speculative philosophy higher.

Plato and *Aristotle* were followed by the *Epicureans* and the *Stoics*, who were openly declared mutual enemies. The *former* placed *the highest good* in a *joyful heart*, which they called *pleasure*;[p] the *latter* found it solely in *loftiness and strength of soul*, whereby one can do without all the comforts of life.

The Stoics, by the way, were *dialectical* in speculative philosophy, *dogmatic* in moral philosophy, and in their practical principles, through which they sowed the seed for the most sublime sentiments[q] that ever existed, they showed uncommonly much dignity. The founder of the Stoic school is *Zeno of Citium*. The most famous men from this school among the Greek philosophers are *Cleanthes* and *Chrysippus*.

The Epicurean school was never able to achieve the same repute that the Stoic did. Whatever one may say of the Epicureans, however, this much is certain: they demonstrated the greatest moderation in enjoyment and were the *best natural philosophers* among all the thinkers of Greece.

We note here further that the foremost Greek schools bore particular names. Thus Plato's school was called the *Academy*, Aristotle's the *Lyceum*, the Stoics' school *porticus* (στοά), a covered walkway, from which the name Stoic is derived; Epicurus's school was called *horti*, because Epicurus taught in *gardens*.

Plato's Academy was followed by three other Academies, which were founded by his disciples. *Speusippus* founded the first, *Arcesilaus* the second, *Carneades* the third.

These Academies inclined toward skepticism. *Speusippus* and *Arcesilaus* both adjusted their mode of thought to skepticism, and in this *Carneades* went still further. On this account the skeptics, these subtle, dialectical thinkers, are also called *Academics*. Thus the Academics followed the first great doubter, *Pyrrho*, and his successors. Their teacher *Plato* had himself given them occasion for this by expounding many of his doctrines *dialogically*, so that the grounds *pro* and *contra* were put forth, without his deciding about the matter himself, although he was otherwise very *dogmatic*.

31 If we begin the epoch of skepticism with Pyrrho, then we get a whole school of skeptics, who are essentially distinct from the *dogmatists* in their mode of thought and method of philosophizing, in that they made it the first maxim for all philosophizing use of reason *to withhold one's judgment*

[p] "*Wollust*."

[q] "Gesinnungen."

even when the semblance[r] *of truth is greatest*; and they advanced the principle that *philosophy consists in the equilibrium of judgment and teaches us to uncover false semblance.*[s] From these skeptics nothing has remained for us, however, but the two works of Sextus Empiricus, in which he brought together all doubts.

When philosophy subsequently passed from the Greeks to the Romans, it was not extended; for the Romans always remained just *disciples*.

Cicero was a disciple of Plato in speculative philosophy, a Stoic in morals. The Stoic sect included as the most famous *Epictetus*, *Antonius the Philosopher*, and *Seneca*. There were no *naturalists* among the Romans except for *Pliny the Elder*,[15] who left a natural history.

Finally culture disappeared among the Romans too, and *barbarism* arose until the *Arabs* began in the 6th and 7th centuries to apply themselves to the sciences and to revive Aristotle again. Then the sciences rose in the occident again, and in particular the regard for Aristotle, who was followed, however, in a slavish way. In the 11th and 12th centuries the *scholastics* appeared; they *elucidated* Aristotle and pursued his subtleties to infinity. They occupied themselves with nothing but abstractions. This scholastic method of pseudo-philosophizing was pushed aside at the time of the Reformation, and now there were *eclectics* in philosophy, i.e., thinkers who thought for themselves, who acknowledged no school, but who instead sought the truth and accepted it where they found it.

Philosophy owes its improvement in modern times *partly* to the greater study of nature, *partly* to the combination of mathematics with natural science. The order that arose in thought through the study of these sciences was also extended over the particular branches and parts of philosophy proper. The first and greatest investigator of nature in modern time was *Bacon of Verulam*. In his investigations he followed the path of experience and called attention to the importance and indispensability of *observations* and *experiments* for the discovery of truth. It is hard to say, by the way, from whence the improvement of speculative philosophy really comes. *Descartes* rendered it no small service, in that he contributed much to *giving distinctness to thought* by advancing his criterion of truth, which he placed in the *clarity and evidence of cognition*.

32

Leibniz and *Locke* are to be reckoned among the greatest and most meritorious reformers of philosophy in our times. The latter sought to analyze the human understanding and to show which powers of the soul and which of its operations belonged to this or that cognition. But he did not complete the work of his investigation, and also his procedure is very

[r] "*Scheine.*"

[s] "*Schein.*"

dogmatic, although we did gain from him, in that we began to study the nature of the soul better and more thoroughly.

As for what concerns the special dogmatic method of philosophizing peculiar to *Leibniz* and *Wolff*, it was quite mistaken. Also, there is so much in it that is deceptive that it is in fact necessary to suspend the whole procedure and instead to set in motion another, the *method of critical philosophizing*, which consists in investigating the procedure of reason itself, in analyzing the whole human faculty of cognition and examining how far its *limits* may go.

In our age *natural philosophy* is in the most flourishing condition, and among the investigators of nature there are great names, e.g., *Newton*. Modern philosophers cannot now be called excellent and lasting, because everything here goes forward, as it were, in flux. What one builds the other tears down.

In moral philosophy we have not come further than the ancients. As for what concerns metaphysics, however, it seems as if we had been stopped short in the investigation of metaphysical truths. A kind of *indifferentism* toward this science now appears, since it seems to be taken as an honor to speak of metaphysical investigations contemptuously as mere *cavilling*.[t] And yet metaphysics is the real, true philosophy!

33 Our age is the age of *critique*, and it has to be seen what will come of the critical attempts of our time in respect to philosophy and in particular to metaphysics.

V.

Cognition in general – Intuitive and discursive cognition; intuition and concept and in particular their difference – Logical and aesthetic perfection of cognition

All our cognition has a *twofold* relation, *first* a relation to the *object*, *second* a relation to the subject. In the former respect it is related to *representation*, in the latter to *consciousness*, the universal condition of all cognition in general. – (Consciousness is really a representation that another representation is in me.)

In every cognition we must distinguish *matter*, i.e., the object, and form, i.e., *the way in which* we cognize the object. If a savage sees a house from a distance, for example, with whose use he is not acquainted, he admittedly has before him in his representation the very same object as someone else who is acquainted with it determinately as a dwelling established for men. But as to form, this cognition of one and the same object is different in the

[t] "*Grübeleien.*"

two. With the one it is *mere intuition*, with the other it is *intuition* and *concept* at the same time.

The difference in the form of the cognition rests on a condition that accompanies all cognition, on *consciousness*. If I am conscious of the representation, it is *clear*; if I am not conscious of it, *obscure*.

Since consciousness is the essential condition of all logical form of cognitions, logic can and may occupy itself only with clear but not with obscure representations. In logic we do not see how representations arise, but merely how they agree with logical form. In general logic cannot deal at all with mere representations and their possibility either. This it leaves to metaphysics. Logic itself is occupied merely with the rules of thought in concepts, judgments, and inferences, as that through which all thought takes place. Something precedes, of course, before a representation becomes a concept. We will indicate that in its place, too. But we will not investigate how representations arise. Logic deals with cognition too, to be sure, because in cognition there is already thought. But representation is not yet cognition, rather, cognition always presupposes representation. And this latter cannot be explained at all. For we would always have to explain *what representation is* by means of yet another representation. 34

All clear representations, to which alone logical rules can be applied, can now be distinguished in regard to *distinctness* and *indistinctness*. If we are conscious of the whole representation, but not of the manifold that is contained in it, then the representation is indistinct. First, to elucidate this, an example in intuition.

We glimpse a country house in the distance. If we are conscious that the intuited object is a house, then we must necessarily have a representation of the various parts of this house, the windows, doors, etc. For if we did not see the parts, we would not see the house itself either. But we are not conscious of this representation of the manifold of its parts, and our representation of the object indicated is thus itself an indistinct representation.

If we want an example of indistinctness in concepts, furthermore, then the concept of beauty may serve. Everyone has a clear concept of beauty. But in this concept many different marks occur, among others that the beautiful must be something that (1.) strikes the senses and (2.) pleases universally. Now if we cannot explicate the manifold of these and other marks of the beautiful, then our concept of it is still indistinct.

Wolff's disciples call the indistinct representation a *confused* one. But this expression is not fitting, because the opposite of confusion is not distinctness but order. Distinctness is an effect of order, to be sure, and indistinctness an effect of confusion; and every confused cognition is thus also an indistinct one. But the proposition does not hold conversely; not every indistinct cognition is a confused one. For in the case of cognitions in which there is no manifold at hand, there is no order, but also no confusion.

35 This is the situation with all *simple* representations, which never become distinct, not because there is confusion in them, but rather because there is no manifold to be found in them. One must call them indistinct, therefore, but not confused.

And even with compound representations, too, in which a manifold of marks can be distinguished, indistinctness often derives not from confusion but from *weakness of consciousness*. Thus something can be distinct as to *form*, i.e., I can be conscious of the manifold in the representation, but the distinctness can diminish as to *matter* if the degree of consciousness becomes smaller, although all the order is there. This is the case with abstract representations.

Distinctness itself can be of two sorts:

First, sensible. This consists in the consciousness of the manifold in intuition. I see the Milky Way as a whitish streak, for example; the light rays from the individual stars located in it must necessarily have entered my eye. But the representation of this was merely clear, and it becomes distinct only through the telescope, because then I glimpse the individual stars contained in the Milky Way.

Secondly, intellectual; distinctness in concepts or *distinctness of the understanding*. This rests on the analysis of the concept in regard to the manifold that lies contained within it. Thus in the concept of *virtue*, for example, are contained as marks (1.) the concept of freedom, (2.) the concept of adherence to rules (to duty), (3.) the concept of overpowering the force of the inclinations, in case they oppose those rules. Now if we break up the concept of virtue into its individual constituent parts, we make it distinct for ourselves through this analysis. By thus making it distinct, however, we add nothing to a concept; we only explain it. With distinctness, therefore, concepts are improved not as to *matter* but only *as to form*.

If we reflect on our cognitions in regard to the two essentially different 36 basic faculties, sensibility and the understanding, from which they arise, then here we come upon the distinction between intuitions and concepts. Considered in this respect, all our cognitions are, namely, either *intuitions* or *concepts*. The former have their source in *sensibility*, the faculty of intuitions, the latter in the *understanding*, the faculty of concepts. This is the *logical* distinction between understanding and sensibility, according to which the latter provides nothing but intuitions, the former on the other hand nothing but concepts. The two basic faculties may of course be considered from another side and defined in another way: sensibility, namely, as a faculty of *receptivity*, the understanding as a faculty of *spontaneity*. But this mode of explanation is not logical but rather *metaphysical*. It is also customary to call sensibility the *lower* faculty, the understanding on the other hand the *higher* faculty, on the ground that sensibility gives the mere material for thought, but the understanding rules over this material and brings it under rules or concepts.

The difference between *aesthetic* and *logical perfection* of cognition is grounded on the distinction stated here between *intuitive* and *discursive* cognitions, or between intuitions and concepts.

A cognition can be perfect either according to laws of sensibility or according to laws of the understanding; in the former case it is *aesthetically* perfect, in the other *logically* perfect. The two, aesthetic and logical perfection, are thus of different kinds; the former relates to sensibility, the latter to the understanding. The logical perfection of cognition rests on its agreement with the object, hence on *universally valid* laws, and hence we can pass judgment on it according to norms *a priori*. Aesthetic perfection consists in the agreement of cognition with the subject and is grounded on the particular sensibility of man. In the case of aesthetic perfection, therefore, there are no objectively and universally valid laws, in relation to which we can pass judgment on it *a priori* in a way that is universally valid for all thinking beings in general. Insofar as there are nonetheless universal laws of sensibility, which have validity subjectively for the whole of humanity although not objectively and for all thinking beings in general, we can think of an aesthetic perfection that contains the ground of a subjectively universal pleasure. This is *beauty*, that which pleases the senses in *intuition* and can be the object of a universal pleasure just because the laws of intuition are universal laws of sensibility. 37

Through this agreement with the universal laws of sensibility *the really, independently beautiful*, whose essence consists in *mere form*, is distinguished in kind from the *pleasant*,[u] which pleases[v] merely in sensation through stimulation or excitement, and which on this account can only be the ground of a merely private pleasure.[w]

It is this essential aesthetic perfection, too, which, among all [perfections], is compatible with logical perfection and may best be combined with it.

Considered from this side, aesthetic perfection in regard to the essentially beautiful can thus be advantageous to logical perfection. In another respect it is also disadvantageous, however, insofar as we look, in the case of aesthetic perfection, only to the *non-essentially* beautiful, the *stimulating* or the *exciting*, which pleases the senses in mere sensation and does not relate to mere form but rather to the matter of sensibility. For stimulation and excitement, most of all, can spoil the logical perfection in our cognitions and judgments.

In general, however, there always remains a kind of conflict between the

[u] "dem *Angenehmen*."
[v] "gefällt."
[w] "eines bloßen Privat-Wohlgefallens."

aesthetic and the logical perfection of our cognition, which cannot be fully removed. The understanding wants to be instructed, sensibility enlivened; the first desires insight, the second comprehensibility. If cognitions are to instruct then they must to that extent be thorough; if they are to entertain at the same time, then they have to be beautiful as well. If an exposition is beautiful but shallow, then it can only please sensibility but not the understanding, but if it is thorough yet dry, only the understanding but not sensibility as well.

Since the needs of human nature and the end of popularity in cognition demand, however, that we seek to unite the two perfections with one another, we must make it our task to provide aesthetic perfection for those cognitions that are in general capable of it, and to make a scholastically 38 correct, logically perfect cognition popular through its aesthetic form. But in this effort to combine aesthetic with logical perfection in our cognitions we must not fail to attend to the following rules, namely: (1.) that logical perfection is the basis of all other perfections and hence cannot be wholly subordinated or sacrificed to any other; (2.) that one should look principally to *formal* aesthetic perfection, the agreement of a cognition with the laws of intuition, because it is just in this that the essentially beautiful, which may best be combined with logical perfection, consists; (3.) that one must be very cautious with *stimulation* and *excitement*, whereby a cognition affects sensation and acquires an interest for it, because attention can thereby so easily be drawn from the object to the subject, whence a very disadvantageous influence on the logical perfection of cognition must evidently arise.

To acquaint us better with the essential differences that exist between the logical and the aesthetic perfection of cognition, not merely in the universal but from several particular sides, we want to compare the two with one another in respect to the four chief moments of quantity, quality, relation, and modality, on which the passing of judgment as to the perfection of cognition depends.

A cognition is perfect (1.) as to quantity if it is *universal*; (2.) as to quality if it is *distinct*; (3.) as to relation if it is *true*; and finally (4.) as to modality if it is *certain*.

Considered from the viewpoints indicated, a cognition will thus be logically perfect as to quantity if it has objective universality (universality of the concept or of the rule), as to quality if it has objective distinctness (distinctness in the concept), as to relation if it has objective truth, and finally as to modality if it has objective certainty.

To these logical perfections correspond now the following aesthetic perfections in relation to those four principal moments, namely

1. *aesthetic universality*. This consists in the applicability of a cognition to a multitude of objects that serve as examples, to which application of it can be made, and whereby it becomes useful at the same time for the end of popularity; 39
2. *aesthetic distinctness*. This is distinctness in intuition, in which a concept thought abstractly is exhibited or elucidated *in concreto* through examples;
3. *aesthetic truth*. A merely subjective truth, which consists only in the agreement of cognition with the subject and the laws of sensory illusion, and which is consequently nothing more than a universal semblance.[x]
4. *aesthetic certainty*. This rests on what is necessary in consequence of the testimony of the senses, i.e., what is confirmed through sensation and experience.

With the perfections just mentioned two things are always to be found, which in their harmonious union make up perfection in general, namely, *manifoldness* and *unity*. Unity in the concept lies with the understanding, unity of intuition with the senses.

Mere manifoldness without unity cannot satisfy us. And thus truth is the principal perfection among them all, because it is the ground of unity through the relation of our cognition to the object. Even in the case of aesthetic perfection, truth always remains the *conditio sine qua non*, the foremost negative condition, apart from which something cannot please taste universally. Hence no one may hope to make progress in the belles lettres[y] if he has not made logical perfection the ground of his cognition. It is in the greatest possible unification of logical with aesthetic perfection in general, in respect to those cognitions that are both to instruct and to entertain, that the character and the art of the genius actually shows itself.

VI. PARTICULAR LOGICAL PERFECTIONS OF COGNITION

40

A) Logical perfection of cognition as to quantity – Quantity – Extensive and intensive quantity – Extensiveness and thoroughness or importance and fruitfulness of cognition – Determination of the horizon of our cognition

The quantity of cognition can be understood in two senses, either as *extensive* or as *intensive* quantity. The former relates to the *extension* of cognition and thus consists in its multitude and manifoldness; the latter

[x] "ein allgemeiner Schein."
[y] "in schönen Wissenschaften."

relates to its *content*,[z] which concerns the *richness*[a] or the logical importance and fruitfulness of a cognition, insofar as it is considered as ground of many and great consequences (*non multa sed multum.*[b])

In expanding our cognitions or in perfecting them as to their extensive quantity it is good to make an estimate as to how far a cognition agrees with our ends and capabilities. This reflection concerns the determination of the *horizon* of our cognitions, by which is to be understood *the congruence*[c] *of the quantity of all cognitions with the capabilities and ends of the subject.*

The horizon can be determined

1. *logically*, in accordance with the faculty or the powers of cognition in relation to the *interest of the understanding.* Here we have to pass judgment on how far we can go in our cognitions, how far we must go, and to what extent certain cognitions serve, in a logical respect, as means to various principal cognitions as our ends;
2. *aesthetically*, *in accordance with taste* in relation to the interest of feeling. He who determines his horizon aesthetically seeks to arrange science according to the taste of the public, i.e., to make it *popular*, or in general to attain only such cognitions as may be universally communicated, and in which the class of the unlearned, too, find pleasure and interest;
3. 41 *practically*, in accordance with *use* in relation to the *interest* of the *will.* The practical horizon, insofar as it is determined according to the influence which a cognition has on our morality, is *pragmatic* and is of the greatest importance.

Thus the horizon concerns passing judgment on, and determining, what man *can* know, what he *is permitted* to know, and what he *ought* to know.

Now as for what concerns the theoretically or logically determined horizon in particular – and it is of this alone that we can speak here – we can consider it either from the *objective* or from the *subjective* viewpoint.

In regard to *objects*, the horizon is either *historical* or *rational.* The former is much broader than the other, indeed, it is immeasurably great, for our historical cognition has no limits. The rational horizon, on the other hand, may be fixed, e.g., it may be determined to what kind of objects mathematical cognition cannot be extended. So too in respect of philosophical cognition of reason, as to how far reason can go here *a priori* without any experience.

In relation to the *subject* the horizon is either the *universal* and *absolute*, or a *particular* and *conditioned* one (a private horizon).

By the absolute and universal horizon is to be understood the congru-

[z] "*Gehalt.*"

[a] "*Vielgültigkeit.*"

[b] Not many but much.

[c] "*Angemessenheit.*"

ence[d] of the limits of human cognitions with the limits of the whole of human perfection in general. And here, then, the question is: In general, what can man, as man, know?

The determination of the private horizon depends upon various empirical conditions[e] and special considerations, e.g., age, sex, station, mode of life, etc. Every particular class of men has its particular horizon in relation to its special powers of cognition, ends, and standpoints, every mind its own horizon according to the standard of the individuality of its powers and its standpoint. Finally, we can also think a horizon of *healthy reason* and a horizon of *science*, which latter still requires *principles*, in accordance with which to determine *what we can and cannot know*.

42

What we *cannot* know is *beyond*[f] our horizon, what we do not need to know[g] is *outside*[h] our horizon. This latter can hold only *relatively*, however, in relation to various particular private ends, to whose accomplishment certain cognitions not only do not contribute anything but could even be an obstacle. For no cognition is, absolutely and for every purpose, useless and unusable, although we may not always be able to have insight into its use. Hence it is an objection as unwise as it is unjust that is made to great men who labor in the sciences with painstaking industry when shallow minds ask, *What is the use of that?*[i] We must simply never raise this question if we want to occupy ourselves with the sciences. Even granted that a science could give results only concerning some possible object, it would still for that reason alone be useful enough. Every logically perfect cognition always has some possible use, which, although we are as yet unacquainted with it, will perhaps be found by posterity. If in the cultivation of the sciences one had always looked only to material gain, their use, then we would have no arithmetic or geometry. Besides, our understanding is so arranged that it finds satisfaction in mere insight, even more than in the use that arises therefrom. *Plato* noted this. Man feels in this his own excellence, he senses what it means to have understanding. Men who do not sense this must envy the animals. The *inner* worth that cognitions have through logical perfection is not to be compared with the *outer*, their worth in application.

Like that which lies *outside* our horizon, insofar as we, in accordance with our purposes, do not *need* to know it, as dispensable for us, that which

[d] "Congruenz."

[e] Ak, "empirischen und speciellen Rücksichten"; 1st ed., "empirischen Bedingungen und speciellen Rücksichten."

[f] "*über.*"

[g] "was wir nicht wissen *dürfen* oder nicht zu wissen brauchen."

[h] "*außer.*"

[i] Reading "*wozu das nütze*" for "*wozu ist das nütze*," in accordance with the published list of printer's errors (KI, xli).

lies *beneath*[j] our horizon, insofar as we *ought* not to know it as *harmful* to us, is to be understood in a *relative* sense but never in an absolute one.

With respect to the extension and the demarcation of our cognition, the following rules are to be recommended:

One must

43 1. determine his horizon *early*, but of course only when one can determine it oneself, which usually does not occur before the 20th year;
2. not alter it lightly or often (not turn from one thing to another);
3. not measure the horizon of others by one's own, and not consider as useless what is of no use *to us*; it would be presumptuous to want to determine others' horizons, because one is not sufficiently acquainted, in part with their capabilities, in part with their purposes;
4. neither extend it too far nor restrict it too much. For he who wants to know too much ends by knowing nothing, and conversely, he who believes of some things that they do not concern him, often deceives himself; as when, e.g., the philosopher believes of history that it is dispensable for him[.]

One should also seek

5. to determine in advance the absolute horizon of the whole human race (as to past and to future time), as well as also
6. to determine, in particular, the position that our science occupies in the whole of cognition. The *Universal Encyclopedia* serves for this as a universal map (*mappe-monde*[k]) of the sciences[.]
7. In determining his own particular horizon one should carefully consider for which part of cognition one has the greatest capability and pleasure, what is more or less necessary in regard to certain duties, what cannot coexist with the *necessary* duties; and finally
8. one should of course always seek to expand his horizon rather than to narrow it.

As for the extension of cognition, there need be no concern in general about what concerned d'Alembert.[16] For the burden does not press us down, but rather the volume of space for our cognitions constrains us. Critique of reason, of history and historical writings, a universal spirit that deals with human cognition *en gros* and not merely in *detail*$_F$, will always make the extension smaller, without diminishing anything in the content. The metal merely separates from the slag, or the inferior vehicle, the 44 husk, which was necessary for so long. With the extension of natural history, of mathematics, etc., new methods will be invented which will shorten the old and make the multitude of books dispensable. It will be because of the invention of such new methods and principles that we will be able, with their help, to find anything we desire without burdening

[j] "*unter.*"

[k] French: *mappemonde, map of the world.*

memory. Thus he who brings history under ideas that can always remain renders it service as a genius.

Opposed to the logical perfection of cognition in regard to its extension stands *ignorance.*[l] A *negative* imperfection, or imperfection of *lack*, which, on account of the restrictions of the understanding, is inseparable from our cognition.

We can consider ignorance from an *objective* or from a *subjective* viewpoint.

1. Taken objectively, ignorance is either *material* or *formal.* The former consists in a lack of historical cognitions, the other in a lack of rational cognitions. One does not have to be completely ignorant in any field, but one can well restrict historical knowledge in order to devote oneself more to rational knowledge, or conversely.

2. In the *subjective* sense, ignorance is either learned, *scientific*, or is *common.* He who has distinct insight into the restrictions of cognition, hence into the field of ignorance from where it begins, e.g., the philosopher who sees and proves how little one can know of gold in regard to its structure due to a lack of the requisite data, is ignorant *artfully*[m] or in a learned way. He who is ignorant, on the other hand, without having insight into the grounds of the limits of knowledge, and without concerning himself with this, is so in a common, not a scientific way. Such a one does not even know that he knows nothing. For one can never represent his ignorance except through science, as a blind man cannot represent darkness until he has become sighted.

Cognition[n] of one's ignorance presupposes science, then, and makes one at the same time modest, while imagined knowledge puffs one up. Hence Socrates' non-knowledge[o] was a laudable ignorance, really a knowledge of non-knowledge, according to his own admission. It is precisely those who possess very many cognitions,[p] then, and who for all that are astounded at the multitude of what they do not know, who cannot be reproached with their ignorance. 45

Ignorance in things whose cognition lies beyond our horizon is in general *irreproachable* (*inculpabilis*), and in regard to the speculative use of our faculty of cognition it can be *allowed* (although only in the relative sense), insofar as the objects here lie *not beyond* our horizon but yet *outside* it. It is *shameful*, however, in things that it is quite necessary and also easy to know.

[l] "*Unwissenheit.*"
[m] "*kunstmäßig.*"
[n] "Kenntniß."
[o] "Nichtwissen."
[p] "Kenntnisse."

There is a distinction between *not knowing* something and *ignoring* something, i.e., *taking no notice of it*. It is good to ignore much that it is not good for us to know. *Abstracting* is distinct from both of these. One abstracts from a cognition when one ignores its application, whereby one gets it *in abstracto* and can better consider it in the universal as a principle. Such abstraction from what does not belong to our purpose in the cognition of a thing is useful and praiseworthy.

Scholars in matters of reason[q] are commonly ignorant historically.

Historical knowledge without determinate limits is *polyhistory*; this puffs one up. *Polymathy* has to do with cognition of reason. Both historical and rational knowledge, when extended without determinate limits, can be called *pansophy*. Historical knowledge includes the science of the tools of learnedness – *philology*, which comprises a critical acquaintance with books and languages (*literature* and *linguistics*).

Mere polyhistory is *cyclopic* learnedness, which lacks one eye, the eye of philosophy, and a cyclops among mathematicians, historians, natural historians, philologists, and linguists is a learned man who is great in all these matters, but who for all that holds all philosophy to be dispensable.

One part of philology is constituted by the *humaniora*, by which is understood acquaintance with the ancients, which furthers the *unification of science with taste*, which rubs off coarseness and furthers the communicability and urbanity in which *humanity* consists.

46 The *humaniora*, then, concern instruction in what serves the cultivation of taste, in conformity with the models of the ancients. This includes, e.g., eloquence, poetry, wide reading in the classical authors, etc. All these humanistic cognitions[r] can be reckoned in the *practical* part of philology, which aims in the first instance at the cultivation of taste. If we separate the mere philologist from the humanist, however, the two would differ from one another in that the former seeks the tools of *learnedness* among the ancients, the latter the tools for the *cultivation of taste*.

The *belletrist*, or *bel esprit*,[s] is a humanist according to contemporary models in living languages. He is not learned, then, for only *dead languages* are now learned languages, but is rather a mere *dilettante* in cognitions of taste[t] in accordance with *fashion*, with no need for the ancients. We could call him one who *apes* the humanist. The polyhistor must, as philologist, be a *linguist* and a *literator*, and as humanist a *classicist* and expositor of the classics. As philologist he is *cultivated*, as humanist *civilized*.

---

[q] "Vernunftlehrer."

[r] "Kenntnisse."

[s] French: aesthete, belletrist.

[t] "Geschmackskenntnisse."

In regard to the sciences, there are two degenerate forms of prevailing taste: *pedantry* and *gallantry*.[u] The *one* pursues the sciences only for the *school* and thereby restricts them in respect of their use, the *other* pursues them merely for intercourse or for the world and in this way restricts them in respect of their *content*.

The pedant is either opposed, as learned man, to the man of the world, and is to this extent the puffed up man of learning, unacquainted with the world, i.e., with the ways of bringing his science to bear on men; or he is to be considered, in general, as a man of skill, but only in *formalities*, not as to essence and as to his end. In the latter sense he is a *fanatic for formalities*;[v] restricted in regard to the core of things, he looks only to the clothing and the shell. He is the unfortunate imitation or *caricature* of the *methodical* mind. Thus pedantry can also be called cavilling fussiness[w] and useless exactitude (micrology) in formalities. And such formality of scholastic method outside the schools is to be found not merely among learned people and in learned things, but also in other classes and in other things. 47 What is the *ceremonial at court* and in *intercourse* but a *pursuit of formalities*[x] and *hair-splitting*.[y] In the military this is not completely so, although it seems so. But in conversation, in clothing, in diet, in religion, a good deal of pedantry often prevails.

Thoroughness (scholarly, scholastic perfection[z]) is a purposeful exactitude in formalities. Pedantry is thus an *affected* thoroughness, just as gallantry, as a mere courtesan seeking the approval of taste, is nothing but an affected popularity. For gallantry only strives to gain the reader's affection and thus never to insult him with a hard word.

To avoid pedantry requires extensive cognitions[a] not only in the sciences themselves but also in regard to their use. Only the true man of learning, then, can free himself from pedantry, which is always the property of a restricted mind.

In striving to procure for our cognition the perfection of scholastic thoroughness and at the same time of popularity, without falling into the indicated mistakes of affected thoroughness or of affected popularity, we must look above all to the scholastic perfection of our cognition, the scholastically correct form of thoroughness; and only then may we concern ourselves about how we are to make our cognition, methodically learned in school, truly popular, i.e., easily and universally communicable to others, in such a way that thoroughness is not displaced by popularity.

[u] "*Galanterie*."
[v] "*Formalienklauber*."
[w] "grüblerische Peinlichkeit."
[x] "Formalienjagd."
[y] "Klauberei."
[z] "schulgerechte, scholastische Vollkommenheit."
[a] "Kenntnisse."

For scholastic perfection, without which all science is nothing but tricks and trifling,[b] must not be sacrificed for the sake of popular perfection, to please the people.

To learn true popularity, however, one must read the ancients, e.g., Cicero's philosophical writings, the poets *Horace*, *Virgil*, etc., and among the moderns *Hume*, *Shaftesbury*, et. al. Men who have all had a good deal of intercourse with the refined world, without which one cannot be popular. For true popularity demands a good deal of practical acquaintance with the world and with men, acquaintance with men's concepts, taste, and inclinations, to which constant regard must be given in presentation and even in the choice of expressions that are fitting and adequate to popularity. This ability to descend[c] to the public's power of comprehension and to the customary expressions, in which scholastic perfection is not slighted, but in which the clothing of thoughts is merely so arranged that the framework, the *scholastically correct* and *technical* in that perfection, may not be seen (just as one draws lines with a pencil, writes on them, and subsequently erases them) – this truly popular perfection of cognition is in fact a great and rare perfection, which shows much insight into the science. It has this merit, too, in addition to many others, that it can provide a proof of complete insight into a thing. For the merely scholastic examination of a cognition leaves doubt as to whether that examination is not one-sided and whether the cognition itself has a worth admitted by all men. The school has its prejudices, just as does the common understanding. One improves the other here. It is therefore important that a cognition be examined by men whose understanding does not depend on any school.

48

This perfection of cognition, whereby it qualifies for easy and universal communication, could also be called *external extension*,[d] or the extensive quantity of a cognition, insofar as it is widespread *externally* among men.

Since cognitions are so many and manifold, one will do well to make himself a plan, in accordance with which he orders the sciences in the way that best agrees with, and contributes to the furtherance of, his ends. All cognitions stand in a certain natural connection with one another. Now if, in striving to expand his cognitions, one does not look to their connection, then extensive knowledge[e] amounts to nothing more than a mere *rhapsody*. If one makes one principal science his end, however, and considers all other cognitions only as means for achieving it, then he brings a certain systematic character into his knowledge. And in order to go to work on

[b] "Spielwerk und Tändelei."
[c] "Eine solche Herablassung (Condescendenz)."
[d] "*äußere Extension*."
[e] "Vielwissen."

extending his cognitions according to such a well ordered and purposive plan, one must seek, therefore, to become acquainted with this connection of cognitions among themselves. For this, the sciences get guidance from *architectonic*, which is a *system in accordance with ideas*, in which *the sciences are considered in regard to their kinship and systematic connection in a whole of cognition that interests humanity*. 49

Now as for what concerns the *intensive quantity*[f] of cognition – i.e., its content, or its richness[g] and importance, which is essentially distinct from its extensive quantity, its mere *extensiveness*, as we noted above – we want here to add only the following few remarks:

1. A cognition that is concerned with *what is great*, i.e., with *the whole* in the use of the understanding, is to be distinguished from *subtlety in what is small* (micrology).
2. Every cognition that furthers logical perfection *as to form* is to be called *logically important*, e.g., every mathematical proposition, every law of nature into which we have distinct insight, every correct philosophical explanation. *Practical* importance cannot be *foreseen*, one must simply *wait and watch* for it.
3. Importance must not be confused with *difficulty*.[h] A cognition can be difficult without being important, and conversely. Difficulty, then, does not decide either *for* or *against* the worth or the importance of a cognition. This rests on the quantity or multiplicity of its consequences. A cognition is the more important accordingly as it has more or greater consequences, as the use that may be made of it is more. Cognition without important consequences is called *cavilling*;[i] scholastic philosophy, e.g., was of this sort.

VII.

B) Logical perfection of cognition as to relation – Truth – Material and formal, or logical, truth – Criteria of logical truth – Falsehood and error – Illusion, as source of error – Means for avoiding errors

A principal perfection of cognition, indeed, the essential and inseparable condition of all its perfection, is *truth*. Truth, it is said, consists in the agreement of cognition with its object. In consequence of this mere nominal explanation, my cognition, to count as true, is supposed to agree with its object. Now I can compare the object with my cognition, however, only *by cognizing it*. Hence my cognition is supposed to confirm itself, which is far short of being sufficient for truth. For since the object is outside me, 50

[f] Ak, "*intensive* Größe"; 1st ed., "*intensive Größe*."

[g] "Vielgültigkeit."

[h] "*Schwere*."

[i] "*Grübelei*."

the cognition in me, all I can ever pass judgment on is whether my cognition of the object agrees with my cognition of the object. The ancients called such a circle in explanation a *diallelon*.[j] And actually the logicians were always reproached with this mistake by the skeptics, who observed that with this explanation of truth it is just as when someone makes a statement before a court and in doing so appeals to a witness with whom no one is acquainted, but who wants to establish his credibility by maintaining that the one who called him as witness is an honest man. The accusation was grounded, too. Only the solution of the indicated problem is impossible without qualification and for every man.

The question here is, namely, whether and to what extent there is a criterion of truth that is certain, universal, and useful in application. For this is what the question, *What is truth?*, ought to mean.

To be able to decide this important question we must distinguish that which belongs to the *matter* in our cognition and is related to the *object* from that which concerns its *mere form*, as that condition without which a cognition would in general never be a cognition. With respect to this distinction between the *objective*, *material* relation in our cognition and the *subjective*, *formal* relation, the question above thus breaks down into these two particular ones:

1. Is there a universal material, and
2. Is there a universal formal criterion of truth?

A universal material criterion of truth is not possible; it is even self-contradictory. For as a *universal* criterion, valid for all objects in general, it would have to abstract fully from all difference among objects, and yet at the same time, as a material criterion, it would have to deal with just this difference, in order to be able to determine whether a cognition agrees with just that object to which it is related and not just with any object in general, in which case nothing would really be said. Material truth must consist in this agreement of a cognition with just that determinate object to which it is related, however. For a cognition that is true in regard to one object can be false in relation to other objects. Hence it is absurd to demand a universal material criterion of truth, which should abstract and at the same time not abstract from all difference among objects.

51

If the question is about *universal formal* criteria of truth, however, then here it is easy to decide that of course there can be such a thing. For *formal* truth consists merely in the agreement of cognition with itself, in complete abstraction from all objects whatsoever and from all difference among them. And the universal formal criteria of truth are accordingly nothing other than universal logical marks of the agreement of cognition with itself

[j] Ak, "Diallele"; 1st ed., "*Diallele*."

or – what is one and the same – with the universal laws of the understanding and of reason.

These formal, universal criteria are of course not sufficient for objective truth, but they are nonetheless to be regarded as its *conditio sine qua non*.

For the question of whether cognition agrees with its objects must be preceded by the question of whether it agrees with itself (as to form). And this is a matter for logic.

The formal criteria of truth in logic are

1. *the principle of contradiction*,
2. *the principle of sufficient reason*.

Through the former the *logical possibility* of a cognition is determined, through the latter its *logical actuality*.

To the logical actuality of a cognition it pertains, namely:

First: that it be logically possible, i.e., *not contradict itself*. This characteristic of *internal* logical truth is only *negative*, however; for a cognition that contradicts itself is of course false, but if it does not contradict itself it is not always true.

Second: that it be *logically grounded*, i.e., that it (a) have grounds and (b) not have false consequences.

This second criterion of *external* logical truth or of *accessibility to reason*,[k] which concerns the logical connection of a cognition with grounds and consequences, is *positive*. And here the following rules are valid: 52

1. From the *truth of the consequence* we may infer the *truth* of the cognition *as ground*, but only *negatively*: if one false consequence flows from a cognition, then the cognition itself is false. For if the ground were true, then the consequence would also have to be true, because the consequence is determined by the ground.

But one cannot infer conversely that if no false consequence flows from a cognition, then it is true; for one can infer true consequences from a false ground.

2. *If all the consequences of a cognition are true, then the cognition is true too.* For if there were something false in the cognition, then there would have to be a false consequence too.

From the consequence, then, we may infer to a ground, but without being able to determine this ground. Only from the complex of all consequences can one infer *to a determinate ground*, infer that it is the true ground.

The former mode of inference, according to which the consequence

[k] "*Rationabilität*."

can only be a *negatively* and *indirectly* sufficient criterion of the truth of a cognition, is called in logic the *apagogic* mode (*modus tollens*).

This procedure, of which frequent use is made in geometry, has the advantage that I may derive just one false consequence from a cognition in order to prove its falsehood. To show, e.g., that the earth is not flat, I may just infer apagogically and indirectly, without bringing forth positive and direct grounds: If the earth were flat, then the pole star would always have to be at the same height; but this is not the case, consequently it is not flat.

With the other, the *positive* and *direct* mode of inference (*modus ponens*) the difficulty enters that the totality of the consequences cannot be cognized apodeictically, and that one is therefore led by the indicated mode of inference only to a probable and *hypothetically* true cognition (hypotheses), in accordance with the presupposition that where many consequences are true, all the remaining ones[l] may be true too.

Thus we will be able to advance three principles here as universal, merely formal or logical criteria of truth; these are

1. *the principle of contradiction and of identity* (*principium contradictionis and identitatis*), through which the internal possibility of a cognition is determined for *problematic* judgments;
2. *the principle of sufficient reason* (*principium rationis sufficientis*), on which rests the (logical) *actuality* of a cognition, the fact that it is grounded, as material for *assertoric* judgments;
3. *the principle of the excluded middle* (*principium exclusi medii inter duo contradictoria*[m]), on which the (logical) necessity of a cognition is grounded – that we must necessarily judge thus and not otherwise, i.e., that the opposite is false – for *apodeictic* judgments.

53

The opposite of truth is *falsehood*, which, insofar as it is taken for truth, is called *error*. An erroneous judgment – for there is error as well as truth only in judgment – is thus one that confuses the illusion of truth with truth itself.

It is easy to have insight into *how truth is possible*, since here the understanding acts in accordance with its essential laws.

But it is hard to comprehend *how error in the formal sense of the word, i.e.,* how the *form of thought contrary to the understanding* is possible, just as we cannot in general comprehend how any power should deviate from its own essential laws. We cannot seek the ground of errors in the understanding itself and its essential laws, then, just as little as we can in the *restrictions* of the understanding, in which lies the cause of *ignorance*, to be sure, but not in any way the cause of error. Now if we had no other power of cognition but the understanding, we would never err. But besides the understand-

[l] Ak, "auch alle"; 1st ed., "alle auch."
[m] principle of the excluded middle between two contradictories.

ing, there lies in us another indispensable source of cognition. That is *sensibility*, which gives us the material for thought, and in doing this works according to other laws than those the understanding does. Error cannot arise from sensibility in and by itself, however, because the senses simply do not judge.

The ground for the origin of all error will therefore have to be sought simply and solely in the *unnoticed influence of sensibility upon the understanding*, or to speak more exactly, upon *judgment*. This influence, namely, brings it about that in judgment we take merely *subjective* grounds to be *objective*, and consequently confuse *the mere illusion of truth with truth itself*. For it is just in this that the essence of illusion consists, which on this account is to be regarded as a ground for holding a false cognition to be true.

54

What makes error possible, then, is *illusion*, in accordance with which the merely *subjective* is confused in judgment with the *objective*.

In a certain sense, however, one can make the understanding the author of errors, namely, insofar as it allows itself, due to a lack of requisite attention to that influence of sensibility, to be misled by the illusion arising therefrom into holding merely subjective determining grounds of judgment to be objective ones, or into letting that which is true only according to the laws of sensibility hold as true in accordance with its own laws.

In the restrictions of the understanding, then, lies only the responsibility for ignorance; the responsibility for error we have to assign to ourselves. Nature has denied us many cognitions, to be sure, it leaves us in unavoidable ignorance concerning so much, but still it does not cause error. We are misled into this by our own inclination to judge and to decide even where, on account of our limitedness, we are not able to judge and to decide.

Every error into which the human understanding can fall is only *partial*, however, and in every erroneous judgment there must always lie something true. For a *total* error would be a complete *opposition* to the laws of the understanding and of reason. But how could that, as such, in any way come from the understanding and, insofar as it is still a judgment, be held to be a product of the understanding.

In respect to the true and the erroneous in our cognition, we distinguish an *exact* cognition from a *rough* one.

Cognition is *exact* when it is adequate to its object, or when there is not the slightest error in regard to its object, and it is *rough* when there can be errors in it yet without being a hindrance to its purpose.

This distinction concerns the *broader* or *narrower determinateness* of our cognition (*cognitio late vel stricte determinata*). Initially it is sometimes necessary to determine a cognition in a broader extension (*late determinare*),

55

particularly in historical things. In cognitions of reason everything must be determined exactly (*stricte*), however. In the case of broad determination one says that a cognition is determined *praeter propter.*[n] Whether a cognition ought to be determined roughly or exactly always depends on its purpose. Broad determination leaves a certain play for error, which still can have its determinate limits, however. Error occurs particularly where a broad determination is taken for a strict one, e.g., in matters of morality,[o] where everything must be determined *stricte*. Those who do not do this are called by the English *latitudinarians*.

One can distinguish *subtlety*, as a *subjective* perfection of cognition, from exactness, as an objective perfection – since here cognition is fully congruent with its object.

A cognition is subtle when one discovers in it that which usually escapes the attention of others. It requires a higher degree of attention, then, and a greater application of power of the understanding.

Many reprove all subtlety because they cannot attain it. But in itself it always brings honor to the understanding and is even laudable and necessary, insofar as it is applied to an object worthy of observation. When one could have attained the same end with less attention and effort of the understanding, however, and yet one uses more, then one makes a useless expense and falls into subtleties, which are difficult, to be sure, but do not have any use (*nugae difficiles*[p]).

As the rough is opposed to the exact, so is the *crude* to the subtle.

From the nature of error – whose concept, as we noted, contains as an essential mark, besides falsehood, also the illusion of truth – we get the following important rule for the truth of our cognition:

56 To avoid errors – and no error is *unavoidable*, at least not absolutely or without qualification, although it can be unavoidable *relatively*, for the cases where it is unavoidable for us to judge, even with the danger of error – to avoid errors, then, one must seek to disclose and to explain their source, illusion. Very few philosophers have done that, however. They have only sought to refute the errors themselves, without indicating the illusion from which they arise. This disclosure and breaking up of illusion is a far greater service to truth, however, than the direct refutation of errors, whereby one does not block their source and cannot guard against the same illusion misleading one into errors again in other cases because one is not acquainted with it. For even if we are convinced that we have erred, then in case the illusion that grounds our error has not been

[n] approximately.

[o] Ak, "Modalität"; 1st ed., "Moralität."

[p] difficult trivialities.

removed we still have *scruples*, however little we can bring forth in justification of them.

Through the explanation of illusion, furthermore, one grants to the one who erred a kind of fairness. For no one will admit that he erred without any illusion of truth, which might even have deceived someone more acute, because here it is a matter of subjective grounds.

Where the illusion is evident even to the common understanding (*sensus communis*), an error is called a *stupidity* or an *absurdity*. The charge of absurdity is always a personal reproof, which one must avoid, particularly in the refutation of errors.

For to him who maintains an absurdity, the very illusion that lies at the ground of the evident falsehood is not evident. One must first *make* this illusion evident to him. Then if he still persists, he is admittedly stupid; but then nothing more can be undertaken with him either. He has thereby made himself just as incapable of further correction and refutation as he is unworthy of it. For one cannot really *prove* to anyone that he is absurd; here all ratiocination would be vain. If one proves absurdity, then one is no longer speaking with him who erred but with him who is rational. But then the disclosure of the absurdity (*deductio ad absurdum*) is not necessary.

One can also call a *stupid* error one that nothing, *not even illusion*, serves to excuse; just as a *crude* error is an error that proves ignorance in common cognition or a slip in common attentiveness. 57

Error *in principles* is greater than *in their application*.

An *external* mark or an *external* touchstone of truth is the comparison of our own judgments with those of others, because the subjective will not be present in all others in the same way, so that illusion can thereby be cleared up. The *incompatibility* of the judgments of others with our own is thus an external mark of error and is to be regarded as a cue to investigate our procedure in judgment, but not for that reason to reject it at once. For one can perhaps be right *about the thing* but not right *in manner*, i.e., in the exposition.

The common human understanding (*sensus communis*) is also in itself a touchstone for discovering the mistakes of the *artificial* use of the understanding. This is what it means *to orient* oneself *in thought* or in the speculative use of reason by means of the common understanding, when one uses the *common* understanding as a test for passing judgment on the correctness of the *speculative* use.

Universal rules and conditions for avoiding error in general are: 1) to think for oneself, 2) to think oneself in the position of someone else, and 3) always to think in agreement with oneself. The maxim of thinking for oneself can be called the *enlightened mode of thought*; the maxim of putting oneself in the viewpoint of others in thought, the *extended mode of thought*; and the maxim of always thinking in agreement with one self, the *consequent*[q] or *coherent*[r] *mode of thought*.

58

VIII.

C) Logical perfection of cognition as to quality – Clarity – Concept of a mark in general – Various kinds of marks – Determination of the logical essence of a thing – Its distinction from the real essence – Distinctness, a higher degree of clarity – Aesthetic and logical distinctness – Distinction between analytic and synthetic distinctness

From the side of the understanding, human cognition is *discursive*, i.e., it takes place through representations which take as the ground of cognition that which is common to many things, hence through *marks*[s] as such. Thus we cognize things *through marks* and that is called *cognizing*,[t] [the German word for which] comes from [the German word for] *being acquainted.*[u]

A *mark is that in a thing which constitutes a part of the cognition of it*, or – what is the same – a *partial representation, insofar as it is considered as ground of cognition of the whole representation*. All our *concepts* are marks, accordingly, and all *thought* is nothing other than a representing through marks.

Every mark may be considered from two sides:

First, as a representation in itself;

Second, as belonging, as a partial concept, to the whole representation of a thing, and thereby as ground of cognition of this thing itself.

All marks, considered as grounds of cognition, have *two* uses, either an *internal* or an *external* use. The *internal* use consists in *derivation*, in order to cognize the thing itself through marks as its grounds of cognition. The external use consists in *comparison*, insofar as we can compare one thing with others through marks in accordance with the rules of *identity* or *diversity*.

There are many specific differences among marks, on which the following classification of them is grounded.

[q] "*consequente.*"
[r] "*bündige.*"
[s] "*Merkmale.*"
[t] "*Erkennen.*"
[u] "*Kennen.*"

1. *Analytic* or *synthetic* marks. *The former* are partial concepts of my *actual* concept (marks that I already think therein), while the latter are partial concepts of the *merely possible* complete concept (which is supposed to *come to be* through a synthesis of several parts). The former are all *concepts of reason*, the latter can be *concepts of experience*. 59
2. *Coordinate* or *subordinate*. This division of marks concerns their connection *after*[v] or *under*[w] one another.

Marks are *coordinate* insofar as each of them is represented as an *immediate* mark of the thing and are *subordinate* insofar as one mark is represented in the thing only by means of the other. The combination of coordinate marks to form the whole of a concept is called an *aggregate*, the combination of subordinate concepts a *series*. The former, the aggregation of coordinate marks, constitutes the totality of the concept, which, in regard to synthetic empirical concepts, can never be completed, but rather resembles a straight line *without limits*.

The series of subordinate marks terminates *a parte ante*, or on the side of the grounds, in concepts which cannot be broken up, which cannot be further analyzed on account of their simplicity; *a parte post*, or in regard to the consequences, it is *infinite*, *because we have a highest genus* but no lowest *species*.

With the synthesis of every new concept in the aggregation of coordinate marks, the *extensive* or *extended* distinctness grows, as *intensive* or *deep* distinctness grows with the further analysis of the concept in the series of subordinate marks. This latter kind of distinctness, since it necessarily contributes to *thoroughness* and *coherence* of the cognition, is thus principally a matter of philosophy and is pursued to the highest degree in metaphysical investigations in particular.

3. *Affirmative* or *negative* marks. Through the former we cognize what the thing is, through the latter what it is not.

Negative marks serve to keep us from errors. Hence they are unnecessary *where it is impossible to err*, and are necessary and of importance only in those cases where they keep us from an important error into which we can easily fall. Thus in regard to the concept, e.g., of a being like *God*, negative marks are quite necessary and important.

Through affirmative marks we seek *to understand something*, through negative marks – into which all marks can be transformed – we only seek not to *misunderstand* or not to *err*, even if we should not thereby become acquainted with anything. 60

4. *Important* and *fruitful*, or *empty* and *unimportant*, marks.

[v] "*nach*."

[w] "*unter*."

A mark is important and fruitful if it is a ground of cognition for great and numerous consequences, *partly* in regard to its internal use, its use in derivation, insofar as it is sufficient for cognizing thereby a great deal in the thing itself, *partly* in respect to its *external* use, its use in comparison, insofar as it thereby contributes to cognizing both the *similarity* of a thing to many others and its difference from many others.

We have to distinguish *logical* importance and fruitfulness from *practical*, from *usefulness* and *utility*, by the way.

5. *Sufficient*[x] *and necessary* or *insufficient and accidental* marks.

A mark is *sufficient* insofar as it suffices always to distinguish the thing from all others; otherwise it is insufficient, as the mark of barking is, for example, for dogs. The sufficiency[y] of marks, as well as their importance, is to be determined only in a relative sense, in relation to ends that are intended through a cognition.

Necessary marks, finally, are those that must always be there to be found in the thing represented. Marks of this sort are also called *essential* and are opposed to *extra-essential* and *accidental* marks, which can be separated from the concept of the thing.

Among necessary marks there is another distinction, however.

Some of them belong to the thing *as grounds* of other marks of one and the same thing, while *others* belong only *as consequences* of other marks.

The former are *primitive* and *constitutive* marks (*constitutiva, essentialia in* 61 *sensu strictissimo*[z]), the others are called *attributes* (*consectaria, rationata*[a]) and belong admittedly to the essence of the thing, but only insofar as they must first be derived from its essential points, as the three angles follow from the three sides in the concept of the triangle, for example.

Extra-essential marks are again of *two kinds*; they concern either *internal* determinations of a thing (*modi*) or its external relations (*relationes*). Thus the mark of *learnedness* signifies an inner determination of a man, but *being a master or a servant* only an external relation.

The complex of all the essential parts of a thing, or the sufficiency of its marks as to coordination or subordination, is the *essence* (*complexus notarum primitivarum, interne conceptui dato sufficientium; s. complexus notarum, conceptum aliquem primitive constituentium*[b]).

In this explanation, however, we must not think at all of the *real* or

[x] "*Zureichende.*"

[y] "Hinlänglichkeit."

[z] things that are constitutive, things that are essential in the strictest sense.

[a] things that follow, things grounded.

[b] the complex of primitive marks internally sufficient for a given concept, or the complex of marks that primitively constitute a certain concept.

natural essence of things, into which we are never able to have insight. For since logic abstracts from all content of cognition, and consequently also from the thing itself, in this science the talk can only be of the *logical* essence of things. And into this we can easily have insight. For it includes nothing further than the cognition of all the predicates in regard to which an object is determined *through its concept*; whereas for the real essence of the thing (*esse rei*) we require cognition of those predicates on which, as grounds of cognition, everything that belongs to the existence of the thing depends. If we wish to determine, e.g., the logical essence of body, then we do not necessarily have to seek for the data for this in nature; we may direct our reflection to the marks which, as essential points (*constitutiva, rationes*) originally constitute the basic concept of the thing. For the logical essence is nothing but *the first basic concept of all the necessary marks of a thing* (*esse conceptus*).

The first stage of the perfection of our cognition as to quality is thus its clarity. A second stage, or a higher degree of clarity, is *distinctness*. This consists in *clarity of marks*. 62

First of all we must here distinguish logical distinctness in general from aesthetic distinctness. Logical distinctness rests on objective clarity of marks, aesthetic distinctness on subjective clarity. The former is a clarity *through concepts*, the latter a clarity through *intuition*. The latter kind of distinctness consists, then, in a mere *liveliness* and *understandability*, i.e., in a mere clarity through examples *in concreto* (for much that is not distinct can still be understandable, and conversely, much that is hard to understand can still be distinct, because it goes back to remote marks, whose connection with intuition is possible only through a long series).

Objective distinctness frequently causes subjective obscurity, and conversely. Hence logical distinctness is often possible only to the detriment of aesthetic distinctness, and conversely aesthetic distinctness through examples and similarities which do not fit exactly but are only taken according to an analogy often becomes harmful to logical distinctness. Besides, examples are simply not marks and do not belong to the concept as parts but, as intuitions, to the use of the concept. Distinctness through examples, mere understandability, is hence of a completely different kind than distinctness through concepts as marks. *Lucidity* consists in the combination of both, of aesthetic or popular distinctness and of scholastic or logical distinctness. For one thinks of a *lucid mind* as the talent for a luminous presentation of abstract and thorough cognitions that is congruent with the *common understanding's* power of comprehension.

Next, as for what concerns logical distinctness in particular, it is to be called *complete* distinctness insofar as all the marks which, taken together, make up the whole concept have come to clarity. A *completely*[c] distinct concept can be so, again, either in regard to the totality of its *coordinate* marks or in respect to the totality of its *subordinate* marks. *Extensively* complete or sufficient distinctness of a concept consists in the total clarity of its coordinate marks, which is also called *exhaustiveness*. Total clarity of subordinate marks constitutes *intensively* complete distinctness, *profundity*.

63 The former kind of logical distinctness can also be called the *external completeness* (*completudo externa*) of the clarity of marks, the other the *internal completeness* (*completudo interna*). The latter can be attained only with pure concepts of reason and with arbitrary concepts, but not with empirical concepts.

The extensive quantity of *distinctness*, insofar as it is not superfluous,[d] is called *precision*.[e] *Exhaustiveness*[f] (*completudo*) and precision (*praecisio*) together constitute *adequacy*[g] (*cognitio, quae rem adaequat*[h]); and *the completed perfection of a cognition* (*consummata cognitionis perfectio*) consists (as to quality) in *intensively adequate* cognition, *profundity*, combined with *extensively adequate* cognition, *exhaustiveness* and *precision*.

Since, as we have noted, it is the business of logic *to make clear concepts distinct*, the question now is *in what way* it makes them distinct.

Logicians of the *Wolffian* school place the act of making cognitions distinct[i] entirely in mere analysis of them. But not all distinctness rests on analysis of a given concept. It arises thereby only in regard to those marks that we already thought in the concept, but not in respect to *those* marks that are first added to the concept as parts of the whole possible concept.

The kind of distinctness that arises not through analysis but through synthesis of marks is *synthetic* distinctness. And thus there is an essential difference between the two propositions: *to make a distinct concept* and *to make a concept distinct*.

For when I make a distinct concept, I begin with the parts and proceed from these toward the whole. Here there are no marks as yet at hand; I acquire them only through synthesis. From this synthetic procedure emerges synthetic distinctness, then, which actually extends my concept as to content through what is added as a mark *beyond*[j] the concept in (pure

[c] "*vollständig* oder *complet*."
[d] "abundant."
[e] "*Präcision* (Abgemessenheit)."
[f] "*Ausführlichkeit*."
[g] "*Angemessenheit*."
[h] cognition that is adequate to the thing.
[i] "alle Deutlichmachung der Erkentnisse."
[j] "*über*."

or empirical) intuition. The mathematician and the natural philosopher make use of this synthetic procedure in making distinctness in concepts.[k] For all distinctness of properly mathematical cognition, as of all cognition based on experience, rests on such an expansion of it through the synthesis of marks. 64

When I make a concept distinct, however, my cognition does not grow at all as to content through this mere analysis. The content remains the same, only the form is altered, in that I learn to distinguish better, or to cognize with clearer consciousness, what lay in the given concept already. As nothing is added to a map through the mere illumination[l] of it, so a given concept is not in the least increased through its mere illumination[m] by means of the analysis of its marks.

To synthesis pertains the making distinct of *objects*,[n] to analysis the making distinct of *concepts*.[o] In the latter case *the whole precedes the parts*, in the former *the parts precede the whole*. The philosopher only makes given concepts distinct. Sometimes one proceeds synthetically even when the concept that one wants to make distinct in this way is already *given*. This is often the case with propositions based on experience, in case one is not yet satisfied with the marks already thought in a given concept.

The analytic procedure for creating distinctness, with which alone logic can occupy itself, is the first and principal requirement in making our cognition distinct. For the more distinct our cognition of a thing is, the stronger and more effective it can be too. But analysis must not go so far that in the end the object itself disappears.

If we were conscious of all that we know, we would have to be astonished at the great multitude of our cognitions.

In regard to the objective content of our cognition in general, we may think the following *degrees*, in accordance with which cognition can, in this respect, be graded:

The *first* degree of cognition is: *to represent* something;[p]

The *second*: to represent something with consciousness, or *to perceive*[q] (*percipere*);

The *third*: *to be acquainted*[r] with something (*noscere*), or to represent 65

[k] "Deutlichmachung der Begriffe."
[l] "Illumination."
[m] "Aufhellung."
[n] "Deutlichmachung der *Objecte*."
[o] "Deutlichmachung der *Begriffe*."
[p] "sich etwas *vorstellen*."
[q] "*wahrnehmen*."
[r] "*kennen*."

something in comparison with other things, both as to *sameness*[s] and as to *difference*;[t]

The *fourth*: to be acquainted with something *with consciousness*, i.e., to *cognize*[u] it (*cognoscere*). Animals are *acquainted* with objects too, but they do not *cognize* them.

The *fifth*: *to understand*[v] something (*intelligere*), i.e., to cognize something *through the understanding by means of concepts*, or to *conceive*.[w] One can conceive[x] much, although one cannot comprehend[y] it, e.g., a *perpetuum mobile*, whose impossibility is shown in mechanics.

The *sixth*: to cognize something through reason, or *to have insight*[z] into it (*perspicere*). With few things do we get this far, and our cognitions become fewer and fewer in number the more that we seek to perfect them as to content.

The *seventh, finally*: *to comprehend*[a] something (*comprehendere*), i.e., to cognize something through reason or *a priori* to the degree that is sufficient for our purpose. For all our comprehension is only *relative*, i.e., sufficient for a certain purpose; we do not comprehend anything *without qualification*. Nothing can be comprehended more than what the mathematician demonstrates, e.g., that all lines in the circle are proportional. And yet he does not comprehend how it happens that such a simple figure has these properties. The field of understanding or of the understanding is thus in general much greater than the field of comprehension or of reason.

IX.

D) Logical perfection of cognition as to modality certainty – Concept of holding-to-be-true in general – Modi of holding-to-be-true: opining, believing and knowing – Conviction and persuasion – Reservation and deferral of a judgment – Provisional judgments – Prejudices, their sources and principal kinds

Truth is an *objective property* of cognition; the judgment through which 66 something is *represented* as true, the relation to an understanding and thus to a particular subject, is, *subjectively*, *holding-to-be-true*.[b]

[s] "*Einerleiheit.*"
[t] "*Verschiedenheit.*"
[u] "*erkennen.*"
[v] "*verstehen.*"
[w] "*concipiren.*"
[x] "Concipiren."
[y] "begreifen."
[z] "*einsehen.*"
[a] "*begreifen.*"
[b] "*Fürwahrhalten.*"

Holding-to-be-true is in general of two kinds, *certain* or *uncertain*. Certain holding-to-be-true, or *certainty*, is combined with consciousness of necessity, while uncertain holding-to-be-true, or *uncertainty*, is combined with consciousness of the contingency or the possibility of the opposite. The latter is again either *subjectively as well as objectively* insufficient, or *objectively insufficient* but *subjectively sufficient*. *The former* is called *opinion*,[c] *the latter* must be called *belief*.[d]

Accordingly, there are *three kinds or modi* of holding-to-be-true: *opining*,[e] *believing*,[f] and *knowing*.[g] Opining is *problematic* judging, believing is *assertoric* judging, and knowing is *apodeictic* judging. For what I merely opine I hold in judging, with consciousness, only to be problematic; what I believe I hold to be *assertoric*, but not as objectively necessary, only as subjectively so (holding only for me); what I *know*, finally, I hold to be *apodeictically certain*, i.e., to be universally and objectively necessary (holding for all), even granted that the object to which this certain holding-to-be-true relates should be a merely empirical truth. For this distinction in holding-to-be-true according to the three *modi* just named concerns only the *power of judgment* in regard to the subjective criteria for subsumption of a judgment under objective rules.

Thus, for example, our holding-to-be-true of immortality would be merely problematic in case we only act *as if we were immortal*, but it would be *assertoric in case we believe that we are immortal*, and it would be *apodeictic, finally, in case we all knew* that there is another life after this one.

There is an essential difference, then, between opining, believing, and knowing, which we wish to expound more exactly and in more detail here.

1. *Opining*. Opining, or holding-to-be-true based on a ground of cognition that is neither subjectively nor objectively sufficient, can be regarded as *provisional* judging (*sub conditione suspensiva ad interim*) that one cannot easily dispense with. One must first opine before one accepts and maintains, but in doing so must guard oneself against holding an opinion to be something more than mere opinion. For the most part, we begin with opining in all our cognizing. Sometimes we have an obscure premonition of truth, a thing seems to us to contain marks of truth; we *suspect* its truth even before we cognize it with determinate certainty. 67

But now where does mere opining really occur? Not in any sciences that contain cognitions *a priori*, hence neither in mathematics nor in metaphysics nor in morals, but merely in *empirical* cognitions: in physics, psychology, etc. For it is absurd *to opine a priori*. In fact, too, nothing could be more ridiculous than, e.g., only to opine in mathematics. Here, as in

[c] "*Meinung*."
[d] "*Glaube*."
[e] "*Meinen*."
[f] "*Glauben*."
[g] "*Wissen*."

metaphysics and in morals, the rule is *either to know or not to know*. Thus *matters of opinion* can only be objects of a cognition by experience, a cognition which is possible *in itself* but impossible *for us* in accordance with the restrictions and conditions of our faculty of experience and the attendant degree of this faculty that we possess. Thus, for example, the *ether* of modern physicists is a mere matter of opinion. For with this as with every opinion in general, whatever it may be, I see that the opposite could perhaps yet be proved. Thus my holding-to-be-true is here both objectively and subjectively insufficient, although it can become complete, considered in itself.

2. *Believing*. Believing, or holding-to-be-true based on a ground that is objectively insufficient but subjectively sufficient, relates to objects in regard to which we not only cannot know anything but also cannot opine anything, indeed, cannot even pretend there is probability, but can only be certain that it is not contradictory to think of such objects as one does think of them. What remains here is a *free* holding-to-be-true, which is necessary only in a practical respect given *a priori*, hence a holding-to-be-true of what I accept on *moral* grounds, and in such a way that I am certain that the *opposite* can never be proved.*

* Believing is not a special source of cognition. It is a kind of incomplete holding-to-be-true with consciousness, and if considered as restricted to a particular kind of object (which pertains only to believing), it is distinguished from opining not by its degree but rather by the relation that it has as cognition to action. Thus the businessman, for example, to strike a deal, needs not just to opine that there will be something to be gained thereby, but to believe it, i.e., to have his opinion be sufficient for an undertaking into the uncertain. Now we have theoretical cognitions (of the sensible) in which we can come to certainty, and in regard to everything that we can call human cognition this latter must be possible. We have just such certain cognitions, and in fact completely *a priori*, in practical laws, but these are grounded on a supersensible principle (of freedom) and in fact *in us ourselves*, as a principle of practical reason. But this practical reason is a causality in regard to a likewise supersensible object, *the highest good*, which is not possible through our faculty in the sensible world. Nature as object of our theoretical reason must nonetheless agree with this, for the *consequence* or *effect* of this idea is supposed to be met with in the world of the senses. Thus we ought to act so as to make this end actual.

68

Now in the world of the senses we also find traces of an *artistic wisdom*,[h] and we believe that the cause of the world also works with *moral* wisdom toward the highest good. This is a holding-to-be-true that is enough for action, i.e., a *belief*. Now we do not need this for action in accordance with moral laws, for *these* are given through practical reason alone, but we need to accept a highest wisdom as the object of our moral will, an object beyond the mere legitimacy of our actions, toward which we cannot avoid directing our ends. Although *objectively* this would not be a necessary relation of our faculty of choice, *subjectively* the highest good is still necessarily the object of a good (even of a human) will, and hence belief in its attainability is necessarily presupposed.

There is no mean between the acquisition of a cognition through experience (*a posteriori*) and through reason (*a priori*). But there is a mean between the cognition of an object and the mere presupposition of its possibility, namely, an empirical ground or a ground of reason for

[h] "*Kunstweisheit.*"

Matters of belief are thus I) not objects of *empirical* cognition. Hence so-called historical belief cannot really be called belief, either, and cannot be opposed as such to knowledge, since it can itself be knowledge. Holding-to-be-true based on testimony is not distinguished from holding-to-be-true through one's own experience either as to degree or as to kind. 68

II) [N]or [are they] objects of cognition by reason (cognition *a priori*), whether theoretical, e.g., in mathematics and metaphysics, or practical, in morals.

One can believe mathematical truths of reason on testimony, to be sure, partly because error here is not easily possible, partly, too, because it can easily be discovered, but one cannot know them in this way, of course. But

accepting this possibility in relation to a necessary extension of the field of possible objects beyond those whose cognition is possible for us. This necessity occurs only in regard to that in which the object is cognized as practical and, through reason, as practically necessary, for to accept something on behalf of the mere extension of theoretical cognition is always *contingent*. This practically necessary presupposition of an object is the presupposition of the possibility of the highest good as object of choice, hence also of the condition of this possibility (God, freedom, and immortality). This is a subjective necessity to accept the reality of the object for the sake of the necessary determination of the will. This is the *casus extraordinarius*, without which practical reason cannot maintain itself in regard to its necessary end, and here a *favor necessitatis* proves useful to it in its own judgment. It cannot acquire an object logically, but can only oppose what hinders it in the use of this idea, which belongs to it practically. 69

This belief is the necessity to accept the objective reality of a concept (of the highest good), i.e., the possibility of its object, as *a priori* necessary object of choice. If we look merely to actions, we do not need this belief. But if we wish to extend ourselves through actions to possession of the end that is thereby possible, then we must accept that this end is completely possible. Hence I can only say that *I* see myself necessitated through my end, in accordance with laws of freedom, to accept as possible a highest good in the world, but I *cannot necessitate anyone else through grounds* (the belief is free).

A belief of reason can never aim at theoretical cognition, then, for there objectively insufficient holding-to-be-true is merely opinion. It is merely a presupposition of reason for a subjective though absolutely necessary practical purpose. The sentiment toward moral laws leads to an object of choice, which [choice] is determinable through pure reason. The acceptance of the feasibility of this object, and hence of the reality of its cause, is a moral belief, or a free holding-to-be-true that is necessary for moral purposes for completion of one's ends.

Fides is really good faith[i] in the *pactum*, or subjective trust[j] in one another, that one will keep his promise to the other, with full faith and credit.[k] The first when the *pactum* is made, the second when it is to be concluded.

In accordance with the analogy, practical reason is, as it were, the *promisor*,[l] man the *promissee*,[m] the good expected from the deed the *promised*.[n]

[i] "Treue."
[j] "subjectives Zutrauen."
[k] "Treue und Glauben."
[l] "der *Promittent*."
[m] "der *Promissarius*."
[n] "das *Promissum*."

philosophical truths of reason may not even be believed, they must simply be known; for philosophy does not allow mere persuasion. And as for what concerns in particular the objects of practical cognition by reason in morals, rights and duties, there can just as little be mere belief in regard to them. One must *be fully certain* whether something is right or wrong, in accordance with duty or contrary to duty, allowed or not allowed. In moral things one cannot *risk anything* on the uncertain, one cannot decide anything *on the danger of trespass against the law*. Thus it is not enough for the judge, for example, that he *merely believe* that someone accused of a crime actually committed this crime. He must know it (juridically), or he acts unconscientiously.

70

III) The only objects that are matters of belief are those in which holding-to-be-true is necessarily free, i.e., is not determined through objective grounds of truth that are independent of the nature and the interest of the subject.

Thus also on account of its merely subjective grounds, believing yields no conviction that can be communicated and that commands universal agreement, like the conviction that comes from knowledge. Only *I myself* can be certain of the validity and unalterability of my practical belief, and my belief in the truth of a proposition or the actuality of a thing is what takes the place of a cognition only in relation to me without itself being a cognition.

He who does not accept what it is *impossible* to know but *morally necessary* to presuppose is morally *unbelieving*. At the basis of this kind of unbelief lies always a lack of moral interest. The greater a man's moral sentiment,[o] the firmer and more lively will be his belief in all that he feels himself necessitated to accept and to presuppose out of moral interest, for practically necessary purposes.

3. *Knowing*. Holding-to-be-true based on a ground of cognition that is objectively as well as subjectively sufficient, or certainty, is either *empirical* or *rational*, accordingly as it is grounded either on *experience* – one's own as well as that communicated by others – or on *reason*. This distinction relates, then, to the two sources from which the whole of our cognition is drawn: *experience* and *reason*.

Rational certainty, again, is either mathematical or philosophical certainty. The former is *intuitive*,[p] the latter *discursive*.

Mathematical certainty is also called *evidence*,[q] because an intuitive cognition is clearer than a discursive one. Although the two, mathematical and philosophical cognition of reason, are in themselves equally certain, the certainty is different in kind in them.

71

[o] "moralische Gesinnung."

[p] "*intuitiv*."

[q] "*Evidenz*."

Empirical certainty is original (*originarie empirica*) insofar as I become certain of something *from my own* experience, and *derived* (*derivative empirica*) insofar as I become certain through *someone else's* experience. The latter is also usually called *historical* certainty.

Rational certainty is distinguished from empirical certainty by the consciousness of *necessity* that is combined with it; hence it is *apodeictic* certainty, while empirical certainty is only *assertoric*. We are rationally certain of that into which we would have had insight *a priori* even without any experience. Hence our cognitions can concern objects of experience and the certainty concerning them can still be both empirical and rational at the same time, namely, insofar as we cognize an empirically certain proposition from principles *a priori*.

We cannot have rational certainty of everything, but where we can have it, we must put it before empirical certainty.

All certainty is either *unmediated* or *mediated*, i.e., it either requires a proof, or it is not capable of and does not require any proof. Even if so much in our cognition is certain only mediately, i.e., through a proof, there must still be something *indemonstrable* or *immediately certain*, and the whole of our cognition must proceed from *immediately certain* propositions.

The proofs on which any mediated or mediate certainty of a cognition rests are either *direct* proofs or *indirect*, i.e., *apagogical* ones. When I prove a truth from its grounds I provide a direct proof for it, and when I infer the truth of a proposition from the falsehood of its opposite I provide an indirect one. If this latter is to have validity, however, the propositions must be opposed *contradictorily* or *diametraliter*. For two propositions opposed only as contraries (*contrarie opposita*) can both be false. A proof that is the ground of mathematical certainty is called a *demonstration*, and that which is the ground of philosophical certainty is called an *acroamatic* proof. The essential parts of any proof in general are its *matter* and its *form*, or the *ground of proof* and the *consequentia*.

From [the German word for] *knowing*[r] comes [the German word for] *science*,[s] by which is to be understood the complex of a cognition as a *system*. It is opposed to *common* cognition, i.e., to the complex of a cognition as *mere aggregate*. A system rests on an idea of the whole, which precedes the parts, while with common cognition on the other hand, or a mere aggregate of cognitions, the parts precede the whole. There are *historical* sciences and sciences *of reason*. 72

In a science we often *know* only the *cognitions* but not the *things repre-*

[r] "*Wissen*."

[s] "*Wissenschaft*."

sented through them; hence there can be a science of that of which our cognition is not knowledge.

From the foregoing observations concerning the nature and the kinds of holding-to-be-true we can now draw the universal result that all our conviction is thus either *logical* or *practical*. When we know, namely, that we are free of all subjective grounds and yet the holding-to-be-true is sufficient, then we are *convinced*, and in fact *logically* convinced, or convinced on *objective* grounds (the object is certain).

Complete holding-to-be-true on subjective grounds, which in a *practical relation* hold just as much as objective grounds, is also conviction, though not logical but rather *practical* conviction (*I am certain*). And this practical conviction, or this *moral belief of reason*,[t] is often firmer than all knowledge. With knowledge one still listens to opposed grounds, but not with belief, because here it does not depend on objective grounds but on the moral interest of the subject.*

73 Opposed to conviction stands *persuasion*, a holding-to-be-true on insufficient grounds, of which one does not know whether they are merely subjective or also objective.

Persuasion often precedes conviction. We are conscious of many cognitions only in such a way that we cannot judge whether the grounds of our holding-to-be-true are objective or subjective. To be able to pass from mere persuasion to conviction, then, we must first of all *reflect*, i.e., see to which power of cognition a cognition belongs, and then *investigate*, i.e., test whether the grounds are sufficient or insufficient in regard to the object. Many remain with persuasion. Some come to reflection, few to investigation. He who knows what pertains to certainty will not easily mix up persuasion and conviction, and hence will not let himself be easily

* This practical conviction is thus *moral belief of reason*,[u] which alone can be called a belief in the proper sense and be opposed as such to knowledge and to all theoretical or logical conviction in general, because it can never elevate itself to knowledge. So-called historical belief, on the other hand, as already observed, may not be distinguished from knowledge, since as a kind of theoretical or logical holding-to-be-true it can itself be knowledge. We can accept an empirical truth on the testimony of others with the same certainty as if we had attained it through *facta* of our own experience. In the former kind of empirical knowledge there is something deceptive, but also with the latter kind.

Historical or mediate empirical knowledge rests on the reliability of testimony. The requirements of an irrefutable witness include *authenticity*[v] (competence[w]) and *integrity*.[x]

[t] "*moralische Vernunftglaube.*"
[u] "der *moralische Vernunftglaube.*"
[v] "*Authenticität.*"
[w] "Tüchtigkeit."
[x] "*Integrität.*"

persuaded, either. There is a ground of determination to approval, which is composed of objective and subjective grounds, and most men do not analyze[y] this mixed effect.

Although all persuasion is false as to form (*formaliter*), namely, insofar as an uncertain cognition appears here to be certain, it can nonetheless be true as to matter (*materialiter*). And thus it is distinct from opinion, too, which is an uncertain cognition, *insofar as it is held to be uncertain*.

The sufficiency of holding-to-be-true (in belief) can be put to the test by *betting* and by *taking oaths*. For the first *comparative* sufficiency of *objective* grounds is necessary, for the second *absolute* sufficiency, instead of which, if this is not available, a merely subjectively sufficient holding-to-be-true nevertheless holds.

It is customary to use the expressions, *to agree with someone's judgment, to reserve, to defer, or give up one's judgment*. These and similar expressions seem to indicate that there is something arbitrary[z] in our judging, in that we hold something to be true because we want to hold it to be true. The question arises, accordingly, *whether willing has an influence on our judgments*.

The will does not have any influence immediately on holding-to-be-true; this would be quite absurd. When it is said that *we gladly believe what we wish*, this means only our benign wishes, e.g., those of a father for his children. If the will had an immediate influence on our conviction concerning what we wish, we would constantly form for ourselves chimeras of a happy condition, and always hold them to be true, too. But the will cannot struggle *against* convincing proofs of truths that are contrary to its wishes and inclinations. 74

Insofar as the will either impels the understanding toward inquiry into a truth or holds it back therefrom, however, one must grant it an influence on the *use of the understanding*, and hence mediately on conviction itself, since this depends so much upon the use of the understanding.

As for what concerns in particular the *deferral* or *reservation* of our judgment, however, this consists in the resolution not to let a merely *provisional* judgment become *determining*. A provisional judgment is one in which I represent that while there are more grounds for the truth of a thing than against it, these grounds still do not suffice for a *determining* or *definitive* judgment, through which I simply decide for the truth. Provisional judging is thus merely problematic judging with consciousness.

Reservation of judgment can happen for two purposes: *either* in order to seek for the grounds of the determining judgment, *or* in order *never* to

[y] "setzen . . . nicht aus einander."

[z] "etwas Willkürliches."

judge. In the former case the deferral of judgment is called *critical* (*suspensio judicii indagatoria*), in the latter *skeptical* (*suspensio judicii sceptica*). For the skeptic refrains from all judgment, while the true philosopher merely suspends his judgment in case he does not yet have sufficient grounds for holding something to be true.

To suspend one's judgment *in accordance with maxims* requires a practiced faculty of judgment, which is found only in advancing age. In general, reservation of our approval is a very hard thing, partly because our understanding is so desirous of expanding itself and enriching itself with cognitions[a] by judging, partly because our inclination is always directed more toward certain things than toward others. He who has often had to retract his approval, however, and who has thereby become smart and 75 cautious, will not give it so quickly, out of fear of having subsequently to retract his judgment again. This *revocation* is always mortifying and causes one to mistrust all other cognitions.[b]

We observe here further that leaving one's judgment *in dubio* is something different from leaving it *in suspenso*. In the latter case I always have an interest in the thing, in the former it is not always in conformity with my end and interest to decide whether the thing is true or not.

Provisional judgments are quite necessary, indeed, indispensable, for the use of the understanding in all meditation and investigation. For they serve to guide the understanding in its inquiries and to provide it with various means thereto.

When we meditate concerning an object, we must always judge provisionally and, as it were, get the scent of the cognition that is partly to come to us through the meditation. And when we go after inventions or discoveries, we must always make a provisional plan, otherwise our thoughts go on at random. We can think of provisional judgments, therefore, as *maxims* for the investigation of a thing. We could also call them *anticipations*, because we anticipate our judgment of a thing even before we have the determining judgment. Judgments of this sort have their good use, then, and rules can even be given for how we ought to judge provisionally concerning an object.

Prejudices must be distinguished from provisional judgments.

Prejudices are provisional judgments *insofar as they are accepted as principles*. Every prejudice is to be regarded as a principle of erroneous judgments, and from prejudices arise not prejudices, but rather erroneous judgments. Hence one must distinguish the false cognition that arises from prejudice from its source, the prejudice itself. Thus the interpreta-

[a] "Kenntnissen."
[b] "Kenntnisse."

tion of dreams, for example, is not in itself a prejudice, but rather an error, which arises from the assumed universal rule that what happens a few times happens always, or is always to be held to be true. And this principle, under which the interpretation of dreams belongs, is a prejudice.

Sometimes prejudices are true provisional judgments; what is wrong is only that they hold for us as principles or as *determining* judgments. The 76 cause of this deception is to be sought in the fact that subjective grounds are falsely held to be objective, *due to a lack of reflection*, which must precede all judging. For even if we can accept some cognitions, e.g., immediately certain propositions, without *investigating* them, i.e., without examining the conditions of their truth, we still cannot and may not judge concerning anything without *reflecting*, i.e., without comparing a cognition with the power of cognition from which it is supposed to arise (sensibility or the understanding). If we accept judgments without this reflection, which is necessary even where no investigation occurs, then from this prejudices arise, or principles for judging based on subjective causes that are falsely held to be objective grounds.

The principal sources of prejudices are: *imitation*, *custom*, and *inclination*.

Imitation has a universal influence on our judgments, for there is a strong ground for holding to be true what others have put forth as true. Hence the prejudice that what the whole world does is right. As for what concerns prejudices that have arisen from custom, they can only be rooted out in the course of time, as the understanding, having little by little been held up and slowed down in judging by opposing grounds, is thereby gradually brought to an opposite mode of thought. If a prejudice of custom has arisen at the same time from imitation, however, then the man who possesses it is very hard to cure. The *inclination toward passive use of reason*, or *toward the mechanism of reason rather than toward its spontaneity under laws*, can also be called a prejudice of imitation.

Reason is an active principle, to be sure, which ought not to derive anything from the mere authority of others, nor even, when its *pure* use is concerned, from experience. But the indolence of many men is such that they prefer to follow in the footsteps of others rather than strain their own powers of understanding. Men of this sort can only be copies of others, and if everyone were of this kind, the world would remain eternally in one and the same place. Hence it is most necessary and important not to confine youths to mere imitation, as customarily happens.

There are so many things that contribute to accustoming us to the maxim of imitation, and thereby to making reason a fruitful ground of 77 prejudices. Such aids to imitation include:

1. *Formulas.*[c] These are rules whose expression serves as a model for imitation. They are uncommonly useful, by the way, for making complicated proposi-

[c] "*Formeln.*"

tions easier, and the most enlightened mind therefore seeks to discover such things.

2. *Sayings*,[d] whose expression has the great precision of pregnant meaning, so that it seems one could not capture the sense with fewer words. Pronouncements of this sort (*dicta*$_L$), which must always be borrowed from others whom one trusts to have a certain infallibility, serve, on account of this authority, as rules and as laws. The pronouncements of the bible are called sayings κατ' ἐξοχήν.[e]
3. *Sentences*,[f] i.e., propositions which recommend themselves and which, through the force of the thoughts lying within them, often retain their prestige through centuries as products of a mature power of judgment.
4. *Canones*. These are universal rules[g] that serve as foundations for the sciences and indicate something sublime and thought through. One can express them in a sententious way, too, so that they are the more pleasing.
5. *Proverbs*[h] (*proverbia*). These are popular rules of the common understanding, or expressions for signifying its popular judgments. Since provincial propositions of this sort serve only the common crowd as sentences and canons, they are not to be found among people of finer upbringing.

From the three universal sources of prejudices stated above, and from imitation in particular, many particular prejudices arise, among which we wish to touch here upon the following as the most common.

1. *Prejudices of prestige*. Among these are to be reckoned:

a) The *prejudice of the prestige of the person*. If, in things that rest on experience and on testimony, we build our cognition on the prestige of other persons, we are not thereby guilty of any prejudice; for in matters of 78 this kind, since we cannot experience everything ourselves and comprehend it with our own understanding, the prestige of the person must be the foundation of our judgments. When we make the prestige of others the ground of our holding-to-be-true in respect of cognitions of reason, however, we accept these cognitions merely on the basis of prejudice. For truths of reason hold anonymously; the question here is not, *Who* said it? but rather, *What* did he say? It does not matter at all whether a cognition is of noble descent; but the inclination toward the prestige of great men is nonetheless very common, partly because of the restrictedness of our own insight, partly due to a desire to imitate what is described to us as *great*. Added to this is the fact that the prestige of the person serves to flatter our vanity in an indirect way. Just as the subjects of a powerful despot are proud of the fact that they are all just treated *equally* by him, since to this

[d] "*Sprüche.*"
[e] par excellence.
[f] "*Sentenzen.*"
[g] "Lehrsprüche."
[h] "*Sprüchwörter.*"

extent the least can fancy himself the equal of the foremost, as they are both nothing over against the unrestricted power of their ruler, so too do the admirers of a great man judge themselves to be equal, insofar as the superiorities that they may have compared to one another are to be regarded as insignificant when considered against the merit of the great man. For more than one reason, therefore, highly prized great men contribute not a little to the inclination toward the prejudice of the prestige of the person.

b) The *prejudice of the prestige of the multitude*. It is principally the *crowd* who are inclined to this prejudice. For since they are unable to pass judgment on the merits, the capabilities, and the cognitions[i] of the person, they hold rather to the judgment of the multitude, under the presupposition that what everyone says must surely be true. This prejudice among the vulgar relates only to historical matters, however; in matters of religion, where they are themselves interested, they rely on the judgment of the learned.

It is in general noteworthy that the ignorant man has a prejudice for learnedness, while the learned man, on the other hand, has a prejudice for the common understanding.

If, after a learned man has nearly run the course of the sciences, he does not procure appropriate satisfaction from all his efforts, he finally acquires a mistrust of learnedness, especially in regard to those specula- 79 tions where the concepts cannot be made sensible, and whose foundations are unsettled, as, e.g., in metaphysics. Since he still believes, however, that it must be possible to find the key to certainty concerning certain objects somewhere, he seeks it now in the common understanding, after he had sought it so long in vain on the path of scientific inquiry.

But this hope is quite deceptive, for if the cultivated faculty of reason can accomplish nothing in respect to the cognition of certain things, the uncultivated faculty will certainly do so just as little. In metaphysics the appeal to pronouncements of the common understanding is completely inadmissible, because here no case can be exhibited *in concreto*. With morals, however, the situation is admittedly different. Not only can all rules in morals be given *in concreto*, but practical reason even manifests itself in general more clearly and more correctly through the organ of the common use of the understanding than through that of its speculative use. Hence the common understanding often judges more correctly concerning matters of morality and duty than does the speculative.

c) The *prejudice of the prestige of the age*. Here the prejudice of *antiquity* is one of the most significant. We do have reason to judge kindly of antiquity, to be sure, but that is only a ground for moderate respect, whose limits we all too often overstep by treating the ancients as treasurers of cognitions

[i] "Kenntnisse."

and of sciences, elevating the *relative* worth of their writings to an *absolute* one and trusting blindly to their guidance. To esteem the ancients so excessively is to lead the understanding back into its childhood and to neglect the use of one's own talent. We would also err greatly if we believed that everyone in antiquity had written as classically as those whose writings have come down to us. For since time sifts everything and preserves only what has an inner worth, we may assume, not without reason, that we only possess the best writings of the ancients.

There are several *causes* by which the prejudice of antiquity is created and sustained.

80 If something exceeds expectation as a universal rule, one initially *wonders* at this, and this wonder then often turns to admiration. This is the case with the ancients when one finds something in them that, in respect of the circumstances of time in which they lived, one did not seek. Another cause lies in the circumstance that acquaintance with the ancients and with antiquity proves learnedness and wide reading, which always brings respect, however common and insignificant in themselves the things may be that one has drawn from the study of the ancients. A third cause is the gratitude we owe to the ancients for the fact that they blazed the path toward many cognitions.[j] It seems fair to show them special esteem, whose measure we often overstep, however. A fourth cause, finally, is to be sought in a certain *envy* toward our contemporaries. He who cannot contend with the moderns extols the ancients at their expense, so that the moderns cannot raise themselves above him.

The opposite of this is the prejudice of *modernity*. Sometimes the prestige of antiquity and the prejudice in its favor declined, particularly at the beginning of this century, when the famous Fontenelle[17] took the side of the moderns. In the case of cognitions that are capable of extension, it is quite natural that we place more trust in the moderns than in the ancients. But this judgment has ground only as a mere provisional judgment. If we make it a determining one, it becomes a prejudice.

2. *Prejudices based on self-love* or *logical egoism*, in accordance with which one holds the agreement of one's own judgment with the judgments of others to be a dispensable criterion of truth. They are opposed to the prejudices of prestige, since they express themselves in a certain preference for that which is the product of one's own understanding, e.g., one's own system.

Is it good and advisable to let prejudices stand or even to encourage them? It
81 is astonishing that in our age such questions can still be advanced, especially that concerning the encouragement of prejudices. Encouraging some-

[j] "Kenntnissen."

one's prejudices amounts to deceiving someone with good intent. It would be permissible to leave prejudices untouched, for who can occupy himself with exposing and getting rid of every prejudice? But it is another question whether it would not be advisable to work toward rooting them out with all one's powers. Old and rooted prejudices are admittedly hard to battle, because they justify themselves and are, as it were, their own judges. People also seek to excuse letting prejudices stand on the ground that disadvantages would arise from rooting them out. But let us always accept these disadvantages; they will subsequently bring all the more good.

X.

Probability – Explanation of the probable – Distinction between probability and plausibility – Mathematical and philosophical probability – Doubt – Subjective and objective doubt – Skeptical, dogmatic, and critical mode of thought or method of philosophizing – Hypotheses

To the doctrine concerning the certainty of our cognition pertains also the doctrine of the cognition of the probable, which is to be regarded as an approximation to certainty.

By probability is to be understood a holding-to-be-true based on insufficient grounds which have, however, a greater relation to the sufficient grounds than do the grounds of the opposite. By this explanation we distinguish probability[k] (*probabilitas*) from mere *plausibility*[l] (*verisimilitudo*), a holding-to-be-true based on insufficient grounds insofar as these are greater than the grounds of the opposite.

The ground of holding-to-be-true, that is, can be either *objectively* or *subjectively* greater than that of the opposite. Which of the two it is one can only discover by comparing the grounds of the holding-to-be-true with the sufficient grounds; for then the grounds of the holding-to-be-true are greater than the grounds of the opposite *can be*. With probability, then, the ground of the holding-to-be-true is *objectively valid*, while with mere plausibility it is only *subjectively valid*. Plausibility is merely quantity of persuasion, probability is an approximation to certainty. With probability there must always exist a standard in accordance with which I can estimate it. This standard is *certainty*. For since I am supposed to compare the insufficient grounds with the sufficient ones, I must know how much pertains to certainty. Such a standard is lacking, however, with mere plausibility, since here I do not compare the insufficient grounds with the sufficient ones, but only with the grounds of the opposite.

82

"Wahrscheinlichkeit."

"*Scheinbarkeit.*"

The moments of probability can be either *homogeneous* or *heterogeneous*. If they are homogeneous, as in mathematical cognition, then they must be *enumerated*;[m] if they are heterogeneous, as in philosophical[n] cognition, then they must be *weighed*,[o] i.e., evaluated according to their effect, and this according to the overpowering of obstacles in the mind. The latter give no relation to certainty, but only a relation of one plausibility to another. From this it follows that only the mathematician can determine the relation of insufficient grounds to the sufficient ground; the philosopher must content himself with plausibility, a holding-to-be-true that is sufficient merely subjectively and practically. For in philosophical cognition probability cannot be estimated, on account of the heterogeneity of the grounds; here the weights are not all stamped, so to speak. Hence it is only of *mathematical* probability that one can really say *that it is more than half of certainty*.

There has been much talk of a logic of probability (*logica probabilium*). But this is not possible; for if the relation of the insufficient grounds to the sufficient ground cannot be weighed mathematically, then rules do not help at all. Also, one cannot give any universal rules of probability, except that error will not occur on *one* side, but there must rather be a ground of agreement in the object; likewise, that when there are as *many* errors, and errors in equal *degree*, on two *opposed* sides, the truth is in the *middle*.

---

83 *Doubt* is an opposing ground or a mere obstacle to holding-to-be-true, which can be considered either *subjectively* or *objectively*. Doubt is sometimes taken *subjectively*, namely, as a condition of an undecided mind, and *objectively* as cognition of the insufficiency of the grounds for holding-to-be-true. In the latter respect it is called an *objection*, that is, an objective ground for holding to be false a cognition that is held to be true.

A *scruple* is a ground opposed to holding-to-be-true that is merely subjectively valid. In the case of a scruple one does not know whether the obstacle to holding-to-be-true is grounded objectively or only subjectively, e.g., only in inclination, in custom, etc. One doubts without being able to explain the ground of the doubt distinctly and determinately and without being able to have insight into whether this ground lies in the object itself or only in the subject. Now if it is to be possible to remove such scruples, then they must be raised to the distinctness and determinateness of an objection. For it is through objections that certainty is brought to distinctness and completeness, and no one can be certain of a thing unless opposing grounds have been stirred up, through which it can

[m] "*numerirt*."
[n] Ak, "*philosophischen*"; 1st ed., "philosophischen."
[o] "*ponderirt*."

be determined how far one still is from certainty or how close[p] one is to it. Also, it is not enough merely to answer each doubt, one must also *resolve* it, that is, make comprehensible how the scruple has arisen. If this does not happen, the doubt is only *turned back*, but not *removed*, the seed of the doubt still remains. In many cases, of course, we do not know whether the obstacle to holding-to-be-true has only subjective grounds in us or objective ones, and hence we cannot remove the scruple by exposing the illusion, since we cannot always compare our cognitions with the object but often only with each other. It is therefore modesty to expound one's objections only as doubts.

There is a principle of doubting which consists in the maxim that cognitions are to be treated with the intention of making them uncertain and showing the impossibility of attaining certainty. This method of philosophizing is the *skeptical* mode of thought, or *skepticism*. It is opposed to the dogmatic mode of thought, or *dogmatism*, which is a blind trust in the faculty of reason to expand itself *a priori* through mere concepts, without critique, merely on account of seeming success. 84

Both methods are mistaken if they become universal. For there are many cognitions[q] in regard to which we cannot proceed dogmatically, and on the other side skepticism, by renouncing all assertoric cognition,[r] ruins all our efforts at attaining possession of a cognition of the *certain*.

As harmful as this skepticism is, though, the *skeptical* method is just as useful and purposeful, provided one understands nothing more by this than the way of treating something as uncertain and of bringing it to the highest uncertainty, in the hope of getting on the trail of truth in this way. This method is thus really a mere suspension of judging. It is quite useful to the *critical* procedure, by which is to be understood that method of philosophizing in accordance with which one investigates the *sources* of his claims or objections and the grounds on which these rest, a method which gives hope of attaining certainty.

In mathematics and physics skepticism does not occur. The only cognition that can occasion it is that which is neither mathematical nor empirical, *purely philosophical* cognition. Absolute skepticism pronounces everything to be illusion. Hence it distinguishes illusion from truth and must therefore have a mark of the distinction after all, and consequently must presuppose a cognition of truth, whereby it contradicts itself.

---

[p] Reading "wie nahe man" for "wie nahe man noch," with Hinske (KI, xlii).
[q] "Kenntnisse."
[r] "behauptende Erkenntniß."

Concerning probability, we observed above that it is merely an approximation to certainty. Now this is especially the case with *hypotheses*, through which we can never attain apodeictic certainty in our cognition, but always only a greater or lesser degree of probability.

A *hypothesis* is a *holding-to-be-true of the judgment of the truth of a ground for the sake of its sufficiency for given consequences*,[18] or more briefly, *the holding-to-be-true of a presupposition as a ground.*

85 All holding-to-be-true in hypotheses is thus grounded on the fact that the presupposition, as ground, is sufficient to explain other cognitions as consequences. For we infer here from the truth of the consequence to the truth of the ground. But since this mode of inference, as already observed above, yields a sufficient criterion of truth and can lead to apodeictic certainty only when *all possible* consequences of an assumed ground are true, it is clear from this that since we can never determine all possible consequences, hypotheses always remain hypotheses, that is, presuppositions, whose complete certainty we can never attain. In spite of this, the probability of a hypothesis can grow and rise to an *analogue* of certainty, namely, when all the consequences *that have as yet occurred to us* can be explained from the presupposed ground. For in such a case there is no reason why we should not assume that we will be able to explain all possible consequences thereby. Hence in this case we give ourselves over to the hypothesis as if it were fully certain, although it is so only *through induction*.

And in every hypothesis something must be apodeictically certain, too, namely,

1. the *possibility* of the *presupposition itself*. If, for example, to explain earthquakes and volcanoes we assume a subterranean fire, then such a fire must be possible, if not as a flaming body, yet as a hot one. For the sake of certain other appearances, however, to make the earth out to be an animal, in which the circulation of the inner fluids produces warmth, is to put forth a mere invention and not a hypothesis. For realities may be made up, but not possibilities; these must be certain.

2. The *consequentia*. From the assumed ground the consequences must flow correctly; otherwise the hypothesis becomes a mere chimera.

3. The *unity*. It is an essential requirement of a hypothesis that it be only one and that it not need any subsidiary hypotheses for its support. If, in the case of a hypothesis, we have to have several others to help, then it thereby loses very much of its probability. For the more consequences that may be derived from a hypothesis, the more probable it is, the fewer, the more improbable. Thus *Tycho Brahe's* hypothesis, for example, did not suffice for the explanation of many appearances; hence he assumed several new hypotheses to complete it.[19] Now here it is to be surmised that the 86 assumed hypothesis cannot be the real ground. The Copernican system, on the other hand, is an hypothesis from which everything can be ex-

lained that ought to be explained therefrom, *so far as it has yet occurred to s*. Here we do not need any *subsidiary hypotheses* (*hypotheses subsidiarias*).

There are sciences that do not allow any hypotheses, as, for example, nathematics and metaphysics. But in the doctrine of nature they are iseful and indispensable.

APPENDIX

Of the distinction between theoretical and practical cognition

A cognition is called *practical* as opposed to *theoretical*, but also as opposed o *speculative* cognition.

Practical cognitions are, namely, either

1. *imperatives*, and are to this extent opposed to *theoretical* cognitions; or they contain
2. the *grounds for possible imperatives* and are to this extent opposed to *speculative* cognitions.

By an *imperative* is to be understood in general every proposition that expresses a possible free action, whereby a certain end is to be made real. Every cognition that contains imperatives is practical, then, and is to be called practical in opposition to *theoretical* cognition. For theoretical cognitions are ones that express not what ought to be but rather what is, hence they have as their object *not an acting*[s] but rather a *being*.[t]

On the other hand, if we oppose practical to *speculative* cognitions, then they can also be *theoretical, provided only that imperatives can be derived from them*. Considered in this respect they are then practical as to *content* (*in potentia*) or *objectively*. By speculative cognitions we understand, namely, ones from which no rules for proceeding can be derived, or which contain no grounds for possible imperatives. There is a multitude of such speculative propositions in *theology*, for example. Speculative cognitions of this sort are always theoretical, then, but it is not the case, conversely, that every theoretical cognition is speculative; it can also be at the same time practical, considered in another respect.

87

In the end everything comes down to the *practical*, and the practical worth of our cognition consists in this tendency of everything theoretical and all speculation in regard to its use. This worth is *unconditioned*, however, only if the *end* toward which the practical use of the cognition is directed is an *unconditioned* end. The sole, unconditioned, and final end (ultimate end) to which all practical use of our cognition must finally relate is *morality*, which on this account we may also call the practical *without qualification or the absolutely practical*. And that part of philosophy

"*kein Handeln*."
"ein *Sein*."

which has morality as its object would accordingly have to be called practical philosophy κατ' ἐξοχήν;[a] although every other philosophical science always has its *practical* part, i.e., can contain a directive from the theories advanced for their practical use for the realization of certain ends.

[a] par excellence.

I. Universal doctrine of elements

FIRST SECTION

91

Of concepts

§1

The concept in general and its distinction from intuition

All cognitions, that is, all representations related with consciousness to an object, are either *intuitions* or *concepts*. An intuition is a *singular*[v] representation (*repraesentatio singularis*), a concept a universal (*repraesentatio per notas communes*) or *reflected*[w] representation (*repraesentatio discursiva*).

Cognition through concepts is called *thought* (*cognitio discursiva*).

Note 1. A concept is opposed to intuition, for it is a universal representation, or a representation of what is common to several objects, hence a representation *insofar as it can be contained in various ones*.[20]

2. It is a mere tautology to speak of universal or common[x] concepts – a mistake that is grounded in an incorrect division of concepts into *universal*, *particular*, and *singular*. Concepts themselves cannot be so divided, but only *their use*.

§2

Matter and form of concepts

With every concept we are to distinguish *matter* and *form*. The matter of concepts is the *object*, their form *universality*.

v "*einzelne*."

w "*reflectirte*."

x "gemeinsamen."

92

§3

Empirical and pure concept

A concept is either an *empirical* or a *pure* concept (*vel empiricus vel intellectualis*). A *pure* concept is one that is not abstracted[y] from experience but arises rather from the understanding even *as to content*.

An *idea* is a concept of reason whose object simply cannot be met with in experience.

Note 1. An empirical concept arises from the senses through comparison of objects of experience and attains through the understanding merely the form of universality. The reality of these concepts rests on actual experience, from which, as to their content, they are drawn.[z] But whether there are *pure concepts of the understanding* (*conceptus puri*), which, as such, arise merely from the understanding, independently of all experience, must be investigated by metaphysics.

2. Concepts of reason, or ideas, simply cannot lead to actual objects, because these latter must all be contained in a possible experience. But they serve to lead the understanding by means of reason in regard to experience and to the use of its rules in the greatest perfection, or also to show that not all possible things are objects of experience, and that the principles of the possibility of the latter do not hold of things in themselves, nor of objects of experience as things in themselves.

An idea contains the *archetype* for the use of the understanding, e.g., the idea of the *world whole*, which idea must necessarily be, *not as constitutive* principle for the empirical use of the understanding, but as *regulative* principle for the sake of the thoroughgoing connection[a] of our empirical use of the understanding. Thus it is to be regarded as a necessary basic concept, either for *objectively completing* the understanding's actions of subordination or for regarding them as *unlimited*. – The idea *cannot* be attained *by composition*, either, for the whole is prior to the part. There are ideas, however, to which an approximation occurs. This is the case with *mathematical* ideas, or ideas of the *mathematical production of a whole*, which differ essentially from *dynamical* ideas, which are completely *heterogeneous* from all concrete concepts, because the whole is different from concrete concepts not as to quantity (as with the mathematical ideas) but rather as to *kind*.

93

One cannot provide objective reality for any theoretical idea, or prove it, except for the idea of freedom, because this is the condition of the *moral*

[y] "abgezogen."
[z] "geschöpft."
[a] "des durchgängigen Zusammenhanges."

law, whose reality is an axiom. The reality of the idea of *God* can only be proved by means of this idea, and hence only with a *practical* purpose, *i.e., to act as if there is a God*, and hence only *for* this purpose.

In all sciences, above all in those of reason, the idea of the science is its universal *abstract* or *outline*, hence the extension of all the cognitions[b] that belong to it. Such an idea of the whole – the first thing one has to look to in a science, and which one has to seek – is *architectonic*, as, e.g., the idea of jurisprudence.[c]

Most men lack the idea of humanity, the idea of a perfect republic, of a happy life, etc. Many men have no idea of what they want, hence they proceed according to instinct and authority.

§4

Concepts that are given (a priori *or* a posteriori) *and concepts that are made*

All concepts, *as to matter*, are either *given* (*conceptus dati*) or *made* (*conceptus factitii*). The former are given either *a priori* or *a posteriori*.

All concepts that are given empirically or *a posteriori* are called *concepts of experience*,[d] all that are given *a priori* are called *notions*.

Note. The form of a concept, as that of a discursive representation, is always made.

§5

Logical origin of concepts

The origin of concepts as to *mere form* rests on reflection and on abstraction from the difference among things that are signified by a certain representation. And thus arises here the question: *Which acts of the understanding constitute a concept?* or what is the same, *Which are involved in the generation of a concept out of given representations?*

Note 1. Since universal logic abstracts from all content of cognition through concepts, or from all matter of thought, it can consider a concept only in respect of its form, i.e., only *subjectively*; not how it determines an object through a mark, but only how it can be related to several objects. Hence 94

[b] "Kenntnisse."

[c] "Rechtswissenschaft."

[d] "*Erfahrungsbegriffe.*"

universal logic does not have to investigate the *source* of concepts, not how concepts *arise as representations*, but merely *how given representations become concepts in thought*; these concepts, moreover, may contain something that is derived from experience, or something invented, or borrowed from the nature of the understanding. – This *logical* origin of concepts – the origin as to their mere form – consists in reflection, whereby a representation common to several objects (*conceptus communis*) arises, as that form which is required for the power of judgment. Thus in logic *only the difference in reflection* in concepts is considered.

2. The origin of concepts in regard to their *matter*, according to which a concept is either *empirical* or *arbitrary* or *intellectual*, is considered in metaphysics.

§6

Logical Actus *of comparison, reflection, and abstraction*

The logical *actus* of the understanding, through which concepts are generated as to their form, are:

1. *comparison*[e] of representations among one another in relation to the unity of consciousness;
2. *reflection*[f] as to how various representations can be conceived in one consciousness; and finally
3. *abstraction*[g] of everything else in which the given representations differ.

Note 1. To make concepts out of representations one must thus be able *to compare, to reflect*, and *to abstract*, for these three logical operations of the understanding are the essential and universal conditions for generation of every concept whatsoever. I see, e.g., a spruce, a willow, and a linden. By first comparing these objects with one another I note that they are different from one another in regard to the trunk, the branches, the leaves, etc.; but next I reflect on that which they have in common among themselves, trunk, branches, and leaves themselves, and I abstract from the quantity, the figure, etc., of these; thus I acquire a concept of a tree.

95

2. The expression *abstraction* is not always used correctly in logic. We must not speak of abstracting something (*abstrahere aliquid*), but rather of abstracting *from something* (*abstrahere ab aliquo*). With a scarlet cloth, for example, if I think only of the red color, then I abstract from the cloth; if I abstract from this too and think the scarlet as a material stuff in general, then I abstract from still more determinations, and my concept has in this

[e] "*Comparation*, d.i., die Vergleichung."
[f] "*Reflexion*, d.i. die Überlegung."
[g] "*Abstraction* oder die Absonderung."

way become still more abstract. For the more the differences among things that are left out of a concept, or the more the determinations from which we abstract in that concept, the more abstract the concept is. Abstract concepts, therefore, should really be called *abstracting* concepts (*conceptus abstrahentes*), i.e., ones in which several abstractions occur. Thus the concept *body* is really not an abstract concept, for I cannot abstract from body itself, else I would not have the concept of it. But I must of course abstract from the size, the color, the hardness or fluidity, in short, from all the special determinations of particular bodies. The *most abstract* concept is the one that has nothing in common with any distinct from itself. This is the concept of *something*, for that which is different from it is *nothing*, and it thus has nothing in common with something.

3. Abstraction is only the *negative* condition under which universal representations can be generated, the *positive* condition is comparison and reflection. For no concept *comes to be* through abstraction; abstraction only perfects it and encloses it in its determinate limits.

§7

Content and extension of concepts

Every concept, *as partial concept*, is contained in the representation of things; as *ground of cognition*, *i.e.*, *as mark*,[h] these things are contained *under* it. In the former respect every concept has a *content*, in the other an *extension*.

The content and extension of a concept stand in inverse relation to one another. The more a concept contains *under* itself, namely, the less it contains *in* itself, and conversely.

Note. The universality or universal validity of a concept does not rest on the fact that the concept is a *partial concept*, but rather on the fact that it is a *ground of cognition*.

§8

96

Quantity of the extension of concepts

The more the things that stand under a concept and can be thought through it, the greater is its extension or *sphere*.

---

[h] Ak, "*d.i.* als *Merkmal*"; 1st ed., "*d.i. als Merkmal.*"

Note. As one says of a *ground* in general that it contains the *consequence* under itself, so can one also say of the concept that as *ground of cognition* it contains all those things under itself from which it has been abstracted, e.g., the concept of metal contains under itself gold, silver, copper, etc. For since every concept, as a universally valid representation, contains that which is common to several representations of various things, all these things, which are to this extent contained under it, can be represented through it. And it is just this that constitutes the *usefulness* of a concept. The more the things that can be represented through a concept, the greater is its sphere. Thus the concept *body*, for example, has a greater extension than the concept *metal.*

§9

Higher and lower concepts

Concepts are called *higher* (*conceptus superiores*) insofar as they have other concepts under themselves, which, in relation to them, are called *lower* concepts. A mark of a mark – a *remote* mark – is a higher concept, the concept in relation to a remote mark is a lower one.

Note. Since higher and lower concepts are so called only *relatively* (*respective*$_{L}$), one and the same concept can, in various relations, be simultaneously a higher one and a lower one. Thus the concept *man* is a higher one in relation to the concept *Negro*,[i] but a lower one in relation to the concept *animal.*

§10

Genus and species

The higher concept, in respect to its lower one, is called genus,[j] the lower concept in regard to its higher one *species.*[k]

97 Like higher and lower concepts, *genus* and *species concepts* are distinguished not as to their nature, then, but only in regard to their relation to one another (*termini a quo* or *ad quod*[l]) in logical subordination.

[i] Ak, "Neger"; 1st ed., "Pferd."
[j] "*Gattung* (*genus*)."
[k] "*Art* (*species*)."
[l] terms from which [or] to which.

§11

Highest genus and lowest species

The *highest* genus is that which is not a species (*genus summum non est species*), just as the *lowest* species is that which is not a genus (*species, quae non est genus, est infima*).

In consequence of the law of continuity, however, there cannot be either a *lowest* or a *next* species.

Note. If we think of a series of several concepts subordinated to one another, e.g., iron, metal, body, substance, thing, then here we can attain ever higher genera – for every *species* is always to be considered at the same time as *genus* in regard to its lower concept, e.g., the concept *learned man* in regard to the concept *philosopher* – until we finally come to a *genus* that cannot in turn be a *species*. And we must finally be able to attain such a one, because in the end there must be a highest concept (*conceptus summus*), from which, as such, nothing further may be abstracted without the whole concept disappearing. – But in the series of species and genera there is no lowest concept (*conceptus infimus*) or lowest species, under which no other would be contained, because such a one cannot possibly be determined. For even if we have a concept that we apply *immediately* to individuals, there can still be specific differences in regard to it, which we either do not note, or which we disregard. Only *comparatively for use* are there lowest concepts, which have attained this significance,[m] as it were, through convention, insofar as one has agreed not to go deeper here.

In respect to the determination of species and genus concepts, then, the following universal law holds: *There is a genus that cannot in turn be a species, but there is no species that should not be able in turn to be a genus.*

§12

98

Broader and narrower concept – Convertible concepts

The higher concept is also called a *broader* concept, the lower concept a *narrower* one.

Concepts that have one and the same sphere are called *convertible concepts*[n] (*conceptus reciproci*).

[m] "Bedeutung."

[n] "*Wechselbegriffe.*"

§13

Relation of the lower concept to the higher, of the broader to the narrower

The lower concept is not contained *in* the higher, for it contains *more* in itself than does the higher one; it is contained *under* it, however, because the higher contains the ground of cognition of the lower.

Furthermore, one concept is not *broader* than another because it contains *more* under itself – for one cannot know that – but rather insofar as it contains under itself the *other concept* and *besides this still more.*

§14

Universal rules in respect of the subordination of concepts

In regard to the logical extension of concepts, the following universal rules hold:

1. What belongs to or contradicts higher concepts also belongs to or contradicts all lower concepts that are contained under those higher ones; and
2. conversely: What belongs to or contradicts *all* lower concepts also belongs to or contradicts their higher concept.

Note. Because that in which things agree flows from their *universal* properties, and that in which they are different from one another flows from their *particular* properties, one cannot infer that what belongs to or contradicts *one* lower concept also belongs to or contradicts *other* lower concepts, which belong with it to one higher concept. Thus one cannot infer, e.g., that what does not belong to man does not belong to angels either.

99

§15

Conditions for higher and lower concepts to arise: Logical abstraction and logical determination

Through continued logical abstraction higher and higher concepts arise, just as through continued logical determination, on the other hand, lower and lower concepts arise. The greatest possible abstraction yields the highest or most abstract concept – that from which no determination can be further thought away. The highest, completed determination would yield a *thoroughly determinate* concept (*conceptus omnimode determinatus*), i.e., one to which no further determination might be added in thought.

Note. Since only individual things,[o] or individuals,[p] are thoroughly determinate, there can be thoroughly determinate cognitions only as *intuitions*, but not *as concepts*; in regard to the latter, logical determination can never be regarded as completed (§ 11, Note).

§16

Use of concepts in abstracto *and* in concreto

Every concept can be used *universally* or *particularly* (*in abstracto* or *in concreto*). The lower concept is used *in abstracto* in regard to its higher one, the higher concept *in concreto* in regard to its lower one.

Note 1. Thus the expressions *abstract* and *concrete* relate not to concepts in themselves – for every concept is an abstract concept – but rather only to their *use*. And this use can in turn have various degrees, accordingly as one treats a concept more or less abstractly or concretely, i.e., as one either leaves aside or adds more or fewer determinations. Through abstract use a concept comes closer to the highest genus, through concrete use, on the other hand, to the individual. 100

2. Which use of concepts, the abstract or the concrete, has an advantage over the other? Nothing can be decided about this. The worth of the one is not to be valued less than the worth of the other. Through very abstract concepts we cognize *little* in *many* things, through very concrete concepts we cognize *much* in *few* things; what we win on the one side, then, we lose again on the other. A concept that has a large sphere is very useful insofar as one can apply it to many things; but in return for that, there is that much less contained in it. In the concept *substance*, for example, I do not think as much as in the concept *chalk*.

3. The *art of popularity* consists in finding the relation between representation *in abstracto* and *in concreto* in the same cognition, hence between concepts and their exhibition, through which the maximum of cognition is achieved, both as to extension and as to content.

SECOND SECTION

101

Of judgments

§17

Definition[q] *of a judgment in general*

A judgment is the representation of the unity of the consciousness of various representations, or the representation of their relation insofar as they constitute a concept.

[o] "einzelne Dinge."

[p] "Individuen."

[q] "*Erklärung.*"

§18

Matter and form of judgments

Matter and *form* belong to every judgment as essential constituents of it. The *matter* of the judgment consists in the given representations that are combined in the unity of consciousness in the judgment, the *form* in the determination of the way that the various representations belong, as such, to one consciousness.

§19

Object of logical reflection the mere form of judgments

Since logic abstracts from all real or objective difference of cognition, it can occupy itself as little with the matter of judgments as with the content of concepts. Thus it has only the difference among judgments in regard to their mere form to take into consideration.

102

§20

Logical forms of judgments: Quantity, quality, relation, and modality

The distinctions among judgments in respect of their form may be traced back to the four principal moments of *quantity*, *quality*, *relation*, and *modality*, in regard to which just as many different kinds of judgments are determined.

§21

Quantity of judgments: Universal, particular, singular

As to quantity, judgments are either *universal* or *particular* or *singular*, accordingly as the subject is either *wholly in*cluded in or *ex*cluded from the notion of the predicate or is only *in part in*cluded in or *ex*cluded from it. In the *universal* judgment, the sphere of one concept is wholly enclosed within the sphere of another; in the *particular*, a part of the former is enclosed under the sphere of the other; and in the *singular* judgment, finally, a concept that has no sphere at all is enclosed, merely as part then, under the sphere of another.

Note 1. As to logical form, singular judgments are to be assessed as like universal ones in use, for in both the predicate holds of the subject without exception. In the singular proposition, Caius is mortal, for example, there can just as little be an exception as in the universal one, All men are mortal. For there is only one Caius.

2. In respect of the universality[r] of a cognition, there exists a real distinction between *general*[s] and *universal*[t] propositions, which of course does not have to do with logic, however. *General* propositions, namely, are those that contain merely something of the universal regarding certain objects, and consequently do not contain sufficient conditions of subsumption, e.g., the proposition that one must make proofs thorough. *Universal*[u] propositions are those that maintain something universally[v] of an object.

3. Universal rules are either *analytically* or *synthetically* universal. The *former* abstract from differences, the *latter* attend to distinctions and consequently determine in regard to them too. The more simply an object is thought, the more possible is analytic universality in consequence of a concept. 103

4. If we cannot have insight into universal propositions in their universality without cognizing[w] them *in concreto*, then they cannot serve as a standard and hence cannot hold *heuristically* in application, but are only assignments to investigate the universal grounds for that with which we first became acquainted in particular cases. For example, the proposition, *He who has no interest in lying and who knows the truth will speak the truth*; we cannot have insight into this proposition in its universality, because we are acquainted with the restriction to the condition of the disinterested – namely, that men can lie out of interest, which comes because they do not hold fast to morality – only through experience. An observation that teaches us the weakness of human nature.

5. Of *particular judgments* it is to be noted that if it is to be possible to have insight into them through reason, and hence for them to have a rational, not merely intellectual (abstracted) form, then the subject must be a broader concept (*conceptus latior*) than the predicate. Let the predicate always = ○, the subject □, then

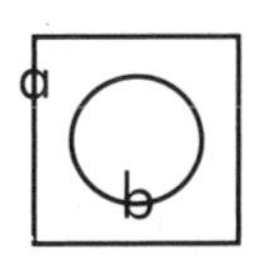

is a particular judgment, for some of what belongs under *a* is *b*, some not *b* – that follows from reason. But let it be

[r] "Allgemeinheit."
[s] "*generalen*."
[t] "*universalen*."
[u] "*Universale*."
[v] "allgemein."
[w] "kennen."

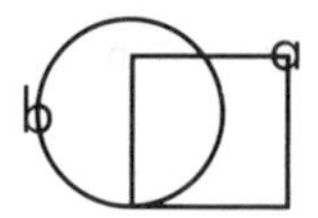

then at least all *a* can be contained under *b*, if it is smaller, but not if it is greater, hence it is particular only by accident.

§22

Quality of judgments: Affirmative, negative, infinite

As to *quality*, judgments are either *affirmative* or *negative* or *infinite*. In the *affirmative* judgment the subject is thought *under* the sphere of a predicate, in the *negative* it is posited *outside* the sphere of the latter, and in the *infinite* 104 it is posited in the sphere of a concept that lies outside the sphere of another.

Note 1. The infinite judgment indicates not merely that a subject is not contained under the sphere of a predicate, but that it lies somewhere in the infinite sphere outside its sphere; consequently this judgment represents the sphere of the predicate as restricted.

Everything possible is either *A* or *non A*. If I say, then, something is *non A*, e.g., the human soul is *non-mortal*, some men are non-learned, etc., then this is an infinite judgment. For it is not thereby determined, concerning the finite sphere *A*, under which *concept* the object belongs, but merely that it belongs in the sphere outside *A*, which is really no sphere at all but only *a sphere's sharing of a limit with the infinite*,[x] or the *limiting itself*.[y] Now although exclusion is a negation, the restriction[z] of a concept is still a positive act. Therefore limits[a] are positive concepts of restricted[b] objects.

2. According to the principle of the excluded middle[c] (*exclusi tertii*), the sphere of one concept relative to another is either exclusive or inclusive. Now since logic has to do merely with the form of judgment, not with concepts as to their content, the distinction of infinite from negative judgments is not proper to this science.

3. In negative judgments the negation always affects the copula; in infinite ones it is not the copula but rather the predicate that is affected, which may best be expressed in Latin.

[x] "*die Angrenzung einer Sphäre an das Unendliche.*"
[y] "die *Begrenzung selbst.*"
[z] "Beschränkung."
[a] "Grenzen."
[b] "beschränkter."
[c] "Principium der Ausschließung jedes Dritten."

§23

Relation of judgments: Categorical, hypothetical, disjunctive

As to relation, judgments are either *categorical* or *hypothetical* or *disjunctive*. The given representations in judgment are subordinated one to another for the unity of consciousness, namely, either as *predicate* to *subject*, or as *consequence* to *ground*, or as *member of the division* to the *divided concept*. Through the first relation *categorical* judgments are determined, through the second *hypothetical*, and through the third *disjunctive*.

§24

105

Categorical judgments

In categorical judgments, subject and predicate constitute their matter; the form, through which the relation (of agreement or of opposition) between subject and predicate is determined and expressed, is called the *copula*$_{\text{L}}$.

Note. Categorical judgments constitute the matter of the remaining judgments, to be sure, but one must not on this account believe, as several logicians do, that both hypothetical and disjunctive judgments are nothing more than various clothings of categoricals and hence may be wholly traced back to these latter. All three kinds of judgments rest on essentially different logical functions of the understanding and must therefore be considered according to their specific difference.

§25

Hypothetical judgments

The matter of *hypothetical* judgments consists of two judgments that are connected with one another as ground and consequence. One of these judgments, which contains the ground, is the *antecedent*[d] (*antecedens, prius*), the other, which is related to it as consequence, is the *consequent*[e] (*consequens, posterius*), and the representation of this kind of connection of two judgments to one another for the unity of consciousness is called the *consequentia*, which constitutes the *form* of hypothetical judgments.

---

[d] "*Vordersatz.*"
[e] "*Nachsatz.*"

Note 1. What the *copula*$_L$ is for categorical judgments, then, the *consequentia* is for hypotheticals – their form.

2. Some believe it is easy to transform a hypothetical proposition into a categorical. But this will not do, because the two are wholly different from one another as to their nature. In categorical judgments nothing is problematic, rather, everything is assertoric, but in hypotheticals only the *consequentia* is assertoric. In the latter I can thus connect two false judgments with one another, for here it is only a matter of the correctness of the connection – the form of the *consequentia*, on which the logical truth of these judgments rests. There is an essential difference between the two propositions, All bodies are divisible, and, If all bodies are composite, then they are divisible. In the former proposition I maintain the thing directly, in the latter only under a condition expressed problematically.

106

§26

Modes of connection in hypothetical judgments: modus ponens *and* modus tollens

The form of the connection in hypothetical judgments is of two kinds: the positing[f] (*modus ponens*) and the denying[g] (*modus tollens*).

1. If the ground (*antecedens*) is true, then the consequence (*consequens*) determined by it is true too; called *modus ponens.*
2. If the consequence (*consequens*) is false, then the ground (*antecedens*) is false too; *modus tollens.*

§27

Disjunctive judgments

A judgment is *disjunctive* if the parts of the sphere of a given concept determine one another in the whole or toward a whole[h] as complements (*complementa*).

§28

Matter and form of disjunctive judgments

The several given judgments of which the disjunctive judgment is composed constitute its *matter* and are called the *members of the disjunction or opposition.* The *form* of these judgments consists in the *disjunction* itself,

[f] "*setzende.*"
[g] "*aufhebende.*"
[h] "in dem Ganzen oder zu einem Ganzen."

i.e., in the determination of the relation of the various judgments as members of the whole sphere of the divided cognition which mutually exclude one another and complement one another.

Note. Thus all disjunctive judgments represent various judgments *as in the community of a sphere* and produce each judgment only through the restriction of the others in regard to the whole sphere; they determine each judgment's relation to the whole sphere, then, and thereby at the same time the relation that these various members of the division (*membra disjuncta*) have among themselves. Thus one member determines every other here only insofar as they stand together in community as parts of a whole sphere of cognition, *outside of which, in a certain relation, nothing may be thought.* 107

§29

Peculiar character of disjunctive judgments

The peculiar character of all disjunctive judgments, whereby their specific difference from others, in particular from categorical judgments, is determined as to the moment of relation, consists in this: that the members of the disjunction are all problematic judgments, of which nothing else is thought except that, taken together as parts of the sphere of a cognition, each the complement of the other toward the whole (*complementum ad totum*), they are equal to the sphere of the first. And from this it follows that in one of these problematic judgments the truth must be contained or – what is the same – that one of them must hold *assertorically*, because outside of them the sphere of the cognition includes nothing more under the given conditions, and one is opposed to the other, consequently neither something *outside* them *nor* more than one *among* them can be true.

Note. In a categorical judgment the thing whose representation is considered as a part of the sphere of another, subordinated representation is considered as contained under this, its higher concept; thus here, in the subordination of the spheres, the part of the part is compared with the whole. But in disjunctive judgments I go from the whole to all the parts taken together. What is contained under the sphere of a concept is also contained under one of the parts of this sphere. Accordingly, the sphere must first be divided. If, for example, I make the disjunctive judgment, A learned man is learned either historically or in matters of reason, I thereby determine that these concepts are, as to the sphere, parts of the sphere of the learned man, but not in any way parts of one another, and that taken together they are all complete.

The following schema of comparison between categorical and disjunc- 108 tive judgments may make it more intuitive that in disjunctive judgments the sphere of the divided concept is not considered as contained in the sphere of the divisions, but rather that which is contained under the divided concept is considered as contained under one of the members of the division.

In categorical judgments *x*, which is contained under *b*, is also under *a*:

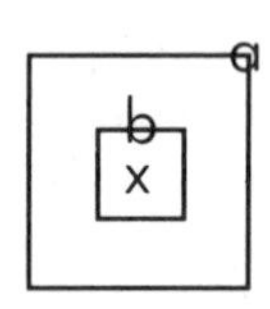

In disjunctive ones *x*, which is contained under *a*, is contained either under *b* or *c*, etc.:

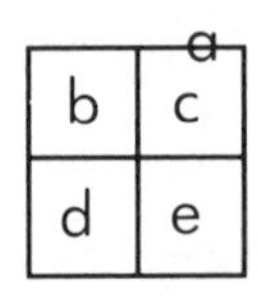

Thus the division in disjunctive judgments indicates the coordination not of the parts of the whole concept, but rather all the parts of its sphere. Here I think *many things through one concept*, there *one thing* through[i] *many concepts*, e.g., the *definitum* through all the marks of coordination.

§30

Modality of judgments: Problematic, assertoric, apodeictic

As to modality, through which moment the relation of the whole judgment to the faculty of cognition is determined, judgments are either *problematic* or *assertoric* or *apodeictic*. The problematic ones are accompanied with the consciousness of the mere possibility of the judging, the assertoric ones with the consciousness of its actuality, the apodeictic ones, finally, with the consciousness of its necessity.

Note 1. This moment of modality indicates, then, only the way in which something is maintained or denied in judgment: whether one does not settle 109 anything concerning the truth or untruth of a judgment, as in the problematic judgment, The soul of man may be immortal; or whether one determines something concerning it, as in the assertoric judgment, The human soul is immortal; or, finally, whether one even expresses the truth of a judgment with the dignity of necessity, as in the apodeictic judgment,

[i] Ak, "*durch*"; 1st ed., "durch."

The soul of man must be immortal. This determination of merely possible or actual or necessary truth concerns only *the judgment itself*, then, not in any way *the thing* about which we judge.

2. In problematic judgments, which one can also explain as ones whose material is given with the possible relation between predicate and subject, the subject must always have a smaller sphere than the predicate.
3. On the distinction between problematic and assertoric judgments rests the true distinction between judgments and *propositions*, which is customarily placed, wrongly, in the mere expression through words, without which one simply could not judge at all. In judgment the relation of various representations to the unity of consciousness is thought merely as problematic, but in a proposition as assertoric. A problematic proposition is a *contradictio in adjecto*. Before I have a proposition I must first judge; and I judge about much that I cannot decide, which I must do, however, as soon as I determine a judgment *as a proposition*. It is good, by the way, first to judge problematically, before one accepts the judgment as assertoric, in order to examine it in this way. Also, it is not always necessary to our purpose to have assertoric judgments.

§31

Exponible judgments

udgments in which an affirmation and a negation are contained simultaneously, but in a covert way, so that the affirmation occurs distinctly but he negation covertly, are *exponible propositions*.

Note. In the exponible judgment, Few men are learned, for example lies (1.), but in a covert way, the negative judgment, Many men are not learned, and (2.) the affirmative one, Some men are learned. Since the nature of exponible propositions depends merely on conditions of language, in accordance with which one can express two judgments briefly at once, the observation that in our language there can be judgments that must be expounded belongs not to logic but to grammar.

§32

110

Theoretical and practical propositions

Those propositions that relate to the object and determine what belongs or does not belong to it are called *theoretical*; *practical* propositions, on the other hand, are those that state the action whereby, as its necessary condition, an object becomes possible.

Note. Logic has to deal only with propositions that are practical *as to form*, which are to this extent opposed to *theoretical* ones. Propositions that are practical *as to content*, and to this extent are distinct from *speculative* ones, belong to morals.

§33

Indemonstrable and demonstrable propositions

Demonstrable propositions are those that are capable of a proof; those not capable of a proof are called *indemonstrable*.

Immediately certain judgments are indemonstrable and thus are to be regarded as *elementary propositions*.

§34

Principles

Immediately certain judgments *a priori* can be called principles,[j] insofar as other judgments are proved from them, but they themselves cannot be subordinated to any other. On this account they are also called *principles*[k] (beginnings[l]).

§35

Intuitive and discursive principles: Axioms and acroamata

Principles are either *intuitive* or *discursive*. The former can be exhibited in intuition and are called *axioms* (*axiomata*), the latter may be expressed only through concepts and can be called *acroamata*.

111

§36

Analytic and synthetic propositions

Propositions whose certainty rests on *identity* of concepts (of the predicate with the notion of the subject) are called *analytic* propositions.[m] Propositions whose truth is not grounded on identity of concepts must be called *synthetic*.

---

[j] "Grundsätze."
[k] "*Principien.*"
[l] "Anfänge."
[m] Ak, "*Sätze*"; 1st ed., "Sätze."

Note 1. An example of an *analytic* proposition is, To everything x, to which the concept of body $(a + b)$ belongs, belongs also *extension* (b)

An example of a *synthetic* proposition is, To everything x, to which the concept of body $(a+b)$ belongs, belongs also *attraction* (c). Synthetic propositions increase cognition *materialiter*, analytic ones merely *formaliter*. The former contain *determinations* (*determinationes*), the latter only *logical*[n] *predicates*.

2. Analytic principles are not axioms, for they are *discursive*. And even synthetic principles are axioms only if they are *intuitive*.

§37

Tautological propositions

The identity of the concepts in analytic judgments can be either *explicit* (*explicita*) or *non-explicit* (*implicita*). In the first case the analytic propositions are *tautological*.

Note 1. Tautological propositions are empty *virtualiter*, or *empty of consequences*,[o] for they are without value or use. The tautological proposition, *Man is man*, is of this sort, for example. For if I do not know anything more to say of man except that he is a man, then I know nothing more of him at all.

Propositions that are identical *implicite*, on the other hand, are not empty of consequences or fruitless, for they make clear the predicate that lay undeveloped (*implicite*) in the concept of the subject through *development*[p] (*explicatio*).

2. Propositions that are empty of consequences must be distinguished from ones that are *empty of sense*,[q] which are empty in meaning[r] because they concern the determination of so-called *hidden properties* (*qualitates occultae*).

§38

112

Postulate and problem

A *postulate* is a practical, immediately certain proposition, or a principle that determines a possible action, in the case of which it is presupposed that the way of executing it is immediately certain.

Problems (*problemata*) are demonstrable propositions that require a direc-

[n] Ak, "logische"; 1st ed., "*logische.*"
[o] "*folgeleer.*"
[p] "*Entwickelung.*"
[q] "*sinnleeren.*"
[r] "leer an Verstand."

tive, or ones that express an action, the manner of whose execution is not immediately certain.

Note 1. There can also be *theoretical* postulates on behalf of practical reason. These are theoretical hypotheses that are necessary for a practical purpose of reason, like those of the existence of God, of freedom, and of another world.

2. A problem involves (1.) the *question*,[s] which contains what is to be accomplished, (2.) the *resolution*, which contains the way in which what is to be accomplished can be executed, and (3.) the *demonstration* that when I have proceeded thus, what is required will occur.

§39

Theorems, corollaries, lemmas, and scholia

Theorems are theoretical propositions that are capable of and require proof. *Corollaries* are immediate consequences from a preceding proposition. Propositions that are not indigenous to the science in which they are presupposed as proved, but rather are borrowed from other sciences, are called *lemmas* (*lemmata*). *Scholia*, finally, are mere *elucidative propositions*,[t] which thus do not belong to the whole of the system as members.

Note. Essential and universal moments of every theorem are the *thesis* and the *demonstration*. Furthermore, one can place the distinction between theorems and corollaries in the fact that *the latter* are inferred immediately, but *the former* are drawn through a series of consequences from immediately certain propositions.

114

§40

Judgments of perception and of experience

A *judgment of perception* is merely *subjective*, an objective judgment from perceptions is a *judgment of experience*.

Note. A judgment from mere perceptions is really not possible, except through the fact that I express my representation *as perception*: I, who perceive a

[s] "*Quästion.*"
[t] "*Erläuterungssätze.*"

tower, perceive in it the red color. But I cannot say: *It is red.* For this would not be merely an empirical judgment, but a *judgment of experience*, i.e., an empirical judgment through which I get a concept of the object. E.g., *In touching the stone I sense warmth*, is a judgment of perception: but on the other hand, *The stone is warm*, is a judgment of experience. It pertains to the latter that I do not reckon to the object what is merely in my subject, for a judgment of experience is perception from which a concept of the object arises; e.g., whether points of light move on *the moon* or in *the air* or in *my eye*.

THIRD SECTION

114

Of inferences

§41

Inference in general

By *inferring* is to be understood that function of thought whereby one judgment is derived from another. An inference is thus in general the derivation of one judgment from the other.

§42

Immediate and mediate inferences

All inferences are either *immediate* or *mediate.*

An *immediate* inference (*consequentia immediata*) is the derivation (*deductio*) of one judgment from the other without a mediating judgment (*judicium intermedium*). An inference is *mediate* if, besides the concept that a judgment contains in itself, one needs still others in order to derive a cognition therefrom.

§43

Inferences of the understanding, inferences of reason, and inferences of the power of judgment

Immediate inferences are also called *inferences of the understanding*; all mediate inferences, on the other hand, are either *inferences of reason* or *inferences of the power of judgment*. We deal here first with immediate inferences, or inferences of the understanding.

115

I. INFERENCES OF THE UNDERSTANDING

§44

Peculiar nature of inferences of the understanding

The essential character of all immediate inferences and the principle of their possibility consists simply in an alteration of the *mere form* of judgments, while the *matter* of the judgments, the subject and predicate, remains *unaltered, the same.*

Note 1. By virtue of the fact that in immediate inferences only the form of judgments is altered and not in any way the matter, these inferences differ essentially from all mediate inferences, in which the judgments are distinct *as to matter* too, since here a new concept must be added as mediating judgment or as middle concept (*terminus medius*) in order to deduce the one judgment from the other. If I infer, e.g., All men are mortal, hence Caius is mortal too, this is not an immediate inference. For here I need for the deduction the mediating judgment, Caius is a man; through this new concept, however, the matter of the judgments is altered.

2. With inferences of the understanding a *judicium intermedium* may also be made, to be sure, but then this mediating judgment is merely *tautological.* As, for example, in the immediate inference, All men are mortal, *some men are men*, hence some men are mortal, the middle concept is a tautological proposition.

§45

Modi *of inferences of the understanding*

Inferences of the understanding run through all the classes of the logical functions of judgment and consequently are determined in their principal kinds through the moments of quantity, quality, relation, and modality. On this rests the following division of these inferences.

116

§46

1. *Inferences of the understanding* (in relation to the *quantity* of judgments) per judicia subalternata

In inferences of the understanding *per judicia subalternata* the two judgments are distinct as to *quantity*, and here the particular judgment is derived from the universal in consequence of the principle: *The inference from the universal to the particular is valid* (*ab universali ad particulare valet consequentia*).

Note. A *judicium* is called *subalternatum* insofar as it is contained *under* the other, as, e.g., *particular* judgments are under *universal* ones.

§47

2. *Inferences of the understanding* (in relation to the *quality* of judgments) per judicia opposita

In inferences of the understanding of this kind, the alteration concerns the *quality* of the judgments, and this considered in relation to *opposition*. Now since this opposition can be *of three kinds*, the following particular division of immediate inference results: through *contradictorily opposed*, through *contrary*, and *subcontrary* judgments.[u]

Note. Inferences of the understanding through *equivalent*[v] judgments (*judicia aequipollentia)* cannot really be called inferences, for there is no consequence here; they are rather to be regarded as a mere substitution of words that signify one and the same concept, where the judgments themselves also remain unaltered as to form. E.g., Not all men are virtuous, and, Some men are not virtuous. The two judgments say one and the same thing.

§48

a. *Inferences of the understanding* per judicia contradictorie opposita

In inferences of the understanding through judgments which are opposed to one another contradictorily and which, as such, constitute genuine, pure opposition, the truth of one of the contradictorily opposed judgments is deduced from the falsehood of the other, and conversely. For genuine opposition, which occurs here, contains no more and no less than what belongs to opposition. In consequence of the *principle of the excluded middle*,[w] the two contradicting judgments cannot both be true, and just as little can they both be false. If the one is true, then the other is false, and conversely.

117

[u] Ak, "durch *conträre* und durch *subconträre* Urtheile"; 1st ed., "durch *conträre* und *subconträre* Urtheile."

[v] "*gleichgeltende*."

[w] "*Princip des ausschließenden Dritten*."

§49

b. *Inferences of the understanding* per judicia[x] contrarie opposita

Contrary or conflicting judgments (*judicia contrarie opposita*) are judgments of which the one is universally affirmative, the other universally negative. Now since one of them says more than the other, and since in the excess – that it says more than the mere negation of the other – there can lie falsehood, they cannot both be true, of course, but they can both be false. In regard to these judgments, therefore, only the inference *from the truth of the one to the falsehood of the other holds, but not conversely.*

§50

c. *Inferences of the understanding* per judicia subcontrarie opposita

Subcontrary judgments are ones of which the one affirms or denies *in particular* (*particulariter*) what the other denies or affirms in particular.

Since they can both be true but cannot both be false, only the following inference holds in regard to them: *If one of these propositions is false, the other is true, but not conversely.*

Note. In the case of subcontrary judgments there is no pure, strict opposition, for what is affirmed or denied in the one is not denied or affirmed of *the same* objects in the other. In the inference, e.g., Some men are learned, hence some men are not learned, what is denied in the second judgment is not affirmed of *the same* men in the first.

118

§51

3. *Inferences of the understanding (with respect to the relation of judgments)* per judicia conversa sive per conversionem

Immediate inferences through *conversion* concern the relation of judgments and consist in the transposition of subject and predicate in the two judgments, so that the subject of the one judgment is made the predicate of the other judgment, and conversely.

[x] Ak, "judica"; 1st ed., "judicia."

§52

Pure and altered conversion

In conversion the quantity of the judgments is either altered or it remains unaltered. In the first case the converted (*conversum*) is distinct from what converts (*convertens*) as to quantity, and the conversion is said to be *altered*[y] (*conversio per accidens*); in the latter case the conversion is called *pure* (*conversio simpliciter talis*).

§53

Universal rules of conversion

With respect to inferences of the understanding through conversion, the following rules hold:

1. *Universal affirmative*[z] judgments may be converted only *per accidens*; for the predicate in these judgments is a broader concept and thus only some of it is contained in the concept of the subject.
2. But all *universal negative*[a] judgments may be converted *simpliciter*; for here the subject is removed from the sphere of the predicate. Thus too, finally,
3. All *particular affirmative* propositions may be converted *simpliciter*; for in these judgments a part of the sphere of the subject has been subsumed under the predicate, hence a part of the sphere of the predicate may be subsumed under the subject.

Note 1. In universal affirmative judgments the subject is considered as a *contentum* of the predicate, since it is contained under its sphere. Therefore I may only infer, e.g., All men are mortal, hence some of those who are contained under the concept mortal are men. The cause of the fact that universal negative judgments may be converted *simpliciter* is that two concepts that contradict one another universally contradict each other *in the same extension*. 119

2. Some universal affirmative judgments may be converted *simpliciter*, to be sure. But the ground of this lies not in their form but in the particular character of their *matter*; as, e.g., the two judgments, Everything unalterable is necessary, and everything necessary is unalterable.

[y] Ak, "*veränderte*"; 1st ed., "veränderte."
[z] Ak, "*Allgemein bejahende*"; 1st ed., "Allgemein bejahende."
[a] Ak, "*allgemein verneinenden*"; 1st ed., "allgemein verneinenden."

§54

4. *Inferences of the understanding (in relation to the modality of judgments)* per judicia contraposita

The immediate mode of inference through contraposition consists in that transposition (*metathesis*$_{L}$) of judgments in which merely the quantity remains the same while the *quality* is altered. They concern only the modality of judgments, since they transform an assertoric into an apodeictic judgment.

§55

Universal rule of contraposition

With respect to contraposition, the universal rule holds:

All universal affirmative judgments may be contraposed simpliciter. For if the predicate, as that which contains the subject under itself, is denied, and hence the whole sphere, then a part of it must also be denied, i.e., the subject.

Note 1. The *metathesis*$_{L}$ of judgments through conversion and that through contraposition are thus opposed to one another to the extent that the former alters merely quantity, the latter merely quality.

2. The immediate modes of inference mentioned relate merely to *categorical* judgments.

120

II. INFERENCES OF REASON

§56

Inference of reason in general

An inference of reason is the cognition of the necessity of a proposition through the subsumption of its condition under a given universal rule.

§57

Universal principle of all inferences of reason

The universal principle on which the validity of all inference through reason rests may be determinately expressed in the following formula:

What stands under the condition of a rule also stands under the rule itself.

Note. The inference of reason premises a *universal rule* and a *subsumption* under its *condition*. Through this one cognizes the conclusion *a priori*, not in the individual, but as contained in the universal and as necessary under a certain condition. And this, that everything stands under the universal and is determinable in universal rules, is just the principle of *rationality* or of *necessity* (*principium rationalitatis sive necessitatis*).

§58

Essential components of the inference of reason

To every inference of reason belong the following essential three parts:

1. a universal rule, which is called the *major proposition*[b] (*propositio major*),
2. the proposition which subsumes a cognition under the condition of the universal rule, and which is called the *minor proposition*[c] (*propositio minor*), and finally
3. the proposition which affirms or denies the rule's predicate of the subsumed cognition: the *conclusion*[d] (*conclusio*).

The first two propositions, in their combination with one another, are called *premises*.[e] 121

Note. A rule is an assertion under a universal condition. The relation of the condition to the assertion, namely, how the latter stands under the former, is the exponent[f] of the rule.

The cognition that the condition (somewhere) exists is the *subsumption*.

The combination of that which is subsumed under the condition with the assertion of the rule is the *inference*.

[b] "*Obersatz.*"
[c] "*Untersatz.*"
[d] "*Schlußsatz.*"
[e] "*Vordersätze* oder *Prämissen.*"
[f] "*Exponent.*"

§59

Matter and form of inferences of reason

The *matter* of inferences of reason consists in the antecedent propositions or premises, the *form* in the conclusion insofar as it contains the *consequentia*.

Note 1. In every inference of reason, then, the truth of the premises is to be examined first, and then the correctness of the *consequentia*. In rejecting an inference of reason, one must never reject the conclusion first, but rather one must first reject either the premises or the *consequentia*.

2. In every inference of reason the conclusion is given as soon as the premises and the *consequentia* are given.

§60

Division of inferences of reason (as to relation) *into categorical, hypothetical, and disjunctive*

All rules (judgments) contain objective unity of consciousness of the manifold of cognition, hence a condition under which one cognition belongs with another to one consciousness. Now only three conditions of this unity may be thought, however, namely: as subject of the inherence of marks, or as ground of the dependence of one cognition on another, or, finally, as combination of parts in a whole (logical division). Consequently 122 there can only be just as many kinds of universal rules (*propositiones majores*), through which the *consequentia* of one judgment from another is mediated.

And on this is grounded the division of all inferences of reason into *categorical*, *hypothetical*, and *disjunctive*.

Note 1. Inferences of reason can be divided *neither* as to *quantity*, for every $major_L$ is a rule, hence something universal; *nor* in regard to *quality*, for it is equivalent whether the conclusion is affirmative or negative; *nor*, finally, in respect of *modality*, for the conclusion is always accompanied with the consciousness of necessity and consequently has the dignity of an apodeictic proposition. Thus only *relation* remains as the sole possible ground of division of inferences of reason.

2. Many logicians hold only categorical inferences of reason to be *ordinary*, the others to be *extraordinary*. But this is groundless and false. For all three of these kinds are products of equally correct, though equally essentially different functions of reason.

§61

Peculiar difference between categorical, hypothetical and disjunctive inferences of reason

The distinguishing feature among the three mentioned kinds of inferences of reason lies in the *major premise*. In *categorical* inferences of reason the *major*$_L$ is a categorical proposition, in *hypothetical* ones it is a hypothetical or problematic proposition, and in *disjunctive* ones it is a disjunctive proposition.

§62

1. Categorical inferences of reason

In every categorical inference of reason there are three *principal concepts*[g] (*termini*), namely:

1. the predicate in the conclusion, which concept is called the *major concept*[h] (*terminus major*), because it has a larger sphere than the subject,
2. the *subject* (in the conclusion), whose concept is called the *minor concept*[i] (*terminus minor*), and
3. a mediating mark (*nota intermedia*), which is called the *middle concept*[j] (*terminus medius*), because through it a cognition is subsumed under the condition of the rule. 123

Note. This distinction among the mentioned *termini* exists only in categorical inferences of reason, because these alone infer through a *terminus medius*; the others, on the other hand, infer only through the subsumption of a proposition represented problematically in the *major*$_L$ and assertorically in the *minor*$_L$.

§63

Principle of categorical inferences of reason

The principle on which the possibility and validity of all categorical inferences of reason rests is this:

What belongs to the mark of a thing belongs also to the thing itself; and what

[g] "*Hauptbegriffe.*"
[h] "*Oberbegriff.*"
[i] "*Unterbegriff.*"
[j] "*Mittelbegriff.*"

contradicts the mark of a thing contradicts also the thing itself (*nota notae est nota rei ipsius; repugnans notae, repugnat rei ipsi*).

Note. From the principle just set forth the so-called *dictum de omni et nullo* may easily be deduced, and hence it can hold as the first principle neither for inferences of reason in general nor for the categorical in particular.

Genus and *species concepts* are universal marks of all things that stand under these concepts. Accordingly, the rule holds here: *What belongs to or contradicts the genus or species belongs to or contradicts all the objects that are contained under that genus or species.* And this rule is called just the *dictum de omni et nullo.*

§64

Rules for categorical inferences of reason

From the nature and the principle of categorical inferences of reason flow the following rules for them:

124

1. In no categorical inference of reason can either more or fewer than *three principal concepts* (*termini*) be contained; for here I am supposed to combine two concepts (subject and predicate) through a mediating mark.
2. The antecedent propositions or premises may not be wholly negative *(ex puris negativis nihil sequitur*[k]); for the subsumption in the minor premise must be affirmative, as that which states that a cognition stands under the condition of the rule.
3. The premises may also not be wholly *particular*[l] propositions (*ex puris particularibus nihil sequitur*[m]); for then there would be no rule, i.e., no universal proposition, from which a particular cognition could be deduced.
4. *The conclusion always follows the weaker part of the inference*, i.e., the negative and the particular proposition in the premises, as that which is called the weaker part of the categorical inference of reason (*conclusio sequitur partem debiliorem*[n]). If, therefore,
5. one of the premises is a negative proposition, then the conclusion must be negative too, and
6. if one premise is a particular proposition, then the conclusion must be particular too.
7. In all categorical inferences of reason the *major*$_{\mathrm{L}}$ must be a universal proposition (*universalis*), the *minor*$_{\mathrm{L}}$ an affirmative one (*affirmans*), and from this it follows, finally,

[k] From purely negative [premises] nothing follows.

[l] "*besondere* (particulare)."

[m] From purely particular [premises] nothing follows.

[n] The conclusion follows the weaker part.

8. that the conclusion must follow the *major premise* in regard to *quality*, but the *minor premise* as to *quantity*.

Note. It is easy to see that the conclusion must in every case follow the negative and the particular proposition in the premises.

If I make the minor premise only particular, and say, Some is contained under the rule, then I can only say in the conclusion that the predicate of the rule belongs to some, because I have *not* subsumed *more than this* under the rule. And if I have a negative proposition as the rule (major premise), then I must also make the conclusion negative. For if the major premise says that this or that predicate must be denied of everything that stands under the condition of the rule, then the conclusion must also deny the predicate of that (subject) which has been subsumed under the condition of the rule. 125

§65

Pure and mixed categorical inferences of reason

A categorical inference of reason is *pure*[o] (*purus*) if no immediate inference is mixed in with it, nor is the legitimate order of the premises altered; in the contrary case it is called *impure* or *mixed* (*ratiocinium impurum* or *hybridum*).

§66

Mixed inferences of reason through conversion of propositions – Figures

Those inferences which arise through the conversion of propositions and in which the position of these propositions is thus not the legitimate one are to be counted as mixed inferences. This case occurs in the three latter so-called figures of the categorical inference of reason.

§67

Four figures of inferences

By figures are to be understood those four modes of inferring whose difference is determined through the particular position of the premises and their concepts.

[o] Ak, "*rein*"; 1st ed., "rein."

§68

Ground of the determination of their distinction through the different position of the middle concept

The middle concept, namely, on whose position things really depend here, can occupy either (1.) the place of the subject in the major premise and the place of the predicate in the minor premise, or (2.) the place of the predicate in both premises, or (3.) the place of the subject in both, or finally (4.) the place of the predicate in the major premise and the place of the subject in the minor premise. Through these four cases, the distinction among the four figures is determined. If we let *S* signify the subject of the conclusion, *P* its predicate, and *M* the *terminus medius*, then the schema for the four mentioned figures may be exhibited in the following table:

126

M P	P M	M P	P M
S M	S M	M S	M S
S P	S P	S P	S P

§69

Rules for the first figure, as the only legitimate one

The rule of the *first figure* is that the *major*$_{L}$ be a *universal* proposition, the *minor*$_{L}$ an *affirmative*. And since this must be the universal rule of all categorical inferences of reason in general, it results from this that the first figure is the only legitimate one, which lies at the basis of all the others, and to which all the others must be traced back through conversion of premises (*metathesis praemissorum*), insofar as they are to have validity.

Note. The first figure can have a conclusion of any quantity and quality. In the other figures there are conclusions only of a certain kind; some *modi* of them are excluded here. This already indicates that these figures are not perfect, that there are certain restrictions in them which prevent the conclusion from occurring in all *modi*, as in the first figure.

§70

Condition of the reduction of the three latter figures to the first

The condition of the validity of the three latter figures, under which a correct modus of inference is possible in each of them, amounts to this: 127 that the *medius terminus* occupies a place such that from it, through immediate inferences (*consequentias immediatas*), their position in accordance with the rules of the first figure can arise. – From this the following rules for the three latter figures emerge.

§71

Rules of the second figure

In the second figure the *minor*$_L$ stands rightly, hence the *major*$_L$ must be *converted*, and in such a way that it remains *universal* (*universalis*). This is possible only if it is *universally negative*; but if it is *affirmative*, then it must be contraposed. In both cases the conclusion becomes *negative* (*sequitur partem debiliorem*).

Note. The rule of the second figure is, What is contradicted by a mark of a thing contradicts the thing itself. Now here I must first convert and say, What is contradicted by a mark contradicts this mark; or I must convert the conclusion, What is contradicted by a mark of a thing is contradicted by the thing itself, consequently it contradicts the thing.

§72

Rule of the third figure

In the third figure the *major*$_L$ stands rightly, hence the *minor*$_L$ must be converted, yet in such a way that an affirmative proposition arises therefrom. This is only possible, however, when the affirmative proposition is *particular*, consequently the *conclusion* is *particular*.

Note. The rule of the third figure is, What belongs to or contradicts a mark also belongs to or contradicts some things under which this mark is contained. Here I must first say, It belongs to or contradicts everything that is contained under this mark.

128

§73

Rule of the fourth figure

If in the fourth figure the *major*$_L$ is universal negative, then it may be converted purely (*simpliciter*), just as the *minor*$_L$ may be as particular; hence the conclusion is negative. If, on the other hand, the *major*$_L$ is universal affirmative, then it may either be converted only *per accidens* or it may be contraposed; hence the conclusion is either particular or negative. If the conclusion is not to be converted (*P S* transformed into *S P*), a transposition of the premises (*metathesis praemissorum*) or a conversion (*conversio*) must occur.

Note. In the fourth figure it is inferred that the *predicate* depends on the *medius terminus*, the *medius terminus* on the *subject* (of the conclusion), consequently the *subject* on the *predicate*; this simply does not follow, however, but at most its converse. To make this possible, the *major*$_L$ must be made the *minor*$_L$ and *vice versa*, and the conclusion must be converted, because in the first alteration the *terminus minor* is transformed into the *major*$_L$.

§74

Universal results concerning the three latter figures

From the rules stated for the three latter figures it is clear

1. that in none of them is there a universal affirmative conclusion, but rather the conclusion is always either negative or particular;
2. that in every one an *immediate inference* (*consequentia immediata*) is mixed in, which is not expressly signified, to be sure, but still must be silently included; that on this account, too,
3. these three latter *modi* of inference must all be called impure inferences (*ratiocinia hybrida, impura*), not pure ones, since no pure inference can have more than three principal propositions (*termini*).

129

§75

2. *Hypothetical inferences of reason*

A hypothetical inference is one that has a hypothetical proposition as *major*$_L$. Thus it consists of two propositions, (1.) an *antecedent proposition*[p] (*antecedens*) and (2.) a *consequent proposition*[q] (*consequens*), and

[p] "*Vordersatze.*"
[q] "*Nachsatze.*"

here the deduction is either according to *modus ponens* or to *modus tollens*.

Note 1. Hypothetical inferences of reason have no *medius terminus*, then, but instead the *consequentia* of one proposition from another is only indicated in them. In their *major*$_L$, namely, the *consequentia* of two propositions from one another is expressed, of which the first is the premise, the second a conclusion. The *minor*$_L$ is a transformation of the problematic condition into a categorical proposition.

2. From the fact that the hypothetical inference consists only of two propositions, without having a middle concept, it may be seen that it is really not an inference of reason, but rather only an immediate inference, to be proved from an antecedent proposition and a consequent proposition, as to matter or form (*consequentia immediata demonstrabilis [ex antecedente et consequente] vel quoad materiam vel quoad formam*).

Every inference of reason is supposed to be a proof. But the hypothetical carries with it only the *ground* of proof. It is clear from this, consequently, that it cannot be an inference of reason.

§76

Principle of hypothetical inferences

The principle of hypothetical inferences is the *principle of the ground:*[r] *a ratione ad rationatum; a negatione rationati ad negationem rationis valet consequentia.*[s]

§77

3. *Disjunctive inferences of reason*

In disjunctive inferences, the *major*$_L$ is a *disjunctive* proposition and as such must therefore have members of division or disjunction.

Here we infer either (1.) from the truth of one member of the disjunction to the falsehood of the others, or (2.) from the falsehood of all members but one to the truth of this one. The former occurs through the *modus ponens* (or *ponendo tollens*), the latter through the *modus tollens* (*tollendo ponens*). 130

---

[r] "*Satz des Grundes.*"

[s] The *consequentia* from the ground to the grounded, and from the negation of the grounded to negation of the ground, is valid.

Note 1. All the members of the disjunction but one, taken together, constitute the contradictory opposite of this one. Here there is a dichotomy, then, according to which, if one of the two is true, the other must be false, and conversely.

2. All disjunctive inferences of reason of more than two members of disjunction are thus really *polysyllogistic*. For every true disjunction can only be *bimembris*, and logical division is also *bimembris*, but for brevity's sake the *membra subdividentia* are posited among the *membra dividentia*.

§78

Principle of disjunctive inferences of reason

The principle of disjunctive inferences is the *principle of the excluded middle:*[t]

A contradictorie oppositorum negatione unius ad affirmationem alterius, a positione unius ad negationem alterius valet consequentia.[u]

§79

Dilemma

A dilemma is a hypothetical-disjunctive inference of reason, or a hypothetical inference, whose *consequens* is a disjunctive judgment. The hypothetical proposition whose *consequens* is disjunctive is the major proposition; the minor proposition affirms that the *consequens* (*per omnia membra*) is false, and the conclusion affirms that the *antecedens* is false. (*A remotione consequentis ad negationem antecedentis valet consequentia.*[v])

131

Note. The ancients made a great deal of the dilemma and named this inference *cornutus*. They knew how to drive an opponent into a corner by rehearsing everything to which he could turn and then contradicting everything, too. They showed him many difficulties with any opinion he accepted. But it is a sophistical trick, not to refute propositions directly but rather only to show difficulties, which is feasible with many, indeed, most things.

Now if we wish to declare as false everything with which we find difficulties, then it is an easy game to reject everything. It is good, to be sure, to show the impossibility of the opposite, only there still lies something decep-

[t] "*Grundatz des ausschließenden Dritten.*"

[u] From the negation of one contradictory opposite to the affirmation of the other, and from the positing of one to the negation of the other, the *consequentia is valid.*

[v] From the denial of the consequence to the negation of the antecedent the consequence is valid.

tive in this in case one takes the *incomprehensibility* of the opposite for its *impossibility*. Hence *dilemmata* have much that is captious in them, even though they infer correctly. They can be used to defend true propositions, but also to attack true propositions by means of difficulties that one throws up against them.

§80

Formal and covert inferences of reason (ratiocinia formalia *and* cryptica)

A *formal* inference of reason is one that not only contains everything required as to matter but also is expressed correctly and completely as to form. Opposed to formal inferences of reason are *covert* ones (*cryptica*), to which all those can be reckoned, in which either the premises are transposed, or one of the premises is left out, or, finally, the middle concept alone is combined with the conclusion. A covert inference of reason of the second kind, in which one premise is not expressed but only thought, is called a *truncated*[w] one or an *enthymeme*. Those of the third kind are called *contracted*[x] inferences.

III. INFERENCES OF THE POWER OF JUDGMENT

§81

Determinative and reflective power of judgment

The power of judgment is of two kinds: the *determinative*[y] or the *reflective*[z] power of judgment. The former goes *from the universal to the particular*, the second *from the particular to the universal*. The latter has only *subjective* validity, for the universal to which it proceeds from the particular is only *empirical* universality – a mere analogue of the *logical*. 132

§82

Inferences of the (reflective) power of judgment

Inferences of the power of judgment are certain modes of inference for coming from particular concepts to universal ones. They are not functions

[w] *"verstümmelter."*
[x] *"zusammengezogene."*
[y] *"bestimmende."*
[z] *"reflectirende."*

of the *determinative* power of judgment, then, but rather of the *reflective*; hence they also do not determine the *object*, but only the *mode of reflection* concerning it, in order to attain its cognition.

§83

Principle of these inferences

The principle that lies at the basis of these inferences of the power of judgment is this: *that the many will not agree in one without a common ground, but rather that which belongs to the many in this way will be necessary due to a common ground.*

Note. Since such a principle lies at the basis of the inferences of the power of judgment, they cannot, on that account, be held to be *immediate* inferences.

§84

Induction and analogy – The two modes of inference of the power of judgment

The power of judgment, by proceeding from the particular to the universal in order to draw from experience (empirically) universal – hence not *a priori* – judgments, infers *either* from *many* to *all* things of a kind, *or* from *many* determinations and properties, in which things of one kind agree, *to the remaining ones, insofar as they belong to the same principle.* The former mode of inference is called inference *through induction*, the other inference *according to analogy*.

---

133 *Note 1.* *Induction* infers, then, from the particular to the universal (*a particulari ad universale*) according to the principle of *universalization*:[a] *What belongs to many things of a genus belongs to the remaining ones too. Analogy* infers from *particular* to *total* similarity of two things, according to the principle of *specification*: Things of one genus, which we know to agree in much,[b] also agree in what remains, with which we are familiar in some things of this genus but which we do not perceive in others. Induction extends the empirically given from the particular to the universal in regard to *many objects*, while analogy extends the *given properties* of one thing to several [other properties] *of the very same thing*[.] – *One in many*, hence in all: *Induction*; *many in one* (which are also in others), hence also what remains

[a] "Princip der *Allgemeinmachung*."
[b] "von denen man vieles Uebereinstimmende kennt."

in the same thing: *Analogy*. Thus the ground of proof for immortality from the complete development of natural dispositions of each creature is, for example, an inference according to analogy.

In the inference according to analogy, however, *identity of the ground* (*par ratio*) is not required. In accordance with analogy we infer only rational inhabitants of the moon, not men. Also, one cannot infer according to analogy beyond the *tertium comparationis*.

2. Every inference of reason must yield necessity. *Induction and analogy* are therefore not inferences of reason, but only logical *presumptions*, or even empirical inferences; and through induction one does get general propositions, but not universal ones.
3. The mentioned inferences of the power of judgment are useful and indispensable for the sake of the extending of our cognition by experience.[c] But since they give only empirical certainty, we must make use of them with caution and care.

§85

Simple and composite inferences of reason

An inference of reason is called *simple* if it consists of one inference of reason, *composite* if of several.

§86

Ratiocinatio polysyllogistica

A composite inference, in which the several inferences of reason are combined with one another not through mere coordination but through *subordination*, i.e., as grounds and consequences, is called a chain of inferences of reason (*ratiocinatio polysyllogistica*). 134

§87

Prosyllogisms and episyllogisms

In the series of composite inferences one can infer in two ways, either from the grounds down to the consequences, or from the consequences up to the grounds. The first occurs through *episyllogisms*, the other through *prosyllogisms*.

An episyllogism is that inference, namely, in the series of inferences, whose premise becomes the conclusion of a *prosyllogism*, hence of an inference that has the premises of the former as conclusion.

[c] "Erfahrungserkenntnisses."

§88

Sorites or chain inference

An inference consisting of several inferences that are shortened and combined with one another for one conclusion is called a *sorites* or a *chain inference*, which can be either *progressive* or *regressive*, accordingly as one climbs from the nearer grounds up to the more distant ones, or from the more distant grounds down to the nearer ones.

§89

Categorical and hypothetical sorites

Both progressive and regressive chain inferences can in turn be either *categorical* or *hypothetical*. *The former* consists of *categorical* propositions, as a series of predicates, *the latter* of *hypothetical* ones, as a series of consequences.

§90

Fallacy – Paralogism – Sophism

An inference of reason that is wrong as to form, although it has for itself the illusion of a correct inference, is called a *fallacy* (*fallacia*). Such an
135 inference is a *paralogism* insofar as one deceives oneself through it, a *sophism* insofar as one intentionally seeks to deceive others through it.

Note. The ancients occupied themselves very much with the art of making such sophisms. Therefore many of this kind have emerged, e.g., the *sophisma figurae dictionis*, in which the *medius terminus* is taken in different meanings – *fallacia a dicto secundum quid ad dictum simpliciter, sophisma heterozeteseos, elenchi*[d] *ignorationis*,[e] etc.

§91

Leap in inference

A leap (*saltus*) in inference or proof is the combination of a premise with the conclusion so that the other premise is left out. Such a leap is *legitimate*

[d] Reading "elenchi" for "elenchi,".

[e] the fallacy [of inferring] from what is said with qualification to what is said *simpliciter*, the sophism of misdirection, the *ignoratio elenchis*, etc.

legitimus) if everyone can easily add the missing premise in thought, but *illegitimate* (*illegitimus*) if the subsumption is not clear. Here a distant mark is connected with a thing without an intermediate mark (*nota intermedia*).

§92

Petitio principii – Circulus in probando

By a *petitio principii* is understood the acceptance of a proposition as ground of proof as an immediately certain proposition, although it still requires a proof. And one commits a *circle in proof* if one lays at the basis of its *own* proof the very proposition that one wanted to prove.

Note. The circle in proof is often hard to discover, and this mistake is usually most frequently committed where the proofs are hard.

§93 136

Probatio plus and minus probans

A proof can prove *too much*, but also *too little*. In the *latter* case it proves only a part of what is to be proved, in the *former* it also goes on to that which is false.

Note. A proof that proves too little can be true and thus is not to be rejected. But if it proves too much, then it proves more than is true, and that is then false. Thus, for example, the proof against suicide, that he who has not given life cannot take it either, proves too much; for on this ground we would not be permitted to kill animals. Thus it is false.

II. Universal doctrine of method

139

§94

Manner and method

All cognition, and a whole of cognition, must be in conformity with a rule. (Absence of rules is at the same time unreason.) But this rule is either that of *manner* (free) or that of *method* (compulsion).

§95

Form of science – Method

Cognition, as science, must be arranged in accordance with a method. For science is a whole of cognition as a system, and not merely as an aggregate. It therefore requires a systematic cognition, hence one composed in accordance with rules on which we have reflected.

§96

Doctrine of method – Its object and end

As the doctrine of elements in logic has for its content the elements and conditions of the perfection of a cognition, so the universal doctrine of method, as the other part of logic, has to deal with the form of a science in general, or with the ways of acting so as to connect the manifold of cognition in a science.

§97

Means for furthering the logical perfection of cognition

The doctrine of method is supposed to expound the way for us to attain 140 the perfection of cognition. Now one of the most essential logical perfections of cognition consists in its distinctness, thoroughness, and systematic ordering into the whole of a science. Accordingly, the doctrine of method will have principally to provide the means through which these perfections of cognition are furthered.

§98

Conditions of the distinctness of cognition

The distinctness of cognitions and their combination in a systematic whole depends on the distinctness of concepts both in regard to what is contained *in* them and in respect of what is contained *under* them.

The distinct consciousness of the *content* of concepts is furthered by *exposition* and *definition* of them, while the distinct consciousness of their *extension*, on the other hand, is furthered through *logical division* of them. – First of all, then, of the means for furthering the distinctness of concepts in *regard to their content*.

I. FURTHERING LOGICAL PERFECTION OF COGNITION THROUGH DEFINITION, EXPOSITION, AND DESCRIPTION OF CONCEPTS

§99

Definition

A definition is a sufficiently distinct and precise concept (*conceptus rei adaequatus in minimis terminis, complete determinatus*[f]).

Note. The definition alone is to be regarded as a logically perfect concept, for in it are united the two essential perfections of a concept: distinctness, and completeness and precision in distinctness (quantity of distinctness).

§100

141

Analytic and synthetic definition

All definitions are either analytic or synthetic. The former are definitions of a concept that is *given*, the latter of one that is *made*.

[f] A concept adequate to the thing, in minimal terms, completely determined.

§101

Concepts that are given and made a priori *and* a posteriori

The given concepts of an analytic definition are given either *a priori* or *a posteriori*, just as the concepts of a synthetic definition, which are made are made either *a priori* or *a posteriori.*

§102

Synthetic definitions through exposition or construction

The synthesis of concepts that are made, out of which synthetic definitions arise, is either that of *exposition*[g] (of appearances) or that of *construction*. The latter is the synthesis of concepts that are made *arbitrarily*, the former the synthesis of concepts that are made empirically, i.e., from given appearances as their matter (*conceptus factitii vel a priori vel per synthesin empiricam*[h]). Concepts that are made arbitrarily are the *mathematical* ones.

Note. All definitions of mathematical concepts and – provided that definitions could exist in the case of empirical concepts – of concepts of experience must be made synthetically, then. For even in the case of concepts of the latter kind, e.g., the empirical concepts water, fire, air, etc., I ought not to analyze what lies *in them*, but to become acquainted, through experience with what belongs *to them*. All empirical concepts must thus be regarded as concepts that are made, whose synthesis is not arbitrary, however, but empirical

§103

Impossibility of empirically synthetic definitions

Since the synthesis of empirical concepts is not arbitrary but rather is 142 empirical and as such can never be complete (because one can always discover in experience more marks of the concept), empirical concepts cannot be defined, either.

Note. Thus only arbitrary concepts may be defined synthetically. Such definitions of arbitrary concepts, which are not only always possible but also necessary, and which must precede all that is said by means of an arbitrary

[g] "*Exposition.*"

[h] concepts that are made either a priori or through empirical synthesis.

concept, could also be called *declarations*, insofar as through them one declares his thoughts or gives account of what one understands by a word. This is the case among *mathematicians*.

§104

Analytic definitions through analysis of concepts given a priori *or* a posteriori

All *given* concepts, be they given *a priori* or *a posteriori*, can be defined only through *analysis*. For one can make given concepts distinct only insofar as one successively makes their marks clear. If *all* the marks of a given concept are made clear, then the concept becomes *completely* distinct; if it does not contain too many marks, then it is at the same time precise, and from this there arises a definition of the concept.

Note. Since one cannot become certain through any test whether one has exhausted all the marks of a given concept through a complete analysis, all analytic definitions are to be held to be uncertain.

§105

Expositions and descriptions

Not all concepts *can* be defined, and not all *need* to be.

There are approximations to the definition of certain concepts; these are partly *expositions*[i] (*expositiones*), partly *descriptions* (*descriptiones*).

The *expounding*[j] of a concept consists in the connected (successive) representation[k] of its marks, insofar as these are found through analysis. 143

Description is the exposition of a concept, insofar as it is not precise.

Note 1. We can expound either a *concept* or *experience*. The first occurs through analysis, the second through synthesis.

2. Exposition occurs only with *given* concepts, then, which are thereby made distinct; it is thereby distinct from *declaration*, which is a distinct representation of concepts that are *made*.

Since it is not always possible to make analysis complete, and since in general an analysis must first be incomplete before it becomes complete, an incomplete exposition, as part of a definition, is also a true and useful

[i] "*Erörterungen*."
[j] "*Exponiren*."
[k] "in der an einander hängenden (successiven) Vorstellung."

exhibition of a concept. Definition always remains here only the idea of a logical perfection that we must seek to attain.

3. Description can occur only with empirically given concepts. It has no determinate rules and contains only the materials for definition.

§106

Nominal and real definitions

By mere *definitions of names,*[l] or *nominal definitions*, are to be understood those that contain the meaning that one wanted arbitrarily to give to a certain name, and which therefore signify only the logical essence of their object, or which serve merely for distinguishing it from other objects. *Definitions of things,*[m] or *real definitions*, on the other hand, are ones that suffice for cognition of the object according to its inner determinations, since they present the possibility of the object from inner marks.

Note 1. If a concept is internally sufficent for distinguishing the thing then it certainly is externally sufficient too, but if it is not internally sufficient then it can be externally sufficient merely in *a certain relation*, namely, in the comparison of the *definitum* with other things. But *unrestricted* external sufficiency is not possible without internal sufficiency.

144 2. Objects of experience allow only nominal explanations. Logical nominal definitions of given concepts of the understanding are derived from an attribute, real definitions, on the other hand, from the essence of the thing, the first ground of possibility. Thus the latter contain what always belongs to the thing – its real essence. Merely *negative* definitions cannot be called real definitions either, because negative marks can serve just as well as affirmative ones for distinguishing one thing from others, but not for cognition of the thing according to its inner possibility.

In matters of morals real definitions must always be sought; all our striving must be directed toward this. There are real definitions in mathematics, for the definition of an arbitrary concept is always *real.*

3. A definition is *genetic* if it yields a concept through which the object can be exhibited *a priori in concreto*; all mathematical definitions are of this sort

§107

Principal requirements of definition

The essential and universal requirements that pertain to the completeness of a definition in general may be considered under the four principal moments of quantity, quality, relation, and modality:

[l] "*Namen-Erklärungen.*"
[m] "*Sach-Erklärungen.*"

. as to *quantity* – what concerns the sphere of the definition – the definition and the *definitum* must be *convertible concepts*[n] (*conceptus reciproci*), and hence the definition must be neither *broader* nor *narrower* than its *definitum*;
. as to *quality*, the definition must be a *detailed* and at the same time *precise* concept,
. as to *relation*, it must not be *tautological*, i.e., the marks of the *definitum* must, as *grounds of its cognition*, be different from it itself, and finally
. as to *modality*, the marks must be *necessary*, and hence not such as are added through experience.

Note. The condition that the genus concept and the concept of the specific difference (*genus* and *differentia specifica*) ought to constitute the definition holds only in regard to nominal definitions in *comparison*, but not for real definitions in *derivation*. 145

§108

Rules for testing definitions

n the testing of definitions four acts are to be performed; it is to be nvestigated, namely, whether the definition

. considered as a proposition *is true*, whether
. as a concept it is *distinct*,
. whether as a distinct concept it is also *detailed*, and finally whether
. as a detailed concept it is at the same time *determinate*, i.e., adequate to the thing itself.

§109

Rules for preparation of definitions

The very same acts that belong to the testing of definition are also to be performed in the preparation of them. Toward this end, then, seek (1.) true propositions, (2.) whose predicate does not presuppose the concept of the thing; (3.) collect several of them and compare them with the concept of the thing itself to see if they are adequate; and finally (4.) see whether one mark does not lie in another or is not subordinated to it.

Note 1. These rules hold, as is surely understood without any reminder, only of analytic definitions. But now since one can never be certain here whether the analysis has been complete, one may put forth the definition only as

"*Wechselbegriffe.*"

an experiment and make use of it only as if it were not a definition. Unde this restriction one can still use it as a distinct and true concept and drav corollaries from the concept's marks. I will be able to say, namely, that t that to which the concept of the *definitum* belongs, the definition belong too, but of course not conversely, since the definition does not exhaus the whole *definitum*.

2. To make use of the concept of the *definitum* in the explanation, or t make the *definitum* the basis of the definition, is called explaining throug a *circle* (*circulus in definiendo*).

146

II. FURTHERING THE PERFECTION OF COGNITION THROUGH LOGICAL DIVISION OF CONCEPTS

§110

Concept of logical division

Every concept contains a manifold *under* itself insofar as the manifol agrees, but also insofar as it is different. The determination of a concep in regard to everything possible that is contained under it, insofar a things are opposed to one another, i.e., are distinct from one another, i called the *logical division of the concept*. The higher concept is called the *divided concept* (*divisus*), the lower concepts the *members of the divisio* (*membra dividentia*).

Note 1. To *take apart*[o] a concept and to *divide*[p] it are thus quite different things. In taking a concept apart I see what is contained *in* it (through analysis), ir dividing it I consider what is contained *under* it. Here I divide the spher of the concept, not the concept itself. Thus it is a great mistake t suppose that division is the taking apart of the concept; rather, the members of the division contain more in themselves than does the divided concept.

2. We go up from lower to higher concepts, and afterward we can go down from these to the lower ones – through division.

§111

Universal rules of logical division

In every division of a concept we must see to it:

[o] "*theilen.*"
[p] "*eintheilen.*"

1. that the members of the division exclude or are opposed to one another, that furthermore they
2. belong under one higher concept (*conceptus communis*), and finally that
3. taken together they constitute the sphere of the divided concept or are equal to it.

Note. The members of the division must be separated from one another through *contradictory* opposition, not through mere contrariety[q] (*contrarium*). 147

§112

Codivision and subdivision

Various divisions of a concept, which are made in various respects, are called *codivisions*, and division of the members of division is called a *subdivision* (*subdivisio*).

Note 1. Subdivision can be carried on to infinity, but comparatively it can be finite. Codivision, especially with concepts of experience, always goes to infinity; for who can exhaust all the relations of concepts?

2. *Codivision* can also be called a division according to the variety of concepts of the same object (viewpoints), as *subdivision* can be called a division of the viewpoints themselves.

§113

Dichotomy and polytomy

A division into *two* members is called *dichotomy*; but if it has *more than two* members, it is called *polytomy*.

Note 1. All polytomy is empirical; dichotomy is the only division from principles *a priori*, hence the only *primitive* division. For the members of a division are supposed to be opposed to one another, but for each *A* the opposite is nothing more than *non A*.

2. Polytomy cannot be taught in logic, for it involves *cognition of the object*. Dichotomy requires only the *principle of contradiction*, however, without being acquainted, *as to content*, with the concept one wants to divide. Polytomy requires *intuition*, either *a priori*, as in mathematics (e.g., in the division of conic sections), or empirical intuition, as in description of nature. However, division based on the *principle of synthesis*[r] *a priori* has

[q] "Widerspiel."
[r] "*Princip der Synthesis*."

148 *trichotomy*, namely: (1.) the concept as condition, (2.) the conditioned and (3.) the derivation of the latter from the former.

§114

Various divisions of method

Now as for what concerns in particular *method* itself in working up and treating scientific cognitions, there are various principal kinds of it, which we can present in accordance with the following division.

§115

1. *Scientific or popular method*

Scientific[s] or *scholastic* method differs from *popular* method through the fact that the former proceeds from basic and elementary propositions, but the latter from the *customary* and the interesting. The former aims for *thoroughness* and thus removes everything foreign, the latter aims at *entertainment*.

Note. These two methods differ as to *kind*, then, and not merely as to exposition, and popularity in method is hence something other than popularity in exposition.

§116

2. *Systematic or fragmentary method*

Systematic method is opposed to *fragmentary* or *rhapsodic* method. If one has thought in accordance with a method and then also expressed this method in the exposition, and if the transition from one proposition to another is distinctly presented, then one has treated a cognition systematically. If, on the other hand, one has thought according to a method but has not arranged the exposition methodically, such a method is to be called *rhapsodic*.

Note. *Systematic* exposition is opposed to the *fragmentary* as *methodical* exposition
149 is to the *tumultuous*. He who thinks methodically can expound systemati-

[s] "*scientifische*."

cally or fragmentarily, that is. Exposition that is outwardly fragmentary but in itself methodical is *aphoristic*.

§117

3. *Analytic or synthetic method*

Analytic is opposed to *synthetic* method. The former begins with the conditioned and grounded and proceeds to principles (*a principiatis ad principia*), while the latter goes from principles to consequences or from the simple to the composite. The former could also be called *regressive*, as the latter could *progressive*.

Note. Analytic method is also called the method of *invention*. Analytic method is more appropriate for the end of popularity, synthetic method for the end of scientific and systematic preparation of cognition.

§118

4. *Syllogistic* [*or*] *tabular method*

Syllogistic method is that according to which a science is expounded in a chain of inferences.

That method in accordance with which a finished system is exhibited in its complete connection is called *tabular*.

§119

5. *Acroamatic or erotematic method*

Method is *acroamatic* insofar as someone only teaches, *erotematic* insofar as he asks as well. The latter method can be divided in turn into *dialogic* or *Socratic* method and *catechistic* method, accordingly as the questions are directed either to the *understanding* or merely to *memory*.

Note. One cannot teach erotematically except through the *Socratic dialogue*, in which both must ask and also answer one another in turn, so that it seems as if the pupil is also himself teacher. The Socratic dialogue teaches, that is, through questions, by acquainting the learner with his own principles of reason and sharpening his attention to them. Through common *catechism*, however, one cannot teach but can only elicit what one has taught acroamatically. Catechistic method also holds, then, only for empirical and historical cognitions, while the dialogic holds for rational cognitions.

150

§120

Meditation

By meditation is to be understood reflection, or methodical thought. Medi tation must accompany all reading and learning, and for this it is requisit that one *first* undertake provisional investigations and *then* put hi thoughts in order, or connect them in accordance with a method.

PART V

Appendixes

A. German-English glossary

German terms are given in their contemporary spellings. Where a German term is translated by more than one English term, but the English terms are used interchangeably, they are separated by commas. Where a German term is translated by more than one English term, with distinct meanings, the English terms are separated by semicolons.

Abgemessenheit: precision
abgeschmackt: stupid
ableiten: derive
abnehmen: conclude
Abschnitt: section
Absicht: purpose, intention; respect
absondern: separate; abstract
abweisen: reject, turn back
Aggregat: aggregate
allgemein: universal
analysieren: analyze
Analysis: analysis
analytisch: analytic
anbringen: set forth
angeben: state, indicate
angemessen: adequate; congruent
angenehm: pleasant
angewandt: applied
Anleitung: guidance, directive
annehmen: accept; suppose
anschaulich: intuitive
Anschauung: intuition
Ansehen: prestige
Ansehung: regard
anstellen: obtain, arrange
antworten: answer
Anweisung: directive
Art: kind, way, mode; species
Artigkeit: politeness
Aufgabe: problem, task
aufheben: remove
auflösen: resolve, break up
Auflösung: resolution; solution
aufschieben: defer
aufstellen: put forth
Auftrag: commission
augenscheinlich: evident
Augenscheinlichkeit: evidence
Ausbreitung: extensiveness
Ausdehnung: extension
auseinandersetzen: explicate
ausfindig machen: discover
ausführlich: exhaustive
Ausführlichkeit: exhaustiveness
ausgebreitet: extensive
ausgedehnt: extended
ausmachen: settle, decide; constitute
ausrichten: accomplish
äußer: external
außerwesentlich: extra-essential
ausüben: employ
Ausübung: employment
Auszug: selection, excerpt

beantworten: to provide an answer
Bedeutung: meaning, sense
bedingt: conditioned
Bedingung: condition
befördern: further, promote
Begehrungsvermögen: faculty of desire
begreifen: comprehend
Begriff: concept
behandeln: deal with, treat

beharren: persist
Beifall: approval
beilegen: attribute, attach
bejahend: affirmative
belegen: provide evidence for, show
Belieben: wish
Beraubung: deprivation
Beredsamkeit: oratory
Beschaffenheit: character
beschränken: restrict
besonder: particular; special
besonders: in particular; especially
beständig: constant, lasting
bestimmen: determine
bestimmend: determinative, determining
bestimmt: determinate
Bestimmung: determination
betrachten: consider
Betrachtung: consideration
beurteilen: pass judgment on
Beweis: proof
beweisen: prove
Beweisgrund: ground of proof
Beweistum: ground of proof
bezeichnen: signify, designate
Bezeichnung: signification
beziehen (*sich . . . auf*): relate to
Bild: image
bilden: cultivate
billig: fair
Billigkeit: fairness
bündig: coherent
Bündigkeit: coherence

darlegen: display
darstellen: exhibit; present
dartun: show
definieren: define
Definition: definition
denken: think
Denken: thought, thinking
Denkspruch: motto
deutlich: distinct
Deutlichkeit: distinctness
dichten: fabricate
Dichtung: fabrication
dissimulieren: conceal
dunkel: obscure
Dunkelheit: obscurity

Eigendunkel: self-conceit
Eigenschaft: property
eigentlich: actual(ly), real(ly); proper(ly)
Einbildungskraft: imagination
einfach: simple
Einheit: unity; unit
einig: in agreement
einschränken: restrict
einsehen: have insight into
Einsicht: insight
einteilen: divide
Einteilung: division
Einwurf: objection
Eitelkeit: vanity
empfinden: sense
Empfindung: sensation
Endzweck: ultimate end
entdecken: discover
Entdeckung: discovery
entlehnen: derive, borrow
entscheiden: decide
entstehen: arise
Entstehen: genesis
entwerfen: sketch
erdichten: fabricate
Erdichtung: fabrication
erfahren: experience
Erfahrung: experience
erfinden: discover, invent
erfordern: require
erforschen: investigate
erhalten: attain
erkennen: cognize
Erkenntnis: cognition
erklären: explain, illuminate; define
Erklärung: explanation, illumination; definition
erkünsteln: fabricate
erläutern: elucidate
erlangen: acquire, attain
erscheinen: appear
Erscheinung: appearance
erweisen: prove
erweislich: provable
erweitern: extend

Erweiterung: extension
erwerben: acquire
erzeugen: create, generate
Evidenz: evidence

Fähigkeit: capacity
fassen: comprehend, grasp
Fasslichkeit: comprehensibility
Fehler: mistake
Fehlschluß: mistaken inference
Fertigkeit: skill, accomplishment; readiness
Folge: consequence
folgern: deduce
Folgerung: deduction
Form: form
förmlich: formal
forschen: inquire, investigate
fruchtleer: fruitless
füglich: suitable
Fürwahrhalten: holding-to-be-true

Gattung: genus
Gebrauch: use
gebrauchen: use
gefallen: please
Gefühl: feeling
gegeben: given
Gegenteil: opposite
gekünstelt: affected
gelehrt: learned
Gelehrter: learned man
Gelehrtheit: learnedness
gemäß: conformable to; in conformity with
gemein: common; general
Gemüt: mind
genau: exact
gesamt: entire, whole
geschehen: take place, occur
Geschmack: taste
gesellig: sociable
gesellschaftlich: social
Gesinnung: sentiment
gesund: healthy
Gewißheit: certainty
Gewohnheit: custom

glauben: believe
Glaube: belief
gleichartig: homogeneous
Glückseligkeit: happiness; blessedness
Grad: degree
Grenze: limit, boundary
grob: crude
Grübelei: cavilling
gründlich: thorough
Gründlichkeit: thoroughness
Grund: ground, reason
Grund- [as prefix]: basic

handeln: act
Handlung: action
hellig: lucid
Helligkeit: lucidity
herrlich: excellent
hervorbringen: produce
hinlänglich: sufficient
Hinlänglichkeit: sufficiency
Hochmut: pride
Horizont: horizon

Inbegriff: complex
Inhalt: content
innewerden: become aware
inner: internal
Irrtum: error

kennen: be acquainted with
Kenntnis: acquaintance, familiarity
Kennzeichen: characteristic
klar: clear
Klarheit: clarity
kongruent: congruent
Konsequenz: *consequentia*
Körper: body
körperlich: corporeal
künsteln: cultivate
künstlich: artificial; artful
Kunst: art

Lehnsatz: lemma
Lehre: doctrine
Lehrsatz: dogma; thesis
Lehrspruch: rule

listig: cunning
locken: attract
Lust: pleasure

machen: make
Mangel: lack
mannigfaltig: manifold
Mannigfaltige: manifold
Materie: matter
meinen: opine
Meinung: opinion
Menge: multitude, collection
Merkmal: mark
mittelbar: mediate
mutmaßen: conjecture

nach: according to, as to
Nachahmung: imitation
nachdenken: reflect
nachforschen: inquire
Nachteil: detriment, disadvantage
Natur: nature
Nebenbegriff: coordinate concept
Nebeneinteilung: codivision
Neigung: inclination
notwendig: necessary
Nutzen: use, gain, profit

Obersatz: major proposition

Peinlichkeit: fussiness
Phantasie: imagination
Pöbel: the crowd
Profundität: profundity
Pünktlichkeit: meticulousness

Quell: source
Quelle: source

Raum: space
Recht: justice
rechtmäßig: rightful
rechtschaffen: honest
Rechtschaffenheit: honesty, righteousness
Rechtsgelehrsamkeit: jurisprudence
Rechtsgelehrter: jurist
redlich: sincere, honest
Regel: rule
Reihe: series
rein: pure
Reiz: stimulation
reizen: stimulate
roh: rough
Rücksicht: respect
rühren: excite
Rührung: excitement

Sage: rumor
Satz: proposition; principle
Scharfsinn: acuity
Schein: illusion
scheinbar: plausible
Scheinbarkeit: plausibility
schließen: infer
Schluß: inference
Schlußfolgerung: deduction
Schmuck: ornament
schön: beautiful, fine
Schranke: restriction
seicht: shallow
sicher: sure, certain
simulieren: pretend
Sinn: sense
sinnleer: meaningless
sinnlich: sensible
Sinnlichkeit: sensibility
Sinnspruch: aphorism
sollen: ought, be supposed to
Spruch: saying
Sprichwort: proverb
stattfinden: occur; exist
Stoff: material
Stufe: gradation
stumpf: dull
Synthesis: synthesis
synthetisch: synthetic

tabellarisch: tabular
tadelhaft: blameworthy
tadeln: blame, reprove
Teil: part
teilen: take apart, partition
Tiefsinn: profundity

Treue: fidelity, good faith
treu: faithful
Triebfeder: motive
Trugschluß: fallacy
Tüchtigkeit: competence

üben: practice, exercise
übereinstimmen: agree
Übereinstimmung: agreement
überhaupt: in general
überlegen: reflect
überreden: persuade
Überredung: persuasion
überzeugen: convince
Überzeugung: conviction
Uebung: practice, exercise
Umfang: extension
umgekehrt: conversely
umkehren: convert
unauflöslich: irreducible
Unbeständigkeit: inconstancy
unendlich: infinite
ungereimt: absurd
Unlust: displeasure
unmittelbar: immediate
unstreitig: indisputable
Untersatz: minor proposition
unterscheiden: distinguish
Unterschied: distinction, difference
Untereinteilung: subdivision
unvollkommen: imperfect
Unvollkommenheit: imperfection
Unwissenheit: ignorance
Urbild: archetype
Urteil: judgment
urteilen: judge
Urteilskraft: power of judgment

verachten: despise
verändern: alter
Veränderung: alteration
verbinden: combine
Verbindung: combination
Verdienst: merit, gain
vereinbar: compatible
verfahren: proceed
Verfahren: procedure
vergänglich: perishable
vergnügen: please
Verhalten: conduct
verkehrt: absurd
verknüpfen: connect
verlegen: perplexed
Vermessenheit: arrogance
Vermögen: faculty; wealth
vermuten: surmise, suppose
verneinend: negative
vernünfteln: engage in reasoning
Vernunft: reason
Vernunftkünstler: artist of reason
versetzen: transpose
Versetzung: transposition
Verstand: the understanding
verständlich: understandable
versteckt: covert
Versuch: trial, attempt; experiment
verträglich: social
vertragen (*sich*): be compatible
verwerfen: reject
verworren: confused
Vielgültigkeit: richness
vollkommen: perfect
Vollkommenheit: perfection
vollständig: complete
Vollständigkeit: completeness
vorausgesetzt: presupposed, given
voraussetzen: presuppose
Vorbild: prototype
vorläufig: provisional
vornehm: excellent, noble, foremost
Vorsatz: intention; resolve
Vorschrift: precept
vorstellen (*sich etwas . . .*): represent
Vorteil: benefit, advantage
Vortrag: exposition
vortragen: expound
vortrefflich: excellent
Vorurteil: prejudice
Vorzug: advantage, superiority

wahr: true
Wahrheit: truth
Wahrnehmung: perception
Wahrscheinlichkeit: probability
wanken: waver

Wechselbegriff: convertible concept
weitläufig: extensive
Weitläufigkeit: extensiveness
Werth: worth
Wesen: essence; nature
widerlegen: refute
widersprechen: contradict
Widerstreit: conflict
Wille: will
Willkür: faculty of choice
willkürlich: arbitrary
wirken: act upon, affect
wirklich: actual(ly), real(ly)
Wirklichkeit: actuality
wissen: know
Wissen: knowledge
Wissenschaft: science
Wohlgefallen: satisfaction
Wohlredenheit: eloquence
Würde: dignity

Zahl: number
zählen: count
zergliedern: analyze
Zeuge: witness
Zeugnis: testimony
zufällig: contingent
zureichend: sufficient
zurückhalten: withhold, reserve
zusammenhängen: be connected
Zusammenhang: connection
zusammensetzen: put together, compound
zusammengesetzt: composite
Zusatz: corollary
Zweck: end

B. English-German glossary

abstract: absondern
absurd: ungereimt, verkehrt
accept: annehmen
accomplish: ausrichten
according to: nach
acquaintance: Kenntnis
acquainted (*be . . . with*): kennen
acquire: erlangen, erwerben
act: handeln
act upon: wirken
action: Handlung
actual: wirklich
actuality: Wirklichkeit
actually: wirklich
acuity: Scharfsinn
adequate: angemessen
advantage: Vorteil; Vorzug
affect: wirken
affirmative: bejahend
agree: übereinstimmen
agreement: Uebereinstimmung
alter: verändern
alteration: Veränderung
analysis: Analysis
analytic: analytisch
analyze: analysieren, zergliedern
answer: beantworten
answer (*to provide an . . .*): beantworten
aphorism: Sinnspruch
appear: erscheinen
appearance: Erscheinung
applied: angewandt
approval: Beifall
arbitrary: willkürlich
archetype: Urbild
arise: entstehen
arrange: anstellen
art: Kunst
artful: künstlich
artificial: künstlich
artist of reason: Vernunftkünstler
as to: nach
attain: erhalten; erlangen
attempt: Versuch; versuchen
attract: locken
attribute: beilegen
aware (*become . . .*): innewerden

basic: Grund- [*as prefix*]
beautiful: schön
belief: Glaube
believe: glauben
benefit: Vorteil
blame: tadeln
blameworthy: tadelhaft
blessedness: Glückseligkeit
body: Körper
borrow: entlehnen
break up: auflösen

capacity: Fähigkeit
certain: gewiß, sicher
certainty: Gewißheit
character: Beschaffenheit
characteristic: Kennzeichen
choice (*faculty of . . .*): Willkür
clarity: Klarheit
clear: klar
codivision: Nebeneinteilung
cognition: Erkenntnis
cognize: erkennen
coherent: bündig
coherence: Bündigkeit
collection: Menge
combination: Verbindung
combine: verbinden

commission: Auftrag
common: gemein
compatible: vereinbar
competence: Tüchtigkeit
complete: vollständig
completeness: Vollständigkeit
complex: Inbegriff
composite: zusammengesetzt
compound: zusammensetzen
comprehend: begreifen; fassen
comprehensibility: Begreiflichkeit; Fasslichkeit
comprehensible: begreiflich; fasslich
concept: Begriff
conclude: abnehmen
condition: Bedingung
conduct: Verhalten
conflict: Widerstreit
conformable to: gemäß
confused: verworren
congruent: kongruent; angemessen
conjecture: mutmaßen
connect: verknüpfen
connected (be . . . with): zusammenhängen
connection: Verknüpfung; Zummenhang
consequence: Folge
consider: betrachten
consideration: Betrachtung
constant: beständig
constitute: ausmachen
content: Inhalt
contingent: zufällig
contradict: widersprechen
conversely: umgekehrt
convert: umkehren
convertible concept: Wechselbegriff
conviction: Ueberzeugung
convince: überzeugen
coordinate concept: Nebenbegriff
corollary: Zusatz
corporeal: körperlich
count: zählen
create: erzeugen
crowd: Pöbel
crude: grob
cultivate: bilden künsteln
cunning: listig
custom: Gewohnheit

deal with: behandeln
decide: entscheiden
deduce: folgern
deduction: Folgerung; Schlußfolgerung
defer: aufschieben
define: definieren; erklären
definition: Definition; Erklärung
degree: Grad, der
deprivation: Beraubung
derive: ableiten; entlehnen
designate: bezeichnen
desire (faculty of . . .): Begehrungsvermögen
despise: verachten
determinate: bestimmt
determination: Bestimmung
determinative: bestimmend
determine: bestimmen
determining: bestimmend
detriment: Nachteil
difference: Unterschied
dignity: Würde
directive: Anleitung; Anweisung
disadvantage: Nachteil
discover: entdecken; erfinden
discovery: Entdeckung; Erfindung
display: darlegen
displeasure: Unlust
distinct: deutlich
distinction: Unterschied
distinctness: Deutlichkeit
distinguish: unterscheiden
divide: einteilen
division: Einteilung
doctrine: Lehre
dogma: Lehrsatz

eloquence: Wohlredenheit
elucidate: erläutern
elucidation: Erläuterung
employ: ausüben
employment: Ausübung
end: Zweck
entire: gesamt
error: Irrtum

especially: besonders
essence: Wesen
evidence: Augenscheinlichkeit; Evidenz
evidence (*provide . . . for*): belegen
evident: augenscheinlich
exact: genau
excerpt: Auszug
excite: rühren
excitement: Rührung
exercise: üben; Uebung
exhaustive: ausführlich
exhaustiveness: Ausführlichkeit
exhibit: darstellen
exist: stattfinden
experience: erfahren; Erfahrung
experiment: Versuch
explain: erklären
explanation: Erklärung
explicate: auseinandersetzen
exposition: Vortrag
expound: vortragen
extend: erweitern
extended: ausgedehnt
extension: Umfang; Erweiterung; Ausdehnung
extensive: ausgebreitet; weitläufig
extensiveness: Weitläufigkeit; Ausbreitung
external: äußer
extra-essential: außerwesentlich

fabricate: erdichten, dichten; erkünsteln
fabrication: Erdichtung; Dichtung
faculty: Vermögen
fair: billig
fairness: Billigkeit
faith (*good . . .*): Treue
faithful: treu
fallacy: Trugschluß
familiarity: Kenntnis
feeling: Gefühl
fidelity: Treue
fine: schön
form: Form
formal: förmlich
fruitless: fruchtleer
further: fördern
fussiness: Peinlichkeit

gain: Nutzen
general (*in . . .*): überhaupt
generate: erzeugen
genesis: Entstehen, das
genus: Gattung
given: gegeben
given that: vorausgesetzt
gradation: Stufe
grasp: fassen
ground: Grund
ground of proof: Beweisgrund; Beweistum
guidance: Anleitung

happiness: Glückseligkeit
healthy: gesund
holding-to-be-true: Fürwahrhalten
homogeneous: gleichartig
honest: rechtschaffen; redlich
honesty: Rechtschaffenheit
horizon: Horizont

ignorance: Unwissenheit
illuminate: erklären
illumination: Erklärung
illusion: Schein
image: Bild, das
imagination: Einbildungskraft; Phantasie
imitation: Nachahmung
immediate: unmittelbar
in general: überhaupt
in particular: besonders
inclination: Neigung
inconstancy: Unbeständigkeit
indisputable: unstreitig
infer: schließen
inference: Schluß
inference (*mistaken . . .*): Fehlschluß
inquire: forschen, nachforschen
insight: Einsicht
insight (*have . . . into*): einsehen
intention: Absicht; Vorsatz
internal: inner
intuition: Anschauung
intuitive: anschaulich
invent: erfinden
invention: Erfindung

investigate: erforschen, forschen
irreducible: unauflöslich

judge: urteilen
judgment: Urteil
judgment (pass . . . on): beurteilen
judgment (power of . . .): Urteilskraft
jurisprudence: Rechtsgelehrsamkeit
jurist: Rechtsgelehrte

kind: Art
know: wissen
knowledge: Wissen

lack: Mangel
lasting: beständig
learned: gelehrt
learnedness: Gelehrtheit
lemma: Lehnsatz
limit: Grenze
lucid: hellig
lucidity: Helligkeit

major proposition: Obersatz
make: machen
manifold: mannigfaltig; Mannigfaltige
mark: Merkmal
material: Stoff
matter: Materie
meaning: Bedeutung
meaningless: sinnleer
mediate: mittelbar
merit: Verdienst
meticulousness: Pünktlichkeit
mind: Gemüt
minor proposition: Untersatz
mistake: Fehler
modality: Modalität
mode: Art
motive: Triebfeder
motto: Denkspruch
multitude: Menge

nature: Natur; Wesen
necessary: notwendig
negative: verneinend
number: Zahl

objection: Einwurf
obscure: dunkel
obtain: anstellen
occur: geschehen; stattfinden
opine: meinen
opinion: Meinung
opposite: Gegenteil
oratory: Beredsamkeit
ought: sollen

part: Teil
particular: besonder
perceive: wahrnehmen
perception: Wahrnehmung
perfect: vollkommen
perfection: Vollkommenheit
perishable: vergänglich
perplexed: verlegen
persist: beharren
persuade: überreden
persuasion: Ueberredung
plausibility: Scheinbarkeit
plausible: scheinbar
pleasant: angenehm
please: gefallen
pleasure: Lust
politeness: Artigkeit
practice: üben; Uebung
precept: Vorschrift
precise: abgemessen
precision: Abgemessenheit
prejudice: Vorurteil
present: darstellen
prestige: Ansehen
presuppose: voraussetzen
pride: Hochmut
principle: Satz
probable: wahrscheinlich
probability: Wahrscheinlichkeit
problem: Aufgabe
procedure: Verfahren
proceed: verfahren
produce: hervorbringen
profit: Nutzen
profundity: Tiefsinn; Profundität
promote: befördern
proof: Beweis
proper(ly): eigentlich
property: Eigenschaft
proposition: Satz

prototype: Vorbild
provable: erweislich
prove: beweisen; erweisen
proverb: Sprichwort
provisional: vorläufig
pure: rein
purpose: Absicht
put together: zusammensetzen

readiness: Fertigkeit
real(ly): eigentlich; wirklich
reason: Vernunft
reflect: überlegen; nachdenken
refute: widerlegen
regard: Ansehung
reject: abweisen; verwerfen
relate to: beziehen (sich . . . auf)
remove: aufheben
represent: vorstellen (sich etwas . . .)
reprove: tadeln
require: erfordern
reserve: zurückhalten
resolve: auflösen; Vorsatz
respect: Absicht; Rücksicht
restrict: beschränken
restriction: Schranke
richness: Vielgültigkeit
righteousness: Rechtschaffenheit
rough: roh
rule: Regel; Lehrspruch
rumor: Sage

satisfaction: Wohlgefallen
saying: Spruch
science: Wissenschaft
section: Abschnitt
sensation: Empfindung
sense: empfinden
sensible: sinnlich
sensibility: Sinnlichkeit
sentiment: Gesinnung
separate: absondern
series: Reihe
settle: ausmachen
settled: ausgemacht
shallow: seicht
show: belegen; dartun
signification: Bezeichnung
signify: bezeichnen
simple: einfach
sincere: redlich
sketch: entwerfen
skill: Fertigkeit
sociable: gesellig
social: gesellschaftlich; verträglich
source: Quell; Quelle
space: Raum
special: besonder
species: Art
state: angeben
stimulate: reizen
stimulation: Reiz
stupid: abgeschmackt
subdivision: Untereinteilung
sufficiency: Hinlänglichkeit
sufficient: zureichend; hinlänglich
superiority: Vorzug
suppose: vermuten; annehmen
supposed (*be . . . to*): sollen
surmise: vermuten
suitable: füglich
sure: sicher
synthesis: Synthesis
synthetic: synthetisch

tabular: tabellarisch
take apart: teilen
take place: geschehen
task: Aufgabe
taste: Geschmack
testimony: Zeugnis
thesis: Lehrsatz
think: denken
thinking: Denken
thought: Denken
thorough: gründlich
thoroughness: Gründlichkeit
time: Zeit
transpose: versetzen
transposition: Versetzung
treat: behandeln
trial: Versuch
true: wahr
truth: Wahrheit
turn back: abweisen

ultimate end: Endzweck
understandable: verständlich
understanding: Verstand
unit: Einheit
unity: Einheit
universal: allgemein
use: gebrauchen; Gebrauch; Nutzen

vanity: Eitelkeit

waver: wanken
way: Art
wealth: Vermögen
whole: gesamt
will: Wille
wish: Belieben
withhold: zurückhalten
witness: Zeuge
worth: Wert

C. A concordance of G. F. Meier's Excerpts from the Doctrine of Reason *(with Kant's reflections) and the* Jäsche logic

What follows is a table which summarizes the contents of Kant's handwritten notes on Meier's *Excerpts from the Doctrine of Reason* and correlates them with the related pages of the *Jäsche logic.* These notes, or reflections, were inscribed in Kant's personal copy of the text, from which he lectured. They were edited by Erich Adickes and published in Volume 16 of the Academy edition.

The main headings (in bold-face and italics) are taken from Meier's text. The subsidiary headings were provided by Adickes for Volume 16, and they reflect the content of Kant's reflections rather than of Meier's text. Next to each heading are: the numbers of the corresponding paragraphs of Meier's text; the page numbers in Volume 16 where both Kant's reflections and the relevant sections of Meier's text are printed; and the page numbers in Volume 9 of the corresponding portion of the *Jäsche logic.*

This table is derived from the table of contents for Volume 16 and from the correlations established by Adickes and printed at the beginning of each section within that volume. Note that not all paragraphs of Meier's text appear in this table, and that not all entries in the table find a place in the *Jäsche logic.*

Contents:	Paragraph in Meier	Pagination of Vol. 16	Pagination of Vol. 9
Introduction to the doctrine of reason	§§ 1–9	3–75	11–87
Concept, task, and division of logic	§§ 1–4	3–50	11–21
Concept and division of logic	§ 5	51–71	21–3
Analytic–dialectic. Theoretical–practical logic. Value of logic	§§ 6–9	71–5	16–20

Contents:	Paragraph in Meier	Pagination of Vol. 16	Pagination of Vol. 9
The first main part: Of learned cognition	§§ 10–413	76–775	33–136
The first section: Of learned cognition in general	§§ 10–40	76–169	33–9
Representation. Object of representation. Kinds of representation. Clarity. Distinctness	§§ 10–14	76–91	33–5
Ground and consequence	§§ 15–16	91–3	
Cognition of reason, historical cognition	§§ 17–18	93–9	21–2
Logical and aesthetic perfection of cognition	§§ 19–35	99–162	35–9
Imperfections of cognition	§ 36	162–6	44–5
The second section: Of the extensiveness of learned cognition	§§ 41–65	170–218	40–9
Ignorance. Horizon of cognition	§§ 41–9	170–90	40–4
Praiseworthy and blameworthy ignorance	§§ 50–2	190–5	44–5
Polyhistory, *humaniora*	§§ 53–4	195–202	45–6
Pedantry, gallantry	§ 65	206–18	46–8
The third section: Of the quantity of learned cognition	§§ 66–91	219–36	49
The fourth section: Of the truth of learned cognition	§§ 92–114	237–95	49–57
Nature[1] and criteria of truth and falsity	§§ 92–8	237–61	49–54
Logical, aesthetic and practical truth; total and partial truth. Exact and subtle cognition, rough and crude cognition	§§ 99–103	262–75	54–5
Dogmatic and historical truths. System	§§ 104–5	275–80	
Nature[2] of error	§§ 109–10	282–88	53–7
Kinds of error	§§ 111–13	288–94	55–7
The fifth section: Of the clarity of learned cognition.	§§ 115–54	296–358	58–65
Mark	§ 115	296–300	58
Analytic and synthetic	§ 116	300–4	58–9

Contents:	Paragraph in Meier	Pagination of Vol. 16	Pagination of Vol. 9
marks, coordinated and subordinated marks			
Affirmative and negative marks	§ 117	305–7	59–60
Important and unimportant, fruitful and unfruitful marks	§ 118	307–9	60
Sufficient and insufficient marks	§ 119	309–310	60
Necessary and contingent marks	§ 120	310	60
External and internal marks. *Modi, attributa, essentia*	§ 121	311–15	60–1
Clear, distinct and obscure cognition	§§ 122–31	315–26	61–2
Degrees of clarity. Distinctness	§§ 132–4	327–32	61–4
Liveliness of cognition	§ 135	333–8	62
Analytic and synthetic distinctness. Degrees of cognition	§§ 139–40	340–46	63–5
Degrees of distinctness	§ 147–54	349–58	62–3
The sixth section: Of the certainty of learned cognition	§§ 155–215	359–515	65–86
Certainty of cognition. Opining, believing, knowing	§§ 155–67	359–96	65–73
Reservation of judgment. Provisional judgments	§ 168	396–400	73–5
Prejudice in general	§§ 168–9	400–12	75–7
Kinds of prejudices. Procedure against prejudices	§ 170	412–27	77–81
Probability, plausibility, moral certainty	§§ 171–5	427–43	81–2
Doubt, scruple, objection	§ 176	444–6	83
True and false doubts. Resolution of doubts. Settled and unsettled truths	§ 177	446–51	83
Dogmatism. Skepticism. Skeptical method	§§ 178–80	452–61	83–4
Hypothesis	§§ 181–3	461–72	84–6
Persuasion	§ 184	473–5	73
Science. System	§ 185	476–8	72
Kinds and degrees of certainty	§§ 186–9	479–82	70–1

Contents:	Paragraph in Meier	Pagination of Vol. 16	Pagination of Vol. 9
Arbitrary truths	§ 190	482–3	
Proof	§§ 191–200	483–92	71
Experience. Reason. Belief.	§§ 201–6	493–504	66–71
Witness. Disbelief. Moral belief	§§ 207–15	504–15	67–72
The seventh section: Of practical learned cognition	§§ 216–48	516–32	86–87
Practical, speculative, theoretical	§§ 216–17	516–19	86–87
The eighth section: Of learned concepts	§§ 249–91	533–623	91–100, 140–148
Concept in general. Idea	§§ 249–53	533–41	91–4
Kinds of concepts. Concepts of experience	§§ 254–58	541–9	92–4
Abstraction, comparison, reflection	§§ 259–60	549–558	94–5
Contents, extension of concepts. Higher, lower Concept. Genus, species	§§ 261–5	559–67	95–100
Arbitrarily made concepts	§§ 266–7	568–72	93
Definition, exposition, description	§§268–9	572–89	140–3
Requirements for a definition	§§ 270–9	589–600	144–5
Nominal and real definitions	§§ 280–4	601–11	143–5
Logical division of a concept	§§ 285–91	612–23	146–8
The ninth section: Of learned judgments	§§ 292–352	624–703	100–19
Nature[3] of judgment. Matter and form	§§ 292–3	624–35	101–4
Quality of judgments	§§ 294–6	635–41	102–4
Condition, determination, analysis of judgments	§§ 297–300	642–6	
Quantity of judgments	§§ 301–3	647–51	102–3
Simple and composite judgments	§ 304	651–2	
Hypothetical and disjunctive judgments	§§305–8	653–62	104–8
Modality of judgments	§ 309	662–3	108–9
Exponible judgments	§ 310	663–4	109
Theoretical and practical judgments	§§ 311–12	664–7	110

Contents:	Paragraph in Meier	Pagination of Vol. 16	Pagination of Vol. 9
ʾrovable and unprovable empty) judgments. Axioms ınd postulates. Analytic and ynthetic judgments	§§ 313–18	667–74	110–12
udicia intuitiva – discursiva	§§ 319–322	674–7	
udgments of perception ınd of experience	§ 323	678–9	113
Corollaries. Theorems. ʾroblems. Lemmas. Scholia. *Qualitates occultae*	§§ 324–340	679–690	112
nferences of the understanding: equipollence, subılternation, opposition, conersion, contraposition of udgments	§§ 341–352	691–703	114–19
The tenth section: Of learned nferences of reason	§§ 353–413	704–75	114, 120–36
Nature,[4] constituent parts, cinds of inferences	§§ 353–6	704–10	114, 120–3, 132
Termini, matter and form of he inference of reason	§§ 357–9	710–12	121, 122–3
Jniversal rules for inferences of reason of all kinds	§§ 360–66	712–19	123, 125, 129, 130
Ordinary and extraordinary nferences of reason. Major ınd minor in ordinary (cateçorical) inferences of reason	§§ 367–8	719–20	120, 122
The four figures of inferences	§§ 369–73	721–9	125–8
Jniversal rules for categorical inferences	§§ 374–82	729–34	123–5
Particular rules for the variəus figures of categorical inferences. *Modi* of these figures	§§ 383–91	734–44	126–8
Hypothetical inferences of reason	§§ 392–4	745–8	129
Disjunctive inferences of reason	§§ 395–6	748–50	129–30
Dilemma	§ 397	750–1	130–1
Immediate deductions. Fornal and covert inferences of reason	§§ 398–400	751–2	131

Contents:	Paragraph in Meier	Pagination of Vol. 16	Pagination of Vol. 9
Induction and analogy	§ 401	753–61	131–3
Fallacies	§§ 402–5	762–7	134–5
Composite inferences of reason	§§ 406–9	768–72	133–4
Proofs and mistakes in proof	§§ 410–13	773–5	135–6
The second main part: Of the method of learned cognition	§§ 414–38	776–813	139–40, 148–50
Method in general. Various kinds of method	§§ 414–21	776–85	139–40, 148–9
Analytic and synthetic method	§§ 422–6	786–98	149
Scientific and popular method	§ 427	798–800	148
Further kinds of methods	§§ 428–33	800–9	149–50
Doctrine, discipline, science	§ 434	809–10	
Methodical and tumultuous	§435	810–11	148–9
Meditation	§§ 436–8	811–13	150
The third main part: Of learned exposition	§§ 439–63	814–64	
The first section: Of the usage of words	§§ 439–63	814–30	
The second section: Of the learned way of writing	§§ 464–78	831–7	
The third section: Of a learned speech	§§ 479–517	838–59	
The fourth section: Of learned writings	§§ 518–26	860–64	
The fourth main part: Of the character of a learned man	§§ 527–63	865–72	

[1] "Wesen."
[2] "Wesen."
[3] "Wesen."
[4] "Wesen."

D. A concordance of the translated transcripts with G. F. Meier's Excerpts from the Doctrine of Reason

Meier's Text	Ak., Vol. 16	Blomberg	Wiener	Hechsel	Dohna-Wndl.
§ 1	5	26–27	790; 792	–	693
§ 2	5	28	791–2	–	693–4
§ 3	5	29	–	–	–
§ 4	5	–	–	–	–
§ 5	51–2	29–31	797–9	–	697–8
§ 6	72	38	793–4	–	695
§ 7	72–3	38	794	–	700
§ 8	73	38–9	–	–	–
§ 9	74	–	–	–	–
§ 10	76	39–40	797–8	–	701
§ 11	76–7	40	797–8	–	–
§ 12	79	40	797–8	–	–
§ 13	80	40–1	797–8	–	702
§ 14	80–1	41–2	797–8	–	702–3
§ 15	91	42–3	–	–	703
§ 16	92	43	–	–	703
§ 17	93–4	43	–	–	703–4
§ 18	94	43–9	–	–	704
§ 19	99	43–9	808–12	–	705
§ 20	100–1	49	–	–	–
§ 21	101	49–50	–	–	–
§ 22	101–2	50–2	809–10	–	705–7
§ 23	103–4	52–4	813–14	–	708
§ 24	104	54–5	–	–	–
§ 25	105	55–6	–	–	711–12
§ 26	106	55–6	–	–	709
§ 27	106	56	–	–	709
§ 28	107	56–7	–	–	709
§ 29	107	57	–	–	–
§ 30	108	58–9	815	–	–
§ 31	109	59–60	–	–	–

Meier's Text	Ak., Vol. 16	Blomberg	Wiener	Hechsel	Dohna-W
§ 32	109	60	–	–	–
§ 33	109–110	60	–	–	–
§ 34	110	61–3	–	–	–
§ 35	111	63	–	–	–
§ 36	163	63–4	813	–	710
§ 37	167–8	64–5	–	–	–
§ 38	168	65	–	–	–
§ 39	168–9	65	–	–	–
§ 40	169	65–6	–	–	–
§ 41	170–1	66	–	–	–
§ 42	171	66	–	–	710
§ 43	172	66–7	–	–	–
§ 44	173	67–9	814–17	–	711–12
§ 45	174	67–9	815–16	–	711
§ 46	175–6	69–70	816	–	711
§ 47	176–7	70	–	–	712
§ 48	177	71	–	–	–
§ 49	178	–	–	–	–
§ 50	190–1	71	–	–	713
§ 51	194–5	–	817	–	–
§ 52	195	71–2	–	–	–
§ 53	195–6	72	818	–	713–14
§ 54	197–8	–	818	–	714
§ 55	202	72–3	–	–	–
§ 56	202	73	–	–	–
§ 57	202	73	–	–	–
§ 58	203	73–4	–	–	–
§ 59	203	74–5	–	–	–
§ 60	203	–	–	–	–
§ 61	204	75	–	–	–
§ 62	204–5	–	–	–	717
§ 63	205	–	819	–	–
§ 64	206	–	–	–	–
§ 65	206	75–6	820	–	714–16
§ 66	219	76		–	
§ 67	2119–20	–		–	
§ 68	220–1	76–7	822	–	717–18
§ 69	223	77	–	–	–
§ 70	223–4	77	–	–	–
§ 71	224	77–8	–	–	–
§ 72	224–25	77–8	–	–	–
§ 73	225	77–8	–	–	–
§ 74	225	77–8	–	–	–
§ 75	227	77–8	–	–	–
§ 76	228	–	–	–	–

Meier's Text	Ak., Vol. 16	Blomberg	Wiener	Hechsel	Dohna-Wndl.
§ 77	228	–	–	–	–
§ 78	228	–	–	–	–
§ 79	228–9	–	–	–	–
§ 80	229–30	78	–	–	–
§ 81	230	–	–	–	–
§ 82	231	78	–	–	–
§ 83	232	78–9	–	–	–
§ 84	233	79	–	–	–
§ 85	233	–	–	–	–
§ 86	234	79	–	–	–
§ 87	234	79	–	–	–
§ 88	235	79	–	–	–
§ 89	235	79	–	–	–
§ 90	236	79	–	–	–
§ 91	236	80	–	–	–
§ 92	237	80–8	–	–	–
§ 93	238	80–8	823	–	718
§ 94	238–9	88	823–4	–	718–19
§ 95	239–40	89	823–4	–	–
§ 96	241	89–90	823–4	–	–
§ 97	242	89–90	823–4	–	718
§ 98	243	89–90	823–4	–	–
§ 99	262	89–90	823–4	–	718–19
§ 100	262–4	93–96	825f./828	–	722
§ 101	264–5	–	–	–	–
§ 102	265–6	96–7	829–30	–	722–3
§ 103	267	97–9	–	–	–
§ 104	275–6	99–100	830–1	–	724
§ 105	277	–	–	–	–
§ 106	281	100–1	832	–	723
§ 107	282	–	–	–	–
§ 108	282	–	–	–	–
§ 109	282–3	101–4	832–3	–	719–20
§ 110	287	104	–	–	–
§ 111	288–9	104–5	832	–	724
§ 112	289	–	–	–	–
§ 113	290–1	105–6	832–3	–	724
§ 114	295	106	–	–	723–4
§ 115	296–7	106–8	834	–	725
§ 116	301	108–10	834–5	–	726
§ 117	305	110–11	836–7	–	726
§ 118	307–8	111–12	837–8	–	726
§ 119	309–10	112–13	838	–	726
§ 120	310	113	838	–	727
§ 121	311–12	113–18	838–40	–	727–8

Meier's Text	Ak., Vol. 16	Blomberg	Wiener	Hechsel	Dohna-W
§ 122	315	–	–	–	–
§ 123	316	–	–	–	–
§ 124	316	118–19	840–1	–	729–30
§ 125	316–18	119–22	841–42	–	729–30
§ 126	320–1	–	–	–	–
§ 127	321–2	–	–	–	–
§ 128	322	–	–	–	–
§ 129	323–4	–	–	–	–
§ 130	324	–	–	–	–
§ 131	324–6	123	–	–	729–30
§ 132	327	123–5	–	–	729–30
§ 133	328	125–6	–	–	–
§ 134	329–30	–	–	–	–
§ 135	333	126–30	842–3	–	730
§ 136	338	–	–	–	–
§ 137	338–9	–	–	–	–
§ 138	339	–	–	–	–
§ 139	340–1	130–4	842–5	–	730
§ 140	341–2	134–7	845–7	–	730–1
§ 141	346–47	–	–	–	–
§ 142	348	–	–	–	–
§ 143	348	–	–	–	–
§ 144	349	137	847–8	–	–
§ 145	349	–	–	–	–
§ 146	349	–	–	–	–
§ 147	349–50	137–8	848–9	–	731
§ 148	351–2	141–2	847	–	731
§ 149	353	138–40	847	–	731
§ 150	354	–	–	–	–
§ 151	355–6	141–2	849	–	731
§ 152	356	–	–	–	–
§ 153	357	–	–	–	–
§ 154	357–8	142	848	–	731
§ 155	359	142–51	849	–	731–2
§ 156	360	142–51	–	–	–
§ 157	361	151–2	856–7	–	–
§ 158	361–2	152	–	–	–
§ 159	362	152	–	–	–
§ 160	363–4	–	–	–	–
§ 161	364	153	857	–	734; 735
§ 162	365	–	–	–	–
§ 163	366–7	–	–	–	–
§ 164	368	–	–	–	–
§ 165	368–9	–	–	–	–
§ 166	370–1	–	–	–	–

Meier's Text	Ak., Vol. 16	Blomberg	Wiener	Hechsel	Dohna-Wndl.
§ 167	371	154–5	859	–	–
§ 168	396–401	155–61	859–61	–	735–6
§ 169	401–2	161–94	–	–	–
§ 170	412–17	161–94	863–79	–	737–42
§ 171	427–8	194–7	879–84	–	742–3
§ 172	428–9	–	–	–	–
§ 173	429	–	–	–	–
§ 174	429–30	–	–	–	–
§ 175	430–2	198–201	–	–	742
§ 176	444	201–3	884	–	743
§ 177	446–51	203–4	884	–	743–4
§ 178	452	204–18	–	–	743–4
§ 179	453–4	204–18	–	–	–
§ 180	454–5	204–18	–	–	–
§ 181	461	218–25	886–9	–	746
§ 182	462	225–6	–	–	–
§ 183	463–4	225–6	–	–	–
§ 184	473–5	226–7	889–90	–	747
§ 185	476	227–8	891	–	747
§ 186	479	–	–	–	–
§ 187	479–80	–	–	–	–
§ 188	480	–	–	–	–
§ 189	480–1	229–30	892	–	748
§ 190	482–3	230	892	–	748
§ 191	483–5	230–3	892	–	748
§ 192	485–6	230–3	893	–	748
§ 193	487	–	–	–	–
§ 194	488	–	–	–	–
§ 195	488	–	–	–	–
§ 196	488–9	233–4	893	–	748–9
§ 197	491	234	893–894	–	749
§ 198	492	–	–	–	–
§ 199	492	234	–	–	–
§ 200	492–3	235	–	–	–
§ 201	493	235–6	–	–	749–50
§ 202	493–4	–	–	–	749–50
§ 203	495	236–40	–	–	749–50
§ 204	496	236–40	–	–	749–50
§ 205	496	240–1	–	–	749–50
§ 206	496–7	241–6	895–897	–	750
§ 207	504	241–6	898–899	–	750
§ 208	505	246–7	900	–	750
§ 209	505	–	–	–	–
§ 210	506	247–8	900	–	750
§ 211	506–7	–	–	–	–

Meier's Text	Ak., Vol. 16	Blomberg	Wiener	Hechsel	Dohna-W
§ 212	507	–	–	–	–
§ 213	507–8	248–9	900	–	750
§ 214	509	249	–	–	–
§ 215	509–10	249–50	–	–	–
§ 216	516–17	250	900–903	–	751
§ 217	517	250–1	900–903	–	751
§ 218	520	–	–	–	–
§ 219	520	–	–	–	–
§ 220	520	–	–	–	–
§ 221	520	–	–	–	–
§ 222	520–1	–	–	–	–
§ 223	521	–	–	–	–
§ 224	521	–	–	–	–
§ 225	521–2	–	–	–	–
§ 226	522	–	–	–	–
§ 227	523	–	–	–	–
§ 228	523	–	–	–	–
§ 229	524	–	–	–	–
§ 230	524	–	–	–	–
§ 231	524–5	–	–	–	–
§ 232	525	–	904	–	–
§ 233	526	–	–	–	–
§ 234	526	–	–	–	–
§ 235	527	–	–	–	–
§ 236	527	–	–	–	–
§ 237	528	–	904	–	–
§ 238	528–9	–	–	–	–
§ 239	529	–	–	–	–
§ 240	529	–	–	–	–
§ 241	530	–	–	–	–
§ 242	530	–	–	–	–
§ 243	531	–	–	–	–
§ 244	531	–	–	–	–
§ 245	531	–	–	–	–
§ 246	532	–	–	–	–
§ 247	531	–	–	–	–
§ 248	532	–	–	–	–
§ 249	533	251		–	752
§ 250	534	252		–	753
§ 251	534	–	–	–	–
§ 252	535	–	–	–	–
§ 253	535–6	–	–	–	–
§ 254	541	252–4	–	–	–
§ 255	542	254–5	905	–	753
§ 256	542–3	254–5	–	–	–

Meier's Text	Ak., Vol. 16	Blomberg	Wiener	Hechsel	Dohna-Wndl.
§ 257	544	255	–	–	–
§ 258	545	–	–	–	–
§ 259	549–50	255–6	907–9	–	753–4
§ 260	551	256–9	907–9	–	753–4
§ 261	559–60	259–60	910–11	–	754–6
§ 262	560–1	260–1	911–12	–	754–6
§ 263	562	261	–	–	–
§ 264	562–3	261	–	–	–
§ 265	563	–	–	–	–
§ 266	58	261–3	–	–	–
§ 267	569	–	–	–	–
§ 268	572	263–70	912–13	–	756–60
§ 269	573	270–2	920–1	–	757–8
§ 270	589–90	–	–	–	–
§ 271	591	–	–	–	–
§ 272	591–2	–	–	–	–
§ 273	592	–	–	–	–
§ 274	593	–	921	–	–
§ 275	594	–	920	–	–
§ 276	595	–	–	–	–
§ 277	596	265	924	–	760
§ 278	597	–	–	–	–
§ 279	597–8	–	–	–	–
§ 280	601–2	268–72	919–20	–	760
§ 281	602–3	–	–	–	–
§ 282	603–4	–	–	–	–
§ 283	604	–	–	–	–
§ 284	605	–	–	–	–
§ 285	612–13	272–3	925–8	–	760–1
§ 286	613	272–3	925–8	–	761
§ 287	614–15	272–3	925–8	–	761–2
§ 288	615–17	272–3	925–8	–	761–2
§ 289	618	–	–	–	–
§ 290	618	–	–	–	–
§ 291	619	–	–	–	–
§ 292	624–5	273–5	928	–	762–3
§ 293	625–6	273–5	–	–	763
§ 294	635–6	273–5	929–30	–	764
§ 295	636	–	–	–	–
§ 296	636–7	–	–	–	–
§ 297	642	275	932	–	764
§ 298	642–4	–	–	–	764
§ 299	645	–	–	–	–
§ 300	646	–	932	–	–
§ 301	647–8	275–6	929/31/32	–	765

Meier's Text	Ak., Vol. 16	Blomberg	Wiener	Hechsel	Dohna-W
§ 302	648–9	–	–	–	–
§ 303	649	–	–	–	–
§ 304	651–2	–	–	–	–
§ 305	653	276	933–5	–	765
§ 306	653	–	–	–	–
§ 307	654	276–7	932/333/335	–	765
§ 308	654	–	–	–	–
§ 309	662–3	–	–	–	766
§ 310	663	277–8	936	–	766
§ 311	664	–	936	–	766
§ 312	665–6	278	936	–	766
§ 313	667	278–9	936	–	767
§ 314	668	–	936–7	86	767
§ 315	668	–	–	87	767–8
§ 316	669	–	–	87	–
§ 317	669–70	–	–	87	–
§ 318	670	279	–	87	–
§ 319	674–5	279–80	–	87	767
§ 320	676	–	–	–	–
§ 321	676–7	–	–	–	–
§ 322	677	–	–	–	–
§ 323	678	–	–	87	767
§ 324	679	280	–	88	767–8
§ 325	680	280	938	87	767
§ 326	680–1	–	–	88	–
§ 327	681	–	–	–	–
§ 328	681	280	938	88	767–8
§ 329	682–3	–	–	–	–
§ 330	683–4	–	–	–	–
§ 331	684–5	–	–	–	–
§ 332	685	–	–	–	–
§ 333	685	–	–	–	–
§ 334	686	–	–	–	–
§ 335	686–7	–	–	–	–
§ 336	687	–	–	–	–
§ 337	688	–	–	–	–
§ 338	688–9	–	938	88	768
§ 339	690	280	938	–	769
§ 340	690	280	938	88	768
§ 341	691–2	281	938	89	769
§ 342	693	281	938	89–90	769
§ 343	694–5	281	938	90	770
§ 344	696	281	939	91–2	770
§ 345	697	281–2	939	91–2	770
§ 346	698–9	282	939	91–2	770–1

Meier's Text	Ak., Vol. 16	Blomberg	Wiener	Hechsel	Dohna-Wndl.
§ 347	699	282	–	91–2	771
§ 348	699	282	–	91–2	–
§ 349	700	282	–	91–2	771
§ 350	700	282	–	91–2	771
§ 351	701	282	–	91–2	–
§ 352	702–3	282	939	92	771
§ 353	704	–	–	–	–
§ 354	705	282–4	939	93	771
§ 355	706	–	–	–	–
§ 356	706	284	939	93	771–2
§ 357	710–11	283	939	95	771–2
§ 358	711–12	–	–	–	–
§ 359	712	284	939	93–4, 96	772
§ 360	712–13	284	–	93–4, 96	772
§ 361	714	–	–	–	–
§ 362	714	–	–	97	773
§ 363	715	284	–	97–9, 101	773
§ 364	718	–	–	99	–
§ 365	718	–	–	99	–
§ 366	719	–	–	88–9	–
§ 367	719	284–5	939–40	–	–
§ 368	720	–	–	95–6	773
§ 369	721	–	–	99–103	774
§ 370	721	–	–	99–103	774
§ 371	722	–	–	99–103	774
§ 372	722–3	–	–	99–103	774
§ 373	723	–	–	99–103	–
§ 374	729–30	284	–	104	775
§ 375	730	–	–	104	775
§ 376	730–1	–	–	104	775
§ 377	731	–	–	104	775
§ 378	732	–	–	104	775
§ 379	732–3	–	–	104	775
§ 380	733	–	–	104	775
§ 381	733	–	–	–	–
§ 382	733–4	–	–	–	–
§ 383	734	–	–	105	775
§ 384	735	–	–	105	775
§ 385	735	–	–	103–4, 105–6	–
§ 386	736	–	–	103–4, 105–6	776
§ 387	736	–	–	103–4, 105–6	776
§ 388	736–7	–	–	103–4, 105–6	–
§ 389	737	–	–	103–4, 105–6	–
§ 390	737–8	–	–	103	–
§ 391	738	–	–	–	–

Meier's Text	Ak., Vol. 16	Blomberg	Wiener	Hechsel	Dohna-W
§ 392	745	284–6	939–40	107	776
§ 393	745–6	284–6	–	107	776
§ 394	746–7	–	–	107	–
§ 395	748–9	286	939–40	107	772–3
§ 396	749–50	286	–	107	–
§ 397	750	286	–	107	776
§ 398	751	286	–	88–9	–
§ 399	751–2	286–7	–	109	776
§ 400	752	287	–	109	776
§ 401	752–4	287	–	109	776–7
§ 402	762	287–8	–	110	777
§ 403	762–3	–	–	110–11	–
§ 404	763–4	–	–	111	–
§ 405	764–5	288	–	111–12	778
§ 406	768	288	–	112	778
§ 407	769	288	–	112	778
§ 408	769–70	288	–	112	778
§ 409	770–3	288	–	112	–
§ 410	773	288	–	113	778
§ 411	774	289	–	113	778
§ 412	775	289	–	113	778
§ 413	775	289	–	–	–
§ 414	776	289–90	–	114	779
§ 415	777	290	–	114	779
§ 416	777	–	–	–	–
§ 417	777	–	–	–	–
§ 418	777–8	–	–	–	–
§ 419	778	–	–	–	–
§ 420	778	–	–	115	–
§ 421	778	290	–	115	–
§ 422	786	291	–	115–16	779
§ 423	786–7	291	–	115–16	–
§ 424	788	291	–	115–16	–
§ 425	788	291	–	–	–
§ 426	788–9	–	–	–	779
§ 427	798	291–2	–	116	779
§ 428	800–2	292	–	116	780
§ 429	802	292	–	–	–
§ 430	802–3	292	–	116–17	780
§ 431	803–4	–	–	–	–
§ 432	804–5	292	–	117	–
§ 433	805	–	–	–	–
§ 434	809–10	293	–	–	–
§ 435	810	293	–	117	780
§ 436	811–12	293	–	117	783

Meier's Text	Ak., Vol. 16	Blomberg	Wiener	Hechsel	Dohna-Wndl.
§ 437	812–13	293	–	117	–
§ 438	813	–	–	117	–
§ 439	814	–	–	117	–
§ 440	814–15	294	–	117	–
§ 441	815	–	–	117	–
§ 442	815	–	–	117–18	–
§ 443	816	–	–	–	–
§ 444	816	–	–	–	–
§ 445	816	–	–	–	–
§ 446	816–19	–	–	117	781
§ 447	820	–	–	–	–
§ 448	820	–	–	–	–
§ 449	820–1	294	–	117	781
§ 450	821	294	–	117	781
§ 451	821–2	–	–	–	–
§ 452	822–3	294	–	117	781
§ 453	823	–	–	–	–
§ 454	824	294	–	–	–
§ 455	824	–	–	–	–
§ 456	824–5	–	–	–	–
§ 457	825	294	–	–	781
§ 458	825	–	–	–	–
§ 459	826	–	–	–	–
§ 460	826–7	–	–	–	–
§ 461	827–8	–	–	–	–
§ 462	828–9	–	–	–	781
§ 463	829–30	–	–	–	781
§ 464	831	294–5	–	117	781
§ 465	832	–	–	–	781
§ 466	832	–	–	–	–
§ 467	832–3	–	–	–	–
§ 468	833	–	–	–	–
§ 469	833	–	–	–	781
§ 470	833–4	–	–	–	–
§ 471	834	–	–	–	781
§ 472	835	–	–	–	–
§ 473	836	295	–	–	781
§ 474	837	–	–	–	781
§ 475	837	295	–	–	781
§ 476	837	–	–	–	–
§ 477	837	295	–	–	–
§ 478	837	–	–	–	–
§ 479	838–9	–	–	117–18	781
§ 480	839	–	–	117–18	–
§ 481	840	–	–	117–18	–

Meier's Text	Ak., Vol. 16	Blomberg	Wiener	Hechsel	Dohna-W
§ 482	841	–	–	117–18	–
§ 483	841	–	–	117–18	–
§ 484	842	–	–	117–18	–
§ 485	842	–	–	117–18	–
§ 486	843	–	–	117–18	–
§ 487	843	–	–	117–18	–
§ 488	843–4	–	–	117–18	–
§ 489	844	–	–	117–18	–
§ 490	844	295	–	117–18	–
§ 491	844–5	295	–	118	–
§ 492	845	–	–	–	–
§ 493	845	295–6	–	–	782
§ 494	846	–	–	–	–
§ 495	846	–	–	–	–
§ 496	846	–	–	–	–
§ 497	846	–	–	–	–
§ 498	846	–	–	–	–
§ 499	846–7	–	–	118	782
§ 500	847	–	–	118	782
§ 501	847	296	–	–	782
§ 502	848	–	–	–	–
§ 503	849	–	–	–	–
§ 504	849–50	296	–	118	–
§ 505	850	–	–	–	–
§ 506	850–1	–	–	–	–
§ 507	851–2	–	–	–	–
§ 508	852–4	296	–	–	782
§ 509	855	296	–	118	782
§ 510	856	–	–	–	–
§ 511	856	–	–	118	782
§ 512	856	296	–	118	782
§ 513	856	–	–	–	–
§ 514	857–8	296	–	–	782–3
§ 515	858	–	–	–	–
§ 516	859	–	–	–	–
§ 517	859	–	–	–	783
§ 518	869–71	296–7	–	–	783
§ 519	862	297	–	–	–
§ 520	863	297–8	–	–	783
§ 521	863	–	–	–	–
§ 522	864	–	–	–	–
§ 523	864	–	–	–	–
§ 524	864	–	–	–	–
§ 525	864	298	–	–	783
§ 526	864	298	–	–	783

Meier's Text	Ak., Vol. 16	Blomberg	Wiener	Hechsel	Dohna-Wndl.
§ 527	865	298	–	–	783
§ 528	865–6	–	–	–	–
§ 529	866	–	–	–	–
§ 530	866	299	–	–	–
§ 531	866	–	–	–	–
§ 532	866	–	–	–	–
§ 533	866–7	299	–	–	–
§ 534	867	–	–	–	–
§ 535	867	–	–	–	–
§ 536	867	–	–	–	–
§ 537	867	–	–	–	783
§ 538	868	–	–	–	–
§ 539	868	299	–	–	–
§ 540	868	299	–	–	–
§ 541	868–9	300	–	–	–
§ 542	869–70	–	–	–	–
§ 543	870	–	–	–	–
§ 544	870	300	–	–	–
§ 545	870	–	–	–	–
§ 546	870	300	–	–	–
§ 547	870	–	–	–	–
§ 548	870	300	–	–	–
§ 549	870–1	300	–	–	783
§ 550	871	–	–	–	–
§ 551	871	–	–	–	–
§ 552	871	–	–	–	–
§ 553	871	300–1	–	–	–
§ 554	871	301	–	–	–
§ 555	871	301	–	–	–
§ 556	871–2	301	–	–	–
§ 557	872	–	–	–	–
§ 558	872	–	–	–	–
§ 559	872	–	–	–	–
§ 560	872	–	–	–	–
§ 561	872	–	–	–	–
§ 562	872	–	–	–	–
§ 563	872	–	–	–	–

Explanatory notes

PART I. THE BLOMBERG LOGIC

1 Giovani Alfonso Borelli (1608–1679), *De motu animalium* (*On the Motion of Animals*), 1679.

2 Francis Bacon (1561–1626), often referred to as Lord Chancellor (an office he held from 1618 to 1621) and as Baron Verulam.

3 Johann Heinrich Samuel Formey (1711–1797) published his *Histoire abrégée de la philosophie* (*Abridged History of Philosophy*) in Amsterdam in 1760. Kant, however, or at least the author of the Blomberg Logic, seems to have relied on the German translation of this work, *Kurzgefassete Historie der Philosophie von Herrn Formey*, Berlin, 1763, since at many points the text of the MS corresponds closely to the latter. See Hinske, KI, lxxv-lxxvi.

4 Friedrich Gentzke (1678–1757), *Historia philosophiae* (*History of Philosophy*), Hamburg, 1724.

5 MS pagination; cf. 24:31, above.

6 The MS reads: "Hipparener, Babylonier, Orchenier, Marsyper Borsippener etc." The references are apparently to schools that existed in ancient Babylon and were identified with the cities of Sippar, Uruk, and Borsippa. See Lehmann's explanatory note (24:990).

7 A variant spelling of the name for Zoroaster.

8 "Janzu" may refer to Chuang-tze, 4th century B.C. Taoist. The reference to a 3-headed idol appears to be based on a confusion. See Lehmann's explanatory note (24:991).

9 See note 3 to 24:28, above.

10 The reference is presumably to the ebb and flow of the tides, and not merely to its occurrence but rather to its explanation as an effect of the moon's gravitation attraction, which Newton's theory of gravity made possible.

11 Petrus Ramus, or Pierre de La Ramée (1515–72), *Dialecticae Institutiones* (*Principles of Dialectic*), 1543.

12 Jacob Bernoulli (1654–1705), *Ars coniecturandi* (*The Art of Conjecture*), Basel, 1713.

13 Christian August Crusius (1715–1775), *Weg zur Gewißheit und Zuverlässigkeit der menschlichen Erkenntnis (The Way to Certainty and Reliability of Human Congition)*, Leipzig, 1747.

14 Alexander Gottlieb Baumgarten (1714–62), *Meditationes philosophicae de nonnullis ad poema pertinentibus* (*Philosophical Meditations Concerning Some Things Pertaining to a Poem*), Halle, 1735, and *Aesthetica*, 2 vols., Frankfurt an der Oder, 1750–58.

15 Not a day without lines. Attributed to the Greek sculptor Apelles, the saying is apparently meant to emphasize that the sculptor must be able to draw well, and that this requires regular practice. See the explanatory notes of Lehmann (24:993) and Hinske (KI, lxxvii).

16 The reference is probably to Johann Hübner (1668–1731), *Kurze Fragen aus der alten und neuen Geographie* (*Short Questions from Ancient and Modern Geography*), published in numerous editions.

17 White areas on a map denoted territory that was unmapped. Such areas were of course uncultivated, and in many cases not capable of cultivation.

18 Johann Matthias Gesner (1691–1761), *Primae lineae Isagoges in eruditionem universalem*, which was published by Niclas in two volumes in 1774–5, but which was also published by Gesner himself in 1756 and 1760, as Lehmann notes (24:978). If the *Blomberg Logic* dates from 1772 or earlier, as seems likely, then the earlier editions must be the ones referred to.

19 Pierre Louis Moreau de Maupertuis (1698–1759) suggested in his *Lettre sur le progres des sciences* (in *Les Oeuvres de Mr. de Maupertuis*, Dresden, 1752, pp. 327–52) that instead of building pyramids, the Egyptians could have better used their manpower to dig holes in the earth, so as to discover something of its internal structure. Voltaire ridiculed Maupertuis's suggestions. Some of Voltaire's satirical writing against Maupertuis was translated into German under the title of *Maupertuisiana* (published by Samuel König, Leipzig, 1753), though it is unclear whether this is the source to which Kant referred.

20 See note 13 to 24:38, above.

21 The place inhabited by the Israelites during their captivity in Egypt, where they were spared the plagues, including the darkness, visited upon the Egyptians.

22 Reading "Pythias" for "Phintias." The reference is to Damon and Pythias, two young Pythagoreans whose loyalty to one another epitomizes true friendship. Pythias was condemned to death for plotting against Dionysius I of Syracuse, but he was allowed to leave to settle his affairs when Damon offered to die in his place if his friend did not return. Pythias returned just in time, and Dionysius was so moved by their friendship that he set both men free.

23 See note 21 to 24:94, above.

24 A digest of the corpus juris civilis, the codification of Roman civil law prepared by order of the Byzantine emperor Justinian I in the 6th century A.D.

25 Laurent Angliviel de la Beaumelle (1726–1773), *Mes pensées*, published anonymously in 1750 or 1751.

26 Bernard le Bovier de Fontenelle (1657–1757), a proponent and interpreter of modern science who paved the way for the ideas of the Enlightenment.

27 Cf. Mark 5:25–34, Luke 8:43–48.

28 Edward Young (1683–1765), English poet and dramatist.

29 Friedrich Gottlieb Klopstock (1724–1803), German poet.

30 Johann Wilhelm Ludwig Gleim (1719–1803), German poet.

31 Jean Terrasson (1670–1750), *La philosophie applicable à tous les objets de l'esprit*

et de la raison (*Philosophy Applicable to all the Objects of the Mind and of Reason*), Paris, 1754.

32 Pierre Bayle (1647–1706), French philosopher whose views influenced Enlightenment thinkers, especially the authors of the *Encyclopédie*.

33 The reference is to Hume, *Vermischte Schriften* (*Miscellaneous Writings*), 4 volumes, Hamburg, 1754–6. Volume II contains the *Enquiry Concerning Human Understanding*, translated by J. G. Sulzer.

34 Geronimo Cardano (1501–1576) wrote nothing with this or any similar title. The reference is probably to Heinrich Cornelius Agrippa von Nettesheim (1486–1535), *De incertitudine et vanitate scientiarum* . . . (*On the Uncertainty and Vanity of the sciences* . . .), Cologne, 1527.

35 The reference is to J. H. S. Formey, *Le triomphe de l'evidénce. Avec un discours préliminaire de Mr. de Haller* (*The Triumph of Evidence. With an Introduction by M. de Haller.*), Berlin, 1756. A German translation, entitled *Prüfung der Secte, die an allem zweifelt, mit einer Vorrede von Herrn von Haller* (*Examination of the Sect that Doubts Everything, with a Preface by Mr. von Haller.*), appeared at Göttingen in 1757.

36 E. Pontopiddans, *Versuch einer natürlichen Historie von Norwegen* (*Attempt at a Natural History of Norway*), translated from Danish, Flensburg and Leipzig, 1769.

37 The example is obviously supposed to illustrate reduction of fractions to miminum terms, as the identity "$1/3 = 4/12$" does. In the rest of the example, however, the text is apparently corrupt.

38 Kant's Inaugural Dissertation, *De mundi sensibilis atque intelligibilis forma et principiis* (*Concerning the Form and the Principles of the World that is both Sensible and Intelligible*), was defended on August 21, 1770, on the occasion of his appointment as Ordinary Professor of Logic and Metaphysics. See 2:385–419

39 The reference is probably to a transcript of Kant's lectures on metaphysics (*Dicta metaphysica*) that had been bound together in one volume with a copy of the Inaugural Dissertation.

40 See 2:412–13.

PART II (A). THE VIENNA LOGIC

1 See note 11 to 24:37 in the *Blomberg Logic*.

2 Alexander Gottlieb Baumgarten (1714–1762), *Acroasis Logica* (*Hearkening to Logic*), Halle, 1761.

3 J. P. Reusch (1691–1758), *Systema logicum* (*A System of Logic*), 1734.

4 M. Knutzen (1713–1751), *Elementa philosophiae rationalis seu logicae* . . . (*Elements of Rational Philosophy or Logic* . . .), 1747.

5 Malebranche's *De la recherche de la vérité* (*Of the Search for Truth*) appeared in 1674. The reason for the mistaken dating is unclear.

6 See note 13 to 24:38, in the *Blomberg Logic*.

7 Johann Heinrich Lambert (1728–1777), *Neues Organon* (*New Organon*), 1764.

8 Pierre Daniel Huet (1630–1721), French philologist and philosopher.

9 See note 32 to 24:211, in the *Blomberg Logic.*
10 See note 2 to 24:28, in the *Blomberg Logic.*
11 Johann Joachim Spalding (1714–1804), German Protestant theologian, whose sermons were published both singly and in collections.
12 The reference may be to the *Spectator*, published by J. Addison and R. Steele, 1711–14, or to the *Spectateur*, edited by P. Marivaux, 1721–24.
13 Johann Georg Sulzer (1720–1779), *Allgemeine Theorie der Schönen Künste – nach alphabetischer Ordnung* (*Universal Theory of the Fine Arts – In Alphabetical Order*), Leipzig, 1771–4.
14 Christoph Martin Wieland (1733–1813), German poet and novelist known for his elegant, playful style.
15 See note 18 to 24:74, in the Blomberg Logic.
16 Claude Adrien Helvétius (1715–1771), French philosopher and Encyclopedist.
17 Johann Kaspar Lavater (1741–1801), Swiss theologian and mystic; *Aussichten in die Ewigkeit, in Briefen an Dr. Zimmermann* (*Prospects for Eternity, in Letters to Dr. Zimmermann*), 4 vols., 1768.
18 MS Pagination; see 24:825–6.
19 Marie-Thérèse Rodet Geoffrin (1699–1777), supporter of the Encyclopedists, whose salon was an international meeting place for artists and men of letters.
20 Caius Maecenas (d. 8 B.C.), Roman statesman, patron of Horace and Virgil.
21 The first clause of this sentence appears to be corrupt. As it stands, the sentence translates as follows: Ideas [are] concepts because they are grounds[;] essential [marks] are not in the least derived. Reading "Notae" for "Ideae" and "quae" for "quia" would yield the following translation: Essential marks are marks of a concept which are grounds, not in the least derived.
22 The pronoun refers to "essentiales" (essential [marks]).
23 See note 13 to 24:811, above.
24 This sentence and the next seem to be corrupt, and their meaning is unclear. They read in full: "Also muß man doch Alles aus der Erfahrung herkommen, und ist also doch nie etwas evident, als wenn es die Vernunft allein gemacht hatte. Wenn du dich durch Verstand allein überzeugen willst, woher willst du das nehmen?"
25 In fact there are only five winning combinations out of the thirty-six that are possible. The example is developed correctly in the *Dohna-Wundlacken Logic* (24:742).
26 The sentence seems to be corrupt. It reads in full: "Es kann dawider kein Zweifel gemacht werden, weil sie eben so wohl das Gegentheil behauptet."
27 MS pagination; see 24:826–7.
28 Tycho Brahe (1546–1601) attempted a compromise between the Copernican and the Ptolemaic systems, positing that the earth was immobile, that the sun revolved around it, and that the five planets then known revolved around the sun.
29 James Jurin (1684–1750), English physician and physicist.
30 Apollonius of Tyana (fl. 1st century A.D.), a neo-Pythagorean philosopher,

was exalted after his death as a prophet and worker of miracles, e.g., in a biography by the Greek sophist and writer Philostratus (fl. c. 217). Alexander the Paphlagonian (fl. 2nd century A.D.) founded an oracle of the god of healing and was able to amass an enormous amount of money by performing apparent miracles.

31 Longinus (fl. 1st century A.D.?), Περὶ ὕπους (*On the Sublime*). In Kant's day this treatise was still wrongly ascribed to Cassius Longinus (c. 213–273), rhetorician and member of the neoplatonic school.

32 Friedrich Christian Baumeister (1709–1785), *Institutiones metaphysica* (*Metaphysical Principles*), 1738, which Kant used temporarily as a text for his lectures on metaphysics.

33 Johann Kaspar Lavater (1741–1801), Swiss theologian and mystic, in *Sämtliche Prosaische Schriften vom Jahr 1763–1783* (*Collected Prose Writings from the Years 1763–1783*), Winterthur, 1784.

34 MS pagination; see 24:795.

35 MS pagination; see 24:911.

PART II (B). THE HECHSEL LOGIC

1 Batto was apparently a stutterer (reading "Batto" for "Bathos," with Pinder).

2 The sentence reads in full: "Ein unmittelbares *wahrnehmungs Urtheil* ist, wenn wir allgemeine Erfahrungen so unterscheiden, daß viele unmittelbare Erfahrungen zuletzt eine Regel der Erkenntnis heißen." Like Pinder, I can find no way to emend this to make sense of it.

3 The other case, where one judgment denies universally and the other affirms particularly, has inadvertently been omitted.

4 Throughout this passage, "conversum" and "convertens" are confused. The judgment that is to be converted should be labeled the "conversum," its converse the "convertens." The terms are defined and used correctly in the *Blomberg Logic* (24:282) and in the *Dohna-Wundlacken Logic* (24:770).

5 Whatever holds of the genus or the species holds also of all the things contained under the genus or the species (reading "specie valet quoque de omnibus sub isto genere vel specie contentis" for "specie contentis," with Pinder). The negative portion of the formula, which is omitted, would run thus: Quidquid non valet de genere vel specie, valet quoque de nullis sub isto genere vel specie contentis (whatever does not hold of the genus or of the species does not hold, either, for anything contained under the genus or the species).

6 The corresponding negative proposition – What does not belong to a mark of a thing does not belong to any of the things contained under that mark – has been omitted.

7 The writer has evidently gotten the example confused. Put properly, as Pinder notes, it would run thus: To be indivisible contradicts the composite, but being composite belongs to all bodies, consequently being indivisible also contradicts all bodies themselves.

8 As it appears in the text, the table contains several abbreviations and errors. I have made the needed additions and corrections.

9 The abbreviation "pp" occurs three times in the portion of the Hechsel manuscript translated here. Each time it plainly bears the sense of "and so forth," though I have been unable to trace its origin.

10 Pinder identifies the passage as *Institutiones oratoriae*, V, 12, 5.

11 There is no evident meaning in this. Perhaps it is a fragment of a misunderstood quotation. Pinder calls attention to 8:189, where Kant quotes this passage from Quintilian at length.

12 As Pinder notes in his commentary on this passage, Leonhard Euler (1707–1783) tried to explain gravitation as an effect of the ether pressing down on bodies closer to the surface of the earth, implying that the ether itself is not subject to gravitation. See Euler, *De magnete*, in *Opuscula varii argumenti*, vol. 3, Berlin, 1751, p. 17f. This helps to explain why Kant cites the judgment that bodies are heavy as an example of a synthetic judgment (*Critique of Pure Reason*, A7 = B11 ff.).

13 Pinder reports that the quotation comes not from Horace but from the Jesuit general Aquaviva.

14 According to Pinder, a segment of roughly eight words is missing from the MS here.

15 Johann Christoph Gottsched (1700–1766), *Erste Gründe der gesammten Weltweisheit* (*The First Grounds of All Philosophy*), Leipzig, 1734.

16 Friedrich Gedike, *Vier Dialogen des Plato: Menon, Kriton, und beyde Alkibiades* (*Four Dialogues of Plato: Meno, Crito, and both Alcibiades*), Berlin, 1780.

17 Pinder conjectures that the dashes indicate that a paragraph (of Meier's text) has been left out.

18 This sentence is plainly garbled, as is the following sentence ("Gelegentlich kann er sich aber auch zu ihm hinzuwenden."), which I omit. As an indication of what was probably said, Pinder quotes the following sentence from the *Warsaw Logic* (p. 165): "Those who do not have it in their power do better if they devote themselves more to the art of ascending than to that of descending, even if a few may actually lose something in the process."

PART III. THE DOHNA-WUNDLACKEN LOGIC

1 The Academy edition is based on Kowalewski's edition, as this note indicates. The present translation is based, in turn, on the Academy edition, with corrections. See Section 4 of the Translator's Introduction.

In the Kowalewski edition and in the Academy edition, brackets ("[," "]") are used to mark the inserted marginal notes. In this volume braces ("{," "}") are used instead, since brackets are used throughout to indicate minor emendations made by the translator.

2 Kowalewski omits the "}." He also places this note in the middle of the present paragraph, not at the end, as the MS indicates. On grounds of content his placement seems justified, and I follow him.

3 The distinctions drawn here refer to the division of the university into higher and lower faculties. The faculties of religion (blessedness), jurisprudence (freedom and property), and medicine (life and health) were conventionally classified as higher. Philosophy was conventionally regarded as the lower

faculty, despite the fact that it is concerned with the betterment of life (*melius esse*), not just with its maintenance (*esse*). Kant argues against the conventional classification in *Der Streit der Fakultäten* (*The Conflict among the Faculties*, 7:1–116). The connection of this matter with Rabanus Maurus Magnentius (c. 780–856), a leading figure in the Carolingian renaissance, is unclear.

4 Johannes Peter Reusch (1691–1758), *Systema logicum* (*System of Logic*), Jena, 1734.

5 Christian Johann Anton Corvin (d. 1739), *Institutiones philosophiae rationalis methodo scientifica conscriptae* (*Methods of Rational Philosophy Composed in accordance with Scientific Method*), Jena, 1742(?).

6 See note 13 to 24:38 in the *Blomberg Logic*.

7 Ak, "K"; MS, "P." The reference is to MS pagination; see 24:702–04.

8 In the MS there is no paragraph break here. It was introduced by Kowalewski when he inserted marginal note below.

9 I have inserted the " . . . " to indicate that the passage is apparently corrupt, lacking a term for what corresponds to the *literatus*.

10 Antonio Magliabecchi (1633–1714), librarian to the grand duke of Tuscany in Florence. His library formed the foundation for the National Library of Italy.

11 The reference is to p. 24 of the MS (24:714), where § 65 of Meier's text is discussed.

12 What is meant is perhaps "Doctor umbraticus," a teacher who speaks in a shadowy, obscure way.

13 See note 19 to 24:829, in the *Vienna Logic*.

14 The sentence reads: "Dieser kann eingetheilt werden, z.B. quid." I read "quidquam" for "quid," and punctuate the sentence as indicated. The point, it seems, is that in breaking a concept into its partial concepts, one finally reaches simple concepts, ones that have no further partial concepts, like the concept of *quidquam* (something). But while this concept has no partial concepts, it can be divided, i.e., its extension can be partitioned. See the *Jäsche Logic*, § 6, Note 2 (9:95), § 11, Note (9:97), and § 110 with Notes (9:146).

15 The idea is perhaps that it is logically better (*melius esse logicum*) to be lawfully entitled to happiness (*beatitudo juridica*) in possessing things than it is to be happy in the actual possession of them (*beati possidentes*) – that removing the former also removes the latter.

16 The point seems to be that extension ("Ausdehnung") is an essential mark of body.

17 Reference is to the MS pagination; see 24:729.

18 I omit the following sentence, which appears in the MS as a marginal note: "{Geist, Geischt <noch in der Schweiz>, Gescht, Dunst.}" The words listed are dialectal variations of "Geist," meaning spirit or mind. Aside from the difficulty of rendering this in English, it is also unclear what bearing this has on the discussion.

19 Lehmann suggests (24:1017) that the reference is to Milton, *Paradise Lost*, VIII 148–52. This is supported by a letter from Kant to Schiller dated

March 30, 1795 (12:10–12), though Kant's interpretation of the passage, as stated in the letter, seems doubtful.

20 Louis-Sébastian Mercier (1740–1814), French dramatist and author, known for his portrayals of Parisian life.

21 MS pagination; see 24:739.

22 Themistocles (c. 525-c. 460 B.C.), Athenian statesman and naval commander, masterminded the defeat of the Persians at Salamis in 480. Many of his opponents were ostracized, including Aristides (d. 468 B.C.), who was famed for his uprightness in public life. The precise point of the reference is uncertain, however.

23 The reference is to § 176 of Meier's text, p. 55 of the MS (24:737–8).

24 MS pagination; see 24:746.

25 The reference is to § 181 of Meier's text, p. 57 of the MS (24:738–9).

26 On the hypothesis of a central fire, meant to explain volcanoes, earthquakes, etc., see the *Jäsche Logic*, 9:85.

27 The reference is unclear.

28 See Hermann Conring (1606–1681), *De hermetica Aegyptiorum vetere et nova Paracelsiorum medicina* (*Concerning the Ancient Hermetics of the Egyptians and the New Medicine of the Paracelsians*), Helmstedt, 1648, pp. 7f. and 115.

29 The reference is to § 184 of Meier's text, p. 58 of the MS (24:739–40).

30 Joseph Priestley (1733–1804), English chemist and theologian; Richard Price (1723–1791), English nonconformist minister and moral and political philosopher. For further information see Lehmann's explanatory note (24:1017–18).

31 MS pagination; see 24:705.

32 The middle letter may be something other than "P"; the MS is difficult to read at this point. In any case, the significance of the letters is unclear.

33 The letters are evidently meant as abbreviations of proper names, perhaps "Caius" (which Kant frequently uses as at 9:102 and 9:115 in the *Jäsche Logic*) and "Julius."

34 The first two lines in the example are presumably meant to represent the fact that "divisible" is the term through which "alterable" is related to "bodies." The last three lines are presumably meant to suggest the same point by representing schematically the syllogism:

All divisible things are changeable.

All bodies are divisible.

All bodies are changeable.

35 Johann Peter Reusch (1691–1754), *Systema logicum* (*System of Logic*), 1734.

36 MS pagination; see 24:771.

37 The names refer to standard arguments. The text in question is J. G. Darjes (1714–1791), *Via ad veritatem . . .* (*The Way to Truth . . .*), Jena, 1755.

38 The idea is probably that one might prove, e.g., that the soul continues after death without thereby proving that it is immortal, i.e., that it continues to live after death. See the discussion of the *sophisma heterozeteseos* in the *Hechsel Logic*, MS p. 111.

39 August Hermann Francke (1663–1727), German Protestant leader, educator, and social reformer.

40 Johann Heinrich Lambert (1728–1777), German-French mathematician, scientist, and philosopher who was a frequent correspondent of Kant's.

PART IV. THE JÄSCHE LOGIC

1 In his *Nachricht von der Einrichtung seiner Vorlesungen in dem Winterhalbjahre 1765–1766* (*Announcement of the Arrangement of his Lectures for the Winter Semester, 1765–1766*), which was widely read, Kant says that he will take Meier's manual as his text. Apparently, however, he used Meier's *Excerpts* throughout his career, beginning in 1755.

2 The reference is to the eighth section of the First Main Part of Meier's *Selections*. The Eighth Section deals with concepts, the Ninth with judgments, and the Tenth with inferences, and it is with these sections, on Kant's view, that the proper subject matter of logic begins.

3 Ludwig Heinrich Jakob (1759–1827), *Grundriss der Allgemeinen Logik* (*Outline of Universal Logic*), 1788.

4 The reference is to the view of Johann Gottlieb Fichte (1762–1814), a form of idealism whose first principle is supposed to be both formal and material. Fichte's views are developed in *Ueber den Begriff der Wissenschaftslehre* (*Concerning the Concept of the Doctrine of Science*) and *Grundlage der gesamten Wissenschaftslehre* (*Foundation of the Complete Doctrine of Science*), the reference below being to the latter work. Both works were published at Leipzig in 1794, appearing subsequently in various revised and altered versions.

5 Friedrich Wilhelm Joseph Schelling (1775–1854) defended a form of idealism resembling Fichte's in his early work, *Vom Ich als Prinzip der Philosophie, oder Ueber das Unbedingte im menschlichen Wissen* (*Of the I as Principle of Philosophy, or Concerning the Unconditioned in Human Knowledge*), Tübingen, 1795.

6 Christoph Bardili (1761–1808) published his *Grundriss der ersten Logik, gereinigt von den Irtümmern bisheriger Logiken überhaupt* (*Outline of Primary Logic, Altogether Purified of the Errors of Previous Logics*) in 1800.

7 It has been argued that this is erroneous, on the grounds that only metaphysics, not logic, is a science of reason as to its matter. (Cf. Kinkel's edition of the *Logic*, Leipzig: Felix Meiner, 1924, p. 15.) But the text seems correct. Logic does have reason as its object, and is a science of reason as to its matter, on Kant's view, since it investigates acts of reason through which concepts originate as to form. Cf. § 5, Note 1 (9:94, below).

8 See the note 14 to 24:49, in the *Blomberg Logic*.

9 Henry Home (Lord Kames, 1696–1782), *Elements of Criticism*, in 3 vols., Edinburgh, 1762–5.

10 Johann Heinrich Lambert (1728–1777), *Neues Organon, oder Gedanken über die Erforschung und Bezeichnung des Wahren und dessen Unterscheidung von Irrtum und Schein* (*New Organon, or Thoughts Concerning the Investigation and Designation of the True and Its Distinction from Error and Illusion*), 2 vols., Leipzig, 1764.

11 Christian Wolff (1679–1754), *Philosophia rationalis sive logica* (*Rational Philosophy, or Logic*), 1728.

12 Johann Peter Reusch (1691–1754), *Systema logicum* (*A System of Logic*), Jena.

13 Alexander Gottlieb Baumgarten (1714–1762), *Acroasis logica* (*Hearkening to Logic*), Halle, 1761.

14 Christian August Crusius (1712–1775), *Weg zur Gewißheit und Zuverlässigkeit der menschlichen Erkenntnis* (*The Path to Certainty and Reliability of Human Cognition*), Leipzig, 1747.

15 Reading "Plinius dem ältern" for "Plinius dem jüngern." Pliny the Elder (Caius Plinius Secundus, c. 23–29) wrote a *Historia naturalis* in thirty-seven volumes. Pliny the Younger (Caius Plinius Caecilius Secundus, 62(?)-113) was an orator and statesman, not a naturalist. Jäsche's mistake may have been caused by the fact that both share the name "Secundus," which also suggests "younger," as Heinze suggests (9:506).

16 Jean-Baptiste le Rond d'Alembert (1717–1783), French mathematician and philosopher, who wrote a "preliminary discourse" to the *Encyclopédie* (1751).

17 See the note 26 to 24:186, in the Blomberg Logic

18 Reading "um der Zulänglichkeit desselben zu gegebenen Folgen willen" for "um der Zulänglichkeit der Folgen willen," following Reflexion 2694 (16: 472). See also Reflexionen 2678 and 2690, and the corresponding discussion in the Blomberg Logic (24:220–22).

19 Tycho Brahe (1546–1601) did not fully accept the Copernican hypothesis. He proposed instead that the earth was immobile, that the sun revolved about the earth, and that the planets revolved about the sun.

20 The German leaves it unclear whether "various ones" refers to various objects or to various representations. Hartman and Schwarz suggest the former (*Logic*, p. 96, n. 2) but the latter is suggested by the first paragraph of § 7, below.

Name index

Subject index